# The Gun Digest Book Of
# MODERN GUN VALUES
## Third Edition

## By Jack Lewis
## Edited by Harold A. Murtz

DBI BOOKS, INC., NORTHFIELD, ILLINOIS

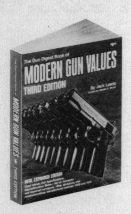

**THE COVER**

The ten Colt .45 automatics appearing on the cover were loaned by Tom Goss of The Fix-It Shop, Northfield, Illinois, from his personal collection. Photograph by John Hanusin.

**Art Director**
John Vitale

**Technical Editor**
Wayne F. Novak

**Production Editor**
Sonya Kaiser

**Production Coordinator**
Betty Burris

**Copy Coordinator**
Dorine Imbach

**Publisher**
Sheldon L. Factor

Produced by
Charger Productions

ISBN 0-910676-19-4
Library of Congress Catalog Card Number 75-10067

# WITH OUR THANKS . . .

A book like this doesn't just happen. Although my name is on the cover, a lot of credit must go to a lot of individuals, each of them expert in their own way.

First, I must thank Harold Murtz of the DBI staff for his personal research and sometimes painful editing, to Bob Anderson of DBI for running down many of the new firearms photos contained in this new updated version, which goes back to 1900 and brings us forward to 1978. Too, the contributions of Wayne Novak, who advised on much of the current pricing, as well as Jack Mitchell and Dean Grennell for technical help cannot be ignored. Without each of them making his contribution, this book would be far less complete.

The Buffalo Bill Museum of Cody, Wyoming, for its photos of aged Winchesters and Larry Goodstall of Remington's museum also must be credited for their help in getting this volume in shape. Thanks also go to Triple K Manufacturing for permission to reproduce illustrations of automatic pistols included in the handguns section.

Finally, the long hours devoted to production by Betty Burris, Dorine Imbach and John Vitale cannot be evaluated in any terms other than their professionalism. I feel lucky to be surrounded by such a crew and offer each and every one my thanks.

Jack Lewis,
Capistrano Beach, California

# CONTENTS

RIFLES: Some used rifles are higher than their original new
price, but cost has little to do with whether it is a good buy!

**SHOTGUNS:** In buying a used shotgun, there are many items to
check to determine whether you are buying wisely . . . . . . . . . . . . . . . . . . . . . . . . . . . . . . . . . . . .**229**

**COMMEMORATIVES:** Is there too much of a good thing in the
commemorative market, as opposed to supply and demand? . . . . . . . . . . . . . . . . . . . . . . . . . . . . .**361**

# CURRENT
# AMERICAN ARMSMAKERS

AMT (Arcadia Machine & Tool), 11666 McBean Dr., El Monte, CA 91732

A.R. Sales Co., 9624 Alpaca St., South El Monte, CA 91733

Accuracy Systems, Inc., 2105 S. Hardy Dr., Tempe, AZ 85282

ArmaLite, 118 E. 16th St., Costa Mesa, CA 92627

Auto-Ordnance Corp., Box ZG, West Hurley, NY 12491

Bauer Firearms, 34750 Klein Ave., Fraser, MI 48026

Bortmess Gun Co., Inc., R.D. 2, Box 3, Scenery Hill, PA 15360 412-945-5175

Brown Precision Co., P.O. Box 270W, 7786 Molinos Ave., Los Molinos, CA 96055/916-384-2506

Browning (Gen. Offices), Rt. 1, Morgan, UT 84050/801-876-2711

Champlin Firearms, Inc., Box 3191, Enid, OK 73701

Charter Arms Corp., 430 Sniffens Ln., Stratford, CT 06497

Colt, 150 Huyshope Ave., Hartford, CT 06102

Commando Arms, Inc., Box 10214, Knoxville, TN 37919

Coonan Arms, Inc., 570 S. Fairview, St. Paul, MN 55116 612-699-5639

Crown City Arms, P.O. Box 1126, Cortland, NY 13045

Cumberland Arms, Rt. 1, Shafer Rd., Blanton Chapel, Manchester, TN 37355

Day Arms Corp., 2412 S.W. Loop 410, San Antonio, TX 78227

Detonics 45 Associates, 2500 Seattle Tower, Seattle, WA 98101

DuBiel Arms Co., 1724 Baker Rd., Sherman, TX 75090/214-893-7313

EMF Co., Inc., Box 1248, Studio City, CA 91604

FTL Marketing Corp., 12521-3 Oxnard St., No. Hollywood, CA 91601/213-985-2939

Firearms Imp. & Exp. Corp., 4530 NW 135th St., Opa-Locka, FL 33054/305-685-5966 (FIE)

Freedom Arms Co., Freedom, WY 83120

Gwinn Firearms, No. 19 Freedom Industrial Park, Bangor, ME 04401/207-848-3333

Harrington & Richardson, Industrial Rowe, Gardner, MA 01440

High Standard Sporting Firearms, 31 Prestige Park Circle, East Hartford, CT 06108

Hopkins & Allen Arms, No. 1 Melnick Rd., Monsey, NY 10952

Hyper-Single Precision SS Rifles, 520 E. Beaver, Jenks, OK 74037

Ithaca Gun Co., Ithaca, NY 14850

Iver Johnson Arms Inc., P.O. Box 251, Middlesex, NJ 08846

Kimber of Oregon, Inc., 9039 S.E. Jannsen Rd., Clackamas, OR 97015/503-656-1704

H. Koon, Inc., 1602 Stemmons, Suite D, Carrollton, TX 75006

L.E.S., 2301 Davis St., North Chicago, IL 60064/312-473-9484

Ljutic Ind., Inc., P.O. Box 2117, Yakima, WA 98902 (Mono-Gun)

Ljutic Intl., 101 Carmel Dr., Suite 120, Carmel, IN 46032/ 317-848-5051

M&N Distributors, 23535 Telo St., Torrance, CA 90505/ 213-530-9000

Marlin Firearms Co., 100 Kenna Dr., New Haven, CT 06473

Merrill Co., Inc., 704 E. Commonwealth, Fullerton, CA 92631/ 714-879-8922

O.F. Mossberg & Sons, Inc., 7 Grasso St., No. Haven, CT 06473

Mowrey Gun Works, Box 28, Iowa Park, TX 76367

Navy Arms Co., 689 Bergen Blvd., Ridgefield, NJ 07657

Numrich Arms Corp., W. Hurley, NY 12491

Plainfield Inc., 292 Vail Ave., Piscataway, NJ 08854

RG Industries, 2485 N.W. 20th SE, Miami, FL 33142

Raven Arms, 1300 Bixby Dr., Industry, CA 91745

Remington Arms Co., Bridgeport, CT 06602

Savage Arms Corp., Westfield, MA 01085

Sears, Roebuck & Co., 825 S. St. Louis, Chicago, IL 60607

Semmerling Corp., P.O. Box 400, Newton, MA 02160

Sharps Rifle Co., 3428 Shakertown Rd., Dayton, OH 45430

Shiloh Products, 37 Potter St., Farmingdale, NY 11735 (Sharps)

Smith & Wesson, Inc., 2100 Roosevelt Ave., Springfield, MA 01101

Springfield Armory, 111 E. Exchange St., Geneseo, IL 61254

Sterling Arms Corp., 211 Grand St., Lockport, NY 14094/ 716-434-6631

Sturm, Ruger & Co., Southport, CT 06490

Thompson-Center Arms, Box 2405, Rochester, NH 03867

Universal Firearms, 3740 E. 10th Ct., Hialeah, FL 33013

Ward's, 619 W. Chicago, Chicago, IL 60607 (Western Field brand)

Weatherby's, 2871 E. Firestone Blvd., South Gate, CA 90280

Dan Wesson Arms, 293 S. Main St., Monson, MA 01057

Wichita Arms, 333 Lulu, Wichita, KS 67211

Wildey Firearms Co., Inc., P.O. Box 4264, New Windsor, NY 12250/ 203-272-7215

Winchester Repeating Arms Co., New Haven, CT 06504

# CURRENT
# FIREARMS IMPORTERS,
# FOREIGN ARMSMAKERS

Abercrombie & Fitch, 2302 Maxwell Lane, Houston, TX 77023

Action Arms, 4567 Bermuda, Philadelphia, PA 19124/215-744-3400

Alpha Arms, Inc., 1602 Stemmons, Suite D, Carrollton, TX 75006/ 214/245-3115

American Arms International, P.O. Box 11717, Salt Lake City, UT 84147/801-531-0180

AYA (Aguirre y Aranzabal) see: IGI Domino or Wm. L. Moore

Pedro Arrizabalaga, Eibar, Spain

Armoury Inc., Rte. 202, New Preston, CT 06777

Armsport, Inc., 3590 N.W. 49th St., Miami, FL 33142/305-592-7850

Beretta U.S.A., 17601 Indian Head Hwy., Accokeek, MD 20007/ 301-283-2191

Britarms, Ltd., Unit 1, Raban's Close, Raban's Lane Industrial Estate, Aylesbury, Bucks, England

Browning (Gen. Offices), Rt. 1, Morgan, UT 84050/801-876-2711

Browning (parts & service), Rt. 4, Box 624-B, Arnold, MO 63010/ 314-287-6800

Century Arms Co., 3-5 Federal St., St. Albans, VT 05478
Champlin Firearms, Inc., Box 3191, Enid, OK 73701
Commercial Trading Imports, Inc., 2125 Center Ave., Suite 201, Fort Lee, NJ 07024/201-461-8833
Connecticut Valley Arms Co., Saybrook Rd., Haddam, CT 06438
Walter Craig, Inc., Box 927-A, Selma, AL 36701
Creighton & Warren, P.O. Box 15723, Nashville, TN 37215
Morton Cundy & Son, Ltd., P.O. Box 315, Lakeside, MT 59922
Charles Daly (see: Outdoor Sports HQ.)
Dikar s. Coop. (see: Connecticut Valley Arms Co.)
Dixie Gun Works, Inc., Hwy. 51, South, Union City, TN 38261/901-885-0561
Dynamit Nobel of America, Inc., 105 Stonehurst Court, Northvale, NJ 07647/201-767-1660
Excam Inc., 4480 E. 11 Ave., P.O. Box 3483, Hialeah, FL 33013
F.E.T.E. Corp., 2867 W. 7th St., Los Angeles, CA 90005
Ferlach (Austria) of North America, P.O. Box 430435, S. Miami, FL 33143
Firearms Center Inc. (FCI), 308 Leisure Lane, Victoria, TX 77901
Firearms Imp. & Exp. Corp., 4530 NW 135th St., Opa-Locka, FL 33054/305-685-5966
Flaig's Lodge, Millvale, PA 15209
Freeland's Scope Stands, Inc., 3737 14th Ave., Rock Island, IL 61201
J.L. Galef & Son, Inc., 85 Chambers, New York, NY 10007
Hawes National Corp., 15424 Cabrito Rd., Van Nuys, CA 91406
Healthways, Box 45055, Los Angeles, CA 90061
Gil Hebard Guns, Box 1, Knoxville, IL 61448
Heckler & Koch Inc., 933 N. Kenmore St., Suite 218, Arlington, VA 22201
Heym, Friedr. Wilh., Box 861, Bolton, Ont. L0P 1A0, Canada
Hunting World, 16 E. 53rd St., New York, NY 10022
IGI Domino Corp., 200 Madison Ave., New York, NY 10016/212-889-4889
Incor, Inc., P.O. Box 132, Addison, TX 75001/214-386-7000
Interarmco, see: Interarms
Interarms Ltd., 10 Prince St., Alexandria, VA 22313
International Distr., Inc., 7290 S.W. 42nd St., Miami, FL 33155
Paul Jaeger, Inc., 211 Leedom St., Jenkintown, PA 19046
Jana Intl. Co., Box 1107, Denver, CO 80201 (Parker-Hale)
J.J. Jenkins Enterprises, Inc., 375 Pine Ave. No. 25, Goleta, CA 93017/805-967-1366
Kassnar Imports, 5480 Linglestown Rd., Harrisburg, PA 17110
Kleinguenther's, P.O. Box 1261, Seguin, TX 78155
Knight & Knight, 5930 S.W. 48 St., Miami, FL 33155
L.A. Distributors, 4 Centre Market Pl., New York, NY 10013
La Paloma Marketing, 4500 E. Speedway Blvd., Suite 93, Tucson, AZ 85712/602-881-4750 (K.F.C. shotguns)
Lever Arms Serv. Ltd., 771 Dunsmuir, Vancouver, B.C., Canada V6C 1M9
Liberty Arms Organization, Box 306, Montrose, CA 91020
Mandall Shtg. Suppl. Corp., 3616 N. Scottsdale Rd., Scottsdale, AZ 85251/602-945-2553

Mannlicher Div., Steyr Daimler Puch of Amer., 85 Metro Way, Secaucus, NJ 07094
Mitchell Arms Corp., 116 East 16th St., Costa Mesa, CA 92627/714-548-7701
Wm. Larkin Moore, 31360 Via Colinas, Suite 109, Westlake Village, CA 91360/213-889-4160
Navy Arms Co., 689 Bergen Blvd., Ridgefield, NJ 07657
Outdoor Sports Headquarters, Inc., 2290 Arbor Blvd., Dayton, OH 45439/513-294-2811
P.M. Air Services, Ltd., P.O. Box 1573, Costa Mesa, CA 92626
Pachmayr Gun Works, 1220 S. Grand Ave., Los Angeles, CA 90015
Pacific Intl. Merch. Corp., 2215 "J" St., Sacramento, CA 95816
Rob. Painter, 2901 Oakhurst Ave., Austin, TX 78703
Ed Paul Sptg. Goods, 172 Flatbush Ave., Brooklyn, NY 11217
Pragotrade, a Div. of Molokov Canada, Inc., 307 Humberline Dr., Rexdale, Ont. M9W 5V1, Canada/416-675-1322
Precise, 3 Chestnut, Suffern, NY 10901
Precision Sports, 798 Cascadilla St., Ithaca, NY 14850/607-273-2993
Premier Shotguns, 172 Flatbush Ave., Brooklyn, NY 11217
Leonard Puccinelli Co., 11 Belle Ave., San Anselmo, CA 94960/415-456-1666
RG Industries, Inc., 2485 N.W. 20th St., Miami, FL 33142
L. Joseph Rahn, Inc., First Natl. Bldg., Room 502, 201 S. Main St., Ann Arbor, MI 48104
Ravizza Caccia Pesca Sport, s.p.a., Via Volta 60, 20090 Cusago, Italy
Richland Arms Co., 321 W. Adrian St., Blissfield, MI 49228
Rottweil, see: Dynamit Nobel of America
Ruko Sporting Goods Inc., 195 Sugg Rd., Buffalo, NY 14225
Sanderson's, 724 W. Edgewater, Portage, WI 53901
Sarco, Inc., 323 Union St., Stirling, NJ 07980/201-647-3800
Savage Arms Corp., Westfield, MA 01085 (Anschutz)
Security Arms Co., see: Heckler & Koch
Service Armament, 689 Bergen Blvd., Ridgefield, NJ 07657
Sherwood Intl. Export Corp., 18714 Parthenia St., Northridge, CA 91324
Shore Galleries, Inc., 3318 W. Devon Ave., Chicago, IL 60645
Shotguns of Ulm, 7 Forest Glen, Highland Park, NJ 08904/201-297-0573
Sile Distributors, 7 Centre Market Pl., New York, NY 10013
Simmons Spec., Inc., 700 Rogers Rd., Olathe, KS 66061
Sloan's Sprtg. Goods, Inc., 10 South St., Ridgefield, CT 06877
Solersport, 23629 7th Ave., West, Bothell, WA 98011
Steyr-Daimler-Puch of America, Inc., see: Mannlicher
Stoeger Industries, 55 Ruta Ct., S. Hackensack, NJ 07606/201-440-2700
Tradewinds, Inc., P.O. Box 1191, Tacoma, WA 98401
Valmet Sporting Arms Div., 7 Westchester Plaza, Elmsford, NY 10523/914-347-4440
Valor Imp. Corp., 5555 N.W. 36th Ave., Miami, FL 33142
Ventura Imports, P.O. Box 2782, Seal Beach, CA 90740
Weatherby's, 2781 Firestone Blvd., So. Gate, CA 90280

# FOREIGN ARMS MANUFACTURERS

**AUSTRALIA**

Slazengers (Australia) Pty., Ltd., Alexandria, N.S.W.

**AUSTRIA**

Sport und Waffen — Dschulnigg, Griesgasse 8, 5020 Salzburg
Johann Fanzoi, Postfach 25, 9100 Ferlach, Kaernten
Hirtenberger Ratronen, Zundhutchen und Metallwarenfabrik, A.G., 2552 Hirtenberg
Gottfried Juch, 9100 Ferlach, Kaernten
Josef Just, 9100 Ferlach, Kaernten
Richard Mahrholdt & Sohn, Postfach 177, 6020 Innsbruck
Franz Sarnitz, 10 Osterleitengasse, 1190 Vienna 19
Franz Sodia, Gartengasse 6, 9170 Ferlach, Kaernten
Johann Springer's Erben, 10 Josefsgasse, 1010 Vienna 8
Steyr-Daimler-Puch A.G., Postfach 4, 4400 Steyr
Vereinigte Ferlacher Jagdwaffenerzeuger G.m.b.H., 9100 Ferlach, Kaernten
Voare Tiroler Jagd u. Sportwaffenfabrik, 6330 Kufstein
Benedikt-Winkler, Postgasse 1, 9100 Ferlach, Kaernten

**BELGIUM**

Armaf S.A. — Manufacture Liegeoise, 54 Rue du Vertbois, Liege
A. Jos. Defourny, Herstal
Delcour S.A., 315 Rue des Allies, Nessonvaux, Fraipont
Jean Duchateau, Rue Louis Fraigneux, 8 Liege
Dumoulin & Fils, 16-18 Rue du Tilleul, 4411 Milmort (Liege)
Dumoulin Frs. & Cie, 2 Rue Thier de la Fontaine, Liege
Fabrique Nationale Herstal, 4400 Herstal (Liege)
Auguste Francotte & Cie, 61 Rue Mont Saint Martin, Liege
N. Lajot & Cie, Rue aux Chevaux, 33, Liege
Etablissements Georges Laloux, 3, Rue des Urbanistes, Liege
Lebeau-Couraliy, 386 Rue St. Gilles, Liege
Lecocq & Hoffmann, 31 Rue de L'Ecuyer, Brussels
Ancienne Maison H. Mahi'lon S.A., 208, Rue Royale, Brussels
Anciens Etablissements Pieper, S.A., Herstal, Liege
Manufacture d'Armes de Chasse "Masquelier", 88 Rue de la Cathedrale, Liege
Neumann & Co., Rue Cheri 39, Liege
Manufacture Generale d'Armes J. Saive, 10, Rue Theodore Schwann, Liege
Maison Fernand Thonon, 51, Rue Monulphe, 51, Liege

**BRAZIL**

Farma S.A., Rua Antonio de Godoi, Sao Paulo
Forjas Taurus S.A., Caixa Postal 44, Porto Alegre, Rio Grande do Sul
Fundicao E Industria De Armas "Lerap" Ltda., Rua Sao Leopoldo 833, Sao Paulo
Industria Nacional de Armas S.A., Rua Coronel Xavier Toledo 123, 60, cj, 63, Sao Paulo
Lisariturri & Cia., Ltda., Rua Tobias Barreto 621, Sao Paulo
Metalurgica Serrana Ltda., Caixa Postal 464, Erechim, Rio Grande do Sul
Amadeo Rossi & Cia., Caixa Postal 28, 93000 Sao Leopoldo, Rio Grande do Sul

**CANADA**

Canadian Industries, Ltd. (Ammunition Div.), Howard House, Brownsburg, Quebec J0V 1A0
Sevelot of Canada Ltd., Saskatoon, Sask.
Ithaca Gun Co. of Canada, 211 Park Ave., Dunnville, Ontario
Remington Arms of Canada, Ltd., 36 Queen Elizabeth Blvd., Toronto, Ontario
Valcartier Industries Inc., P.O. Box 790, Courcelette, Co. Portneuf, P.Q.
Winchester-Western (Canada) Ltd., Coburg, Ontario

**CZECHOSLOVAKIA**

Povazske Strojarne, Narodni Podnik, Povazska Bystrica (Kovo Ltd., Metal & Engineering Products and Raw Materials Trading Co.), P.O. Box 889, Prague
Sellier & Bellot, Vlasim, Merkvria, P.O. Box 18, 17005, Prague 7
Zbrojovka Brno — Jan Sverma Works, National Corp., Merkvria, P.O. Box 18, 17005, Prague 7

**DENMARK**

Haerens Ammunitionsarsenalet, Copenhagen (Danish Government)
Schultz & Larsen Gevaerfabrik, Otterup
Dansk Industri Syndikat, Compagnie Madsen, Copenhagen

**FINLAND**

Lepuan Patrunatehdas, Lapua
Oy Sako Ab, 11100 Riihimaki
Oy Tikkakoski Ab, 41160 Tikkakoski
Valmet Oy, Valmet Building, Punanotkonkatu 2, Helsinki

**FRANCE**

Verney-Carron, 17 Cours Favriel, 42010 St. Etienne Cedex (Loire)
Charlin Cie, 16 a 20 rue Beranger, St. Etienne (Loire)
Etablissements Damon & Cie, 7, rue des Francs-Macons, St. Etienne Darne, 71 Cours Favriel, 42010 St. Etienne
Gastinne-Renette, 39, Avenue Roosevelt, Paris 8e (Champs-Elysees)
J. Gaucher Armes, St. Etienne, (Loire)
Gevelot, 50, rue Ampere, 75017 Paris
Manufacture d'Armes Automatiques, 35, Allees Marines, Bayonne
Manufacture de Machines du Haut-Rhin (Manurhin), 68200 Mulhouse-Bourtzwiller
Manufacture Nationale d'Armes de Chatellerault, Chatellerault
Manufacture d'Armes des Pyrenees Francaises, 647 Hendaye
Manufrance, St. Etienne, (Loire)
Manufacture d'Armes de Chasse Kerne, 18 rue des Etats Generaux, Versailles
Societe Francaise d'Armes at Cycles de St. Etienne, St. Etienne
Societe Generale de Mecanique, 21 rue Clemont Forissier, St. Etienne, (Loire)
Societe Moderne de Fabrications Mecaniques, 56 rue Tarentaize, St. Etienne, (Loire)

**EAST GERMANY**

Buhag G.m.b.H., Suhl
PGH Hubertus, Suhl

VEB Fahrzeug und Geratwerk Simson, 60 Suhl
VEB Sprengstoffwerk 1, Schonebeck (Elbe)
VEB Ernst-Thalmann Werk, 60 Suhl (Thur.) (Fortuna; Merkel)
Albert Wilhelm Wolf K.G., Suhl

## WEST GERMANY

J.G. Anschutz G.m.b.H., Daimlerstrasse 12, 7900 Ulm/Donau
B.S.F. Bayerische-Sportwaffenfabrik, Postfach 121, 8520 Erlangen
Wilhelm Brenneke K.G., Ilmenauweg 32, 3012 Langenhagen/Kr. Hannover
Gewehrfabrik H. Burgsmuller & Sohne G.m.b.H., Postfach 5, 3350 Kreiensen
Deutsche Jagdpatronenfabrik G.m.b.H., 7210 Rottweil/Neckar
Dianawerk Mayer & Grammelspacher, Murgtalstrasse 34, 7550 Rastatt/Baden
Dynamit Nobel A.G., P.O. Box 1209, 5210 Troisdorf-Oberlar
Em-GE Sportgerate K.G., Gerstenberger & Eberwein, 7921 Gerstetten-Gussenstadt/Wurtt
Erma Werke B. Geipel G.m.b.H., Johann Ziegler Strasse 13/15, 8060 Dachau
Feinwerkbau Westinger & Altenburger G.m.b.H., 7238 Oberndorf/Neckar
Walter Gehmann, Karlstrasse 41-43, 7500 Karlsruhe
Heckler & Koch G.m.b.H., 7238 Oberndorf/Neckar
Hege Jagd und Sportwaffen G.m.b.H., 7170 Schwabisch Hall
Friedrich Wilhelm Heym, 8732 Munnerstadt
Industrie-Werke Karlsruhe A.G., 7500 Karlsruhe
Albrecht Kind G.m.b.H. & Co., 5270 Gummerbach-Hunstig bei Dieringhausen (Rhld.)
Krico-Kriegeskorte & Co. G.m.b.H., 7000 Stuttgart-Hedelfingen
Heinrich Krieghoff G.m.b.H., Bosch Str. 22, 7900 Ulm/Donau
Mauser Werke A.G., 7238 Oberndorf/Neckar
Mayer & Riem G.m.b.H. 5760 Neheim-Husten 2, Am Wagenberg
Mayer & Sons, P.O. Box 4340, 5760 Arnsberg 1
Reck Sportwaffenfabrik, Karl Arndt K.G., 8560 Lauf/Pegnitz
Remington Arms G.m.b.H., Winterhausen Str. 85, 8700 Wurzburg
Rheinmetall G.m.b.H., Abteilung VA, 4000 Dusseldorf 1
Rhoner Sportwaffenfabrik G.m.b.H., Weisbach/Rhon, Kr. Bad Neustadt/Saale
Rohm G.m.b.H., Kreis Heidenheim/Brenz, 7927 Sontheim/Brenz
J.P. Sauer & Sohn A.G., P.O. Box 1408, 2330 Eckernforde
Herbert Schmidt Waffenfabrik, 8745 Ostheim/Rhon
Voere G.m.b.H., 7741 Vohrenbach/Schw.
Carl Walther G.m.b.H., P.O. Box 4325, 7900 Ulm/Donau
Lothar Walther, 7923 Konigsbronn (Wurtt.)
Hermann Weihrauch Sportwaffenfabrik, 8744 Mellrichstadt/Bayern
Winchester G.m.b.H., Grafenberger Allee 66, 4000 Dusseldorf
Wischo KG, 8520 Erlangen

## GREAT BRITAIN

Atkin, Grant & Lang Ltd., 7 Bury St., St. Jame's, London, S.W.1
Thomas Bland & Sons Ltd., 4/5 William IV Street, Strand, London W.C. 2
Boss & Co. Guns, 13-14 Cork St., Picadilly, London, W.1
Charles Boswell Ltd., P.O. Box 433, Wrethem Works, Strafford Road, London, W.3
BSA Guns, Ltd., Birmingham B11 2PX
E.J. Churchill, Ltd., Orange St., Gun Works, Leicester Square, London, W.C.2
John Dickson & Son, 21 Frederick St., Edinburgh
Eley, P.O. Box 216, Witton, Birmingham B6 7DA
G.E. Fulton & Son, Ltd., Bisley Camp, Brookwood, Surrey
Stephen Grant & Joseph Lang, Ltd., 7 & 8 Bury Street, St. James's, London, S.W.1
W.W. Greener, Ltd., St. Mary's Row, Birmingham 16
Holland & Holland, Ltd., 13 Bruton St., London, W1X 8JS
Imperial Metal Industries (Kynoch) Ltd., Witton, Birmingham 6
W.J. Jeffery & Co. Ltd., 13 Bruton Street, London, W.1
Parker-Hale Ltd., Bisley Works, Golden Hillock Road, Sparbrook, Birmingham B11 2PZ
William Powell & Son, 35 Carr's Lane, Birmingham 4
James Purdey & Sons, Ltd., 57-58 South Audley St., London, W1Y 6ED
John Rigby & Co., 43 Sackville St., London, W.1
Webley & Scott, Ltd., Park Lane, Handsworth, Birmingham B21 8LU
Westley Richards & Co., Ltd., 13 Bruton St., London, W1X 8JS

## GREECE

Greek Powder & Cartridge Co., Ltd., Athens

## HOLLAND

Nederlandsche Wapen-en Munitiefabriek N.V., De Kruithoorn's-Hertogenbosch

## HUNGARY

Artex, Via Hador 31, Budapest

## ITALY

Armigas-Comega, Via Valle Inzino 34, 25063 Gardone V.T., (Brescia)
Luigi Belleri, Via Convento 27, 25063 Gardone V.T., (Brescia)
Andrea Benetti, Via Matteotti, 60, 25063 Gardone V.T., (Brescia)
Pietro Beretta S.p.A., 25063 Gardone V.T., (Brescia)
L. Santina Bernardelli, Via Zanardelli 9/E, 25063 Gardone V.T., (Brescia)
Vincenzo Bernardelli, 25063 Gardone V.T., (Brescia)
Angelo & Emilio Boniotti, 25063 Gardone V.T., (Brescia)
Breda Meccanica Bresciana, Via Lunga 2, 25100 Brescia
Fabbrica Bresciana Armi, Brescia
Bruno Castellani, Via S. Giovanni Bosco 4, 25063 Gardone V.T., (Brescia)
Rodolfo Cosmi & Figli, Via Flaminia 307, Torrete, (Ancona)
Libero Daffini, Vicolo Tri Archi 9, Brescia
Fratelli Di Maggio, Via Leonardo da Cinvi, 29, 25063 Gardone V.T., (Brescia)
Armi Famars, Via Cinelli 29, 25063 Gardone V.T. (Brescia)
Guilio Fiocchi, 22053 Lecco
Luigi Franchi S.p.A., Via Calatafimi 18, Brescia
Fratelli Galesi, Via Trento 10/A, Collebeato, (Brescia)
Rigarmi di Rino Galesi, Via Italia 1/3, Brescia
Le Armerie Italiane Dei Fratelli Gamba, 25063 Gardone V.T., Brescia
Armi Renato Gamba, Via Artigiani 89, 25063 Gardone V.T. (Brescia)
Armotecnica Gardonese, Via C. Battisi 8, 25063 Gardone V.T., (Brescia)
Fabbrica Pietro Giacomelli di Giov., Magno di Gardone V.T., (Brescia)
Giuseppe Gitti & Figli, Via Matteotti, 2 b-c, 25063 Gardone V.T., (Brescia)
Pierino Gitti, Via Leonardo da Vinci 2, 25063 Gardone V.T. (Brescia)
Umberto Gitti, 25063 Gardone V.T., (Brescia)
Armi San Marco di Buffoli Giuseppe, Via A. Canossi, 2, 25063 Gardone V.T., (Brescia)
Gnali Graziano, Via Puccini 4, 25063 Gardone V.T. (Brescia)
F.A.V.S.-Fabbrica Armi Valle Susa di Guglielminotti, Via Nazionale 19, Villarfocchiardo (Torino)
Lames, S.p.A., Via San Rufina 29, 16043 Chiavari
Luigi Maffi, Via San Mario 8, 25063 Gardone V.T. (Brescia)
Stefano Marocchi & Figli, 25063 Gardone V.T. (Brescia)
Davide Pedersoli, Vicolo Bolognini 2, 25063 Gardone V.T. (Brescia)
Pedretti & Ongaro, Via Convento 54, 25063 Gardone V.T. (Brescia)
Manifattura Armi Perazzi, Via S. Orsola 98, S. Eufemia, Brescia
Fabbrica Italiana Armi Pietro Perugini, Nuvolera, Brescia
Fratelli Piotti, Via Magno 37, 25063 Gardone V.T., (Brescia)
Jager Armi di Armando Piscetta, Via Campazzino 55/b, Torino
Armi San Marco di Ruffoli, Via A. Canossi 2, Brescia
Fabbrica Italiana Armi Sabatti, Via A. Volta 32-A, 25063 Gardone V.T. (Brescia)
Fratelli Serena, Brescia
Manifattura Riunite Armi di Enrico Salvinelli, Via 2 Giugno 8, 25063 Gardone V.T., (Brescia)
Fabbrica d'Armi Sarezzo, Via Mantova 6, Brescia
Manifattura Bresciana Armi Stocchetta, Brescia
Fratelli Tanfoglio, Via Pratello 8, 25063 Gardone V.T., (Brescia)
Fratelli Toschi, Villa San Martino Di Lugo, Ravenna
Aldo Uberti & Figli, Via XX Settembre 7, 25063 Gardone V.T. (Brescia)
Pietro Zanoletti "IAPZ", Via Guglielmo, 4, Brescia
Fabio Zanotti, Via XXV Aprile, 25063 Gardone V.T., (Brescia)
Angelo Zoli & Figli, Via Matteotti 5, 25063 Gardone V.T., (Brescia)
Antonio Zoli, Via Zanardelli 9/D, 25063 Gardone V.T., (Brescia)

## JAPAN

Arakawa Kogyo K.K., 1969, Itsukaichi, Itsukaichi-machi, Nishitama-gun, Tokyo (air rifles)
Asahi Chemical Industry Co., Ltd., Hibiya-Mitsui Building, 12, 1-chome Yuraku-cho, Chiyoda-ku, Tokyo (gunpowder, percussion caps)
Goshi Kaisha Nitto Enkan Seizosho, 20, Fukagawa Tokiwa-cho, Koto-ku, Tokyo (shot)
Hasuike Seisakusho Co., Ltd., 16, 5-chome Oimazato-honmachi, Higashinari-ku, Osaka (air rifle pellets)
Heirinkan Arms Co., Ltd., 10, 3-chome Kanda-Ogawamachi, Chiyoda-ku, Tokyo (rifles, air rifles, shotguns)
Hoshino Shito Kogyo K.K., 80, Shinsakamoto-cho, Daito-ku, Tokyo (sporting rifles)
Howa Machinery Ltd., Sukaguchi, Shinkawa-cho, Nishikasugai-gun, Aichi-ken (sporting rifles)
Kawaguchiya Firearms Co., Ltd., 3, 4-chome Muromachi, Nihonbashi, Chuo-ku, Tokyo (shotguns, shotgun shells)
Keiheisha Honten, Gose-mochi, Gose-shi, Nara-ken (air rifles)
K.K. Jinmeisha, 36, 1-chome Ueshio-machi, Minami-ku, Osaka (shot)

K.K. Kohame Seisakusho, 1, 1-chome Ishihari-machi, Sumida-ku, Tokyo (shot)

Kunii Shokai, 65, Tsutsumishita-machi, Koriyama-shi, Fukushima-ken (air rifle pellets)

K.K. Nihon Ryoju Seiki Seisakusho, 12, Aza Minamigahara Onishi-machi, Okazaki-shi, Aichi-ken (automatic shotguns)

K.K. Sanshin Shojuki Seisakusho, 634, 3-chome Nippori, Arakwa-ku, Tokyo (shotguns)

K.K. Yamamoto Juho Seisakusho, 88, 4-chome Imasato-machi, Higashinari-ku, Osaka (shotguns)

Marusan Seiki Yugen Kaisha, 29, 2-chome Higashiobase Kitano-cho, Higashinari, Osaka (shotguns, air rifles)

Miroku Firearms Mfg., Co., 180, Inari-cho, Kochi-shi, Kochi-ken (shotguns, pistols)

Naniwa Kogyo K.K., 423, Nonogami, Hahikino-shi, Osaka-fu (shotguns, air rifles)

Nihon Juho Kogyosho, Shimogo, Iwama-machi, Nishi Ibaragi-gun, Ibaragi-ken (air rifles, shotguns)

Nikkosha Ryodan Kogyo K.K., 27, 1-chome Miyakojima-hondori, Miyakojima-ku, Osaka (shot)

Nippo Kogyo Co. Ltd., 118, Kami-cho, Idogaya, Minami-ku, Yokohama (shotgun shells)

Nippon Juki Co., Ltd., 22, Ikenouchi-cho, Nishinokyo, Nakayo-ku, Kyoto (shotguns, rifles, air rifles)

Nippon Oils & Fats Co., Ltd., Tokyo Building, 2, 3-chome Marunouchi, Chiyoda-ku, Tokyo (gunpowder)

Olin-Kodensha Co., Ltd., 1225, Sonobe-cho, Tochigi-shi, Tochigi-ken (shotguns)

Sanwa Seisakusho, 1618, Ohhasu, Fuse-shi, Osaka-fu (air rifle pellets)

Sasaki Seiju Kayakuten, 34-18, 1-chome Amanuma, Suginami-ku, Tokyo (shotguns, air rifles)

Sharp Rifle Mfg. Co., Ltd., 8, 2-chome Yotsuya, Shinjuku-ku, Tokyo (rifles, air rifles, rifle scopes)

Shimada Seisakusho, 1396, Ohhasu, Fuse-chi, Osaka-fu (pellets)

Shimaya Seisakusho, 51, 2-chome Nishiimazato-cho, Higashinari-ku, Osaka (air rifles)

Shinbisha Air-Rifle Mfg. Co., 319, 2-chome Komagome, Toshima-ku, Tokyo (rifles, air rifles)

Shin Chuo Kogyo K.K., 18-18, 4-chome Omori-Nishi, Ota-ku, Tokyo (shotguns, pistols)

SKB Arms Co., Sampuku Building, 5, 4-chome Ginza, Chuo-ku, Tokyo (shotguns, air rifles)

Teikoku Kahohin Mfg. Co., Ltd., 18, 2-chome Marunouchi, Chiyoda-ku, Tokyo (percussion caps)

Washino Kinzoku Kogyosho, 11, 3-chome Ajiro, Fuse-chi, Osaka-fu (air rifle pellets)

Watanabe Seisakusho Co., Ltd., 231, Koun-cho, Maebashi-shi, Gunma-ken (shotgun parts)

Yoshizawa Shoten Co., Ltd., 8, Saya-cho, Takasaki-chi, Gunma-ken (shotgun shells)

Yugen Kaisha Shoki Seisakusho, 1146, Higashiura-machi, Utsunomiya-shi, Tochigi-ken (shot)

YSS Fire Arms Co., Ltd., 635, Ohsone-cho, Kohoku-ku, Yokohama (rifles)

## MEXICO

Armamex, S.A., Mexico, D.F.
Cartuchos Deportivos de Mexico, S.A., Cuernavaca, Morelos
Fabrica de Armas Llama, S.A., Mexico, D.F.
Fabrica Nacional de Armas, Mexico, D.F. (Government)
La Cazadora, S.A., Mexico, D.F.
Productos Mendoza, S.A., Mexico, D.F.
Sucesor de Angel Adame Laje, Mexico, D.F.

## NEW ZEALAND

Colonial Ammunition Co., Ltd., Normandy Road, Mt. Eden C3, Auckland

## NORWAY

Kongsberg Vapenfabrikk, Kongsberg
Raufoss Ammunisjonsfabrikker, Raufoss

## PHILIPPINES

Squires Bingham Mfg. Co., Inc., Marikina, Rizal

## SPAIN

Pedro Arosa Aguirre, Santa Ana 10, Elgoibar
Alkatsuna Fabrica de Armas, Guernica
Hijos de v. Armaberri y Cia, P.O. Box 55, Eibar
Aguirre y Aranzabal, Eibar (Guipuzcoa)
Eusebio Arizaga, 30 Fuenterrabia St., San Sebastian
Echaza Echave Arizmendi y Cia S.A., Ubicha, Eibar
Norberto Arizmendi y Cia., S.R.C., Apartado 68, Eibar (Guipuzcoa)
Union Armeria S.L., Eibar
Astra Unceta y Cia, Apartado 3, Guernica (Vizcaya)
Armas Bost, S.L., P.O. Box 47, Eibar
Centro de Estudios Tecnicos de Materiales Especiales, Madrid
Industrias Danok, Barrio San Lorenzo, 38-Vergara, Guipuzcoa
Star Bonifacio Echeverria S.A., Eibar
Egan, Elqueta, Eibar
Armas EGO, Macharia 1, Eibar
Trust Eibarres S.A., Apartado De Correos 32, Eibar (Guipuzcoa)
Armas Erbi, S.C.I., P.O. Box 45, Elgoibar
Gabilondo y Cia, P.O. Box 2, Elgoibar
El Gamo, Industias, San Baudilio de Leobrezat
La Industrial Guipuzcoana, Elgoibar
Crucelegui Hermanos, P.O. Box 13, Eibar
Zabala Hermanos, S.R.C., P.O. Box 97, Eibar
Armas "Jacob," Elgueta, Eibar
Miguel Larranaga, Guipuzcoa
Laurona, Muzatequi, Eibar
Armas Marixa, Eibar
Felix Sarasqueta y Cia, Apartado 233, Eibar
Victor Sarasqueta, S.A., Apartado 25, Eibar
Sarriugarte, Elgoibar
I. Ugartechea, Eibar
Jose Uriquen, Urquizu 2, Eibar
Armas de Tiro y Caza, Eibar

## SWEDEN

Carl Gustafs Stads Gevarsfaktori, Eskilstuna (Swedish Government)
Nitro Nobel, A.B., 71030 Gyttorp
Norma Projektilfabrik; 67040 Amotfors
Vanasverken, Karlsborg (Swedish Government)
Husqvarna Vapenfabriks Aktiebolag, Huskvarna

## SWITZERLAND

W. Glaser, Loewenstrasse, 8001 Zurich
Hammerli Jagd und Sportwaffenfabrik A.G., 5600 Lenzburg
Schweizerische Industrie-Gesellschaft, 8212 Neuhausen am Rheinfall
Eidgenossische Waffenfabrik, 3000 Bern 22
Eidgenossischen Munitionsfabrik Altdorf, Altdorf (Swiss Government)
Eidgenossischen Munitionsfabrik Thun, 3600 Thun (Swiss Government)
Andrae Tanner, Werkst. f. Prazisionswaffen, 4854 Fulenbach
W. Wuthrich Jagd. v. Sportwaffen, 3432 Lutzelfluh

## URUGUAY

Armeria El Cazador, Uruguay 868, Montevideo
Armeria "El Ciervo", Sarandi 683, Montevideo

# INTRODUCTION

## Used Firearms Prices Are On The Rise Like Everything Else, But There Are Ways To Avoid Being Burned!

IN PAST editions of this volume, we have attempted to offer realistic selling prices for used guns. Keep in mind that the prices listed throughout are *retail* prices at the time the book went to press.

In the two earlier editions of this book, incidentally, no firearms manufactured prior to 1925 were listed. The theory then was that any gun more than fifty years old was more likely to be considered a collector item than a proper usin' firearm. That theory still holds true to a degree, of course, and a number of the firearms listed in this edition do have collector value, which we have noted in most cases.

Collector interest, however, does not always keep those firearms from being used in the field or kept in a nightstand for self-protection should the need arise. Any number of the firearms manufactured in the first quarter of this century are not likely to be found in the used gun racks of your local gun shop, but they do turn up occasionally and no doubt there are literally thousands of them still tucked away in attics, behind farmhouse doors and in the backs of closets. That much has been made obvious by some of the mail we have received, the writers wanting to know why a specific firearm was not included in our reviews.

We have, however, drawn some other parameters as to what should and should not be included in this volume. For example, we deliberately have ignored most of the military arms that ended up in the surplus warehouses of two decades ago. Today, the vast majority of these are in the hands of military collectors. For the most part, we have ignored the paramilitary arms that resemble military automatic weaponry, even though they may be limited to semiauto fire. We choose to feel that the average citizen walking into a gun shop to seek out a firearm for sport or self-protection is not interested in replacing the late John Wayne via neighborhood image or looking like a refugee from a mercenary rabble. Call it a matter of personal taste, if you like.

In developing input for this edition, we noted with something approaching awe the manner in which some firearms had jumped in price since our last edition was published. Not only have prices increased, but from one geographic area to another there often is a broad price spread. And the more desirable or rare the firearm involved, the broader the price range is likely to be.

In this era of rapid inflation, the value of used firearms seems to have escalated rapidly for several reasons. Obviously, prices have increased to match the climb of the inflation spiral as is the case with virtually any mechanical device. More important, perhaps, is the current high price tag for newly manufactured firearms. One has only to compare the original retail prices of 1970 or even 1975 firearms with the over-the-counter asking prices of today for identical models.

As a result, anyone who has not kept pace with what is happening with prices and who has been contemplating the purchase of a new shotgun, rifle or handgun usually is stunned by the retail price tag. That is when a potential buyer checks the used firearms market in an effort to lower the expense of his purchase.

And, as with most other consumer goods, value in used guns always is influenced by the law of supply and demand. Any time demand tends to increase, the value of the available supply will show an increase in nearly direct ratio. Therefore, as more people buy used firearms, the available supply diminishes and, consequently, the price increases more rapidly than would be normally expected.

The recent announcement that Olin Industries is putting the firearms manufacturing segment of Winchester on the block is creating a run on classic Winchester designs. No one knows what will happen to the current designs once the name is purchased by a new entity. Thus, if some designs eventually no longer are manufactured, it is felt that collector value of those currently in manufacture will increase severalfold.

In contacting gun dealers about the country to aid in determining current price structures, it was emphasized that the prices would be based upon "NRA Very Good" guidelines.

In some areas, geographic considerations do affect the sale price. For example, the theory in Texas seems to be that the more it shoots, the better it is. A single-shot rifle or shotgun may go begging on Texas gun shop shelves, while an autoloader that shoots lots and fast will be well above the national norm in price. In areas that feature deer hunting as the primary game each Fall, a bolt-action rifle in deer calibers will bring up to $75 more than in a state which limits deer hunting to the use of shotguns.

In many cases, used firearms dealers themselves have created a mystique that may be imaginary. The pre-1964 Winchester Model 70 is a prime example. Some firearms dealers and collectors, as a result of their campaigns, have given this particular rifle super powers.

Admittedly, the Model 70s manufactured after 1964 were different in design, but the shooting qualities changed little. In the pre-1964 era, one gunmaker produced the entire rifle. If you had a good gunmaker, you had a good rifle. If he was relatively new to the business, you might have a less than adequate rifle. We remember one pre-'64 Model 70 that wouldn't hit a bull in the proverbial posterior at fifty yards!

Although not considered to be on the used firearms market at this writing, the 1981 Model 70 is prettier, lighter and probably shoots as well as the average Model 70 of pre-'64 manufacture. It will be interesting to see whether this new version has any effect upon the profit-made mystique that had resulted in the pre-'64 version bringing premium prices.

This volume in all of its three editions has been produced with the shooter rather than the collector in mind. In the matter of collector items, refinishing or adding devices not originally furnished with the firearm, such as variable chokes,

*As the prices of new firearms have tended to skyrocket, the demand for good used guns has increased in proportion.*

or muzzle brakes, may reduce value.

Many of the used guns we see have been modified in some way. Recoil pads are changed often on trap guns; sling swivels often are added to the stocks of both high-power and smallbore rifles, and grips — custom-made or whittled out of the nearest available two-by-four — have been changed on many handguns on the used gun racks of the country.

In most cases, these efforts detract from the ultimate value of the gun, especially if not installed correctly. If corrective gunsmithing work is evident, it should be noted how well the work has been accomplished. Poor work in either repair or refinishing reduces resale value.

Customized firearms, however, always appear to be a hot item. For obvious reasons, we have not attempted to list these in this volume: the variations can be endless. However, the more famous and respected the individual who has worked on a fine firearm, the more valuable it becomes. This gun becomes, in many cases, a personalized work of art. One only has to look to recognize the beautiful lines of a Jerry Fisher stock or the graceful yet functional appearance and feel of a .45 auto reworked by Armand Swenson. These master gunsmiths integrate their knowledge and skills into final products that become valuable because of their beauty.

If you are buying a piece that is alleged to be a product of a famed customizer, be certain you are buying the genuine article. Demand full documentation and, if not certain, check with those familiar with the craftsman's work.

There probably is no greater destroyer of value than the act of rebluing a gun. Especially from the collector's standpoint, this is a disaster that greatly reduces value. The average shooter may not care whether a firearm has been reblued, but he should — and here's why:

Resale of the blued gun — whether rifle, shotgun or handgun — will prove more difficult, as the potential buyer will be asking why it was reblued in the first place. In most instances, guns are reblued either because of carelessness or long use. If the exterior was damaged, what about the inside?

When purchasing a used firearm, check carefully for buffed-down lettering, rounded corners and blued-over scratches and dents. If you find such indications, it's not the greatest deal in the world.

**The author and publishers of this book are in no position to offer individual advice as to the value of that old gun you dug out of the closet. You'll find qualified folks a lot closer to home who can give you a proper appraisal. Please — repeat, please — do not ask us to evaluate your rusty old gun that came out of the family well!**

**Nor are we in the gun business; we are in the publishing field. Therefore, none of the prices included herein constitute an offer by either author or publishers to buy the guns listed at prices quoted.**

**Finally, keep in mind that the prices of virtually all of these firearms will continue to rise as inflation continues. A fair rule of thumb is to add ten percent a year to values shown. It will be noted of course, that some firearms have not increased by that percentage. A poor gun still is a poor gun and no amount of increased inflation is going to make it particularly valuable.**

# HANDGUNS

# The Realistic Value Of A Handgun Is The Result Of Many Complex Interacting Factors

**B**ROWSING THROUGH old gun catalogs of the Thirties or Forties, is apt to prove a painful experience for the present-day handgun aficionado. A great many of the guns illustrated in such yellowing pages have become discontinued long since and now eagerly sought by collectors. Even beyond the pangs of nostalgia aroused by re-encountering the choice old classics, there is the startling effect of the prices quoted for them.

If you happen to have been around in those troubled times, a bit of recollection can serve to put those old, low prices back into reasonably plausible perspective. At the time when a brand new Colt Single Action Army revolver was offered for $34, you could buy six, eight, sometimes ten pounds of bananas for a quarter, and choice steak was perhaps two bits a pound, with hamburger proportionately

*A vintage example of the Colt SAA in .45 Colt, with 4¾" barrel and genuine mother-of-pearl grips.*

less. Average incomes were in line with the same scale. As a result, some of those eye-popping prices represented the greater part of a month's wages, or more, for the would-be buyer of the time. As you stop to think about it, not too many guns down to the present carry price tags larger than what a typical wage-earner is paid in a month.

Even so, if you had the foresight to purchase some carefully selected handguns over the course of the past few decades, a thoughtful examination of a gundealer's handgun display counter can make your head swim a little. The identical twin to a gun you may have purchased for twenty-five to sixty dollars may carry an asking price of $300, $450, or even more.

The complication of assigning a firm value to a given gun lies in the condition of the gun, to a considerable degree, and makes the further assumption that there is someone, somewhere, who might go as high as the quoted figure. As has been noted elsewhere, the prices assigned to the various guns in this book presume that the gun, if used, is

still in what the trade terms "NRA Very Good" condition. Given that assumption, the quoted price represents approximately the upper retail level of the price structure.

That does not mean that you are apt to be able to take a gun to a dealer and exchange it for the full price quoted here. The dealer must put the gun on display for some indeterminate time and, when he sells it, must get more money than he paid for it. Failure to do so in the majority of transactions will put a dealer out of business in short order.

As an illustrative example, the Colt Officers' Model revolver in .38 Special, with a six-inch heavy barrel, in 1935, was listed new at $40.75. In the

*A Colt .38 Special Officers' Model, with heavy barrel, produced about 1935, as discussed in nearby text.*

previous edition of the present book, its value was given as $220 to $230. The gun illustrated here is not quite up to NRA VG status. It shows a minor amount of holster wear, with the admirable Colt bluing turning a bit silver at the sides of the muzzle and on the sharper edges. The action is just a bit loose, so as to require competent professional attention to restore the impressive accuracy for which the original gun was noted.

Under the conditions noted, the gun had languished in the display case of a Southern California dealer since some point prior to 1978. It carried a price tag of $245, probably representing quite close to the top obtainable dollar for that particular gun. Potential buyers came and went past the display case, adding up to platoons and regiments. Some asked to see it, then handed it back to the clerk with a request to view some other gun. The asking price was so high that no one wanted it, quite that badly.

Now, a gun on display doesn't consume much hay, and no oats at all — not even if it's a Colt — but you cannot display one indefinitely without out-of-pocket expense. For but one item, there is the matter of annual inventory tax, which may have been paid three or four times on the gun under discussion. In addition, there is that highly tangible consideration known as overhead: heat, lights, other utilities, insurance, store rental and so on, endlessly.

Thus it came at length to pass that a member of this book's production staff visited the store. Having more than the usual appreciation for Colt guns of nearly any nature, with special emphasis upon those of Thirties' vintage, the staffer had mooned over the HB Officers' Model on each of several prior visits. Entering the store, there was always the speculation as to whether the gun would still be there. Eventually — partially for the sake of eliminating the agonizing suspense — upon finding it still there, he launched spirited negotiations, of the sort highly familiar to dedicated guntraders, and was able to talk the asking price down to the level where it was within reach, although just barely so.

When the gun first went on display, suggestions as to a lowered price would have been dismissed brusquely. If you're prepared to gamble that some well-heeled shopper might snap it away beyond your reach, it's effective strategy to let it age on the dealer's shelf for a few years; it makes them much more prone to take interest in the discussion.

Apart from individual condition and preservation, as well as the esteem and charisma that the gun-buying public attaches to a given make and model, another factor affecting the value of a given gun is its caliber: the cartridge for which it is designed and chambered. In certain instances, that can make a substantial difference. It is a consideration of much less importance to a collector than to the potential buyer who may be considering the gun from the viewpoint of a shooter.

An example of the difference that the caliber can make would be the Colt Pocket Model auto pistols, sometimes termed the Model 1903. Made with minor changes in barrel length and specifications for

*Re-bluing reduces value, but .380 auto is preferred caliber for the Colt Model 1903 Pocket Model; photo is an old one.*

some forty-two years, they were offered in two chamberings: .32 auto and .380 auto. The .32 version seems to have been vastly more popular, perhaps because the .380 cartridge had not achieved its current level of acceptance in the 1903 to 1945 interlude of the gun's production. It is still reasonably common to see Model 1903 pistols displayed for sale in dealers' displays, even down to the present. If you spot one, however, it's an attractive bet that it will turn out to be of the .32 chambering. The .380 version is much scarcer, and usually commands a somewhat better price, as a result.

As a single factor, age alone has no more than limited bearing upon the realistic value of a handgun. As one dealer puts it, "Junk is junk, and it remains junk forever!" The amount of talent, artistry and dogged dedication to the highest possible level of quality is a factor that exerts a direct and powerful effect upon the value set upon a gun by the buying public. If the design and workmanship are of the highest standards, the intrinsic desirability of the gun can be given a further substantial boost if some external factor adds further to its glamor and charisma in the mind of the gunbuying public.

Consider the example of the S&W Model 29 .44 magnum revolver. Introduced in 1956 as a slightly elongated and beefed-up offshoot of the .44

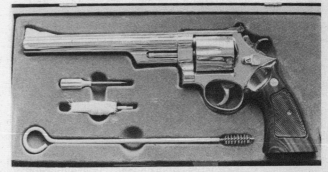

*The S&W M29, here with 8-3/8" barrel and nickel finish, commands a premium price for reasons noted.*

Special — in much the same manner that the .357 magnum was derived from the .38 Special, twenty-one years earlier — the .44 magnum was touted as the "World's most powerful handgun," and with a reasonable degree of justification. That gave it a considerable amount of clout, in its own right, although dealers became accustomed to buyers who'd fetch the new gun back, along with most of the cartridges still in the first box of ammo they'd bought. Could they, perhaps, trade it back in on some slightly less devastating caliber? Preferably, something with considerably less blast and kick?

After some fourteen or fifteen years of doing

fairly well in the marketplace, a film called *Dirty Harry* was released, starring Clint Eastwood and co-starring the .44 magnum Model 29 Smith & Wesson. As an advertising boost for the Model 29, it was a real stunner. For the next few years after the film's release, it was fairly common practice for dealers to tack another few hundred dollars onto the suggested retail price of any Model 29s they could get. Even so, the guns sold, and didn't seem to be brought back for swapping-in purposes as often as before, although it usually took a lengthy while for the buyer to use up the first box of cartridges. The .44 magnum is not exactly your ideal fun-and-plinking cartridge, Clint Eastwood notwithstanding!

A similar factor probably influenced the singular — no pun intended — fluctuation in value of the Colt Single Action Army (SAA) revolvers during the Fifties. Television had become a powerful new influence in moulding the public tastes and fancies. Among the viewing offerings, there were a number of highly popular shows built around the Early West motif, featuring the Colt SAA with rather heavy emphasis. It was hardly surprising, under the circumstances, that a great many devotees of the boob-tube began yearning to have a Frontier sixshooter of their own.

Faring forth to pick one up, they discovered that the legendary Peacemaker hadn't been returned to production after WWII had come to its cataclysmic conclusion. There simply was nowhere nearly as many Colt SAA revolvers as there were eager shoppers. Prices on the available guns went absurdly berserk: ranging to around $400 or $500 at a time when that was still an impressively substantial amount of money.

Foreign makers commenced production of reasonably plausible facsimiles of the Colt SAA, and those sold briskly. Colt saw the handwriting on the wall, sighed and dug out the tooling to put the venerable hogleg back on the line. The day of the $34 brand-new Colt SAA, however, had vanished with the era of the free lunch and the nickel beer. At press time for this edition, the suggested retail price for new Colt SAAs ranges across a span from $480 to $572, and Colt is now phasing it back out of production for the second time. As to what manner of prices well-preserved Colt SAAs may bring in the decades ahead, that's anyone's starry-eyed guess.

The presence of an organized and eager cadre of brand-oriented collectors can and does exert considerable influence upon the value of that maker's products, and even upon some of the unshootable spinoffs of the operation. A salient example of that would be the Ruger Collectors of America (RCA), with an evergrowing number of members intently bent upon accumulating not only Ruger firearms, but the myriad assortment of artifacts associated with the operations of Sturm, Ruger & Company.

A recent edition of the RCA Journal listed the going market values of collectible memorabilia, with $250 as the figure set for one of the little necktie clips featuring a small model of the .22 Standard Ruger auto, with movable bolt. In light of the fact that the forty-five-year-old Colt OM/HB, mentioned earlier, had languished unbought in the case for years, carrying a price tag slightly lower, that may seem more than slightly inexplicable, but it serves to point up the considerable disparity in viewpoints between the shooter and the collector. To an outsider, the rationale of the collector is difficult to fathom, with stamp collectors sometimes paying $1000 or more for a specimen that won't even carry a letter through the postal system!

Does rarity correlate with value, then? Not necessarily, by any means. Getting a new gun into production and making a profit on it is a game with steep stakes, and many hopefuls don't last for more than a few hands. There are any number of guns that never saw but limited production, but it's unusual to find them bringing prices much in excess of their intrinsic value as shooting equipment. Indeed, their exotic status may be reflected in a reluctance on the part of the potential buyer to pay a reasonable market price, due to the probably difficulty of obtaining spare parts or repairs in the event of a breakdown.

From the viewpoint of the potential buyer, shooters in particular, an operative consideration is, "Handsome is as handsome shoots." This is seldom more pertinent than in the example of the Colt Government Model auto, variously known as the Model 1911, 1911A1 or by Colt's own designation, the O-frame. The primary handgun of this country's military forces for the past seventy years, a large number of shooters have been exposed to the M1911 in the course of duty with the armed forces. Some — though by no means all — experience a desire to buy one for their own use, and a large number of surplus military guns found new owners via distribution through the Director of Civilian Marksmanship (DCM) at super-friendly costs down around $20 apiece, or a bit less.

Even as recently as fifteen or twenty years ago, it was not uncommon to take over ownership of a Model 1911 or its improved version, the M1911A1 for prices that seem a bit incredible in retrospect. Even the more desirable commercial version, with its prefix or suffix letter -C on the serial number, brought around $45 in good, used condition, and not too briskly, either. By the end of the Seventies, values had escalated about tenfold, so that almost any operational M1911/A1 seemed about as eminently grabbable at $250 as it had been at $25, a decade or two earlier.

The typical GI .45 auto, as issued, tends to be pretty casual as to grouping abilities, as many a chagrined recruit can testify. More, it is a difficult and challenging gun to fire accurately, even at best. Despite that, it can be made to deliver performance that beggars belief, although it takes a lot of doing. The process of improving guns such as the M1911 series is known by the informal and somewhat dubious term of "accurizing," a word you may have difficulty finding in most dictionaries.

A gun that has been efficiently and effectively accurized is worth considerably more than one of its unmodified contemporaries. That constitutes one of the few exceptions to the general rule that any departure from out-of-the-box newness tends to decrease the value of a gun.

Regional variations have a decided effect upon the going market price for certain guns, in many instances. Guns made of stainless steel tend to bring markedly higher prices in coastal regions or areas subject to heavy rain or humidity, where their superior resistance to corrosion puts a premium upon their value. In Alaska, as another example, the .44 magnum revolver, or other handguns of approximately equal capability, is considered to be a basic necessity by many, if venturing amid the domains of bears or similarly hostile fauna. As you might expect, such guns bring higher prices in light of special conditions of that nature.

Barrel length, as a factor in its own right, can and does affect the value of those guns that are available with barrels of different lengths. The

shorter barrels, prized for their compactness and superior concealability, tend to be in short supply and command a modest premium in price as a result. In some instances, such as the S&W M27 and M29, the longer barrel 8-3/8 inches, or even more — likewise bring higher prices.

There has been a fairly recent trend to make considerable modifications on existing revolvers, thereby converting them into what is usually termed a customized combat gun, for use in simulated combat target competition. The modification consists of replacing the factory barrel with a considerably heavier bull barrel,

*A custom combat conversion by Austin F. Behlert on a S&W K-38 is typical of such guns, as discussed.*

circular or square in cross-section. Such barrels usually are of premium grade and may employ a pitch of rifling different from the factory barrels. The usual pitch used in S&W .38 Special barrels is one turn in 18.75 inches, or 1:18.75, as it's customarily written. Custom barrels with a 1:14 rifling pitch have been found to deliver substantially better accuracy in many instances. In addition to re-barreling, combat customization usually includes meticulous adjustment of the cylinder timing and smoothing of the trigger mechanism.

The cost of combat customizing frequently runs from $200 to $400 or more, when performed upon a gun supplied by the customer. If we assume a base price on the gun of $250 or so, that results in an investment of several hundred dollars, not all of which may prove easily recoverable if the gun is put up for sale. Another modification usually made in such guns is replacing the sights, and it's fairly often the practice to install sights designed so that, when aiming at the head area of the silhouette target, the bullet strikes the high scoring area of the target near what would be the solar plexus on an actual adversary.

It is obvious that such a wall-eyed sight system would be disconcerting and impractical for handgunning applications other than the specialized field of combat competition, and the prospective purchaser of guns thus modified would do well to find out whether the sights are for

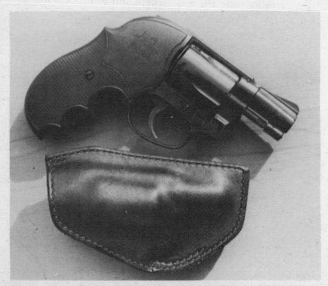

*Shorter barrels remain in brisk demand, as in this Chiefs Special by S&W, with Bianchi grips, Safariland holster.*

point-of-aim, or diverging in the manner described.

Several other handgun modifications are possible and are becoming increasingly popular. Again, as in accurized .45 autos and combat customized revolvers, the buyer should realize and accept that the total investment may not be easily recoverable if the gun is sold. In other words, give sober thoughts to the purchase of such guns unless you plan to keep them and use them over an extended period of time. By retaining them, you have the use of them and the opportunity to amortize the cost over several months and, in addition, the painfully reliable forces of inflation will be working for you instead of against you.

One such revolver modification is performed by Leon Smith (TLS Gunsmithing, Box 773, Redding, California 96001) upon the heavy, N-frame, S&W revolvers such as the Model 28 Highway Patrolman. Smith uses barrel shrouds from Dan Wesson Arms to fit the N-frame S&W with interchangeable barrels of assorted lengths. In the process, he can re-chamber and convert the gun to handle larger cartridges, such as the .41 or .44 magnums, .45 Long Colt, et al. If the basic gun is the Model 28 S&W — usually the least expensive of the N-frames — its slightly shorter cylinder may impose a modest handicap when converted to .41 or .44 magnum by requiring that the longer bullets be seated to a sufficiently short length overall (LOA) to prevent them from projecting out the front of the chambers.

A further factor that may sometimes affect the value of the gun is its serial number, if it's unusually low or impressive and significant in some other manner. Logically, this would have the greatest appeal to the collector rather than the shooter, although even the latter may attach some amount of sentimental value to it, particularly if it complements the serial number of some other similar or identical gun or guns. It is generally agreed that two guns with consecutive serial numbers have a total value somewhat higher than twice the value of either.

In conclusion, though, the individual gunowner who wishes to sell one or more faces the same problem as the gundealer: finding a customer who's willing to pay the asking price. If it's bartered for another gun, that helps bypass the ravages of inflation, as in the example of the boy who traded two $15,000 kittens to another boy for a $30,000 pup!

# ASTRA

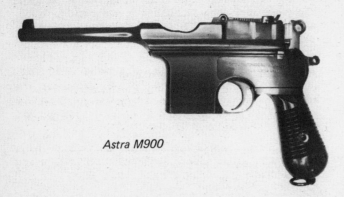

*Astra M900*

**ASTRA Model 900:** Automatic; 7.63mm; 5½" barrel; 11½" overall length; 10-rd. fixed magazine; adjustable rear sight, fixed front; small ring hammer on early models, larger hammer on later; grooved walnut grips; lanyard ring. Based upon design of "broomhandle" Mauser, but has barrel, barrel extension as two parts rather than one as in German Mauser, different lockwork, etc. Introduced in 1928, dropped, 1940. Originally priced at $37; has collector value. Used value, $650 to $750.

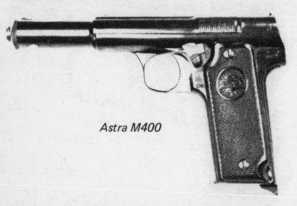

*Astra M400*

**ASTRA Model 400:** automatic; 9mm Bergmann-Bayard; 6" barrel, 10" overall length; 9-rd. magazine; fixed sights; blowback action; some will also chamber and fire 9mm Luger and .38 ACP but it isn't recommended; blued finish; hard rubber or walnut grips. Introduced in 1921; dropped, 1946. Used value, $135 to $150.

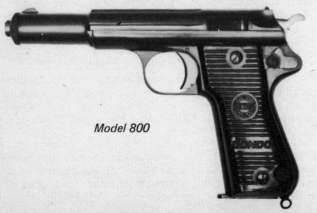

*Model 800*

**ASTRA Model 800:** automatic; also called Condor; 9mm Luger; tubular-type design; 5-5/16" barrel; 8¼" overall length; 8-rd. magazine; fixed sights; blued finish; grooved plastic grips. Based on Model 400 design. Introduced in 1958; dropped, 1968. Few imported; produced primarily for European police, military use. Used value, $400 to $500.

**ASTRA Model 200:** vest pocket automatic; advertised as the Firecat; .25 ACP only; 2¼" barrel, 4-3/8" overall length; 6-rd. magazine; fixed sights; blued finish; plastic grips. Introduced in 1920; still in production; U.S. importation dropped in 1968. Used value, $125 to $165.

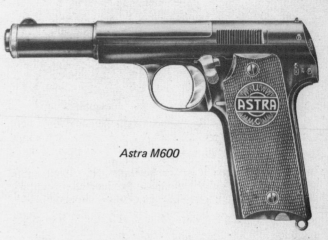

*Astra M600*

**ASTRA Model 600:** military, police automatic; 9mm Luger; 5¼" barrel, 8" overall length; 8 rds.; fixed sights; blued finish, hard rubber or walnut grips. Introduced in 1942; dropped, 1946. Used value, $135 to $150.

**ASTRA 4000:** advertised as Falcon; automatic; .22 LR, .32 auto, .380 auto; 3-2/3" barrel; 6½" overall length; 10-rd. magazine in .22, 8 rds. in .32, 7 rds. in .380; thumb safety; exposed hammer; fixed sights; checkered black plastic grips; blued. Introduced in 1956; U.S. importation dropped, 1968. Used value, $165 to $200; .22 model, $200 to $225.

*Astra M300/3000*

**ASTRA Model 300/3000:** pocket automatic; .32 auto, .380 auto; 4" barrel; 5-3/8" overall length; 7-rd. magazine in .32, 6-rd. in .380; fixed sights, blued finish, hard rubber grips. Introduced in 1922; dropped, 1958. Used value, $175 to $225.

**ASTRA Camper:** Same basic design as Cub, but has 4" barrel, overall length, 6¼"; chambered for .22 short only. Spanish-made. Manufactured 1953 to 1960. Used value, $120 to $125.

*Astra Cub*

**ASTRA Cub:** pocket automatic; .22 short, .25 auto; 2¼" barrel; 4-7/16" overall length; 6-rd. magazine; fixed sights; blued or chrome finish; plastic grips. Introduced in 1957; still in production, but U.S. importation dropped, 1968. Used value, $145 to $165.

*Astra Cadix*

**ASTRA Cadix:** revolver, double action; .22 caliber, 9-rd. cylinder; 5 rds. in .38 Special; 4" or 6" barrel; blued finish; adjustable rear sight, ramp front; checkered plastic stocks. Manufactured 1960 to 1968. Used value, $130 to $140.

*Constable*

**ASTRA Constable:** automatic; .22 LR, .32 ACP, .380 ACP; 3½" barrel; 10-rd. magazine in .22 LR, 8-rd. in .32 ACP, 7 rds. in .380 ACP; adjustable rear sight, fixed front; moulded plastic grips; double action; nonglare rib on slide; quick, no-tool takedown feature; blued or chrome finish except .32, which is no longer available. Current importer is Interarms. Introduced in 1969; still in production. Used values, blued finish, $145 to $165; chrome, $150 to $175.

**ASTRA 357:** revolver; .357 magnum; 3", 4", 6", 8½" barrels; 6-rd. swing-out cylinder; integral rib, ejector rod; click-adjustable rear sight, ramp front; target hammer; checkered walnut grips; blued. Imported by Interarms. Introduced in 1972; still in production. Used value, $125 to $135.

Note: Astra also produced a number of .32 pocket automatics loosely resembling the Colt 1908, .32. Values $100 to $125; and S&W type revolvers, values $75 to $100.

# BAYARD

*Model 1908*

**BAYARD Model 1908:** pocket automatic; .25 auto, .32 auto, .380 auto; 2¼" barrel; 4-7/8" overall length; 6-rd. magazine; fixed sights, blued finish; hard rubber grips. Introduced in 1908; dropped, 1939. Used value, $150 to $225.

**BAYARD Model 1923:** larger model pocket auto; .32 auto, .380 auto, 3-5/16" barrel; 4-5/16" overall length; 6-rd. magazine; fixed sights; blued finish, checkered grips of hard rubber. Introduced in 1923; dropped, 1930. Used value, $150 to $175.

**BAYARD Model 1923:** small model pocket auto; .25 auto only; 2-1/8" barrel; 4-5/16" overall length; fixed sights, blued finish; checkered grips of hard rubber. Scaled-down model of large Model 1923. Introduced in 1923; dropped, 1940. Used value, $175 to $200.

**BAYARD Model 1930:** pocket auto; .25 auto; has same general specifications as small Model 1923 auto pistol with improvements in finish, internal mechanism. Introduced in 1930; dropped, 1940. Used value, $200 to $225.

# BERETTA

*Beretta M1915*

**BERETTA Model 1915:** automatic; .32 auto; 9mm Glisenti; 8-rd. magazine; 6" overall; 3-1/3" barrel; blued finish, fixed sights; grooved wooden stocks. Italian-made. Smaller caliber manufactured 1915 to 1930; 9mm Glisenti, 1915 to 1919. Used value, $185 to $200.

*Beretta 1919*

**BERETTA 1919:** pocket-type automatic; .25 auto only; 3½" barrel; 5¾" overall length; 8-rd. magazine; fixed sights; plastic grips; blued. Introduced in 1919, with several modifications (later version pictured); dropped, 1945. Used values: pre-WWII commercial model, $150 to $175; WWII model, $135 to $150.

**BERETTA Model 1923:** automatic; 9mm Glisenti; 8-rd. magazine; 6½" overall; 4" barrel; blued finish, fixed sights; plastic stocks. Manufactured 1923 to 1936. Used value, $185 to $200.

**BERETTA Model 318:** automatic; .25 Auto; 8-rd. magazine; 4½" overall; 2½" barrel; weighs 14 ounces; blued finish, fixed sights; plastic stocks. Manufactured 1934 to 1939. Used value, $145 to $150.

*Beretta Cougar*

**BERETTA Cougar also Model 1934 or 934:** pocket-type automatic; .380 auto, .32 auto; 3-3/8" barrel, 5-7/8" overall length; 7-rd. magazine; fixed sights; plastic grips; thumb safety; blued or chrome finish. Official Italian service sidearm in WWII; wartime version lacks quality of commercial model. Introduced in 1934; not legally importable; still in production. Used values: WWII model, $150 to $175; commercial model, blued, $175 to $225; nickel finished, $200 to $225.

*Beretta M70 Puma*

**BERETTA Model 70 Puma:** pocket-type automatic; .32 auto only; 4" barrel; 6" overall length; 8-rd. magazine; fixed sights; plastic grips; crossbolt safety; blued, chrome-finish. Introduced in 1934; dropped, 1968. Used values: blued, $125 to $150; chrome finish, $140 to $160.

**BERETTA 25:** pocket-type automatic; .25 auto only; 2½" barrel; 4½" overall length; 8-rd. magazine; fixed sights; plastic grips; blued. Introduced in 1948; not importable, dropped, 1968. Used value, $140 to $175.

*949 Olympian*

**BERETTA Model 949 Olympionico:** target automatic; .22 short only; 8¾" barrel; 12½" overall length; 5-rd. magazine; target sights; adjustable barrel weight; muzzle brake; hand-checkered walnut thumbrest grips; blued. Introduced in 1949; dropped, 1968. Used value, $250 to $275.

*Beretta M950B*

**BERETTA Model 950B Minx M2:** automatic; .22 short only; 2-3/8" barrel; 4¾" overall length; 6-rd. magazine; rear sight milled in slide; fixed front; black plastic grips; blued. Introduced in 1950. Used value, $150 to $165.

Minx M4 has the same specifications as Model M2, except for 4" barrel. Introduced in 1956. Used value, $150 to $165. Neither model importable since 1968.

*Beretta M950*

**BERETTA Model 950B Jetfire:** automatic; .25 auto; 2-3/8" barrel; 4¾" overall length; 7-rd. magazine; has the same general specifications as Minx M2. Introduced in 1950; not importable since 1968. Used value, $145 to $165.

*Beretta M951*

**BERETTA Model 951:** automatic; 9mm Luger; 4½" barrel; 8" overall length; advertised originally as Brigadier model; 8-rd. magazine; external hammer; cross-bolt safety; slide stays open after last shot; fixed sights; moulded grooved plastic grips; blued. Introduced in 1951; still in production. Used value, $250 to $265.

*Beretta M71*

**BERETTA Model 71 and Model 72 Jaguar Plinker:** automatic; .22 LR only; 3½" (Mod. 71), or 6" (Mod. 72) barrels; 8-rd. magazine; rear sight milled in slide, fixed front; checkered plastic grips; blued. Introduced in 1956; dropped, 1968. Used value, $135 to $150.

Jaguar Model 101 has the same general specifications as Jaguar Plinker, except for 6" barrel only; overall length, 8¾"; adjustable rear sight; wrap-around checkered plastic grips; lever thumb safety. Introduced in 1969; still in production. Used value, $150 to $165.

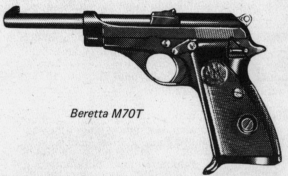

*Beretta M70T*

**BERETTA Model 70T:** automatic; .32 auto; 6" barrel; 8½" overall length; 9-rd. magazine; adjustable rear sight, fixed front; external hammer; slide stays open after last shot; checkered plastic wrap-around grips. Introduced in 1969; dropped, 1975. Used value, $135 to $145.

*Beretta M90*

**BERETTA Model 90:** double-action automatic; .32 auto; 3-5/8" barrel; 6¾" overall length; 8-rd. magazine; fixed sights, matted rib on slide; chamber-loaded indicator; external hammer; stainless steel barrel; moulded plastic wrap-around grips; blued. Introduced in 1969; still in production. Used value, $165 to $170.

**BERETTA Model 70S:** automatic; .380 auto; 3-5/8" barrel; 6½" overall length; 7-rd. magazine; external hammer; fixed sights; checkered plastic wrap-around grips; blued. Introduced in 1971; still in production. Used value, $135 to $145.

*Beretta M76*

# BERNARDELLI

*Bernardelli Vest Pocket Model*

**BERETTA Model 76:** automatic; .22 LR only; 6" barrel; 9½" overall length; 10-rd. magazine; adjustable rear sight, interchangeable blade front; non-glare, ribbed slide; heavy barrel; external hammer; checkered plastic wraparound grips; blued. Introduced in 1971; still in production. Used value, $225 to $245.

**BERETTA Model 81:** automatic, double-action; .32 Auto; 12-rd. magazine; 6.8" overall; 3.8" barrel; blued finish, fixed sights; plastic stocks. Introduced in 1976. Still in production. Used value, $180 to $190.

**BERNARDELLI Vest Pocket Model:** automatic; .22 LR, .25 auto; 2-1/8" barrel; 4-1/8" overall length; 6-rd. magazine in .22, 5-rd. in .25; 8-rd. extension magazine also available in .25; no sights, but sighting groove milled in slide; plastic grips; blued. Introduced in 1948; U.S. importation dropped, 1968. Used value, $150 to $165.

**BERNARDELLI Standard:** automatic; .22 LR only, 6" 8", 10" barrels; with 10" barrel, 13" overall length; 10-rd. magazine; target sights; adjustable sight ramp; walnut target grips; blued. Introduced in 1949; still in production. Used value, $150 to $165.

*Beretta M84*

*Bernardelli M80*

**BERETTA Model 84:** automatic; same as Model 81, except in .380 Auto, with 13-rd. magazine. Introduced in 1976. Still in production. Used value, $180 to $190.

*Beretta M92*

**BERNARDELLI Model 80:** automatic; .22 LR, .32 Auto, .380 Auto; .22 magazine holds 10 rds., .32 holds 8, .380 holds 8; 6½" overall, 3½" barrel; blued finish, adjustable rear sight, white dot front, thumb-rest plastic stocks. Introduced 1968 as modification of Model 60 to meet U.S. import requirements. Used value, $135 to $155.

    **Model 90** has same specs, except for 9" overall length, 6" barrel. Introduced, 1968. Still in production. Used value, $120 to $130.

*Model 100*

**BERETTA Model 92:** automatic, double-action; 9mm Luger; 15-rd. magazine; 8½" overall; 5" barrel; blued finish, fixed sights, plastic stocks. Introduced in 1976. Still in production. Used value, $260 to $275.

**BERNARDELLI Model 100:** automatic, target model; .22 LR only; 10-rd. magazine; 9" overall; 6" barrel; blued finish, adjustable rear sight, interchangeable front; checkered thumb-rest walnut stocks. Introduced in 1969 as Model 68; still in production. Used value, $215 to $235.

*Browning 380*

*Bernardelli Match 22*

**BERNARDELLI Match 22:** automatic .22 LR only; 5¾" barrel; 9" overall length; 10-rd. magazine; manual, magazine safeties; external hammer; adjustable rear sight, post front; hand-checkered thumbrest walnut grips; blued. Introduced in 1971; replaced by Model 100. Used value, $125 to $140.

# BROWNING

*Browning Hi-Power 9mm*

**BROWNING Hi-Power 9mm:** automatic; 9mm Luger only; 4-5/8" barrel, 7¾" overall length; based on Browning-Colt .45 auto; adjustable or fixed rear sight; checkered walnut grips; thumb, magazine safeties; external hammer with half-cock safety feature; blued finish; 13-rd. magazine. Introduced in 1935; still in production. Used value, $350 to $375; with adjustable rear sight, $400 to $425.

**Hi-Power Renaissance** model has the same specifications as standard model, except for chrome-plated finish, full engraving, polyester pearl grips. Introduced in 1954; still in production. Used value, $1200 to $1250.

**BROWNING 380:** automatic; .380, .32 ACP, 3-7/16" barrel, 6" overall length; 9-rd. magazine; pre-'68 models, fixed sights, now adjustable; hard rubber grips; blued finish. Introduced 1910, and a longer barreled version in 1922, redesigned in 1968; still in production. Used value, $275 to

$285 except WWII manufacture, $225 to $235. Current models have 4½" barrel, are 7" overall.

**The 380 Renaissance** model has the same specifications as the standard Browning 380, except for chrome-plated finish, full engraving, polyester pearl grips. Introduced in 1954, still in production. Used value, $1100 to $1150.

*Browning M1906*

**BROWNING Model 1906 .25 Automatic:** .25 ACP only; 2" barrel; 4½" overall length; 6-rd. magazine; fixed sights; blued or nickel finish; hard rubber grips. Almost identical to Colt Vest Pocket .25 auto. Introduced in 1906; dropped, 1940. Used value, $300 to $325.

*Browning 25 "Baby"*

**BROWNING 25 "Baby":** automatic; .25 ACP only; 2-1/8" barrel; 4" overall length; 6-rd. magazine; fixed sights, hard rubber grips; blued finish. Introduced in 1940; dropped, not importable, 1968. Used value, $265 to $275.

**Browning 25 Lightweight** has the same general specifications as the standard model, except that it is chrome plated, has polyester pearl grips, alloy frame. Introduced in 1954; dropped, 1968. Used value, $265 to $275.

**Browning 25 Renaissance Model** has the same specifications as the standard Browning 25, except for chrome-plated finish, polyester pearl grips, full engraving. Introduced in 1954; dropped, 1968. Used value, $1200 to $1250.

*Browning Medalist*

**BROWNING Renaissance Set:** includes Renaissance versions of Hi-Power 9mm, 380 Automatic, 25 Automatic in a specially fitted walnut case. Oddly, value depends to a degree upon condition of the case. Introduced in 1954; dropped, 1968. Used value, $3500 to $4000.

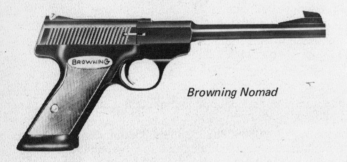

*Browning Nomad*

**BROWNING Nomad:** automatic; .22 LR only; 4½", 6¾" barrels; overall length, 8-15/16" with 4½" barrel; 10-rd. magazine; screw adjustable rear sight, removable blade front; brown plastic grips; blued finish. Introduced in 1962; dropped, 1973. Used value, $200 to $225.

**BROWNING Challenger:** automatic; .22 LR only; 4½", 6¾" barrels; overall length, 11-7/16" with 6¾" barrel; 10-rd. magazine; screw-adjustable rear sight, removable blade front; hand-checkered walnut grips, blued finish. Introduced in 1962; dropped, 1974. Used value, $275 to $300. Reintroduced as Challenger II in 1978. Same values.

    **Challenger Gold Model** has the same general specifications as standard Browning Challenger, except for gold wire inlays in metal; figured, hand-carved, checkered walnut grips. Introduced in 1971; dropped, 1974. Used value, $650 to $700.

    **Challenger Renaissance Model** has the same exact specifications as standard Challenger, except for chrome-plated finish, full engraving, top-grade, hand-carved, figured walnut grips. Introduced in 1971; dropped, 1974. Used value, $1100 to $1250.

**BROWNING Medalist:** automatic; .22 LR only; 6¾" barrel; 11-1/8" overall length; 10-rd. magazine; vent rib; full wrap-around grips of select walnut; checkered with thumb rest; matching walnut forend; left-hand model available; screw adjustable rear sight, removable blade front; dry-firing mechanism; blued finish. Introduced in 1962; dropped, 1974. Used value, $475 to $500.

    **International Medalist** has same general specifications as standard Medalist, but is sans forend; 5.9" barrel, overall length, 10-15/16"; meets qualifications for International Shooting Union regulations. Introduced in 1964; dropped, 1974. Used value, $450 to $475.

    **Medalist Gold Model** has the same specifications as standard Browning Medalist, except for gold wire inlays; better wood in grip. Introduced in 1963; dropped, 1974. Used value, $1500 to $1550.

    **Medalist Renaissance Model** has the same specifications as standard Medalist, except for finely figured, hand-carved grips, chrome plating, full engraving. Introduced in 1964; dropped, 1974. Used value, $2000 to $2500.

*Browning BDA*

**BROWNING BDA:** automatic; 9mm Luger, .38 Super Auto, .45 ACP; 9-rd. magazine in 9mm, .38 Super Auto; 7 rds. in .45 ACP; 7-4/5" overall; 4-2/5" barrel; blued finish, fixed sights, plastic stocks; manufactured by Sauer, also known as SIG-Sauer P220. Imported 1977 to 1979. Browning now imports only .45 ACP version. Used value, $300 to $320.

    **BDA 380:** automatic; .380 auto; 12-rd. magazine; 3-13/16" barrel; 6¾" overall length; blade front sight, windage adjustable rear; combination safety, de-cocking lever; inertia firing pin; uncheckered walnut grips. Manufactured in Italy. Introduced 1978, still in production. Used value, $210 to $220.

# CHARTER ARMS

*Undercoverette*

*Charter Arms Undercover*

**CHARTER ARMS Undercover:** double-action revolver; swing-out 5-rd. cylinder; .38 Special; 2″, 3″ barrels; with 2″ barrel, 6¼″ overall length; walnut standard or bulldog grips; fixed rear sight, serrated ramp front; blued or nickel finish. Introduced in 1965; still in production. Used values, blued, with regular grips, $125 to $135; bulldog grips, $130 to $140; nickel finish, $140 to $150.

*.44 Special Bulldog*

*Charter Arms Pathfinder*

*Police Bulldog*

**CHARTER ARMS Pathfinder:** double-action revolver; has the same general specifications as Undercover model, except in .22 LR only; 3″ barrel only, adjustable rear sight, ramp front; blued finish only. Introduced in 1971; still in production. Used value, $100 to $110.

**Dual Pathfinder** has the same general specifications as standard Pathfinder model, except an extra cylinder is chambered for .22 WRM cartridge; hand-checkered walnut grips. Introduced in 1971; dropped, 1971. Used value, $110 to $120.

**CHARTER ARMS Undercoverette:** double-action revolver; has same general specifications as Undercover, but with 6-rd. .32 S&W long chambering, 2″ barrel only; designed for policewomen or ladies' purse; blued only. Introduced in 1969; still in production. Used value, $90 to $100.

**CHARTER ARMS Bulldog:** revolver, double-action; .44 Special; 5-rd. swing-out cylinder; 3″ barrel only; chrome-moly steel frame; wide trigger, hammer; square notch fixed rear sight, Patridge-type front; checkered walnut grips; blued only. Introduced in 1973. Used value, $120 to $125.

**Police Bulldog** is .38 Special, has 6-rd. cylinder, 4″ barrel; adjustable rear sight, ramp front. Introduced in 1976; still in production. Used value, $125 to $130.

**Target Bulldog** is .357 magnum, .44 Special; adjustable rear sight, ramp front. Introduced in 1976; still in production. Used value, $125 to $130.

**Bulldog 357** has same general specifications as .44 Special model, except for .357 caliber, 6″ barrel. Introduced in 1977; still in production. Used value, $120 to $125.

# COLT

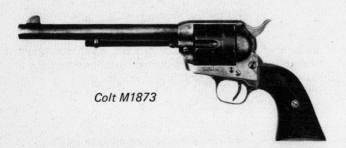

*Colt M1873*

**COLT Model 1873:** also known as Frontier, Peacemaker, Single-Action Army; single-action revolver; originally made in black powder calibers; .22 LR, long, short; .22 WRF, .32 Colt, .32-20, .32 S&W, .32 rimfire, .38 Colt, .38 S&W, .38 Special, .38-40, .357 magnum, .41 Colt, .44 rimfire, .44 Russian, .44-40, .44 Special, .45 Colt, .45 ACP, .450 Boxer, .450 Eley, .455 Eley, .476 Eley; currently made in .357 magnum, .45 Long Colt only; barrels, 3″, 4″ sans ejector, dropped; 4¾″, 5½″, 7½″ with ejector; overall length, 10¼″ with 4¾″ barrel; one-piece uncheckered walnut grip or checkered black rubber; standard model has fixed sights; target model has target sights, flat top strap; blued finish, case-hardened frame or nickel-plated. Those with serial numbers after 165,000 fire smokeless powder; black powder only should be used in lower numbered guns. Change was made in 1896, when spring catch was substituted for cylinder pin screw. Introduced in 1873; dropped, 1942. New production began in 1955 with serial number 1001SA. Used values for pre-WWII models, .22 Target Model, sans ejector, $1900 to $2000; other calibers, $780 to $825; Storekeeper Model, sans ejector, $725 to $750; .45 Artillery Model with 5½″ barrel, $700 to $750; .45 Cavalry Model, 7½″ barrel, $750 to $775; .44-40 Frontier Model, $675 to $700; standard model, $475 to $500. Post-1955 model, $225 to $300.

    **Colt .45 Buntline Special** is same as post-1955 standard Model 1873, except for 12″ barrel; .45 Long Colt only; designed after guns made as presentation pieces by author Ned Buntline. Introduced in 1957; dropped, 1975. Used value, $450 to $500.

    **New Frontier** Single-Action Army has the same specifications as Model 1873, except for flat-top frame, smooth walnut grips, 5½″, 7½″ barrel; .357 magnum, .45 Long Colt; adjustable target-type rear sight, ramp front. Introduced in 1961; still in production. Used value, $325 to $350.

    **New Frontier Buntline Special** has the same specifications as New Frontier Single-Action Army model, except for 12″ barrel. Introduced in 1962; dropped, 1966. Used value, $425 to $450.

**COLT Bisley:** revolver, single-action; same general specifications and calibers as Single Action Army (1873) Model, with trigger, hammer and grips redesigned for target shooting. Target model features target sights, flat-top frame. Manufactured from 1894 to 1915; sought after by collectors. Used values: standard model, $650 to $750; target model, $1750 to $1900.

**COLT Lightning:** revolver, double-action; .38 and .41 calibers; 6-rd. cylinder; with ejector, barrel lengths are 4½, 6″; sans ejector, 2½″, 3½″, 4½″, 6″; fixed sights, blued or nickel finish; hard rubber grips, Manufactured 1877 to 1909. Used value, $350 to $400.

**COLT Double Action Army:** revolver, double action; .38-40, .44-40, .45 Colt; similar to Lightning model, but with heavier frame; 6-rd. cylinder; barrel lengths, with ejector, 4¾″, 5½″, 7½″; sans ejector, 3½″, 4″; lanyard ring in butt; hard rubber grips, fixed sights; blued or nickel finish. Manufactured 1878 to 1905. Used value, $375 to $450.

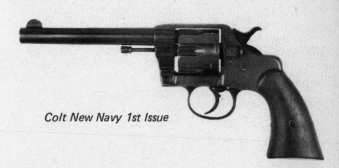

*Colt New Navy 1st Issue*

**COLT New Navy (First Issue):** revolver, double action; .38 Short Colt, .38 Long Colt, .41 Short, Long Colt; left-revolving 6-rd. cylinder; 3″, 4½″, 6″ barrel lengths; fixed blade front sight, V-notched rear; Colt's first solid-frame, swing-out cylinder model; hard rubber or walnut grips, blued or nickel; also called the New Army, adopted by both Army and Navy. Manufactured 1889 to 1894. In demand by collectors. Used value, $250 to $300.

*Colt New Navy 2nd Issue*

**COLT New Navy (Second Issue):** revolver; same general specs as First Issue, except for double cylinder notches, double locking bolt; added calibers: .38 Special, .32-20; does not fire modern high-velocity loads safely. Manufactured 1892 to 1905. Used value, $200 to $250.

**COLT New Pocket Model:** revolver, double action; .32 Short Colt, Long Colt; 6-rd. cylinder; 2½″, 3½″, 6″ barrel lengths; hard rubber grips; fixed blade front sight, notched V rear. Manufactured 1895 to 1905. Used value, $225 to $250.

**COLT New Police:** revolver, double-action; .32 caliber; built on New Pocket Model frame, with larger hard rubber grips; 2½″, 4″, 6″ barrels; same sights as New Pocket Colt, blued or nickel finish. Manufactured 1896 to 1905. Used value, $240 to $260.

*New Police*

New Police Target Model has same specifications, except for target sights, 6" barrel only. Manufactured 1896 to 1905. Used value, $250 to $275.

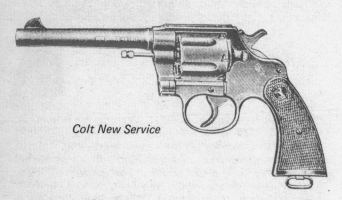

*Colt New Service*

**COLT New Service:** double-action revolver; large frame, swing-out 6-rd. cylinder; .38 Special, .357 magnum, .38-40, .38-44, .44 Russian, .44 Special, .44-40, .45 Long Colt, .45 ACP, .450 Ely, .455 Ely, .476 Ely; 4", 4½", 5", 5½", 6", 7½" barrels. Special run in .45 Auto during WWI was designated as Model 1917 Revolver under government contract. Fixed open notch rear sight milled in top strap, fixed front; hand-checkered walnut grips; lanyard loop on most variations; blued, nickel finish. Introduced in 1897; dropped, 1943. Used values, 1917 military model, $175 to $200; .357 magnum, which was introduced in 1936, $275 to $300; other models, $250 to $275.

**New Service Target Model** has the same general specifications as standard New Service model, except for rear sight adjustable for windage, front adjustable for elevation; top strap is flat; action is hand finished; 5", 6", 7½" barrels; .44 Special, .44 Russian, .45 Long Colt, .45 ACP, .450 Eley, .455 Eley, .476 Ely; blued finish, hand-checkered walnut grips. Introduced in 1900; dropped, 1940. Used value, $425 to $450.

**COLT Model 1900:** automatic; .38 ACP; 7-rd. magazine; 6" barrel; 9" length overall; fixed sights, plain walnut stocks, spur hammer; blued finish. Dangerous to fire modern high-velocity loads. Manufactured 1900 to 1903. Used value, $425 to $475.

**COLT Model 1902 Military:** automatic; .38 ACP; 8-rd. magazine; 9" overall; 6" barrel; fixed sights; fixed blade front sight, notched V rear; checkered hard rubber grips, round back hammer (changed to spur type in 1908), sans safety, blued finish. Do not fire modern high-velocity loads. Manufactured from 1902 to 1929. Used value, $375 to $400.

**COLT Model 1902 Sporter:** automatic; .38 ACP; 8-rd. magazine; 6" barrel, 9" overall; sans safety; checkered hard rubber grips, blade front sight, fixed notch V rear, round hammer. Not safe with modern loads. Manufactured 1902 to 1929. Used value, $450 to $475.

**COLT Model 1903:** pocket automatic; .38 ACP; same general specs as Model 1902 Sporter, except for 4½" barrel, 7½" overall length; round back hammer changed to spur type in 1908. Not safe with modern ammo. Manufactured 1903 to 1929. Used value, $224 to $250.

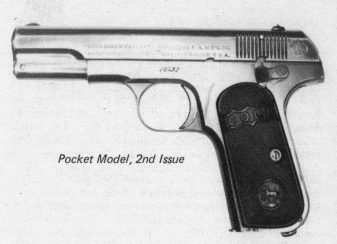

*Pocket Model, 2nd Issue*

**COLT Pocket Model 32, First Issue:** automatic; .32 Auto; 8-rd. magazine; 3¾" barrel, 7" overall; fixed sights, hammerless, slide lock, grip safeties, hard rubber stocks, blued finish, barrel locking bushing. Manufactured from 1903 until 1911. Used value, $185 to $200.

**Second Issue** is same as original issue, except for redesign without barrel bushing. Made from 1911 until 1945. Used value, $175 to $200.

**Model 32 (Third Issue)** has same specifications as second issue, except for 3¾" barrel; overall length, 6¾"; machine-checkered walnut grips. On all guns above serial No. 468097, safety disconnector prevents firing cartridge in chamber if magazine is removed. Introduced in 1926; dropped, 1945. Used value, $185 to $200.

**COLT Pocket Model 380 (First Issue):** automatic; .380 Auto; 7-rd. magazine; 4" barrel, 7" overall. Same general design, specs as Pocket Model 32. Manufactured from 1908 to 1911. Used value, $200 to $225.

**Second Issue** is same as first issue, sans barrel bushing. Manufactured from 1911 to 1945. Used value, $200 to $225.

**Model 380 (Third Issue)** has same specifications as second issue Model 380, except for 3¾" barrel; overall length, 6¾"; machine-checkered walnut grips. Safety disconnector installed on guns with serial numbers above 92,894. Introduced in 1926; dropped, 1945. Used value, $200 to $225.

**COLT Marine Corps Model:** revolver, same specs as Second Issue New Navy, except for round butt, 6" barrel only. Made in .38 Short, Long Colt, .38 Special. Manufactured 1905 to 1909. Used value, $550 to $600.

*Colt Marine*

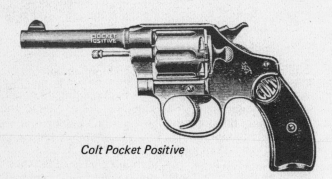

*Colt Pocket Positive*

**COLT Pocket Positive:** double-action revolver, based upon New Pocket model; dropped in 1905; .32 Short Colt, .32 Long Colt, .32 Colt New Police (interchangeable with .32 S&W long, S&W short cartridges); 2½″, 3½″, 6″ barrels; overall length, 7½″ with 3½″ barrel; 6-rd. cylinder; rear sight groove milled in top strap, rounded front sight; positive lock feature; hard rubber grips; blued or nickel finish. Introduced in 1905; dropped, 1940. Used value, $150 to $175.

*Colt Police Positive*

**COLT Police Positive:** double-action revolver; 6-shot swing-out cylinder; replaced New Police model; dropped in 1905; .22 LR, .22 WRF, .32 Short Colt, .32 Long Colt, .32 Colt New Police, .38 S&W; 2½″, 4″, 5″, 6″ barrels; overall length, 8½″ with 4″ barrel; fixed sights; checkered walnut, plastic, hard rubber grips; top of frame matted to reduce glare. Introduced in 1905; dropped, 1947. Used value, $165 to $175.

Police Positive Target model has same general specifications as standard Police Positive. Chambered for .32 Short Colt, .32 Long Colt, .32 New Police, .32 S&W short, .32 S&W long; .22 LR. Introduced in 1910; in 1932, cylinder was modified by countersinking chambers for safety with high-velocity .22 ammo; those with noncountersunk cham-

bers should be fired only with standard velocity .22 LR ammo. Has 6″ barrel, overall length, 10½″; rear sight adjustable for windage, front for elevation; checkered walnut grips; blued; backstrap, hammer spur, trigger checkered. Introduced in 1905; dropped, 1940. Used value, $300 to $325.

Police Positive Special has generally the same specifications as standard Police Positive, except that frame is lengthened to accommodate a longer cylinder, permitting chambering of .38 Special, .32-20; also made in .32 and .38 Colt New Police; 4″, 5″, 6″ barrels; with 4″ barrel, overall length, 8¾″; blued or nickel. Introduced in 1907; dropped, 1973. Used values, blued, $150 to $165; nickel finish, $165 to $175.

*Colt Officers' Model Target*

**COLT Officer's Model Target:** double-action revolver; second issue replaced first issue, discontinued in 1908; .22 LR, .32 Police Positive, .38 special; 6″ barrel in .22 LR and .32 PP, 4″, 4½″, 5″, 6″, 7½″, in .38 Special; overall length, 11¼″ with 6″ barrel; hand-finished action; 6-rd. cylinder; hand-checkered walnut grips; adjustable rear target sight, blade front; blued finish. The .38 Special was introduced in 1908, .22 LR in 1930, .32 PP in 1932; .32 PP dropped in 1942; model dropped, 1949. Used values, .22 LR, $275 to $300; .32 PP, $250 to $265; .38 Special, $250 to $275.

Officers' Model Special is basically the same as second issue Officer's Model Target gun, but with heavier barrel, ramp front sight, Coltmaster adjustable rear sight, redesigned hammer; checkered plastic stocks; 6″ barrel, .22 LR, .38 Special; blued finish. Introduced in 1949; dropped, 1953. Used value, $300 to $325.

Officers' Model Match has the same general specifications as Officers' Model Special, which it replaced. Exceptions are target grips of checkered walnut, tapered heavy barrel, wide hammer spur. Introduced in 1953; dropped, 1970. Used value, $300 to $325.

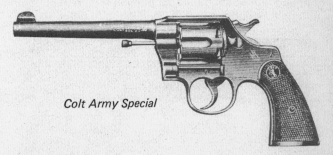

*Colt Army Special*

**COLT Army Special:** double-action revolver, .41 caliber frame; .32-20, .38 Special, .41 Colt; 6-rd. cylinder; barrel lengths, 4″, 4½″, 5″, 6″; overall length, 9¼″ with 4″ barrel; hard rubber grips; fixed sights; blued or nickel finish. Not safe for modern .38 Special high velocity loads in guns chambered for that caliber. Introduced in 1908; dropped, 1928. Used value, $200 to $220.

*Colt Pocket M25*

*Model 1911*

**COLT Pocket Model 25:** advertised as vest pocket model; hammerless automatic; .25 ACP only; 2" barrel, 4½" overall length; 6-rd. magazine; hard rubber or checkered walnut grips; fixed sights, milled in top of slide; incorporates straight-line striker, rather than pivoting hammer, firing pin; slide-locking safety, grip safety; magazine disconnector added in 1917 at serial No. 141,000; blued, with case-hardened safety lever, grip safety, trigger, or nickel finished. Introduced in 1908; dropped, 1941. Used values, blued, $215 to $225; nickel finish, $240 to $250.

*1911 Commercial Model*

*Model 1911A1*

**COLT Model 1911:** automatic, also known as Government Model; .45 ACP only; 5" barrel, 8½" overall length; 7-rd. magazine; checkered walnut grips; fixed sights; military versions have Parkerized or nonglare blued finish; commercial versions have blued finish with letter "C" preceding serial number. Introduced in 1911; produced from 1923 on as Model 1911A1. Used value, $350 to $375.

**Model 1911A1** has the same specifications as Model 1911, except for a longer grip safety spur, checkered, arched mainspring housing; plastic grips. During WWI and WWII, other firms produced the Government Model under Colt license; included were Remington UMC, Remington-Rand, Ithaca Gun Co., North American Arms of Canada (rare), Singer Sewing Machine (rare), Union Switch & Signal Co. and Springfield Armory. These government models bear imprint of licensee on slide. Model was redesigned and redesignated as Government Model MKIV Series 70 in 1970; approximately 850 1911A1 guns were equipped with split-collet barrel bushing — this adds to their collector value. Introduced in 1923. Used values, military model, $275 to $300; commercial model, $350 to $375; nickel finish, $365 to $385.

**COLT Model 1917 Army:** double-action, swing-out 6-rd. cylinder; based upon New Service revolver to fire .45 ACP cartridge with steel half-moon clips; later, shoulder permitted firing ammo sans clip; .45 Auto Rim cartridge can be fired in conventional manner; 5½" barrel, 10.8" overall length; smooth walnut grips; fixed sights; dull finish. Should be checked for damage by corrosive primers before purchase. Introduced in 1917; dropped, 1925. Used value, $225 to $250.

**COLT Camp Perry Model (First Issue):** target single-shot; built on frame of Colt Officers' Model; .22 LR only, with countersunk chamber for high velocity ammo after 1930; 10" barrel, 13¾" overall length; checkered walnut grips; hand-finished action; adjustable target sights; trigger, backstrap, hammer spur checkered; blued finish, with top, back of frame stippled to reduce glare. Resembles Colt revolvers, but chamber, barrel are single unit, pivoting to side for loading and extraction when latch is released. Introduced in 1926; dropped, 1934. Used value, $475 to $500.

**Camp Perry Model (Second Issue)** has the same general specifications as first issue, except for 8" barrel, 12" overall length; shorter hammer fall. As only 440 were produced, it has collector value over original version. Introduced in 1934; dropped, 1941. Used value, $625 to $650.

*1972 Detective Special*

*Woodsman 2nd Issue*

*Woodsman 3rd Issue*

**COLT Detective Special:** swing-out cylinder; double-action revolver; 6-rd. capacity; .32 New Police, .38 New Police, .38 Special; 2″ barrel, 6¾″ overall length. Other specifications are identical to those of Police Positive Special, with rounded butt introduced in 1933. Introduced in 1926; dropped, 1972. Used values, .32 variations, $175 to $185; .38 Special, $185 to $200.

Detective Special (1972) is revamp of original with heavier barrel; integral protective shroud enclosing ejector rod; frame, side-plate, cylinder, barrel, internal parts are of high-tensile alloy steel; .38 Special only; walnut bulldog-type grips; rear sight is fixed; notch milled in top strap, serrated ramp front; checkered hammer spur; blued, nickel finish. Introduced in 1972; still in production. Used values, blued, $165 to $175; nickel finish, $170 to $185.

Woodsman Second Issue has basically the same specifications as first issue, except for substitution of heat-treated mainspring housing for use with high velocity cartridges, heavier barrel. Introduced in 1932; dropped, 1948. Used value, $250 to $275.

Woodsman Third Issue has the same basic specifications as earlier Woodsman issues, except for longer grip, larger thumb safety, slide stop, magazine disconnector, thumb rest, plastic or walnut grips, magazine catch on left side; click adjustable rear sight, ramp front. Introduced in 1948; dropped, 1977. Used value, $200 to $235.

*Colt Bankers Special*

*Colt Woodsman Sport Model*

**COLT Bankers Special:** double-action revolver; swing-out 6-rd. cylinder essentially the same as pre-1972 Detective Special, but with shorter cylinder of Police Positive rather than that of Police Positive Special; .22 LR, with countersunk chambers after 1932, .38 New Police, .38 S&W; 2″ barrel, 6½″ overall length; a few produced with Fitzgerald cutaway trigger guard; checkered hammer spur, trigger; blued or nickel finish. Low production run on .22 gives it collector value. Introduced in 1926; dropped, 1940. Used values, .22, blued, $725 to $750; nickel finish, $750 to $775; .38 blued, $300 to $325; nickel, $325 to $350.

**COLT Woodsman (First Issue):** target automatic; .22 LR standard velocity; 6½″ barrel, 10½″ overall length; 10-rd. magazine; prior to 1927, designated as .22 Target Model. Designation, "The Woodsman," added after serial No. 34,000; adjustable sights, checkered walnut grips. Introduced in 1915; dropped, 1932. Used value, $235 to $250.

**COLT Woodsman Sport Model (First Issue):** has the same general specifications as second issue Woodsman Target model, except for adjustable rear sight, adjustable or fixed front; 4½″ barrel, 8½″ overall length; fires standard or high velocity .22 LR ammo. Introduced in 1933; dropped, 1948. Used value, $250 to $265.

Woodsman Sport Model (Second Issue) has the same specifications as the third-issue Woodsman Target model, except for 4½" barrel, overall length of 9"; plastic grips. Introduced in 1948; dropped, 1976. Used value, $165 to $185.

Woodsman Targetsman has generally the same specifications as third-issue Woodsman Target model, except for no automatic slide stop, less expensive adjustable rear sight. Introduced 1969; dropped, 1976. Used value, $145 to $165.

*Match Target 1st Issue*

**COLT Match Target (First Issue):** target automatic; .22 LR only; 6½" flat-sided barrel, 11" overall length; adjustable rear sight, blade front; checkered walnut one-piece extension grips; blued; same basic design as earlier Woodsman models. Introduced in 1938; dropped, 1942. Used value, $400 to $425.

**Match Target (Second Issue)** has the same general specifications as third-issue Target Woodsman. Flat-sided 6" heavy barrel, 10½" overall length; .22 LR, standard or high velocity ammo; checkered walnut or plastic grips; click adjustable rear sight, ramp front; blued. Introduced in 1948; dropped, 1976. Used value, $325 to $350.

**Match Target 4½** has the same specifications as second-issue Match Target, except for 4½" barrel; measures 9" overall. Introduced in 1950; dropped, 1976. Used value, $250 to $275.

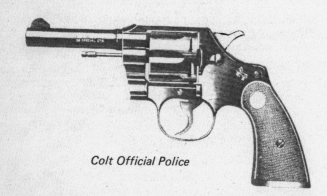

*Colt Official Police*

**COLT Official Police:** double-action revolver; .22 LR, .32-20, .38 Special, .41 Long Colt; 2", 6" heavy barrels in .38 Special only; 4", 6", in .22 LR only; 4", 5", 6", in other calibers; checkered walnut grips, plastic grips on post-WWII models. Version made to military specs in WWII was called Commando model, had sand-blasted blue finish. Introduced in 1928 as replacement for Army Special; dropped, 1969. Used values, standard model, $185 to $200; military model, $150 to $165.

**COLT Super 38:** identical to Government Model or 1911A1 automatic, except for capacity of magazine, caliber; .38 Colt Super; 9-rd. magazine; fixed sights. Introduced in 1928; still in production as Government Model MKIV/Series 70. Used value, $250 to $265. From 1935 to 1941 a few "Super Match" Super .38s were made with adjustable target sights. Used value, $450 to $500.

*Service Model Ace*

**COLT Ace:** automatic; built on same frame as Government Model .45 automatic; .22 LR only, standard or high velocity; does not have floating chamber; 4¾" barrel, 8¼" overall length; adjustable rear sight, fixed front; target barrel, hand-honed action. Introduced in 1930; dropped, 1947. Used value, $375 to $400.

**Service Model Ace** has specifications identical to those of National Match Model 45 automatic, except for magazine capacity, caliber; .22 LR, standard or high velocity; 10-rd. magazine; specially designed chamber increases recoil four-fold to approximate that of .45 auto. Introduced in 1935; dropped, 1945; reintroduced, 1978. Collector interest affects value. Used value, $475 to $500.

*Colt Shooting Master*

**COLT Shooting Master:** double-action revolver; swing-out 6-rd. cylinder; deluxe target version of New Service; .38 Special, .357 magnum, .45 ACP/Auto Rim; .45 Long Colt; 6" barrel, 11¼" overall length; checkered walnut grips, rounded butt; rear sight adjustable for windage, front for elevation; blued. Introduced in 1932; dropped, 1941. Used value, $475 to $500.

**COLT National Match:** target automatic; .45 ACP; has same specifications as Government Model .45 automatic, except for adjustable rear sight, ramp front; match-grade barrel, hand-honed action. Also available with fixed sights. Introduced in 1932; still in production. Used values, fixed sights, $225 to $240; target sights, $295 to $320.

*Colt Challenger*

**COLT Challenger:** automatic; .22 LR only; has same basic specifications of third-issue Target Woodsman, with fewer features; slide does not stay open after last shot; fixed sights; 4½", 5" barrels; overall length, 9" with 4½" barrel; checkered plastic grips; blued finish. Challenger introduced in 1950; dropped, 1955. Used value, $135 to $150.

**Huntsman** has exactly the same specifications as Challenger model, with name change for marketing purposes. Introduced in 1955; dropped, 1976. Used value, $135 to $150.

**COLT Commander:** lightweight automatic; .45 ACP; .38 Super auto; 9mm Luger; 4¼" barrel, 8" overall length; 7-rd. magazine for .45, 9 rds. for other calibers; basic design of Government Model auto, but is of lightweight alloy, reducing weight; early versions had plastic checkered grips, present production have checkered walnut; fixed sights; rounded hammer spur; blued, nickel finish. Introduced in 1950; still in production. Used value, $250 to $275.

*Colt Cobra*

**COLT Cobra:** double-action revolver; 6-rd. swing-out cylinder; .32 New Police, .38 New Police, .38 Special; based upon design of pre-1972 Detective Special, except that frame, side plate are of Coltalloy, high-tensile aluminum alloy; 2", 3", 4", 5" barrels; Coltwood plastic grips on later

guns, checkered wood on early issues; square butt was on early issued, replaced by round butt; optional hammer shroud; blue finish, matted on top, rear of frame. Old model shown. Introduced in 1951; dropped, 1972; 3", 4", 5" barrel styles were special order. Used value, $200 to $225.

**Cobra 1973 Model,** like original version, has frame, side plate of alloy, steel cylinder, barrel; integral protective shroud enclosing ejector rod; other specifications are identical to 1972 Detective Special, with exception of heavier Cobra barrel, blued, nickel finish. Introduced in 1973; still in production. Used values, blued, $165 to $175; nickel finish, $170 to $180.

**COLT Viper:** revolver; double action; .38 Special; has same general specifications as Colt Cobra, except for 4" barrel; 9" overall length. Introduced in 1977; dropped 1978. Used $145 to $160.

**COLT Three-Fifty-Seven:** double-action revolver; 6-rd. swing-out cylinder; .357 magnum only; 4", 6" barrels; 9¼" overall length with 4" barrel; available as service revolver or in target version; latter has wide hammer spur, target grips; checkered walnut grips; Accro rear sight, ramp front; blued finish. Introduced in 1953; dropped, 1961. Used values, standard model, $235 to $250; target model, $250 to $275.

*Colt Agent*

**COLT Agent:** double-action revolver; 6-rd. swing-out cylinder; .38 Special only; 2" barrel, 6¾" overall length; minor variation of Cobra Model with shorter, stub grip for maximum concealment; Coltalloy frame, side plate; steel cylinder, barrel; no housing around ejector rod; square butt; blued finish. Old model shown. Introduced in 1955; dropped, 1972. Used value, $200 to $225.

**Agent 1973 Model** closely resembles 1973 Cobra model, except for grip design, which extends just below bottom of frame; 2" barrel, overall length, 6-5/8"; checkered walnut grips; .38 Special only; blued finish. Introduced in 1973; still in production. Used value, $175 to $200.

**COLT Python:** double-action revolver, 6-rd. swing-out cylinder; .357 magnum only, but will handle .38 Special; made first appearance in 6" barrel, later with 2½", 4"; checkered walnut grips contoured for support for middle finger of shooting hand; vent rib barrel; ramp front sight, rear adjustable for windage, elevation; full-length ejector rod shroud; wide-spur hammer, grooved trigger; blued, nickel finish; hand-finished action. Introduced in 1955; still in production. Used values, blued, $325 to $335; nickel finish, $340 to $350.

to $165; interchangeable magnum cylinder, add $35.

**Scout Buntline** has same specifications as Frontier Scout with steel frame, wood grips, except for 9½" barrel. Introduced in 1959; dropped, 1971. Used value, $175 to $225.

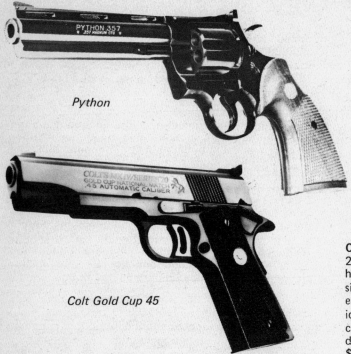

*Python*

*Colt Gold Cup 45*

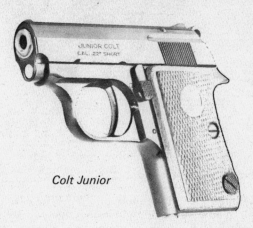

*Colt Junior*

**COLT Gold Cup 45:** National Match grade automatic; .45 ACP only; same general specifications as Government Model .45 auto; has match grade barrel, bushing; long, wide trigger; adjustable trigger stop; flat mainspring housing; adjustable rear sight, target front; hand-fitted slide; wider ejection port; checkered walnut grips. Introduced in 1957; still in production. Used value, $300 to $350.

**Gold Cup 38 Special** has same general specifications as Gold Cup 45, except it is chambered only for .38 Special mid-range ammo. Introduced in 1960; dropped, 1974. Used value, $325 to $375.

**COLT Junior:** pocket model automatic; .22 short, .25 ACP; 2¼" barrel; overall length, 4-3/8"; 6-rd. magazine; exposed hammer with round spur; checkered walnut stocks; fixed sights; blued. Initially produced in Spain by Astra, with early versions having Spanish markings as well as Colt identity; parts were assembled in U.S., sans Spanish identification after GCA '68 import ban. Introduced in 1958; dropped, 1973. Used values: Spanish versions, $125 to $150; U.S.-made versions, $200 to $225.

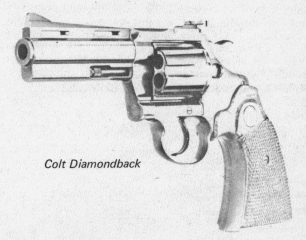

*Colt Diamondback*

*Colt Frontier Scout*

**COLT Diamondback:** double-action revolver; swing-out 6-rd cyl.; scaled-down version of Python; .38 Special, .22 magnum; .22 LR; 2½", 4" barrel; available in nickel, .22 with 4" only; vent rib barrel; target-type rear sight adjustable for windage, elevation; ramp front; full checkered walnut grips; integral rounded rib beneath barrel shrouds ejector rod; broad checkered hammer spur. Introduced in 1966; still in production. Used values, .38 nickel-plated with 4" barrel, $225 to $235; .22 magnum, $275 to $300; .22 LR, $235 to $250.

**COLT Frontier Scout:** single-action revolver; scaled-down version of Model 1873 Army; .22 LR, long, short; interchangeable cylinder for .22 WRF magnum; 4½" barrel, 9-15/16" overall length; originally introduced with alloy frame; steel frame, blue finish introduced in 1959; fixed sights; plastic or wooden grips. Introduced in 1958; dropped, 1971. Used values, alloy frame, $135 to $145; blue finish, plastic grips, $145 to $155; nickel finish, wood grips, $155

**COLT Metropolitan MKIII:** double-action revolver; swing-out 6-rd. cylinder; designed for urban law enforcement; 4" barrel, .38 Special only; fixed sights; choice of service, target grips of checkered walnut; blued finish, standard; nickel, optional. Introduced in 1969; dropped, 1972. Used values, blued, $150 to $165; nickel finish, $155 to $170.

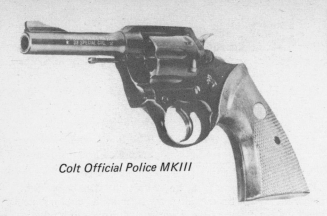

*Colt Official Police MKIII*

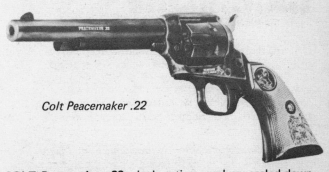

*Colt MK IV/Series '70 45 Govt. Model*

**COLT Official Police MKIII:** double-action revolver; an old name, but a renewed design, incorporating coil mainsprings in place of leaf springs; .38 Special only; 4″ barrel, 9-3/8″ overall length; square-butt, checkered walnut grips; fixed rear sight notch milled in top strap, fixed ramp front; grooved front surface on trigger, checkered hammer spur. Introduced in 1969; dropped, 1975. Used value, $165 to $175.

**COLT Lawman MKIII:** similar to Official Police MKIII, but beefed up to handle .357 Magnum; will also chamber .38 Special; 2″, 4″ barrels; with 4″ barrel, overall length, 9-3/8″; choice of square, round-butt walnut grips; fixed sights; blued, nickel finish. Introduced in 1969; still in production. Used values, Blued, $150 to $165; nickel, $155 to $170.

**COLT Trooper MKIII:** double-action revolver; .357 magnum only; chambers .38 Special as well; 4″, 6″ barrels; with 4″ barrel, overall length, 9½″; rear sight adjustable for windage/elevation, ramp front; shrouded ejector rod; checkered walnut target grips; target hammer, wide target trigger; blued, nickel finish. Introduced in 1969; still in production. Used values, blued, $175 to $185; nickel, $185 to $195.

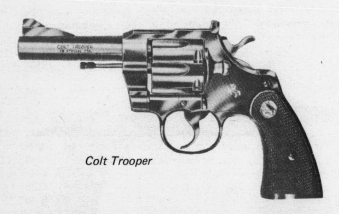

*Colt Trooper*

**COLT Trooper:** double-action revolver; swing-out 6-rd. cylinder; has the same specifications as Officer's Match model, except for 4″ barrel; .38 Special, .357 Magnum; ramp front sight; choice of standard hammer, service grips, wide hammer spur, target grips. Introduced in 1953; dropped, 1969. Used values, standard service model, $175 to $200; target model, $225 to $235.

**COLT MK IV/Series '70 45 Govt. Model:** .45 ACP, 9mm Luger, .38 Super; is identical to .38 Super and previous .45 Government Model, except for improved collet-type barrel bushing and reverse taper barrel to improve accuracy. Introduced in 1970; still in production. Used value, $250 to $260.

*Colt New Frontier .22*

**COLT New Frontier .22:** single-action revolver; scaled-down version of New Frontier .45; 6-rd. capacity; furnished with dual cylinders for .22 LR, .22 WMRF ammo; 4-3/8″, 6″, 7½″ barrels; with 6″ barrel, overall length, 11½″; target-type rear sight adjustable for windage, elevation, ramp front; checkered black plastic grips; flat top strap; color case-hardened frame, rest blued. Introduced in 1973; dropped, 1975. Used values, 7½″ barrel, $145 to $165; others, $145 to $155.

*Colt Peacemaker .22*

**COLT Peacemaker .22:** single-action revolver; scaled-down version of century-old Model 1873; 6-rd. capacity; furnished with dual cylinders for .22 LR, .22 WMRF ammo; rear sight notch milled into rounded top strap, fixed blade front; color case-hardened frame, rest blued; black plastic grips; 4-3/8″, 6″, 7½″ barrels; overall length with 6″ barrel, 11¼″. Introduced in 1973; dropped, 1975. Used values, 7½″ barrel, $155 to $165; others, $145 to $165.

# CZ

*CZ Model 38*

*CZ Pocket Duo*

**CZ Pocket Duo:** automatic; .25 Auto; 6-rd. magazine; 2-1/8'' barrel; 4½'' overall; manufactured in Czechoslovakia; plastic stocks; fixed sights; blued or nickel finish. Manufactured 1926 to 1960. Used value, $100 to $110.

**CZ Model 38:** automatic, double-action; .380 Auto; 9-rd. magazine; 3¾'' barrel, 7'' overall; plastic stocks, fixed sights, blued finish. Also listed as CZ Pistole 39(t) during German occupation. Manufactured 1939 to 1945. Used value, $145 to $155.

**CZ Model 1945:** automatic, double-action; .25 Auto; 8-rd. magazine; 2'' barrel, 5'' overall; plastic stocks, fixed sights, blued finish. Manufactured 1945 to approximately 1960. Used value, $125 to $130.

*CZ New Model .006*

*CZ Model 27*

**CZ Model 27:** automatic; .32 Auto; 8-rd. magazine; 4'' barrel, 6'' overall; plastic stocks, fixed sights, blued finish. Manufactured 1927 to 1951. Used value, $145 to $155.

**CZ New Model .006:** automatic, double-action; .32 Auto; 8-rd. magazine; 3-1/8'' barrel, 6½'' overall; plastic stocks, fixed sights, blued finish. Issue;to Czech police as Model VZ50. Manufactured 1951 to approximately 1967. Used value, $160 to $175.

---

# HAMMERLI

**HAMMERLI Model 33MP:** single-shot competition free pistol; .22 LR; Martini-type action, set trigger; 11½'' octagonal barrel, 16½'' overall length; micrometer rear sight, interchangeable front; European walnut stocks, forearm, blued finish. Manufactured in Switzerland, 1933 to 1949. Used value $525 to $575.

**HAMMERLI Model 100 Free Pistol:** single-shot, slow-fire target model; .22 LR only; 11½'' barrel; adjustable set trigger; micrometer rear sight, interchangeable post or bead front; European walnut grips, forearm; blued. Introduced in 1947; redesignated as Model 101 in 1960; dropped, 1962. Used value, $500 to $600.

*Model 200 Olympia*

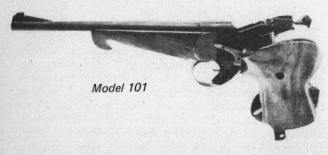

*Model 101*

**HAMMERLI WALTHER Model 200 Olympia:** automatic; also advertised as Quickfire model; .22 LR, short; 7½'' barrel; 8-rd. magazine; muzzle brake; adjustable barrel weights; walnut thumbrest grip; micrometer rear sight;

ramp front; blued. Based on 1936 Olympia with some parts interchangeable. Introduced in 1950. In 1957, muzzle brake was redesigned. Dropped, 1963. Used value, $400 to $450.

**Model 201** has the same specifications as Model 200, except for standard adjustable sights and adjustable custom grip. Introduced in 1950; dropped, 1957. Used value, $400 to $450.

**Model 202** has the same specifications as Model 201, except for 9½" barrel. Introduced in 1957; dropped, 1959. Used value, $400 to $450.

**Model 203** called the American Model, has the same general specifications as Model 201, except for micrometer rear sight, slide stop. Introduced in 1957; dropped, 1959. Used value, $475 to $550.

**Model 204** is the same as the Model 203, except is equipped with the standard thumbrest grips. Introduced in 1947; dropped, 1963. Used value, $475 to $550.

**Model 205** has the same specifications as Model 204, except for hand-checkered French walnut grip; detachable muzzle brake. Introduced in 1960; dropped, 1964. Used value, $550 to $600.

**HAMMERLI Model 110 Free Pistol:** single-shot, slow-fire target model. Has exactly the same specifications as Model 100, except for highly polished, blued barrel. Introduced in 1957; redesignated as Model 102 in 1960; dropped, 1962. Used value, $440 to $460.

*Hammerli Model 103 Free Pistol*

**HAMMERLI Model 103 Free Pistol:** single-shot, slow-fire target model. Has the same specifications as Model 102, except for deluxe carving of wood. Introduced in 1960; dropped, 1963. Used values, $550 to $600; with inlaid ivory carvings, $575 to $625.

*Hammerli International Model 206*

**HAMMERLI International Model 206:** automatic; rapid-fire target model; .22 LR and short; 7-1/16" barrel; 8-rd. magazine; muzzle brake; slide stop; checkered walnut thumbrest grips; adjustable trigger, blued. Cartridges not interchangeable. Introduced in 1964; dropped, 1967. Used value, $450 to $475.

*Model 207*

**International Model 207** has exactly the same specifications as Model 206, except for uncheckered walnut grips, with adjustable grip plates. Introduced in 1964; dropped, 1969. Used value, $475 to $500.

**Hammerli Model 208** has the same specifications as Model 207, except that barrel is shortened to 6", no muzzle brake, adjustable trigger pull; .22 LR only. Introduced in 1958; still in production. Used value, $500 to $525.

*Model 104*

**HAMMERLI Match Pistol Model 104:** single-shot free pistol; .22 LR only; 11½" barrel; micrometer rear sight; post front; uncheckered selected walnut grips with trigger-finger ramp, adjustable hand plate, custom finish; blued. Introduced in 1963; dropped, 1965. Used value, $525 to $550.

**Match Pistol Model 105** has exactly the same specifications as Model 104, except for octagonal barrel, highly polished metal, French walnut grip plates. Introduced in 1963; dropped, 1965. Used value, $575 to $600.

**Model 106** has the same general specifications as Model 104, but with matte blue finish on barrel to reduce glare; other minor changes. Replaced Model 106. Introduced in 1966; dropped, 1972. Used value, $550 to $600.

**Model 107** has the same specifications as Model 105, which it replaced. Has matte blue finish on barrel to reduce glare, other minor improvements. Introduced in 1966; dropped, 1972. Used value, $600 to $650.

**HAMMERLI International Model 210:** automatic; .22 short only; has the same general design as Model 207, but with lightweight bolt to reduce the recoil movement; six gas-escape ports in rear of barrel; barrel vents, adjustable muzzle brake to reduce muzzle jump, adjustable grip plates. Introduced in 1967; dropped, 1970. Used value, $550 to $575.

**Model 209** has exactly the same specifications as Model 210, except for nonadjustable grips. Introduced in 1967; dropped, 1970. Used value, $525 to $550.

*Hammerli Model 230-1*

*Hammerli International Model 211*

**HAMMERLI Model 230-1:** automatic; .22 short; 5-rd. magazine; 6-1/3" barrel, 11-3/5" overall length; micrometer rear sight, post front; uncheckered European walnut thumbrest grips; blued finish. Designed for rapid fire International competition. Introduced in 1970; still in production. Used value, $475 to $500.

**Model 230-2** has same specifications as Model 230-1, except for partially checkered stocks, adjustable heel plate. Introduced in 1970; still in production. Used value, $500 to $525.

**HAMMERLI International Model 211:** automatic; .22 LR only; 5-9/10" barrel, 10" overall length; micrometer bridged rear sight, post ramp front; externally adjustable trigger with backlash stop; hand-checkered European walnut thumbrest grips; blued. Introduced in 1973; still in production. Used value, $475 to $500.

*Model 120 Standard*

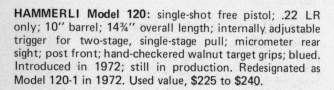

*Hammerli Model 150*

**HAMMERLI Model 150:** single-shot free pistol; .22 LR only; 11-3/8" barrel; 15-3/8" overall length; moveable front sight on collar, micrometer rear; Martini-type action; straight-line firing pin, no hammer; adjustable set trigger; uncheckered adjustable palm-shelf grip. Introduced in 1973; still in production. Used value, $425 to $450.

**HAMMERLI Model 120:** single-shot free pistol; .22 LR only; 10" barrel; 14¾" overall length; internally adjustable trigger for two-stage, single-stage pull; micrometer rear sight; post front; hand-checkered walnut target grips; blued. Introduced in 1972; still in production. Redesignated as Model 120-1 in 1972. Used value, $225 to $240.

**Model 120-2** has the same general specifications as Model 120-1, except for special contoured walnut hand rest. Both sights can be moved forward or rearward; blued. Introduced in 1973; still in production. Used value, $270 to $300.

**Model 120 Heavy Barrel Style** was designed for sale in Great Britain to conform with existing laws governing sporting handgun specs. It has the same specifications as Model 120-1, except for 5¾" barrel. Introduced in 1973; still in production. Used values, with standard grips, $170 to $180; with adjustable grips, $195 to $210.

*Hammerli Virginian*

**HAMMERLI Virginian:** revolver, single-action; .357 magnum, .45 Colt; 6-rd. cylinder; 4-5/8", 5½", 7½" barrels; same general design as Colt SAA, except for base pin safety feature. Has grooved rear sight, blade front; barrel and cylinder are blued, frame case-hardened, with chromed grip frame, trigger guard, one-piece European walnut grip. Manufactured in Europe, 1973 to 1976, for exclusive Interarms importation. Used value, $180 to $190.

# HARRINGTON & RICHARDSON

*H&R American*

**HARRINGTON & RICHARDSON American:** double-action solid-frame revolver; .32 S&W Long, .38 S&W; 2½", 4½", 6" barrels; 6-rd. cylinder in .32, 5-rd. in .38; fixed sights, hard rubber grips; blued, nickel finish. Introduced in 1883; dropped during WWII. Used value, $45 to $65.

*H&R Young America*

**HARRINGTON & RICHARDSON Young America:** double-action solid-frame revolver; .22 L R, .32 S&W Short; 2" 4½", 6" barrels; 7-rd. cylinder in .22, 5-rd, in .32; fixed sights, hard rubber grips; blued, nickel finish. Introduced in 1885; dropped during WWII. Used value, $45 to $65.

*H&R Vest Pocket Model*

**HARRINGTON & RICHARDSON Vest Pocket Model:** double-action solid-frame revolver; .22 long, .32 S&W Short; 1-1/8" barrel; spurless hammer; 7-rd. cylinder in .22, 5-rd. in .32; no sights except for milled slot in top frame; hard rubber grips; blued, nickel finish. Introduced in 1891; dropped during WWII. Used value, $65 to $75.

*H&R Automatic Ejecting Model*

**HARRINGTON & RICHARDSON Automatic Ejecting Model:** double-action hinged-frame revolver; .32 S&W Long, .38 S&W; 3¼", 4", 5", 6" barrels; 6-rd. cylinder in .32, 5-rd. in .38; fixed sights; hard rubber grips; blued, nickel finish. Introduced in 1891; dropped, 1941. Used value, $55 to $65.

*H&R Premier Model*

**HARRINGTON & RICHARDSON Premier Model:** double-action hinged-frame revolver; .22 LR, .32 S&W Short; 2", 3", 4", 5", 6" barrels; 7-rd. cylinder in .22, 5-rd. in .32; fixed sights; hard rubber grips; blued, nickel finish. Introduced in 1895; dropped, 1941. Used value, $60 to $70.

*H&R Model 40 Hammerless*

**HARRINGTON & RICHARDSON Model 40 Hammerless:** double-action small hinged-frame revolver; .22 LR, .32 S&W Short; 2", 3", 4", 5", 6" barrels; 7-rd. cylinder in 22, 5-rd. in .32; fixed sights; hard rubber stocks; blued, nickel finish. Also listed during late production as Model 45. Introduced in 1899; dropped, 1941. Used value, $65 to 75.

**HARRINGTON & RICHARDSON Model 50 Hammerless:** double-action large hinged-frame revolver; .32 S&W Long, .38 S&W; 3¼", 4", 5", 6" barrels; 6-rd. cylinder in .32, 5-rd. in .38; fixed sights; hard rubber grips; blued, nickel finish. Also listed in later production as Model 55. Introduced in 1899; dropped, 1941. Used value, $75 to $85.

*H&R Model 4*

**HARRINGTON & RICHARDSON Model 4:** double-action solid-frame revolver; .32 S&W Long, .38 S&W; 2½", 4½", 6" barrels; 6-rd. cylinder for .32, 5-rd. for .38; fixed sights, hard rubber grips; blued, nickel finish. Introduced in 1905; dropped, 1941. Used value, $50 to $60.

*H&R Model 5*

**HARRINGTON & RICHARDSON Model 5:** double-action solid-frame revolver; .32 S&W Short only; 2½", 4½", 6" barrels; 5-rd. cylinder; fixed sights; hard rubber grips; blued nickel finish. Introduced in 1905; dropped, 1939. Used value, $50 to $60.

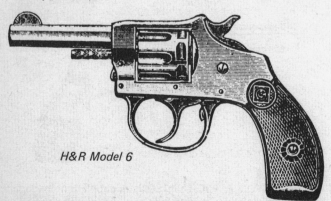

*H&R Model 6*

**HARRINGTON & RICHARDSON Model 6:** double-action solid-frame revolver; .22 LR only; 2½", 4½", 6" barrels; 7-rd. cylinder; fixed sights; hard rubber grips; blued, nickel finish. Introduced in 1906; dropped, 1941. Used value, $75 to $85.

*H&R Trapper Model*

**HARRINGTON & RICHARDSON Trapper Model:** double-action solid-frame revolver; .22 LR only; 6" octagonal barrel; 7-rd. cylinder; fixed sights; checkered walnut stocks; blued. Introduced in 1924; dropped during WWII. Used value, $85 to $95.

*H&R .22 Special*

**HARRINGTON & RICHARDSON .22 Special:** double-action heavy hinged-frame revolver; .22 LR, .22 WRF; 6" barrel, 9-rd. cylinder; fixed rear sight; gold-plated front; checkered walnut grips; blued. Originally introduced as Model 944; later version with recessed cylinder for high speed ammo was listed as Model 945. Introduced in 1925; dropped, 1941. Used value, $90 to $100.

*H&R Model 766*

**HARRINGTON & RICHARDSON Model 766:** double-action target revolver; hinged frame; .22 LR, .22 WRF; 6" barrel; 7-rd. cylinder; fixed sights; checkered walnut grips; blued. Introduced in 1926; dropped, 1936. Used value, $90 to $100.

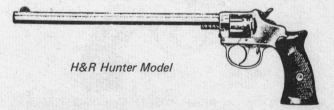

*H&R Hunter Model*

**HARRINGTON & RICHARDSON Hunter Model:** double-action solid-frame revolver; .22 LR only; 10" octagon barrel; 9-rd. cylinder; fixed sights; checkered walnut grips; blued. Introduced in 1926; dropped, 1941. Used value, $90 to $100.

*H&R USRA Model*

*H&R No. 199*

**HARRINGTON & RICHARDSON USRA Model:** single-shot hinged-frame target pistol; .22 LR only; 7", 8", 10" barrels; adjustable target sights; checkered walnut grips; blued. Introduced in 1928; dropped, 1943. Used value, $250 to $275.

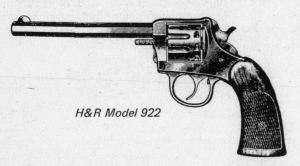

*H&R Model 922*

**HARRINGTON & RICHARDSON Model 922:** double-action solid-frame revolver; .22 LR only; 4", 6", 10" barrels; 9-rd. cylinder; fixed sights; checkered walnut or Tenite grips; blued or chrome finish. Introduced in 1929. Early production had octagon 10" barrel, later dropped. Still in production in 4", 6" lengths. Used value, $60 to $70.
**Model 922 Bantamweight** has the same specifications as standard model, except for 2½" barrel, rounded butt. Introduced in 1951; still in production. Used value, $60 to $70.

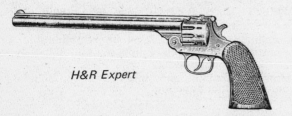

*H&R Expert*

**HARRINGTON & RICHARDSON Expert:** has the same general specifications as the .22 Special Model 945, except for being produced with 10" barrel. Listed as Model 955. Introduced in 1929; dropped, 1941. Used value, $90 to $100.

**HARRINGTON & RICHARDSON Self-Loading 25:** automatic; .25 Auto; 6-rd. magazine; 2" barrel, 4½" overall; checkered hard rubber stocks, fixed sights, blued finish. Variation of Webley & Scott design. Manufactured approximately 1929 to 1941. Used value, $175 to $190.

**HARRINGTON & RICHARDSON Self-Loading 32:** automatic; .32 auto; 8-rd. magazine; 3½" barrel, 6½" overall; checkered hard rubber stocks, fixed sights, blued finish. Variation of Webley & Scott design. Manufactured approximately 1929 to 1941. Used value, $175 to $195.

**HARRINGTON & RICHARDSON No. 199:** advertised as Sportsman Model; single-action hinged-frame revolver; .22 LR only; 6" barrel, 11" overall length; 9-rd. cylinder; adjustable target sights; checkered walnut grips; blued. Introduced in 1933; dropped, 1951. Used value, $90 to $100.

**HARRINGTON & RICHARDSON No. 999:** double-action hinged-frame revolver; .22 LR, .22 WRF. Has the same general specifications as No. 199. Current style is in .22 LR only, has vent-rib barrel, redesigned hammer. Introduced in 1936; still in production. Used value, $75 to $85.

*H&R New Defender*

**HARRINGTON & RICHARDSON New Defender:** also listed as Model 299; double-action hinged-frame revolver; .22 LR only; 2" barrel; 6¼" overall length; has the same basic specifications, except for barrel length, as Model 999; adjustable sights; checkered walnut grips, round butt; blued. Introduced in 1936; dropped, 1941. Used value, $125 to $140.

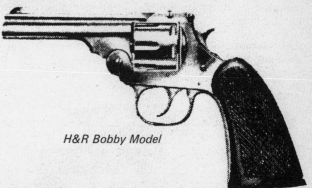

*H&R Bobby Model*

**HARRINGTON & RICHARDSON Bobby Model:** also listed as Model 15; double-action hinged-frame revolver; .32 S&W Long, .38 S&W; 4" barrel; 9" overall length; 6-rd. cylinder in .32, 5-rd. in .38; fixed sights; checkered walnut grips; blued. Designed for use by London police during WWII. Introduced in 1941; dropped, 1943. Used value, $110 to $125.

**HARRINGTON & RICHARDSON Guardsman:** double-action solid-frame revolver; .32 S&W Long only; 2½", 4" barrels; 6-rd. cylinder; fixed sights; checkered Tenite grips; blued, chrome finish. Introduced in 1946; dropped, 1957. Used values, blued, $37.50 to $42.50; chrome finish, $70 to $80.

*H&R Model 929*

*H&R Model 939*

**HARRINGTON & RICHARDSON Model 929:** advertised as Sidekick Model; double-action revolver; solid-frame; swing-out cylinder; .22 LR, short; 2½'', 4'', 6'' barrels; 9-rd. cylinder; fixed sights; checkered plastic grips; blued. Introduced in 1956; still in production. Used value, $60 to $65.

*H&R Model 622*

**HARRINGTON & RICHARDSON Model 622:** double-action revolver; solid-frame; .22 LR, long, short; 2½'', 4'', 6'' barrels; 6-rd. cylinder; fixed sights; checkered plastic grips; blued. Introduced in 1957, 6'' barrel dropped. Others still in production. Used value, $50 to $60.

**Model 623** has exactly the same specifications as Model 622, except for chrome finish. Introduced in 1957; dropped, 1963. Used value, $60 to $70.

*Model 732*

**HARRINGTON & RICHARDSON Model 732:** double-action revolver; solid-frame; 6-rd. swing-out cylinder; .32 S&W, .32 S&W Long; 2½'', 4'' barrels; rear sight adjustable for windage on 4'' model, fixed on shorter barrel; ramp front; plastic checkered grips; blued. Introduced in 1958; still in production. Used value, $50 to $60.

**Model 733** has the same specifications as Model 732, except for nickel finish. Used value, $60 to $70.

**HARRINGTON & RICHARDSON Model 939:** advertised as Ultra Sidekick Model; double-action revolver; solid-frame; swing-out 9-rd. cylinder; 6'' barrel, with vent rib; adjustable rear sight, ramp front; checkered walnut grips; blued. Introduced in 1958; still in production. Used value, $75 to $85.

**HARRINGTON & RICHARDSON Model 949:** advertised as Forty-Niner Model; double-action revolver; solid-frame; side-loading, ejection; 9-rd. cylinder; .22 LR, long, short; 5½'' barrel; adjustable rear sight, blade front; one-piece plain walnut grip; blued, nickel finish. Introduced in 1960; still in production. Used value, $65 to $75.

*Model 900*

**HARRINGTON & RICHARDSON Model 900:** double-action revolver; solid-frame; snap-out, 9-rd. cylinder; .22 LR, long, short; 2½'', 4'', 6'' barrels; fixed sights; high impact plastic grips; blued. Introduced in 1962; dropped, 1973. Used value, $70 to $80.

**Model 901** has the same specifications as Model 900, except for chrome finish, white plastic grips. Introduced in 1962; dropped, 1963. Used value, $75 to $85.

*H&R Model 925*

**HARRINGTON & RICHARDSON Model 925:** advertised as the Defender Model; originally introduced as Model 25. Double-action revolver; hinged-frame; .38 S&W only; 5-rd. cylinder; 2½'' barrel; adjustable rear sight, fixed front; one-piece smooth plastic grip; blued. Introduced in 1964; still in production. Used value, $75 to $85.

**HARRINGTON & RICHARDSON Model 976:** revolver, double-action; hinged frame; .22 LR, with 9-rd. cylinder; .38 S&W, 5 rds.; 4" barrel; fixed front sight, adjustable rear; checkered walnut stocks, blued finish. Introduced 1968, still in production. Used value, $70 to $75.

*H&R Model 926*

**HARRINGTON & RICHARDSON Model 926:** revolver, double-action; hinged frame; .22 LR, with 9-rd. cylinder; .38 S&W, 5 rds.; 4" barrel; fixed front sight, adjustable rear; checkered walnut stocks, blued finish. Introduced 1968; dropped 1980. Used value, $70 to $75.

**HARRINGTON & RICHARDSON Model 666:** revolver, double-action; solid frame; combo with two 6-rd. cylinders; .22 LR, .22 Winchester rimfire magnum; 6" barrel, fixed sights, plastic stocks, blued finish. Introduced 1976; dropped 1980. Used value, $50 to $55.

*H&R Model 649*

**HARRINGTON & RICHARDSON Model 649:** revolver, double-action, solid frame; combo with two 6-rd. cylinders: .22 LR, .22 Winchester rimfire magnum; 5½" barrel; blade front sight, adjustable rear; one-piece walnut grip, blued finish. Introduced in 1976; dropped 1980. Used value, $55 to $60.

**HARRINGTON & RICHARDSON Model 650:** revolver, double-action; solid frame. Has same specifications as Model 649, except is nickel finished. Introduced 1976; dropped 1980. Used value, $55 to $60.

**HARRINGTON & RICHARDSON Model 676:** revolver, double-action; solid frame; combo with two 6-rd. cylinders: .22 LR, .22 Winchester rimfire magnum; 4½", 5½", 7½", 12" barrel lengths; blade front sight, adjustable rear; one-piece walnut grip, color case-hardened frame, blued finish. Introduced 1976, still in production. Used value, $60 to $70.

# HAWES

*Hawes Western Marshal*

**HAWES Western Marshal:** revolver, single-action; 6-rd. cylinder; .357 magnum, .44 magnum, .45 Long Colt, .45 Auto, .22 magnum, .22 LR; 6" barrels for center-fire calibers, 5" for rimfires; rosewood grips in center-fire models, plastic stag grips for rimfires; also available with interchangeable cylinder combos: .357 magnum/9mm Luger, .45 Colt/.45 Auto, .44 magnum/.44-40, .22 LR/.22 Winchester rimfire magnum. Introduced 1968; manufactured in West Germany by Sauer & Sohn exclusively for Hawes. Dropped in 1980. Used values, .357 magnum, $110 to $115; .45 Long Colt, $110 to $115; .44 magnum, $100 to $110; .45 Auto, $100 to $110; .22 LR, $95 to $100. Combo values: .357 magnum/9mm

Luger, $130 to $140; .45 Long Colt/.45 Auto, $130 to $140; .44 magnum/.44-40, $135 to $150; .22 LR/.22 WMRF, $115 to $120.

**HAWES Montana Marshal:** revolver, single-action; has same specs, caliber combinations as Western Marshal, except for brass grip frame. Introduced 1968, dropped 1980. Used value, .357 magnum, $115 to $120; .45 Long Colt, $115 to $120; .44 magnum, $105 to $115; .45 Auto, $105 to $115; .22 LR, $100 to $105. Combo values, .357 magnum/9mm Luger, $140 to $150; .45 Long Colt/.45 Auto, $140 to $150; .44 magnum/.44-40, $140 to $155; .22 LR/.22 WMRF, $125 to $135.

**HAWES Texas Marshal:** revolver, single-action, same specifications, caliber combos as Western Marshal, except for pearlite grips, nickel finish; Introduced 1969; dropped 1980. Used values, same as for Montana Marshal.

**HAWES Federal Marshal:** revolver, single-action, same specifications as Western Marshal, except never manufactured in .22 rimfires; has color case-hardened frame, one-piece European walnut grip, brass grip frame. Introduced 1969; dropped 1980. Used values, .357 magnum, $130 to $140; .45 Colt, $130 to $140; .44 magnum, $145 to $160. Combo values, .357 magnum/9mm Luger, $160 to $165; .45 Colt/.45 Auto, $160 to $165; .44 magnum/.44-40, $165 to $175.

**HAWES Silver City Marshal:** revolver, single-action, same basic specifications as Western Marshal. Differs with pearlite grips, brass grip frame, blued barrel and cylinder, nickel-plated frame. Not made in .22. Introduced 1969; dropped 1980. Used values, .357 magnum, $130 to $140, .45 Colt, $130 to $140; .44 magnum, $140 to $150. Combo values, .357 magnum/9mm Luger, $150 to $165; .44 magnum/.44-40, $160 to $170; .45 Long Colt/.45 auto, $160 to $170.

**HAWES Chief Marshal:** revolver, single-action; same specifications as Western Marshal, except for target-type front sight, adjustable rear, oversize stocks. Not made in .22 RF. Introduced 1969; dropped 1980. Used values, .357 magnum, $130 to $140; .45 Colt, $130 to $140; .44 magnum, $140 to $150. Combo values, .357 magnum/9mm Luger, $150 to $160; .44 magnum/.44-40, $160 to $170; .44 Long Colt/.45 Auto, $160 to $170.

**HAWES Deputy Marshal:** revolver, single-action; .22 LR; also available as combo with .22 Winchester rimfire magnum cylinder; 6-rd. cylinders; 5½" barrel, 11" overall length; blade front sight, adjustable rear, plastic or walnut grips. blued finish. Introduced 1973; dropped 1980. Used values, .22 LR with plastic grips, $50 to $55; with walnut grips, $55 to $60. Combo values, .22 LR/.22 WMRF, with plastic grips, $60 to $65; walnut grips, $65 to $70.

**HAWES Deputy Denver Marshal:** revolver, single-action; same specifications as Deputy Marshal, except for brass frame. Introduced 1973; dropped 1980. Used values, .22 LR with plastic grips, $60 to $65; with walnut grips, $65 to $70. Combo values, .22 LR/.22 WMRF, with plastic grips, $65 to $70; walnut grips, $70 to $75.

**HAWES Deputy Montana Marshal:** revolver, single-action; same specifications as Deputy Marshal, except has walnut grips only, brass grip frame. Introduced 1973; dropped 1980. Used value, .22 LR, $55 to $60. Combo value, .22 LR/.22 WMRF, $70 to $75.

**HAWES Deputy Texas Marshal:** revolver, single-action; same specifications as Deputy Marshal, except for chrome finish. Introduced 1973, dropped 1980. Used values, .22 LR, with plastic grips, $55 to $60; walnut grips, $60 to $65. Combo values, .22 LR/.22 WMRF, $65 to $70 with plastic grips; $70 to $75, with walnut grips.

**HAWES Deputy Silver City Marshal:** revolver, single-action; same specifications as Deputy Marshal, except for brass grip frame, chromed frame, blued barrel and cylinder. Introduced 1973; dropped 1980. Used values, .22 LR with plastic grips, $55 to $60; walnut grips, $60 to $65. Combo values, .22 LR/.22 WMRF, $65 to $70, with plastic grips; $70 to $75, walnut grips.

*Hawes Favorite*

**HAWES Favorite:** single-shot; tip-up action; .22 LR; 8" barrel, 12" overall; target sights, plastic or rosewood stocks, blued barrel, chromed frame. Replica of Stevens No. 35 target model. Manufactured, 1968 to 1976. Used value, $60 to $65.

**HAWES/SAUER Double Action:** automatic; 9mm Luger, .45 ACP; 9-rd. magazine in 9mm, 7 rds. in .45; 4-3/8" barrel, 7¾" overall length; checkered European walnut stocks or black plastic; windage adjustable rear sight, blade front; square combat trigger guard. Manufactured in Germany. Introduced 1977, still in production; dropped by Hawes 1980; also known as Browning BDA. Used value, $180 to $200.

# HIGH STANDARD

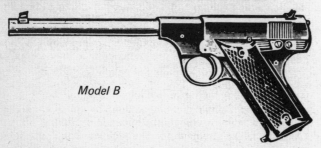

*Model B*

**HI-STANDARD Model B:** automatic; hammerless; .22 LR only; 4¾", 6¾" barrels; 10¾" overall length, with 6¾" barrel; 10-rd. magazine; fixed sights; checkered hard rubber grips, blued. Introduced in 1932; dropped, 1942. Used value, $145 to $175.

Model S-B has the same specifications as Model B, except with 5¾" barrel only; smoothbore for .22 shot cartridge. Introduced in 1939; dropped, 1940. Used value, $275 to $300.

Model H-B has the same general specifications as the Model B, except there is no thumb safety; has visible hammer. Introduced in 1940; dropped, 1942. Used value, $175 to $200.

**HI-STANDARD Model C:** automatic; hammerless; .22 short only. Other specifications are identical to those of Model B Hi-Standard auto. Introduced in 1936; dropped, 1942. Used value, $165 to $175.

*Model A*

**HI-STANDARD Model A:** automatic; hammerless; .22 LR only; 4½", 6¾" barrel; 11½" overall length, with 6¾" barrel; adjustable target-type sights; checkered walnut grips; blued. Actually an updated version of Model B. Introduced in 1938; dropped, 1942. Used value, $175 to $200.

Model H-A has the same specifications as Model A, but has visible hammer, sans thumb safety. Introduced in 1940; dropped, 1942. Used value, $200 to $225.

**HI-STANDARD Model D:** automatic; hammerless; .22 LR only; has the same specifications as Model A, except with heavy barrel. Introduced in 1938; dropped, 1942. Used value, $215 to $235.

Model H-D has the same specifications as Model D, except for visible hammer, sans thumb safety. Introduced in 1940; dropped in 1942. Used value, $225 to $250.

Model H-DM has the same general specifications as Model H-D, but with thumb safety added. Introduced in 1946; dropped, 1951. Used value, $160 to $200.

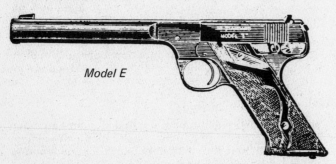

*Model E*

**HI-STANDARD Model E:** automatic; hammerless; .22 LR only; has same general specifications as Model A, except for thumb rest grips, heavy barrel. Introduced in 1937; dropped, 1942. Used value, $200 to $225.

Model H-E has the same specifications as Model E, except for visible hammer, sans thumb safety. Introduced in 1941; dropped, 1942. Used value, $225 to $250.

**HI-STANDARD Model G-380:** automatic; takedown; .380 auto only; 5″ barrel; visible hammer; thumb safety; fixed sights; checkered plastic grips; blued. Introduced in 1947; dropped, 1950. Used value, $175 to $225.

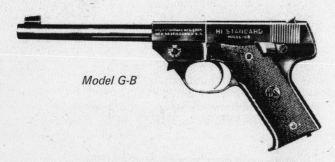

*Model G-B*

**HI-STANDARD Model G-B:** automatic; hammerless; takedown; .22 LR only; interchangeable barrels of 4½″, 6¾″; with 6¾″ barrel, overall length, 10¾″; fixed sights; checkered plastic grips; blued. Introduced in 1949; dropped, 1951. Used values, with two barrels, $200 to $225; one barrel, $150 to $175.

Model G-D has same general specifications as Model G-B, including interchangeable barrels; except for target sights, checkered walnut grips. Introduced in 1949; dropped, 1951. Used values, with two barrels, $235 to $250; one barrel, $175 to $200.

Model G-E has same general specifications as Model G-D, except for thumb-rest walnut grips, heavy barrels. Introduced in 1949; dropped, 1951. Used values, with both barrels, $250 to $275; one barrel, $200 to $225.

*First Model Olympic*

**HI-STANDARD Olympic (First Model):** automatic hammerless; .22 short only; light alloy slide; other specifications are same as Model G-E, including interchangeable barrels. Introduced in 1950; dropped, 1951. Used values, with both barrels, $275 to $300; one barrel, $225 to $250.

Olympic (Second Model) is hammerless, takedown automatic; .22 short only; interchangeable 4½″, 6¾″ barrels; with 6¾″ barrel, 11½″ overall length; 10-rd. magazine; target sights; adjustable barrel weights; alloy slide; checkered plastic thumb-rest grips; blued. Introduced in 1951; dropped, 1958. Used values, with both barrels, $250 to $275; one barrel, $235 to $250.

*Supermatic*

*Supermatic Tournament*

**HI-STANDARD Supermatic:** automatic; hammerless; takedown; .22 LR only; 4½″, 6¾″ interchangeable barrels; 10-rd. magazine; late models have recoil stabilizer on longer barrel; 11½″ overall length, with 6¾″ barrel; 2, 3-oz. adjustable barrel weights; target sights; checkered plastic thumb-rest grips; blued. Introduced in 1951; dropped, 1958. Used values, with both barrels, $200 to $225; one barrel, $150 to $175.

Supermatic Tournament model is .22 LR only, with

*Supermatic Citation*

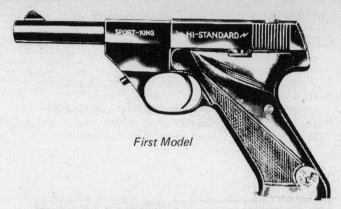

*First Model*

same specifications of standard Supermatic, except for interchangeable 5½'' bull barrel, and 6¾'' barrel; barrels drilled, notched for stabilizer, weights; click adjustable rear sight, undercut ramp front; checkered walnut grips; blued finish. Introduced in 1958; dropped, 1963. Used values, both barrels, $250 to $275; one barrel, $200 to $225.

**Supermatic Citation** has the same general specifications as Tournament model, except for choice of 5½'' bull barrel, 6¾'', 8'', 10'' tapered barrels, with stabilizer, 2 removable weights; adjustable trigger pull; click adjustable rear sight; ramp front; checkered laminated wood grips; bull barrel model has checkered walnut grips with thumb rest. Introduced in 1958; dropped, 1966. Used values, tapered barrel, $200 to $250; bull barrel, $200 to $225.

**Supermatic Standard Citation** is a simplified version of original Citation, but with 5½'' bull barrel only; 10'' overall length; over-travel trigger adjustment; rebounding firing pin; click adjustable square notch rear sight, undercut ramp front; checkered walnut grips with or without thumb rest, right or left-hand. Dropped, 1977. Used value, $150 to $175.

**Supermatic Citation Military** model has same specs as Standard Citation model, except for military-style grip, positive magazine latch, stippled front, backstraps; 5½'' bull barrel or 7¾'' fluted barrel. Still in production. Used value, $140 to $150.

**Supermatic Trophy** has the same specifications as original Citation model, except for choice of 5½'' bull barrel, 7¼'' fluted style; extra magazine; high-lustre blue finish. Introduced in 1963; dropped, 1966. Used value, $175 to $200.

**Supermatic Trophy Military** model has same general specifications as standard Trophy model, except that grip duplicates feel of Government Model .45; trigger adjustable for pull, over-travel; stippled front, backstrap; checkered walnut grips with or without thumb rest; right or left-hand; frame-mounted click adjustable rear sight; undercut ramp front. Still in production. Used value, $165 to $175.

**HI-STANDARD Sport-King (First Model):** automatic; hammerless; .22 LR only; 4½'', 6¾'' interchangeable barrels; with 6¾'' barrel, 11½'' overall length; 10-rd. magazine; fixed sights; checkered thumb-rest plastic grips; blued. Introduced in 1951; dropped, 1958. Used values, with both barrels, $150 to $165; one barrel, $135 to $145.

**Lightweight Sport-King** has the same specifications as the standard Sport-King model, except frame is of forged aluminum alloy. Introduced in 1954; dropped, 1965. Used values, both barrels, $150 to $165; one barrel, $135 to $140.

**Sport-King (Second Model)** is all-steel, .22 LR; minor interior design changes from first model Sport-King, interchangeable barrel retained. Introduced in 1958; still in production. Used values, both barrels, $125 to $135; one barrel, $85 to $95.

**HI-STANDARD Flight-King (First Model):** automatic; hammerless; .22 short only; other specifications are identical to those of Sport-King model, except for aluminum alloy frame, slide. Introduced in 1953; dropped, 1958. Used values, with both barrels, $150 to $175; one barrel, $125 to $135.

**Flight-King (Second Model)** has the same general specifications as first-model Flight-King, except for all-steel construction; .22 LR only. Introduced in 1958; dropped, 1966. Used values, with both barrels, $175 to $185; one barrel, $135 to $150.

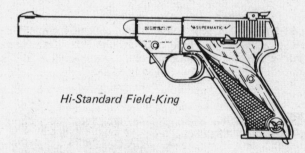

*Hi-Standard Field-King*

**HI-STANDARD Field-King:** automatic; hammerless .22 LR only; has the same general specifications as Sport-King model, but with target sights, heavier 6¾'' barrel; late model with recoil stabilizer. Introduced in 1951; dropped, 1958. Used value, $150 to $165.

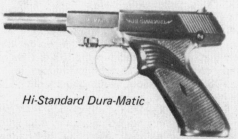

*Hi-Standard Dura-Matic*

**HI-STANDARD Dura-Matic:** automatic; hammerless takedown; .22 LR only; 4½'', 6½'' interchangeable barrels; with 6½'' barrel, overall length, 10-7/8''; usually sold with one barrel only; fixed sights; checkered plastic grips; blued. Introduced in 1955; dropped, 1969. Used value, $100 to $125.

*Hi-Standard Olympic ISU*

*Hi-Standard Victor*

**HI-STANDARD Olympic ISU:** target automatic; hammerless; .22 short only; 6¾" barrel; (5½" bull, 8" tapered; dropped, 1964) 10-rd. magazine; detachable weights, integral stabilizer; trigger adjustable for pull, over-travel; click adjustable square notch rear sight; undercut ramp front; checkered walnut grips with or without thumb rest; left, right-hand; blued finish. Meets International Shooting Union regulations. Introduced in 1958; dropped, 1977. Used value, $200 to $225.

**HI-STANDARD Victor:** automatic; hammerless; .22 LR only; 4½", 5½" barrels; 8¾" overall length with shorter barrel; vent or solid aluminum rib; 10-rd. magazine; interchangeable barrel feature; rib-mounted click-adjustable rear sight, undercut ramp front; checkered walnut grips with thumb rest; blued. Introduced in 1973; still in production. Used values, solid rib, $200 to $225; vent rib, $250 to $275.

*Hi-Standard Plinker*

**HI-STANDARD Plinker:** automatic; hammerless; .22 LR only; interchangeable 4½", 6½" barrels; 9" overall length with 4½" barrel; 10-rd. magazine; grooved trigger; checkered plastic target grips; fixed square notch rear sight; ramp front; blued. Introduced in 1972; dropped, 1975. Used value, $75 to $100.

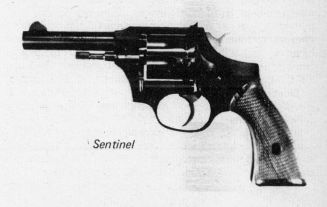

*Sentinel*

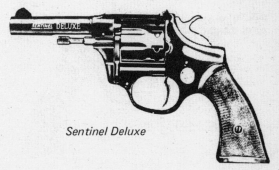

*Sentinel Deluxe*

*Hi-Standard Sharpshooter*

**HI-STANDARD Sharpshooter:** automatic; hammerless; .22 LR only; 5½" barrel; 9-rd. magazine; push-button takedown feature; scored trigger; adjustable square notch rear sight, ramp front; slide lock; checkered laminated plastic grips; blued. Introduced in 1972; still in production. Used value, $135 to $145.

**HI-STANDARD Sentinel:** double-action revolver; solid aluminum alloy frame; 9-rd. swing-out cylinder; .22 LR only; 3", 4", 6" barrels; with 4" barrel, overall length, 9"; fixed sights; checkered plastic grips; blued, nickel finish. Introduced in 1955; dropped, 1974. Used values, blued, $60 to $65; nickel $65 to $70.

**Sentinel Deluxe** has the same specifications as the standard Sentinel; exceptions are movable rear sight, two-piece square-butt checkered walnut grips, wide trigger; 4", 6" barrels only. Introduced in 1957; dropped, 1974. Used value, $75 to $80.

**Sentinel Snub** model has same specifications as Sentinel Deluxe, except for checkered bird's-head-type grips, 2-3/8" barrel. Introduced in 1957; dropped, 1974. Used value, $70 to $75.

**Sentinel Imperial** has the same general specifications as standard Sentinel model, except for ramp front sight, two-piece checkered walnut grips, onyx-black or nickel finish. Introduced in 1962; dropped, 1965. Used values, black finish, $60 to $65; nickel finish, $70 to $75.

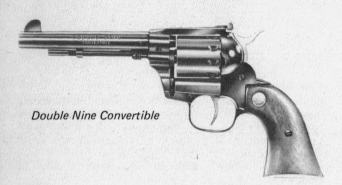

*Double-Nine Convertible*

**HI-STANDARD Double-Nine:** double-action revolver; Western-styled version of Sentinel; .22 short or LR; 5½" barrel; 11" overall length; 9-rd. swing-out cylinder; dummy ejection rod housing; spring-loaded ejection; rebounding hammer; movable notch rear sight, blade front; plastic grips; blued, nickel finish. Introduced in 1959; dropped, 1971. Used values, blued, $60 to $65; nickel, $65 to $70.

**Double-Nine Convertible** model has the same general specifications as original Double-Nine, except primary cylinder is chambered for .22 LR, long, short; extra cylinder fires .22 Win. rimfire magnum; smooth frontier-type walnut grips; movable notched rear sight, blade front; blued, nickel finish. Introduced in 1972; still in production. Used values, blued, $85 to $90; nickel, $95 to $100.

*Hi-Standard Kit Gun*

**HIGH STANDARD Kit Gun:** double action; .22 LR, long, short; 4" barrel; 9" overall length; 9-rd. swing-out cylinder; micro-adjustable rear sight, target ramp front; checkered walnut grips; blued. Introduced in 1970; dropped, 1973. Used value, $42.50 to $46.50.

**HI-STANDARD Natchez:** double-action revolver; same general specifications as Double-Nine, except for 4½" barrel; 10" overall length; ivory-like plastic bird's-head grips; blued. Introduced in 1961; dropped, 1966. Used value, $60 to $65.

**HI-STANDARD Posse:** double-action revolver; same general design as Double-Nine, except for 3½" barrel; 9" overall length; uncheckered walnut grips; brass grip frame, trigger guard; blued. Introduced in 1961; dropped, 1966. Used value, $70 to $75.

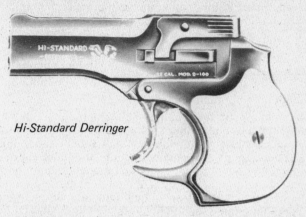

*Hi-Standard Derringer*

**HI-STANDARD Derringer:** double-action; hammerless; over/under 2" barrels; 5" overall length; 2-shot; .22 LR, long, short; .22 rimfire magnum; plastic grips; fixed sights; standard model has blue, nickel finish. Presentation model is gold plated, introduced in 1965; dropped, 1966. Presentation model has some collector value. Standard model, introduced in 1963, .22 long rifle version dropped in 1977, .22 magnum still in production. Used values, standard model, $90 to $100; presentation model, $175 to $200; matched pair, presentation model, consecutive serial numbers, $400 to $450; .22 magnum, $100 to $125.

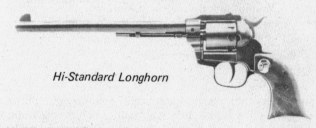

*Hi-Standard Longhorn*

**HI-STANDARD Longhorn:** double-action revolver; same general specifications as Double-Nine; original version has 4½" barrel, pearl-like plastic grips; model with 5½" barrel has plastic staghorn grips; later model has walnut grips, 9½" barrel; aluminum alloy frame; blued finish. Long barreled model introduced in 1970; dropped, 1971. Other models introduced in 1961; dropped, 1966. Used values, 9½" barrel, walnut grips, $90 to $95; other models, $80 to $85.

**Longhorn Convertible** has the same general specifications as standard Longhorn, but with 9½" barrel only; smooth walnut grips; dual cylinder to fire .22 Win. rimfire magnum cartridge. Introduced in 1971; still in production. Used value, $95 to $100.

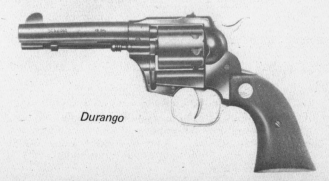

*Durango*

**HI-STANDARD Durango:** double-action revolver; has the same general specifications as the Double-Nine model; .22 LR, long, short; 4½", 5½" barrels; 10" overall length with shorter barrel; brass-finished trigger guard, backstrap; uncheckered walnut grips; blued only in shorter barrel length; blued, nickel in 5½" barrel. Introduced in 1972; dropped, 1975. Used values, blued, $60 to $65; nickel, $65 to $70.

*Mark II*

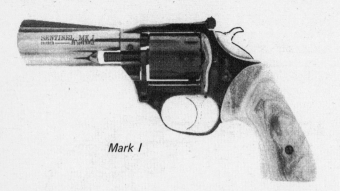

*Mark I*

**HIGH STANDARD Sentinel Mark IV:** double-action revolver; .22 WMRF; except for caliber, has same specifications as Sentinel Mark I. Introduced in 1974, dropped 1979. Used value, $85 to $95.

**HIGH STANDARD Sentinel Mark I:** double-action revolver; .22 LR; 9-rd. cylinder; 2", 3", 4" barrel lengths; uncheckered walnut stocks, ramp front sight, fixed or adjustable rear, blued or nickel finish. Introduced 1974, still in production. Used value: $85 to $95.

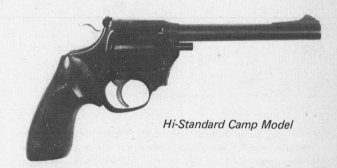

*Hi-Standard Camp Model*

**HIGH STANDARD Sentinel Mark II:** double-action revolver; .357 magnum, 6-rd. cylinder; 2½", 4", 6" barrel lengths; walnut combat grips, fixed sights, blued finish. Manufactured 1974 to 1976. Used value, $95 to $105.

**HIGH STANDARD Sentinel Mark III:** double-action revolver; has the same specifications as Sentinel Mark II, except for ramp front sight, adjustable rear. Manufactured 1974 to 1976. Used value, $100 to $110.

**HIGH STANDARD Camp Model:** double-action revolver; .22 LR, .22 WMRF; has same specifications as Sentinel Mark IV, except for target-type checkered walnut grips, 6" barrel, adjustable rear sight. Introduced 1976; dropped 1979. Used value, $90 to $95.

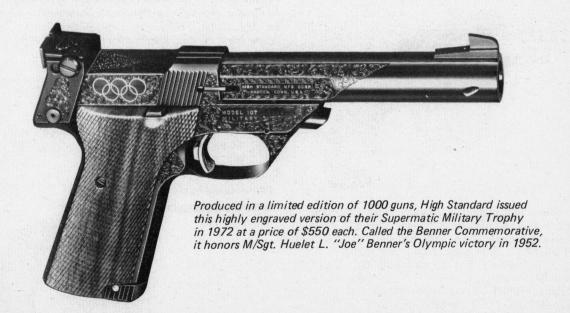

*Produced in a limited edition of 1000 guns, High Standard issued this highly engraved version of their Supermatic Military Trophy in 1972 at a price of $550 each. Called the Benner Commemorative, it honors M/Sgt. Huelet L. "Joe" Benner's Olympic victory in 1952.*

# IVER JOHNSON

*Iver Johnson Safety Hammer Model*

**IVER JOHNSON Safety Hammer Model:** double-action revolver; hinged frame; .22 LR, .32 S&W long, .32 S&W; 2", 3", 3¼", 4", 5", 6" barrels; in .22 LR, 7-rd. cylinder; in .32 S&W long, 6 rds., 5-rd. capacity in others; fixed sights; hard rubber grips with round butt, square butt with rubber or walnut; heavier frame for .32 S&W long, .38 S&W; blued, nickel finish. Introduced in 1892; dropped, 1950. Used value, $50 to $55.

**IVER JOHNSON Safety Hammerless Model:** double-action revolver; hinged frame; basic design comparable to Safety Hammer model; .22 LR, .32 S&W Long, .32 S&W, .38 S&W; 2", 3", 3¼", 4", 5", 6" barrels; in .22 LR, 7-rd. cylinder; in .32 S&W long, 6 rds., 5-rd. capacity in others; fixed sights, hard rubber grips with round butt, square butt with rubber or walnut; heavier frame for .32 S&W Long, .38 S&W; blued, nickel finish. Introduced in 1895; dropped, 1950. Used value, $55 to $60.

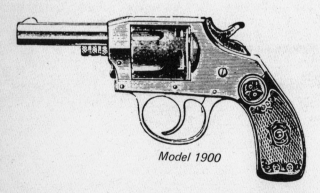

*Model 1900*

**IVER JOHNSON Model 1900:** double-action revolver; solid frame; .22 rimfire, .32 S&W Long, .32 S&W, .38 S&W; 2½", 4½", 6" barrels; 7-rd. cylinder in .22, 6 rds. in .32 S&W, 5 rds. in .32 S&W long; fixed sights; hard rubber grips; blued, nickel finish. Introduced in 1900; dropped, 1947. Used value, $40 to $45.

**Model 1900 Target** utilizes same frame as standard model; .22 LR only; 6", 9" barrels; 7-rd. cylinder; fixed sights; checkered walnut grips; blued finish. Introduced in 1925; dropped, 1942. Used value, $65 to $70.

**IVER JOHNSON 22 Supershot:** double-action revolver; hinged frame; .22 LR only; 6" barrel; 7-rd. cylinder; fixed sights; checkered walnut grips; blued finish. Introduced in 1929; dropped, 1949. Used value, $60 to $65.

**Supershot 9-shot** has hinged frame, .22 LR only, 9-rd. cylinder; pre-WWII model has adjustable finger rest. Other specifications are same as standard model. Introduced in 1929; dropped, 1949. Used value, $75 to $85.

**IVER JOHNSON Target 9-Shot:** double-action revolver; solid frame; .22 LR only; 6", 10" barrels; 10¾" overall length with 6" barrel; 9-rd. cylinder; fixed sights; checkered diamond panel walnut grips; blued finish. Introduced in 1929; dropped, 1946. Used value, $60 to $65.

*Sealed 8 Target*

*Supershot*

**IVER JOHNSON Sealed Eight Supershot:** double-action revolver; hinged frame; .22 LR only; 6" barrel; 8-rd. cylinder counterbored for high velocity ammo; 10¾" overall length; pre-WWII version has adjustable finger rest; adjustable target sights; checkered diamond panel walnut grips; blued finish. Introduced in 1931; dropped, 1957. Used value, $80 to $90.

**Sealed Eight Target** has solid frame; 6", 10" barrels; fixed sights. Other specifications are same as Sealed Eight Supershot. Introduced in 1931; dropped, 1957. Used value, $60 to $65.

**Sealed Eight Protector** has hinged frame; 2½" barrel; 7¼" overall length; fixed sights, checkered walnut grips; blued finish. Introduced in 1933; dropped, 1949. Used value, $65 to $70.

*Champion*

**IVER JOHNSON Champion:** single-action target revolver; hinged frame; .22 LR only; 6'' barrel; 10¾'' overall length; 8-rd. cylinder; countersunk chambers for high velocity ammo; adjustable finger rest; adjustable target-type sights; checkered walnut grips; blued finish. Introduced in 1938; dropped, 1948. Used value, $75 to $85.

*Iver Johnson Trigger-Cocking Model*

**IVER JOHNSON Trigger-Cocking Model:** single-action target revolver; hinged frame; .22 LR only; 6'' barrel; 10¾'' overall length; 8-rd. cylinder, with countersunk chambers; adjustable target sights, grips; blued finish; checkered walnut grips. First pull on the trigger cocks the hammer; second releases hammer. Introduced in 1940; dropped, 1947. Some collector value. Used value, $90 to $100.

**IVER JOHNSON Supershot Model 844:** double-action revolver; hinged frame; .22 LR only; 4½'', 6'' barrels; 9¼'' overall length, with 4½'' barrel; 8-rd. cylinder; adjustable sights; one-piece checkered walnut grip; blued finish. Introduced in 1955; dropped, 1956. Used value, $65 to $70.

**IVER JOHNSON Armsworth Model 855:** single-action revolver; hinged frame; .22 LR only; 6'' barrel; 10¾'' overall length; adjustable finger rest; adjustable sights; one-piece checkered walnut grip; blued finish. Introduced in 1955; dropped, 1957. Used value, $85 to $95.

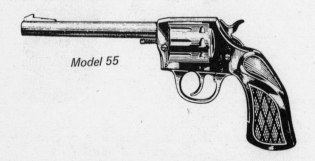

*Model 55*

**IVER JOHNSON Model 55:** double-action target revolver; solid frame; .22 LR, long, short; 4½'', 6'' barrels; 10¾'' overall length, with 6'' barrel; 8-rd. cylinder; fixed sights; checkered walnut grips; blued finish. Introduced in 1955; dropped 1961. Used value, $35 to $40.

**Model 55A** has the same specifications as Model 55, except for incorporation of a loading gate. Introduced in 1962; still in production. Used value, $40 to $45.

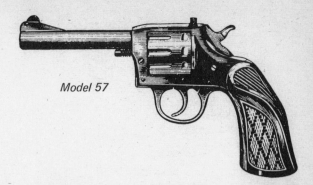

*Model 57*

**IVER JOHNSON Model 57:** double-action target revolver; solid frame; .22 LR, long, short; 4'', 5'' barrels; 8-rd. cylinder; 10¾'' overall length with 6'' barrel; adjustable sights, checkered plastic grip, with thumb channel; blued finish. Introduced in 1956; dropped, 1961. Used value, $45 to $50.

**Model 57A** has the same specifications as Model 57, except for addition of loading gate. Introduced in 1962; still in production. Used value, $45 to $50.

*Model 66 Trailsman*

**IVER JOHNSON Model 66 Trailsman:** double-action revolver; hinged frame; .22 LR, long, short; 6'' barrel; 11'' overall length; 8-rd. cylinder; rebounding hammer; adjustable sights checkered plastic grips with thumb channel; blued finish. Introduced in 1958; still in production. Used value, $45 to $50.

**Trailsman 66 Snubby** model has same general specifications as standard Model 66, except for 2¾'' barrel; 7'' overall length; smooth, rounded plastic grips; also available in .32 S&W, .38 S&W with 5-rd. cylinder; Introduced in 1961; dropped, 1972. Used value, $55 to $60.

*Iver Johnson Model 50A Sidewinder*

**IVER JOHNSON Model 50A Sidewinder:** frontier-style double action revolver; solid frame; .22 LR, long short; 6'' barrel; 11¼'' overall length; 8-rd cylinder; fixed sights; plastic staghorn grips; blued finish. Introduced in 1961; still in production in varying configurations as Models 524, 624, 724, 824, some with adjustable sights. Used value, $45 to $50.

Model 55S-A

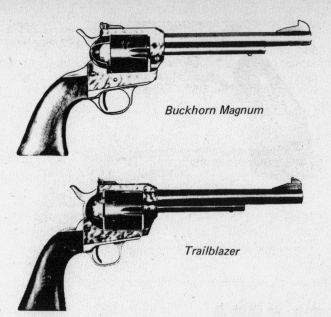

Buckhorn Magnum

Trailblazer

**IVER JOHNSON Model 55S Cadet:** double-action revolver; solid frame; .22 LR, long, short, .32 S&W, .38 S&W; 2½" barrel; 7" overall length; .22 has 8-rd. cylinder, others, 5-rd. capacity; fixed sights; plastic grips; blued finish. Introduced in 1955; dropped, 1961. Used value, $40 to $45.

**Model 55S-A** has the same specifications as Model 55S, except for addition of a loading gate. Introduced in 1962; still in production. Used value, $50 to $55.

**Cattleman Buntline** has same specifications as Cattleman Buckhorn, except for 18" barrel, shoulder stock with brass fittings. Introduced in 1973; dropped 1980. Used values, $225 to $250.

**Cattleman Trailblazer** has same general specifications as Cattleman Buckhorn, except .22 caliber; has combo .22 LR, .22 WMRF cylinders, 5½, 6½" barrel lengths. Introduced in 1973; dropped 1980. Used value, $100 to $110.

Model 67S

Iver Johnson American Bulldog

**IVER JOHNSON Model 67 Viking:** double-action revolver; hinged frame; .22 LR, long, short; 4½", 6" barrels; 11" overall length, with 6" barrel; 8-rd. cylinder; adjustable sights; plastic grips with thumb channel. Introduced in 1964; dropped, 1974. Used value, $55 to $60.

**Model 67S Viking Snubby** has the same general specifications as standard Model 67, except for 2¾" barrel, 7" overall length; small plastic grips; also available in .32 S&W, .38 S&W, with 5-rd. cylinder. Introduced in 1964; dropped, 1974. Used value, $60 to $65.

**IVER JOHNSON Cattleman:** single-action revolver; .357 magnum, .44 magnum, .45 Colt; 6-rd. cylinder; 4¾",5 ½", 6" barrel lengths; one-piece uncheckered walnut grip, fixed sights, brass grip frame, color case-hardened frame, blued barrel and cylinder. Manufactured in Italy. Introduced 1973; dropped 1980. Used value, $120 to $140.

**Cattleman Buckhorn** has the same specifications as Cattleman, except for ramp front sight, adjustable rear, additional barrel lengths of 5½" and 12". Introduced in 1973; dropped 1980. Used value, $140 to $160, depending on caliber, barrel length.

**IVER JOHNSON American Bulldog:** double-action revolver; solid frame; .22 LR, .22 WMRF, .38 Special; in .22, 6-rd. cylinder, in .38 Special, 5 rds.; 2½", 4" barrel lengths; checkered plastic stocks, adjustable rear sight, fixed front, blued or nickel finish. Manufactured 1974 to 1976. Used value, $60 to $70.

**IVER JOHNSON Sportsman:** double-action revolver; solid frame; .22 LR; 6-rd. cylinder; 4¾", 6" barrel lengths; checkered plastic stocks, fixed sights, blued finish. Manufactured 1974 to 1976. Used value, $50 to $55.

*Iver Johnson Rookie*

**IVER JOHNSON Rookie:** double-action revolver; solid frame; .38 Special; 5-rd. cylinder; 4" barrel, 9" overall length; checkered plastic stocks, fixed sights, blued finish. Introduced 1975; dropped 1976. Used value, $50 to $55.

**IVER JOHNSON Deluxe Target Model:** double-action revolver; solid frame; .22 LR. Same specifications as Sportsman model, except for substitution of adjustable sights. Manufactured 1975 to 1976. Used value, $60 to $65.

**IVER JOHNSON Swing Out Model:** double-action revolver; .22 LR, .22 WMRF, .32 S&W Long, .38 Special; in .22, 6-rd. cylinder; in center-fire calibers, 5 rds.; plain barrels are 2", 3", 4"; with vent rib, 4", 6", 8¾"; fixed sights with plain barrel, adjustable sights with vent rib barrel; walnut stocks, blued or nickel finish. Introduced in 1977; dropped 1979. Used values: plain barrel, $70 to $80; vent rib barrel, $110 to $115.

# LLAMA

*Llama M-IIIA*

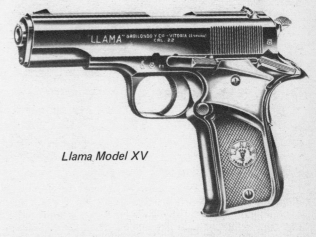

*Llama Model XV*

*Llama Model VIII*

**LLAMA Model IIIA:** automatic; .380 auto only; 3-11/16" barrel; 6½" overall length; 7-rd. magazine; checkered thumbrest plastic grips; adjustable target sights; vent rib; grip safety; blued. Early versions were sans vent rib, had lanyard ring, no thumbrest on grips. Imported by Stoeger. Introduced in 1951; still in production. Used value, $100 to $115.

**LLAMA Model XA:** automatic; .32 auto only; 3-11/16" barrel; 6½" overall length; 8-rd. magazine; checkered thumbrest plastic grips; adjustable target sights; grip safety; blued. Imported by Stoeger. Introduced in 1951; still in production. Used value, $100 to $110.

**LLAMA Model XV:** automatic; .22 LR only; 3-11/16" barrel; 6½" overall length; 8-rd. magazine; checkered thumbrest plastic grips; adjustable target sights; vent rib; grip safety; blued. Imported by Stoeger. Introduced in 1951; still in production. Used value, $120 to $125.

**LLAMA Model VIII:** automatic; .38 Super only; 5" barrel; 8½" overall length; 9-rd. magazine; hand-checkered walnut grips; fixed sights; vent rib; grip safety; blued. Imported by Stoeger. Introduced in 1952; still in production. Used value, $135 to $145.

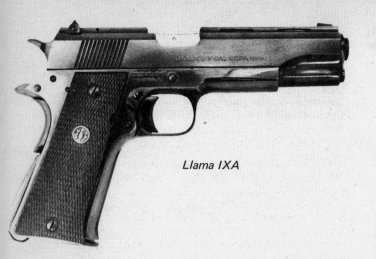

Llama IXA

Llama Martial

**LLAMA Model IXA:** automatic; .45 auto only; 5'' barrel; 8½'' overall length; 7-rd. magazine; hand-checkered walnut grips; vent rib; fixed sights; grip safety; blued. Introduced in 1952; still in production. Used value, $145 to $155.

**LLAMA Martial:** double-action revolver; .22 LR, .22 magnum, .38 Special; 4'' barrel in .38 only, 6'' in .22; 11¼'' overall length with 6'' barrel; hand-checkered walnut grips; target sights; blued. Imported by Stoeger. Introduced in 1969; still in production. Used value, $110 to $120.

Llama Model XI

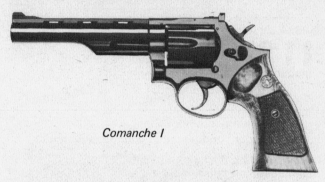

Comanche I

**LLAMA Comanche I:** double-action revolver; .22 LR; 6-rd. cylinder; 6'' barrel, 11¼'' overall length; checkered walnut stocks, target-type sights, blued finish. Introduced in 1977, replacing Martial .22 model; still in production. Used value, $150 to $155.

**Comanche II** has same general specifications as Comanche I, except chambered in .38 Special, 4'' barrel. Introduced in 1977, still in production. Used value, $150 to $155.

**Comanche III** was introduced in 1975 as original Comanche; .357 magnum; 6-rd. cylinder, 4'' barrel, 9¼'' overall, ramp front sight, adjustable rear, checkered walnut stocks, blued finish. Still in production. Used value, $160 to $165.

**LLAMA Model XI:** automatic; 9mm Parabellum; 5'' barrel; 8½'' overall length; 8-rd. magazine; checkered thumbrest plastic grips; adjustable rear sight, fixed front; vent rib; grip safety; blued. Imported by Stoeger Arms. Introduced in 1954 by Stoeger; still in production. Used value, $135 to $145.

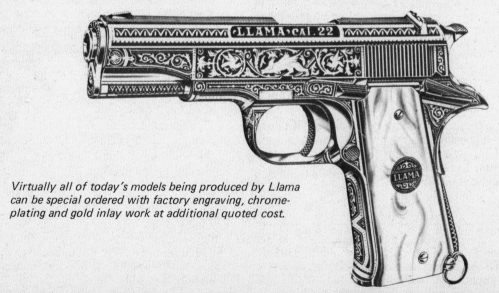

*Virtually all of today's models being produced by Llama can be special ordered with factory engraving, chrome-plating and gold inlay work at additional quoted cost.*

# MAB

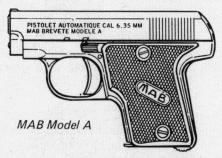

*MAB Model A*

**MAB Model A:** automatic; .25 auto; 2½″ barrel; 4½″ overall length; based on Browning design; 6-rd. magazine; no rear sight, fixed front; checkered plastic or hard rubber grips; blued. Introduced in 1921; production suspended in 1942. Production resumed in 1945 for importation into U.S. as WAC Model A or Le Defendeur; importation dropped in 1968. Manufactured by Manufacture d'armes de Bayonne, France. Used value, $115 to $125.

**MAB Model B:** automatic; .25 auto; 2″ barrel; 4½″ overall length; 6-rd. magazine; no rear sight; fixed front; hard rubber grips; blued. Introduced in 1932; dropped in 1967. Never imported into U.S. Used value, $115 to $125.

*MAB Model C*

**MAB Model C:** automatic; .32, .380 auto; 3¾″ barrel; 6″ overall length; 7-rd. magazine in .32, 6 rds. in .380; push-button magazine release behind trigger; fixed sights; checkered black hard rubber grips; blued. Introduced in 1933; made under German supervision during WWII. Importation dropped, 1968. Used value, $85 to $95.

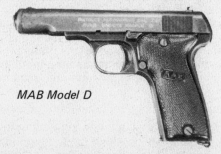

*MAB Model D*

**MAB Model D:** automatic; .32, .380 auto; 3½″ barrel; 7″ overall length; 9-rd. magazine in .32, 8 rds. in

.380; push-button magazine release; fixed sights; checkered black hard rubber grips; blued. Introduced in 1933; made under German supervision in WWII. Imported to U.S. as WAC Model D or MAB Le Gendarme. Importation dropped, 1968. Used value, $100 to $115.

*MAB Model E*

**MAB Model E:** automatic; .25 auto; 3¼″ barrel; 6.1″ overall length; 10-rd. magazine; fixed sights; plastic grips; blued. Introduced in 1949; imported into U.S. as WAC Model E. Importation dropped, 1968. Used value, $115 to $125 to $145.

**MAB Model R:** automatic; .22 LR, 4½″ or 7″ barrel; external hammer; 10-rd. magazine. Introduced in 1950; never imported into U.S. Still in production. Used value, $90 to $100.

*MAB Model P-15*

**MAB Model P-15:** 9mm Parabellum; 4½″ barrel; 8″ overall length; 15-rd. magazine; fixed sights; checkered plastic grips; blued; still in production. Used value, $145 to $165.

*MAB Model F*

**MAB Model F:** automatic; .22 LR; 3¾″, 6″, 7¼″ barrels; 10¾″ overall length; 10-rd. magazine; windage adjustable rear sight, ramp front; plastic thumbrest grips; blued. Introduced in 1950; variation imported into U.S. as Le Chasseur model. Importation dropped, 1968. Used value, $80 to $90.

# MAUSER

*Mauser Model 1910 Pocket Pistol*

**MAUSER Model 1910 Pocket Pistol:** automatic; .25 auto, 3-3/16'' barrel; 5-3/8'' overall length; 9-rd. magazine; fixed sights; checkered hard rubber or walnut grips; blued. Introduced in 1910; dropped, 1939. Used value, $140 to $160.

**MAUSER Model 1914 Pocket Pistol:** .32 Auto; 8-rd. magazine; 3-2/5'' barrel, 6'' overall length; checkered walnut, hard rubber stocks; fixed sights, blued finish. Similar in design to Model 1910. Manufactured 1914 to 1935. Used value, $160 to $170.

**MAUSER Model 1934 Pocket Pistol:** .32 Auto; has the same general specifications as Model 1914, except for substitution of one-piece walnut stock. Manufactured 1934 to 1939. Used value, $160 to $170.

*Mauser Bolo Model 96*

**MAUSER Bolo Model 96:** automatic; 7.63mm Mauser; locked-bolt design; 4'' barrel; 10¾'' overall length; 10-rd. box magazine; adjustable rear sight, fixed front; serrated walnut grips. Based upon original Model 96 design, but barrel reduced in length in accordance with Versailles Treaty. Introduced in 1922 for export; dropped, 1930. Used value, $425 to $450.

**MAUSER Model 1930:** 7.63mm Mauser, 5¼'' barrel, serrated walnut grips; introduced in 1930, dropped, ca. 1939. Used value, $465 to $485.

*Mauser WTP 1st Model*

**MAUSER WTP (First Model):** automatic; advertised as Westentaschen-Pistole or vest-pocket pistol; .25 auto only;

2½'' barrel; 4½'' overall length; 6-rd. magazine; checkered hard rubber grips; blued. Introduced in 1922; dropped, 1938. Used value, $200 to $225.

*Second Model WTP*

**Second Model WTP** is smaller, lighter in weight. Introduced in 1938; dropped during WWII. Used value, $210 to $225.

*Mauser Model HSc*

**MAUSER Model HSc:** double-action automatic; .32 auto, .380 auto; 3-3/8'' barrel; 6.05'' overall length; 7-rd. magazine; fixed sights; checkered walnut grips; blued, nickel finish. Introduced in 1939; dropped 1978. Imported by Interarms. Used values, blued, $165 to $175; nickel, $200 to $225.

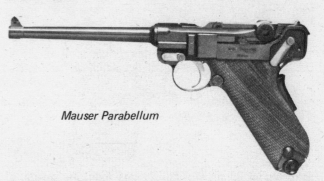

*Mauser Parabellum*

**MAUSER Parabellum:** automatic; .30 Luger, 9mm Parabellum; 4'' barrel in 9mm, 4'', 6'' in .30; with 4'' barrel, overall length, 8.7''; fixed sights; manual, grip safeties; checkered walnut grips; blued. American eagle over chamber; follows Swiss Luger style. Imported by Interarms. Introduced in 1966; dropped 1978. Used value, $350 to $375.

**Parabellum P-08** has the same general specifications as 1906 model, except for redesigned takedown lever; curved front strap, improved safety, trigger; Mauser banner on toggle. Introduced in 1908; resurrected in 1975; dropped 1978. Imported by Interarms. Used value, $325 to $350.

**Pre-WWII MAUSER Lugers:** 9mm (rarely 7.65mm) marked ''Mauser,'' ''S/42,'' or ''byf'' on toggle. Prices often reflect collector interest. Used values, $325 up.

# NAVY ARMS

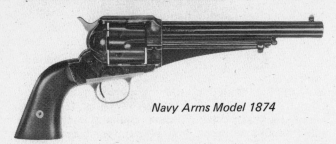

*Navy Arms Model 1874*

*Frontier SA*

*Buntline Frontier*

**NAVY ARMS Model 1874:** single-action revolver; .357 magnum, .44-40, .45 Colt; 6-rd. cylinder; 7½'' barrel, 13½'' overall length; smooth European walnut grips; fixed sights, blued or nickel finish. Manufactured in Italy. Introduced 1955, still in production. Replica of Remington Model 1874. Used value, $125 to $130.

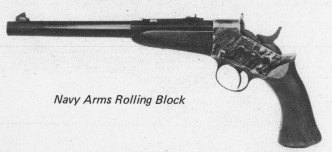

*Navy Arms Rolling Block*

**NAVY ARMS Rolling Block:** single-shot; .22 LR, .22 Hornet, .357 magnum; 8'' barrel, 12'' overall length; color case-hardened frame; brass trigger guard; uncheckered walnut stocks, forearm; blued barrel, adjustable sights. Manufactured in Italy. Hornet chambering dropped 1975. Introduced 1965, still in production. Used value, $110 to $115.

**NAVY ARMS Frontier Model:** .22 LR, .22 WMRF, .357 magnum, .45 Colt; 6-rd. cylinder; 4½'', 5½'', 7½'' barrels. brass grip frame, color case-hardened frame, blued barrel and cylinder, fixed sights; one-piece uncheckered walnut grip. Manufactured in Italy. Introduced 1975, still in production. Used value, $110 to $115.

**Frontier Target Model** has the same specifications as Frontier, except for ramp front sight, adjustable rear. Introduced 1975; still in production. Used value, $120 to $125.

**Frontier Buntline** has same general specifications as Frontier Target Model; made in .357 magnum and .45 Colt only; has 16½'' barrel, detachable shoulder stock. Introduced 1975, still in production. Used value, $150 to $160.

# REMINGTON

*Remington Model 95*

**REMINGTON Model 95:** superposed double-barrel derringer; single-action; .41 short rimfire; 3'' barrels, 4-7/8'' overall length. Introduced in 1866; dropped, 1935. Prior to 1888, the model was stamped E. Remington & Sons; from 1888 to 1910, the derringers were marked Remington Arms Co.; from 1910 to 1935, guns were marked Remington Arms-U.M.C. Co. The early styles have a two-armed extrac-

tor, long hammer spur. In later models, a few have no extractor; majority have sliding extractor, short hammer spur. Available with all-blued finish; full nickel plate, blued barrels, nickel-plated frame; factory engraving; choice of checkered hard rubber, walnut, mother-of-pearl, ivory grips; fixed rear groove sight, front blade cast on top barrel. Value of gun on modern market is primarily as collector item. Used value, plain model, $275 to $325; all nickel, $350 to $375; engraved model with mother-of-pearl or ivory grips, $500 to $750.

**REMINGTON Model 1901:** single-shot, rolling block action; .22 Short, .22 LR, .44 S&W Russian; 10'' barrel; 14'' overall length; checkered walnut grips, forearm; target sights, blued finish. Manufactured 1901 to 1909. Collector value. Used value, $400 to $425.

**REMINGTON Model 51:** automatic pistol; .32 auto, .380 auto; 7-rd. magazine; 3½'' barrel, 3-5/8'' overall length; fixed sights, blued finish; hard rubber grips. Introduced in 1918; dropped, 1934. Used value, $200 to $225.

*Model 51*

**REMINGTON Model XP-100:** single-shot pistol; bolt-action; .221 Remington Fireball only; 6½" barrel, 15¾" overall length; vent rib; blade front sight, adjustable rear; receiver drilled, tapped for scope mounts; one-piece brown nylon stock; blued finish. Introduced in 1963; still in production. Used value, $175 to $185.

# RUGER

*Ruger Standard Model*

**RUGER Standard Model:** automatic; .22 LR only; 4¾", 6" barrels; with 4¾" barrel, 8¾" overall length; 9-rd. magazine; checkered hard rubber grips, walnut optional; square-notch rear sight adjustable for windage only, fixed wide blade front; blued. Introduced in 1949; still in production. Until 1951, featured red eagle insignia in grips; changed to black upon death of Alex Sturm. This type has considerable collector value. Used values: red eagle model, $450 to $500; current model, $90 to $100.

*Ruger Mark I*

**RUGER Mark I:** automatic, target model; .22 LR only; 5¼" bull barrel, 6-7/8" tapered; with 6-7/8" barrel, 10-1/8" overall length; 9-rd. magazine; adjustable micrometer rear sight, fixed 1/8" blade front; checkered hard rubber grips, walnut optional; blued. Basically the same design as Standard model. Introduced in 1951; still in production.

Early issue had red eagle in grips; changed to black late in 1951. Former has collector value. Used values: red eagle model, $550 to $600; current model, $110 to $120.

*Lightweight Model*

**RUGER Single Six:** single-action revolver; .22 LR, .22 rimfire magnum; 4-5/8", 5½", 6½", 9½" barrels; with 4-5/8" barrel, overall length, 10"; 6-rd. cylinder; checkered hard rubber grips on early production, uncheckered walnut on later versions; rear sight adjustable for windage only; blued. Introduced in 1953; dropped, 1972. Used value, $135 to $150.

**Lightweight Single Six** has same specifications as standard model, except cylinder, cylinder frame, grip frame are of alloy, 4-5/8" barrel only. Aluminum cylinder has Moultin Hard Coat finish. Some guns have blued steel cylinder. Introduced in 1956; dropped, 1958. Used value, $225 to $250.

**Single Six Convertible** has the same general specifications as standard model, except for interchangeable cylinders, one handling .22 LR, long, short, the other .22 rimfire magnum cartridges; 5½", 6½" barrels only. Introduced in 1962; dropped, 1972. Used value, $145 to $165.

**Super Single Six Convertible** has same general specifications as standard model, except for interchangeable .22 LR, .22 rimfire magnum cylinders; ramp front sight, click adjustable rear sight with protective ribs. Introduced in 1964; dropped, 1972. Used value, $150 to $175.

**New Model Super Single Six** is improved version of original model, with new Ruger interlocked mechanism, independent firing pin, music wire springs throughout, hardened chrome-moly steel frame, other improvements; .22 LR, long, short; .22 rimfire magnum in extra cylinder; fully adjustable rear sight, ramp patridge front; 4-5/8", 5½", 6½", 9½" barrels. Introduced in 1973; still in production. Used values, 9½" barrel, $115 to $125; other lengths, $90 to $100.

New Model Blackhawk

Super Blackhawk

**RUGER .357 Magnum Blackhawk:** single-action revolver; .357 magnum; 4-5/8'', 6½'', 10'' barrels; with 6½'' barrel, 12'' overall length; 6-rd. cylinder; checkered hard rubber or uncheckered walnut grips; click adjustable rear sight, ramp front; blued. Introduced in 1955; dropped, 1972. Used value, $150 to $175.

**Ruger New Model Blackhawk** has same general outward specs as original .357 model, but is chambered for .357 magnum, .41 magnum; 6-rd. cylinder; new Ruger interlocked mechanism; transfer bar ignition; hardened chrome-moly steel frame; wide trigger, music wire springs, independent firing pin; blued. Introduced in 1973; still in production. Used value, $140 to $155.

**Ruger .357/9mm** has the same specifications as .357 magnum, except furnished with interchangeable cylinders for 9mm Parabellum, .357 magnum cartridges. Introduced in 1967; still in production. Used value, $175 to $190.

**RUGER 44 Magnum Blackhawk:** single-action revolver; .44 magnum; 6½'', 7½'', 10'' barrels; 12-1/8'' overall length; 6-rd. cylinder; adjustable rear sight, ramp front; uncheckered walnut grips; blued. Introduced in 1956; dropped, 1963. Used value, $350 to $375.

Super Bearcat

**RUGER Bearcat:** single-action revolver; .22 LR, long, short; 4'' barrel, 8-7/8'' overall length; 6-rd. nonfluted cylinder; fixed sights; uncheckered walnut grips; blued. Introduced in 1958; dropped, 1971. Used value, $200 to $250.

**Super Bearcat** is improved version of original, but with same general specifications. All-steel construction; music wire coil springs throughout; nonfluted engraved cylinder. Introduced in 1971; dropped, 1975. Used value, $185 to $225.

**RUGER Super Blackhawk:** single-action revolver; .44 magnum; 7½'' barrel, 13-3/8'' overall length; 6-rd. unfluted cylinder; steel, brass grip frame; uncheckered walnut grips; click adjustable rear sight, ramp front; square-back trigger guard; blued. Introduced in 1959; dropped, 1972. Used value, $275 to $350.

**New Model Super Blackhawk** has the same exterior specifications as original, but fires .44 Special as well as .44 magnum cartridge. Has new interlocked mechanism, steel grip frame, wide trigger, wide hammer spur, nonfluted cylinder. Introduced in 1973; still in production. Used value, $165 to $175.

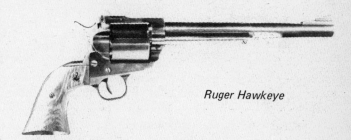

Ruger Hawkeye

**RUGER Hawkeye:** single-shot, single-action pistol; standard frame with cylinder replaced with rotating breech block; 8½'' barrel; 14½'' overall length; chambered for short-lived .256 magnum cartridge; uncheckered walnut grips; click adjustable rear sight, ramp front; barrel drilled, tapped for scope mounts; blued. Introduced in 1963; dropped, 1964. Used value, $700 to $750.

**RUGER 41 Magnum Blackhawk:** single-action revolver; .41 magnum; 4-5/8'', 6½'' barrels; with 6½'' barrel, 12'' overall length. Has same general specifications as Ruger Blackhawk .357 magnum, except for chambering, smaller frame. Introduced in 1965; dropped, 1972. Used value, $150 to $175.

**RUGER 30 Carbine Blackhawk:** single-action revolver; has the same general specifications as other pre-1972 Blackhawk models, except for chambering for .30 military carbine cartridge; 7½'' barrel only, has fluted cylinder; round-back trigger guard. Introduced in 1967; still in production. Used value, $145 to $165.

**RUGER .45 Colt:** single-action revolver; .45 Long Colt only; 4-5/8'', 7½'' barrels; with 7½'' barrel, 13-1/8'' overall; adjustable micro click rear sight, 1/8'' ramp front; uncheckered walnut grips; Ruger interlocked mechanism; similar in design to Super Blackhawk. Introduced in 1971; still in production. Used value, $150 to $165.

**Ruger .45 Colt/.45 ACP** convertible has the same specifications as .45 Colt, but is furnished with interchangeable .45 ACP cylinder. Introduced in 1971; still in production. Used value, $165 to $185.

*Model 107*

**RUGER Security Six Model 117:** double-action revolver; .357 magnum; 2¾", 4", 6" barrels; with 4" barrel, 9¼" overall length; 6-rd. cylinder; externally has same general appearance as Model 107. Has hand-checkered semitarget walnut grips, adjustable rear sight, patridge-type front on ramp; music wire coiled springs throughout. Introduced in 1974; still in production. Used value, $140 to $150.

**RUGER Security Six Model 717:** double-action revolver; .357 magnum. Has exactly the same specifications as Model 117, except that all metal parts except sights are of stainless steel. Sights are black alloy for visibility. Introduced in 1974; still in production. Used value, $160 to $175.

**RUGER Police Service-Six Model 107:** double-action revolver; .357 magnum; 2¾", 4", 6" barrels; 6" barrel dropped in 1973; with 4" barrel, 9¼" overall length; 6-rd. cylinder; solid frame with barrel, sighting rib, ejector rod housing in single integral part; semitarget-type checkered walnut grips; early model had choice of fixed or adjustable rear sight; blued. Introduced in 1972; still in production. Used value, $145 to $165.

**RUGER Speed Six Model 207:** double-action revolver; .357 magnum; 2¾", 4" barrel; 9¼" overall length; square-notch fixed rear sight, patridge-type front; all-steel construction; music wire coil springs throughout; round-butt, diamond-pattern checkered walnut grips; blued. Also available without hammer spur. Introduced in 1974; still in production. Used value, $135 to $150.

*Model 108*

*Speed Six Model 208*

**RUGER Police Service-Six Model 108:** double-action revolver; .38 Special. Has exactly the same specifications as Model 107, except for chambering. Introduced in 1972; still in production. Used value, $135 to $150.

**RUGER Speed Six Model 208:** double-action revolver; .38 Special. Has exactly the same specifications as Model 207, except for chambering. Introduced in 1974; still in production. Used value, $135 to $150.

# RG

*RG-57*

*RG 38S*

**RG 57:** revolver, double-action; .357 magnum; 4" barrel, 9½" overall length; 6-rd. swing-out cylinder, checkered plastic stocks, fixed sights, steel frame. Manufactured in Germany, imported by RG Industries. Introduced 1977, still in production. Used value, $100 to $105.

**RG 38S:** revolver, double-action; .38 Special; 6-rd. swing-out cylinder, 3", 4" barrel lengths; windage adjustable rear sight, fixed front, checkered plastic stocks, blued or nickel finish. Introduced 1977, still in production. Used values, blued, $55 to $60; nickel, $65 to $70.

*RG-30 .32 S&W Cal.*

**RG 30:** revolver, double-action; .22 LR, .32 S&W; 6-rd. swing-out cylinder; 4'' barrel, 9'' overall length; windage-adjustable rear sight, fixed front; checkered plastic stocks, blued or nickel finish. Introduced 1977, still in production. Used values, blued, $45 to $50; nickel, $50 to $52.50.

*RG 63*

**RG 63:** revolver, double-action; .22 LR, .38 Special; 8-rd. cylinder in .22, 6 rds. in .32; 5'' barrel, 10¼'' overall length; checkered plastic stocks, fixed sights; Western configuration with slide ejector rod; blued or nickel finish. Introduced 1976, still in production. Used values, .22 LR, $35 to $40; .38 Special, blued, $45 to $50; .38 Special, nickel, $50 to $55.

*RG-88*

**RG Model 88:** revolver, double-action; .38 Special, .357 magnum; 6-rd. swing-out cylinder; 4'' barrel, 9'' overall length; checkered walnut stocks, fixed sights, wide spur hammer, trigger; blued. Introduced 1977, still in production. Used value, $110 to $115.

**RG Super 66:** revolver, single-action; .22 LR, .22 magnum; 6-rd. cylinder; 4¾'' barrel, 10'' overall length; checkered plastic stocks, adjustable rear sight, fixed front; slide ejector rod, blued or nickel finish. Introduced 1977, still in production. Used values, blued, $40 to $45; nickel, $50 to $55.

# SAUER

*Sauer Model 1913*

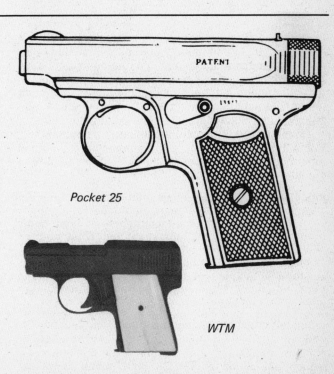

*Pocket 25*

*WTM*

**SAUER Model 1913:** pocket automatic; .32 auto; 3'' barrel; 5-7/8'' overall length; 7-rd. magazine; fixed sights; checkered hard rubber black grips; blued finish. Introduced in 1913; dropped, 1930. Used value, $100 to $125.

**SAUER Pocket 25:** automatic; same general design as Model 1913, but smaller in size; .25 auto; 2½'' barrel; 4¼'' overall length; improved grip, safety features. Introduced about 1920; dropped, 1930. Used value, $150 to $165.

**SAUER WTM:** automatic; .25 auto; 4-1/8'' overall length; top ejection; 6-rd. magazine; fixed sights; checkered hard rubber grips; fluted slide; blued. Introduced about 1924; dropped about 1927. Used value, $150 to $165.

**SAUER Model 28:** automatic; .25 auto; 3-15/16" overall length; slanted serrations on slide; top ejection; same general design as WTM, but smaller in size; checkered black rubber grips with Sauer imprint; blued. Introduced about 1928; dropped, about 1938. Used value, $150 to $165.

*Sauer Model 38 (H)*

*Sauer Model 1930
(Behorden Modell)*

**SAUER Model 1930 (Behorden Modell):** improved version of the Model 1913; .32 auto; black plastic grips; blued finish. Introduced, 1930; dropped, 1938. Used value, $145 to $155.

**SAUER Model 38(H):** double-action automatic; .32 auto; 3¼" barrel; 6¼" overall length; 7-rds., fixed sights; black plastic grips; blued. Introduced in 1938; dropped, 1944. Used value, $135 to $145. Note: .22 and .380 very rare, very valuable.

# SIG

*SIG Model P210-1*

*Model P220*

*SIG-Sauer Model P230*

**SIG Model P210-1:** automatic; .22 LR, 7.65 Luger, 9mm Luger; 6-rd. magazine; 4¾" barrel, 8½" overall length; checkered hardwood stocks; fixed sights, polished blued finish. Introduced in 1949, still in production. Manufactured in Switzerland. Used value, $325 to $350.

**Model P210-2** has the same general specifications as Model P210-1, except it is not chambered for .22 LR cartridge, has plastic stocks and a sandblasted finish. Still in production. Used value, $290 to $315.

**SIG Model 210-5 Target Model:** automatic; .22 LR, 7.65 Luger, 9mm Luger; has same specifications as Model P210-2, except for 6" barrel, adjustable rear sight, target front, adjustable trigger stop. Introduced 1950, dropped 1960. Used value, $375 to $400.

**Model P210-6** target model has the same specifications as Model P210-2, except for micrometer rear sight, target front, adjustable trigger stop. Still in production. Used value, $335 to $350.

**SIG-Sauer Model P220:** automatic, double-action; .22 LR, 7.65mm Luger, 9mm Luger, .38 Super, .45 Auto; 10-rd. magazine in .22 LR, 7-rds. in .45 Auto, 9-rds. in other calibers; 4-2/5" barrel, 7-4/5" overall length; checkered plastic stocks, fixed sights, blued. Sold in U.S. as Browning BDA. Also sold by Hawes. Introduced 1976, still in production. Manufactured in West Germany. Used value, $275 to $290.

**SIG-Sauer Model P230:** automatic, double-action; .22 LR, .32 Auto, .380 Auto; 9mm Police; 10-rd. magazine in .22 LR, 8 rds. in .32 Auto, 7 rds. in other calibers; 3-3/5" barrel, 6¾" overall length; checkered plastic stocks, fixed sights, blued finish. Introduced 1976, still in production. No longer imported. Manufactured in West Germany. Used value, $235 to $250.

**SIG-Hammerli Model P240:** automatic; .38 Special; 5-rd. magazine; 6" barrel, 10" overall length; uncheckered European walnut stocks with target thumb rest; micrometer rear sight, post front, blued finish. Manufactured in Switzerland. Introduced 1975, still in production. Used value, $600 to $625.

# SMITH & WESSON

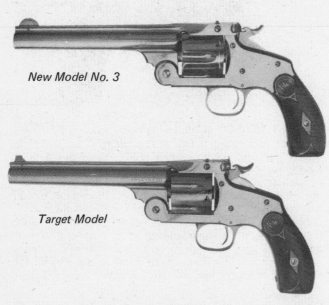

*New Model No. 3*

*Target Model*

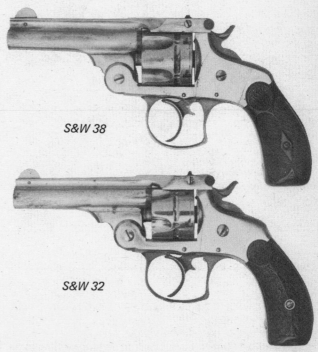

*S&W 38*

*S&W 32*

**SMITH & WESSON New Model No. 3:** revolver, single action; hinged frame; .44 Russian; 4", 5", 6", 6½", 7", 7½", 8" barrel lengths; rounded hard rubber or walnut stocks, fixed or target sights, blued or nickel finish; manufactured 1878 to 1908; has broad collector value. Used value, $400 to $650.

**No. 3 Frontier** model has same general specifications as New Model, but chambered for .44-40 Winchester only; made in barrel lengths of 4", 5", 6¾". Manufactured 1885 to 1908. Great collector interest. Used value, $700 to $750.

**No. 3 Target** model has same specifications as New Model, but is made with 6½" barrel only; available in .32-44 S&W, .38-44 S&W calibers only. Collector interest. Manufactured 1887 to 1910. Used value, $450 to $500.

**SMITH & WESSON 38:** revolver, double action; hinged frame, .32 S&W; 5-rd. cylinder; 4", 4½", 5", 6", 7", 10" lengths; hard rubber checkered stocks; fixed sights, blued or nickel. Several design variations. Manufactured 1880 to 1911. Some collector value. Used values: serial numbers through 4000, $300 to $350; guns with 8, 10" barrels, $300 to $350; other versions, $160 to $175.

**SMITH & WESSON 32:** revolver, double-action; hinged frame; .32 S&W; 5-rd. cylinder; 3", 3½", 6" barrel lengths; hard rubber stocks, fixed sights, blued or nickel. Manufactured 1880 to 1919. Early serial numbers have great collector significance, with numbers through 50 bringing as high as $2500. Used value, standard model, $150 to $175.

*S&W 44*

**SMITH & WESSON 44:** revolver, double-action; .44 Russian, .38-40; 6-rd. cylinder; 4", 5", 6", 6½" barrel lengths; hard rubber stocks, fixed sights, blued or nickel finish. Manufactured 1881 to 1913. Collector interest based upon number manufactured. Used values, .44 Russian, $350 to $400; .38-40, $900 to $950.

Frontier 44 model has same specifications as standard 44 except being chambered for .44-40 cartridge only. Manufactured 1881 to 1910. Collector interest. Used value, $400 to $450.

Favorite 44 has same specifications as standard model, except for lightweight frame. Manufactured 1881 to 1913. Collector interest. Used value, $1900 to $2000.

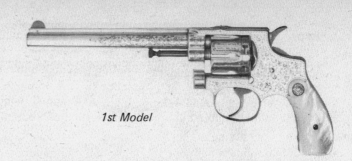

*1st Model*

*Model 1891 Single Shot*

*Model 1891 Target*

SMITH & WESSON Model 1891: revolver, single-action; hinged frame; .38 S&W; 3¾", 4", 5", 6" barrel lengths; hard rubber stocks, blued or nickel finish, fixed sights. Also available with .22 LR single-shot target barrel. Manufactured 1891 to 1911. Used values: $400 to $425; with single-shot barrel, $750 to $800.

Model 1891 Target model, First Issue, was built on same frame as standard Model 1891; .22 LR, .32 S&W, .38 S&W; 6, 8, 10" barrel lengths; target sights, square butt hard rubber stocks, blued finish only. Also furnished with .38 S&W barrel, cylinder to convert to single-action revolver. Manufactured 1893 to 1905. Collector interest. Used values: .22 LR single-shot, $250 to $300; .32 S&W single-shot, $350 to $400; .38 S&W single-shot, $350 to $400; combo set with single-shot barrel, single-action conversion unit, $750 to $800.

Model 1891 Target Model, Second Issue, is basically the same specifications as First Issue, except that it cannot be converted to revolver configuration; redesigned adjustable rear sight; 10" barrel only; .22 LR only. Collector interest. Manufactured 1905 to 1909. Used value, $275 to $300.

SMITH & WESSON Olympic Model: single-shot target model; .22 LR; hinged frame; same general specifications as Model 1891 Target, Second Issue, except incorporates lockwork of S&W double-action; 10" barrel; prior to 1920, was known as Perfected Target model, but was used by Olympic team that year, leading to name; target-type checkered walnut stocks. Produced 1909 to 1923. Collector interest. Used values: Perfected Target model, $250 to $275; Olympic model, $400 to $450.

SMITH & WESSON Model I: revolver, double-action, hand-ejector; .32 S&W Long; 3¼", 4¼", 6" barrel lengths; fixed sights, blued or nickel finish, hard rubber stocks. First S&W solid-frame revolver with swing-out cylinder. Manufactured 1896 to 1903. Collector interest. Used value, $325 to $350.

*S&W Safety Hammerless*

SMITH & WESSON Safety Hammerless: produced for nearly 60 years; discontinued at the start of WWII; also called the New Departure; was the last of S&W's top-break designs. Having no exposed hammer, it was a true pocket gun and would not snag on the draw; could be fired without removing from the pocket. Capacity, 5 rds.; chambered for .32 S&W and .38 S&W; 17 oz., with overall length of 6¼"; antisnag type sights with fixed blade front and U-notch rear; checkered Circassian walnut or hard rubber grips with S&W monogram; blued or nickel finish; featured grip safety and the action provided a distinct pause prior to let-off, giving the effect of single-action pull. Used value, $225 to $265.

*S&W Model 10
Military & Police*

SMITH & WESSON Model 10 Military & Police: the backbone of S&W's line; basic frame is termed S&W's K-frame, the derivative source of the K-38, et al. It is, quite possibly, the most popular, widely accepted police duty revolver ever made. Introduced about 1902. Has been made with square-butt checkered walnut stocks and in round-butt pattern with choice of hard rubber or checkered walnut, in barrel lengths from 2" to 6½", as well as Airweight version.

Currently made in .38 Special, capacity, 6 rds.; with 6"

barrel, overall length is 11-1/8" in square butt, about ¼" less for round butt type; weight is 31 oz; sights, 1/10" service type front and square notch rear, nonadjustable; finishes, blued or nickel. Currently available in standard or heavy-barrel version, nickel or blue finish. Used value, blue, $125 to $145; nickel, $135 to $155. A version of the Military & Police was offered in .32 WCF (also called .32-20), from the introduction of the design to the beginning of WWII; current used value, $150 to $160.

**SMITH & WESSON Military & Police Target Model:** from the early Twenties to 1941, S&W introduced various versions of their M&P, refined for target work; modifications included rear sights adjustable for windage and elevation; with few, if any, exceptions, barrel lengths were 6". Calibers, .38 Special, .32 S&W Long, .22 LR; a few were made up on a custom basis in .32 WCF. All had 6-shot cylinders, with overall lengths of 11-1/8"; weights spanned from 32 oz. for the .38 to 35 oz. for the .22 versions. Pre-WWII target models are identifiable by the absence of a rib on the barrel. Stocks, checkered walnut, but not of the later magna pattern. Used value, $225 to $245 for the .32 S&W Long and .22 LR; $255 to $265 for the .38 Special; up to $350 for the .32 WCF from original factory production.

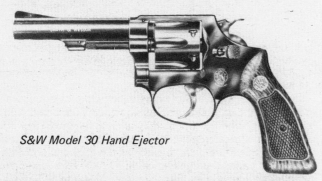
*S&W Model 30 Hand Ejector*

**SMITH & WESSON Model 30 Hand Ejector:** early swing-out cylinder design. Chambered for .32 S&W Long; will accept the .32 S&W and the .32 S&W Long wadcutter load; capacity, 6 rds. Currently made with 2", 3" and 4" barrels; 6" was available at one time; checkered walnut with medallion; formerly hard rubber; fixed sights, with 1/10" serrated ramp front and square notch rear; overall length, 8" with 4" barrel; weight, 18 oz; finish, blue or nickel. Introduced in 1903; still in production. Used value, $150 to $165.

*S&W Perfected Model 38*

**SMITH & WESSON Perfected Model 38:** revolver, double action; hinged frame; .38 S&W; 5-rd. cylinder; 3¼", 4", 5", 6" barrel lengths; hard rubber stocks, fixed sights, blued or nickel. Same general appearance as S&W 38, except has heavier frame, side latch. Manufactured 1909 to 1920. Some collector value. Used value, $300 to $350.

*S&W .22/32 Target*

**SMITH & WESSON .22/32 Target:** a forerunner of the Model 35; made for the .22 LR, capacity 6 rds.; chambers were countersunk at the heads around 1935, for the high-velocity cartridges introduced at that time; furnished only in blued finish; 6" barrel, with overall length of 10½"; won the "Any Revolver" event of the U.S.R.A. matches several times; sights, 1/10" or 1/8" Patridge front, square notch rear sight adjustable for windage and elevation; stocks, special, oversize, square-butt pattern in checkered Circassian walnut, with S&W monogram. Introduced in 1911; superseded by the Model 35 in 1953. Retail price, new, just before WWII, $35. Used value, $275 to $285.

*S&W .35 Auto*

**SMITH & WESSON 35:** automatic; .35 S&W Auto; 7-rd. magazine; 3½" barrel, 6½" overall length; uncheckered walnut stocks, fixed sights, blued or nickel finish. Manufactured 1913 to 1921. Collector interest. Used value, $325 to $350.

*S&W Military Model of 1917*

**SMITH & WESSON Military Model of 1917:** entry of the U.S. into WWI found facilities unable to produce sufficient quantities of the recently adopted Government Model auto pistol, so approximately 175,000 Smith & Wesson revolvers were manufactured, being chambered to fire the .45 ACP cartridge by means of the two 3-rd. steel clips; also fires the .45 Auto Rim round, introduced after the war without clips. The wartime units had a duller blued finish and smooth walnut grips, with 5½" barrel; overall length, 10¼"; weight, 36¼ oz., with lanyard ring in the butt. A commercial version remained in production after the end of WWI to the start of WWII, distinguished by a bright blue finish and checkered walnut stocks. Used value, $200 to $225 for military; $250 to $275 for commercial.

*Police Target Model*

*S&W Model 31 Regulation Police*

*S&W Straightline Single-shot Target*

**SMITH & WESSON Straightline Single-shot Target:** chambered for the .22 LR cartridge, the S&W Straightline was made from 1925 through 1936; had a 10" barrel and was 11-5/16" in overall length, weighing 34¼ oz.; was made only in blued finish, with target sights; stocks were of walnut, usually not checkered. As with many long-discontinued pistols, the current market value is weighted by the interest of dedicated collectors, rather than shooters, most of whom would be disappointed by the accuracy potential of typical examples. Used value, $550 to $575, if complete with original metal case and accessories; $400 to $450 without.

*S&W Model 33 Regulation Police*

**SMITH & WESSON Model 33 Regulation Police:** similar to Model 31, except for its caliber; chambered for the .38 S&W, it will accept the .38 Colt New Police; capacity, 5 rds.; 4" barrel; overall length, 8½"; weight, 18 oz; fixed sights, with 1/10" serrated ramp front and square notch rear; stocks, checkered walnut, with medallion; blue, nickel finish. Introduced in 1917; dropped, 1974. Used value, $140 to $155.

**SMITH & WESSON Regulation Police, Target Model:** target version of the Model 31; 6" barrel and adjustable target sights; made only in .32 S&W Long (accepting .32 S&W and .32 Colt New Police); length, 10¼"; weight, 20 oz; checkered walnut stocks and blued finish; capacity, 6 rds. Introduced, 1917; dropped, 1941. Used value, $240 to $260.

*S&W Model 1926 .44 Military*

**SMITH & WESSON Model 1926 .44 Military:** modified version of S&W's earlier New Century hand-ejector, minus the triple-lock feature, but retaining the heavy shroud around the ejector rod; primarily produced in .44 Special, sometimes encountered in .45 Long Colt, .455 Webley or .455 Eley; barrel lengths, 4", 5" and 6½"; overall length, 11¾" with 6½" barrel; weight, 39½ oz. with 6½" barrel; capacity, 6 rds.; sights, 1/10" service-type front and fixed square notch rear; stocks, checkered walnut, square or magna-type, with S&W medallion; finish, blued or nickel. Discontinued at the start of WWII; replaced after the war by the 1950 model. Used value, $275 to $290 in blue; $285 to $300 in nickel.

S&W Model 1926 Target

S&W Model 27 .357 Magnum

**SMITH & WESSON Model 1926 Target:** a target version of the 1926 Model; rear sight adjustable for windage and elevation; produced from 1926 to the beginning of WWII; replaced after the war by the 1950 Target Model 24. Used value, $350 to $365.

S&W Model 20 .38/44 Heavy Duty

**SMITH & WESSON Model 20 .38/44 Heavy Duty:** six-shot, .38 Special revolver, built on the S&W .44 frame, often termed their N-frame, hence the .38/44 designation; designed to handle high-velocity .38 Special ammunition; barrel lengths, 4", 5" and 6½"; with 5" barrel, overall length, 10-3/8" and weight, 40 oz.; fixed sights, with 1/10" service-type (semi-circle) front and square notch rear; stocks, checkered walnut, magna-type with S&W medallion; finish, blued or nickel. Introduced in 1930; discontinued, 1967. Used value, $245 to $265.

S&W .38/44 Outdoorsman Model 23

**SMITH & WESSON .38/44 Outdoorsman Model 23:** introduced in 1930 as a companion to the Model 20; reintroduced about 1950 with ribbed barrel and magna-type stocks; was made only in blue, with 6½" barrel; plain Patridge 1/8" front sight, S&W micrometer click rear adjustable for windage and elevation; capacity, 6 rds. of .38 Special; overall length, 11¾"; weight, 41¾ oz. Discontinued, 1967. Used value, $300 to $325.

**SMITH & WESSON Model 27 .357 Magnum:** introduced with the .357 magnum cartridge in 1935; essentially the same as the .38 Special, except case is lengthened by 0.135", loaded to substantially higher pressures in order to obtain higher velocities (The case was lengthened to prevent its use in guns chambered for the .38 Special round); Pre-WWII Model 27s offered in barrel lengths of 3½", 5", 6", 6½", 8-3/8" and 8¾"; could be custom-ordered with barrels of any length up to 8¾"; weights were 41 oz. for 3½", 42½ oz. for 5", 44 oz. for 6", 44½ oz. for 6½" and 47 oz. for 8-3/8"; overall length, 11-3/8" for 6" barrel; could be ordered with any of S&W's standard target sights; the 3½" version usually was furnished with a Baughman quick-draw sight on a plain King ramp; finely checkered top strap matched barrel rib, with vertically grooved front and rear grip straps and grooved trigger; capacity, 6 rds. of .357 mag; also could fire .38 Special; S&W bright blue or nickel finishes; checkered Circassian walnut stocks, with S&W medallion in choice of square or magna type. Retail price at beginning of WWII, $60. Post-WWII production was similar, with the hammer redesigned to incorporate a wider spur and inclusion of the present pattern of S&W click micrometer rear sight; blue or nickel finish. Still in production. Model 27 was the first center-fire revolver with recessed cylinders; the .357 required registration with registration no. stamped in yoke of frame; about 6000 made before registration stopped. The papers, themselves, have some collector value without the gun!

Used value, up to $650 for pre-WWII model with registration papers furnished at that time; $270 to $290 for post-war versions.

S&W .22/32 Kit Gun

**SMITH & WESSON .22/32 Kit Gun:** a compact, outdoorsman's revolver, based on the .22/32 Target, modified by a round-butt stock pattern and 4" barrel; made with 1/10" Patridge or pocket revolver front sight, with rear sight adjustable for elevation and windage; checkered Circassian walnut or hard rubber stocks; blued or nickel finishes; barrel length, 4"; overall length, 8" with round butt (small or special oversized target square-butt stocks were offered on special order); weight, 21 oz.; capacity, 6 rds.; chambered only for the .22 LR. Introduced in 1935; replaced, 1953 by the Model 34. Used value, $250 to $275.

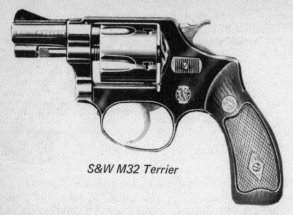

*S&W M32 Terrier*

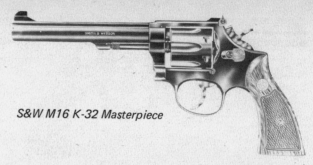

*S&W M16 K-32 Masterpiece*

**SMITH & WESSON Model 32 Terrier:** essentially a 2″ version of the Model 30 Hand Ejector; stocks, round-butt pattern in checkered walnut with medallion; blued finish standard, nickel at extra cost; length, 6¼″; weight, 17 oz; capacity, 5 rds. of .38 S&W (or .38 Colt New Police); fixed sights, with 1/10″ serrated ramp front and square notch rear. Introduced in 1936, discontinued, 1974. Used value, $175 to $200.

**SMITH & WESSON Model 16 K-32 Masterpiece:** Originating as a target version of the hand-ejector in .32 S&W Long, about 1935 and dropped at the beginning of WWII, the Model 16 appeared in its present form in the late Forties, designated the K-32 as a companion to the K-22 and K-38. A double-action revolver, holding 6 rds. of .32 S&W Long, it was made only with 6″ barrel and blued finish. Walnut, magna-pattern stocks with medallions were standard, factory target stocks in exotic woods available as options. Other options included target hammer, target trigger, red insert front sight, white outline rear sight and choice of Patridge or Baughman front sights. Dropped in 1973. Used values: .32 hand-ejector model, $450 to $500; post-war version, $240 to $250.

*S&W M17 K-22 Masterpiece*

*S&W M14 K-38 Masterpiece*

**SMITH & WESSON Model 17 K-22 Masterpiece:** redesigned version of Model 16. Introduced around 1947; still in production. Postwar production added the refinement of a broad barrel rib, intended to compensate for weight variations between the three available calibers: .38 Special, .32 S&W Long and .22 LR. Likewise added were the redesigned hammer, with its broad spur and thumb-tip relief notch, an adjustable anti-backlash stop for the trigger and the magna-type grips developed in the mid-Thirties to help cushion the recoil of the .357 Magnum. 6″ barrel is standard, with 8-3/8″ available. Capacity, 6 rds.; overall length, 11-1/8″ with 6″ barrel; loaded weight, 38½ oz. for 6″, 42½ oz. for 8-3/8″. Blue finish only. Currently offered in .22 LR only. Used value, 6″ barrel, $165 to $185; 8-3/8″ barrel, $175 to $225.

**SMITH & WESSON Model 14 K-38 Masterpiece:** double-action revolver; .38 Special only; 6″, 8-3/8″ barrels; with 6″ barrel, 11-1/8″ overall length; 6-rd. swing-out cylinder; built on S&W K frame; micrometer rear sight; 1/8″ Patridge-type front; hand-checkered service-type walnut grips; blued. Introduced in 1947; still in production. Used value, 6″ barrel, $150 to $175; 8-3/8″ barrel, $165 to $195.

**Model 14 Masterpiece Single Action** has the same general specifications as standard Model 14, except for being single action only; has target hammer, target trigger. Used value, 6″ barrel, $190 to $200; 8-3/8″ barrel, $210 to $225.

*S&W M48 K-22 Masterpiece WMRF*

**SMITH & WESSON Victory Model:** WWII version of the Model 10; usually in 4″ barrel length, Parkerized with sandblasted or brushed finish, smooth (non-magna) walnut stocks and lanyard ring in square butt; usually in .38 Special, though a version termed the .38-200 was made for the British forces. The Victory Model is inferior in external fit, finish to commercial production, though collectors may be willing to pay prices slightly higher than those listed for the standard Model 10 revolver. Used value, $150 to $160.

**SMITH & WESSON Model 48 K-22 Masterpiece WMRF:** a modification of the K-22 Model 17; chambered to accept the .22 WMRF cartridge; available with 4″ barrel, without being distinctly designated as a Combat Masterpiece, and in the 6" and 8-3/8" lengths, as well; weight, with the 6" barrel, 39 oz.; auxiliary cylinder was offered to permit the use of this model with the .22 LR cartridge. The quoted price of this accessory was $35.50, as of 1969. Used value, with 6" barrel, $225 to $235; $250 to $260 for 8-3/8" barrel; add $40, if equipped with .22 LR as well as .22 WMRF cylinder.

*S&W M21 1950 .44 Military*

**SMITH & WESSON Model 21 1950 .44 Military:** post-WWII version of the S&W Model 1926 with minor design refinements; made in 5½" barrel; chambered for the .44 Special (also handles the .44 Russian); length, 10¾"; weight, 36¼ oz.; fixed sights; finish, blued or nickel; stocks, checkered walnut, magna-type, with S&W medallion. Discontinued, 1967. Used value, $225 to $235.

*S&W M22 1950 Army*

**SMITH & WESSON Model 22 1950 Army:** post-WWII version of the Model '17, with minor design refinements; remained in production until 1967; has the usual semi-circular front sight and U-shaped notch rear sight milled in the top of the receiver strap, the same as the M'17. A target version was made, having adjustable rear sight. Used value, $200 to $225.

*S&W 1950/1955 M25 .45 Target*

**SMITH & WESSON 1950/1955 Model 25 .45 Target:** introduced in 1950 as a companion to the 1950 Model 24 .44 Target; identical except being chambered for .45 ACP/Auto Rim. The 1950 .45 Target was redesigned in 1955 to become the 1955 .45 Target, superseding the 1950 version. Modifications consisted of a heavier barrel with broad rib,

similar to that of the K-38, S&W target stocks in place of the magna-type, a target hammer and broad, target-type trigger. Standard barrel length, 6½"; no factory production of 4" has been reported, although some owners have had them cut down to 4" length; capacity, 6 rds.; overall length, 11-7/8"; weight, 45 oz.; sights, 1/8" plain Patridge front, S&W micrometer click rear, adjustable for windage and elevation; finish, blue; stocks, checkered walnut, pattern as noted, with S&W medallion. Continues in production, though in limited quantities. Used value, $350 to $425. The .45 Long Colt made on special order only.

*S&W M24 1950 .44 Target*

**SMITH & WESSON Model 24 1950 .44 Target:** introduced in 1950 as a refined version of the 1926 Target Model; customarily produced with 6½" barrel and Patridge-type front sight having vertical rear blade surface, with S&W micrometer click rear sight adjustable for windage and elevation; limited quantity was produced in a 4" barreled version, with Baughman quick-draw front sight on serrated ramp, with the same type of rear sight. As with most S&W target models, blued finish was standard, although a few specimens may have been custom-ordered in nickel. Chambered for the .44 Special (also handles the shorter .44 Russian cartridge); capacity, 6 rds.; with 4" barrel, overall length is 9¼" and weight is 40 oz. Discontinued about 1966. Used value, $275 to $295 for the 6½" barrel; $550 to $600 for the 4" barrel.

*S&W M15 .38 Combat Masterpiece*

**SMITH & WESSON Model 15 .38 Combat Masterpiece:** it took some years after WWII to reestablish commercial production and begin catching up with civilian demands at S&W. By the early Fifties, the situation was bright enough to warrant introducing a 4" version of the K-38, which was designated the .38 Combat Masterpiece. Its only nominal companion was the .22 Combat Masterpiece and no attempt was made to match loaded weights, as in the K-series; the .38 weighing 34 oz. empty, compared to 36½ oz. for the .22 version. Barrel ribs were more narrow than the K-series and front sights were of the Baughman, quick-draw ramp pattern, replacing the vertical surface of the K-series Patridge type; overall length, 9-1/8"; finish, blue or nickel; capacity, 6 rds.; chambered for .38 Special. Used value, $135 to $150; $145 to $155, nickel.

*S&W M18 .22 Combat Masterpiece*

**SMITH & WESSON Model 18 .22 Combat Masterpiece:** companion to the .38 Combat Masterpiece Model 15, with Baughman 1/8" quick-draw front sight on plain ramp and S&W micrometer click rear sight adjustable for windage and elevation; chambered for .22 LR, handling .22 long and .22 short, as well; capacity, 6 rds.; length of barrel, 4"; overall length, 9-1/8"; loaded weight, 36½ oz.; stocks, checkered walnut, magna-type, with S&W medallion; finish, blue only; available options include broad-spur target hammer, wide target trigger, hand-filling target stocks, red front sight insert and white outlined rear sight notch. Still in production. Used value, $165 to $185.

**SMITH & WESSON Model 12 Military & Police Airweight:** similar to the Model 10, except for the incorporation of an aluminum alloy frame; made only in .38 Special, with capacity of 6 rds.; barrel lengths, 2" and 4"; stocks, checkered walnut magna-type, round or square butt; weight, 18 oz.; with 2" barrel and round butt; overall length 6-7/8" (2", round butt); sights, fixed 1/8" serrated ramp front, square notch rear. Introduced about 1952; still produced. Used value, $165 to $175, blue; $170 to $185, nickel.

**SMITH & WESSON Model 34 1953 .22/32 Kit Gun:** updated version of the earlier .22/32 Kit Gun, the 1953 version — still in production — features a ribbed varrel, micrometer rear sight adjustable for elevation and windage, magna-type stocks; flattened cylinder latch employed on many of S&W's later small pocket designs. Available barrel lengths, 2" and 4"; overall length, 8" with 4" barrel and round butt; weight, 22½ oz. in 4" barrel; stocks, checkered walnut, round or square butt; sights, 1/10" serrated ramp front, square notch rear adjustable for windage and elevation. Used value, $165 to $175.

*Model 36 Chiefs Special*

**SMITH & WESSON Model 36 Chiefs Special:** double action revolver; descended from Model 32 Terrier Model, with longer cylinder. Round butt pattern of grips is most common; although square butt design was available. Barrel lengths, 2", 3"; with 3" barrel, 7½" overall length; fixed square-notch rear sight, 1/10" serrated ramp front; 5-rd. cylinder; .38 Special only; blued or nickel. Introduced in 1952; still in production. Used values, blued, $175 to $200; nickel, $190 to $225.

*Model 37*

**SMITH & WESSON Model 37 Chiefs Special Airweight:** lightweight version of the Model 36, incorporating aluminum alloy frame, reducing weight to 14 oz.; general specs are the same as for Model 36; finish, blue, nickel. Used values, blue, $175 to $200; nickel, $190 to $210.

*Model 43*

**SMITH & WESSON Airweight Kit Gun Model 43:** identical to Model 34, except for aluminum alloy frame; made only in 3½" barrel; weight, 14¼ oz.; square-butt stocks of checkered walnut; overall length, 8". Discontinued about 1974; blue or nickel finish. Used value, respectively, $200 to $215 and $225 to $235.

*Model 40 Centennial*

**SMITH & WESSON Model 40 Centennial:** swing-out version of earlier, top-break Safety Hammerless; has hammerless design, with grip safety. In .38 Special only, with capacity of 5 rds.; barrel length 2", with overall length of 6½"; weight, 19 oz.; fixed sights with 1/10" serrated ramp front and square notch rear. Introduced in 1953; dropped, 1974. Airweight (Model 42), blue, $225 to $250; nickel, $265 to $275.

*S&W M35 1953 .22/32*

**SMITH & WESSON Model 35 1953 .22/32:** a redesign of the .22/32, which had been developed on the .32 Hand Ejector. Departing from the .22/32 Target Model, it added the post-war magna stocks, a rib atop the barrel, and modern S&W front sight and micrometer rear sight. Chambered for the .22 LR, capacity, 6 rds.; barrel length, 6", with 10½" overall length; weight 25 oz., finished only in blue. Introduced in 1953; dropped, 1974. Used value, $175 to $200.

*S&W M28 Highway Patrolman*

**SMITH & WESSON Model 28 Highway Patrolman:** introduced in 1954 as a functional version of the Model 27 minus the cost-raising frills such as the checkered top strap; made only in 4" and 6" barrel lengths; overall length, 11¼" with 6" barrel; weight, 41¾ oz. with 4" barrel; 44 oz. with 6" barrel; sights, 1/8" Baughman quick-draw front on plain ramp, S&W micrometer click rear, adjustable for elevation and windage; stocks, checkered walnut, magna-type, with S&W medallion; target stocks at extra cost; finish, blued, with sandblast stippling of barrel rib and frame edging. Still in production. Used value, $150 to $175.

**SMITH & WESSON Model 38 Bodyguard Airweight:** features a shrouded hammer that can be cocked manually for single-action firing; .38 Special only; capacity, 5 rds.; length of barrel 2"; overall length, 6-3/8"; weight, 14½ oz.; fixed sights, with 1/10" serrated ramp front and square notch rear. Introduced in 1955; still in production. Used values, blue, $175 to $225; nickel, $160 to $235.

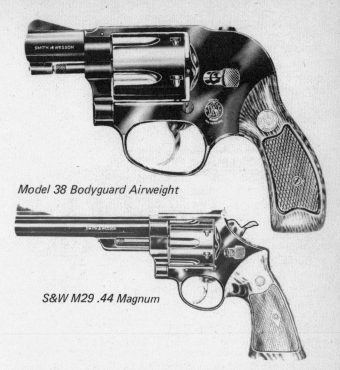

*Model 38 Bodyguard Airweight*

*S&W M29 .44 Magnum*

**SMITH & WESSON Model 29 .44 Magnum:** introduced in 1956; still in rather limited production; nominal retail price of the Model 29 is listed at $310 for most versions, $319.50 for the 8-3/8" barrel. Supply has lagged so far behind demand that Model 29s have been reported selling for up to twice the suggested retail, with used guns in good condition selling for nearly as much. As with the Model 27, the Model 29 was developed to take a new cartridge developed by lengthening the .44 Special case by 0.125" — this being intended to prevent use of .44 mag ammo in guns chambered for the .44 Special. The .44 mag is loaded to pressures approximately twice that of the .44 Special. The six-shot cylinder also will handle .44 Special or .44 Russian. Barrel lengths, 4", 5", 6½", 8-3/8"; length, 11-7/8" with 6½" barrel; weights, 43 oz. with 4", 47 oz. with 6½" and 51½ oz. with 8-3/8" barrel; sights, 1/8" red ramp front, S&W micrometer click rear, adjustable for elevation and windage; stocks, target type of goncalo alves, with S&W medallion. Broad, grooved target trigger, wide-spur target hammer. Finish, bright blue or nickel. Used value, up to $425 for 4" or 6½" barrel; up to $550 for 8-3/8" barrel. In this instance, largely a matter of supply and demand, some going for $1000!

*S&W M19 Combat Magnum*

**SMITH & WESSON Model 19 Combat Magnum:** introduced about 1956; built on the lighter S&W K-frame, as used on the K-38, et al., rather than on the heavier N-frame, used for the Model 27 and 28; its six-shot cylinder is chambered for the .357 magnum cartridge; capable of firing .38 Special ammo; finish, S&W bright blue or nickel; stocks, checkered goncalo alves with S&W medallion; sights, 1/8" Baughman quick-draw front plain ramp, S&W micrometer click rear, adjustable for windage and elevation; available with 2½", 4" or 6" barrel; with 4" barrel, length is 9½" and weight is 35 oz. Used value, $185 to $215.

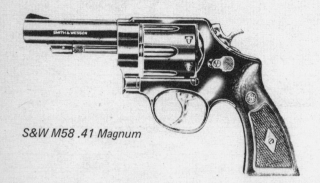

*S&W M58 .41 Magnum*

**SMITH & WESSON Model 58 .41 Magnum:** also known as the .41 Military & Police, this is a fixed-sight version of the Model 57; available only in 4" barrel, in blue or nickel; capacity, 6 rds.; overall length, 9¼"; weight, 41 oz.; sights, 1/8" serrated ramp front, square notch rear; stocks, checkered walnut, with S&W medallion, in magna pattern. Used values, blue, $200 to $215; nickel, $220 to $235.

*S&W M49 Bodyguard*

**SMITH & WESSON Model 49 Bodyguard:** identical to the Model 38; except for all-steel frame, rather than aluminum alloy, increasing the weight to 20½ oz. Finished in blue, nickel. Introduced about 1959; still in production. Used values, blue, $185 to $220; nickel, $195 to $235.

**SMITH & WESSON Model 53 .22 Magnum:** starting in the late Fifties, there was considerable interest in converting K-22s to center-fire wildcat (i.e., nonstandard cartridge) configurations, usually being chambered for a shortened version of the .22 Hornet, known as the .22 Harvey K-Chuck. With the intent of capitalizing on this interest, S&W introduced the .22 Remington CFM or center-fire magnum cartridge — also termed the .22 Jet — and the Model 53, chambered for it. The .22 magnum was a necked-down .357 case, designed to use a bullet of .222-.223" diameter. The Model 53 was supplied with six chamber bushings, adapting it for firing .22 rimfire ammo, by means of repositioning the striker on the hammer. Alternatively, a standard

*Model 53*

.22 LR cylinder was offered as a factory-fitted accessory, at about $35.30, for interchanging with the .22 Jet cylinder. Capacity, 6 rds.; barrel, 4", 6" and 8-3/8"; with 6" barrel, length was 11¼" and weight, 40 oz.; finish, blued only; stocks, checkered walnut with S&W medallion; sights, 1/8" Baughman ramp front, S&W micrometer click rear, adjustable for elevation and windage; Model 53 was dropped from production in 1974, having been introduced about 1960. Used value, $325 to $350, if complete with chamber inserts and/or fitted .22 LR cylinder; $50 to $60 higher with 8-3/8" barrel.

*S&W M51 1950 .22/32 Kit Gun M.R.F.*

**SMITH & WESSON Model 51 1960 .22/32 Kit Gun M.R.F.:** identical to the Model 43, except that it is chambered for the .22 Winchester magnum rimfire cartridge and weighs 24 oz.; has an all-steel frame, 3½" barrel. Introduced in 1960; dropped, 1974. Retail, new, was $105.50 in blue, $113.50 in nickel. Used value, $200 to $225, blue; $225 to $250, nickel.

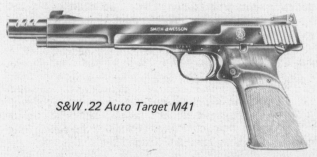

*S&W .22 Auto Target M41*

**SMITH & WESSON .22 Auto Target Model 41:** introduced about 1957; still in production; chambered for the .22 LR, the Model 41 is also available in .22 short for international competition; capacity, either caliber, 10 rds. in magazine; barrel lengths, 5" or 7-3/8". With 7-3/8" barrel, overall length is 12", weight is 43½ oz. Sights, 1/8" undercut Patridge type in front, S&W micrometer click rear, adjustable for windage and elevation; stocks, checkered walnut with modified thumb rest, usable by right- or left-handed shooters; finish, S&W bright blue, only; trigger, 3/8" wide, grooved, with adjustable stop; detachable muzzle brake supplied with 7-3/8" barrel only. Used value, $245 To $265.

The Model 41 was also made in a heavy-barrel variant, with or without an extendible front sight and in a less elaborate version, called the Model 46, with moulded nylon stocks. Values are approximately the same as quoted here.

*S&W M57 .41 Magnum*

**SMITH & WESSON Model 57 .41 Magnum:** introduced as a deluxe companion to the Model 58, both being chambered for a new cartridge developed especially for them at that time, carrying a bullet of .410" diameter. The old .41 Long Colt cartridge cannot be fired in guns chambered for the .41 magnum, nor can any other standard cartridge. Ammo is loaded by Rem-Peters and by Win-Western, with 210-grain lead or 210-grain JSP bullets, respectively to medium and high velocities. Capacity, 6 rds.; barrel lengths, 4", 6" and 8-3/8"; finish, bright blue or nickel; with 6" barrel, length is 11-3/8" and weight is 48 oz. Sights, 1/8" red ramp front, S&W micrometer click rear, adjustable for elevation and windage, with white outline notch; stocks, special over-size target-type of goncalo alves, with S&W medallion; wide, grooved target trigger and broad-spur target hammer. Introduced in 1964; still in production; blued, nickel. Used values, 4" and 6" barrels, $265 to $285; 8-3/8" barrel, $300 to $325.

*S&W M60 Stainless Chiefs Special*

**SMITH & WESSON Model 60 Stainless Chiefs Special:** identical to Model 36 Chiefs Special, except that all metal parts are of corrosion-resistant steel alloys. Introduced in 1965, still in production. Used value, $245 to $275.

**SMITH & WESSON Model 61 Escort:** automatic; hammerless; .22 LR only; 2.175" barrel; 4-13/16" overall length; 5-rd. magazine; thumb safety on left side of grip; fixed sights; cocking indicator; checkered plastic grips; blued or nickel finish. Introduced in 1970; dropped, 1973. Used values, blued, $145 to $150; nickel finish, $150 to $160.

*Model 61*

*.32 Auto*

**SMITH & WESSON .32 Auto:** successor to S&W's original auto pistol, which was chambered for the caliber .35 S&W Auto cartridge, this gun was chambered for the common .32 Auto or 7.65mm cartridge, having a magazine capacity of 8 rds., barrel length of 4" and weight of about 28 oz., measuring 7" overall; stocks, walnut, not checkered; finish, blued or nickel. Features included an unusual grip-safety, just below the trigger guard. Introduced in 1924; discontinued, 1937. Used value, $575 to $650.

*S&W M39 9mm Auto*

**SMITH & WESSON Model 39 9mm Auto:** introduced in 1954; still in production; furnished with two 8-rd. magazines; barrel length, 4"; length overall 7-7/16"; weight, 26½ oz., without magazine; sights, 1/8" serrated ramp front, rear sight adjustable only for windage, with square notch; stocks, checkered walnut, with S&W medallion; finish, S&W bright blue or nickel. During the first dozen years of its production, a limited number of Model 39s were made with steel frames, rather than the standard aluminum alloy type, currently commanding premium prices, as noted here. Used value, blued, $200 to $220; nickel, $220 to $250. Steel-frame model, $800 to $850.

*S&W M52 .38 Target Auto*

*S&W M59 9mm Auto*

**SMITH & WESSON Model 52 .38 Target Auto:** introduced in 1961; still in production; designed to fire a mid-range loading of the .38 Special cartridge, requiring a wadcutter bullet seated flush with the case mouth; action is straight blowback, thus not suited for firing of high-velocity .38 Special ammo; magazine holds 5 rds.; barrel, 5", length overall, 8-5/8"; weight, 41 oz.; sights, Patridge-type front on ramp, S&W micrometer click rear, adjustable for elevation and windage; stocks, checkered walnut, with S&W medallion; available only in blue. Used value, $325 to $365.

**SMITH & WESSON Model 59 9mm Auto:** introduced in the early Seventies; similar to the Model 39, except for incorporation of a staggered-column magazine holding 14 rds.; weight, 27½ oz., without magazine; stocks, checkered, high-impact moulded nylon. Like the Model 39, the 59 offers the option of carrying a round in the chamber, with hammer down, available for firing via a double-action pull of the trigger. Other specs are the same as for the Model 39. Blue or nickel finish. Used value, $230 to $240 for blue finish; $240 to $250, nickel.

# STAR

*Star Model A*

*Star Model CO*

**STAR Model A:** automatic; 7.63mm Mauser, 9mm Bergmann (9mm Largo), .45 auto; modified version of Colt Model 1911 .45 auto, appearing almost identical to Browning patent; 5" barrel; 8½" overall length; 8-rd. magazine; checkered walnut grips; fixed sights; blued. The first locked breech pistol manufactured commercially by Bonifacio Echeverria, S.A., in Eibar, Spain. Currently designated as Model AS, in .38 Super auto only. Not currently imported. Introduced in 1922; still in production. Used value, $165 to $170.

**STAR Model B:** automatic; 9mm Parabellum; 9-rd. magazine; has the same design, other specifications as Model A. Early versions, had choice of barrel lengths: 4-3/16", 4-1/8" or 6-5/16". Introduced in early Twenties, dropped in WWII. Used value, $145 to $160.

**STAR Model CO:** automatic, pocket model; .25 auto only; 2¾" barrel; 4½" overall length; fixed sights; 6-rd. magazine; checkered plastic grips; blued. Introduced in 1934; dropped, 1957. Engraved models, pearl-like grips were available at added cost. Used value, $115 to $125.

**STAR Model H:** pocket automatic; .32 auto; 7-rd. magazine. Identical in design to Model CO, except for caliber, magazine capcity. Introduced in 1934; dropped, 1941. Used value, $110 to $125.

**Model HN** has same general specifications as Model H, except for .380 auto chambering, 6-rd. magazine. Manufactured 1934 to 1941. Used value, $150 to $120.

*Star Model I*

*Model S*

**STAR Model I:** automatic, police model; .32 auto; 4¾" barrel; 7½" overall length; 9-rd. magazine; fixed sights, checkered plastic grips; blued. Not imported into U.S. Introduced in 1934; dropped, 1945. Used value, $115 to $135.

    **Model IN** has the same general specifications as Model I, except chambered for .380 auto only; 8-rd. magazine. Introduced in 1934; still in production, but importation prohibited by Firearms Act of 1968. Used value, $135 to $145.

*Star Model M*

**STAR Model M:** automatic; .380 auto, 9mm Luger, 9mm Bergmann, .45 auto; 5" barrel, 8½" overall length; 7-rd. magazine for .45 auto, 8 rds. for all other calibers; modification of Model 1911 Colt automatic model; fixed sights; checkered walnut grips; blued. Not imported into U.S. Introduced in 1935; still in production and marketed abroad. Used value, $140 to $145.

**STAR Model S:** automatic; .380 auto only; 4" barrel, 6½" overall length; 7-rd. magazine; fixed sights; checkered plastic grips, blued. Scaled-down modification of Colt 1911 automatic. Introduced in 1941; still in production, but importation into U.S. banned in 1968. Used value, $135 to $145.

    **Model SI** has the same general specifications as Model S, except for chambering in .32 auto only, 7-rd. magazine. Introduced in 1941; still in production, but importation banned in 1968. Used value, $130 to $140.

    **Super S** has the same general specifications as standard Model S, but with improved luminous sights for aiming in

darkness, magazine safety, disarming bolt, indicator to show number of unfired cartridges. Introduced in 1942; dropped, 1954. Used value, $145 to $155.

    **Super SI** has the same specifications as Super S, except for being chambered in .32 auto only. Introduced in 1942; dropped, 1954. Used value, $140 to $150.

**STAR Super Star Model:** 9mm Parabellum, .38 Super auto, .380 auto; has the same general specifications as the Model M, except for addition of disarming bolt, improved luminous sights, magazine safety, indicator for number of unfired cartridges. Introduced in 1942; dropped, 1954. Not imported. Used value, $140 to $165.

    **Super Star Target Model** has the same general specifications as Super Star model, except for substitution of adjustable target-type rear sight. Introduced in 1942; dropped, 1954. Used value, $155 to $175.

*Model F Target*

**STAR Model F:** automatic; .22 LR only; 4½" barrel, 7¼" overall length; 10-rd. magazine; fixed sights; checkered thumbrest plastic grips; blued. Introduced in 1942; dropped, 1969. Used value, $95 to $100.

    **Model F Sport** model has the same general specifications as standard Model F, but with substitution of 6" barrel, adjustable target-type rear sight. Introduced in 1942; dropped, 1969. Used value, $115 to $125.

    **Model F Target** model has the same general specifications as standard Model F, except for substitution of adjustable target sights, 7" barrel, weights. Introduced in 1942; dropped, 1969. Used value, $125 to $135.

    **Model FRS** is improved version of Model F, replacing the original version, but with same general specifications; 6" barrel; alloy frame. Available in blued, chrome finish, with checkered walnut grips. Introduced in 1969; still in production. No longer imported. Used values, blued, $100 to $115; chrome, $115 to $125.

**Model FM** has the same general specifications as the Model FRS, except for 4¼" barrel. Introduced in 1969; still in production. No longer imported. Used values, blued, $100 to $115; chrome, $115 to $125.

Model BKS

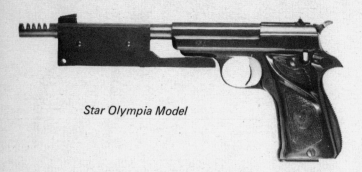

Star Olympia Model

**STAR Olympia Model:** automatic; designed for International rapid-fire target competition; .22 short only; 7" barrel; 11-1/16" overall length; 9-rd. magazine; alloy slide; muzzle brake; adjustable barrel weights; adjustable rear target sight; checkered plastic grips. Introduced in 1950; still in production. Not currently imported. Used value, $145 to $165.

**Model BKM** has same specifications as Model BKS, except for 4" barrel, hand-checkered walnut stocks, checkered backstrap. Introduced in 1976, still in production. Used value $165 to $170.

Star Super SM

Star Model HK

**STAR Super SM:** automatic; .380 ACP; 10-rd. magazine; 4" barrel, 6-5/8" overall length; checkered plastic stocks, adjustable rear sight, blade front; blued or chromed finish; thumb safety, loaded chamber indicator. Manufactured in Spain. Introduced 1977, still in production. Used values: blued, $160 to $165; chromed, $170 to $175.

**STAR Model HK:** automatic; .32 auto, .380 auto; 2¾" barrel; 5-9/16" overall length; 6-rd. magazine in .380, 7 rds. in .32; fixed sights, plastic grips; blued. Introduced in 1955; still in production. Never imported into U.S. Used value, $115 to $125.

**STAR Model DK:** automatic; .380 auto; overall length, 5-11/16" has aluminum alloy frame. Designation originally used for long discontinued .22 pistol. New .380 version introduced in 1958; never imported into United States. Used value, $125 to $135.

Star Model PD

**STAR Model BKS:** automatic; advertised as Star Starlight model; 9mm Parabellum only; 4½" barrel; 8-rd. magazine; fixed sights; magazine, manual safeties; checkered plastic grips; blued, chrome finish. Introduced in 1970; still in production as BKM with duraluminum frame. Model BM, with steel frame. Imported by Interarms. Used values, blued $130 to $145; chrome finish, $140 to $150.

**STAR MODEL PD:** automatic; .45 Auto; 6-rd. magazine; 3¾" barrel, 7" overall length; checkered walnut stocks, adjustable rear sight, ramp front, blued finish. Introduced 1975, still in production. Used value, $190 to $200.

# STERLING

**STERLING Model 283:** also designated as the Target 300; automatic; .22 LR only; 4½" 6", 8" barrels; overall length, 9" with 4½" barrel; 10-rd. magazine; micrometer rear sight, blade front; checkered plastic grips; external hammer; adjustable trigger; all steel construction; blued finish. Introduced in 1970; dropped, 1972. Used value, $85 to $95.

*Model 300*

*Sterling Model 284*

**STERLING Model 284:** also designated as Target 300L; automatic; .22 LR only; 4½", 6" tapered barrel; overall length, 9" with 4½" barrel; 10-rd. magazine; micrometer rear sight, blade front; checkered plastic grips; external spur hammer; adjustable trigger; all-steel construction; blued finish. Introduced in 1970; dropped, 1972. Used value, $85 to $95.

**STERLING Model 285:** advertised as the Husky; automatic; .22 LR; has the same specifications as the Model 283, but manufactured only with 4½" barrel, has fixed sights. Manufactured 1970 to 1971. Used vaue, $85 to $90.

*Sterling Model 286*

**STERLING Model 286:** advertised as the Trapper Model; automatic; .22 LR only; 4½", 6" tapered barrel; overall length, 9" with 4½" barrel; 10-rd. magazine, fixed rear sight, serrated ramp front; checkered plastic grips; external hammer; target-type trigger; all-steel construction; blued finish. Introduced in 1970; dropped, 1972. Used value, $70 to $80.

**STERLING Model 295:** advertised as Husky Model; automatic; .22 LR only; 4½" heavy barrel; overall length, 9"; 10-rd. magazine; fixed rear sight, serrated ramp front; checkered plastic grips; external hammer; target-type trigger; all-steel construction; blued finish. Introduced in 1970; dropped, 1972. Used value, $85 to $90.

**STERLING Model 300:** automatic; blow-back action; .25 auto; 2½" barrel; overall length, 4½"; 6-rd. magazine; no sights; black, white plastic grips; blue, satin nickel finish; all-steel construction. Introduced in 1971; still in production. Used values, blued, $65 to $70; nickel, $75 to $80.

**Model 300S** has same specifications as Model 300, except is manufactured from stainless steel. Introduced 1976, still in production. Used value, $80 to $90.

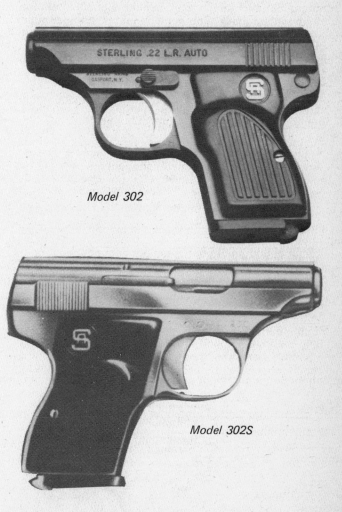

*Model 302*

*Model 302S*

**STERLING Model 302:** automatic; blow-back action; .22 LR; other specifications are generally the same as those of the Model 300, except that grips are available only in black plastic. Introduced in 1972; still in production. Used values, blued, $55 to $60; nickel, $60 to $65.

Model 302S has same specifications as Model 302, except is manufactured from stainless steel. Introduced 1976, still in production. Used value, $65 to $70.

Model 400

Sterling Model 400

STERLING Model 400: automatic; blow-back double-action; .380 ACP; 3½" barrel; overall length, 6½"; micrometer rear sight, fixed ramp front; checkered rosewood grips; blue, satin nickel finish; thumb-roll safety; all-steel construction. Introduced in 1973; still in production as Model 400 MKII. Used values, blued, $115 to $125; nickel, $125 to $130.

Model 400S has same specifications as Model 400, except is manufactured of stainless steel. Introduced 1977, still in production. Used value, $130 to $140.

STERLING Model 402: automatic; blow-back double-action; .22 LR only; other specifications are generally the same as those of the Model 400. Introduced in 1973; dropped, 1974. Used values, blued, $115 to $125; nickel, $125 to $130.

Model 450

STERLING Model 450: automatic, double-action; .45 Auto; 8-rd. magazine; 4" barrel, 7½" overall length; uncheckered walnut stocks, blued finish, adjustable rear sight. Introduced 1977, not yet in production.

# TAURUS

TAURUS Model 74: revolver; double-action; .32 S&W Long; 6-rd. cylinder; 3" barrel, 8¼" overall length; hand-checkered walnut stocks, blued or nickel finish, adjustable rear sight, ramp front. Manufactured in Brazil. Imported by International Distributors. Introduced 1971, still in production. Used value, $55 to $60.

TAURUS Model 80: revolver, double-action; .38 Special; 6-rd. cylinder; 3", 4" barrel lengths; hand-checkered walnut stocks, blued or nickel finish, fixed sights. Introduced 1971, still in production. Used value, $50 to $55.

Taurus Model 82

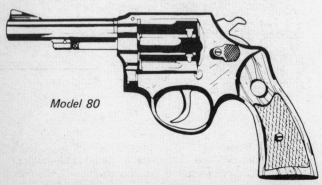

Model 80

TAURUS Model 82: revolver, double-action; .38 Special; has the same specifications as Model 80, except for heavy barrel. Introduced 1971, still in production. Used value, $55 to $60.

*Taurus Model 84*

**TAURUS Model 94:** revolver, double-action; .22 LR; other specifications are the same as those of Model 74, except for 4'' barrel, 9¼'' overall length. Introduced 1971, still in production. Used value, $60 to $65.

**TAURUS Model 96:** revolver, double-action; .22 LR; other specifications are identical to those of Model 86. Introduced 1971, still in production. Used value, $70 to $75.

*Taurus Model 83*

**TAURUS Model 84:** revolver, double-action; .38 Special; has same specifications as Model 83, except for standard weight barrel. Introduced 1971, still in production. Used value, $55 to $60.

**TAURUS Model 86 Target Master:** revolver, double-action; .38 Special; 6-rd. cylinder; 6'' barrel, 11¼'' overall length; hand-checkered walnut stocks; blued finish; adjustable rear sight, Patridge-design front. Introduced 1971, still in production. Used value, $70 to $75.

**TAURUS Model 83:** revolver, double-action; .38 Special; 6-rd. cylinder; 4'' heavy barrel, 9½'' overall length; hand-checkered walnut grips, blued or nickel finish, adjustable rear sight, ramp front. Introduced 1977, still in production. Used value, $65 to $70.

# UNIQUE

*Unique Kriegsmodell*

*Unique Model B/Cf*

**UNIQUE Model B/Cf:** automatic; .32 auto, .380 auto; 9-rd. magazine in .32, 8 rds. in .380; 4'' barrel, 6-2/3'' overall length; thumbrest plastic stocks, fixed sights, blued finish. Manufactured in France. Introduced 1954, still in production, but not imported. Used value, $140 to $154.

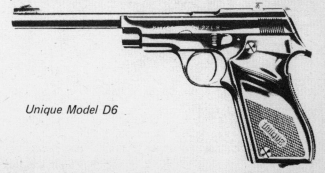

*Unique Model D6*

**UNIQUE Kriegsmodell:** automatic; .32 auto; 9-rd. magazine; 3-2/5'' barrel, 5-4/5'' overall length; grooved plastic stocks, blued finish, fixed sights. Manufactured in France 1940 to 1945 during WWII German occupation. Used value, $110 to $115.

**Model Rr** is the commercial version of Kreigsmodell, with the same specifications, improved finish. Introduced 1951, still in production, but not imported. Used value, $135 to $150.

**UNIQUE Model D2:** automatic; .22 LR; 10-rd. magazine; 4¼" barrel, 7½" overall length; thumbrest plastic stocks, adjustable sights, blued finish. Introduced 1954, still in production, but not imported. Used value, $160 to $165.

**Model D6** has the same specifications as Model D2, except for 6" barrel, 9¼" overall length. Introduced 1954, still in production, but not imported. Used value, $165 to $170.

*Unique Model L*

*Unique Model Mikros*

**UNIQUE Model L:** automatic; .22 LR, .32 auto, .380 auto; 10-rd. magazine in .22 LR, 7 rds. in .32 auto, 6 rds. in .380 auto; 3-1/3" barrel, 5-4/5" overall length; either steel or alloy frame; fixed sights, checkered plastic stocks, blued finish. Introduced 1955, still in production, but not imported. Used value, $110 to $115.

**UNIQUE MODEL Mikros:** automatic, pocket type; .22 short, .22 LR; 6-rd. magazine; 2¼" barrel, 4-7/16" overall length; either alloy or steel frame; fixed sights, checkered plastic stocks, blued finish. Introduced 1957, still in production, but not imported. Used value, $100 to $110.

*Unique Model DES/69*

**UNIQUE Model DES/69:** automatic, match type; .22 LR; 5-rd. magazine; 5-7/8" barrel; 10-2/3" overall length; checkered walnut thumbrest stocks, adjustable handrest; click adjustable rear sight, ramp front; blued finish. Introduced 1969, still in production. Imported by Solersport. Used value, $325 to $340.

**UNIQUE Model DES/VO:** automatic, rapid-fire match type; .22 short, 5-rd. magazine; 5-7/8" barrel, 10-2/5" overall length; adjustable trigger; hand-checkered walnut thumbrest stocks, adjustable handrest; adjustable rear sight, blade front; blued finish. Introduced 1974, still in production. Imported by Solersport. Used value, $340 to $360.

# WALTHER

**WALTHER Model 1:** automatic; .25 auto; 6-rd. magazine; 2" barrel, 4-2/5" overall length; checkered hard rubber stocks, fixed sights, blued finish. Manufactured in Germany, 1908 to 1918. Used value, $180 to $190.

*Model 1*

*Model 2*

WALTHER Model 2: automatic; .25 auto; 6-rd. magazine; 2'' barrel, 4-2/5'' overall length; checkered hard rubber stocks, fixed sights, blued finish. Has same general internal design as Model 1. Manufactured, 1909 to 1918. Used value, $180 to $190.

Walther M6

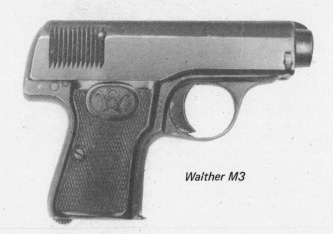

Walther M3

WALTHER Model 3: automatic; .32 auto; 8-rd. magazine; 2-2/3'' barrel; 5'' overall length; checkered hard rubber stocks, fixed sights, blued finish. Manufactured 1909 to 1918. Used value, $180 to $190.

WALTHER Model 4: automatic; .32 auto; 8-rd. magazine; 3½'' barrel, 5-7/8'' overall length; checkered hard rubber stocks, fixed sights, blued finish. Manufactured 1910 to 1918. Used value, $200 to $210.

Walther M7

WALTHER Model 7: automatic; .25 auto; 8-rd. magazine; 3'' barrel, 5-1/3'' overall length; checkered hard rubber stocks, fixed sights, blued finish. Manufactured 1917 to 1918. Used value, $180 to $190.

Walther M5

Walther M8

WALTHER Model 5: automatic; .25 auto; has the same specifications as Model 2, except with better workmanship, improved finish. Manufactured 1913 to 1918. Used value, $200 to $225.

WALTHER Model 6: automatic, 9mm Luger; 8-rd. magazine; 4¾'' barrel, 8¼'' overall length; checkered hard rubber stocks, fixed sights, blued finish. Manufactured 1915 to 1917. Used value, $230 to $245.

WALTHER Model 8: automatic; .25 auto only; 2-7/8'' barrel; 5-1/8'' overall length; 8-rd. magazine; fixed sights; checkered plastic grips; blued. Manufactured by Waffen-fabrik Walther, Zella-Mehlis, Germany. Introduced in 1920; dropped, 1945. Used value, $175 to $200.

Model 8 Lightweight has exactly the same specifications as the standard Model 8, except for use of aluminum alloy in slide, elements of frame. Introduced in 1927; dropped, 1945. Used value, $175 to $200.

*Walther Model 9*

*Post-WWII PPK*

**WALTHER Model 9:** automatic; vest pocket type; .25 auto only; 2" barrel, 3-15/16" overall length; 6-rd. magazine; checkered plastic grips, fixed sights; blued. Introduced in 1921; dropped, 1945. Used value, $200 to $225.

*Walther Model PP*

**WALTHER Model PP:** automatic; designed as law-enforcement model; .22 LR, .25 auto, .32 auto, .380 auto; 3-7/8" barrel, 6-5/16" overall length; 8-rd. magazine; fixed sights, checkered plastic grips, blued. WWII production has less value because of poorer workmanship. Introduced in 1929; dropped, 1945. Used values, wartime models, $250 to $275; .32, .380 calibers, $275 to $300; .22 caliber, $325 to $350; .25 caliber, $500 to $525.

**Model PP Lightweight** has the same specifications as standard model, except for use of aluminum alloy in construction. Introduced in 1929; dropped, 1945. Used values, .32, .380 calibers, $315 to $325; .22 caliber, $380 to $400; .25 caliber, $550 to $575.

**Post-WWII Model PP** is being manufactured currently by Carl Walther Waffenfabrik, Ulm/Donau, West Germany. It has the same specifications as the prewar model except not made in .25. Still in production. Imported by Interarms. Used value, $250 to $275.

**Model PP Mark II** is being made in France by Manufacture De Machines D Haut-Rhin and has the same specifications as the pre-WWII model. Introduced in 1953; still in production, but not imported. Used value, $200 to $225.

**WALTHER Model PPK:** automatic; designated as the detective pistol; .22 LR, .25 auto, .32 auto, .380 auto; 3¼" barrel, 5-7/8" overall length; 7-rd. magazine; checkered plastic grips; fixed sights; blued finish. WWII production has less value due to poorer workmanship. Introduced in 1931; still in production. Used values, wartime models, $250 to $275; .32, .380 calibers, $275 to $300; .22 caliber, $375 to $400; .25 caliber, $650 to $700.

**Model PPK Lightweight** has the same specifications as standard model, except for incorporation of aluminum alloys. Introduced in 1933; dropped, 1945. Used values, .32, .380, $425 to $450; .22, .25, $650 to $700.

**Post-WWII PPK** model is being manufactured in West Germany by Carl Walther Waffenfabrik. It has the same general specifications as the prewar model, with construction either of steel or aluminum alloy. Still in production, although U.S. importation was dropped in 1968. Used value, $300 to $325.

**Model PPK Mark II** is produced in France by Manufacture De Machines Du Haut-Rhin. It has the same specifications as pre-WWII model. Introduced in 1953; still in production, but not imported. Used value, $245 to $265.

**Model PPK Mark II Lightweight** has the same specifications as the standard model, except that the receiver is of Dural and chambering is .22 LR, .32 auto only. Introduced in 1953; still in production, but not imported. Used value, $275 to $300.

**WALTHER Target Model:** automatic; hammerless; .22 LR only; 6", 9" barrels; adjustable trigger; spring-driven firing pin; 10-rd. magazine capacity; safety on rear left side of frame; fixed front sight; rear adjustable for windage; hard rubber grips; Introduced in 1932; dropped during WWII. Used value, $325 to $345.

*Walther Self-Loading Model*

**WALTHER Self-Loading Model:** automatic; sport design; .22 LR only; 6", 9" barrels; with 6" barrel, 9-7/8" overall length; checkered one-piece walnut or plastic grip; adjustable target sights; blued. Introduced in 1932; dropped during WWII. Used value, $290 to $300.

**WALTHER Olympia Sport Model:** automatic; .22 LR only; 7-3/8" barrel; 10-11/16" overall length; checkered plastic grips; adjustable target sights; blued. Available with set of four detachable weights. Introduced in 1936; dropped during WWII. Used value, $425 to $450.

**Olympia Hunting Model** has the same specifications as Sport Model, except for 4" barrel. Introduced in 1936; dropped during WWII. Used value, $425 to $435.

**Olympia Rapid Fire Model** is automatic design; .22 short

*Olympia Rapid Fire Model*

*Walther P-38 Military Model*

only; 7-7/16" barrel; 10-11/16" overall length; detachable muzzle weight; checkered plastic grips; adjustable target sights; blued finish. Introduced in 1936; dropped during WWII. Used value, $435 to $450.

**Olympia Funkampf Model** is automatic design; .22 LR only; 9-5/8" barrel; 13" overall length; set of four detachable weights; checkered plastic grips; adjustable target sights; blued. Introduced in 1937; dropped during WWII. Used value, $600 to $625.

*Walther Model HP*

**WALTHER Model HP:** automatic; 9mm Luger; 5" barrel; 8-3/8" overall length; 10-rd. magazine; checkered walnut or plastic grips; fixed sights; blued. Introduced as commercial handgun in 1939; dropped during WWII. Used value, $475 to $500.

**WALTHER P-38 Military Model:** 9mm Luger; same specifications as the Model HP, but adopted as official German military sidearm in 1938 and produced throughout World

War II by Walther, Mauser and others. Quality, in most cases, is substandard to that of HP due to wartime production requirements. Introduced in 1938; dropped, 1945. Used value, $275 to $300.

*Post-war Model P-38*

Post-war Model P-38 is manufactured currently by Carl Walther Waffenfabrik in West Germany. It has the same general specifications as the WWII military model, except for improved workmanship and use of alloys in construction. Still in production. Imported by Interarms. Used value, $325 to $350.

**WALTHER GSP Match Model:** .22 LR; 5-rd. magazine; 5¾" barrel, 11-4/5" overall length; hand-fitting walnut stocks, adjustable rear sight, fixed front; marketed with spare magazine, barrel weight; blued finish. Imported by Interarms. Introduced 1977, still in production. Used value, $325 to $340.

**GSP-C Match Model** has the same specifications as GSP, but is chambered for .32 S&W wadcutter cartridge. Introduced 1977, still in production. Used value, $450 to $475.

# WEBLEY

*Webley Model 1906*

**WEBLEY Mark III Police Model:** revolver; double action; hinged frame; .38 S&W only; 6-rd. cylinder; 3", 4" barrels; with 4" barrel, overall length, 9½"; fixed sights; checkered Vulcanite or walnut grips; blued finish. Introduced in 1897; dropped, 1945. Used value, $115 to $125.

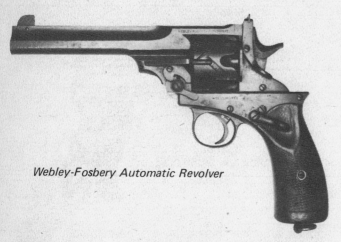

*Webley-Fosbery Automatic Revolver*

**WEBLEY-Fosbery Automatic Revolver:** .455 Webley, .38 Colt Auto; 6-rd. cylinder in .455, 8 rds. in .38 Colt Auto; hinged frame; 6" barrel, 12 inches overall; hand-checkered walnut stocks, fixed sights, blued finish. Recoil revolves cylinder, cocking hammer, leading to automatic terminology. Manufactured 1901 to 1939. Colt Auto version has collector value. Used values: .455 Webley, $210 to $220; .38 Colt Auto, $500 to $550.

*Webley Model 1906*

**WEBLEY Model 1906:** automatic; .380 auto, .32 auto; 3½" barrel; 6¼" overall length; 7-rd. magazine in .380, 8 rds. in .32; exposed hammer; checkered hard rubber grips; checkered walnut grips on special order; blued; popular in Commonwealth for police use; law enforcement version has rear sight; those for civilian consumption have sight groove full length of slide. Introduced in 1905; dropped, 1940. Used value, $150 to $175.

**WEBLEY Model 1906:** automatic; .25 auto only; 2-1/8" barrel; overall length, 4¼"; 6-rd. magazine; checkered hard rubber grips; resembles Model 1913 in appearance, but had no sights, no sight groove on slide, and is much smaller. Introduced in 1906, dropped, 1940. Used value, $200 to $225.

**WEBLEY Police & Civilian Pocket Model:** revolver; double action; hinged frame; .32 S&W only; 3½" barrel; 6¼" overall length; 8-rd. cylinder; checkered plastic grips; fixed sights; blued finish. Introduced in 1906; dropped, 1940. Used value, $125 to $135.

*Webley Model 1909*

**WEBLEY Model 1909:** automatic; hammerless; .25 auto only; 2-1/8" barrel; 4¼" overall length; 6-rd. magazine; front, rear sights mounted on slide; ejection port at top of slide; checkered black composition grips. Introduced in 1909; dropped, 1940. Used value, $250 to $275.

**Model 1909 Improved** is in 9mm Browning Long only; limited production, some for the government of the Union of South Africa. It differs from the original in several features: grip frame is angled more than on other Webley autos; magazine release button is behind trigger guard; no grip safety; lanyard ring mounted at bottom of backstrap; safety lever on left side of slide; checkered black plastic grips. Introduced in 1909; dropped, 1930. Has considerable collector value. Used value, $375 to $395.

*Model 1909 Single-Shot*

**WEBLEY Model 1909:** single-shot; tip-up action; .22, .32 S&W, .38 S&W; 9-7/8" barrel; blade front sight; plastic thumbrest target grips; late versions had ballast chamber in butt to permit weight adjustment; rebounding hammer; matte-finish barrel; blued. Introduced in 1909; dropped, 1965. Used value, $145 to $165.

*Mark IV Police*

*Webley Model 1913*

fitting, blued-over unpolished surfaces. To protect the corporate reputation, most were stamped, "War Finish." Used value, $135 to $145.

**WEBLEY Model 1913:** automatic; .455 Webley only; commercial version of model adopted by Royal Navy in 1913; overall length, 8½"; 7-rd. magazine; grip safety; movable rear sight; fixed blade front; checkered black composition grips; checkered walnut grips on special order. Introduced in 1911; dropped, 1931. Has some collector value. Used value, $285 to $315.

*Webley Mark IV Target Model*

*Model 1911 9-inch barrel*

*Model 1911 4½-inch barrel*

**WEBLEY Mark IV Target Model:** revolver; double action; .22 LR only; built in small quantities on the Mark IV .38 frame; fitted with adjustable rear sight. Introduced in 1931; dropped, 1968. Virtually a custom-produced handgun. Used value, $250 to $275.

**WEBLEY Mark IV .32 Police:** revolver; double action; .32 S&W; has the same specifications as .38 S&W Mark IV Police version, except is chambered for smaller caliber. Introduced in 1929; dropped, 1968. Used value, $115 to $125.

**WEBLEY Model 1911:** single-shot; .22 rimfire only; has appearance of automatic as it is built on Model 1906 frame; 4½" and 9" barrels; originally introduced as police training arm; some were available with removable wooden stock. Introduced in 1911; dropped, 1927. Only a few hundred produced, affording it collector interest. Used value, $250 to $300.

**WEBLEY Mark IV Police Model:** revolver; double action; hinged frame; .38 S&W only; 6-rd. cylinder; 3", 4", 5", 6" barrels; with 5" barrel, overall length, 9-1/8"; fixed or target sights; checkered plastic grips; lanyard ring; blued finish. Introduced in 1929; dropped, 1968. Used value, $150 to $160.

    **Mark IV War Model** has the same general specifications as the Police Model. Built during WWII, it usually has poor

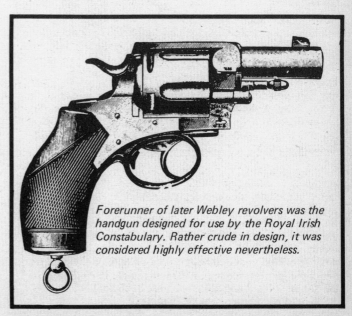

*Forerunner of later Webley revolvers was the handgun designed for use by the Royal Irish Constabulary. Rather crude in design, it was considered highly effective nevertheless.*

# DAN WESSON

*Dan Wesson Model 15*

*Dan Wesson Model 11*

*Dan Wesson Model 12*

**DAN WESSON Model 11:** double-action revolver; .357 magnum only; 2½", 4", 6" interchangeable barrels; with 4" barrel, 9¼" overall length; 6-rd. cylinder; interchangeable grips; adjustable dovetail rear sight, serrated ramp front. Marketed with tools for changing barrels, grips; non-recessed barrel nut, blued. Introduced in 1969; dropped, 1974. Used value, $145 to $165.

**DAN WESSON Model 12:** double-action revolver; .357 magnum only; 2¼", 3¾", 5¾" interchangeable barrels; with grips; 6-rd. cylinder; adjustable target-type rear sight, serrated ramp front. Marketed with tools for changing barrels, grips; blued. Introduced in 1969; dropped, 1974. Used value, $165 to $175.

**DAN WESSON Model 14:** double-action revolver; .357 magnum only; 2¼", 3¾", 5¾" interchangeable barrels; with 3¾" barrel, 9" overall length; 6-rd. cylinder; interchangeable walnut grips; fixed dovetail rear sight, serrated ramp front; wide trigger with adjustable overtravel stop; wide spur hammer; recessed barrel nut; blued, nickel, matte nickel finish. Introduced in 1971; dropped, 1975. Replaced by Model 14-2. Used values, blued, $165 to $175; nickel, $165 to $175; matte nickel, $170 to $190.

Dan Wesson Model 15-2

**DAN WESSON Model 15:** double-action revolver; .357 magnum only; 2¼", 3¾", 5¾" interchangeable barrels; has same general specifications as Model 14, except for rear sight adjustable for windage, elevation. Introduced in 1971; dropped, 1975. Replaced by Model 15-2. Used values, blued, $175 to $190; nickel, $175 to $190; matte nickel, $185 to $195.

Model 15-2H has same specifications as the Model 15-2, except for heavy barrel options. Introduced 1975, still in production. Values depend upon barrel length, ranging from 2" through 15" barrel. Values, $170 to $275; extra barrels, $60 to $150, depending upon length.

Model 15-2HV has same specifications as Model 15-2, except for heavy vent rib barrel, ranging from 2 to 15". Introduced 1975, still in production. Used values comparable to those of Model 15-2H.

**DAN WESSON Model 8-2:** revolver, double-action; .38 Special. Except for caliber, other specifications are the same as the Model 14-2. Introduced 1975, still in production. Used value, $135 to $140.

**DAN WESSON Model 9-2H:** revolver, double-action; .38 Special; has the same general specifications as Model 15-2H, except for caliber. Introduced 1975, still in production. Used value, $170 to $275, depending upon barrel length; extra barrels, $60 to $150, depending upon length.

Model 9-2V has same specifications as Model 9-2H, except for standard vent rib barrel, ranging from 2" to 15". Introduced 1975, still in production. Values are comparable to those of Model 9-2H.

Model 9-2HV has same specifications as Model 9-2, except for heavy vent rib barrel; made in .38 Special only. Introduced 1975, still in production. Used value, comparable to that of 9-2H.

# MISCELLANEOUS HANDGUNS
## U.S.-MADE

*American 25*

**AMERICAN 25:** .25 auto, 8-rd. magazine; 4.4'' overall length, 2.1'' barrel; fixed sights; walnut grips; blued ordnance steel or stainless steel; manufactured by American Firearms Manufacturing Co., Inc. Introduced in 1966; dropped, 1974. Used values, blued steel model, $70 to $75; stainless steel model, $80 to $85.

**AMERICAN FIREARMS Derringer:** 2-shot; .38 Special, .22 LR, .22 WRM; 3'' barrel; fixed open sights; checkered plastic grips; entirely of stainless steel; spur trigger, half-cock safety. Introduced in 1972; dropped, 1974. Used value, $85 to $95.

*American 380 Automatic*

**AMERICAN 380:** automatic; .380 auto; stainless steel; 8-rd. magazine; 5½'' overall; 3½'' barrel; smooth walnut stocks. Limited manufacture, 1972. Used value, $135 to $145.

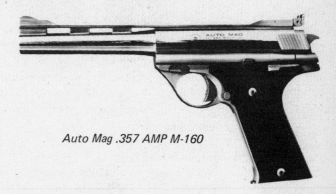

*Auto Mag .357 AMP M-160*

**AUTO MAG:** automatic; .357 Auto Mag., .44 Auto Mag.; 6½'' barrel; 11½'' overall length; 7-rd. magazine; short recoil, rotary bolt system; stainless steel construction; checkered plastic grips. fully adjustable rear sight, ramp front. Manufactured 1970 to 1975. Used value, $575 to $600.

*Bauer Auto .25*

**BAUER 25:** automatic; .25 auto; 2-1/8'' barrel; 4'' overall length; 6-rd. magazine; stainless steel construction; fixed sights; plastic pearl or checkered walnut grips; manual, magazine safeties. Introduced in 1973; still in production. Used value, $75 to $95.

**BAUER 22:** automatic; .22 long rifle only; same design as Bauer 25 except has 5-rd. magazine; 2¼'' barrel, measures 4-1/8'' overall. Manufacture began 1977. Used value, $80 to $90.

**BUDISCHOWSKY TP-70:** double-action automatic; .22 LR, .25 auto; 2-7/16'' barrel; 4-2/3'' overall length; 6-rd. magazine; fixed sights; all stainless steel construction; manual, magazine safeties. Introduced in 1973; still in production. Used value, $135 to $145.

*Budischowsky TP 70*

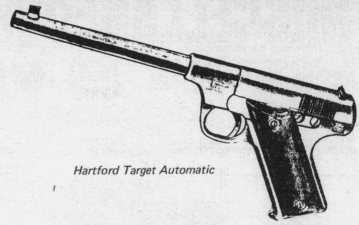

*Hartford Target Automatic*

*Clerke 1st Model*

**CLERKE First Model:** double-action revolver; .32 S&W, .22 LR, long, short; 2¼" barrel, 6¼" overall length; fixed sights; 5-rd. swing-out cylinder in .32, 6 rds. in .22; checkered plastic grips; blued, nickel finish. Introduced in 1973; dropped, 1975. Used value, $10 to $15.

**HARTFORD Target Automatic:** in .22 LR only; 6¾" barrel; 10¾" overall length; 10-rd. magazine; checkered black rubber grips; target sights; blued finish. Bears close resemblance to early High Standard automatic models. Introduced in 1929; dropped, 1930. Has more collector than shooter value. Used value, $200 to $235.

**HARTFORD Repeating Pistol:** has the same general outward design characteristics as target auto; .22 LR only; hand-operated repeater, with slide being moved rearward by hand to eject cartridge case, forward to chamber new round. Introduced in 1929; dropped, 1930. Used value, $200 to $225.

**HARTFORD Target Single-Shot:** same general outward appearance as Hartford target auto, but with 5¾" barrel; 10¾" overall length; .22 LR only; black rubber or walnut grips, target sights, color case-hardened frame, blued barrel. Introduced in 1929; dropped, 1930. Used value, $175 to $200.

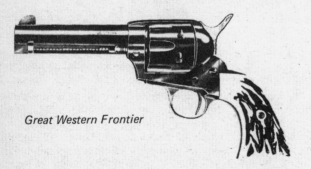

*Great Western Frontier*

*Indian Arms DA*

**GREAT WESTERN Frontier:** revolver, single-action; .22 LR, .38 Special, .357 magnum, .44 Special, .44 magnum, .45 Colt; 6-rd. cylinder; 4¾", 5½", 7½" barrel lengths; grooved rear sight, fixed blade front; imitation stag grips, blued finish. Sold primarily by mail order. Manufactured 1951 to 1962. Used value, $50 to $60.

**GREAT WESTERN Derringer:** over/under, 2-shot; .38 S&W, 3" barrels, 5" overall length; checkered black plastic grips, fixed sights, blued finish. Replica of Remington Double Derringer. Manufactured 1953 to 1962. Used value, $75 to $80.

**INDIAN ARMS Stainless:** automatic, double-action; .380 auto; 6-rd. magazine; 3½" barrel, 6-1/16" overall length; checkered walnut stocks, adjustable rear sight, blade front; made of stainless steel, but with natural or blued finish; optional safety lock. Introduced 1977; dropped 1978. Used value, $160 to $170.

**INTERARMS Virginian Dragoon:** single-action revolver; .357 magnum, .44 magnum, .45 Colt; 6-rd. cylinder; 6", 7½", 8-3/8" barrel lengths; base pin safety system; unchecked walnut grips, ramp front sight, fixed or micrometer rear sight, color case-hardened frame, blued finish. Introduced 1977, still in production. Used values: with fixed sights, $140 to $145; adjustable sight, $145 to $155.

**MERRILL Sportsman:** single-shot; .22 Short, .22 LR, .22 WMR, .22 WRF, .22 Rem Jet, .22 Hornet, .357 magnum, .38 Special, .256 Win magnum, .45 Colt, .30-30, .44 magnum; and many others 9", 12", 14" semi-octagon hinged barrel; unchecked walnut grips with thumb, heel rest; adjustable rear sight, fixed front; hammerless, top rib grooved for scope mounts. Introduced 1972, still in production. Used value, $165 to $175.

*Mossberg Brownie*

**MOSSBERG Brownie:** double-action, pocket pistol; four 2½" barrels; revolving firing pin; .22 LR, long, short; break-open action; steel extractor. Introduced in 1919; dropped, 1932. Has some collector interest. Used value, $125 to $135.

**NORTH AMERICAN ARMS Model 22S:** single-action revolver; .22 Short; 5-rd. cylinder; 1-1/8" barrel, 3½" overall length; made of stainless steel; plastic stocks, fixed sights. Introduced 1975, still in production as Freedom Arms Mini Revolver. Used value, $65 to $70.

**Model 22 LR** has the same general specifications as Model 22S, but chambered for .22 LR cartridge; 3-7/8" overall length. Introduced 1976, still in production. Used value, $75 to $85.

**NORTH AMERICAN ARMS Model 454C:** single-action revolver; .454 Casull; 5-rd. cylinder; 7½" barrel; 14" overall length; made of stainless steel; unchecked hardwood stocks; fixed sights. Introduced in 1977, sporadic production since. Used value, $325 to $350.

**PLAINFIELD Model 71:** automatic; .22 LR, .25 auto; 10-rd. magazine in .22 LR; .25 auto, 8 rds.; 2½" barrel; 5-1/8" overall length; stainless steel slide, frame; fixed sights, checkered walnut stocks. Also made with caliber conversion kit. Introduced 1970, dropped 1980 (approx.) Used values: .22 LR, $65 to $70; .25 auto, $65 to $70; with conversion kit, $75 to $85.

**PLAINFIELD Model 72:** automatic; has the same general specifications as Model 71, except for 3½" barrel, 6" overall length; aluminum slide. Introduced 1970; dropped about 1978. Used values: .22 LR, $65 to $70; .25 auto, $65 to $70; with conversion kit, $75 to $85.

**RAVEN:** automatic; .25 auto; 3" barrel, 5½" overall length; unchecked walnut or pearlite stocks; fixed sights, blued, nickel or satin nickel finish. Manufactured in U.S., marketed by Early and Modern Firearms. Introduced 1977, still in production. Used value, $35 to $40.

*Reising Target Model*

**REISING Target Model:** automatic; hinged frame; .22 LR; 12-rd. magazine; 6½" barrel; external hammer; hard rubber checkered stocks; fixed sights, blued finish. Manufactured 1921 to 1924. Collector Value. Used value, $300 to $325.

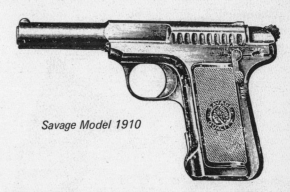

*Savage Model 1910*

**SAVAGE Model 1910:** automatic; .32 auto, .380 auto; .32 auto has 10-rd. magazine, 3¾" barrel, 6½" overall length; .380 auto has 9-rd. magazine, 4½" barrel, 7" overall length; grip safety, either hammerless or with exposed hammer; checkered hard rubber stocks, fixed sights, blued finish. Manufactured 1910 to 1917. Collector value. Used value, $200 to $225.

*Savage Model 1917*

**SAVAGE Model 1917:** automatic pistol; .32 auto, 10-rd. magazine; .380 auto, 9-rd. magazine; 3¾" barrel in .32, 4½" barrel in .380; spurred hammer; blued finish, fixed sights, hard rubber grips. Introduced in 1920 to replace Model 1915; dropped, 1928. Used value, $155 to $160.

*Savage Model 101*

**SECURITY INDUSTRIES Model PM357:** double-action revolver; .357 magnum; 5-rd. cylinder; 2½" barrel, 7½" overall length; made of stainless steel; uncheckered American walnut target stocks; fixed sights. Introduced in 1973, dropped 1977. Used value, $145 to $155.

**SECURITY INDUSTRIES Model PPM357:** double-action revolver; .357 magnum; 5-rd. cylinder; 2" barrel, 6-1/8" overall length; made of stainless steel; checkered American walnut target stocks; fixed sights. Introduced 1976 with spurless hammer; converted to conventional hammer, 1977. Dropped 1977. Used value, $145 to $155.

**SEDGLEY Baby Hammerless Model:** double-action revolver; solid frame; .22 LR; 6-rd. cylinder; folding trigger, 4" overall length; hard rubber stocks, fixed sights, blued or nickel. Manufactured 1930 to 1939. Some collector interest. Used value, $110 to $120.

**SAVAGE Model 101:** single-action single-shot; .22 LR, long, short; 5½" barrel integral with chamber; overall length, 9"; fake cylinder swings out for loading, ejection; manual ejection with spring-rod ejector; compressed, plastic-impregnated wood grips; adjustable slotted rear sight, blade front; blued. Introduced in 1968; dropped 1969. Used value, $65 to $75.

**SHERIDAN Knockabout:** single-shot pistol; tip-up action; .22 short, long, 5" barrel, 8¾" overall length; checkered plastic grips; blued finish; fixed sights. Introduced in 1953; dropped, 1960. Used value, $70 to $80.

*Security Industries Model PSS38*

*Stevens No. 35*

**STEVENS No. 35:** single-shot target pistol; .22 LR only; 6", 8", 12¼" barrels; tip-up action; walnut grips; target sights; blued. Also produced to handle .410 shotshell. Introduced in 1907; dropped, 1939. Has mostly collector value. Used value, $175 to $225.

**SECURITY INDUSTRIES Model PSS38:** double-action revolver; .38 Special; 5-rd. cylinder; 2" barrel, 6½" overall length; made of stainless steel; checkered American walnut stocks; fixed sights. Introduced 1973; dropped 1977. Used value, $125 to $130.

*Stevens No. 10*

*Security Model PM357*

**STEVENS No. 10:** single-shot target model; tip-up action; .22 LR, 8" barrel, 11½" overall length; hard rubber stocks, blued finish, target sights. Manufactured 1919 to 1939. Some collector interest. Used value, $150 to $160.

**STOEGER Luger:** automatic; .22 LR only; 11-rd. magazine; 4½", 5½" barrel; based upon original Luger design, but made in U.S. for Stoeger Arms; checkered or smooth wooden grips; blued. Introduced in 1970; dropped 1978. All steel model reintroduced 1980. Used value, $80 to $85.

*Stoeger Target Luger*

**Luger Target** model has the same specifications as standard Stoeger Luger, except for checkered hardwood stocks, target sights. Introduced 1975; all steel model reintroduced 1980. Used value, $95 to $100.

**TDE Backup:** automatic; .380 ACP, 5-rd. magazine; 2½" barrel, 5" overall length; uncheckered hardwood stocks, recessed fixed sights; concealed hammer, blowback operation; stainless steel. Introduced 1977, still in production. Used value, $120 to $125.

**THOMAS 45:** automatic; double-action; .45 ACP, 6-rd. magazine; 3½" barrel, 6½" overall length; checkered plastic stocks, windage adjustable rear sight, blade front; blued finish, matte sighting surfaces; blow-back action. Introduced 1977; dropped 1978. Only about 600 guns ever made. Used value, $190 to $200.

*Thompson/Center Contender*

**THOMPSON/CENTER Contender:** introduced in 1967; still in production. Single-shot, break-open pistol with exposed hammer, the action being opened by pressing rearward and upward on the tang of the trigger guard. Barrels are interchangeable, permitting the firing of different calibers from the same receiver. A circular insert in the face of the hammer is pivoted one-half turn to switch between the center-fire and rimfire firing pins. Barrels have been factory chambered and custom rechambered for a variety of different cartridges, many of them nonstandard, or "wildcat" numbers. A detachable choke tube was developed originally for a barrel chambered for the .45 Long Colt which, with choke installed, could fire 3" .410 shotshells effectively. Production of this barrel was discontinued at the suggestion of BATF; the .45 LC/.410 barrels have changed hands at prices of $175 or more, due to their scarcity. Currently, two types of choked barrels are made: an external model and an internal choke, the latter being furnished on the vent-ribbed barrel; both being made in .357 magnum and .44 magnum permitting the firing of solid-bullet loads when the choke is removed or T/C's "HotShot" capsules with choke in place.

Rimfire calibers are .22 LR (also handling .22 BB caps, CB caps, short, long or shot loads), .22 WMRF, 5mm Rem.; center-fire calibers are .22 Hornet, .22 K-Hornet, .22 Rem. Jet, .218 Bee, .221 Rem. Fire Ball, .222 Rem., .256 Win. magnum, .25-35 WCF, .30 M-1 Carbine, .30-30 WCF, .38 Super Auto, .38 Special, .357 magnum, .357/44 Bain & Davis, 9mm Parabellum (Luger), .45 ACP, .45 Long Colt, .44 magnum. The .357, .44 and .45 LC can be had with choke or without; unfluted "bull barrels" are offered in .30 Herrett and .357 Herrett, these being two wildcat cartridges based upon the .30-30 case; standard barrel lengths, 8¾" and 10", although a few have been made in 6" length; standard forends snap on, but a special screw-held forend is supplied with the bull barrels; two designs of grips have been furnished, the early type having a decorative metal butt cap and the current one having a black plastic butt cap; decorative game scene etching is standard on both sides of all receivers; later models have adjustable trigger-stop in rear of trigger guard; standard sights consist of an undercut Patridge front sight on a ramp, with square-notch rear sight adjustable for windage or elevation; scope mounts available from T/C and other suppliers to fit the holes drilled and tapped for rear sight; weight, with 10" barrel, about 43 oz.; finish, blued; stocks, checkered walnut forend and handgrip, with thumb rest grips that must be ordered for right-hand or left-hand use, no extra charge for left-hand grips. Most early models embody a receiver design which makes it necessary to reset the action by pulling the trigger guard tang rearward before the hammer can be cocked. Used values, $145 to $155 for standard gun, complete with one barrel; $160 to $170 for gun with ventilated rib/internal choke or full bull barrel less sights; $175 to $180 for gun with bull barrel and iron sights; $50 to $55 for standard barrel alone; $65 to $75 for ventilated rib/internal choke or bull barrel less sights; $65 to $75 for bull barrel alone, fitted with iron sights. Scarce, discontinued barrels in exotic chamberings, may command higher figures.

**U.S. ARMS Abilene Model:** revolver, single-action; .357 magnum, .41 magnum, .44 magnum, .45 Colt; 4-5/8, 5½, 6½, 7½, 8½" barrel lengths; adjustable rear sight, ramp front; uncheckered American walnut stocks, blued finish or stainless steel. Introduced in 1976, still in production. Currently manufactured, marketed by O.F. Mossberg & Sons. Used values: blued finish, $135 to $155; stainless steel, $175 to $200.

**Abilene Convertible** has same general specifications as standard model, except for interchangeable .357 magnum, 9mm Luger cylinders; available only in blued finish. Used value, $140 to $150.

*Warner Infallible Model*

**WARNER Infallible Model:** automatic, pocket configuration; .32 auto; 7-rd. magazine; 3" barrel; 6½" overall length; checkered hard rubber stocks, fixed sights, blued finish. Manufactured 1917 to 1919. Used value, $150 to $165.

**WILKINSON Diane:** automatic; .22 LR, .25 ACP; 8-rd. magazine for .22 LR, 8 rds. for .25 ACP; 2-1/8" barrel, 4½" overall length; checkered styrene stocks, fixed sights integral with slide, matte blued finish, internal hammer, separate ejector. Introduced 1977, still in production. Used value, $80 to $85.

**WHITNEY Wolverine:** autoloader; .22 LR only; 4-4/8" barrel; 9" overall length; aluminum alloy frame; rear sight movable for windage only; 1/8" Patridge-type front; top of

*Whitney Wolverine*

slide serrated to reduce reflection; checkered plastic grips; blued or nickel finish. Introduced in 1956; dropped, 1963. Has some collector interest. Used values, blued finish, $140 to $150; nickel, $165 to $175.

# FOREIGN

*Alkartasuna Ruby*

*Beholla Pocket*

**ALKARTASUNA Ruby:** automatic; .32 auto; 9-rd. magazine; 6-3/8" overall; 3-3/8" barrel; checkered hard rubber or wooden stocks; blued finish, fixed sights. Manufactured in Spain, 1917 to 1922; distributed primarily in Europe; some used by French army in World Wars I, II. Used value, $65 to $70.

**BEHOLLA Pocket Auto:** automatic; .32 auto; 7-rd. magazine; 5½" overall; 3" barrel; blued finish, fixed sights; grooved hard rubber or wooden stocks. German-made. Manufactured 1915 to 1925. Used value, $80 to $90.

**BRONCO Model 1918:** automatic; .32 auto; 6-rd. magazine; 5" overall; 2½" barrel; blued finish, fixed sights, hard rubber stocks. Manufactured in Spain 1918 to 1925. Used value, $60 to $65.

**DOMINO Model SP-601:** automatic, match pistol design; .22 short; 5-rd. magazine; 5½" barrel length; 11¼" overall length; open notch adjustable rear sight, blade front; single lever takedown, European walnut match stocks, adjustable

palm rest; barrel ported to reduce recoil. Manufactured in Italy. Imported by Mandall Shooting Supplies. Introduced 1977, still in production. Used value, $450 to $475.

    **Model SP-602** has same general specifications as Model SP-601, but is chambered for .22 LR, has adjustable one-piece walnut stock, no gas ports, different trigger, sear mechanism. Introduced 1977, still in production. Used value, $400 to $425.

**DREYSE Model 1907:** automatic; .32 auto; 8-rd. magazine; 3½" barrel, 6¼" overall; fixed sights, hard rubber checkered stocks; blued finish. Manufactured in Germany, 1907 to 1914. Used value, $90 to $100.

**DREYSE Vest Pocket Model:** automatic; .25 auto; 6-rd. magazine; 2" barrel, 4½" overall length; fixed sights, checkered hard rubber stocks, blued finish. Manufactured 1909 to 1914. Used value, $90 to $100.

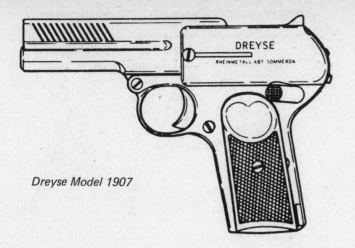

*Dreyse Model 1907*

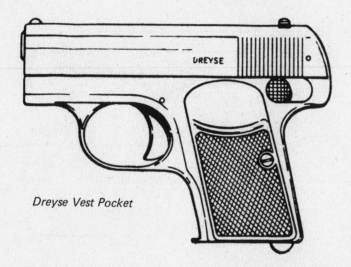

*Dreyse Vest Pocket*

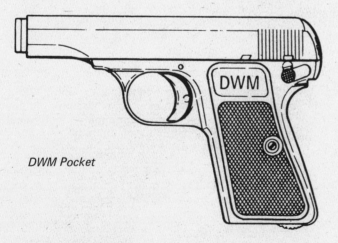

*DWM Pocket*

**DWM Vest Pocket Model:** automatic; .32 auto; 3½" barrel, 6" overall; hard rubber checkered stocks, blued finish. Design resembles Browning FN Model 1910. Manufactured in Germany, 1920 to 1931. Used value, $105 to $115.

**ERMA Automatic:** .22 LR target pistol, 10-rd. magazine, interchangeable 8-3/16", 11¾" barrels; adjustable target sights; checkered plastic grips; blued finish. Used value, $85 to $100.

*Erma KGP 68*

**ERMA KGP 68:** auto pistol; .32 auto (KGP32), 6-rd. magazine; .380 auto (KGP38), 5-rd. magazine; 3½" barrel, overall length, 6¾"; adjustable blade front sight, fixed rear; checkered walnut grips; side-lock manual safety. Imported by Excam. Used value, $80 to $90.

*Erma KGP 69*

**ERMA KGP 69:** auto pistol; .22 LR, 8-rd. magazine; 4" barrel, overall length, 7-5/16"; checkered walnut grips; adjustable blade front sight, fixed rear; slide stays open after last shot; imported from Germany by Excam as the KGP22. Used value, $85 to $80.

**FIE E27 Titan:** automatic; .25 ACP; 6-rd. magazine; 4, 6" barrel lengths; checkered walnut stocks, wide trigger, fixed sights, blued or chromed finish. Manufactured by Firearms Import & Export. Introduced, 1977, still in production. Used values, Blued, $25 to $27.50; chromed, $30 to $32.50.

**FIE G27 Guardian:** automatic; .25 ACP; 6-rd. magazine; 2-7/16" barrel, 4¾" overall length; contoured plastic stocks, fixed sights; blued, gold or chromed finish. Introduced 1977, still in production. Used values, blued, $25 to $25.50; chromed, $30 to $32.50; gold, $35 to $37.50.

**FN BROWNING** Model 1900: automatic; .32 auto; 7-rd. magazine, 4" barrel, 6¾" overall length; checkered hard rubber stocks, fixed sights, blued finish. Manufactured in Belgium, 1899 to 1910. Used value, $130 to $145.

**FN BROWNING** Model 1903: automatic; 9mm Browning; 7-rd. magazine; 5" barrel, 8" overall; hard rubber checkered stocks, fixed sights, blued finish. Designed primarily for military use; design, function similar to Browning FN 380. Manufactured 1903 to 1939. Used value, $150 to $175.

**FN BROWNING Model 1922:** automatic; .32 auto, with 9-rd. magazine; .380 auto, 8 rds.; 4½'' barrel; 7'' overall checkered hard rubber stocks, fixed sights, blued finish. Introduced in 1922; still in production. Used value, $135 to $150.

**FROMMER Stop Pocket Model:** automatic; .32 Auto, with 7-rd. magazine; .380 Auto, with 6 rds.; 3-7/8'' barrel, 6½'' overall length; grooved hard rubber stocks, fixed sights, blued finish. Manufactured in Hungary, 1912 to 1920. Used value, $110 to $115.

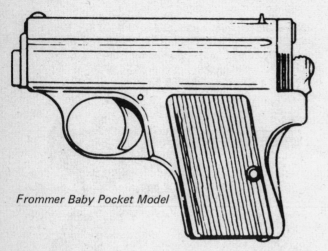

*Frommer Baby Pocket Model*

**FROMMER Baby Pocket Model:** automatic, .32 auto; 6-rd. magazine; smaller version of Stop Pocket model with 2'' barrel, 4¾'' overall. Manufactured from 1919 to approximately 1922. Used value, $140 to $145.

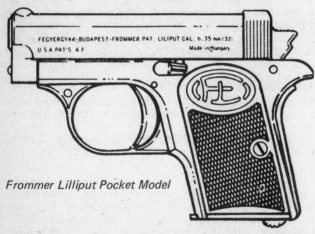

*Frommer Lilliput Pocket Model*

**FROMMER Lilliput Pocket Model:** automatic, blow-back action; .25 auto; 6-rd. magazine; 2-1/8'' barrel, 4-1/3'' overall length; hard rubber stocks, fixed sights, blued finish. Manufactured 1921 to 1924. Used value, $150 to $160.

**GALISI Model 6:** automatic; .25 auto; 6-rd. magazine; 2½'' barrel, 4-3/8'' overall; plastic stocks, fixed sights, blued finish. Manufactured in Italy. Introduced in 1930, still in production. Used value, $85 to $90.

**GALISI Model 9:** automatic; .22 LR, .32 auto, .380 auto; 8-rd. magazine; 3¼'' barrel, plastic stocks, fixed sights, blued finish. Introduced in 1930; still in production. Used value, $80 to $95.

*Galesi Model 6*

*Galesi Model 9*

**GARCIA Regent:** revolver, .22 LR only; 3'', 4'', 6'' barrels; 8-rd. swing-out cylinder; fixed rear sight, ramp front; checkered plastic grips; blued. Introduced in 1972; dropped, 1977. Used value, $45 to $50.

*Garcia/FI Model D*

**GARCIA/FI Model D:** automatic; .380 ACP; 6-rd. magazine; 3-1/8'' barrel, 6-1/8'' overall length; checkered American walnut stocks, windage adjustable rear sight, blade front, blued, lanyard ring. Manufactured by Firearms International, 1977 to 1979. Used value, $120 to $130.

*H&K HK-4*

**HECKLER & KOCH HK-4:** auto double-action pistol; .380 auto; 8-rd. magazine; 3½" barrel, 6" overall length; checkered black plastic grips; rear sight adjustable for windage, front, fixed. Early version was available with interchangeable barrels, magazines for four calibers. Imported from Germany originally by Harrington & Richardson, currently by Heckler & Koch, Inc. Used value, single caliber, $150 to $165; with four barrels as set, $300 to $325.

*H&K P9S*

**HECKLER & KOCH P9S:** 9mm Parabellum; 9-rd. magazine; 4" barrel, 5.4" overall length; fixed sights, checkered plastic grips; double-action; loaded/cocked indicators; hammer cocking lever; originally imported from Germany by Gold Rush Gun Shop, currently by Heckler & Koch, Inc. Used value, $275 to $300.

    **P9S Target Model** has same specifications as Model P9S 9mm, except for adjustable trigger, trigger stop and adjustable rear sight. Used value, $275 to $285.

    **P9S 45** has same specifications as Model P9S 9mm, except for being made for .45 auto cartridge; has 7-rd. magazine. Used value, $280 to $300.

    **P9S Competition Kit** is the same as P9S 9mm, but has interchangeable 5½" barrel, barrel weight, choice of standard plastic or walnut competition stock. Used values: with plastic stock, $310 to $325; with walnut competition stock, $400 to $420.

**KASSNAR M-100D:** revolver; double-action; .22 LR, .22 magnum, .38 Special; 6-rd. cylinder; 3", 4", 6" barrel lengths; target style checkered hardwood stocks, elevation adjustable rear sight, ramp front, vent rib barrel.

Manufactured in the Philippines by Squires Bingham; imported by Kassnar. Introduced 1977, still in production. Used value, $70 to $75.

**KLEINGUENTHER R-15:** revolver, double-action; .22 LR, .22 magnum, .32 S&W; 6-rd. cylinder; 6" barrel; 11" overall length; checkered thumbrest walnut stocks, adjustable rear sight, fixed front, full-length solid barrel rib, adjustable trigger, blued finish. Manufactured in Germany. Introduced 1976, dropped 1978. Used value, $95 to $105.

*Lahti Model 40*

**LAHTI Model 40:** automatic, 9mm Luger; 8-rd. magazine; 4¾" barrel; checkered plastic stocks, fixed sights, blued finish; manufactured in Sweden by Husqvarna. Manufactured 1940 to 1944. Used value, $180 to $200.

    **Model L-35** is basically the same as Model 40, but was manufactured on limited basis in Finland from 1935 until World War II. Has better finish, quality and, because of limited number, has greater value to collectors. Used value, $375 to $425.

*LeFrancais Policeman Model*

**LE FRANCAIS Policeman Model:** double-action automatic; .25 auto; 3½" hinged barrel, 6" overall length; 7-rd. magazine; checkered hard rubber stocks, fixed sights, blued finish. Manufactured in France. Introduced 1914, still in production, but not imported. Used value, $85 to $90.

**LE FRANCAIS Staff Officer Model:** double-action automatic; .25 auto; has same general specifications as Policeman Model, except for 2½" barrel, no cocking piece head. Introduced 1914, still in production, but not imported. Used value, $85 to $90.

**LE FRANCAIS Army Model:** double-action automatic; 9mm Browning Long; has same general specifications as Policeman Model, except for 8-rd. magazine, 5" barrel, 7¾" overall length, checkered European walnut stocks. Manufactured 1928 to 1938. Used value, $85 to $90.

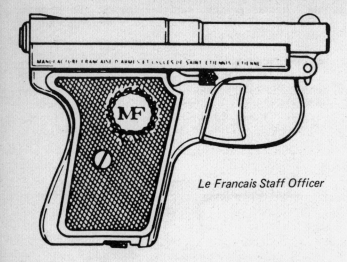

Le Francais Staff Officer

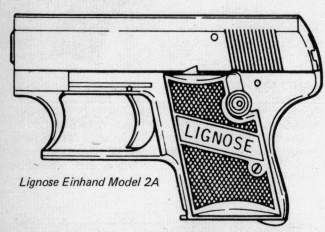

Lignose Einhand Model 2A

Lignose Model 3A

**Lignose Model 3A Einhand** has same specifications as Model 2A, except for extended grip, 9-rd. magazine. Used value, $125 to $140.

Luna Model 300

**LUNA Model 300:** single-shot, free pistol; .22 short; 11" barrel; set trigger; checkered, carved walnut stock, forearm, adjustable palm rest, target sights, blued finish. Manufactured in Germany, approximately 1929 to 1939. Used value, $725 to $750.

MKE Model TPK

**MKE Model TPK:** double-action auto pistol; .32 auto, 8-rd. magazine .380, 7-rd. magazine; 4" barrel, 6½" overall length; adjustable notch rear sight, fixed front; checkered plastic grips; exposed hammer; safety blocks firing pin, drops hammer; chamber loaded indicator pin. Copy of Walther PP. Imported from Turkey by Firearms Center, Inc. Used value, $85 to $95.

Pocket .32

**LIGNOSE Model 2:** pocket automatic; .25 auto; follows conventional Browning design; 2" barrel, 4½" overall length; 6-rd. magazine; checkered hard rubber stocks, blued finish. Manufactured in Germany. Used value, $100 to $120.

**Lignose Model 2A Einhand** has same general specifications as Model 2, except for trigger-type mechanism at front of trigger guard allows trigger finger to retract the slide. Used value, $125 to $140.

**ORTGIES Pocket Pistol:** automatic; blowback action; .32 auto; 3¼" barrel; 6½" overall length; 8-rd. magazine; constructed without screws, uses pins and spring-loaded catches; grip safety protrudes only when firing pin is cocked; fixed sights, uncheckered walnut grips; blued. Introduced about 1919; dropped, 1926. Used value, $65 to $70.

**Ortgies .380 Auto** has same specifications as the .32,

except for additional thumb-operated safety catch; 7-rd. magazine. Introduced in 1922; dropped, 1926. Used value, $80 to $90.

Ortgies .25 Auto is scaled-down version of .32 auto; 6-rd. magazine; 2¾" barrel, 5-3/16" overall length. Introduced in 1920; dropped, 1926. Used value, $65 to $70.

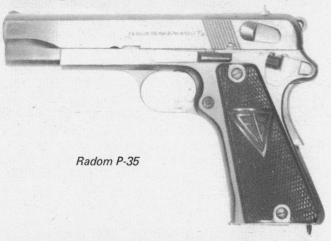

*Radom P-35*

**RADOM P-35:** automatic; 9mm Luger; 8-rd. magazine; 4¾" barrel, 7¾" overall length; checkered plastic stocks, fixed sights, blued finish. Design based on Colt Model 1911A1. Manufactured in Poland 1935 to 1945. Used value, $190 to $200.

**RECORD-MATCH Model 200:** single-shot free pistol; Martini action; .22 short; 11" barrel; micrometer rear sight, target-type front; carved, checkered European walnut stock, forearm, with adjustable hand base; blued finish; set trigger, spur trigger guard. Manufactured in Germany prior to WWII. Used value, $725 to $750.

*Record-Match Model 210*

**RECORD-MATCH Model 210:** single-shot free pistol; has same general design, specifications as Model 210, except for more intricate carving, checkering; button release on set trigger. Manufactured prior to WWII. Used value, $1000 to $1100.

Model 210A is identical to Model 210, except for dual action. Manufactured prior to WWII. Used value, $1000 to $1100.

**ROSSI Double-Action Model:** revolver; .22 LR, .32 S&W Long, .38 Special; 5-rd. cylinder in .38 Special, 6 rds. in other calibers; 3", 6" barrels; wood or plastic stocks; ramp front sight, adjustable rear; blued, nickel finish. Manufactured in Brazil; currently imported by Interarms. Introduced in 1965, still in production. Used value, $75 to $85.

**STEYR Model SP:** automatic; double-action pocket pistol; .32 auto; 7-rd. detachable magazine; revolver-type trigger; movable rear sight, fixed front; checkered black plastic grips; blued finish. Introduced in 1957; still in production, but not imported since 1968 Gun Control Act. Used value, $125 to $150.

**TARGA Model GT27:** automatic; .25 ACP; 6-rd. magazine; 2-7/16" barrel, 4-5/8" overall length; checkered nylon stocks, fixed sights, external hammer with half-cock feature, safety lever takedown; blued, chromed finish. Manufactured in U.S. Introduced 1977, still in production. Used values, blued, $20 to $25; chromed, $25 to $30.

**TARGA Model GT32:** automatic; .32 ACP; 7-rd. magazine; 4-7/8" barrel, 7-3/8" overall length; optional checkered nylon thumbrest or walnut stocks, windage-adjustable rear sight, blade front, external hammer, blued or chromed finish. Introduced 1977, still in production. Used values, Blued, $60 to $70; chromed, $65 to $70.

Model GT380 has the same general specifications as Model GT32, except is chambered for .380 ACP cartridge; introduced 1977, still in production. Made in Italy, imported by Excam, Inc. Used values, blued, $70 to $70; chromed, $70 to $75.

# HANDGUN NOTES

# HANDGUN NOTES

# RIFLES

# Some Used Rifles Are Higher Than Their Original New Price, But Cost Has Little To Do With Whether It Is A Good Buy!

*The prices on the much-ornamented custom-built classics has skyrocketed in recent years and the feeling is that any who'd take one afield would enter a Rolls-Royce in the Demolition Derby; values currently appear comparable.*

WITH EVER-INCREASING inflation, the prices of rifles in the used firearms market have continued to escalate, but as with all things, some have grown more rapidly than others.

Those rifles that come under the heading of collector items have been forced upward by the interest of collectors. So, if you want a hunting rifle in the same model and maker, you may have to pay more on a proportionate basis than for the same caliber in a somewhat similar model by another manufacturer. The so-called classics, most of them of foreign manufacture, seem to have gotten far beyond their value as practical tools for the range or for the hunting fields. One has only to look at the current-day prices placed on the Holland & Hollands, the Rigbys and other firearms of similar ilk to realize that anyone who would take such a gun afield has to be the type who would enter a Rolls-Royce in a Demolition Derby!

As has been stated in past editions of this tome, it is the general rule that a rifle has its highest value when it is new and in unfired condition, fresh off the shelves of your friendly neighborhood gun dealer. At least, that used to be the rule. But again, the cost of new rifles — and any other firearm, for that matter — in this age of continuing inflation has resulted in the fact that numerous using-type rifles now bring more on the used market than they did at the time of initial introduction.

Again, the collector — or if you prefer the term, speculator — is having a definite effect on the firearms market. Old Winchesters, Remingtons and rifles by other well known makers are becoming rare. They are being gobbled up by collectors who intend to sit on them, watching them gain value, placing them on the market, when the value has reached its ultimate peak.

Some of this increase in price, we tend to feel, is planned and the result of continuing publicity. Much of this notoriety, sadly, is from the

contributions of today's firearms writers. As mentioned in the introduction to this volume, the pre-1964 Winchester Model 70 has become a case in point. Those who have this vintage Model 70 insist it is a far superior rifle to anything of similar configuration to come out of New Haven since that magic year. Those who make the claim the loudest all too often are those who have collected a host of Model 70s of 1964 and prior manufacture and now have them for sale at fancy prices.

The truth is that current-day quality control probably is superior to what was offered in those days of two decades past. Winchester has changed its manufacturing techniques to an assembly line approach, with one man on one machine specializing in a particular facet of rifle manufacture and assembly.

In the pre-1964 era, there were good Model 70s, true; there also were some pretty poor specimens of the same model. At that time, one gunsmith worked on the entire gun. It was his personal project. If he was a good craftsman, the ultimate purchaser got a good product. If the gunsmith was not as good as some of his contemporaries, the ultimate purchaser got a rifle that was not as good as some of those with serial numbers only a few digits away.

But the Model 70 mystique goes on — those who have them telling the rest of the world that they're worth a lot of money. The interesting thing is that, so long as this self-interest hue and cry continues, those pre-'64 Model 70s are worth a lot of money. But if you'll check used gun prices overall, any Model 70 is worth a lot of loot compared to its introductory price!

One of the basics of firearms collecting lies in the fact that virtually all discontinued models have a certain increased value simply because they no longer are in production...and they are not likely to be any more.

Incidentally, keep in mind that the used values

included in this volume are listed as "NRA Very Good." That translates to mean that the firearm in question has remained in its original unaltered factory condition. Since most of the so-called "mint" examples on nearly any and every firearm are locked away in private collections, the "very good" range, it is felt, puts the gun in reach of the shooter and hunter.

We have heard many hunters and competitive shooters complain in recent years that many of the fine shooting guns are being hung on a wall as a collector item or socked away in a vault for the sake of speculation. Sadly, the ultimate function — to shoot and hunt — is being overshadowed to a great degree by the increasing value.

Let us take a look at Harrington & Richardson, as an example. This firm has been known for decades as a producer of practical working firearms. In most instances, there has been little fancy about the various models. They have been made at a specific investment to sell for a moderate price. That, over the years, has been the basis for the firm's success. In my youth, virtually every farm and ranch had one of these rifles or shotguns behind the kitchen door.

Today, it looks as though some Harrington & Richardson guns are on the verge of becoming valuable collector items. Part of the reason lies in the fact that some models no longer are made, of course. Another theory advanced by our technical editor, Wayne Novak, is based upon the fact that there is little else left for the neophyte to collect. Savage rifles — some models, at least — have gained increasing value in the past five years as collector

*Used prices on what have been considered the ordinary usin' guns have climbed due to cost of current models.*

items. Yet, there was a day not long ago, when a Savage was considered a behind-the-kitchen-door usin' rifle.

The prices quoted in the pages that follow are today's retail costs, if you try to purchase a used rifle from a reputable gun dealer. Chances are, you'll pay the amount listed — or more. But this dealer also had to get the rifle somewhere, and for less loot than he's asking, if he intends to remain in business.

The difference is that the gun dealer makes a living from his used guns, as well as those that are shiny and new, in boxes, on the shelf. Chances are, he has added one third to one-half his original investment to bring it up to its current asking price. You may be able to do better, if you do a bit of shopping. We've noted of late that a number of the small throw-away shopping guides distributed in local areas carry advertisements both from buyers and sellers. The buyers don't usually talk about what they're willing to pay, but the seller usually has a price he would like to get for his rifle. This, I've found in my own dealings, is his ideal figure, if that is the term, he would like to see come into his coffers. But usually, with a bit of haggling, one can get that rifle for less than is being asked. That, of course, is if a bona fide gun dealer isn't reading the same ads and gets to this individual ahead of you!

A few years ago, a friend of ours was burglarized and lost his collection of hunting rifles. As it turned out, at least in this particular instance, his rifles were being peddled out of the back of a van at a weekend flea market.

Several of the purchasers discovered to their dismay — through official channels — that they were handling stolen goods. Some of the rifles were returned to the rightful owner and the buyer was out his price given the bearded lad, who operated from the rear of his van. So far as I know, the seller never was caught. He was described as "twitchy and sniffled a lot." Those familiar with narcotics may see some correlation here.

But the point is that, if you are going to purchase a gun from a private owner, make certain you know who he is, get a proper bill of sale and it doesn't hurt to clarify that you intend to run the firearm through the local constabulary simply for your own peace of mind to determine that it isn't recent loot! If the individual simply wants to sell his rifle, he shouldn't mind. If the seller tends to take exception to such a plan, we'd suggest you ankle over to the nearest police department, tell of your experience in detail, then keep shopping.

When you purchase a new rifle of reputable make from a local dealer who's been in business for

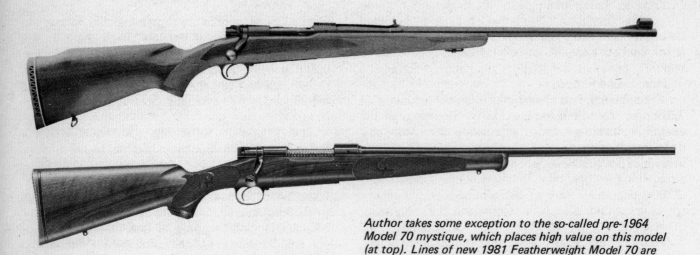

some while and, it is to be hoped, will remain at it, your chances of obtaining your money's worth of satisfaction are at their best. If something goes wrong with the gun, as can happen, you've recourse to the manufacturer's warranty and the dealer's integrity. In itself, that's one of the valuable considerations included in the purchase price.

When buying a rifle from a private party, or a used rifle from any source, it is well to protect your future interests by taking any steps you can arrange to assure your long-term satisfaction with the purchase. There are certain routine precautions and procedures that should be regarded as

*Given the opportunity, anyone considering the purchase of a used rifle should put a few rounds through its bore.*

absolutely mandatory. As but one example, *always* check the bore prior to firing the rifle for the first time. A member of this book's production staff has long made that a rigid practice and, on at least one occasion, the routine check — performed on a rifle that'd been sent to him by another gunwriter to be tested and passed along to yet a third such scribe — turned out to have a jacketed bullet lodged in the bore, about 1½ inches ahead of the front of the chamber! You can check a lot of barrels to avoid such pitfalls, and still feel the minor effort is amply justified.

There is a reasonably natural inclination on the part of the gun-buying public to assume that higher prices equal higher quality. That would be nice if it were true, but it doesn't always hold good. In a quarter-century or so of writing for the firearms press, some of our staffers — indeed, most of them — have encountered impressively-priced rifles whose accuracy performance was impressively wretched. There was one fine flossy fusil, ornately decorated and richly engraved, into whose chamber it was virtually impossible to coax a loaded cartridge of the prescribed caliber and, once that had been done, it proved impossible to fire the cartridge and, a bit later, even harder to extract the cartridge than it had been to chamber it in the first place. The rifle carried a suggested retail price of more than $800, and that was several years ago...

Many hair-raising adventures can accost the unwary rifle shopper. On another occasion, a staffer wandered into a neighborhood pawn shop, saw an old bolt-action military rifle that was identified as a 7x57mm Mauser on its price tag. Its state of preservation was marginal, but the price was quite interesting, so he bought it. Upon firing it for the first time, it was painfully evident that all was not going as optimistically planned.

The innocent purchaser, relying upon the data on the price tag, had chambered a factory round of 7x57mm Mauser ammo. Upon extracting and examining the case, there was clear indication of defunct rodents in the wood pile. Further investigation finally established that some owner along the way had had it rebarreled to accept the .270 Winchester cartridge, with no slightest clue as to its modified diet to be seen on the barrel or other areas.

Now, the .270 Winchester cartridge is considerably longer than that for the 7x57mm Mauser, with enough room up front so that the shorter cartridge could be chambered readily. The crux of the problem lies in the fact that the .270 Winchester uses a bullet of .277-inch diameter, while the 7x57mm Mauser carries a projectile that's .284-inch across its wider portions. When you fire a 7mm bullet through a .277-inch bore, that bullet gets sized down by .007-inch, in one goshawful helluva hurry! The .007-inch dimension may not seem like much on the end of a person's nose, but it is a substantial figure, indeed, in terms of bullet diameter.

Guns that have been converted should be stamped to indicate the new caliber or cartridge, but you can't really depend upon it. When you've bought an extensively used rifle, it is a good idea to check it out carefully and thoughtfully. If you don't feel qualified, take it to a competent and reliable gun dealer and have him perform the inspection. The modest fee he's apt to charge for such a service will seem trifling, insignificant and a great bargain, particularly when compared to the tab for a cornea transplant.

# ANSCHUTZ

Model 64S

**ANSCHUTZ Model 64:** bolt-action, single-shot match rifle; .22 LR only; 26" barrel; walnut-finished hardwood stock; cheekpiece; hand-checkered pistol grip, beavertail forearm; adjustable butt plate; no sights; scope blocks, receiver grooved for Anschutz sights; adjustable single-stage trigger; sliding side safety; forward sling swivel for competition sling. Marketed in U.S. as Savage/Anschutz Model 64. Introduced in 1967; still in production. Used value, $175 to $185.

**Model 64L** has the same specifications as Model 64, except for left-hand action. Still in production. Used value, $180 to $190.

**Model 64S** has the same specifications as standard Model 64, except for addition of Anschutz No. 6723 match sight set. Still in production. Used value, $215 to $225.

**Model 64SL** has the same specifications as Model 64S except for left-hand action. Still in production. Used value, $225 to $245.

Model 1407

**ANSCHUTZ Model 1407:** bolt-action, single-shot match rifle; action based upon that of Savage/Anschutz Model 54; .22 LR only; 26" barrel; length, weight conform to ISU competition requirements, also suitable for NRA matches; French walnut prone-style stock; Monte Carlo, cast-off cheekpiece; hand-stippled pistol grip, forearm; swivel rail, adjustable swivel; adjustable rubber butt plate; no sights; receiver grooved for Anschutz sights; scope blocks; single-stage trigger; wing safety. Marketed in U.S. by Savage. Introduced in 1967; still in production. Used value, right-hand model, $375 to $385; left-hand stock, $390 to $400.

Model 1411

**ANSCHUTZ Model 1411:** bolt-action, single-shot match rifle; built on same action as Savage/Anschutz Model 54; .22 LR only; has same basic specifications as Model 1407, except for longer overall length of 46"; 27½" barrel. Introduced in 1967; still in production. Used value, $395 to $415; left-hand stock, $420 to $430.

Model 1413

**ANSCHUTZ Model 1413:** bolt-action, single-shot match rifle; has the same specifications as Model 1411, except for International-type French walnut stock; adjustable aluminum hook butt plate; adjustable cheekpiece. Introduced in 1967; still in production. Used value, $625 to $650; left-hand stock, $670 to $690.

*Model 1408*

**ANSCHUTZ Model 1408:** bolt-action, sporter; .22 LR; 5 or 10-rd. magazine; 19¾" barrel; receiver grooved for scope mount; folding leaf rear sight, hooded ramp front; European walnut Mannlicher-type stock; hand-stippled pistol grip, forearm; cheekpiece. Introduced in 1976, still in production. Used value, $225 to $240.

**Model 1408-ED** is designated as Super Running Boar version; has same general specifications as Model 1408, except for single-shot only capability, 23" barrel, receiver drilled and tapped for scope mount, no metallic sights; has oversize bolt knob, European walnut thumbhole stock, adjustable comb and buttplate, single-stage adjustable trigger. Introduced in 1976, still in production. Used value, $375 to $400.

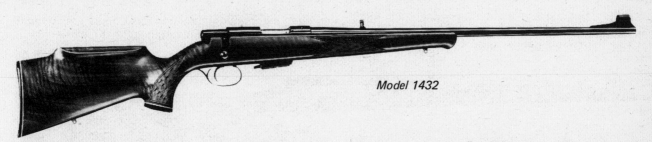

*Model 1432*

**ANSCHUTZ Model 1432:** bolt-action; .22 Hornet; 5-rd. box magazine; 24" barrel; receiver grooved for scope mount; folding leaf rear sight, hooded ramp front; European walnut Monte Carlo-type stock; hand-checkered pistol grip, forearm; cheekpiece. Introduced in 1976, still in production. Used value, $375 to $400.

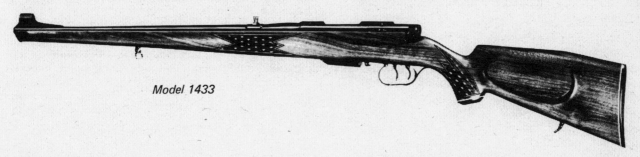

*Model 1433*

**ANSCHUTZ Model 1433:** bolt-action; sporter design; .22 Hornet; 5-rd. box magazine; receiver grooved for scope mount; 19¾" barrel; single-stage or double-set trigger; folding leaf rear sight, hooded ramp front; European walnut Mannlicher-type stock; hand-checkered pistol grip, forearm; cheekpiece. Introduced 1976, still in production. Used value, $375 to $400.

**ANSCHUTZ Model 1533:** bolt-action; .222 Remington; has same general specifications as Model 1433, except for chambering, 3-rd. box magazine. Introduced 1976, still in production. Used value, $375 to $400.

*Model 1518*

**ANSCHUTZ Model 1518:** bolt-action; has same general specifications as Model 1418, except for 4-rd. box magazine; chambered for .22 WRFM cartridge. Introduced 1976, still in production. Used value, $240 to $250.

# BRNO

*Model 21H*

**BRNO Model 21H:** bolt-action, Mauser-type; 6.5x55, 7x57, 8x57mm; 5-rd. box magazine; 20½" barrel; 2-leaf rear sight, hooded ramp front; half-length sporting stock; hand-checkered pistol grip, forearm; sling swivels; double-set trigger. Manufactured prior to World War II. Used value, $500 to $525.

**BRNO Hornet:** bolt-action; .22 Hornet; 5-rd. box magazine; 23" barrel; 3-leaf rear sight, hooded ramp front; double-set trigger; sling swivels; hand-checkered pistol grip, forearm. Manufactured in Czechoslovakia prior to World War II. Used value, $500 to $525.

*Model 22F*

**BRNO Model 22F:** bolt-action, Mauser-type; has same general specifications as Model 21, except for Mannlicher-type stock. Produced prior to World War II. Used value, $500 to $525.

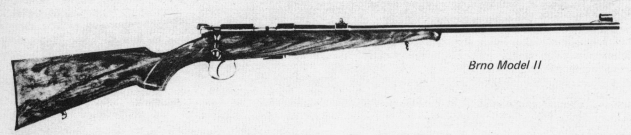

*Brno Model II*

**BRNO Model I:** bolt-action; .22 LR; 5-rd. magazine; 3-leaf rear sight, hooded ramp front; sling swivels; sporting stock, hand-checkered pistol grip. Manufactured prior to World War II. Used value, $250 to $275.

**Model II** has same specifications as Model I, except for better grade of European walnut stock. Manufactured prior to World War II. Used value, $275 to $300.

# BROWNING

*Grade I Autoloader*

**BROWNING Grade I Autoloader .22:** same action as discontinued Remington Model 241A; takedown; .22 LR, .22 short, not interchangeable; 19¼" barrel for LR, 22¼" for short cartridge; butt stock tube magazine, holding 11 LR, 16 short cartridges; select European walnut stock; hand-checkered pistol grip, semi-beavertail forearm; open rear sight, bead front; engraved receiver, grooved for tip-off scope mount; cross-bolt safety. Introduced in 1958. Manufactured in Belgium until 1972; production transferred to

Miroku in Japan; still in production. Used value, (Belgium) $175 to $200; (Japanese) $150 to $165.

**Grade II** has identical specifications to Grade I, except for gold-plated trigger; .22 LR only; 11-rd. capacity; satin chrome-plated receiver, small game animal scenes engraved on receiver. Still in production. Used value, (Belgium) $325 to $350; (Japanese) $275 to $300.

**Grade III** has same specifications as Grade I, except for gold-plated trigger, extra-fancy walnut stock, forearm; skip checkering on pistol grip, forearm; satin chrome-plated receiver; hand-carved, engraved scrolls, leaves, dog/game bird scenes; .22 LR only. Still in production. Used value, (Belgium) $575 to $625; (Japanese) $450 to $475.

*Safari Grade Heavy Barrel*

*Olympian Grade*

**BROWNING High-Power Safari Grade:** standard Mauser-type bolt-action; .270 Win., .30/06, 7mm Rem. magnum, .300 Win. magnum; .308 Norma magnum, .338 Win. magnum, .375 Holland & Holland magnum, .458 Win. magnum; 24" barrel in magnum calibers, 22" in others; 4-rd. magazine capacity for magnum cartridges, 6 rds. for others; European walnut stock; hand-checkered pistol grip, forearm; Monte Carlo cheekpiece; recoil pad on magnum models; folding leaf rear sight, hooded ramp front; quick-detachable sling swivels. Introduced in 1960; dropped, 1974. Used value, $575 to $600.

**Safari grade short action** has the same specifications as standard grade Safari except for short action; .222 Rem., .222 Rem. magnum; 22" lightweight, 24" heavy barrel. Dropped, 1974. Used value, $525 to $550.

**Safari grade medium action** model has same specifications as standard model except for action length; .22-250, .243 Win., .284 Win., .308 Win.; 22" lightweight barrel standard, but available in .22-250, .243 with heavy barrel. Dropped, 1974. Used value, $550 to $575.

**Medallion grade** has the same specifications as standard Safari grade with exception of scroll-engraved receiver, barrel; engraved ram's head on floor plate; select European walnut stock has rosewood grip cap, forearm tip. Dropped 1974. Used value, $875 to $950.

**Olympian grade** High-Power has the same specifications as Safari, except for engraving on barrel; chrome-plated floor plate, trigger guard, receiver, all engraved with game scenes; figured European walnut stock; rosewood forearm tip, grip cap; grip cap is inlaid with 18-karat gold medallion. Discontinued, 1974. Used value, $1850 to $2250.

*Model T-2*

**BROWNING Model T-1 T-Bolt:** straight-pull bolt-action; .22 LR only; 24" barrel; 5-rd. clip magazine; uncheckered walnut pistol-grip stock; peep rear sight, ramped blade front; in either left or right-hand model. Introduced in 1965;

dropped, 1973. Used value, $175 to $200.

**Model T-2** has same specifications as Model T-1, except for figured, hand-checkered walnut stock. Dropped, 1973. Used value, $235 to $250.

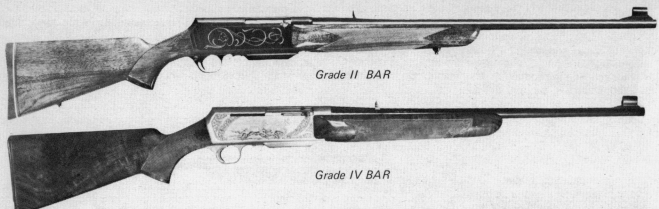

Grade II BAR

Grade IV BAR

**BROWNING BAR:** not to be confused with military Browning selective fire rifle; semiautomatic; .243 Win., .308 Win., .270 Win., .30/06, 7mm Rem. magnum, .300 Win. magnum, .338 Win. magnum; 22" barrel; 4-rd. detachable box magazine for standard calibers, 3-rd. for magnums; adjustable folding leaf rear sight, gold bead hooded ramp front; receiver tapped for scope mounts; checkered walnut

pistol-grip stock, forearm. Grades I, II introduced in 1967; Grades II, III, V still in production. Grades vary according to amount of checkering, carving, engraving, inlay work. Used values, standard calibers Grade I, $400 to $425; II, $465 to $475; III, $625 to $650; IV, $450 to $475; V, $1100 to $1200; magnum calibers, Grade I, $450 to $475; II, $425 to $550; III, $725 to $750; IV, $950 to $1050; V, $1250 to $1350.

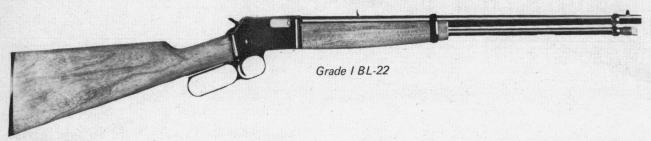

Grade I BL-22

**BROWNING BL-22 Grade I:** lever-action; .22 LR, long, short; 20" barrel; tube magazine holds 22 rds. in .22 short, 17 rds. in long, 15 LR; folding leaf rear sight, bead post front; two-piece uncheckered walnut stock, forearm; barrel band; half-cock safety; receiver grooved for tip-off mounts.

Grade II has engraved receiver, checkered grip, forearm. Produced by Miroku Firearms, Tokyo, Japan, to Browning specifications. Introduced in 1970; still in production. Used values, $145 to $155 for Grade I; $175 to $185 for Grade II.

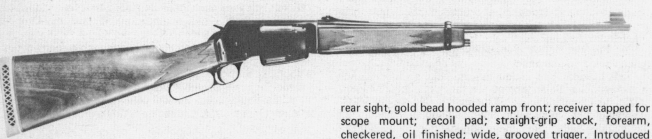

**BROWNING BLR:** lever-action; .308 Win., .243 Win.; 20" barrel; 4-rd. detachable magazine; square-notch adjustable

rear sight, gold bead hooded ramp front; receiver tapped for scope mount; recoil pad; straight-grip stock, forearm, checkered, oil finished; wide, grooved trigger. Introduced 1971; made to Browning specifications by Miroku Firearms, Tokyo, Japan, since May '74; still in production. Used value, $250 to $275.

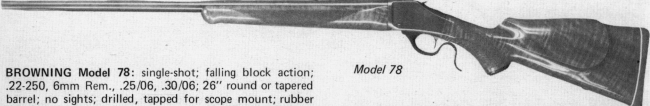

**BROWNING Model 78:** single-shot; falling block action; .22-250, 6mm Rem., .25/06, .30/06; 26" round or tapered barrel; no sights; drilled, tapped for scope mount; rubber recoil pad; select walnut stock, hand checkered, hand rubbed; exposed hammer; automatic ejector, half-cock safety. Produced to Browning specifications by Miroku

Model 78

Firearms, Tokyo Japan. Manufactured 1973 to 1980. Used value, $250 to $265.

BAR-22

**BROWNING BAR-22:** semi-automatic; .22 LR; 15-rd. tubular magazine; 20¼" barrel; receiver grooved for scope mount; folding leaf rear sight, gold bead ramp front; French walnut stock, hand-checkered pistol grip, forearm. Introduced 1977, still in production. Manufactured in Japan. Used value, $115 to $125.

BPR-22 No. 12

**BROWNING BPR-22:** pump action; .22 LR; .22 WRFM hammerless; other specifications generally the same as those of BAR-22, except for magazine capacity of 11 rds. Introduced in 1977, still in production. Used value, $115 to $125.

# BSA

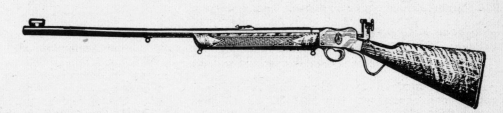

**BSA No. 12:** single-shot Martini-action target rifle; .22 LR only; 29" barrel; straight-grip walnut stock; hand-checkered forearm; Parker-Hale No. 7 rear sight, hooded front. Introduced in 1912; dropped, 1929. Used value, $200 to $225.

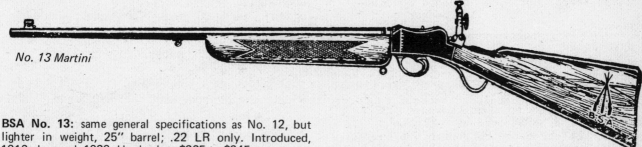

No. 13 Martini

**BSA No. 13:** same general specifications as No. 12, but lighter in weight, 25" barrel; .22 LR only. Introduced, 1913; dropped, 1929. Used value, $235 to $245.

**No. 13 Sporter** has same specs as standard No. 13, except for Parker-Hale Sportarget rear sight, bead front. Available also in .22 Hornet. Dropped, 1932. Used values, .22 LR, $235 to $240; .22 Hornet, $250 to $265.

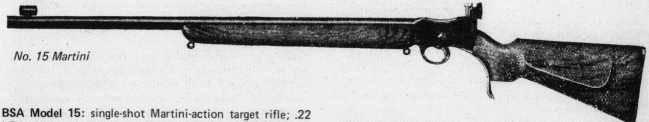

No. 15 Martini

**BSA Model 15:** single-shot Martini-action target rifle; .22 LR only; same general specifications as No. 12; 29" barrel; uncheckered walnut target stock; cheekpiece, pistol grip, long semi-beavertail forearm; BSA No. 30 rear sight, No. 20 front. Introduced in 1915; dropped, 1932. Used value, $235 to $240.

**BSA Centurion:** has the same basic specifications as Model 15, but was outfitted with Centurion match barrel; maker guaranteed 1.5" groups at 100 yards. Dropped, 1932. Used value, $260 to $275.

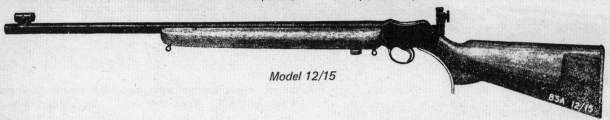

*Model 12/15*

**BSA-Parker Model 12/15:** single-shot Martini-action target rifle; allegedly combined best features of No. 12 and Model 15; .22 LR only; 29" barrel; walnut target stock with high comb, cheekpiece, beavertail forearm; forward sling swivel; Parker-Hale PH-7A rear sight, PH-22 front. Introduced in 1938; dropped at beginning of WWII. Used value, $215 to $225.

value, $187 to $200.

**BSA Model 12/15:** has the same specifications as BSA-Parker Model 12/15, but this was designation given rifle when reintroduced following WWII. Dropped, 1950. Used value, $187 to $200.

**BSA Heavy Model 12/15** has same specifications as standard Model 12/15, except for extra-heavy competition barrel. Used value, $235 to $255.

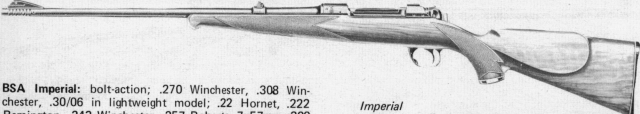

*Martini-International Heavy Pattern*

**BSA Martini-International Heavy Pattern:** single-shot match rifle, Martini-type action; .22 LR only; 29" heavy barrel; uncheckered two-piece target stock; full cheekpiece, pistol grip, broad beavertail forearm; hand stop; swivels; right or left-hand styles. Introduced in 1950; dropped, 1953. Used value, $255 to $265.

**Martini-International Light Pattern** has same general specifications, except for lightweight 26" barrel. Used value, $255 to $265.

**Martini ISU Match** model has same general specs except for 28" barrel; flat cheekpiece; available with standard or heavy barrel; adjustable trigger; modified PH-1 Parker tunnel front sight, PH-25 Aperture rear. Imported by Freelands.

Used values, standard barrel, $500 to $525; heavy barrel, $510 to $535.

**Martini-International Mark II** has same specifications as 1950 model, with choice of light, heavy barrel. Improvements to original include redesigned stock, forearm, trigger mechanism, ejection system. Introduced in 1953; dropped, 1959. Used value, $265 to $275.

**Martini-International Mark III** has same specifications as Mark II heavy barrel model, plus redesigned stock, forearm, free-floating barrel, longer frame with alloy strut to attach forearm. Introduced in 1959; dropped, 1967. Used value, $285 to $300.

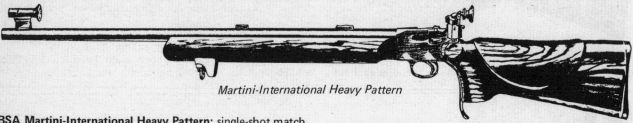

*Imperial*

**BSA Imperial:** bolt-action; .270 Winchester, .308 Winchester, .30/06 in lightweight model; .22 Hornet, .222 Remington, .243 Winchester, .257 Roberts, 7x57mm, 300 Savage and .30/06 in standard weight; 22" barrel; recoil reducer cut into muzzle; fully adjustable trigger; European walnut cheekpiece stock; hand-checkered pistol grip, schnabel forearm; black butt plate, pistol grip cap with white spacers; drilled, tapped for scope mounts. Introduced in 1959; dropped, 1964. Used value, $200 to $225.

*Majestic Deluxe*

**BSA Majestic Deluxe:** Mauser-type bolt-action; .22 Hornet, .222 Rem., .243 Win., .308 Win., .30/06, 7x57mm; 22" barrel; 4-rd. magazine; European walnut stock; checkered pistol grip, forearm; cheekpiece, schnabel forearm; folding leaf rear sight, hooded ramp front; sling swivels. Introduced in 1959; dropped, 1965. Used value, $265 to $275.

**Majestic Deluxe Featherweight** has the same general specifications as standard Majestic Deluxe, except for recoil pad, lightweight barrel, recoil reducer; .243 Win., .270 Win., .308 Win., .30/06, .458 Win. magnum. Used value, .458 Win. magnum, $325 to $350; other calibers, $250 to $275.

*Monarch Deluxe*

**BSA Monarch Deluxe:** Mauser-type bolt-action; .222 Rem., .243 Win., .270 Win., 7mm Rem. magnum, .308 Win., .30/06; 22″ barrel. Has same general specifications as Majestic Deluxe standard model, except for redesigned stock, with hardwood forearm tip, grip cap. Introduced in 1965; dropped, 1977. Used value, $200 to $225.

**Monarch Deluxe Varmint** model has same specifications as standard Monarch Deluxe except for 24″ heavy barrel; .222 Rem., .243 Win. Used value, $200 to $225.

# COLT

**COLT Lightning:** slide-action; .32-20, .38-40, .44-40; 26″ round or octagonal barrel; 15-rd. tubular magazine; open rear sight, blade front; American walnut stock, forearm. Manufactured 1884 to 1902. Collector value. $250 to $500.

**Lightning Carbine** has same specifications except for 20″ barrel, adjustable military-type sights, 12-rd. magazine. Collector value. Manufactured 1884 to 1902. Used value, $375 to $950.

**Lightning Baby Carbine** has same specifications as Lightning Carbine, except lighter in weight; 22″ rounm barrel; weighs 8 pounds. Collector value. Manufactured 1885 to 1900. Used value, $1100 to $2500.

**Lightning Small Frame** model .22 Short, .22 Long; 24″ round or octagonal barrel; tubular magazine holds 16 Shorts, 15 Longs; open rear sight, bead front; American walnut stock, forearm. Collector value. Manufactured 1887 to 1904. Used value, $200 to $450.

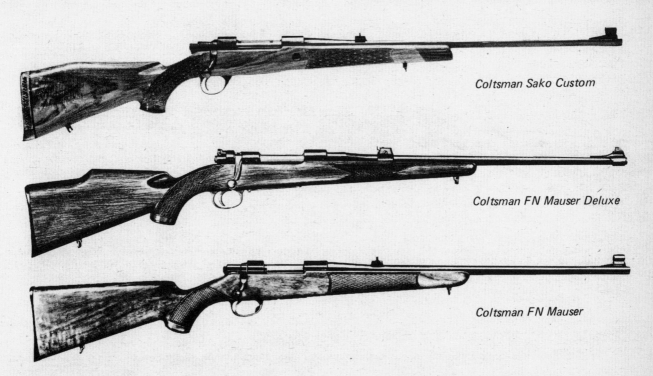

*Coltsman Sako Custom*

*Coltsman FN Mauser Deluxe*

*Coltsman FN Mauser*

**COLT Standard Coltsman:** bolt-action; FN Mauser action; .30/06, 300 Holland & Holland magnum; 22″ barrel; hand-checkered pistol-grip walnut stock; 5-rd. box magazine; no rear sight, ramp front; quick-detachable sling swivels. Introduced in 1957; replaced in 1962 by Sako action model; dropped, 1965. Used value, $275 to $285.

**Coltsman Deluxe** model has the same specifications as standard model, except for better checkering, wood. Adjustable rear sight, ramp front. Introduced in 1957; dropped in 1962. Used value, $300 to $325.

**Coltsman Custom** model has same specifications as standard model, except for fancy walnut stock, Monte Carlo comb, cheekpiece, engraved floor plate. Introduced in 1957; replaced in 1962 by Sako action; dropped, 1965. Used value, $365 to $375.

**Coltsman Sako short-action Standard** model is bolt-action; made from 1957 to 1961 in .243 Winchester, .308 Winchester; from 1962 to 1966, in .222, .222 magnum only; other specifications are virtually the same as those of the FN Mauser model. Used value, $275 to $285.

**Coltsman Sako short-action Deluxe** model has same general specifications as FN Mauser version except made in .243, .308 Winchester calibers only from 1957 to 1961. Dropped in this grade in 1961. Action had integral scope blocks. Used value, $295 to $315.

**Coltsman Sako short-action Custom** model has same general specifications as FN Mauser version except for action; made in .243, .308 Winchester calibers only from 1957 to 1961; in .222, .222 magnum from 1962 to 1966; dropped, 1966. Used value, $355 to $375.

**Coltsman medium-action Sako Standard** model has hinged floor plate, hand-checkered walnut stock, standard sling swivels; bead front sight on hooded ramp, folding leaf rear; sliding safety; in .243 Winchester, .308 Winchester. Introduced in 1962; dropped, 1966. Used value, $255 to $265.

**Coltsman Custom medium-action Sako** has same specifications, calibers as Standard, except for fancy Monte Carlo stock, recoil pad, dark wood forearm tip, pistol-grip cap, skip-line checkering. Introduced in 1962; dropped, 1966. Used value, $325 to $350.

**Coltsman Standard long-action Sako** model is chambered for .264 Winchester, .270 Winchester, .30/06, .300 Holland & Holland, .375 Holland & Holland. With exception of action, calibers, other specifications are same as those of Standard Sako medium-action version. Introduced in 1962; dropped, 1966. Used value, $265 to $275.

**Coltsman Custom long-action Sako** is the same as Standard version, except for fancy Monte Carlo stock, recoil pad, dark wood forearm tip and pistol-grip cap, skip-line checkering. Introduced in 1962; dropped, 1966. Used value, $325 to $350.

*Colteer 1-22*

**COLT Colteer 1-22:** single-shot bolt-action; .22 LR, long short; 20", 22" barrels; open rear sight, ramp front; un-checkered walnut pistol-grip Monte Carlo stock. Introduced in 1957; dropped 1967. Used value, $65 to $75.

*Colteer*

**COLT Colteer:** autoloader; .22 LR only; 19-3/8" barrel; 15-rd. tube magazine; open rear sight, hooded ramp front; uncheckered straight Western-style carbine stock; barrel band; alloy receiver. Introduced in 1964; dropped, 1975. Used value, $85 to $95.

*Stagecoach*

**COLT Stagecoach:** autoloader; .22 LR only; has the same general specifications as Colteer model, except for saddle ring, 16½" barrel, 13 rd. magazine, engraved receiver. Introduced in 1965; dropped, 1975. Used value, $90 to $95.

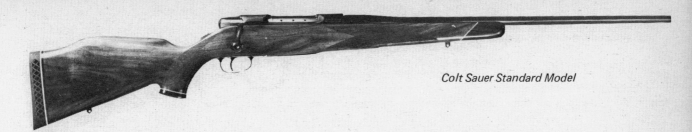

*Colt Sauer Standard Model*

**COLT Sauer Sporter:** bolt-action; standard model uses long action made in Germany by Sauer and Sohn; .25/06, .270 Win., .30/06, 7mm Rem. magnum, .300 Weatherby magnum, .300 Win. magnum; 24'' barrel; 3-rd. detachable box magazine; no sights; hand-checkered American walnut pistol-grip stock; rosewood pistol grip, forearm caps; recoil pad; quick-detachable sling swivels. Introduced in 1971; still in production. Used value, $425 to $450.

**Colt-Sauer short action** has the same general specifications as standard long action model, except chambering for .22-250, .243 Win., .308 Win. Introduced in 1974; still in production. Used value, $475 to $500.

**Colt-Sauer Grand African** has the same general specifications, except for .458 Win. chambering only; bubinga wood stock; finer checkering, adjustable sliding rear sight, ivory bead front. Still in production. Used value, $625 to $650.

# ERMA

*Erma Model EM1 22*

*Erma Model EGM1*

**ERMA Model EM1:** semi-automatic; .22 LR; 10 or 15-rd. magazine; 18'' barrel; patterned after U.S. Cal. .30 MI carbine; M1-type sights; receiver grooved for scope mounts; sling swivel in barrel band, oiler slot in stock; European walnut M1-Carbine-type stock. Introduced 1966, still in production. Used vlaue, $100 to $110.

**Model EGM1** has same specifications as Model EM1, but no oiler slot in stock; has ramp front sight, 5-rd. magazine. Introduced 1970, still in production. Used value, $100 to $110.

*Erma Model EG72*

**ERMA EG72:** pump-action; .22 LR; 15-rd. magazine; 18½'' barrel; visible hammer; open rear sight, hooded ramp front; grooved slide handle, straight hardwood stock; receiver grooved for scope mounts. Manufactured 1970 to 1976. Used value, $75 to $80.

*Model EG712*

**ERMA Model EG712:** lever-action; .22 Short, Long, LR.; tubular magazine holds 21 Shorts, 17 Longs, 15 LR; 18½" barrel; near replica of Model 94 Winchester; open rear sight, hooded ramp front; Carbine-style stock, forearm of European hardwood, barrel band; receiver grooved for scope mount. Introduced in 1976, still in production. Used value, $100 to $110.

**ERMA Model EG73:** lever-action; has same general specifications as Model EG712, except for .22 WMRF chambering, 19.3" barrel; magazine holds 12 rds. Introduced in 1973, still in production.

---

# HAMMERLI

*Model Olympia*

**HAMMERLI Model Olympia:** bolt-action, single-shot designed for 300-meter event; chambered in Europe for 7.5mm, marketed in U.S. in .30/06, .300 H&H magnum; other calibers on special order; 29½" heavy barrel, double-pull or double set trigger; micrometer peep rear sight, hooded front; free-type rifle stock with full pistol grip, thumbhole; cheekpiece, palm rest, beavertail forearm; swivels, Swiss-type butt plate. Introduced in 1949; dropped, 1959. Used value, $625 to $650.

*Model 45*

**HAMMERLI Model 45:** bolt-action, single-shot match type; .22 LR; 27½" barrel; free-rifle stock with full pistol grip, thumbhole, cheekpiece; palm rest, beavertail forearm; Swiss-type butt plate, sling swivels; micrometer peep rear sight, blade front; pistol-grip hardwood stock; knob forearm Used value, $500 to $525.

**HAMMERLI Model 54:** bolt-action, single-shot; match rifle; .22 LR, 21½" barrel; micrometer peep rear sight, globe front; European walnut free-rifle stock; cheekpiece, adjustable hook buttplate, palm rest, thumbhole, swivel. Manufactured 1954 to 1957. Used value, $400 to $425.

*Hammerli Model 503*

**HAMMERLI Model 503:** bolt-action, single-shot; free rifle; .22 LR; 27½" barrel; micrometer rear sight, globe front; European walnut free-rifle stock; cheekpiece, adjustable hook buttplate, palm rest, thumbhole, swivel. Manufactured 1957 to 1962. Used value, $400 to $425.

*Hammerli-Tanner 300M*

**HAMMERLI**-Tanner 300 Meter: bolt-action, single-shot; free rifle design; 7.5mm Swiss; 29½'' barrel; micrometer peep rear sight, globe front; uncheckered European walnut free-rifle stock; cheekpiece, adjustable hook buttplate, thumbhole, palm rest, swivel. Manufactured in Switzerland. Introduced 1962, still in production. Used value, $625 to $640.

*Hammerli Model 506*

**HAMMERLI** Model 506: bolt-action, single-shot; match rifle; .22 LR; 26¾'' barrel; micrometer peep rear sight, globe front; European walnut free-rifle stock; cheekpiece, adjustable hook buttplate, palm rest, thumbhole, swivel. Manufactured 1963 to 1966. Used value, $425 to $450.

# HARRINGTON & RICHARDSON

*Model 60*

**HARRINGTON & RICHARDSON** Reising Model 60: semi-automatic; .45 Auto; 12, 20-rd. detachable box magazines; 18¼'' barrel; open rear sight, blade front; uncheckered hardwood pistol grip stock. Manufactured 1944 to 1946. Some collector value. Used value, $260 to $275.

*Model 65*

**HARRINGTON & RICHARDSON** Model 65: semi-automatic; .22 LR; 10-rd. detachable box magazine; 23'' barrel; rear peep sight, blade front; uncheckered hardwood pistol grip stock; used as training rifle by the Marine Corps in WWII, has same general dimensions as M-1 Garand. Manufactured 1944 to 1946. Used value, $150 to $165.

*Model 165*

**HARRINGTON & RICHARDSON Model 165:** called the Leatherneck Model, it was a variation of Model 65 military autoloader used to train Marines in basic marksmanship during WWII. Blow-back autoloader; .22 LR only; 23" barrel; 10-rd. detachable box magazine; uncheckered hardwood pistol-grip stock; Redfield No. 70 rear peep sight, blade front on ramp; sling swivels, web sling. Introduced in 1945; dropped, 1961. Used value, $125 to $145.

*Model 265*

**HARRINGTON & RICHARDSON Model 265:** called the Reg'lar Model in advertising; bolt-action repeater; .22 LR only; 22" barrel; 10-shot detachable box magazine; uncheckered hardwood pistol-grip stock; Lyman No. 55 rear peep sight, blade front on ramp. Introduced in 1946; dropped, 1949. Used value, $90 to $100.

**HARRINGTON & RICHARDSON Model 365:** called the Ace in advertising; bolt-action single-shot; .22 LR only; 22" barrel; uncheckered hardwood pistol-grip stock; Lyman No. 55 rear peep sight, blade front on ramp. Introduced in 1946; dropped, 1947. Used value, $50 to $55.

*Model 465*

**HARRINGTON & RICHARDSON Model 465:** advertised as Targeteer Special; bolt-action repeater; .22 LR only; 25" barrel; 10-shot detachable box magazine; uncheckered walnut pistol-grip stock; Lyman No. 57 rear peep sight, blade front on ramp; sling swivels, web sling. Introduced in 1946; dropped, 1947. Used value, $95 to $100.

**Targeteer Jr.** has the same basic specifications as Model 465, except for 20" barrel; shorter youth stock; 5-rd. detachable box magazine; Redfield No. 70 rear peep sight, Lyman No. 17A front. Introduced in 1948; dropped, 1951. Used value, $95 to $100.

**HARRINGTON & RICHARDSON Model 450:** bolt-action repeater; .22 LR only; 26" barrel; 5-shot detachable box magazine; uncheckered walnut target stock with full pistol grip, thick forearm; scope bases; no sights; sling swivels, sling. Introduced in 1948; dropped, 1961. Used value, $115 to $125.

**HARRINGTON & RICHARDSON Model 451:** advertised as Medalist Model; has the same specifications as Model 450, except for addition of Lyman 524F extension rear sight, Lyman No. 77 front sight. Introduced in 1948; dropped, 1961. Used value, $135 to $145.

**HARRINGTON & RICHARDSON Model 250:** advertised as the Sportster Model; bolt-action repeater; .22 LR only; 23" barrel; 5-rd. detachable box magazine; uncheckered hardwood pistol-grip stock; open rear sight, blade front on ramp. Introduced in 1948; dropped, 1961. Used value, $75 to $85.

**HARRINGTON & RICHARDSON Model 251:** has the same specifications as Model 250, except for addition of Lyman No. 55H rear sight. Introduced in 1948; dropped, 1961. Used value, $85 to $95.

**HARRINGTON & RICHARDSON Model 765:** bolt-action, single-shot; .22 LR, long, short; 24″ barrel; uncheckered hardwood pistol-grip stock; open rear sight, hooded bead front. Introduced in 1948; dropped, 1954. Used value, $45 to $55.

*Model 865*

**HARRINGTON & RICHARDSON Model 865:** bolt-action repeater; .22 LR, long, short; 24″ barrel; 5-rd. detachable box magazine; uncheckered hardwood pistol-grip stock; open rear sight, bead front. Introduced in 1949; still in production. Used value, $45 to $55.

**HARRINGTON & RICHARDSON Model 150:** autoloader; .22 LR only; 22″ barrel; 5-rd. detachable box magazine; uncheckered pistol-grip stock; open rear sight, blade front on ramp. Introduced in 1949; dropped, 1953. Used value, $65 to $70.

**HARRINGTON & RICHARDSON Model 151:** has the same specifications as Model 150, except for substitution of Redfield No. 70 peep rear sight. Introduced in 1949; dropped, 1953. Used value, $75 to $80.

**HARRINGTON & RICHARDSON Model 852:** bolt-action repeater; .22 LR, long, short; 24″ barrel; tube magazine with capacity of 15 LR, 17 long, 21 short cartridges; uncheckered pistol-grip hardwood stock; open rear sight, bead front. Introduced in 1952; dropped, 1953. Used value, $60 to $65.

**HARRINGTON & RICHARDSON Model 422:** slide-action repeater; .22 LR, long, short; 24″ barrel; tube magazine, capacity of 15 LR, 17 long, 21 short cartridges; uncheckered walnut pistol-grip stock, grooved slide handle; open rear sight, ramp front. Introduced in 1952; dropped, 1958. Used value, $75 to $85.

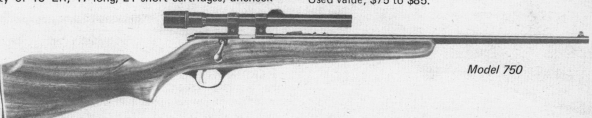

*Model 750*

**HARRINGTON & RICHARDSON Model 750:** bolt-action single-shot; .22 LR, long, short; 24″ barrel; uncheckered hardwood stock; open rear sight, bead front, double extractors; feed ramp. Introduced in 1954; still in production. Used value, $45 to $50.

**HARRINGTON & RICHARDSON Model 800:** autoloader; .22 LR only; 22″ barrel; 5, 10-rd. clip-type magazine; unchecked checkered walnut pistol-grip stock; open rear sight, bead ramp front. Introduced in 1958; dropped, 1960. Used value, $70 to $75.

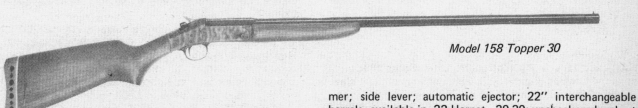

*Model 158 Topper 30*

**HARRINGTON & RICHARDSON Model 158 Topper 30:** single-shot combo rifle; shotgun-type action; visible hammer; side lever; automatic ejector; 22″ interchangeable barrels, available in .22 Hornet, .30-30; uncheckered walnut pistol-grip stock, forearm; recoil pad; Lyman folding adjustable open rear sight, ramp front. Introduced in 1963; still in production. Used value, $75 to $85.

Model 158 Topper Jet has the same general specifications as Model 158 Topper 30, except standard caliber is .22 Rem. Jet, interchangeable with 20-ga., .410-ga., .30-30

barrels. Introduced in 1963; dropped, 1967. Used values, standard .22 Rem. Jet, $50 to $65; additional .30-30 barrel, $35 to $40; 20-ga. barrel, $35 to $40; .410 barrel, $35 to $40.

*Model 755*

**HARRINGTON & RICHARDSON Model 755:** advertised as the Sahara Model; single-shot .22 LR, long, short; 22" barrel; blow-back action; automatic ejection; hardwood

Mannlicher-type stock; open rear sight, military front. Introduced in 1963; dropped, 1971. Some collector interest. Used value, $75 to $85.

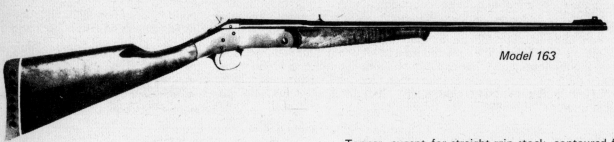

*Model 163*

**HARRINGTON & RICHARDSON Model 163:** single-shot, break-open action; has the same specifications as Model 158

**HARRINGTON & RICHARDSON Model 164:** single-shot; has same specifications as Model 158, except for straight-

Topper, except for straight-grip stock, contoured forearm, gold-plated hammer, trigger. Manufactured 1964 to 1967. Advertised as the Mustang. Used value, $45 to $50.

grip uncheckered walnut stock, contoured forearm; gold-plated hammer, trigger. Introduced in 1964; dropped, 1967. Used value, $90 to $95.

*Model 760*

**HARRINGTON & RICHARDSON Model 760:** single-shot; has the same specifications as Model 755, except for substitution of conventional hardwood sporter stock. Introduced in 1965; dropped, 1970. Used value, $70 to $75.

*Model 300*

**HARRINGTON & RICHARDSON Ultra Model 300:** bolt-action, FN Mauser action; .22-250, .243 Win., .270 Win., .30/06, .308 Win., .300 Win. magnum, 7mm Rem. magnum; 22" barrel; 3-rd. magazine for magnums, 5-rd. for others; hand-checkered American walnut stock; cheekpiece, full pistol grip; pistol-grip cap, forearm tip of contrasting exotic wood; open rear sight, ramp front; rubber butt plate, sling

swivels. Manufactured 1965 to 1978. Used value, $250 to $265.

**Model 30** has same general specs as Model 300; .243 Winchester, .270 Winchester, .30/06, .308 Winchester, 7mm Remington magnum, .300 Winchester magnum; less checkering on stock, no sling swivels, forend tip, or pistol grip cap. Advertised as Hunters Model. Manufactured 1967 to 1972. Used value, $190 to $200.

**Model 333** has same general specs as Model 300; 7mm Remington magnum, .30/06; 22" barrel; uncheckered hardwood stock, no sights. Manufactured 1974 only. Used value, $155 to $165.

*Model 301*

**HARRINGTON & RICHARDSON Ultra Model 301:** bolt-action carbine; has the same general specifications as Ultra Model 300, except for 18" barrel, Mannlicher-style stock; metal forearm tip. Not available in .22-250. Introduced in 1978; still in production. Used value, $275 to $290.

*Ultra Model 317*

**HARRINGTON & RICHARDSON Ultra Model 317:** advertised as the Ultra Wildcat; .17 Rem., .222 Rem., .223 Rem., .17/223 handloads; 20" tapered barrel; same general specifications as Ultra Model 300, except for 6-rd. magazine, no sights; receiver dovetailed for integral scope mounts. Introduced in 1966; dropped, 1976. Used value, $250 to $265.

**Ultra Model 317P** has same specifications as Model 317, except for better grade of walnut, basket-weave checkering. Dropped, 1976. Used value, $325 to $335.

*Ultra Model 370*

**HARRINGTON & RICHARDSON Ultra Model 370:** advertised as Ultra Medalist; built on Sako action; .22-250, .243 Win., 6mm Rem.; 24" heavy target/varmint barrel; uncheckered, oil-finished walnut stock; roll-over comb; no sights; tapped for open sights and/or scope mounts; adjustable trigger; recoil pad, sling swivels. Introduced in 1967; dropped, 1974. Used value, $275 to $285.

**HARRINGTON & RICHARDSON Model 308:** autoloader, gas operated; .264 Win., .308 Win.; 22" barrel; 3-rd. detachable box magazine; hand-checkered walnut stock; roll-over cheekpiece, full pistol grip, exotic wood pistol-grip cap, forearm tip; sling swivels; open adjustable rear sight, gold bead front. Introduced in 1967; dropped, 1973. Used value, $175 to $180.

*Ultra Model 360*

**HARRINGTON & RICHARDSON Ultra Model 360:** has exactly the same specifications as Model 308, except chambered for .243 Win., .308 Win. Introduced in 1967; still in production. Used value, $200 to $210.

**Model 361** has same general specifications as Model 360, except for full roll-over cheekpiece. Manufactured 1970 to 1973. Used value, $230 to $235.

*Model 866*

**HARRINGTON & RICHARDSON Model 866:** bolt-action; .22 Short, Long, LR; has the same specifications as the

**HARRINGTON & RICHARDSON Model 751:** bolt-action, single-shot; .22 Short, Long, LR. Has same specifications as

Model 865, except for Mannlicher stock. Manufactured in 1971 only. Used value, $85 to $95.

Model 750, except for Mannlicher stock. Manufactured only in 1971. Used value, $35 to $40.

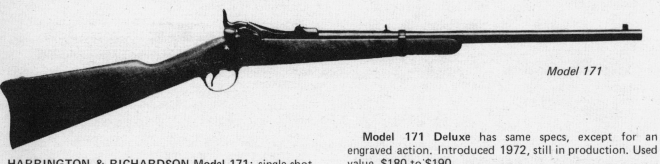

*Model 155*

**HARRINGTON & RICHARDSON Model 155:** single-shot; .45-70; 24'' or 28'' barrel; folding leaf rear sight, blade front; uncheckered straight grip hardwood stock, forearm,

barrel band; built on Model 158 action, has brass cleaning rod. Introduced 1972, still in production. Used value, $55 to $60.

*Model 171*

**HARRINGTON & RICHARDSON Model 171:** single-shot, trap door action; .45-70; 22'' barrel; leaf rear sight, blade front; uncheckered walnut stock. Replica of Model 1873 Springfield cavalry carbine. Introduced 1972, still in production. Used value, $150 to $155.

**Model 171 Deluxe** has same specs, except for an engraved action. Introduced 1972, still in production. Used value, $180 to $190.

**Model 172** has same specs as Model 171 Deluxe, except for fancy checkered walnut stock, tang-mounted aperture sight, silver-plated hardware. Introduced 1972, still in production. Used value, $875 to $950.

*Model 173*

**HARRINGTON & RICHARDSON Model 173:** single-shot, trapdoor action; .45-70; 26'' barrel; replica of Model 1873

**HARRINGTON & RICHARDSON Model 178:** single-shot, trapdoor action; .45-70; 32'' barrel; replica of Model 1873 Springfield infantry rifle; uncheckered full length walnut

Springfield Officer's Model; engraved breech block, receiver, hammer, barrel band, lock, buttplate; checkered walnut stock; ramrod; peep rear sight, blade front. Introduced 1972, still in production. Used value, $215 to $225.

stock; leaf rear sight, blade front; barrel bands, sling swivels, ramrod. Manufactured 1973 to 1975. Used value, $210 to $220.

*Model 157*

**HARRINGTON & RICHARDSON Model 157:** single-shot; .22 WRFM, .22 Hornet, .30-30; 22″ barrel; folding leaf rear sight, blade front; uncheckered hardwood pistol grip buttstock, full length forearm; swing swivels; built on Model 158 action. Introduced 1976, still in production. Used value, $55 to $60.

*Model 700*

**HARRINGTON & RICHARDSON Model 700:** autoloader; .22 WRFM; 5 or 10-rd. magazine; 22″ barrel; folding leaf rear sight, blade front on ramp; American walnut Monte Carlo stock; white line butt plate. Introduced 1977, still in production. Used value, $100 to $110.

# HIGH STANDARD

*Sport King*

**HIGH STANDARD Sport King:** autoloader; standard version was advertised as Field Model; .22 LR, long, short; 22¼″ barrel; tube magazine has capacity of 15 LR, 17 long, 21 short cartridges; uncheckered pistol-grip stock; open rear sight, bead post front. Introduced in 1960; still in production. Used value, $60 to $65.

**Sport King Special** has the same specifications as the standard or Field Model, except for Monte Carlo stock, semi-beavertail forearm. Introduced in 1950; dropped, 1966. Used value, $65 to $75.

**Sport King Deluxe** has the same specifications as Special Model, except for impressed checkering on stock. Introduced in 1966; dropped, 1975. Used value, $75 to $85.

**Sport King carbine** has the same action as Sport King Special; 18¼″ barrel; open rear sight, bead post front; straight grip stock; brass buttplate; sling swivels. Tube magazine holds 12 LR, 14 long, 17 short cartridges; receiver grooved for scope mounts; golden trigger guard, trigger, safety. Introduced in 1962; dropped, 1972. Used value, $70 to $75.

*Hi-Power Field*

**HIGH STANDARD Hi-Power:** bolt-action; standard model was advertised as Field Model; built on Mauser-type action; .270, .30/06; 22″ barrel; 4-rd. magazine; uncheckered walnut field-style pistol-grip stock; sliding safety; quick-detachable sling swivels; folding leaf open rear sight, ramp front.

Introduced in 1962; dropped, 1966. Used value, $185 to $195.

**Hi-Power Deluxe** model has the same specifications as the standard version, except for impressed checkering on Monte Carlo stock, sling swivels. Introduced in 1962; dropped, 1966. Used value, $210 to $220.

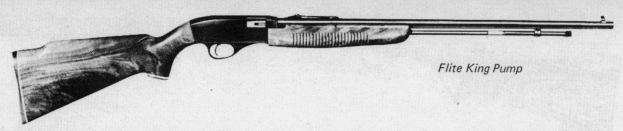

*Flite King Pump*

**HIGH STANDARD Flite King:** pump action; hammerless; .22 LR, long, short; 24" barrel; tube magazine holds 17 LR, 19 long, 24 short cartridges; uncheckered hardwood Monte Carlo pistol-grip stock, grooved semi-beavertail forearm; patridge-type rear sight, bead front. Manufactured 1962 to 1975. Used value, $60 to $65.

# HUSQVARNA

**HUSQVARNA Hi-Power:** Mauser-type bolt-action; .220 Swift, .270 Win., .30/06, 6.5x55, 8x57, 9.3x57; 23¾" barrel; 5-rd. box magazine; hand-checkered pistol-grip beech stock; open rear sight, hooded ramp front; sling swivels. Introduced in 1946; dropped, 1959. Used value, $185 to $195.

**HUSQVARNA Model 1950:** Mauser-type bolt-action; has the same specifications as Hi-Power model, except chambered only in .220 Swift, .270 Win., .30/06. Introduced in 1950; dropped, 1952. Used value, $215 to $225.

*Model 1951 Hi-Power*

**HUSQVARNA Model 1951 Hi-Power:** has the same specifications as the Model 1950, except for a high-comb stock, low safety. Produced under model designation only in 1951. Used value, $220 to $230.

*Series 1100*

**HUSQVARNA Series 1100:** Mauser-type bolt-action sporter; .220 Swift, .30/06, 6.5x55, 8x57, 9.3x57; 23½" barrel; other specifications generally the same as Model 1951 except for European walnut stock, jeweled bolt. Introduced in 1952; dropped, 1956. Used value, $265 to $275.

**HUSQVARNA Series 1000:** Mauser-type bolt-action; has the same general specifications as Model 1951, except for substitution of European walnut stock, with cheekpiece, Monte Carlo comb. Introduced in 1952; dropped, 1956. Used value, $250 to $265.

*Series 3100*

**HUSQVARNA Series 3100:** advertised as Crown Grade; Husqvarna improved Mauser action; .243 Win., .270 Win., 7mm Rem., .30/06, .308 Win.; 23¾" barrel; 5-rd. box magazine; hand-checkered European walnut pistol-grip stock; cheekpiece; black forearm tip, pistol-grip cap; open rear sight, hooded ramp front; sling swivels. Introduced in 1954; dropped, 1976. Used value, $275 to $285.

**HUSQVARNA Series 3000:** Husqvarna improved Mauser action; has the same specifications as Series 3100, except for substitution of Monte Carlo-style stock. Introduced in 1954; dropped, 1976. Used value, $265 to $275.

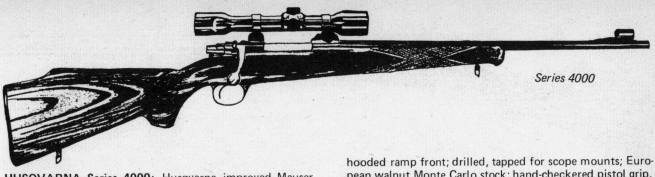

*Series 4000*

**HUSQVARNA Series 4000:** Husqvarna improved Mauser action; .243 Win., .270 Win., .30/06, .308 Win., 7mm Rem. magnum; 20½'' barrel; 5-rd. box magazine; no rear sight, hooded ramp front; drilled, tapped for scope mounts; European walnut Monte Carlo stock; hand-checkered pistol grip, forearm; sling swivels. Introduced in 1954; dropped, 1976. Used value, $275 to $285.

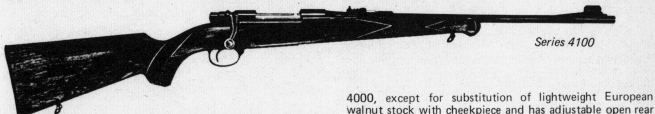

*Series 4100*

**HUSQVARNA Series 4100:** bolt-action; Husqvarna improved action; specifications identical to those of Series 4000, except for substitution of lightweight European walnut stock with cheekpiece and has adjustable open rear sight. Introduced in 1954; dropped, 1976. Used value, $265 to $275.

*Model 456*

**HUSQVARNA Model 456:** full-stock bolt-action sporter; has the same general specifications as Series 4000, except for full-length sporter stock, open adjustable rear sight, metal forearm cap, slope-away cheekpiece. Introduced in 1959; dropped, 1970. Used value, $295 to $315.

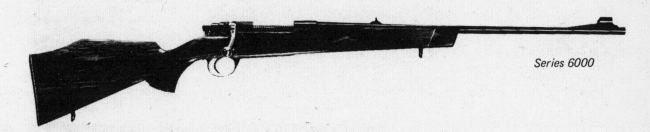

*Series 6000*

**HUSQVARNA Series 6000:** advertised as Imperial Custom Grade; .243 Win., .270 Win., .30/06, .308 Win., 7mm Rem. magnum; other specifications the same as Series 3100, except for fancy walnut stock, adjustable trigger, three-leaf folding rear sight. Introduced in 1968; dropped, 1970. Used value, $325 to $335.

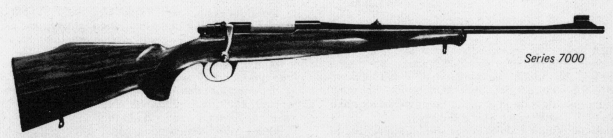

*Series 7000*

**HUSQVARNA Series 7000:** advertised as Imperial Monte Carlo Lightweight Model; .243 Win., .270 Win., .30/06, .308 Win.; other specifications are identical to those of Series 4000, except for fancy walnut stock, adjustable trigger, three-leaf folding rear sight. Introduced in 1968; dropped, 1970. Used value, $325 to $335.

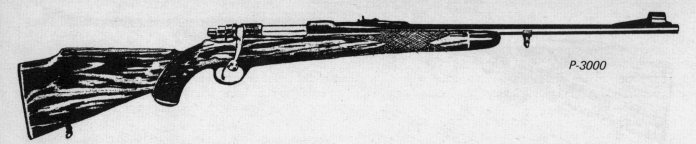

*P-3000*

**HUSQVARNA Series P-3000:** advertised as Presentation grade; .243 Win., .270 Win., .30/06, 7mm Rem. magnum; other specifications identical to those of Series 3000,

except for engraved action, adjustable trigger, top grade walnut stock. Introduced in 1968; dropped, 1970. Used value, $625 to $650.

**HUSQVARNA Model 8000:** advertised as Imperial grade; improved Husqvarna bolt-action; .270 Win., .30/06, .300 Win. magnum, 7mm Rem. magnum; 23¾" barrel; jeweled bolt; hand-checkered deluxe French walnut stock; Monte

Carlo cheekpiece, rosewood forearm tip, pistol-grip cap; adjustable trigger; 5-rd. box magazine, hinged engraved floor plate; no sights. Introduced in 1971; dropped, 1972. Used value, $375 to $400.

**HUSQVARNA Model 9000:** advertised as Crown grade; has the same specifications as Model 8000, except for folding leaf rear sight, hooded ramp front; Monte Carlo cheekpiece

stock, no jeweling on bolt, no engraving on floor plate. Introduced in 1971; dropped, 1972. Used value, $265 to $280.

---

# ITHACA

*Model X5-T*

**ITHACA Model X5-C:** takedown autoloader; .22 LR only; 22" barrel; 7-rd. clip-type magazine; uncheckered hardwood pistol-grip stock, grooved forearm; open rear sight, Raybar front. Introduced in 1958; dropped, 1964. Used

value, $70 to $75.

**Model X5-T** has the same specifications as the Model X5-C, except for 16-rd. tube magazine; ungrooved forearm. Introduced in 1959; dropped, 1963. Used value, $75 to $80.

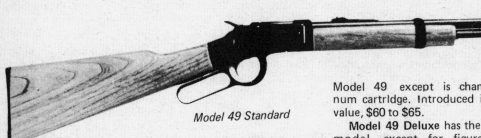

*Model 49 Standard*

**ITHACA Model 49:** advertised as Saddlegun; lever-action single-shot; .22 LR, long, short; 28" barrel; blank tube magazine for appearance only; straight uncheckered Western-style carbine stock; barrel band on forearm; open adjustable rear sight, bead post front. Introduced in 1961; dropped 1976. Used value, $45 to $50.

**Model 49 Youth Saddlegun** has same specifications as the standard model, except for shorter stock. Introduced in 1961; dropped 1976. Used value, $45 to $50.

**Model 49 Magnum** has same specifications as standard

Model 49 except is chambered for .22 rimfire magnum cartridge. Introduced in 1962; dropped, 1976. Used value, $60 to $65.

**Model 49 Deluxe** has the same specifications as standard model, except for figured walnut stock, gold-plated hammer, trigger, sling swivels. Introduced in 1962; dropped, 1975. Used value, $65 to $70.

**Model 49 Presentation** has same specifications as standard Model 49, except for fancy figured walnut stock, gold nameplate inlay, gold trigger and hammer, engraved receiver; in .22 LR, .22 WMR only. Introduced in 1962; dropped, 1974. Used value, $135 to $155.

**Model 49R** has same general specs as Model 49 single-shot, but is repeater; .22 Shorts, Longs, LR; tubular magazine; 20" barrel; open rear sight, bead front; checkered grip. Manufactured 1968 to 1971. Used value, $80 to $90.

*Model X-15*

**ITHACA Model X-15:** autoloader; .22 LR; has same specifications as Model X5-C, except that forearm is not grooved. Manufactured 1964 to 1967. Used value, $60 to $65.

*Model 72*

**ITHACA Model 72:** lever-action repeater; .22 LR, .22 rimfire magnum; 18½" barrel; uncheckered Western-style straight American walnut stock, barrel band on forearm; 15-rd. tube magazine; half-cock safety; step-adjustable open rear sight, hooded ramp front; receiver grooved for scope mounts. Introduced in 1972; dropped, 1977. Used value, .22 LR, $92 to $95; .22 WMR, $106 to $112.

**Model 72 Deluxe** has same specs as Model 72, but receiver is engraved, silver-finished; has octagonal barrel, higher grade American walnut stock, forearm. Manufactured 1974 to 1976. Used value, $150 to $160.

**Model 72 Magnum** has same specs as Model 72, except for .22 WRFM chambering, 11-rd. tubular magazine, 18½" barrel. Manufactured 1975 to 1977. Used value, $115 to $120.

*Model LSA-55 Standard*

**ITHACA LSA-55:** bolt-action repeater; .243 Win., .308 Win., .22-250, .222 Rem., 6mm Rem., .25/06, .270 Win., .30/06; 23" free-floating barrel; European walnut pistol-grip Monte Carlo stock. Early versions had impressed checkering on pistol grip, forearm; as of 1974, stocks are hand checkered. Removeable adjustable rear sight, hooded ramp front; 3-rd. detachable box magazine; adjustable trigger; re-

ceiver drilled, tapped for scope mounts. Introduced in 1972; dropped about 1976. Used values, $225 to $235; with heavy barrel .222, .22-250 only, $285 to $300.

**LSA Deluxe** has same specifications as standard model, except pre-'74 version had hand-checkered stock; also, roll-over cheekpiece, rosewood forearm tip, grip cap, white spacers; sling swivel, no heavy barrel. Used value, $265 to $285.

**LSA-55 Heavy Barrel** has same specs as standard model, except for 23" barrel; no sights, redesigned stock, beavertail forearm; made in .22-250, .222 Remington. Manufactured 1974 to 1976. Used value, $300 to $310.

**ITHACA MODEL LSA-65:** bolt-action repeater; has same specifications as standard grade Model LSA-55, except for 4-rd. magazine; made in .25/06, .270 Winchester, .30/06. Manufactured 1969 to 1976. Used value, $240 to $250.

**Model LSA-65 Deluxe** has same specs as standard model,

except for roll-over cheekpiece, skip-line checkering, rosewood grip cap, forend tip, no sights, scope mount included. Manufactured 1969 to 1976. Used value, $270 to $280.

**ITHACA BSA CF2:** bolt-action; 7mm Remington magnum, .300 Winchester magnum; 3-rd. magazine; Mauser-type action; 23-3/5" barrel; adjustable rear sight, hooded ramp

front; checkered American walnut Monte Carlo stock, roll-over cheekpiece; rosewood forend tip; sling swivels; recoil pad. Manufactured in England. Imported 1976 only. Used value, $250 to $260.

# MANNLICHER

*Model 1903*

**MANNLICHER-SCHOENAUER Model 1903:** bolt-action carbine sporter; 6.5x53mm only; 17.7" barrel; full-length uncheckered European walnut Mannlicher-style stock; metal forearm cap; pistol grip; cartridge trap in butt plate; 5-rd. rotary magazine; double-set trigger; two-leaf rear sight, ramp front; flat bolt handle; sling swivels. Introduced in 1903; dropped, 1937. Used value, $445 to $465.

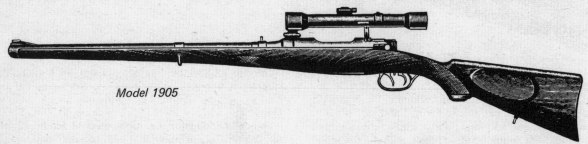

*Model 1905*

**MANNLICHER-SCHOENAUER Model 1905:** bolt-action carbine sporter; 9x56mm only; 19.7" barrel. Other specifications identical to those of Model 1903. Introduced in 1905; dropped, 1937. Used value, $500 to $525.

**MANNLICHER-SCHOENAUER Model 1908:** bolt-action carbine; 7x57mm and 8x56mm; all other specifications identical to those of Model 1905. Introduced in 1908; dropped, 1937. Used value, $535 to $565.

**MANNLICHER-SCHOENAUER Model 1910:** bolt-action sporting carbine; 9.5x57mm only; other specifications identical to those of Model 1908. Introduced in 1910; dropped, 1937. Used value, $500 to $525.

*High Velocity*

**MANNLICHER-SCHOENAUER High Velocity:** bolt-action sporting rifle; .30/06, 7x64 Brenneke, 8x60 magnum, 9.3x62, 10.75x57mm; 23.6" barrel; hand-checkered traditional sporting stock of European walnut; cheekpiece, pistol grip; 5-rd. rotary magazine; British-type three-leaf open rear sight, ramp front; sling swivels. Introduced in 1922; dropped, 1937. Used value, $575 to $600.

**MANNLICHER-SCHOENAUER Model 1924:** bolt-action carbine; .30/06 only; aimed at American market; other specifications identical to those of Model 1908. Introduced in 1924; dropped, 1937. Used value, $640 to $675.

**MANNLICHER-SCHOENAUER Model 1950:** bolt-action sporter; designed primarily for the U.S. market; .257 Roberts, .270 Win., .30/06; 24" barrel; standard hand-checkered European walnut sporting stock; pistol grip, cheekpiece; ebony forend tip; 5-rd. rotary magazine; single or double-set trigger; flat bolt handle; folding leaf open rear sight, hooded ramp front; shotgun-type safety; sling swivels. Introduced in 1950; dropped, 1952. Used value, $600 to $625.

*Model 1950 Standard*

*Model 1950 Carbine*

**Model 1950 carbine** has the same specifications as standard Model 1950 rifle, except for full-length Mannlicher-type stock, metal forearm cap; 20″ barrel. Introduced in 1950; dropped, 1952. Used value, $635 to $650.

**Model 1950 6.5 carbine** has same specifications as Model 1950 carbine, except for 18¼″ barrel chambered for 6.5x53mm only. Introduced in 1950; dropped, 1952. Used value, $625 to $640.

*Model 1952*

*Model 1952 Carbine*

**MANNLICHER-SCHOENAUER Model 1952:** bolt-action sporting rifle; .257 Roberts, .270 Win., .30/06, 9.3x62mm; improved version of Model 1950; has same specifications, except for swept-back bolt handle, improved stock design. Introduced in 1952; dropped, 1956. Used value, $450 to $465.

**Model 1952 carbine** has the same specifications as the Model 1950 carbine, except for full-length Mannlicher stock design, swept-back bolt handle; .257 Roberts, .270 Win., .30/06, 7mm Rem. mag. Introduced in 1952; dropped, 1956. Used value, $550 to $575.

**Model 1952 6.5 carbine** has the same specifications as Model 1950 6.5 carbine, except for swept-back bolt handle, improved stock design. Chambered for 6.5x53mm only. Introduced in 1952; dropped, 1956. Used value, $525 to $550.

*Model 1956*

*Model 1956 Carbine*

**MANNLICHER-SCHOENAUER Model 1956:** bolt-action sporting rifle; .243 Win., .30/06; has the same general specifications as Model 1952 rifle, except for high-comb improved walnut stock, 22″ barrel. Introduced in 1956; dropped, 1960. Used value, $475 to $500.

**Model 1956 carbine** has the same general specifications as Model 1952 carbine, except for redesigned high-comb walnut stock; .243 Win., .257 Roberts, .270 Win., .30/06; dropped, 1960. Used value, $500 to $525.

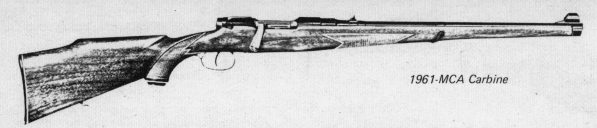

*1961-MCA Carbine*

**MANNLICHER-SCHOENAUER Model 1961-MCA:** bolt-action rifle; .243 Win., .270 Win., .30/06; has the same specifications as Model 1956 rifle, except for substitution of Monte Carlo-style walnut stock. Introduced in 1961; dropped, 1971. Used value, $585 to $600.

**1961-MCA carbine** has the same general specifications as Model 1956 carbine, except for substitution of walnut Monte Carlo stock; .243 Win., .270 Win., .30/06, .308 Win., 6.5x53mm. Introduced in 1961; dropped, 1971. Used value, $635 to $650.

*Model SL Rifle*

**MANNLICHER Model SL:** bolt-action; .222 Remington, .222 Remington magnum, .223 Remington; 5-rd. detachable rotary magazine, 23" barrel; interchangeable single or double-set trigger; open rear sight, hooded ramp front; Steyr-Mannlicher SL action; European walnut half-stock, Monte Carlo comb, cheekpiece; skip-chekcered

pistol grip, forearm; detachable sling swivels, butt pad. Introduced 1967, still in production. Used value, $330 to $340.

**Model SL Carbine** has same specs as Model SL rifle, except for full-length stock, 20" barrel. Introduced 1968, still in production. Used value, $350 to $360.

**Model SL Varminter** has same specs as Model SL rifle, except in .222 Remington only, no sights, 25-5/8" barrel. Introduced 1969, still in production. Used value, $330 to $350.

*Model L Carbine*

**MANNLICHER Model L:** bolt-action; .22-250, 5.6x57mm, .243 Winchester, 6mm Remington, .308 Winchester; built on L action; other specifications are the same as the Model SL. Introduced 1968, still in production. Used value, $340 to $350.

**Model L Carbine** has same specifications as Model SL

carbine, except for L-type action; .222 Remington, .222 Remington magnum, .223 Remington. Introduced 1968, still in production. Used value, $365 to $375.

**Model L Varminter** has same general specs as SL Varmint model except for L-type action; chambered for .22-250, .243 Winchester, .308 Winchester. Introduced 1969, still in production. Used value, $330 to $340.

*Model SSG Match*

**MANNLICHER Model SSG Match Target:** bolt-action; .308 Winchester; 5 or 10-rd. magazine; L-type action; 25½" heavy barrel; single-shot plug; single trigger; micrometer peep rear sight, globe front; European walnut target stock;

full pistol grip, wide forearm, swivel rail, adjustable butt plate; also made with high-impact plastic stock. Introduced 1969, still in production. Used values: walnut stock, $480 to $490; plastic stock, $450 to $460.

*Model M Rifle*

**MANNLICHER Model M:** bolt-action; 6.5x57mm, .270 Winchester, 7x57, 7x64, .30/06, 8x57JS, 9.3x62; M-type action; other specifications are the same as Model SL rifle, except for forend tip, recoil pad. Also made in left-hand model, with bolt on left and 6.5x55, 7.5mm Swiss as additional calibers. Standard version introduced 1969, left-hand version 1977; still in production. Used values: standard model, $360 to $375; left-hand model, $380 to $390.

**Model M Carbine** has the same general specifications as the Model SL carbine, except is built on M-type action, has recoil pad. Also made in left-hand action, with added 6.5x55mm, 7.5mm Swiss chamberings. Introduced 1969, still in production. Left-hand version introduced 1977, still in production. Used values: standard carbine, $385 to $400; left-hand model, $400 to $415.

**Model M Professional** has the same specs as standard model, except for Cycolac stock; chambered for 6.5x55mm, 6.5x57mm, .270 Winchester, 7x57mm, 7x64mm, 7.5mm Swiss, .30/06, 8x57JS, 9.3x62. Introduced 1977, still in production. Used value, $290 to $300.

*Model S*

**MANNLICHER Model S:** bolt-action; 6.5x68mm, .257 Weatherby magnum, .264 Winchester magnum, 7mm Remington magnum, .300 Winchester magnum, .300 H&H magnum, .308 Norma magnum, 8x68S, .338 Winchester magnum, 9.3x64mm, .375 H&H magnum; has the same specifications as SL model, except is built on S-type action, forend tip, recoil pad, 25-5/8'' barrel. Introduced 1970, still in production. Used value, $425 to $440.

**Model S/T** has same specs as Model S, except chambered for 9.3x64mm, .375 H&H magnum, .458 Winchester; heavy barrel. Introduced 1975, still in production. Used value, $440 to $450.

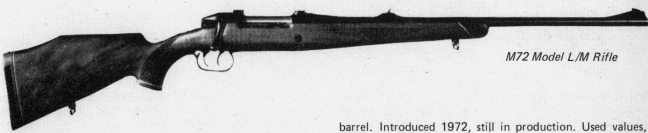

*M72 Model L/M Rifle*

**MANNLICHER-SCHOENAUER M72 Model L/M:** bolt-action; .22-250, 5.6x57mm, 6mm Remington, .243 Winchester, 6.5x57mm, .270 Winchester, 7x57mm, 7x64mm, .308 Winchester, .30/06; 23-5/8'' barrel; L/M receiver, 5-rd. rotary magazine; front-locking bolt; open rear sight, hooded ramp front; interchangeable single or double-set trigger; European walnut half-stock, hand-checkered pistol grip forearm, rosewood forend tip; recoil pad, detachable sling swivels. Introduced 1972, still in production. Used value, $470 to $485.

**M72 Model L/M Carbine** has same general specs as standard M72 Model L/M, except for full-length stock, 20'' barrel. Introduced 1972, still in production. Used values, $500 to $520.

**M72 Model S** has same general specs as standard M72 Model L/M, except for magnum action; 4-rd. magazine; 25-5/8'' barrel; chambered for 6.5x68, 7mm Remington magnum, 8x68S, 9.3x64mm, .375 H&H magnum. Introduced 1972, still in production. Used value, $535 to $550.

**M72 Model S/T** has same specs as standard M72 Model S, except for optional 25-5/8'' barrel; chambered for .300 Winchester magnum, 9.3x64mm, .375 H&H magnum, 9.3x64mm, .375 H&H magnum, .458 Winchester magnum. Introduced 1975, still in production. Used value, $575 to $590.

# MARLIN

**MARLIN Model 92:** lever-action; .22 Short, Long, LR, .32 Short, Long rimfire or centerfire with interchangeable firing pin; barrel lengths, 16", 24", 26", 28"; tubular magazine; open rear sight, blade front; uncheckered straight-grip stock, forearm. Originally marketed as Model 1892. Manufactured 1892 to 1916. Collector value. Used value, $350 to $375.

*Model 93*

**MARLIN Model 93:** lever action; .25-36 Marlin, .30-30, .32 Special, .32-40, .38-55; solid frame or take-down; 10-rd. tubular magazine; 26", 28", 30", 32" round or octagonal barrel; open rear sight, bead front; uncheckered straight-grip stock, forearm. Originally marketed as Model 1893. Manufactured 1893 to 1936. Collector value. Used value, $325 to $350.

**Model 93 Carbine** has same specs as standard model except for 20" barrel, 7-rd. magazine; chambered for .30-30, .32 Special; carbine sights. Collector value. Used value, $475 to $500.

**Model 93SC,** designated as the Sporter Carbine, has same specs as standard carbine, except for shorter 5-rd. magazine. Collector value. Used value, $475 to $500.

*Model 94*

**MARLIN Model 94:** lever action; .25-20, .32-20, .38-40, .44-40; 10-rd. magazine; 24" round or octagonal barrel; solid frame or take-down; open rear sight, bead front; uncheckered pistol grip or straight stock, forearm. Originally marketed as Model 1894. Manufactured 1894 to 1934. Collector value, $375 to $400.

*Model 95*

**MARLIN Model 95:** lever action; .32 WCF, .38-56, .40-65, .40-70, .40-82, .45-70; 9-rd. tubular magazine; 24" round or octagonal barrel, other lengths on special order; open rear sight, bead front; uncheckered straight or pistol grip stock, forearm. Manufactured 1895 to 1915. Collector value. Used value, $425 to $450.

*Model 97*

**MARLIN Model 97:** lever action; .22 Short, Long, LR; tubular magazine; 16", 24", 26", 28" barrel lengths; open rear sight, bead front; uncheckered straight or pistol grip stock, forearm. Originally marketed as Model 1897. Manufactured 1897 to 1922. Collector value. Used value, $275 to $300.

**MARLIN Model 18:** slide action; .22 Short, Long, LR; tube magazine; round or octagonal 20" barrel; solid frame; exposed hammer; open rear sight, bead front; unchecked straight stock, slide handle. Manufactured 1906 to 1909. Some collector value. Used value, $160 to $175.

*Model 20*

**MARLIN Model 20:** slide action; .22 Short, Long, LR; full-length tubular magazine holds 18 LRs, half-length holds 10 LRs; 24" octagonal barrel; open rear sight, bead front; unchecked straight-grip stock, grooved slide handle. Later versions designated as 20S. Manufactured 1907 to 1922. Some collector value. Used value, $160 to $175.

**MARLIN Model 25:** slide action; .22 Short; 15-rd. tubular magazine; 23" barrel; open rear sight, bead front; unchecked straight-grip stock, slide handle. Manufactured 1909 to 1910. Some collector value. Used value, $185 to $200.

*Model 27*

**MARLIN Model 27:** slide action; .25-20, .32-20; 7-rd. tubular magazine; 24" octagonal barrel; open rear sight, bead front; unchecked straight-grip stock, grooved slide handle. Manufactured 1910 to 1916. Some collector value. Used value, $160 to $175.

Model 27S has the same specifications as standard model, except for round barrel; chambered also for .25 Stevens RF. Manufactured 1920 to 1932. Used value, $160 to $175.

**MARLIN Model 32:** slide action; .22 Short, Long, LR; short tubular magazine holds 10 LRs, full-length magazine holds 18 LRs; 24" octagonal barrel; open rear sight, bead front; unchecked pistol-grip stock, grooved slide handle. Some collector value. Manufactured 1914 to 1915. Used value, $160 to $175.

*Model 38*

**MARLIN Model 38:** slide-action repeater; hammerless takedown; .22 long, .22 LR, .22 short; tube magazine holds 10 LR, 12 long, 15 short cartridges; 24" octagon barrel; open rear sight, bead front; unchecked pistol-grip walnut stock, grooved slide handle. Introduced in 1920; dropped, 1930. Used value, $155 to $170.

*Model 50*

**MARLIN Model 50:** autoloader; takedown; .22 LR only; 6-rd. detachable box magazine; 22" barrel; open rear sight adjustable for elevation, bead front; unchecked pistol-grip walnut stock, grooved forearm. Introduced in 1931; dropped, 1934. Used value, $85 to $95.

Model 50E has same specs as Model 50, except for hooded front sight, peep rear. Used value, $55 to $65.

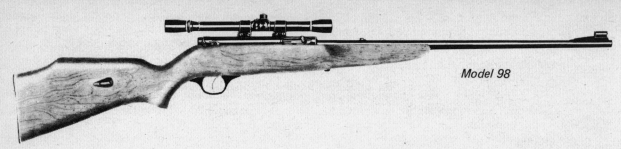

Model 98

**MARLIN Model 98:** solid frame autoloader; .22 LR only; butt stock tube magazine has 15-rd. capacity; 22" barrel; open rear sight, hooded ramp front; uncheckered Monte Carlo stock, cheekpiece. Introduced in 1950; dropped, 1961. Used value, $60 to $65.

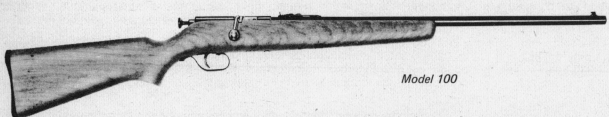

Model 100

**MARLIN Model 100:** bolt-action, takedown single-shot; .22 LR, .22 long, .22 short; 24" barrel; open rear sight adjustable for elevation, bead front; uncheckered walnut pistol-grip stock. Introduced in 1936; dropped, 1960. Used value, $45 to $50.

**Model 100S** was introduced in 1936; dropped, 1946. It is known as the Tom Mix Special, allegedly because Tom Mix used such a rifle in his vaudeville act in the Thirties. It has the same specifications as standard Model 100 except for sling, peep rear sight, hooded front. Value is based largely upon rarity. Used value, $100 to $125.

**Model 100SB** is the same as Model 100, except it is smoothbore for use with .22 shot cartridge; has shotgun sight. Actually, this probably is the version used by Tom Mix in his act, as he used shot cartridges for breaking glass balls and other on-stage targets. Introduced in 1936; dropped, 1941. Used value, $100 to $125.

**MARLIN Model 101:** Improved version of Model 100; current version has improved bolt, redesigned stock, 22" barrel; semi-buckhorn folding sight adjustable for windage, elevation, hooded Wide-Scan front; black plastic trigger guard; T-shaped cocking piece; uncheckered walnut stock has beavertail forearm; receiver grooved for tip-off scope mount. Introduced in 1951; dropped, 1976. Used value, $50 to $55.

**Model 101DL** has same specs as Model 101, except for peep rear sight, hooded front; sling swivels. Manufactured 1952 to 1964. Used value, $50 to $55.

**Marlin-Glenfield Model 101G** has same specs as Model 101, with plainer wood in stock. Manufactured 1960 to 1965. Used value, $40 to $45.

Model 36

**MARLIN MODEL 36:** lever-action, carbine repeater; .32 Special, .30-30; 6-rd. tube magazine; 20" barrel; uncheckered walnut pistol-grip stock, semi-beavertail forearm; carbine barrel band; open rear sight, bead front. Introduced in 1936; dropped, 1948. Used value, $185 to $200.

**Model 36A** has same specs as Model 36 standard, except for shorter tube magazine holding 5 rds.; 24" barrel; hooded front sight. Used value, $185 to $200.

**Model 36A-DL** has same specs as Model 36A, except for sling swivels, hand-checkered walnut stock, forearm. Used value, $210 to $225.

**Model 36 Sporting** carbine has same general specs as Model 30A, except for a 20" barrel. Used value, $225 to $235.

**MARLIN Model 336C:** lever-action repeating carbine; updated version of Model 36 carbine; specs are virtually the same, except for round breech bolt; gold-plated trigger; offset hammer spur; semi-buckhorn adjustable folding rear sight; ramp front with Wide-Scan hood; receiver tapped for scope mounts; top of receiver sand-blasted to reduce glare. Introduced in 1948; still in production, in .30-30, .35 Rem.; latter was introduced in 1953; .32 Win. Special discontinued, 1963. Used value in .32 Win. Special, $185 to $200; other calibers, $150 to $165.

*Model 336C*

**Model 336A** is same as 336C, except it has 24" round barrel; half-length magazine tube; 5-rd. capacity; blued forearm cap, sling swivels; available now only in .30-30; .35 Rem. discontinued in 1963. Introduced in 1950; still in production. Used value, $145 to $155.

**Model 336A-DL** has the same specifications as Model 336A, except for sling, swivels, hand-checkered stock, forearm. Dropped, 1962. Used value, $165 to $185.

**Model 336 Sporting carbine** has same specifications as Model 336A, except for 20" barrel. Dropped, 1963. Used value, $175 to $195.

**Model 336 Zipper** is same as Model 336 sporting carbine, but was chambered only in .219 Zipper. Introduced in 1955; dropped, 1961. Used value, $265 to $275.

**Model 336T**, called the Texan Model, has same specs as Model 336 carbine, except for straight-grip uncheckered walnut stock, squared lever. Introduced in 1953; still in production. Originally chambered in .30-30, .35 Rem.; was chambered in .44 magnum from 1963 to 1967. Produced currently only in .30-30. Used value, $145 to $150.

**Model 336 Marauder** is same as Model 336T, except with 16¾" barrel. Introduced in 1963; dropped, 1964. Used value, $250 to $275.

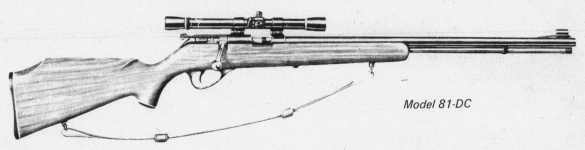

*Model 81-DC*

**MARLIN Model 81:** bolt-action, takedown repeater; .22 LR, .22 long, .22 short; tube magazine holds 18 LR, 20 long, 24 short cartridges; 24" barrel; open rear sight, bead front; uncheckered pistol-grip stock. Introduced in 1937; dropped, 1965. Used value, $70 to $75.

**Model 81E** differs from standard Model 81 only in that it has hooded front sight, peep rear. Used value, $46 to $52.

**Model 81C** is an improved version of standard Model 81; specifications differ only in that the stock has semi-beavertail forearm. Introduced in 1940; dropped, 1970. Used value, $80 to $85.

**Model 81-DC** has same specs as Model 81-C, except for hooded front sight, peep rear, sling swivels. Introduced in 1940; dropped, 1965. Used value, $90 to $95.

**Marlin-Glenfield Model 81G** has same specs as Model 81C, except the stock is of less expensive wood; has bead front sight. Introduced in 1960; dropped, 1965. Used value, $65 to $70.

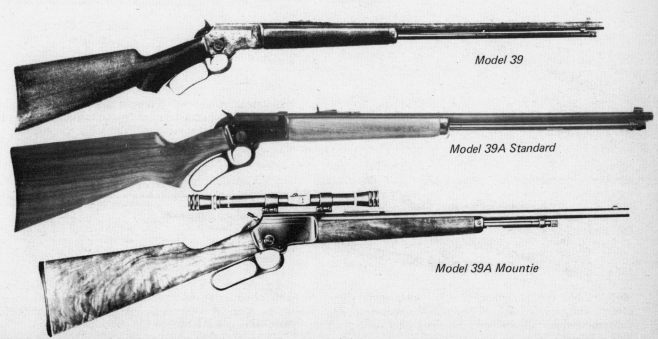

*Model 39*

*Model 39A Standard*

*Model 39A Mountie*

**MARLIN Model 39:** lever-action takedown repeater; .22 LR, .22 long, .22 short; tube magazine holds 18 LR, 20 long, 25 short cartridges; 24" octagon barrel, open rear sight, bead front; unchecked pistol-grip walnut stock, forearm. Introduced in 1938; dropped, 1958. Used $225 to $245.

Model 39A has the same general specs as Model 39, but with heavier stock, semi-beavertail forearm, round barrel.

**MARLIN Model 80:** bolt-action, takedown; .22 LR, .22 long, .22 short; 8-rd. detachable box magazine; 24" barrel; open rear sight, bead front; unchecked walnut pistol-grip stock; black butt plate. Introduced in 1934; dropped, 1939. Used value, $85 to $95.

Model 80E has the same specifications as standard Model 80, except for peep rear sight, hooded front. Used value, $100 to $115.

Introduced in 1939; still in production. Used value, $150 to $165.

Golden Model 39A has gold-plated trigger, other refinements. Used value, $103.50 to $109.

Model 39A Mountie is virtually the same as the Model 39A, but with straight-grip stock, slim forearm; 20" barrel; tube magazine holds 15 LR, 16 long, 21 short cartridges. Introduced in 1953; dropped, 1960. Used value, $103.50 to $109.

Model 80-C replaced standard Model 80 in 1940; dropped in 1970. Has same general specs as Model 80, except that stock has semi-beavertail forearm. Used value, $65 to $75.

Model 80-DL, introduced in 1940, dropped, 1965, has same specifications as the Model 80-C, except for peep rear sight, hooded front; sling swivels. Used value, $75 to $85.

*Model A-1*

**MARLIN Model A-1:** autoloader, takedown; .22 LR only; 6-rd. detachable box magazine; 24" barrel; open rear sight, bead front; unchecked walnut pistol-grip stock. Introduced in 1935; dropped, 1946. Used value, $75 to $85.

Model A1E has the same specifications as standard Model A-1, except for a hooded front sight, peep rear. Used value, $85 to $95.

Model A-1C was introduced in 1940; dropped, 1946; has same specifications as Model A-1, except that stock has semi-beavertail forearm. Used value, $90 to $100.

Model A-1DL has same specs as Model A-1C, except for sling swivels, hooded front sight, peep rear. Used value, $100 to $115.

*Model 88-C*

**MARLIN Model 332:** bolt-action, varmint rifle; .222 Rem. only; short Sako Mauser-type action; 24" barrel; 3-rd. clip-

type magazine; checkered walnut stock; two-position peep sight in rear, hooded ramp front. Introduced in 1954; dropped, 1957. Used value, $225 to $235.

*Model 455*

**MARLIN Model 455:** bolt-action; FN Mauser action; Sako trigger; .308, .30/06, .270 Win.; 5-rd. box magazine; 24" stainless steel barrel; checkered walnut Monte Carlo stock

with cheekpiece; Lyman No. 48 receiver sight, hooded ramp front. Introduced in 1957; dropped, 1959. Used value, $210 to $218.50.

*Model 30A*

**MARLIN-Glenfield Model 30:** lever-action; .30-30; has the same general specs as the Model 336C, except for 4-rd.

magazine; lower-quality stock of American hardwood. Manufactured 1966 to 1968. Used value, $120 to $125.

**Model 30A** has same specs as Model 30, except for impressed checkering on stock, forearm. Introduced in 1969, still in production. Used value, $130 to $140.

*Model 56*

**MARLIN Model 56:** same as Model 57, except equipped

with clip-loading magazine; 8-rd. capacity. Introduced in 1955; dropped, 1964. Used value, $95 to $115.

*Model 57*

**MARLIN Model 57:** lever-action; .22 LR, .22 long, .22 short; tube magazine holds 27 shorts, 21 longs, 19 LR; 22" barrel; unchecked Monte Carlo-type pistol-grip stock; open rear sight, hooded ramp front. Introduced in 1959;

dropped, 1965. Used value, $85 to $90.

**Model 57M** has the same specifications as standard Model 57, except for 24" barrel, 15-rd. magazine, chambered for .22 Win. rimfire magnum cartridge. Introduced in 1959; dropped, 1969. Used value, $100 to $115.

**MARLIN Model 99:** autoloader; .22 LR only; 22" barrel; 18-rd. tube magazine; unchecked walnut pistol-grip stock; open rear sight, hooded ramp front. Introduced in 1959; dropped, 1961. Used value, $60 to $65.

**Model 99C** has same specs as standard Model 99, except for unchecked Monte Carlo stock; grooved receiver for

tip-off scope mounts; gold-plated trigger. Later production features checkering on pistol-grip, forearm. Introduced in 1962; still in production. Used value, $60 to $65.

**Model 99DL** has same specs as standard Model 99, except for unchecked black walnut Monte Carlo stock; jeweled bolt; gold-plated trigger, sling, sling swivels. Intro-

**MARLIN Model 65:** bolt-action single-shot; .22 LR, .22 long, .22 short; 24" barrel; open rear sight, bead front; unchecked walnut pistol-grip stock, grooved forearm.

Introduced in 1932; dropped, 1938. Used value, $55 to $65.

**Model 65E** is the same as Model 65, but is equipped with hooded front sight, peep rear. Used value, $55 to $65.

*Model 89C*

**MARLIN Model 88-C:** takedown autoloader; .22 LR only; tube magazine in butt stock; 14-rd. capacity; open rear sight, hooded front; unchecked pistol-grip stock. Introduced in 1947; dropped, 1956. Used value, $65 to $80.

**MARLIN Model 89C:** same general specifications as Model 88-C, except with clip magazine. Early version had 7-rd. clip; 12-rd. clip in later versions. Introduced in 1950;

**Model 88-DL** was introduced in 1953; dropped, 1956; same specs as Model 88-C, except for hand-checkered stock, sling swivels, receiver peep sight in rear. Used value, $75 to $80.

dropped, 1961. Used value, $65 to $75.

**Marlin Model 89DL** has same specifications as Model 89-C, except for addition of sling swivels, receiver peep sight. Used value, $80 to $85.

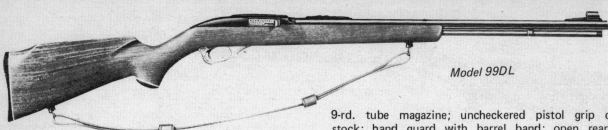

*Model 99DL*

duced in 1960; dropped, 1965. Used value, $70 to $75.

**Model 99M1** carbine, designed after U.S. 30M1 carbine, but otherwise using same action as Model 99C; 18" barrel;

**MARLIN Model 122:** single-shot; bolt-action, junior target model with shortened uncheckered stock; .22 LR, .22 long, .22 short; 22" barrel; open rear sight, hooded ramp front;

9-rd. tube magazine; uncheckered pistol grip carbine stock; hand guard with barrel band; open rear sight, military-type ramp front; sling swivels. Introduced in 1966; still in production. Used value, $65 to $70.

**Model 99G** has same specs as 99C, except for plainer stock, bead front sight. Manufactured 1960 to 1965. Used value, $50 to $55.

walnut Monte Carlo pistol-grip stock; sling, sling swivels. Introduced in 1961; dropped, 1965. Used value, $42.50 to $46.

*Model 980*

**MARLIN Model 980:** bolt-action repeater; .22 Win. rimfire magnum only; 8-rd. clip-type magazine; 24" barrel; open rear sight adjustable for elevation, hooded ramp front; un-

checkered walnut Monte Carlo style stock with white spacers at pistol grip and butt plate; sling, sling swivels. Introduced in 1962; dropped, 1970. Used value, $85 to $95.

*Model 989M2*

**MARLIN 989:** autoloader; .22 LR only; 7-rd clip magazine; 22" barrel; open adjustable rear sight; hooded ramp front; uncheckered Monte Carlo-type pistol-grip stock of black walnut; black butt plate. Introduced in 1962; dropped, 1966. Used value, $37.50 to $40.

**Model 989M2** carbine is the same as the Model 99M1, except for 7-rd. clip-type detachable magazine. Introduced

in 1966; still in production. Used value, $60 to $65.

**Model 989G Marlin-Glenfield** is the same as the Model 989, except for plain stock, bead front sight. Introduced in 1962; discontinued, 1964. Used value, $40 to $50.

**Model 989MC Carbine** has same specs as Model 99M1, except for 7-rd. clip-loading magazine. Introduced 1966, still in production. Used value, $60 to $65.

*Model 62*

**MARLIN Model 62:** lever-action repeater; .256 magnum, .30 carbine; 23" barrel, 4-rd. clip magazine; open rear sight

adjustable for elevation, hooded ramp front; swivels, sling; uncheckered Monte Carlo-type pistol-grip stock. The .256 magnum was introduced in 1963; dropped, 1969. Used value, .256 magnum, $125 to $140; .30 carbine, $120 to $130.

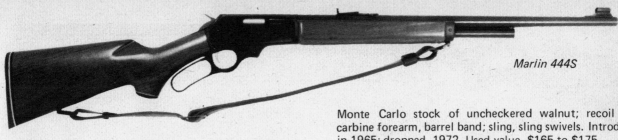

*Marlin 444S*

**MARLIN Model 444:** lever-action repeater; action is strengthened version of Model 336; .444 Marlin cartridge only; 4-rd. tube magazine; 24" barrel; open rear sight adjustable for elevation, hooded ramp front; straight-grip Monte Carlo stock of uncheckered walnut; recoil pad; carbine forearm, barrel band; sling, sling swivels. Introduced in 1965; dropped, 1972. Used value, $165 to $175.

**Model 444 Sporter** has same specs as 444 rifle, except for 22" barrel, Model 336A–type pistol-grip stock, forearm; recoil pad; detachable swivels; sling. Introduced 1972, still in production. Used value, $120 to $130.

*Glenfield M-60 w/200 Scope*

**MARLIN-Glenfield Model 60:** semi-automatic; .22 LR; same general specs as Model 99C, except for checkered or uncheckered walnut-finished hardwood stock. Introduced 1966, still in production. Used value, $45 to $55.

*Model 49DL*

**MARLIN Model 49:** semi-automatic; .22 LR; has same specs as Model 99C, except for checkered or uncheckered hardwood stock. Manufactured 1968 to 1971. Used value, $60 to $70.

**Model 49DL:** autoloader; .22 LR only; same specs as Model 99 standard model, except for capped pistol grip, checkered forearm and pistol grip, gold trigger; scroll-engraved receiver; grooved for tip-off scope mounts. Introduced in 1970; still in production. Used value, $75 to $90.

*Model 70*

**MARLIN-Glenfield Model 70:** semi-automatic; .22 LR; has same specs as Model 989 M2 carbine, except for walnut-finished hardwood stock. Manufactured 1966 to 1969. Used value, $50 to $55.

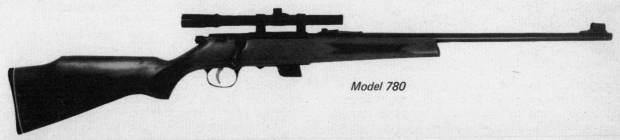

*Model 780*

*Marlin 781*

*Marlin 782*

*Marlin 783 w/200 Scope*

**MARLIN Model 780:** bolt-action; .22 Short, Long, LR; 7-rd. clip magazine; 22'' barrel; open rear sight, hooded ramp front; Monte Carlo stock, checkered pistol grip, forearm; receiver grooved for scope mounts. Introduced 1971, still in production. Used value, $50 to $55.

**Model 781** has same specifications as Model 780, except for tubular magazine holding 17 LRs. Introduced 1971, still

in production. Used value, $55 to $60.

**Model 782** has same specs as Model 780, but has sling swivels, sling; chambered for .22 WRFM. Introduced 1971, still in production. Used value, $55 to $60.

**Model 783** has same specs as Model 782, except for tubular magazine. Introduced 1971, still in production. Used value, $55 to $60.

**MARLIN Model 1894:** .44 magnum only; 10-rd. tube magazine; 20'' carbine barrel; uncheckered straight grip black walnut stock, forearm; gold-plated trigger; receiver tapped for scope mount; offset hammer spur; solid top receiver is sand-blasted to reduce glare; hooded ramp front sight, semi-buckhorn adjustable rear. Supposedly a recreation of the Model 94 of the last century, actually it is built

on the Model 336 action. Introduced, 1971; still in production. Used value, $100.50 to $109.

**Model 1894 Sporter** has same specs as Model 1894 carbine, except for 22'' barrel, 6-rd. magazine. Manufactured 1973. Used value, $100 to $120.

**Model 1894 Octagon** has same specs as 1894 carbine, except for octagonal barrel, bead front sight. Manufactured 1973. Used value, $130 to $140.

*Model 1895*

**MARLIN Model 1895:** .45-70 only; 22'' round barrel; 4-rd. tube magazine; uncheckered straight grip stock, forearm of black walnut; solid receiver tapped for scope mounts, receiver sights; offset hammer spur; adjustable semi-buck-

horn folding rear sight, bead front. Meant to be a recreation of the original Model 1895, discontinued in 1915. Actually built on action of Marlin Model 444. Introduced in 1972; still in production. Used value, $165 to $175.

# MAUSER

*Model 98*

**MAUSER Standard Model 98:** introduced after World War I; commercial version of the German military 98k model; bolt-action repeater; 7mm Mauser, 7.9mm Mauser; 23½" barrel, 5-rd. box magazine; military-style uncheckered

European walnut stock; straight military-type bolt handle; adjustable rear sight, blade front; sling swivels; Mauser trademark on receiver ring. Dropped, 1938. Used value, $165 to $195.

*British Model*

**MAUSER Special British Model:** bolt-action Type A standard Mauser Model 98 action; 7x57, 8x60, 9x57, 9.3x62mm, .30/06; 23½" barrel; 5-rd. box magazine; hand-checkered pistol-grip Circassian walnut sporting stock;

buffalo horn grip cap, forearm tip; Express rear sight, hooded ramp front; military-type trigger; detachable sling swivels. Introduced before WWI, dropped, 1938. Used value, $425 to $450.

*Magnum Model*

**MAUSER Type A Short Model:** has the same general specifications as standard Type A, except for short action, 21½" barrel; 6.5x54, 8x51mm, .250-3000. Introduced before WWI; dropped, 1938. Used value, $325 to $390.

Type A Magnum Model has the same general specifications as standard Type A model, except for heavier magnum action; 10.75x68mm, .280 Ross, .318 Westley Richards Express, .404 Nitro Express. Introduced before WWI; dropped, 1939. Used value, $600 to $625.

*Type B*

**MAUSER Type B:** bolt-action sporter; 7x57, 8x57, 8x60, 9x57, 9.3x62, 10.75x68mm, .30/06; 23½" barrel; 5-rd. box magazine; hand-checkered walnut pistol-grip stock;

schnabel forearm tip; grip cap; double-set triggers; sling swivels; three-leaf rear sight, ramp front. Introduced before WWI; dropped, 1938. Used value, $400 to $425.

*Sporter Model*

**MAUSER Sporter:** bolt-action; 6.5x55, 6.5x58, 7x57, 9x57, 9.3x62, 10.75x68; 5-rd. box magazine; 23½'' barrel; double-set trigger; tangent-curve rear sight, ramp front; uncheckered European walnut stock, pistol grip, Schnabel-tipped forearm; sling swivels. Manufactured in Germany prior to World War I. Used value, $475 to $500.

**Short Model Sporter** has the same specs as the standard rifle, except for 19¾'' barrel; chambered only for 6.5x54, 8x51 cartridges. Manufactured prior to WWI. Used value,

$475 to $500.

**Sporter Carbine** has same specs as standard rifle, except for 19¾'' barrel; chambered only for 6.5x54, 6.5x58, 7x57, 8x57, 9x57. Manufactured prior to WWI. Used value, $475 to $500.

**Military Sporter** has same specs as standard rifle, except for Model 98-type barrel, double-pull trigger, military front sight; chambered for 7x57, 8x57, 9x57. Manufactured prior to WWI. Used value, $425 to $450.

**MAUSER Model EN310:** bolt-action, single-shot; .22 LR only; 19¾'' barrel; fixed open rear sight, blade front; uncheckered European walnut pistol-grip stock.

Manufactured from post World War I era to 1935. Used value, $180 to $190.

*ES350*

**MAUSER Model ES350:** bolt-action repeater; .22 LR rifle only; 27½'' barrel; target-style walnut stock;

hand-checkered pistol grip, forearm; grip cap; open micrometer rear sight, ramp front. Introduced in 1925; dropped, 1935. Used value, $200 to $225.

**MAUSER Model EL320:** bolt-action, single-shot; .22 LR only, 23½'' barrel; sporting-style European walnut stock;

hand-checkered pistol grip; adjustable open rear sight, bead front; sling swivels. Introduced in 1927; dropped, 1935. Used value, $165 to $185.

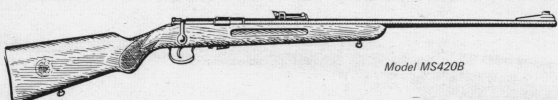

*Model MS420B*

**MAUSER Model MS420:** bolt-action repeater; .22 LR only; 25½'' barrel; 5-rd. detachable box magazine; European walnut sporting stock; hand-checkered pistol grip, grooved forearm, sling swivels; tangent curve open rear sight, ramp

front. Introduced in 1925; dropped, 1935. Used value, $125 to $200.

**Model MS420B** has the same general specifications as MS420, except for better wood, 25¾'' barrel. Introduced in 1935; dropped, 1939. Used value, $225 to $240.

*Model MM410*

**MAUSER Model MM410:** bolt-action repeater; .22 LR only; 23½'' barrel; 5-rd. detachable box magazine; European walnut sporting stock; hand-checkered pistol grip; tangent curve open rear sight, ramp front; sling

swivels. Introduced in 1926; dropped, 1935. Used value, $175 to $200.

**Model MM410B** has the same general specifications as MM410, except for lightweight sporting stock. Introduced in 1935; dropped, 1939. Used value, $225 to $235.

**MAUSER Model DSM34:** bolt-action single-shot; .22 LR only; 26'' barrel; Model 98 Mauser military-type stock; no

checkering; tangent curve open rear sight, barleycorn front; sling swivels. Introduced in 1934; dropped, 1939. Used value, $150 to $185.

**MAUSER Model ES340:** bolt-action single-shot target rifle; .22 LR only; 25½'' barrel; European walnut sporting stock;

hand-checkered pistol grip, grooved forearm; tangent curve rear sight, ramp front; sling swivels. Introduced in 1923; dropped, 1935. Used value, $250 to $275.

**MAUSER Model KKW:** bolt-action single-shot target rifle; .22 LR, 26" barrel; Model 98 Mauser military-type walnut stock; no checkering; tangent curve open rear sight, barley-corn front; sling swivels; improved model was used in training German troops in WWII. Target model introduced in 1935; dropped, 1939. Used value, $200 to $225.

**MAUSER Model EX340B:** bolt-action single-shot target rifle; replaced ES340; has same general specifications, except for 26¾" barrel, uncheckered pistol-grip stock. Introduced in 1935; dropped, 1939. Used value, $235 to $265.

*Model MS350B*

**MAUSER Model MS350B:** bolt-action repeater, replacing Model ES350; same general specifications; .22 LR only; 26¾" barrel; 5-rd. detachable box magazine; target stock of European walnut; hand-checkered pistol grip, forearm; barrel grooved for detachable rear sight/scope; micrometer open rear sight, ramp front; sling swivels. Introduced in 1935; dropped, 1939. Used value, $165 to $185.

**MAUSER Model ES350B:** bolt-action single-shot target rifle; has the same general specifications as Model MS350B, except is single-shot. Introduced in 1935; dropped, 1938. Used value, $275 to $295.

*Standard 660*

*660 Safari*

*660 Deluxe*

**MAUSER Model 660:** bolt-action; .243 Win., .25/06, .270 Win., .308 Win., .30/06, 7x57, 7mm Rem. magnum; 24" barrel; short action; adjustable single-stage trigger; push-button safety; no sights; drilled, tapped for scope mounts; detachable sling swivels; interchangeable barrels; hand-checkered European walnut stock; Monte Carlo roll; white line pistol-grip cap, recoil pad. Introduced in 1973; importation discontinued, 1975. Still in production. Used value, $400 to $425.

**Model 660 Safari** has the same basic specifications as standard 660, except chambered in .458 Win. magnum, .375 Holland & Holland magnum, .338 Win. magnum, 7mm Rem. magnum; 28" barrel, express rear sight, fixed ramp front. Importation discontinued, 1975. Still in production. Used value, $500 to $525.

**Model 660 Ultra** has same specs as standard model, except for 20.9" barrel. Introduced 1965, still in production. Importation discontinued. Used value, $575 to $600.

**Model 660T Carbine** has same specs as standard rifle, except for 29.9" barrel, full-length stock. Introduced 1965, still in production. Importation discontinued. Used value, $625 to $650.

**Model 660SH** has same specs as standard rifle, except for 25-3/5" barrel, chambered for 6.5x68, 7mm Remington magnum, 7mm SE V Hoff, .300 Winchester magnum, 8x68S, 9.3x64. Introduced 1965, still in production. Importation discontinued. Used value, $625 to $650.

**Model 660S Deluxe** has same specs as standard rifle, except available in carbine version also, with engraving, gold/silver inlay work, heavy carving on select walnut stock. Special order only; no longer imported. Used value, $1600 to $1800.

**Model 660P Target** manufactured in .308 Winchester, other calibers on special order; short action; adjustable single-stage trigger; 26-3/5'' heavy barrel, muzzle brake; 3-rd. magazine; dovetail rib for scope mounting; European walnut target stock, with full pistol grip, thumbhole, adjustable cheekpiece, adjustable rubber buttplate. Not imported. Used value, $900 to $950.

**MAUSER Model 2000:** bolt-action; .270 Winchester, .308 Winchester, .30/06; 5-rd. magazine; modified Mauser action; folding leaf rear sight, hooded ramp front; hand-checkered European walnut stock, Monte Carlo comb, cheekpiece; forend tip; sling swivels. Manufactured 1969 to 1971; replaced by Model 3000. Used value, $300 to $325.

*Model 4000*

**MAUSER Model 4000 Varmint:** bolt-action; .222 Remington, .223 Remington; has same general specifications as Model 3000, except for smaller action, rubber buttplate, folding leaf rear sight, hooded ramp front. Manufactured 1971 to 1975. Used value, $325 to $350.

**MAUSER Model 10 Varminter:** bolt-action; .22-250 only; 24'' heavy barrel; no sights; drilled, tapped for scope mounts; externally adjustable trigger; hammer-forged barrel; hand-checkered European walnut Monte Carlo pistol-grip stock; 5-rd. box magazine. Introduced in 1973; importation discontinued, 1975. Still in production. Used value, $275 to $285.

*Model 3000*

**MAUSER Model 3000:** bolt-action; .243 Win., .270 Win., .308 Win., .30/06, .375 Holland & Holland magnum, 7mm Rem. magnum; 22'' barrel in standard calibers, 26'' in magnum; no sights; drilled, tapped for scope mounts; sliding safety; fully adjustable trigger; hand-checkered, European walnut, Monte Carlo stock; white line spacer on pistol-grip cap, recoil pad. Left-hand action at added cost. Introduced in 1973; dropped, 1975. Used values, standard calibers, $275 to $285; left-hand action, $300 to $325; magnums, $300 to $325; left-hand magnums, $325 to $350.

# MOSSBERG

*Model K*

**MOSSBERG Model K:** takedown slide-action repeater; hammerless; .22 LR, long, short; tube magazine holds 14 LR, 16 long, 20 short cartridges; 22'' barrel; uncheckered straight-grip walnut stock, grooved slide handle; open rear sight, bead front. Introduced in 1922; dropped, 1931. Used value, $85 to $95.

**MOSSBERG Model M:** has same specifications as Mossberg Model K, except for 24" octagonal barrel, pistol-grip stock.

Introduced in 1928; dropped, 1931. Used value, $95 to $115.

*Model L*

**MOSSBERG Model L:** takedown, single-shot; .22 LR, long, short; Martini-design falling-block lever-action; 24"

barrel; unchecked walnut pistol-grip stock, forearm; open rear sight, bead front. Introduced in 1929; dropped, 1932. Used value, $175 to $195.

**MOSSBERG Model B:** single-shot, takedown; .22 LR, long, short; 22" barrel; unchecked pistol-grip walnut stock.

Introduced in 1930; dropped, 1932. Used value, $45 to $55.

**MOSSBERG Model R:** bolt-action repeater; takedown; .22 LR, long, short; 24" barrel, tube magazine; unchecked

pistol-grip stock; open rear sight, bead front. Introduced in 1930; dropped, 1932. Used value, $60 to $65.

**MOSSBERG Model 10:** bolt-action, takedown, single-shot; .22 LR, long, short; 22" barrel; unchecked walnut pistol-

grip stock, swivels, sling; open rear sight, bead front. Introduced in 1933; dropped, 1935. Used value, $45 to $50.

**MOSSBERG Model 20:** bolt-action, takedown, single-shot; .22 LR, long, short; 24" barrel; unchecked pistol-grip

stock, forearm with finger grooves; open rear sight, bead front. Introduced in 1933; dropped, 1935. Used value, $45 to $55.

**MOSSBERG Model 30:** bolt-action, takedown, single-shot; .22 LR, long, short; 24" barrel; unchecked pistol-grip

stock, grooved forearm; rear peep sight, hooded ramp bead front. Introduced in 1933; dropped, 1935. Used value, $45 to $55.

**MOSSBERG Model 40:** bolt-action, takedown repeater; has same general specifications as Model 30, except for tube

magazine with capacity of 16 LR, 18 long, 22 short cartridges. Introduced in 1933; dropped, 1935. Used value, $60 to $65.

**MOSSBERG Model 14:** bolt-action, takedown, single-shot; .22 LR, long, short; 24" barrel; unchecked pistol-grip

stock, semi-beavertail forearm; rear peep sight, hooded ramp front; sling swivels. Introduced in 1934; dropped, 1935. Used value, $50 to $55.

**MOSSBERG Model 34:** bolt-action, takedown, single-shot; .22 LR, long, short; 24" barrel; unchecked pistol-grip

stock with semi-beavertail forearm; rear peep sight, hooded ramp front. Introduced in 1934; dropped, 1935. Used value, $45 to $55.

**MOSSBERG Model 44:** bolt-action, takedown, repeater; .22 LR, long, short; 24" barrel; tube magazine, holding 16 LR, 18 long, 22 short cartridges; unchecked walnut

pistol-grip stock, semi-beavertail forearm; rear peep sight, hooded ramp front; sling swivels. Introduced in 1934; dropped, 1935. Used value, $65 to $75.

**MOSSBERG Model 25:** bolt-action, takedown, single-shot; .22 LR, long, short; 24" barrel; unchecked pistol-grip stock, semi-beavertail forearm; rear peep sight, hooded ramp front; sling swivels. Introduced in 1935; dropped,

1936. Used value, $45 to $55.
   **Model 26A** is the same as Model 25, except for minor improvements, including better wood and finish. Introduced in 1936; dropped, 1938. Used value, $55 to $60.

**MOSSBERG Model 42:** bolt-action, takedown, repeater; .22 LR, long, short; 7-rd. detachable box magazine; 24" barrel; unchecked walnut pistol-grip stock; receiver peep sight, open rear sight, hooded ramp front; sling swivels. Introduced in 1935; dropped, 1937. Used value, $65 to $75.

   **Model 42A** has same general specifications as Model 42, with only minor upgrading. Introduced in 1937 to replace dropped Model 42; dropped in 1938. Used value, $75 to $80.
   **Model L42A** is the same as Model 42A, but with left-handed action. Introduced in 1938; dropped, 1941. Used value, $75 to $85.

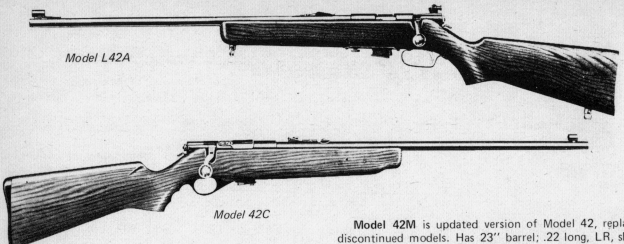

Model L42A

Model 42C

**Model 42B** has same general specs as Model 42A, with minor design improvements and replaced the latter; had micrometer peep sight, with open rear, 5-rd. detachable box magazine. Introduced in 1938; dropped, 1941. Used value, $75 to $80.

**Model 42C** has same specs as Model 42B, except it is sans rear peep sight. Used value, $60 to $65.

**Model 42M** is updated version of Model 42, replacing discontinued models. Has 23" barrel; .22 long, LR, short; 7-rd. detachable box magazine; two-piece Mannlicher-type stock with pistol-grip, cheekpiece; micrometer receiver peep sight, open rear sight, hooded ramp front; sling swivels. Introduced in 1940; dropped, 1950. Used value, $65 to $75.

**Model 42MB** has the same specifications as Model 42; made specifically for Great Britain, British proofmarks. Produced only during World War II. Some collector value. Used value, $100 to $125.

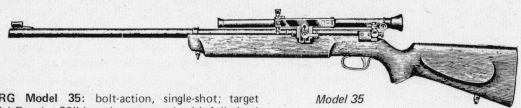

Model 35

**MOSSBERG Model 35:** bolt-action, single-shot; target grade; .22 LR only; 26" barrel, target stock with full pistol grip, beavertail forearm; micrometer rear peep sight; hooded ramp front; sling swivels. Introduced in 1935; dropped, 1937. Used value, $85 to $95.

**Model 35A:** bolt-action, single-shot; .22 LR only; 26" heavy barrel; unchecked target stock with cheekpiece, full pistol grip; micrometer rear peep sight, hood front; sling swivels. Introduced in 1937; dropped, 1938. Used value, $60 to $70.

**Model 35A-LS** is the same as standard Model 35A,

except for substitution of Lyman 17A front sight, Lyman No. 57 rear. Used value, $75 to $85.

**Model 35B** is not a variation of Model 35, as might plausibly be expected. Instead, it has the same specifications as the Model 44B, but is single-shot. Introduced in 1938; dropped, 1940. Used value, $70 to $75.

Model 45 Standard

**MOSSBERG Model 45:** bolt-action, takedown, repeater; .22 LR, long, short; tube magazine holds 15 LR, 18 long, 22 short cartridges; unchecked pistol-grip stock; receiver peep sight, open rear, hooded ramp front; sling swivels. Introduced in 1935; dropped, 1937. Used value, $65 to $75.

**Model 45C** has same specifications as standard Model 45, except that it has no sights; designed for use only with scope sight. Used value, $60 to $65.

**Model 45A** is improved version of discontinued Model

45, with minor design variations. Introduced in 1937; dropped, 1938. Used value, $65 to $75.

**Model 45AC** is the same as the Model 45A, but without receiver peep sight. Used value, $60 to $65.

**Model L45A** is the same as the Model 45A, except for having a left-hand action. Introduced in 1937; dropped, 1938. Used value, $75 to $85.

**Model 45B** has same general specs as Model 45A, but with open rear sight. Introduced in 1938; dropped, 1940. Used value, $60 to $65.

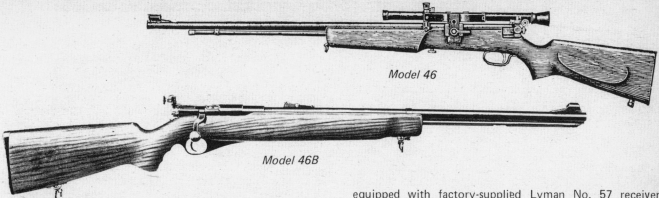

Model 46

Model 46B

**MOSSBERG Model 46:** bolt-action, takedown repeater; .22 LR, long, short; 26" barrel; tube magazine holds 15 LR, 18 long, 22 short cartridges; uncheckered walnut pistol-grip stock with cheekpiece, beavertail forearm; micrometer rear peep sight; hooded ramp front; sling swivels. Introduced in 1935; dropped, 1937. Used value, $65 to $70

**Model 46C** has same specs as standard Model 45, except for heavier barrel. Used value, $75 to $85.

**Model 46A** has virtually the same specifications as discontinued Model 46, but with minor design improvements, detachable sling swivels. Introduced in 1937; dropped, 1938. Used value, $75 to $85.

**Model 46AC** differs from Model 46A only in that it has open rear sight instead of micrometer peep sight. Used value, $60 to $65.

**Model 46A-LS** is the same as the Model 46A, except it is equipped with factory-supplied Lyman No. 57 receiver sight. Used value, $75 to $80.

**Model L-46A-LS** differs from model 46A-LS only in fact that it has left-hand action. Used value, $75 to $85.

**Model 46B** is updated version of Model 46A, but with receiver peep and open rear sights. Introduced in 1938; dropped, 1940. Used value, $60 to $65.

**Model 46BT** differs from Model 46B only in the fact that it has a heavier barrel, target-styled stock. Introduced in 1938; dropped, 1939. Used value, $75 to $85.

**Model 46M** dates back to design of original Model 46, incorporating many of changes in discontinued models. Has 23" barrel; .22 LR, long, short; tube magazine holds 15 LR, 18 long, 22 short cartridges; two-piece Mannlicher-type stock with pistol grip, cheekpiece; micrometer receiver peep sight, open rear, hooded ramp front; sling swivels. Introduced in 1940; dropped, 1952. Used value, $80 to $85.

**MOSSBERG Model 43:** bolt-action repeater; .22 LR only; adjustable trigger, speed lock; 26" barrel, 7-rd. detachable box magazine; target stock with cheekpiece, full pistol grip; beavertail forearm; Lyman No. 57 rear sight, selective aperture front; adjustable front swivel. Introduced in 1937; dropped, 1938. Used value, $75 to $85.

**Model L43** is the same as standard Model 43, except it was made with left-hand action. Used value, $85 to $90.

**Model 43B** is not styled after standard Model 43, but has same specifications as Model 44B, except for substitution of Lyman No. 57 receiver sight, Lyman No. 17A front. Introduced in 1938; dropped, 1939. Used value, $85 to $95.

Model 44B

**MOSSBERG Model 44B:** bolt-action repeater; target configuration; bears little resemblance to standard Model 44; .22 LR only; 26" heavy barrel; 7-rd. detachable box magazine; walnut target stock with cheekpiece, full pistol grip; beavertail forearm; adjustable sling swivels; micrometer receiver peep sight; hooded front. Introduced in 1938; dropped, 1943. Used value, $85 to $95.

Mossberg Model 26B

**MOSSBERG Model 26B:** bolt-action, single-shot; .22 Short, Long, LR; 26" barrel; micrometer peep rear sight, hooded ramp front; uncheckered pistol-grip stock; sling swivels. Manufactured 1938 to 1941. Used value, $30 to $35.

**Model 26C** has same specifications as Model 26B, except for iron sights, no sling swivels. Used value, $25 to $30.

*Model 50*

**MOSSBERG Model 50:** takedown autoloader; .22 LR only; 24" barrel, 15-rd. tube magazine in butt stock; uncheckered walnut pistol-grip stock; finger grooves in grip; open rear sight, hooded ramp front. Introduced in 1939; dropped, 1942. Used value, $65 to $75.

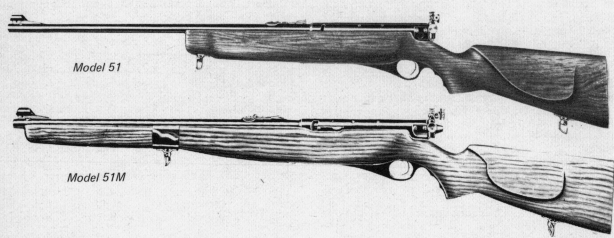

*Model 51*

*Model 51M*

**MOSSBERG Model 51:** has the same general specifications as Model 50, except for addition of receiver peep sight, sling swivels, cheekpiece stock, beavertail forearm. Made only in 1939. Used value, $75 to $85.

**Model 51M** has the same specifications as Model 51, except for substitution of two-piece Mannlicher-style stock, 20" barrel. Introduced in 1946; dropped, 1949. Used value, $85 to $95.

*Model 440US*

**MOSSBERG Model 44US:** bolt-action repeater; redesign of Model 44B, designed primarily for teaching marksmanship to Armed Forces during World War II; .22 LR only; 26" heavy barrel; 7-rd. detachable box magazine; uncheckered walnut target stock; sling swivels; micrometer receiver peep sight, hooded front. Introduced in 1943; dropped, 1948. Collector value. Used value, $100 to $110.

*Model 151M*

**MOSSBERG Model 151M:** takedown autoloader; has same general specifications of Model 51M, with minor mechanical improvements. The action is removable without tools. Introduced in 1946; dropped, 1958. Used value, $65 to $75.

**Model 151K** has same general specifications as Model 151M, except for 24" barrel; is without peep sight, sling swivels. Unchecked stock has Monte Carlo comb, cheekpiece. Introduced in 1950; dropped, 1951. Used value, $60 to $70.

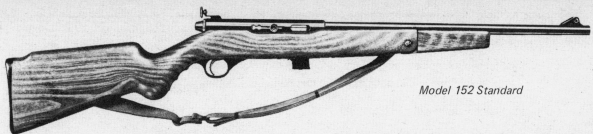

*Model 152 Standard*

**MOSSBERG Model 152:** autoloading carbine; .22 LR only; 18" barrel, 7-rd. detachable box magazine; Monte Carlo pistol-grip stock; hinged forearm swings down to act as forward handgrip; sling swivels are mounted on left side;

rear peep sight, military type ramp front. Introduced in 1948; dropped, 1957. Used value, $75 to $85.

Model 152K has same specifications as Model 152, except peep sight is replaced by open sight. Introduced in 1950; dropped, 1957. Used value, $70 to $75.

**MOSSBERG Model 142:** bolt-action carbine; .22 LR, long, short; 18" barrel, 7-rd. detachable box magazine; walnut Monte Carlo pistol-grip stock; as with Model 52, sling swivels mount on left side of stock, forearm hinges down to act as handgrip; rear peep sight, military style ramp front.

Introduced in 1949; dropped, 1957. Used value, $60 to $65.

Model 142K has same specifications as Model 142, except peep sight is replaced by open sight. Introduced in 1953; dropped, 1957. Used value, $55 to $60.

*Model I44 Standard*

**MOSSBERG Model 144:** bolt-action target model; .22 LR only; 26" heavy barrel; 7-rd. detachable box magazine; pistol-grip target stock; adjustable hand stop; beavertail forearm; sling swivels; micrometer receiver peep sight, hooded front. Introduced in 1949; dropped, 1954. Used

value, $75 to $85.

Model 144LS has the same specs as Model 144, except for substitution of Lyman No. 57MS receiver peep sight, Lyman No. 17A front. Introduced in 1954; still in production. Used value, $85 to $95.

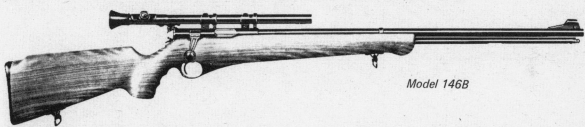

*Model 146B*

**MOSSBERG Model 146B:** bolt-action, takedown repeater; .22 LR, long, short; 26" barrel; tube magazine holds 20 LR, 23 long, 30 short cartridges; uncheckered walnut pistol-grip

stock, Monte Carlo type with cheekpiece; schnabel forearm; micrometer peep sight; hooded front sight; sling swivels. Introduced in 1949; dropped, 1954. Used value, $65 to $70.

**MOSSBERG Model 140K:** bolt-action repeater; .22 LR, long, short; 7-rd. clip magazine; 24½" barrel; uncheckered walnut pistol-grip stock, Monte Carlo with cheekpiece; open rear sight, bead front; sling swivels. Introduced

in 1955; dropped, 1958. Used value, $60 to $65.

Model 140B is target/sporter version of Model 140K; only difference in specifications is substitution of peep rear sight, ramp front. Introduced in 1957; dropped, 1958. Used value, $60 to $65.

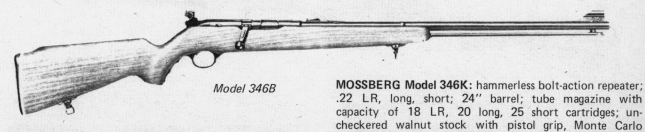

*Model 346B*

**MOSSBERG Model 346K:** hammerless bolt-action repeater; .22 LR, long, short; 24" barrel; tube magazine with capacity of 18 LR, 20 long, 25 short cartridges; uncheckered walnut stock with pistol grip, Monte Carlo comb, cheekpiece; open rear sight, bead front; quick-detachable sling swivels. Introduced in 1958; dropped, 1971. Used value, $60 to $65.

Model 346B has same specifications as Model 346K,

except for hooded ramp front sight, receiver peep with open rear. Introduced in 1958; dropped, 1967. Used value, $65 to $70.

*Model 320 K*

**MOSSBERG Model 320K:** single-shot, hammerless bolt-action; same specifications as Model 346K, except single-shot with drop-in loading platform; automatic safety. Introduced in 1958; dropped, 1960. Used value, $40 to $50.

**Model 320B,** designated by manufacturer as a Boy Scout target model, has the same specifications as the Model 340K, except it is single-shot with automatic safety. Introduced in 1960; dropped, 1971. Used value, $65 to $75.

*Model 340B*

**MOSSBERG Model 340B:** hammerless, bolt-action repeater; target/sporter model is the same as Model 346K, except for clip-type 7-rd. magazine; rear peep sight, hooded ramp front. Introduced in 1958; still in production. Used value, $60 to $65.

**Model 340K** is the same as Model 340B, except for open rear sight, bead front. Introduced in 1958; dropped, 1971.

Used value, $46 to $49.

**340TR** has same general specifications as Model 340K, except for smooth bore; rifled and choke adapters screw on muzzle for shooting bullets or shot. Smooth bore was designed for trap shooting with handtrap. Special device fitted barrel to allow shooter to spring trap. Introduced in 1960; dropped, 1962. Used values, $45 to $50; with Model 1A trap installed, $75 to $85.

**Model 340M** is the same as Model 340K, except for 18½'' barrel, Mannlicher-style stock, sling, sling swivels. Introduced in 1970; dropped, 1971. Used value, $65 to $70.

*Model 342*

**MOSSBERG Model 342:** hammerless bolt-action carbine; .22 LR, long, short; 18'' tapered barrel; 7-rd. clip magazine; uncheckered walnut Monte Carlo pistol-grip stock; two-position forearm that folds down for rest or handgrip; peep

rear sight, bead front; receiver grooved for scope mounts; thumb safety; sling swivels; web sling. Introduced in 1958, still in production. Used value, $55 to $60.

**Model 342K** is the same as Model 342, except with open rear sight. Used value, $50 to $55.

**MOSSBERG Model 350K:** autoloader; .22 LR, long, high-speed short; 23½'' barrel; 7-rd. clip magazine; walnut Monte

Carlo pistol-grip stock; open rear sight, bead front. Introduced in 1958; dropped, 1971. Used value, $60 to $65.

*Model 352K*

**MOSSBERG Model 352:** autoloading carbine; .22 LR, long, short; 18'' barrel; uncheckered walnut Monte Carlo pistol-grip stock; two-position Tenite forearm extension folds down for rest or handgrip; peep rear sight, bead front; sling

swivels, web sling. Introduced in 1958; dropped, 1971. Used value, $60 to $65.

**Model 352K** is the same as Model 352, except with open rear sight. Used value, $55 to $60.

Model 640KS

**MOSSBERG Model 640K:** hammerless bolt-action; .22 rimfire magnum only; 24" barrel, 5-rd. detachable clip magazine; walnut Monte Carlo pistol-grip stock, with cheek-

**MOSSBERG Model 620K:** same as Model 640K, except is

piece; open rear sight, bead front; sling swivels; impressed checkering on pistol grip, forearm. Introduced in 1959; still in production. Used value, $60 to $65.

**Model 640KS** is the same as Model 640K, but with select walnut stock, checkered pistol grip, forearm; gold-plated front sight, rear sight elevator and trigger. Dropped, 1974. Used value, $70 to $75.

single-shot. Introduced in 1958; dropped, 1974. Used value, $40 to $45.

Model 351C

**MOSSBERG Model 351K:** autoloading sporter; .22 LR only; 24" barrel; 15-rd. tube magazine in butt stock; walnut Monte Carlo pistol-grip stock; open rear sight, bead front.

Introduced in 1960; dropped, 1971. Used value, $55 to $60.

**Model 351C** carbine is the same as Model 351K, except for 18½" barrel, straight Western-type carbine stock, with barrel band; sling swivels. Introduced in 1965; dropped, 1971. Used value, $55 to $60.

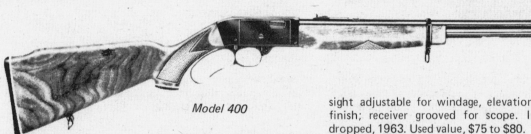

Model 400

**MOSSBERG Model 400 Palomino:** lever action repeater; .22 LR, long, short; 24" barrel; tube magazine has capacity of 15 LR, 17 long, 20 short cartridges; open notch rear

sight adjustable for windage, elevation; bead front; blued finish; receiver grooved for scope. Introduced in 1959, dropped, 1963. Used value, $75 to $80.

**Model 402 Palomino** has same specs as Model 400 except for 18½" or 20" barrel; barrel band on forearm; magazine holds two less rounds in specified .22 RF lengths. Manufactured 1961 to 1971. Used value, $60 to $65.

Model 800

**MOSSBERG Model 800:** bolt-action; .222 Remington, .22-250, .243 Winchester, .308 Winchester; 4-rd. magazine in all but .222; 3 rds. for that caliber; 22" barrel; folding leaf rear sight, ramp front; checkered pistol-grip Monte Carlo stock, forearm; cheekpiece; sling swivels. Manufactured 1967 to 1980. Used value, $140 to $150.

**Model 800VT** for varmint/target shooting, has same specs as standard rifle, except for 24" heavy barrel, no

**MOSSBERG Model 810:** bolt-action; .270 Winchester, .30/06, 7mm Remington magnum, .338 Winchester magnum; 22" barrel in standard calibers, 24" in magnum chamberings; detachable box magazine or internal magazine, hinged floorplate; 4-rd. magazine in standard

sights; chambered for .222 Remington, .22-250, .243 Winchester. Manufactured 1968 to 1980. Used value, $140 to $150.

**Model 800M** has same specs as standard 800, except for Mannlicher-type stock, flat bolt handle, 20" barrel; chambered for .22-250, .243 Winchester, .308 Winchester. Manufactured 1969 to 1972. Used value, $170 to $180.

**Model 800D Super Grade** has same general specs as standard model, except for roll-over comb, cheekpiece; rosewood forend tip, pistol-grip cap; chambered for .22-250, .243 Winchester, .308 Winchester. Manufactured 1970 to 1973. Used value, $170 to $180.

calibers, 3 rds. for magnums; leaf rear sight, ramp front; checkered pistol-grip stock, forearm; Monte Carlo comb, cheekpiece; pistol grip cap, sling swivels. Manufactured 1970 to 1980. Used values, standard calibers, $150 to $160; magnum calibers, $160 to $170.

**MOSSBERG Model 430:** autoloader; .22 LR only; 24″ barrel, 18-rd. tube magazine; walnut Monte Carlo stock; checkered pistol grip, forearm; open rear sight, bead front. Introduced in 1970; dropped, 1971. Used value, $65 to $70.

**MOSSBERG Model 432:** autoloading carbine; same as Model 430, except for unchecked straight-grip carbine stock, forearm; barrel band; sling swivels. 15-rd. tube magazine. Introduced in 1970; dropped, 1971. Used value, $70 to $75.

**MOSSBERG Model 321K:** bolt-action, single-shot; .22 LR, long, short; 24″ barrel; hardwood stock with walnut finish; cheekpiece; checkered pistol grip, forearm; hammerless bolt-action with drop-in loading platform; automatic safety; adjustable open rear sight, ramp front. Introduced in 1972; still in production. Used value, $50 to $55.
**Model 321B** is the same as Model 321K, except with S330 peep sight with ¼-minute click adjustments. Dropped, 1976. Used value, $55 to $60.

*Model 333*

**MOSSBERG Model 333:** autoloader; .22 LR; 20″ barrel; 15-rd. tubular magazine; open rear sight, ramp front; checkered pistol-grip Monte Carlo stock, forearm; barrel band; sling swivels. Manufactured 1972 to 1973. Used value, $60 to $65.

*Model 341*

**MOSSBERG Model 341:** bolt-action; .22 LR, long, short; 24″ barrel; 7-rd. clip magazine; walnut Monte Carlo stock with checkered pistol grip, forearm; plastic butt plate with white line spacer; open rear sight adjustable for windage, elevation; bead post front; sliding side safety. Introduced in 1972; dropped, 1976. Used value, $55 to $60.

*Model 353*

**MOSSBERG Model 353:** autoloader; updated version of Model 352K; specifications are primarily the same; pistol grip, forearm are checkered; receiver is grooved for scope mount. Introduced in 1972; still in production. Used value, $65 to $70.

*Model 472 Carbine (straight grip)*

**MOSSBERG Model 472 Carbine:** lever-action; .30-30, .35 Remington; 6-rd. tubular magazine; 20″ barrel; open rear sight, ramp front; pistol grip or straight stock; barrel band on forearm; sling swivels on pistol-grip style, saddle ring on straight-stock model. Manufactured 1972 to 1980. Used value, $110 to $120.
**Model 472 Rifle** has same specs as carbine except for 24″ barrel, 5-rd. magazine; pistol-grip stock only. Manufactured 1974 to 1976. Used value, $110 to $120.
**Model 472 Brush Gun** has same specs as 472 Carbine, except for 18″ barrel; .30-30 only, 5-rd. magazine; straight

Model 472 "One in Five Thousand" (right side)

stock. Manufactured 1974 to 1976. Used value, $105 to $110.

**Model 472 "1 of 5000"** has same specs as 472 Brush Gun, except for etched frontier scenes on receiver; gold-plated trigger; brass saddle ring, buttplate, barrel bands; selected walnut stock, forearm; limited edition, numbered 1 through 5000. Manufactured 1974. Used value, $185 to $200.

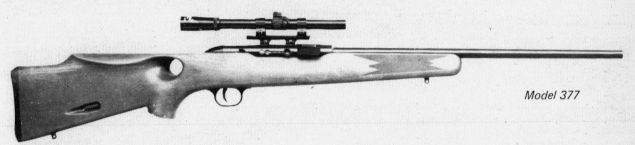

Model 377

**MOSSBERG Model 377:** autoloader; .22 LR; 15-rd. tubular magazine; advertised as the Plinkster; 20" barrel; moulded polystyrene thumbhole stock, roll-over cheekpiece; Monte Carlo comb; no open sights, comes with 4X scope mounted. Introduced 1977. Used value, $45 to $50.

# NAVY ARMS

Model 66

**NAVY ARMS Model 66:** lever-action; reproduction of Winchester Model 1866; .22 short, long, LR; polished brass frame, butt plate, other parts blued; full-length tube magazine; walnut straight-grip stock, forearm; barrel band; open leaf rear sight, blade front. Introduced in 1966; still in production. Used value, $149.50 to $157.50.

**Model 66 Carbine** has same specs as Model 66 rifle, except for 19" barrel, 10-rd. magazine; carbine forearm, barrel band. Introduced 1967, still in production. Used value, $135 to $145.

**Model 66 Trapper** has same specs as carbine version, except for 16½" barrel, magazine holds two rounds less. Used value, $135 to $145.

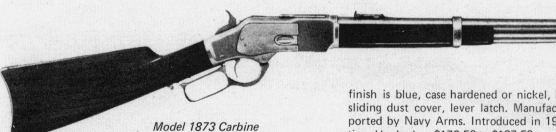

Model 1873 Carbine

**NAVY ARMS Model 1873:** lever-action; .357 magnum, .44-40; barrels, 24" octagon, 20" round carbine, 16½" trapper style; walnut stock, forearm; step adjustable rear sight, blade front; designed after the Winchester '73 model; finish is blue, case hardened or nickel, last in .44-40 only; sliding dust cover, lever latch. Manufactured in Italy; imported by Navy Arms. Introduced in 1973; still in production. Used value, $176.50 to $187.50.

**Model 1873 Carbine** has same specs as rifle, except for 19" round barrel, 10-rd. magazine, carbine forearm, barrel band. Introduced 1973, still in production. Used value, $155 to $165.

**Model 1873 Trapper** has same specs as carbine, except for 16½" barrel, 8-rd. magazine. Used value, $155 to $165.

*Navy Arms Revolving Carbine*

**NAVY ARMS Revolving Carbine:** .357 magnum, .44-40, .45 Colt; 6-rd. cylinder; 20'' barrel; action based on Remington Model 1874 revolver; open rear sight, blade front; straight-grip stock, brass buttplate, trigger guard. Manufactured in Italy. Introduced 1968, still in production. Used value, $130 to $140.

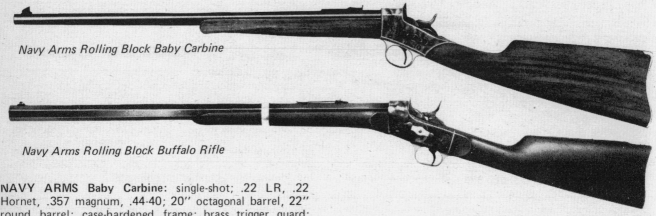

*Navy Arms Rolling Block Baby Carbine*

*Navy Arms Rolling Block Buffalo Rifle*

**NAVY ARMS Baby Carbine:** single-shot; .22 LR, .22 Hornet, .357 magnum, .44-40; 20'' octagonal barrel, 22'' round barrel; case-hardened frame; brass trigger guard; based on Remington rolling-block action; open rear sight, blade front; uncheckered straight-grip stock, forearm; brass buttplate. Introduced 1968, still in production only in .22 LR and .357; other cals. dropped. Used value, $100 to $110.

**Rolling Block Buffalo Rifle** has same general design as Baby Carbine; .444 Marlin, .45-70, .50-70; 26'', 30'' half or full octagonal barrel; open rear sight, blade front; brass barrel band. Introduced 1971, still in production. Used value, $110 to $120.

**Rolling Block Creedmore Model** has same specs as Buffalo Rifle, except for 28'', 30'' heavy half or full octagon barrel; .45-70, .50-70; Creedmore tang peep sight. Used value, $120 to $130.

**Rolling Block Buffalo Carbine** has same specs as Buffalo Rifle, except for 18'' barrel. Used value, $110 to $120.

*Navy Arms Martini Target Rifle*

**NAVY ARMS Martini:** single-shot; .444 Marlin, .45-70; 26'', 30'' half or full octagon barrel; Creedmore tang peep sight, open middle sight, blade front; checkered pistol-grip stock, Schnabel forend, cheekpiece. Introduced 1972, importation dropped 1978. Used value, $150 to $170.

*Navy Arms 45-70 Mauser Rifle*

**NAVY ARMS .45-70 Mauser:** bolt-action; .45-70 Government; 3-rd. magazine; 24'', 26'' barrel; built on Siamese Mauser action; open rear sight, ramp front; hand-checkered Monte Carlo stock. Introduced 1973, still in production. Used value, $110 to $120.

**.45-70 Mauser Carbine** has same specs as rifle, except for 18'' barrel, straight stock. Used value, $110 to $120.

# NOBLE

**NOBLE Model 33:** slide-action hammerless repeater; .22 LR, long, short; 24" barrel; tube magazine holds 15 LR, 17 long, 21 short cartridges; Tenite stock, grooved wood slide handle; open rear sight, bead front. Introduced in 1949;

dropped, 1953. Used value, $40 to $45.

**Model 33A** has the same general specifications as the Model 33, except that the stock and slide handle are of hardwood. Introduced in 1953, as replacement for Model 33. Dropped, 1955. Used value, $50 to $55.

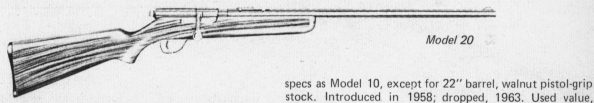

*Model 236*

**NOBLE Model 236:** slide-action hammerless repeater; .22 LR, long, short; 24" barrel; tube magazine holds 15 LR, 17 long, 21 short cartridges; hardwood pistol-grip stock,

grooved wood slide handle; open rear sight, ramp front. Introduced in 1951; dropped, 1973. Used value, $50 to $55.

*Model 10*

**NOBLE Model 10:** bolt-action, single-shot; .22 LR, long, short; 24" barrel; uncheckered hardwood pistol-grip stock;

open rear sight, bead front. Introduced in 1955; dropped, 1958. Used value, $25 to $35.

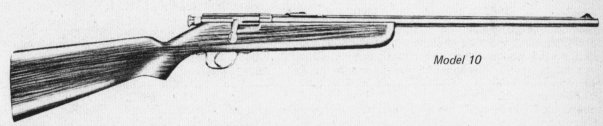

*Model 20*

**NOBLE Model 20:** bolt-action, single-shot; same general

specs as Model 10, except for 22" barrel, walnut pistol-grip stock. Introduced in 1958; dropped, 1963. Used value, $25 to $35.

*Model 222*

**NOBLE Model 222:** bolt-action, single-shot; .22 LR, long,

short. Barrel, receiver milled as integral unit; uncheckered hardwood pistol-grip stock; interchangeable peep and V-notch rear sight, ramp front; scope mounting base. Introduced in 1958; dropped, 1971. Used value, $30 to $35.

*Model 275*

**NOBLE Model 275:** lever-action, hammerless; .22 LR, long, short; 24" barrel; tube magazine holds 15 LR, 17 long, 21

short cartridges; uncheckered hardwood full pistol-grip stock; open rear sight, ramp front. Introduced in 1958; dropped, 1971. Used value, $60 to $65.

# REMINGTON

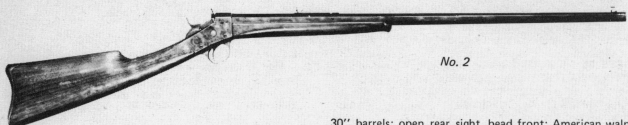

*No. 2*

**REMINGTON No. 2:** single-shot; .22, .25, .32, .38, .44 rimfire or center-fire; rolling block action; 24", 26", 28",

30" barrels; open rear sight, bead front; American walnut straight grip stock, Schnabel forearm. Manufactured 1873 to 1910. Collector value. Used values: .22 through .32 calibers, $130 to $145; .38 and .44 calibers, $275 to $290.

*No. 3*

**REMINGTON No. 3:** single-shot; .22 WCF, .22 Extra Long, .25-20 Stevens, .25-21 Stevens. .25-25 Stevens, .32 WCF, .32 Ballard & Marlin, .32-40 Remington, .38 WCF, .38-40 Remington, .38-50 Remington, .38-55 Ballard & Marlin, .40-60 Ballard & Marlin, .40-60 WCF, .45-60 Remington, .40-82 WCF, .45-70 Government, .45-90 WCF; falling-block action, side lever; 28", 30" half or full-octagon barrel; open

rear sight, blade front; hand-checkered pistol-grip stock. Manufactured 1880 to 1911. Collector value. Used value, $400 to $450.

**No. 3 High Power** has same general specs, action as standard No. 3; .30-30, .30-40, .32 Special, .32-40, .38-55, .38-72 high-power cartridges; 28", 30" barrels; open rear sight, bead front; hand-checkered pistol-grip stock, forearm. Manufactured 1893 to 1907. Collector value. Used values: .38-55 and .38-72, $500 to $525; other calibers, $375 to $400.

*Lee Sporter*

**REMINGTON-Lee Sporter:** bolt-action; 6mm USN, .30-30, .30-40, 7mm Mauser, 7.65 Mauser, .32 Remington, .32-40, .35 Remington, .38-55, .38-72, .405 Winchester, .43 Spanish, .44-77 Sharps, .45-70, .45-90; 5-rd. detachable box magazine; 24", 26" barrel; open rear sight, bead front;

hand-checkered American walnut pistol-grip stock. Collector value. Manufactured 1886 to 1906. Used value, $425 to $450.

**Deluxe Sporter** has same specifications, except for half-octagon barrel, Lyman sights, deluxe walnut stock. Collector value. Manufactured 1886 to 1906. Used value, $650 to $700.

*Baby Carbine*

**REMINGTON Baby Carbine:** single-shot; .44 Winchester, 7x57 Mauser; 20" barrel; rolling-block action; open rear sight, blade front; uncheckered American walnut carbine-

style straight stock, forearm; barrel band. Manufactured 1883 to 1910. Collector value. Used value, $325 to $350.

No. 4

**REMINGTON No. 4:** single-shot, rolling-block action; solid frame or takedown; .22 short, long, LR; 25 Stevens rimfire; .32 short, long rimfire; has 22½" octagonal barrel; 24" barrel available for .32 rimfire only; blade front sight, open rear; plain walnut stock, forearm. Introduced in 1890; dropped, 1933. (1890 to 1901 solid frame; 1901 to 1926 first takedown with lever on right side; 1926 to 1933 second takedown with large screw head.) Used value, $145 to $185.

No. 4S

**REMINGTON No. 4S:** Also known as Model 22 military single-shot rifle; rolling-block action; in .22 short or .22 LR only; 26" barrel; blade front sight, military-type rear; military stock, including stacking swivel, sling; bayonet stud on barrel; bayonet, scabbard originally included. Prior to the time the Boy Scouts of America down-graded militarism for fear of being compared with the Hitler Youth Movement, this was called the Boy Scout rifle and was the official rifle of the BSA. Introduced in 1913; dropped, 1933. Collector value. Used value, $225 to $250.

No. 5

**REMINGTON No. 5:** single-shot; 7mm Mauser, .30-30, .30-40 Krag, .303 British, .32-40, .32 Special, .38-55 high-power cartridges; 24", 26", 28" barrels; rolling-block action; open sporting rear sight, blade front; uncheckered straight-grip stock. Some collector value. Manufactured 1902 to 1918. Used value, $300 to $325.

**No. 5 Military,** also designated as Model 1897 and Model 1902, has same specs as standard No. 5 except for 30" barrel, chambering for 8mm Lebel, 7mm Mauser, 7.62 Russian. Used value, $200 to $215.

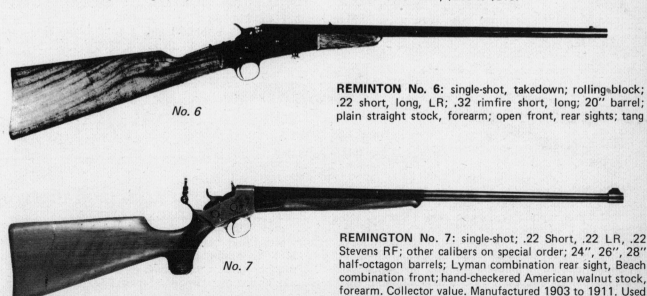

No. 6

No. 7

**REMINTON No. 6:** single-shot, takedown; rolling block; .22 short, long, LR; .32 rimfire short, long; 20" barrel; plain straight stock, forearm; open front, rear sights; tang

**REMINGTON No. 7:** single-shot; .22 Short, .22 LR, .22 Stevens RF; other calibers on special order; 24", 26", 28" half-octagon barrels; Lyman combination rear sight, Beach combination front; hand-checkered American walnut stock, forearm. Collector value. Manufactured 1903 to 1911. Used value, $425 to $450.

*Model 8A*

**REMINGTON Model 8A:** autoloader; takedown; .25, .30, .32, .35 Rem. calibers; detachable box magazine with 5 rd. capacity; 22" barrel; plain walnut straight stock, forearm; bead front sight, open rear. Introduced in 1906; dropped, 1936. Used value, $250 to $275.

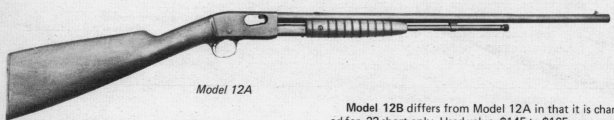

*Model 12A*

**REMINGTON Model 12A:** hammerless, takedown slide action; .22 short, long, LR; tube magazine holds 15 shorts, 12 longs, 10 LR; 22" barrel, bead front sight, open rear; uncheckered straight stock; grooved slide handle. Introduced in 1909; dropped, 1936. Used value, $150 to $175.

**Model 12B** differs from Model 12A in that it is chambered for .22 short only. Used value, $145 to $165.

**Model 12C** is the same as standard Model 12A, except for pistol-grip stock, octagonal barrel. Used value, $165 to $185.

**Model 12CS** is the same as Model 12C, except it is chambered for .22 WRF; magazine holds 12 rds. Used value, $145 to $165.

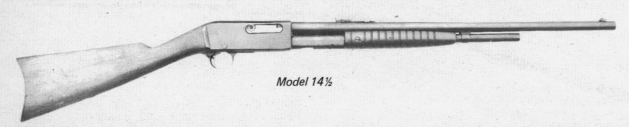

*Model 14½*

**REMINGTON Model 14A:** center-fire slide-action repeater; hammerless, takedown; .25, .30, .32 Rem. calibers; 5-rd. tube magazine; 22" barrel, bead front sight, open rear; uncheckered walnut straight stock, grooved slide handle. Introduced in 1912; dropped, 1935. Used value, $200 to $225.

**Model 14R carbine;** same as standard Model 14A, except for 18" barrel. Used value, $225 to $250.

**Model 14½ rifle** is same as Model 14A, except in .38/40, .44/40 calibers; 11-shot full-length tube magazine; 22½" barrel. Introduced in 1912; dropped, 1925. Used value, $225 to $250.

**Model 14½ carbine** is same as 14½ rifle, except for 9-rd. magazine, 18½" barrel. Used value, $250 to $300.

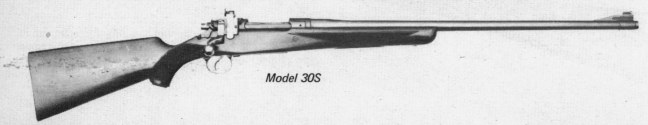

*Model 30S*

**REMINGTON Model 30A:** bolt-action center-fire; modified commercial version of 1917 Enfield action; early models had 24" barrel; military-type double-stage trigger, schnabel forearm tip; later versions have 22" barrel. In .25, .30, .32, .35 Rem., 7mm Mauser, .30/06; 5-rd. box magazine; checkered walnut stock, forearm on later versions, uncheckered on earlier with finger groove in forearm; pistol grip; bead front sight, open rear. Introduced in 1921; dropped, 1940. Used value, $245 to $265.

**Model 30R carbine** is same as Model 30A, except for 20" barrel, plain stock. Used value, $265 to $275.

**Model 30S sporting model** has same action as 30A; .257 Roberts, 7mm Mauser, .30/06; 5-shot box magazine, 24" barrel; bead front sight, No. 48 Lyman receiver sight; has long full forearm, high comb checkered stock. Introduced in 1930; dropped, 1940. Used value, $300 to $325.

*Model 33*

**REMINGTON Model 33:** takedown bolt-action single-shot; .22 short, long, LR; 24" barrel; bead front sight, open rear; unchecked pistol-grip stock, grooved forearm. Introduced in 1931; dropped, 1936. Used value, $65 to $75.

**REMINGTON Model 24A:** takedown autoloader; .22 short only or .22 LR only; tube magazine in butt stock carries 10 LR or 15 short cartridges; 21" barrel; bead front sight, open rear; unchecked walnut stock, forearm. Introduced, 1922; dropped 1935. Used value, $135 to $155.

**Model 33 NRA Junior** target model is same as standard Model 33, except for 7/8" sling, swivels; Patridge front sight, Lyman peep style rear. Used value, $80 to $95.

**Remington Model 24A Speedmaster** replaces standard Model 24A; introduced in 1935; dropped, 1951. Has same general configuration as original model, but with 24" barrel. Used value, $165 to $175.

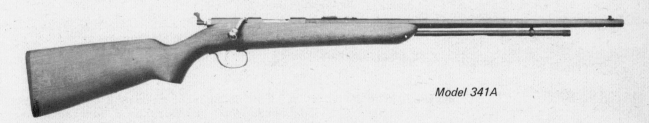

*Model 25A*

**REMINGTON Model 25A:** slide-action repeater; hammerless, takedown; .25/20, .32/20; 10-rd. tube magazine; 24" barrel; blade front sight, open rear; unchecked walnut pistol-grip stock, grooved slide handle. Introduced in 1923; dropped, 1936. Used value, $135 to $150.

**Model 25R carbine** is same as standard Model 25A, except for 18" barrel, 6-rd. magazine; straight stock. Used value, $160 to $175.

*Model 34 Standard*

**REMINGTON Model 34:** bolt-action, takedown repeater; .22 short, long, LR; tube magazine holds 15 LR, 17 longs or 22 shorts; 24" barrel; bead front sight, open rear; unchecked hardwood pistol-grip stock, grooved forearm. In-

troduced in 1932; dropped, 1936. Used value, $110 to $125.

**Model 34 NRA** target model is the same as standard Model 34, except for Patridge front sight, Lyman peep in rear; swivels, 7/8" sling. Used value, $125 to $150.

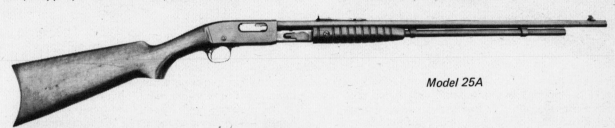

*Model 341A*

**REMINGTON Model 341A:** takedown bolt-action repeater; .22 short, long, LR; tube magazine holds 15 LR, 17 longs, 22 shorts; 27" barrel; bead front sight, open rear; unchecked hardwood pistol-grip stock. Introduced in 1936; dropped, 1940. Used value, $85 to $100.

**Model 341P,** for target shooting, is same as standard

Model 341A, except for hooded front sight, peep rear. Used value, $95 to $115.

**Model 341SB** is same as Model 341A, except it is smoothbore for use with .22 shot cartridges. Used value, $80 to $95.

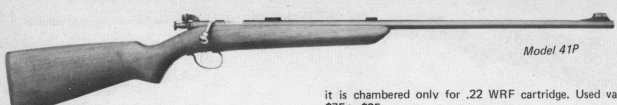

*Model 41P*

REMINGTON Model 41A Targetmaster: takedown bolt-action single-shot; .22 short, long, LR; 27″ barrel; bead front sight; open rear; uncheckered pistol-grip stock. Introduced in 1936; dropped, 1940. Used value, $75 to $95.

Model 41AS differs from 41A Targetmaster only in that it is chambered only for .22 WRF cartridge. Used value, $75 to $85.

Model 41P is same as standard Model 41A, except that it has hooded front sight, peep-type rear. Used value, $85 to $95.

Model 41SB is same as standard 41A Targetmaster, except it is smoothbore only for .22 short cartridges. Used value, $65 to $85.

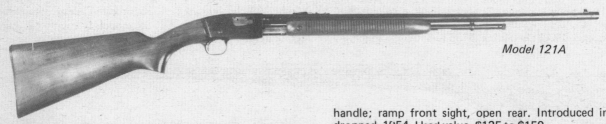

*Model 121A*

REMINGTON Model 121A Fieldmaster: slide-action take-down, hammerless repeater; .22 short, long, LR; tube magazine holds 20 shorts, 15 longs, 14 LR; 24″ round barrel; uncheckered pistol-grip stock, grooved semi-beavertail slide handle; ramp front sight, open rear. Introduced in 1936; dropped, 1954. Used value, $125 to $150.

Model 121S is same as Model 121A, except chambered for .22 WRF; magazine holds 12 rds. Used value, $125 to $150.

Model 121SB; same as Model 121A, except smoothbore for use of .22 shot cartridge. Used value, $110 to $125.

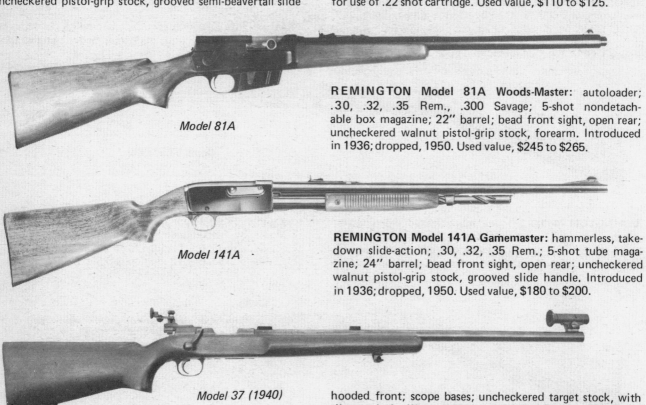

*Model 81A*

REMINGTON Model 81A Woods-Master: autoloader; .30, .32, .35 Rem., .300 Savage; 5-shot nondetachable box magazine; 22″ barrel; bead front sight, open rear; uncheckered walnut pistol-grip stock, forearm. Introduced in 1936; dropped, 1950. Used value, $245 to $265.

*Model 141A*

REMINGTON Model 141A Gamemaster: hammerless, take-down slide-action; .30, .32, .35 Rem.; 5-shot tube magazine; 24″ barrel; bead front sight, open rear; uncheckered walnut pistol-grip stock, grooved slide handle. Introduced in 1936; dropped, 1950. Used value, $180 to $200.

*Model 37 (1940)*

REMINGTON Model 37 Rangemaster: produced in two variations; the first was produced from 1937 to 1940; the second from 1940 to 1954; 1937 model is .22 LR only; 5-shot box magazine; single-shot adapter supplied as standard; 22″ heavy barrel; Remington peep rear sight, hooded front; scope bases; unchecked target stock, with sling, swivels. When introduced, barrel band held forward section of stock to barrel; with modification of forearm, barrel band was eliminated in 1938. Used values, without sights, $250 to $275; with factory sights, $275 to $300.

Model 37 of 1940 has same basic configuration as original; changes include Miracle trigger mechanism; high comb stock, beavertail forearm. Used values, without sights, $275 to $325; with factory sights, $325 to $375.

*Model 510A*

**REMINGTON Model 510A:** takedown bolt-action single-shot; .22 short, long, LR; 25" barrel; bead front sight; open rear; uncheckered walnut pistol-grip stock. Introduced in 1939; dropped, 1962. Used value, $50 to $65.

**Model 510P** is same as standard Model 510, except for Patridge-design front sight on ramp, peep rear. Used value, $65 to $85.

**Model 510SB** is same as standard model, except for being smoothbore for .22 shot cartridge; shotgun bead front sight, no rear sight. Used value, $55 to $65.

**Model 510X** was introduced in 1964; dropped, 1966. Had aspirations to be a target rifle; differed from original model only in improved sights. Used value, $75 to $90.

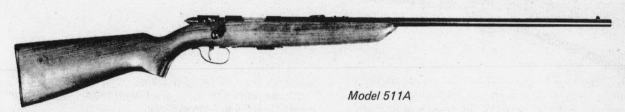

*Model 511A*

**REMINGTON Model 511A:** takedown bolt-action repeater; .22 short, long, LR; 6-rd. detachable box magazine; 25" barrel; bead front sight; open rear; uncheckered pistol-grip stock. Introduced in 1939; dropped, 1962. Used value, $80 to $95.

**Model 511P** is same as standard model, except for peep sight on rear of receiver; Patridge-type ramp blade front. Used value, $80 to $100.

**Model 511X** same as Model 511A, except for clip-type magazine; improved sight. Introduced in 1953; dropped, 1966. Used value, $90 to $115.

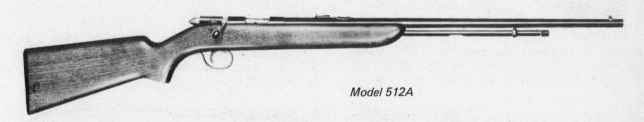

*Model 512A*

**REMINGTON Model 512A:** takedown bolt-action repeater; .22 short, long, LR; tube magazine holds 22 shorts, 17 longs, 15 LR; 25" barrel; bead front sight, open rear; uncheckered pistol-grip stock; semi-beavertail forearm. Introduced in 1940; dropped, 1962. Used value, $80 to $95.

**Model 512P** is same as standard 512A, except for blade front sight on ramp, peep rear. Used value, $80 to $95.

**Model 512X**, same as standard Model 512A, except for improved sight. Introduced in 1964; dropped, 1966. Used value, $100 to $115.

*Model 513TR*

**REMINGTON Model 513TR Matchmaster:** bolt-action target rifle; .22 LR only; 6-shot detachable box magazine; 27" barrel; uncheckered target stock; sling, swivels; globe front sight, Redfield No. 70 peep type rear. Introduced in 1941; dropped, 1969. Used value, $150 to $165.

**Model 513S** differs from 513TR Matchmaster in that it has checkered sporter-style stock; Patridge-type front sight, Marble open rear. Introduced in 1941; dropped, 1956. Used value, $175 to $185.

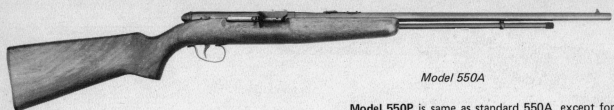

*Model 550A*

**REMINGTON Model 550A:** autoloader; features floating chamber for interchangeable use of .22 short, long, LR ammo; tube magazine holds 22 shorts, 17 longs, 15 LR; 24" barrel; unchecked hardwood pistol-grip stock; bead front sight, open rear. Introduced in 1941; dropped, 1971. Used value, $100 to $115.

**Model 550P** is same as standard 550A, except for blade front sight on ramp, peep-type rear. Used value, $115 to $125.

**Model 550-2G** was originally listed as Gallery Special; same as standard model, except for fired shell deflector; screw eye for counter chain; 22" barrel. Used value, $100 to $120.

*Model 720A*

**REMINGTON Model 720A:** bolt-action; .30/06, .270 Win., .257 Roberts; 5-rd. box magazine; 22" barrel; action is modification of Model 1917 Enfield; checkered pistol-grip stock; bead front sight on ramp, open rear; made only in 1941, as factory facilities were converted to wartime pro-

duction. Used value, $265 to $300.

**Model 720R** is the same as standard 720A, except for 20" barrel. Used value, $265 to $280.

**Model 720S** is same as Model 720A, except for 24" barrel. Used value, $275 to $300.

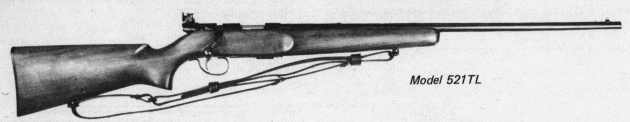

*Model 521TL*

**REMINGTON Model 521TL:** called the Junior Target Model, this is a takedown bolt-action repeater; .22 LR only; 6-rd. detachable box magazine; 25" barrel; unchecked tar-

get stock; came with sling, swivels; blade front sight, Lyman 57RS rear peep type. Introduced in 1947; dropped, 1969. Used value, $115 to $130.

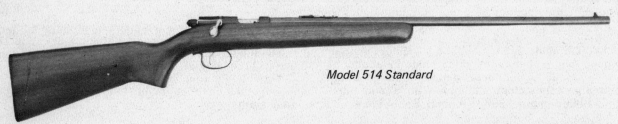

*Model 514 Standard*

**REMINGTON Model 514:** bolt-action single-shot; .22 short, long, LR; 24" barrel; unchecked pistol-grip stock; black plastic butt plate; bead front sight, open rear. Intro-

duced in 1948; dropped, 1971. Used value, $50 to $65.

**Model 514P** is the same as standard 514, except for ramp front sight, peep type in rear. Used value, $60 to $75.

*Model 721A H&H Magnum*

**REMINGTON Model 721A:** standard grade bolt-action; .30/06, .270 Win.; 24" barrel, 4-rd. box magazine; bead front sight on ramp, open rear; unchecked walnut sporter

stock. Introduced in 1948; dropped, 1962. Used value, $200 to $225.

**Model 721ADL** differs from standard grade 721A in that

the wood has deluxe checkering on stock and forearm. Used value, $225 to $250.

Model 721BDL is the same as the Model 721ADL, except that the checkered stock is from more select wood. Used value, $250 to $275.

Model 721 Remington was also offered in .300 Holland & Holland, in all variations. In the case of the 721A Magnum, the changes were a heavy 26" barrel, 3-shot magazine and addition of a recoil pad. Used value, $260 to $300.

Model 721ADL H&H Magnum boasted checkering on walnut stock. Used value, $300 to $325.

.300 H&H Model 721 BDL, with select walnut, has a used value of $325 to $350.

*Model 722A*

REMINGTON Model 722A: same as Model 721 series, except for shorter action; .257 Roberts, .300 Savage, .308 Win. Introduced in 1948; dropped, 1962. Used value, $175 to $200.

Model 722ADL, so-called deluxe grade, is same as standard model, except for checkered stock. Used value, $225 to $250.

Model 722BDL, termed the deluxe special grade, has same checkering as ADL, but has better wood. Used value, $250 to $275.

*Model 722A 222*

REMINGTON Model 722A 222: this series of rifles differs from standard 722A primarily in the fact that it is in .222 Rem.; has 5-shot magazine and 26" barrel. Introduced in 1950; dropped, 1962. Used value, $225 to $235.

Model 722ADL 222 is the same as 722A 222, except for deluxe checkering on walnut stock. Used value, $225 to $250.

Model 722BDL 222 differs from ADL configuration only in that walnut stock is of better grade. Used value, $250 to $275.

REMINGTON Model 722A 244: has same specs as Model 722A 222, except it is .244 Rem. only and magazine capacity is 4 rds. Introduced in 1955; dropped, 1962. Used value, $215 to $225.

Model 722ADL 244 differs from standard model only in checkering on pistol grip, forearm. Used value, $225 to $250.

Model 722BDL 244 is the same as the ADL configuratopn except for better grade walnut. Used value, $250 to $275.

*Model 760 Standard*

REMINGTON Model 760: hammerless slide-action repeater; made originally in .223 Rem., 6mm Rem., .243 Win., .257 Roberts, .270 Win., .30/06, .300 Savage, .308 Win., .35 Rem. Since dropped are .223, .257 Roberts, .300 Savage, .35 Rem. Models from mid-60s to early 70s had impressed checkering; others are hand checkered on pistol grip, slide handle; early versions had no checkering on stock, had grooved slide handle; 4-shot magazine; 22" barrel; bead front sight on ramp, open rear. Introduced in 1952; dropped, 1980. Used value, $165 to $185.

Model 760 carbine; same as standard Model 760, except in .308 Win., .30/06 only; 18½" barrel. Used value, $175 to $200.

Model 760 ADL is same as standard Model 760, except

for deluxe checkered stock, grip cap, sling swivels, choice of standard or high comb. Used value, $175 to $195.

**Model 760 BDL** is same as standard model, except for basket-weave checkering on pistol grip, forearm; black forearm tip; early versions available in right or left-hand styles; .308 Win., .30/06, .270 Win.; Monte Carlo cheekpiece. Used value, $200 to $225; **760BDL(D)**, with fine checkering, engraving, $650 to $700; **760BDL(F)**, with fine checkering, top grade wood, engraving, $1350 to $1500; **760BDL(F)** with gold inlays, $2600 to $2800.

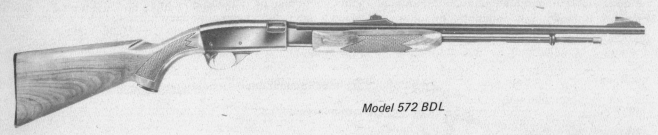

*Model 572 BDL*

**REMINGTON Model 572:** slide-action; .22 rimfire; tube magazine holding 20 short, 17 long, 14 LR cartridges; 24" round tapered barrel; walnut pistol-grip stock, grooved slide handle; step adjustable rear sight, bead post front; cross-bolt safety; receiver grooved for tip-off scope mount. Introduced in 1955; still in production. Used value, $80 to $85.

**Model 572 BDL Deluxe** is same as Model 572, except for pistol-grip cap, RKW wood finish, checkered grip, slide handle; adjustable rear sight, ramp front. Used value, $100 to $110.

**Model 572 SB** is same as Model 572, except has smooth-bore barrel for .22 LR shot cartridge. Used value, $90 to $100.

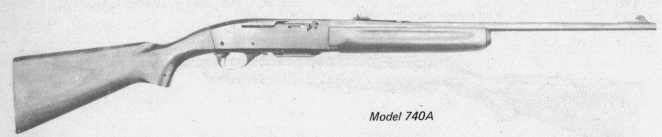

*Model 740A*

**REMINGTON Model 740A:** gas-operated autoloader; .308 Win., .30/06; 4-rd. detachable box magazine; 22" barrel, uncheckered pistol-grip stock; grooved semi-beavertail forearm; ramp front sight, open rear. Introduced in 1955; dropped, 1960. Used value, $175 to $200.

**Model 740ADL** is same as standard model, except for deluxe checkered stock, grip cap, sling swivels, standard or high comb. Used value, $200 to $225.

**Model 740BDL** is same as ADL model, except for selected walnut stock. Used value, $235 to $250.

**REMINGTON Model 40X:** .22 LR single-shot bolt-action target rifle; action is similar to Model 722; adjustable trigger; 28" heavy barrel; Redfield Olympic sights optional; scope bases; target stock; bedding device; adjustable swivel; rubber butt plate. Introduced in 1955; dropped, 1964.

Used value, with sights, $225 to $250; sans sights, $175 to $200.

**Model 40X standard**, with lighter barrel, is same as heavyweight model listed above. Used value, with sights, $235 to $250; sans sights, $175 to $200.

*Model 40-XB Rangemaster*

**REMINGTON Model 40-XB Rangemaster:** rimfire bolt-action single-shot, replacing rimfire Model 40X; .22 LR; 28" barrel, standard or heavyweight; target stock, adjust-able swivel block on guide rail; rubber butt plate; furnished without sights. Introduced in 1964; dropped, 1974. Used value, $285 to $325.

*Model 40X*

**REMINGTON Model 40X Center-fire:** basic specs are same as for 40X rimfire heavy barrel target rifle; standard calibers: .30/06; 7.62 NATO; .222 Rem. magnum, .222 Rem., with other calibers on special request at additional cost. Introduced in 1961; dropped, 1964. Used value, sans sights, $350 to $275; with sights, $400 to $425.

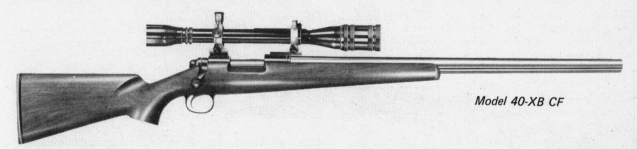

*Model 40-XB CF*

**REMINGTON Model 40-XB Center-fire:** bolt-action single-shot to replace Model 40X center-fire; .308 Win., .30/06, .223 Rem., .222 Rem. magnum, .222 Rem.; 27¼" barrel, standard or heavyweight; target stock; adjustable swivel block on guide rail, rubber butt plate; furnished without sights. Introduced in 1964; still in production. Used value, $325 to $350.

*Model 572A*

**REMINGTON Model 572A Fieldmaster:** hammerless slide-action repeater; .22 short, long, LR; tube magazine holds 20 shorts, 17 longs, 15 LR; 25" barrel; ramp front sight; open rear; uncheckered hardwood pistol-grip stock, grooved forearm. Introduced in 1955; still in production. Used value, $90 to $95.

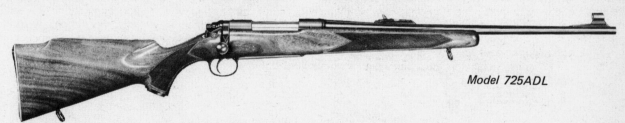

*Model 725ADL*

**REMINGTON Model 725ADL:** bolt action; in .243, .270, .280, .30/06; rifle has 22" barrel, 4-rd. box magazine; in .222, has 24" barrel, 5-rd. magazine; Monte Carlo comb, walnut stock; hand-checkered pistol grip, forearm; swivels; hooded ramp front sight, open rear. Introduced in 1958; dropped, 1961. Used value, $275 to $300.

*Model 552A*

**REMINGTON Model 552A Speedmaster:** standard model autoloader handles .22 short, long, LR cartridges interchangeably; tube magazine holds 20 shorts, 17 longs, 15 LR; 25" barrel, bead front sight, open rear; uncheckered walnut pistol-grip stock, semi-beavertail forearm. Introduced in 1958; still in production. Used value, $80 to $85.

**Model 552C carbine** is the same as standard Model 552A, except for 21" barrel. Used value, $90 to $95.

**Model 552GS Gallery Special** has same specs as standard model, except for being chambered in .22 short only. Used value, $85 to $90.

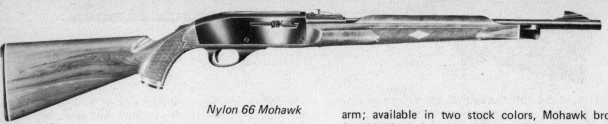

*Nylon 66 Mohawk*

**REMINGTON Nylon 66:** autoloader; .22 LR only; tube magazine in butt stock holds 14 rds.; 19½" barrel; blade front sight, open rear; receiver grooved for tip-off mounts; stock is of moulded nylon, with checkered pistol grip, for-arm; available in two stock colors, Mohawk brown and Apache black; latter has chrome-plated receiver cover. Introduced in 1959; still in production. Used value either color/style, $65 to $70.

**Nylon 66GS** is the same as Nylon 66 Mohawk brown style, except chambered only for .22 shorts. Used value, $70 to $75.

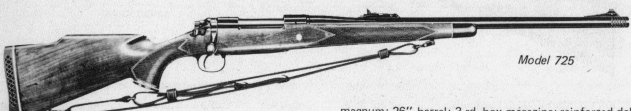

*Model 742 Standard*

**REMINGTON Model 742:** gas-operated semi-auto; 6mm Rem., .243 Win., .280 Rem., .308 Win., .30/06; 4-rd. box magazine; 22" barrel; bead front sight on ramp, open rear; versions of 1960s had impressed checkering on stock, fore-arm; later versions, cut checkering. Introduced in 1960; still in production. Used value, $175 to $185.

**Model 742 carbine** is same as standard model, except has 18½" barrel; .308 Win., .30/06 only. Used value, $185 to $195.

**Model 742BDL** is same as standard 742, except in .308 Win., .30/06 only; available in right, left-hand models; Monte Carlo cheekpiece; black tip on forearm; basket-weave checkering. Used value, $195 to $210.

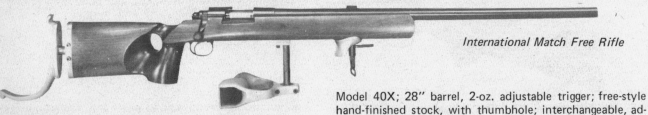

*Model 725*

**REMINGTON Model 725 Kodiak Magnum:** built on the same basic action as 725ADL; .375 H&H magnum, .458 Win. magnum; 26" barrel; 3-rd. box magazine; reinforced deluxe Monte Carlo stock; recoil pad; special recoil reduction device built into barrel; black forearm tip; sling, swivels; made only in 1961. Used value, $550 to $600.

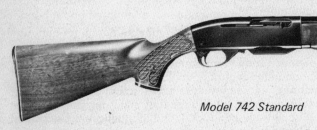

*International Match Free Rifle*

**REMINGTON International Match Free Rifle:** bolt-action single-shot; special order calibers were available, but standard chamberings are .22 LR, .222 Rem., .222 Rem. magnum, .30/06, 7.62mm NATO; used same action as earlier Model 40X; 28" barrel, 2-oz. adjustable trigger; free-style hand-finished stock, with thumbhole; interchangeable, adjustable rubber butt plate and hook-type butt plate; adjustable palm rest; adjustable sling swivel; furnished without sights. Introduced in 1961; dropped, 1964. Used value, $325 to $385.

*Nylon 76*

**REMINGTON Nylon 76:** .22 LR only; same as standard Mohawk brown 66, except has short-throw lever-action. Introduced in 1962; dropped, 1964. Used value, $100 to $120.

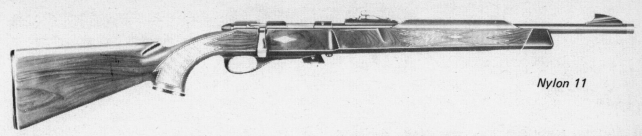

*Nylon 11*

**REMINGTON Nylon 11:** bolt-action repeater; .22 short, long, LR; 6, 10-rd. clip-type magazines; 19-5/8" barrel; blade front sight, open rear; Mohawk brown nylon stock; checkered pistol grip, forearm. Introduced in 1962; dropped, 1964. Used value, $100 to $125.

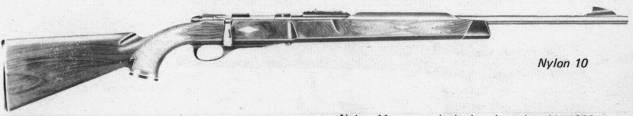

*Nylon 10*

**REMINGTON Nylon 10:** bolt-action single-shot; same as Nylon 11, except single-shot. Introduced in 1962; dropped, 1964. Used value, $60 to $75.

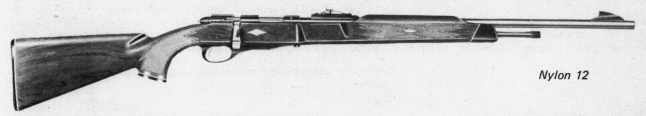

*Nylon 12*

**REMINGTON Nylon 12:** bolt-action repeater; same as Nylon 11 model, except for tube magazine holding 22 shorts, 17 long, 15 LR. Introduced in 1962; dropped, 1964. Used value, $100 to $120.

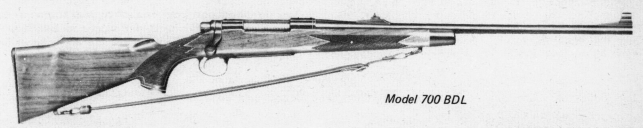

*Model 700 BDL*

**REMINGTON Model 700:** this is another of those guns that verges on being an empire. Introduced in 1962, the Model 700 has been Remington's most recent continuing success and is still a top seller, in spite of price increases each year.

**Model 700 ADL** is bolt-action, .222, .22-250, .243, 6mm Rem., .270, 7mm Rem. magnum, .308, .30/06; 22 and 24" round tapered barrel; walnut Monte Carlo stock, with pistol grip; originally introduced with hand-checkered pistol grip, forearm, was made for several years with RKW finish, impressed checkering; more recent models have computerized cut checkering; removable, adjustable rear sight with windage screw; gold bead ramp front; tapped for scope mounts. Used value, $165 to $175; except for 7mm Rem. mag, $190 to $210.

**Model 700 BDL** is same as 700 ADL, except for black forearm tip, pistol grip cap, fleur-de-lis checkering; matted receiver top; quick release floor plate; quick-detachable swivels, sling; hooded ramp front sight; additional calibers, .17 Rem., 6.5mm Rem. magnum, .350 Rem. magnum, .264 Win. magnum, .300 Win. magnum. Used value, $225 to $245; **Peerless grade**, with better wood, checkering, custom work, $825 to $850; **Premier grade**, with inlays, engraving, $1700 to $1750.

**Model 700 BDL** left-hand is the same as 700 BDL, except for left-hand action, stock; available only in .270 Win., .30/06, 7mm Rem. magnum in current production. Used value, $240 to $255, for .270, .30/06; $265 to $276, for 7mm Rem. magnum.

**Model 700 Safari** is same as Model 700 BDL, except in .458 Win. magnum, .375 Holland & Holland; recoil pad, oil-finished, hand-checkered stock. Used value, $445 to $475.

**Model 700 C** custom rifle is same as Model 700 BDL, except for choice of 20", 22", 24" barrel; with or without sights, hinged floor plate; select walnut, hand-checkered stock; rosewood forearm tip, grip cap; hand-lapped barrel. Used value, in standard calibers, $495 to $525; magnum calibers, $525 to $550; with optional recoil pad, add $15.

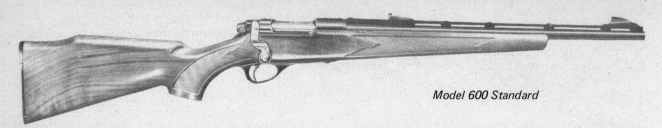

*Model 600 Standard*

**REMINGTON Model 600:** bolt-action carbine; 5-rd. box magazine for 6mm Rem., .243 Win., .308 Win., .350 Rem.; 6-rd. magazine for .222 Rem.; 18½" round barrel, with vent. nylon rib; checkered walnut Monte Carlo pistol-grip stock; blade ramp front sight, open rear; drilled, tapped for scope mounts. Introduced in 1964; dropped, 1967. Used value,

$215 to $225.

   **Model 600 magnum** is the same as Model 600, but with 4-rd. box magazine for 6.5mm Rem. magnum, .350 Rem. magnum; heavy magnum type barrel, stock of laminated walnut/beech; recoil pad; swivels; sling. Introduced in 1965; dropped, 1967. Used value, $350 to $375.

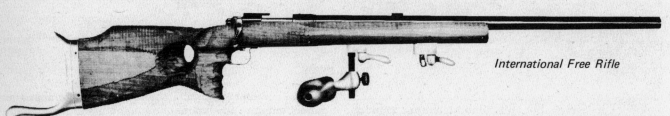

*International Free Rifle*

**REMINGTON International Free Rifle:** in both rimfire, center-fire; has same action as Model 40-XB; .22 LR; .222 Rem., .222 Rem. magnum, .223 Rem., 7.62 NATO, .30/06;

2-oz. adjustable trigger; no sights; hand-finished stock; adjustable butt plate and hook; moveable front sling swivel; adjustable palm rest. Introduced in 1964; dropped, 1974. Used value, $375 to $400.

*Model 581*

**REMINGTON Model 581:** bolt-action, .22 short, long, LR; 5-rd. clip magazine; 24" round barrel; uncheckered hardwood Monte Carlo pistol-grip stock; screw-adjustable open

rear sight, bead post front; side safety; wide trigger; receiver grooved for tip-off mounts. Introduced in 1967; still in production. Used value, $60 to $65; left-hand action, stock, $65 to $70.

*Model 582*

**REMINGTON Model 582:** same as Model 581, except for

tubular magazine holding 20 short, 15 long, 14 LR cartridges. Used value, $70 to $75.

*Model 788*

**REMINGTON Model 788:** bolt-action; .222, .22-250, 6mm Rem., .243, .308; .222 has 5-rd. magazine, others 4-rd.; 24" tapered barrel for .222, .22-250, 22" for other calibers; walnut-finished hardwood pistol-grip stock; uncheckered,

with Monte Carlo roll; open rear sight adjustable for windage, elevation, blade ramp front; thumb safety; detachable box magazine; receiver tapped for scope mounts. Introduced in 1967, still in production. Used value, $115 to $120; left-hand model, $120 to $125.

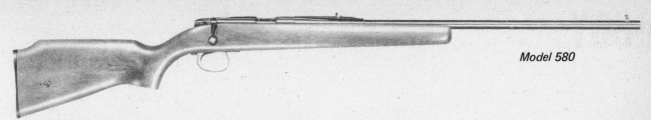

*Model 580*

**REMINGTON Model 580:** single-shot, bolt action; .22 short, long, LR; 24" tapered barrel; hardwood stock with Monte Carlo comb, pistol grip; black composition butt plate; screw-lock adjustable rear sight, bead post front; side safety; integral loading platform; receiver grooved for tip-off mounts. Introduced in 1957; dropped, 1976. Used value, $60 to $65.

**Model 580 SB** is same as standard Model 580, except for smoothbore barrel for shot cartridges. Used value, $60 to $65.

*Model 660*

**REMINGTON Model 660:** bolt-action carbine, replacing Model 600; 5-rd. box magazine for 6mm Rem., .243 Win., .308 Win.; 6-rd. magazine for .222 Rem.; 20" barrel; bead front sight on ramp, open rear; checkered Monte Carlo stock; black pistol-grip cap, forearm tip. Introduced in 1968; dropped, 1971. Used value, $180 to $200.

**Model 660 magnum** is same as 660 standard, except in 6.5mm Rem. magnum, .350 Rem. magnum; 4-rd. magazine; recoil pad; laminated walnut/beech stock for added strength; quick-detachable sling swivels, sling. Introduced in 1968; dropped, 1971. Used value, $290 to $325.

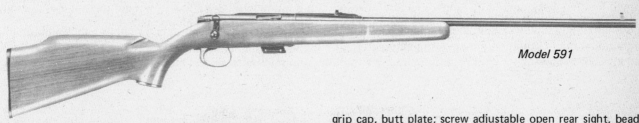

*Model 591*

**REMINGTON Model 591:** bolt-action; 5mm Rem. rimfire; 4-rd. clip magazine; 24" barrel; uncheckered hardwood stock, with Monte Carlo comb; black composition pistol-grip cap, butt plate; screw adjustable open rear sight, bead post front; side safety, wide trigger; receiver grooved for tip-off scope mounts. Introduced in 1970; dropped, 1975. Used value, $110 to $130.

*Model 592*

**REMINGTON Model 592:** same as Model 591, except for tube magazine; holds ten 5mm Rem. rimfire rds. Introduced in 1970; dropped, 1974. Used value, $100 to $130.

*Model 541-S*

**REMINGTON Model 541-S:** bolt-action; .22 long, LR; 24" barrel; walnut stock, with checkered pistol grip, forearm; no sights; drilled, tapped for scope mounts, receiver sights; 10-rd. clip; thumb safety; engraved receiver, trigger guard. Introduced in 1972; still in production. Used value, $165 to $175.

# RIGBY

*Best Quality*

*Second Quality*

**RIGBY Best Quality:** hammerless ejector double rifle; .275 magnum, .350 magnum, .470 Nitro Express; sidelock action; 24'' to 28'' barrels; hand-checkered walnut stock; pistol grip, forearm; folding leaf rear sight, bead front; engraved receiver. Discontinued prior to World War II. Used value, $5500 to $5800.

**Rigby Second Quality** has the same general specifications as the Best Quality model, but features box-lock action. Used value, $4000 to $4250.

**Rigby Third Quality** has the same sepcifications as the Best Quality rifle, except for lower grade wood, not as well finished. Used value, $2800 to $3200.

*350 Magnum*

**RIGBY 350 Magnum:** Mauser-type action; .350 magnum only; 24'' barrel; 5-rd. box magazine; high quality walnut stock with checkered full pistol grip, forearm; folding leaf rear sight, bead front. Still in production. Used value, $1250 to $1350.

**RIGBY 416 Magnum:** Mauser-type action; .416 Big Game only; 24'' barrel; 4-rd. box magazine; walnut sporting stock with checkered pistol grip, forearm; folding leaf rear sight, bead front. Still in production. Used value, $1450 to $1500.

*Rigby 275*

**RIGBY 275:** Mauser-type action; .275 High Velocity, 7x57mm; 25'' barrel; 5-rd. box magazine; walnut sporting stock with hand-checkered full pistol grip; forearm; folding leaf rear sight, bead front. Still in production. Used value, $1150 to $1250.

**Rigby 275 Lightweight** has same specifications as the standard model, except for 21'' barrel. Still in production. Used value, $1150 to $1250.

# RUGER

(Author's Note: In 1976, Ruger marked virtually all then current models with the words: "Made in the 200th yr. of American Liberty." Guns carrying this line command prices twenty-five percent above the standard versions.)

*Standard Model 44*

**RUGER Model 44:** autoloading carbine; .44 magnum only; 18½" barrel; 4-rd. tube magazine; magazine release button incorporated in 1967; uncheckered walnut pistol-grip carbine stock; barrel band; receiver tapped for scope mount; folding leaf rear sight, gold bead front. Introduced in 1961; still in production. Used value, $155 to $165.

**Model 44RS** carbine is the same as the standard Model 44, except for sling swivels, built-in peep sight. Used value,

$165 to $175.

**Model 44 Sporter** is the same as the standard Model 44, except for sling swivels, Monte Carlo sporter stock, grooved forearm, grip cap, flat butt plate. Dropped, 1971. Used value, $175 to $210.

**Model 44 International** is the same as standard Model 44, except for full-length Mannlicher-type walnut stock, sling swivels. Dropped, 1971. Used value, $300 to $350.

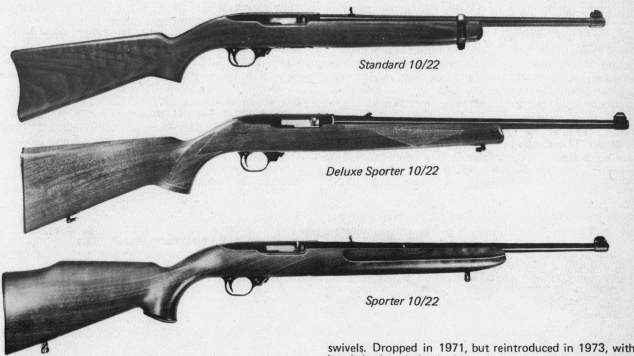

*Standard 10/22*

*Deluxe Sporter 10/22*

*Sporter 10/22*

**RUGER Model 10/22:** autoloading carbine; .22 LR only; 18½" barrel; detachable 10-rd. rotary magazine; uncheckedered walnut carbine stock; barrel band; receiver tapped for scope blocks or tip-off mount; adjustable folding leaf rear sight, gold bead front. Introduced in 1964; still in production. Used value, $70 to $75.

**Model 10/22 Sporter** is the same as Model 10/22, except for Monte Carlo stock with grooved forearm, grip cap, sling

swivels. Dropped in 1971, but reintroduced in 1973, with hand-checkered pistol-grip stock. Dropped 1975. Used value, $85 to $90.

**Model 10/22 Deluxe Sporter** has the same general specs as the standard model, except for checkered stock, flat buttplate, sling swivels. Introduced 1971, still in production. Used value, $100 to $110.

**Ruger Model 10/22 International** has the same specifications as standard model, except for full-length Mannlicher-type stock, sling swivels. Dropped, 1971. Used value, $325 to $350.

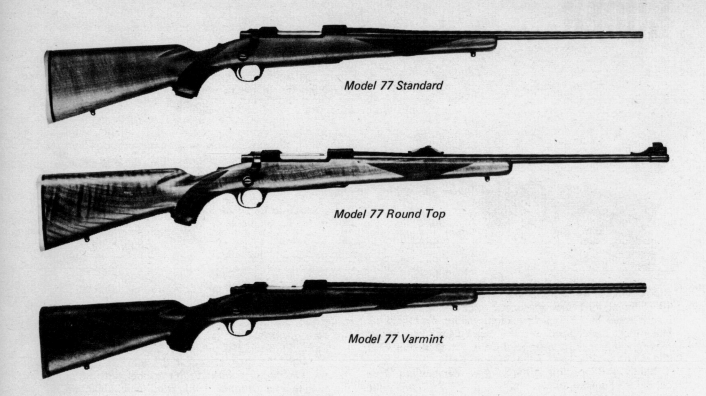

*Model 77 Standard*

*Model 77 Round Top*

*Model 77 Varmint*

RUGER Model 77 Standard (M77R): bolt-action; .22-250, .220 Swift, .243 Win., .25/06, .257 Roberts, .250-3000, 6mm, .270 Win., 7x57mm, 7mm Rem. mag., .30/06; 22" tapered barrel, 3 or 5-rd. capacity, depending upon caliber; hinged floor plate; adjustable trigger; hand-checkered American walnut stock; pistol-grip cap; sling swivel studs; recoil pad; integral scope mount base; optional folding leaf adjustable rear sight, gold bead ramp front. Introduced in 1968; still in production. Used value, $195 to $210; with sights, $215 to $225.

Model 77 magnum-size action, made in .257 Roberts, .25/06, .270 Win., .30/06, 7mm Rem. magnum, .300 Win. magnum, .338 Win. magnum, .458 Win. magnum; magazine capacity, 3 or 5 rds., depending upon caliber; .270, .30/06,

7x57, .280 Rem. have 22" barrels, all others, 24". Used value, $235 to $265, depending upon caliber.

Model 77 Round Top Magnum (77ST) has round top action; drilled, tapped for standard scope mounts, open sights; .25/06, .270 Win., 7mm Rem. mag., .30/06, .300 Win. mag., .338 Win. mag.; other specifications generally the same as Model 77 Standard. Introduced in 1971; still in production. Used value, $220 to $235.

Model 77 Varmint (77V) is made in .22-250, .220 Swift, .243 Win., 6mm, .280 Rem., .25/06 and .308; 24" heavy straight tapered barrel, 26" in .220 Swift; drilled tapped for target scope mounts or integral scope mount bases on receiver; checkered American walnut stock. Introduced 1970; still in production. Used value, $200 to $210.

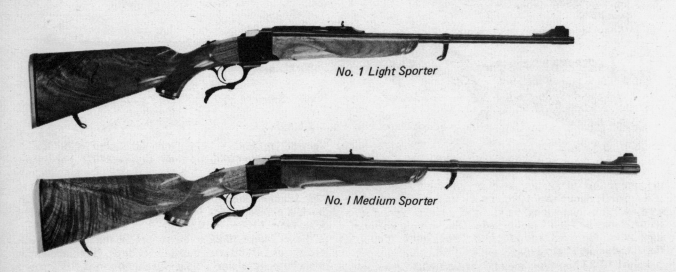

*No. 1 Light Sporter*

*No. I Medium Sporter*

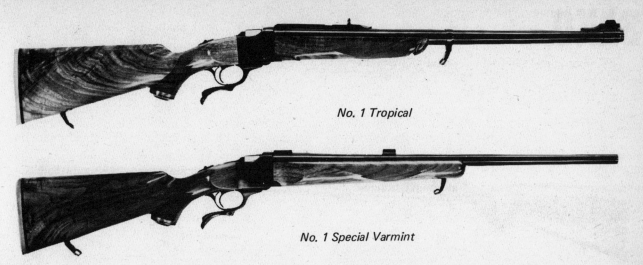

*No. 1 Tropical*

*No. 1 Special Varmint*

**RUGER No. 1 Standard:** under-lever single-shot; .22-250, .220 Swift, .243 Winchester, .223, .257 Roberts, .280, 6mm Remington, .25/06, .270 Winchester, .30/06, 7mm Remington magnum, .300 Winchester magnum, .338 magnum; 26" barrel, with quarter rib; American walnut, two-piece stock; hand-checkered pistol grip, forearm; open sights or integral scope mounts; hammerless falling block design; automatic ejector; top tang safety. Introduced in 1967; still in production. Used value, $250 to $265.

**Number 1 Standard/Light Sporter** has same general specs as standard model, except for 22" barrel, integral mounts for Ruger steel tip-off scope rings; no sights; .223 Remington, .270 Winchester, 7x57mm, .30/06 chambering. Used value, $260 to $285.

**Number 1 Light Sporter** has the same general specifications as standard model, except for 22" barrel, Alex Henry-style forearm, iron sights; .243 Win., .270 Win., .30/06, 7x57mm. Introduced in 1968; still in production. Used value, $250 to $265.

**Number 1 Medium Sporter** has the same specifications as the Light Sporter model, except is chambered in 7mm Rem. mag., .300 Win. mag., .338 Win. mag., .45-70; 26" barrel, except .45-70, with 22" barrel. Introduced in 1968; still in production. Used value, $250 to $265.

**Number 1 Tropical Model** is chambered for .375 H&H mag., .458 Win. mag.; has 24" heavy barrel; open sights. Introduced in 1968; still in production. Used value, $275 to $300.

**Number 1 Special Varminter** has 24" heavy barrel, chambered for .22-250, .220 Swift, .223, .25/06, 6mm, .280 Remington; supplied with target scope bases. Introduced in 1970; still in production. Used value, $250 to $265.

*No. 3 Carbine*

**RUGER No. 3:** under-lever single-shot carbine; .22 Hornet, .223, .30-40 Krag, .375 Win., .45-70; 22" barrel; same action as Ruger No. 1, except for different lever; uncheckered American walnut, two-piece carbine-type stock; folding leaf rear sight, gold bead front; adjustable trigger; barrel band on forearm; automatic ejector. Introduced in 1969; .30-40 chambering dropped 1978; others still in production. Used value, $150 to $165.

*Mini-14*

**RUGER Mini-14:** gas-operated, fixed piston carbine; .223 Rem. only; 18½" barrel; 5-rd. detachable box magazine; uncheckered, reinforced American walnut carbine-type stock; positive primary extraction; fully adjustable rear sight, gold bead front. Introduced in 1973; still in production. Used value, $175 to $190.

**Mini-14 Stainless** has same general specifications as standard model, except that barrel, action are built of stainless steel. Introduced 1978, still in production. Used value, $250 to $275.

# SAKO

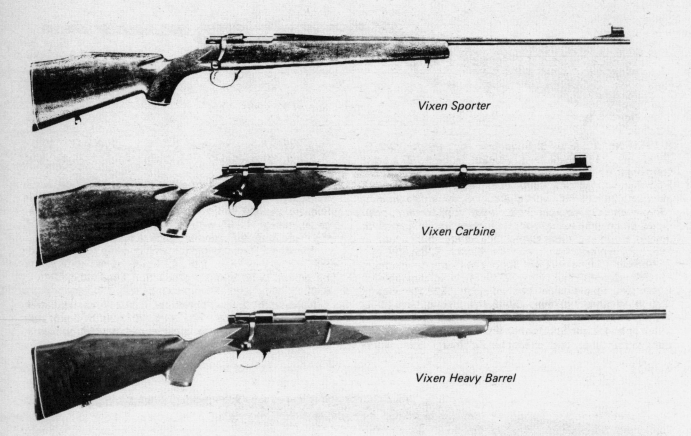

*Vixen Sporter*

*Vixen Carbine*

*Vixen Heavy Barrel*

**SAKO Vixen Sporter:** bolt-action; .218 Bee, .22 Hornet, .222 Rem., .222 Rem. magnum, .223; built on L461 short Mauser-type action; 23½" barrel; checkered European walnut, Monte Carlo, pistol-grip stock; cheekpiece; no rear sight; drilled, tapped for scope mounts; hooded ramp front; sling swivels. Introduced in 1946; dropped, 1976. Used value, $250 to $260.

**Vixen Carbine** has same specifications as the Vixen Sporter, except for Mannlicher-type stock, 20" barrel. Used value, $275 to $300.

**Vixen Heavy Barrel** model has same specifications as sporter, except in .222 Rem., .222 Rem. magnum, .223 only; target-style stock, beavertail forearm; heavy barrel. Used value, $250 to $265.

*Sako Mauser*

**SAKO Mauser:** bolt-action sporter; .270, .30/06; 24" barrel; built on FN Mauser action; 5-rd. magazine; hand-checkered European walnut, Monte Carlo cheekpiece stock; open leaf rear sight, Patridge front; sling swivel studs. Intro-duced in 1946; dropped, 1961. Used value, $350 to $375.

**Magnum Mauser** has same general specifications as standard Sako Mauser; .300 Holland & Holland magnum, .375 Holland & Holland magnum only; recoil pad. Dropped, 1961. Used value, $400 to $425.

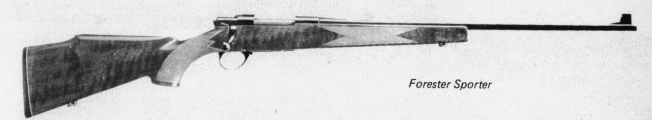

*Forester Sporter*

**SAKO Forester Sporter:** bolt-action; .22-250, .243 Win., .308 Win.; 23″ barrel; built on L579 medium Mauser-type action; 5-rd. magazine; hand-checkered walnut Monte Carlo pistol-grip stock; no rear sight, hooded ramp front; drilled, tapped for scope mounts; sling swivel studs. Introduced in 1957; dropped, 1971. Used value, $375 to $395.

**Forester Carbine** has same specifications as Forester Sporter, except for Mannlicher-type stock, 20″ barrel. Used value, $425 to $450.

**Forester Heavy Barrel** model has same specifications as standard model, except for 24″ heavy barrel. Used value, $380 to $400.

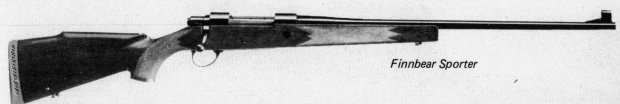

*Finnbear Sporter*

**SAKO Finnbear Sporter:** bolt-action; .25/06, .264 Win. magnum, .270, .30/06, .300 Win. magnum, .338 magnum, 7mm Rem. magnum, .375 Holland & Holland magnum; 24″ barrel; built on L61 long Mauser-type action; magazine holds 5 standard rds., 4 magnums; hand-checkered European walnut, Monte Carlo, pistol-grip stock; recoil pad; sling swivels; no rear sight, hooded ramp front; drilled, tapped for scope mounts. Introduced in 1961; dropped, 1971. Used value, $375 to $400.

*Finnwolf*

**SAKO Finnwolf:** hammerless lever-action; .243 Win., .308 Win. only. 23″ barrel; no rear sight, hooded ramp front; drilled, tapped for scope mounts; hand-checkered European walnut Monte Carlo stock in left or right-hand styling; sling swivels. Introduced in 1964; dropped, 1972. Used value, $275 to $295.

*Model 72*

**SAKO Model 72:** bolt-action; .222 Rem., .223 Rem., .22-250, .243 Win., .25/06, .270 Win., .30/06, 7mm Rem. magnum, .300 Win. magnum, .338 Win. magnum, .375 Holland & Holland magnum; 23″ or 24″ barrel; adjustable trigger; hinged floor plate; short action in .222, .223, long action on all other calibers; adjustable rear sight, hooded front; hand-checkered European walnut stock. Introduced in 1973; dropped, 1976. Used value, standard calibers, $175 to $185; magnums, $185 to $215.

**SAKO Model 73:** lever-action; .243 Winchester, .308 Winchester; has same specifications as Finnwolf model, except for flush floorplate, 3-rd. clip magazine, no cheekpiece. Manufactured 1973 to 1975. Used value, $275 to $290.

*Model 74 Carbine*

**Model 74, Long Action** has same specs as short-action model, except for 24" barrel, 4-rd. magazine for magnum cartridges; chambered for .25/06, .270 Winchester, 7mm Remington magnum, .30/06, .300 Winchester magnum, .338 Winchester magnum, .375 H&H. Heavy-barrel version chambered only for .25/06, 7mm Remington magnum. Introduced 1974, still in production. Used value, $310 to $325.

**Model 74 Carbine** has same specs as long-action Model 74, except for 20" barrel, Mannlicher-design full-length stock; 5-rd. magazine, chambered only for .30/06. Introduced 1974, still in production. Used value, $380 to $400.

**SAKO Model 74, Short Action:** bolt-action; .222 Remington, .223 Remington; 5-rd. magazine; 23½" standard or heavy barrel; no sights; hand-checkered European walnut Monte Carlo stock; Mauser-type action; detachable sling swivels. Introduced, 1974, still in production. Used value, $300 to $310.

**Model 74, Medium Action** has same specs as short-action model, except chambering for .220 Swift, .22-250, .243 Winchester. Introduced 1974, still in production. Used value, $300 to $310.

*Model 78*

**SAKO Model 78:** bolt-action; .22 LR, .22 Hornet; 5-rd. magazine for RF, 4 rds. for Hornet; 22½" barrel; no sights; hand-checkered European walnut Monte Carlo stock. Introduced 1977, still in production. Used values: .22 RF, $200 to $225; .22 Hornet, $215 to $240.

# SAVAGE

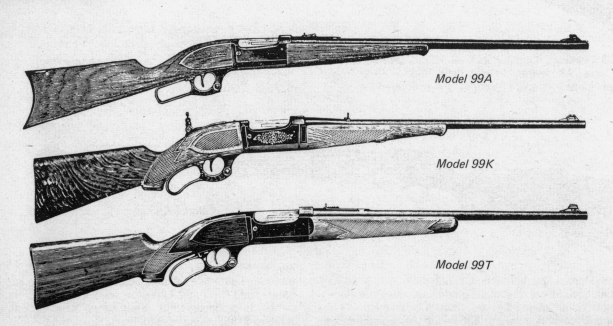

*Model 99A*

*Model 99K*

*Model 99T*

SAVAGE **Model 99A:** lever-action repeater. Every gun company of major proportions seems to have one or two models that have become legend and upon which much of the company's reputation has been built. This is true of the Model 99 — and it's many variations — for the Savage Arms Corporation. The original Model 99 was introduced in 1899 and replaced in 1922 by the Model 99A. The Model 99A is in .30/30, .300 Savage, .303 Savage; hammerless, solid frame; 24" barrel, 5-rd. rotary magazine; unchecked straight-grip American walnut stock, tapered forearm; open rear sight, bead front on ramp. Introduced in 1922; still in production. Used value, $150 to $175.

**Model 99B** is the same as Model 99A, except has takedown design. Dropped, 1937. Used value, $250 to $275.

**Model 99E**, in pre-World War II model had solid frame and was chambered for .22 Hi-Power, .250/3000, .30-30, .300 Savage, .303 Savage; 24" barrel for .300 Savage, 22" for all others; other specifications are the same as Model 99A. Model was dropped in 1940, reintroduced in 1961 and still is in production. The current model is chambered in .243 Win., .300 Savage, .308 Win.; 20" barrel; checkered pistol-grip stock. Used values, pre-WWII, $225 to $250; current model, $160 to $170.

**Model 99H** is solid frame model, with same general specifications as Model 99A, except for carbine stock with barrel band; .250-3000, .30-30, .308 Savage. Used value, $235 to $245.

**Model 99F Featherweight** model was discontinued in 1940, reintroduced in 1955; dropped, 1973. Pre-WWII model was takedown style, with same specifications as prewar Model 99E, except for lighter weight. The 1955 version had solid frame, 22" barrel; .243 Win., .300 Savage, .308 Win.; checkered walnut pistol-grip stock. Used value, pre-WWII model, $255 to $275; 1955 model, $200 to $225.

graved receiver, barrel, Lyman peep rear sight, folding middle sight; fancy grade walnut stock; other specifications identical. Dropped, 1940. Used value, $700 to $750.

**Model 99EG** has same specs as Model G except for unchecked stock in pre-WWII styling. Dropped in 1940, reintroduced in 1955; dropped, 1961. The 1955 version is in .250 Savage, .243 Win., .300 Savage, .308 Win., .358 Win. Used value, pre-WWII, $235 to $250; 1955 model, $175 to $180.

**Model 99T Featherweight** has same general specifications as standard Model 99s; solid frame design; .22 High-Power, .30-30, .303 Savage, .300 Savage; 22" barrel on .300 Savage, 20" for other calibers; hand-checkered walnut pistol-grip stock, beavertail forearm; weighs approximately 1½ lbs. less than standard. Dropped, 1940. Used value, $265 to $285.

**Model 99R** pre-WWII was solid-frame design; .250-3000, .300 Savage; 22" barrel for .250-3000, 24" for .300 Savage; oversize pistol-grip stock, forearm; hand-checkered American walnut. Dropped, 1940; reintroduced, 1951; dropped, 1961. The 1951 version has same specifications as pre-WWII version, except for 24" barrel; sling swivel studs; .243 Win., .250 Savage, .300 Savage, .308 Win., .358 Win. Used value, pre-WWII model, $275 to $295; 1951 model, $185 to $200.

**Model 99RS** was made prior to WWII, dropped in 1940, then reintroduced in 1955, finally being discontinued in 1961. The pre-war model is the same as the pre-war Model 99R, except that it is equipped with quick-detachable sling swivels and sling, a Lyman rear peep sight and a folding middle sight. The pre-war version differs from the 1955 Model 99R only in that it has a Redfield 70LH receiver sight and a milled slot for a middle sight. Used value, pre-WWII model, $275 to $300; 1951 model, $215 to $225.

**Model 99DL Deluxe** has same general specifications as discontinued Model 99F, except for sling swivels, high-

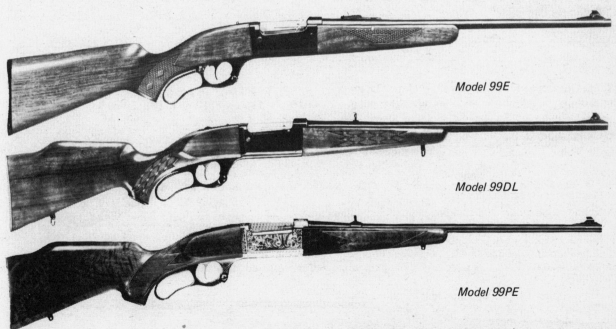

*Model 99E*

*Model 99DL*

*Model 99PE*

**Model 99G** has the same specifications as pre-WWII Model 99E, except for takedown feature; hand-checkered pistol grip, forearm. Dropped, 1940. Used value, $275 to $295.

**Model 99K** is a deluxe version of Model 99G. Has en-

comb Monte Carlo stock; .243 Win., .308 Win. Introduced 1960; dropped, 1974. Used value, $210 to $235.

**Model 99C** has same specifications as Model 99F, except clip magazine replaces rotary type; .243 Win., .284 Win., .308 Win., (.284 dropped in 1974); 4-rd. detachable magazine, 3-rds. for .284. Introduced in 1965; still in production. Used value, $170 to $195.

**Model 99CD** is same as Model 99C, except for removable bead ramp front sight, removable adjustable rear sight, white line recoil pad, pistol-grip cap, hand-checkered pistol grip, grooved forearm, quick-detachable swivels, sling; .250-3000, .308 Win. Used value, $225 to $235.

**Model 99PE Presentation Grade** has same specifications as Model 99DL, plus game scene engraved on receiver sides, engraved tang, lever; fancy American walnut Monte Carlo stock, forearm; hand checkering; quick-detachable swivels; .243 Win., .284 Win., .308 Win. Introduced in 1968; dropped, 1970. Used value, $750 to $800.

**Model 99DE Citation Grade** is same as Model 99PE, but engraving is less elaborate. Introduced in 1968; dropped, 1970. Used value, $400 to $450.

*Model 1903*

**SAVAGE Model 1903:** slide-action; .22 Short, Long, LR; hammerless, takedown detachable box magazine; 24" octagonal barrel; open rear sight, bead front; checkered one-piece straight stock. Manufactured 1903 to 1921. Used value, $100 to $110.

**SAVAGE Model 1904:** bolt-action, single-shot; .22 Short, Long, LR; takedown; 18" barrel; open rear sight, bead front; uncheckered one-piece straight stock. Manufactured 1904 to 1917. Used value, $45 to $50.

**SAVAGE Model 1905:** bolt-action, single-shot; .22 Short, Long, LR; takedown; 22" barrel; open rear sight, bead front; uncheckered one-piece straight stock. Manufactured 1905 to 1918. Used value, $45 to $50.

**SAVAGE Model 1909:** slide-action; .22 Short, Long, LR; has same general specifications as Model 1903, except for uncheckered stock, 20" round barrel. Manufactured 1909 to 1915. Used value, $110 to $120.

*Model 1912*

**SAVAGE Model 1912:** autoloader; .22 LR; 7-rd. detachable box magazine; takedown; open rear sight, bead front; uncheckered straight stock. Manufactured 1912 to 1916. Used value, $110 to $120.

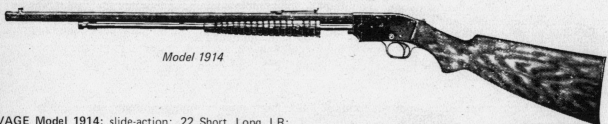

*Model 1914*

**SAVAGE Model 1914:** slide-action; .22 Short, Long, LR; hammerless, takedown; tubular magazine holds 17 LR cartridges; 24" octagonal barrel; open rear sight, bead front; uncheckered pistol-grip stock, grooved slide handle. Manufactured 1914 to 1924. Used value, $110 to $120.

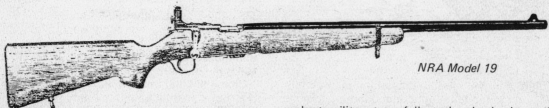

*NRA Model 19*

**SAVAGE NRA Model 19:** bolt-action match rifle; .22 LR only; 25" barrel; 5-rd. detachable box magazine; American walnut military-type full stock, pistol grip, uncheckered; adjustable rear peep sight, blade front. Introduced in 1919; dropped, 1933. Used value, $145 to $155.

**SAVAGE Model 19:** bolt-action target rifle, replacing NRA Model 19; .22 LR only; 25" barrel; 5-rd. detachable box magazine; target-type uncheckered walnut stock, full pistol grip, beavertail forearm. Early versions have adjustable rear peep sight, blade front; later models have hooded front sight, extension rear. Introduced in 1933; dropped, 1946. Used value, $140 to $150.

**Model 19H** is same as 1933 Model 19, except chambered for .22 Hornet only. Used value, $195 to $200.

**Model 19L** has same specifications as 1933 Model 19, except for Lyman 48Y receiver sight, No. 17A front. Used value, $160 to $170.

**Model 19M** has same specifications as 1933 Model 19, except for heavy 28" barrel, with scope bases. Used value, $140 to $150.

**SAVAGE Model 1920:** bolt-action, short Mauser action; .250-3000, .300 Savage; 22" barrel in .250-3000, 24" in .300 Savage; 5-rd. box magazine; hand-checkered American walnut pistol-grip stock, slender schnabel forearm; open rear sight, bead front. Introduced in 1920; dropped, 1926. Used value, $235 to $250.

*Model 20-1926*

**SAVAGE Model 20-1926:** bolt-action; has same specifications as Model 1920, except for redesigned stock, 24" barrel, Lyman No. 54 rear peep sight. Introduced in 1926; dropped, 1929. Used value, $235 to $250.

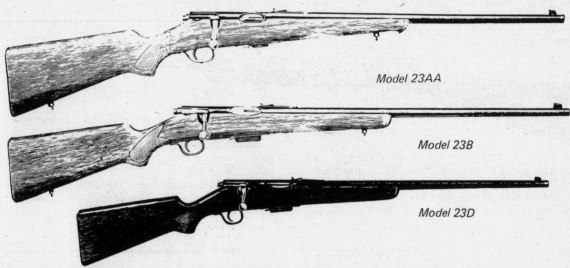

*Model 23AA*

*Model 23B*

*Model 23D*

**SAVAGE Model 23A:** bolt-action; .22 LR only; 23" barrel; 5-rd. detachable box magazine; uncheckered American walnut pistol-grip stock, thin forearm, schnabel tip; open rear sight, blade or bead front. Introduced in 1923; dropped, 1933. Used value, $135 to $145.

**Model 23AA** has the same general specifications as Model 23A, with exception of checkered stock, swivel studs, speed lock. Introduced in 1933; dropped, 1942. Used value, $145 to $165.

**SAVAGE Model 25:** slide-action hammerless takedown repeater; .22 LR, long, short; 24" octagon barrel; tube magazine holds 15 LR, 17 long, 20 short cartridges; uncheckered

**Model 23B** has same specifications as Model 23A, but is chambered for .25-20 cartridge; no schnabel; 25" barrel; swivel studs. Dropped, 1942. Used value, $130 to $140.

**Model 23C** has the same specifications as the Model 23B, except it is chambered for .32-20. Dropped, 1942. Used value, $140 to $150.

**Model 23D** has the same specifications as the Model 23B, except it is chambered for .22 Hornet. Dropped, 1947. Used value, $200 to $215.

American walnut pistol-grip stock; grooved slide handle; open rear sight, blade front. Introduced in 1925; dropped, 1929. Used value, $155 to $165.

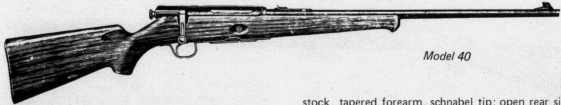

*Model 40*

**SAVAGE Model 40:** bolt-action sporter; .250-3000, .30-30, .300 Savage, .30/06; 24" barrel in .300 Savage, .30/06; 22" in other calibers; uncheckered American walnut pistol-grip stock, tapered forearm, schnabel tip; open rear sight, bead front on ramp; detachable box magazine; release button on right side of stock. Introduced in 1928; dropped, 1940. Used value, $180 to $200.

*Model 45*

**SAVAGE Model 45:** termed Super Sporter, it has same specifications, as Model 40, except for chamberings, hand-checkered pistol grip, forearm. Introduced in 1928; dropped, 1940. Used value, $250 to $275.

*Pre-WWII Model 29*

**SAVAGE Model 29:** slide-action hammerless takedown repeater; .22 LR, long, short; 24″ barrel; tube magazine holds 15 LR, 17 long, 20 short cartridges; open rear sight, bead front. Pre-WWII version had octagon barrel, hand-checkered walnut pistol-grip stock, slide-handle; post-war model had round barrel, unchecked wood. Introduced in 1929; dropped, 1967. Used values, pre-WWII, $160 to $170; post-war, $150 to $160.

*Model 3*

**SAVAGE Model 3:** bolt-action takedown single-shot; .22 LR, long, short; pre-WWII version has 26″ barrel, later models, 24″; unchecked American walnut pistol-grip stock; checkered hard rubber butt plate; open rear sight, bead front. Introduced in 1933; dropped, 1952. Used value, $40 to $50.

Model 3S has same specifications as Model 3, except for substitution of rear peep sight, hooded front sight. Used value, $55 to $60.

Model 3ST has the same specifications as the Model 3S, but was sold with swivels, sling. Dropped, 1941. Used value, $65 to $75.

*Model 4*

**SAVAGE Model 4:** bolt-action takedown repeater; .22 LR, long, short; 24″ barrel, 5-rd. detachable box magazine; pre-WWII version has checkered pistol-grip American walnut stock, grooved forearm; post-war model has unchecked stock; open rear sight, bead front. Introduced in 1933; dropped, 1965. Used values, pre-WWII, $65 to $75; post-war, $50 to $60.

Model 4S has the same specifications as Model 4, except for substitution of rear peep sight, hooded front. Used value, pre-WWII, $70 to $85; post-war, $65 to $70.

Model 4M has same specifications as post-war Model 4, except it is chambered for .22 rimfire magnum cartridge. Introduced in 1961; dropped, 1965. Used value, $85 to $100.

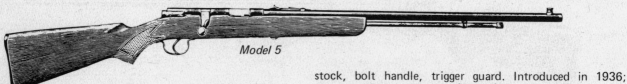

*Model 5*

**SAVAGE Model 5:** bolt-action takedown repeater; has the specifications of Model 4, except for tube magazine with capacity of 15 LR, 17 long, 21 short cartridges; redesigned stock, bolt handle, trigger guard. Introduced in 1936; dropped, 1961. Used value, $65 to $75.

Model 5S has the same specifications as the Model 5, except for substitution of peep rear sight, hooded front. Used value, $75 to $80.

*Model 219*

**SAVAGE Model 219:** hammerless, takedown single-shot; 25" barrel; .22 Hornet, .25-20, .30-30, .32-20; shotgun-type action with top lever; uncheckered walnut pistol-grip stock, forearm; open rear sight, bead front on ramp. Introduced in

**SAVAGE Model 221:** termed a utility gun, it has the same specifications as the Model 219, except for chambering in

**SAVAGE Model 222:** has the same specifications as Model

**SAVAGE Model 223:** has the same specifications as the

**SAVAGE Model 227:** has the same specifications as the

**SAVAGE Model 228:** has same specifications as the Model

**SAVAGE Model 229:** has same specifications as Model 221,

*Model 6*

**SAVAGE Model 6:** takedown autoloader; .22 LR, long, short; 24" barrel; tube magazine has capacity of 15 LR, 17 long, 21 short cartridges; pre-WWII version had checkered pistol-grip stock; post-war style has uncheckered walnut

**SAVAGE Model 7:** autoloader; takedown; same specifications as Model 6, except for 5-rd. detachable box magazine. Introduced in 1939; dropped, 1951. Used

1938; dropped, 1965. Used value, $75 to $85.

    **Savage Model 219L** has same specifications as Model 219 except action is opened with side lever. Introduced in 1965; dropped, 1967. Used value, $65 to $75.

.30-30 only, with interchangeable 30" 12-ga. shotgun barrel. Introduced in 1939; discontinued, 1960. Used value, $125 to $135.

221, except shotgun barrel is 16-ga., 28". Used value, $120 to $125.

Model 221, except that shotgun barrel is 20-ga., 28". Used value, $135 to $145.

Model 221, except that shotgun barrel is 12-ga., 30"; rifle barrel chambered for .22 Hornet. Used value, $125 to $135.

221, except shotgun barrel is 16-ga., 28"; rifle barrel is chambered for .22 Hornet. Used value, $120 to $125.

except shotgun barrel is 20-ga., 28"; rifle barrel is chambered for .22 Hornet. Used value, $125 to $135.

stock; open rear sight, bead front. Introduced in 1938; dropped, 1968. Used value, $65 to $75.

    **Model 6S** has identical specifications to Model 6, except for substitution of peep rear sight. Used value, $145 to $165.

value, $65 to $75.

    **Model 7S** has same specifications as Model 7, except for substitution of peep rear sight, hooded front. Used value, $75 to $85.

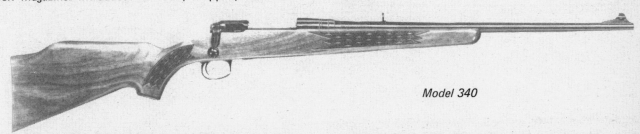

*Model 340*

**SAVAGE Model 340:** bolt-action repeater; .22 Hornet, .222 Rem., .30-30; 24" barrel in .22 Hornet, .222 Rem., 22" in .22 Hornet, .30-30, 20" in .30-30; uncheckered American walnut pistol-grip stock; open rear sight, ramp front. Introduced in 1950; .30-30, .222 Rem. still in production; latter was introduced in 1964; .22 Hornet dropped, 1964. Used values, .30-30, $72 to $75; .222 Rem., $95 to $100; .22 Hornet, $100 to $110.

    **Model 340C** carbine has identical specifications as standard Model 340, except for 18½" barrel, in .30-30 only. Introduced in 1962; dropped, 1965. Used value, $125 to $135.

    **Model 340S** Deluxe has same specifications as Model 340, except for peep rear sight, hooded front; hand-checkered stock, swivel studs. Dropped, 1958. Used value, $145 to $165.

**SAVAGE Model 342:** bolt-action repeater; .22 Hornet only; has same specifications as Model 340 and, after 1953 was incorporated in manufacturer's line as Model 340. Introduced in 1950; dropped, 1953 as model. Used value, $95 to $110.

**Model 342S** has same specifications as Model 340S, but is in .22 Hornet only. Incorporated into Model 340 line in 1953. Used value, $95 to $110.

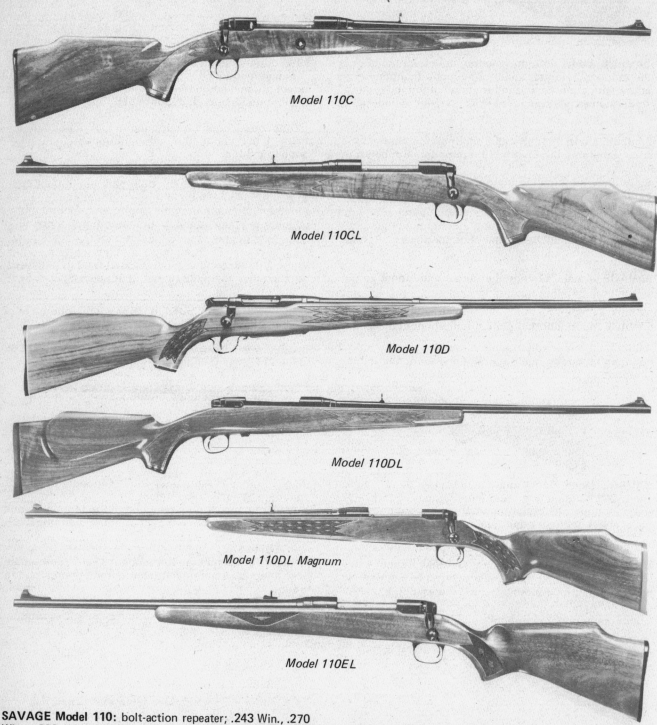

Model 110C

Model 110CL

Model 110D

Model 110DL

Model 110DL Magnum

Model 110EL

**SAVAGE Model 110:** bolt-action repeater; .243 Win., .270 Win., .308 Win., .30/06; 22″ barrel, 4-rd. box magazine; hand-checkered American walnut pistol-grip stock; open rear sight, ramp front. Introduced in 1958; dropped, 1963. This is another of those corporate successes that goes on and on in one variation or another. Used value, $106.50 to $120.

Model 110MC has same specifications as Model 110, except for 24″ barrel, Monte Carlo stock; in .22-250, .243 Win., .270 Win., .308 Win., .30/06. Introduced in 1959; dropped, 1969. Used value, $120 to $130.

Model 110MCL has the same specifications as Model 110MC, except it is built on left-hand action. Introduced in 1959; dropped, 1969. Used value, $125 to $135.

Model 110M magnum has specifications of Model 110MC, except has recoil pad; in .264, .300, .338 Win., 7mm Rem. magnum. Introduced in 1963; dropped, 1969. Used value, $135 to $145.

Model 110ML magnum has same specifications as Model

110M, except for being built on a left-hand action. Used value, $140 to $155.

**Model 110E** has the same general specifications as earlier versions of Model 110; .243 Win., .30/06, 7mm Rem. magnum; 24" stainless steel barrel for magnum, 20" ordnance steel for other calibers; 3-rd. box magazine for magnum, 4-rd. for others; uncheckered Monte Carlo stock on early versions; current models have checkered pistol grip, forearm; 7mm magnum has recoil pad; open rear sight, ramp front. Introduced in 1963; still in production. Used values, 7mm Rem. magnum, $140 to $145; other calibers, $125 to $130.

**Model 110EL** has the same specifications as Model 110E, except in 7mm Rem. magnum, .30/06 only; left-hand action. Used values, 7mm magnum, $145 to $155; .30/06, $135 to $145.

**Model 110P Premier Grade** comes in .243 Win., .30/06, 7mm Rem. magnum; 24" barrel of stainless steel for 7mm magnum, 22" for other calibers; 3-shot box magazine for magnum, 4-shot for others; skip-checkered Monte Carlo French walnut stock, rosewood pistol-grip cap, forearm tip; magnum version has recoil pad; open rear sight, ramp front. Introduced in 1964; dropped, 1970. Used values, 7mm magnum, $325 to $335; other calibers, $295 to $315.

**Model 110PL Premier Grade** has the same specifications as Model 110P, except for left-hand action. Used values, 7mm magnum, $335 to $345; other calibers, $335 to $345.

**Model 110PE Presentation Grade** has same specifications as Model 110P, except for engraved receiver, trigger guard, floor plate; stock is of choice French walnut. Introduced in 1958; dropped, 1970. Used values, 7mm magnum, $535 to $550; other calibers, $475 to $495.

**Model 110EL Presentation Grade** has same specifications as Model 11-PE, except it is built on a left-hand action. Used values, 7mm magnum, $550 to $575; other calibers, $500 to $525.

**Model 110C** was introduced in 1966; still in production; .22-250, .243 Win., .25/06, .270 Win., .30/06, .308 Win., 7mm Rem. magnum, .300 Win. magnum. Magnum calibers have 3-shot detachable box magazine; other calibers, 4-rd. magazine; magnum calibers, .22-250 have 24" barrel, others, 22"; hand-checkered Monte Carlo American walnut pistol-grip stock; magnum has recoil pad; open folding leaf rear sight, ramp front. Offered currently in .243, .270, .30/06, 7mm Rem. magnum. Used values, magnum calibers, $160 to $165; standard calibers, $160 to $165.

**Model 110B** (right-hand bolt) and 110 BL (left-hand bolt) were introduced in 1977 and are same as Model 110E except chambered for .30/06, .270 Win., and .243 Win. and have internal magazines. Used value, Model 110B, $145 to $150; Model 110BL, $150 to $155.

**SAVAGE/ANSCHUTZ Model 153:** bolt-action; .222 Rem. only; 24" barrel; manufactured to Savage specs by J.G. Anschutz, West Germany; skip-checkered French walnut stock; cheekpiece; rosewood grip cap, forearm tip; sling swivels; folding leaf open rear sight, hooded ramp front. Introduced in 1964; dropped, 1967. Used value, $275 to $290.

*Model 65M*

**SAVAGE Model 65:** bolt-action; .22 LR, long, short; 20" free-floating barrel; 5-rd. detachable box magazine; sliding safety; double extractors; American walnut Monte Carlo stock; checkered pistol grip, forearm; step adjustable open rear sight, gold bead ramp front. Introduced in 1965; dropped, 1974. Used value, $60 to $65.

**Model 65M** has same specifications as Model 65, but is chambered for .22 rimfire magnum cartridge. Introduced in 1966; still in production. Used value, $70 to $75.

*Model 73*

*Model 73Y*

**SAVAGE-Stevens Model 73:** bolt-action, single-shot; .22 Short, Long, LR; open rear sight, bead front; uncheckered hardwood pistol-grip stock. Introduced 1965, still in production. Used value, $30 to $35.

**Model 73Y** is Youth version of Model 73; specs are the same except for shorter butt stock, 18" barrel. Introduced 1965, still in production. Used value, $30 to $35.

*Model 164M*

**SAVAGE/ANSCHUTZ Model 164:** bolt-action; .22 LR only; 24" barrel; 5-rd. detachable clip magazine; fully adjustable single-stage trigger; receiver grooved for tip-off mount; European walnut stock, hand-checkered pistol grip, forearm; Monte Carlo comb, cheekpiece, schnabel forearm.

Introduced in 1966; still in production. Used value, $175 to $195.

**Model 164M** has same specifications as Model 164, except magazine holds 4 rds.; chambered for .22 rimfire magnum cartridge. Used value, $175 to $200.

*Model 54*

**SAVAGE/ANSCHUTZ Model 54:** bolt-action; .22 LR only; 23" barrel; 5-rd. clip magazine; adjustable single stage trigger; wing safety; receiver grooved fro tip-off mount, tapped for scope blocks; French walnut stock, with Monte Carlo roll-over comb, schnabel forearm tip. Hand-checkered pistol grip, forearm; folding leaf sight, hooded ramp gold bead front. Introduced in 1966; still in production. Used value, $295 to $315.

**Model 54M** has same specifications as Model 54, except chambered for .22 rimfire magnum. Introduced in 1973; still in production. Used value, $325 to $335.

*Model 184*

**SAVAGE/ANSCHUTZ Model 184:** bolt-action; .22 LR only, 21½" barrel; 5-rd. detachable clip magazine; factory-set trigger; receiver grooved for scope mounts; European walnut stock with Monte Carlo comb, schnabel forearm; hand-checkered pistol grip, forearm; folding leaf rear sight, hooded ramp front. Introduced in 1966; dropped, 1974. Used value, $125 to $135.

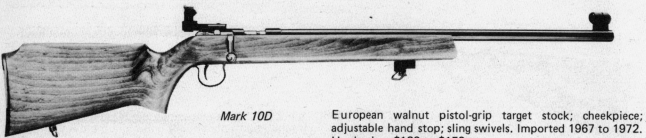

*Mark 10D*

**SAVAGE-Anschutz Mark 10:** bolt-action, single-shot; .22 LR; 26" barrel; micrometer rear sight, globe front; European walnut pistol-grip target stock; cheekpiece; adjustable hand stop; sling swivels. Imported 1967 to 1972. Used value, $130 to $150.

**Mark 10D** has same general specs as standard Mark 10, except for Monte Carlo stock, different rear sight. Imported 1972 only. Used value, $130 to $150.

**SAVAGE-Stevens Model 46:** bolt-action; .22 Short, Long, LR; tubular magazine holds 15 LRs; 20" barrel; uncheckered hardwood pistol-grip stock, or checkered Monte Carlo stock. Manufactured 1969 to 1973. Used value, $45 to $50.

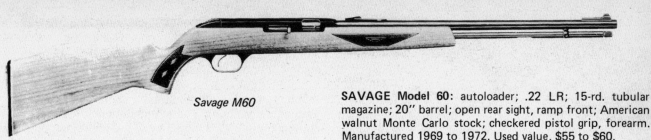

*Savage M60*

SAVAGE Model 88: autoloader; .22 LR; has same general specs as Model 60, except for ramp front sight,

SAVAGE Model 60: autoloader; .22 LR; 15-rd. tubular magazine; 20" barrel; open rear sight, ramp front; American walnut Monte Carlo stock; checkered pistol grip, forearm. Manufactured 1969 to 1972. Used value, $55 to $60.

uncheckered hardwood stock. Manufactured 1969 to 1972. Used value, $40 to $45.

*Savage Model 90*

SAVAGE Model 90 Carbine: autoloader; .22 LR; same general specs as Model 60, except for 10-rd, tubular

magazine, 16½" barrel; folding leaf rear sight, bead front; uncheckered walnut carbine stock; barrel band; sling swivels. Manufactured 1969 to 1972. Used value, $55 to $60.

*Savage Model 63K*

SAVAGE Model 63K: bolt-action, single-shot; .22 Short, Long, LR; 18" barrel; furnished with key to lock trigger; open rear sight, hooded ramp front; full-length hardwood

pistol-grip stock; sling swivels. Manufactured 1970 to 1972. Used value. $35 to $40.

Model 63M has same specs as Model 63K, except chambered for .22 WRFM. Manufactured 1970 to 1972. Used value, $40 to $45.

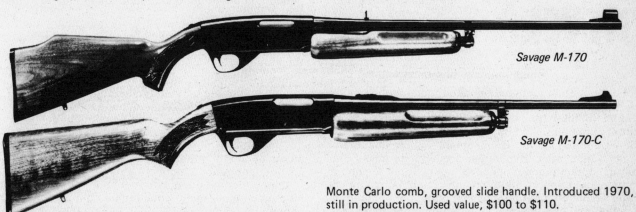

*Savage M-170*

*Savage M-170-C*

SAVAGE Model 170: pump-action; .30-30, .35 Rem.; 3-rd. tubular magazine; 22" barrel; folding leaf rear sight, ramp front; select checkered American walnut pistol-grip stock;

Monte Carlo comb, grooved slide handle. Introduced 1970, still in production. Used value, $100 to $110.

Model 170C Carbine has same specs as Model 170 rifle, except for straight comb stock, 18½" barrel; chambered for .30-30 only. Introduced 1974, still in production. Used value, $100 to $110.

SAVAGE-Stevens Model 72: lever-action, single-shot; .22 Short, Long, LR; 22" octagonal barrel; falling-block action, case-hardened frame; open rear sight, bead front;

uncheckered American walnut straight-grip stock, forearm. Advertised as Crackshot, but differs from original made by Stevens. Manufactured 1972 to 1974. Used value, $45 to $50.

SAVAGE-Stevels Model 74: lever-action, single-shot; same specs as Model 72, except for 22" round barrel,

black-finished frame, hardwood stock. Manufactured 1972 to 1974. Used value, $40 to $45.

*Model 111*

**SAVAGE Model 111:** bolt-action; .243 Win., .270 Win., 7x57, 7mm Rem. magnum, .30/06; 3-rd. clip in 7mm Rem. magnum, 4 rds. in others; 22'', 24'' barrels; leaf rear sight, hooded ramp front; select checkered American walnut pistol-grip stock; Monte Carlo comb, cheekpiece; pistol-grip cap; detachable swivels, sling. Advertised as Chieftain. Introduced 1974, still in production. Used value, $175 to $190.

*Model 112V*

**SAVAGE Model 112V:** bolt-action, single-shot; .220 Swift, .222 Rem., .223 Rem., .22-250, .243 Win., .25/06; 26'' heavy varmint barrel, scope bases; no sights; select American walnut varminter stock; high comb; checkered pistol grip; detachable sling swivels. Introduced 1975, dropped 1979. Used value, $180 to $190.

**Model 112R** has same general design specs as standard model, except for 5-rd. magazine; .22-250, .25/06; 26'' tapered barrel; free-floating American walnut stock; fluted comb, Wundhammer swell at pistol grip; drilled, tapped for scope mounts; top tang safety. Still in production. Used value, $225 to $235.

*Model 80*

**SAVAGE-Stevens Model 80:** autoloader; 15-rd. tubular magazine; 20'' barrel; open rear sight, bead front; checkered American walnut pistol-grip stock; side safety. Introduced 1976, still in production. Used value, $55 to $60.

# STEVENS

*Ideal No. 44*

**STEVENS Ideal No. 44:** single-shot, lever-action, rolling block; takedown; .22 LR, .25 rimfire, .32 rimfire, .25-20, .32-20, .32-40, .38-40, .38-55, .44-40; 24'' or 26'' barrel, round, full octagon, half octagon; uncheckered straight-grip walnut stock, forearm; open rear sight, Rocky Mountain front. Introduced in 1894; dropped, 1932. Primarily of collector interest. Used value, $245 to $255.

**Ideal No. 44½** has the same general specs as No. 44, except for falling-block lever-action replacing rolling block of earlier model. Manufactured 1903 to 1916. Collector interest. Used value, $350 to $375.

**Other Ideal versions**, through No. 56, are virtually identical in basic specs, differing only in type of updated improvements. Prices vary from standard and No. 44½, depending upon improvements. Used values, $275 to $375.

*Favorite No. 17*

**STEVENS Favorite No. 17:** single-shot, lever-action, takedown; .22 LR; .25 rimfire, .32 rimfire; 24'' barrel, with other lengths available on special order; uncheckered walnut straight-grip stock, tapered forearm; open rear sight, Rocky Mountain front. Introduced in 1894; dropped, 1935. Collector value. Used value, $90 to $100.

**STEVENS Favorite No. 18:** has the same specifications as the No. 17, except for substitution of vernier peep rear sight, Beach combination front, addition of leaf middle sight. Introduced in 1894; dropped, 1935. Collector value. Used value, $115 to $125.

**STEVENS Favorite No. 19:** has same specifications as No. 17, except for substitution of Lyman combination rear sight, Lyman front, addition of leaf middle sight. Introduced in 1895; dropped, 1935. Collector value. Used value, $115 to $125.

**STEVENS Favorite No. 20:** has same specifications as No. 17, except for smoothbore barrel for .22 rimfire, .32 rimfire shot cartridges only. Introduced in 1895; dropped, 1935. Collector value. Used value, $120 to $130.

**STEVENS Favorite No. 27:** has the same specifications as No. 17, except for substitution of octagon barrel. Introduced in 1896; dropped, 1935. Collector value. Used value, $115 to $125.

**STEVENS Favorite No. 28:** has same specifications as No. 18, except for substitution of octagon barrel. Introduced in 1896; dropped, 1935. Collector value. Used value, $135 to $145.

**STEVENS Favorite No. 29:** has same specifications as No. 19, except for substitution of octagon barrel. Introduced in 1896; dropped, 1935. Collector value. Used value, $125 to $135.

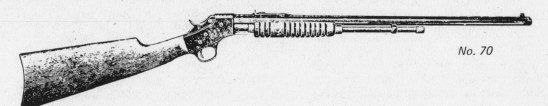

*No. 70*

**STEVENS No. 70:** slide-action repeater; exposed hammer; .22 LR, long, short; 22" barrel; tube magazine holds 11 LR, 13 long, 15 short cartridges; uncheckered straight-grip stock, grooved slide handle; open rear sight, bead front. Introduced in 1907; dropped, 1934. Collector value. Used value, $100 to $125.

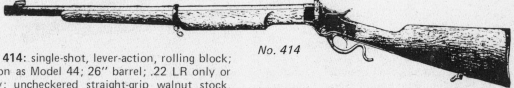

*No. 414*

**STEVENS No. 414:** single-shot, lever-action, rolling block; uses same action as Model 44; 26" barrel; .22 LR only or .22 short only; uncheckered straight-grip walnut stock, military-styled forearm, sling swivels; Lyman receiver peep sight, blade front. Introduced in 1912; dropped, 1932. Known as Armory Model, has some collector value affecting price. Used value, $235 to $250.

*No. 26*

**STEVENS Crack Shot No. 26:** single-shot, takedown, lever-action; .22 LR, .32 rimfire; 18", 22" barrel; uncheckered straight-grip walnut stock, tapered forearm; open rear sight, blade front. Introduced in 1913; dropped, 1939. Collector value. Used value, $95 to $110.

**STEVENS No. 26½:** has the same specifications as No. 26, except for smoothbore barrel for .22, .32 rimfire shot cartridges. Introduced in 1914; dropped, 1939. Collector value. Used value, $95 to $100.

*No. 66*

**STEVENS No. 66:** bolt-action takedown repeater; .22 LR, long, short; 24" barrel; tube magazine holds 13 LR, 15 long, 19 short cartridges; uncheckered walnut pistol-grip stock, grooved forearm; open rear sight, bead front. Introduced in 1931; dropped, 1935. Used value, $60 to $75.

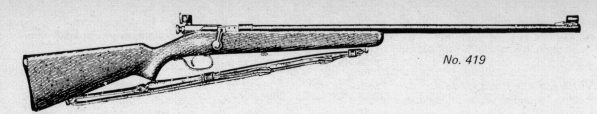

*No. 419*

STEVENS No. 419: bolt-action, takedown single-shot; termed the Junior Target Model; .22 LR only; 26" barrel; uncheckered walnut junior target stock; pistol grip; sling, swivels; Lyman No. 55 peep rear sight, blade front. Introduced in 1932, dropped, 1936. Used value, $60 to $65.

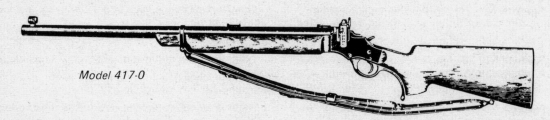

*Model 417-0*

STEVENS Walnut Hill No. 417-0: single-shot lever-action; .22 Hornet, .22 LR only; .22 short only; 28" heavy barrel or 29" extra-heavy; uncheckered walnut target stock; full pistol grip, beavertail forearm; sling swivels, barrel band, sling; Lyman No. 52L extension rear sight, No. 17A front. Introduced in 1932; dropped, 1947. Value largely based upon collector appeal. Used value, $350 to $375.

No. 417-1 Walnut Hill has same specifications as the No. 417-0, except for substitution of Lyman No. 48L receiver sight. Dropped, 1947. Used value, $350 to $375.

No. 417-2 Walnut Hill model has same specifications as No. 417-0, except for substitution of Lyman No. 1441 tang sight. Dropped, 1947. Used value, $375 to $400.

No. 417-3 Walnut Hill has the same specifications as No. 417-0, except that it was sold without sights. Dropped, 1947. Used value, $325 to $350.

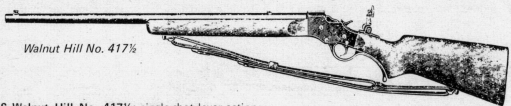

*Walnut Hill No. 417½*

STEVENS Walnut Hill No. 417½: single-shot lever-action; same general specifications as 417-0; .22 Hornet, .25 rimfire, .22 WRF, .22 LR; 28" barrel; uncheckered walnut sporting-style stock; pistol grip, semi-beavertail forearm; swivels, sling; Lyman No. 144 tang peep sight, folding middle sight, bead front. Introduced in 1932; dropped, 1940. Used value, $380 to $400.

*Walnut Hill No. 418*

STEVENS Walnut Hill No. 418: single-shot, takedown lever-action; .22 LR only, .22 short only; 26" barrel; uncheckered walnut stock; pistol grip, semi-beavertail forearm; sling swivels, sling; Lyman No. 144 tang peep sight, blade front. Introduced in 1932; dropped, 1940. Used value, $265 to $275.

*Walnut Hill No. 418½*

STEVENS Walnut Hill No. 418½: has the same general specifications as No. 418, except for availability in .25 Stevens rimfire, .22 WRF also; substitution of Lyman No. 2A tang peep sight, bead front. Introduced in 1932; dropped, 1940. Used value, $215 to $225.

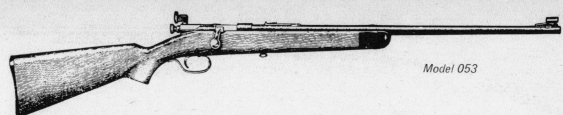

*Model 053*

**STEVENS Buckhorn Model 053:** bolt-action, takedown single-shot; .25 Stevens rimfire, .22 WRF, .22 LR, long, short; 24" barrel; uncheckered walnut stock; pistol grip, black forearm tip; receiver peep sight, open middle sight, hooded front. Introduced in 1935; dropped, 1948. Used value, $65 to $75.

Model 53 has the same specifications as Model 053, except for open rear sight, plain bead front. Used value, $60 to $65.

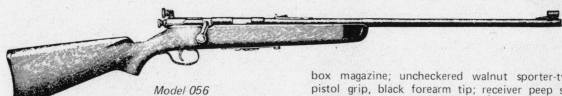

*Model 056*

**STEVENS Buckhorn Model 056:** bolt-action, takedown repeater; .22 LR, long, short; 24" barrel, 5-rd. detachable box magazine; uncheckered walnut sporter-type stock; pistol grip, black forearm tip; receiver peep sight, open middle sight, hooded front. Introduced in 1935; dropped, 1948. Used value, $75 to $85.

Model 56 has same specifications as Model 056, except for open rear sight, plain bead front. Used value, $60 to $70.

*Model 066*

**STEVENS Buckhorn Model 066:** bolt-action, takedown repeater; .22 LR, long, short; 24" barrel; tube magazine holds 15 LR, 17 long, 21 short cartridges; uncheckered walnut sporting stock; pistol grip, black forearm tip; receiver peep sight, open middle sight, hooded front. Introduced in 1935; dropped, 1948. Used value, $65 to $75.

Model 66 has the same specifications as Model 066, except for open rear sight, plain bead front. Used value, $55 to $65.

*Model 82*

**STEVENS Springfield Model 82:** bolt-action, takedown single-shot. Springfield was used as a brand name from 1935 until 1948, with the designation being dropped at that time. It should not be confused in any way with the Springfield Armory, although the name probably was registered with such mistaken identity in mind. After the Springfield brand name was dropped, rifles were known strictly by Stevens name. In .22 LR, long, short; 22" barrel; uncheckered walnut pistol-grip stock, grooved forearm; open rear sight, bead front. Introduced in 1935; dropped, 1939. Used value, $40 to $50.

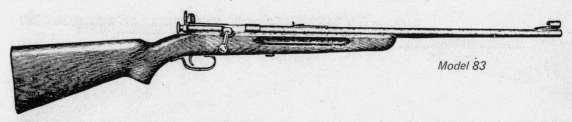

*Model 83*

**STEVENS Springfield Model 83:** bolt-action, takedown single-shot; same basic action as Model 82, but chambered for .25 Stevens, .22 WRF, .22 LR, long, short; 24" barrel; other specifications are identical to those of Model 82. Introduced in 1935; dropped, 1939. Used value, $50 to $55.

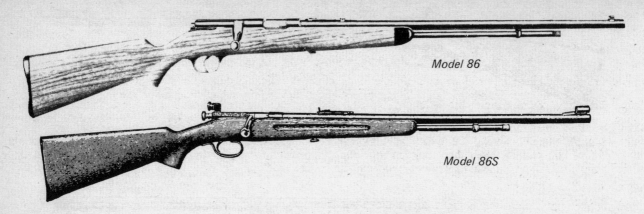

*Model 86*

*Model 86S*

STEVENS-Springfield Model 86: bolt-action, takedown repeater; .22 LR, long, short; 24" barrel; plated bolt, trigger; tube magazine holds 15 LR, 17 long, 21 short cartridges; unchecked military walnut stock; pistol grip, black forearm tip. Introduced in 1935, and produced until 1948 under Springfield brand name; produced from 1948 to 1965 under Stevens name when dropped. Used value, $65 to $70.

Model 086 has the same specifications as Model 86, except for substitution of peep rear sight, hooded front. Marketed under Springfield brand name from 1935 to 1948. Used value, $75 to $80.

Model 86-S is exactly the same as Model 086, but designation was changed when Springfield name was dropped in 1948; marketed as Stevens thereafter, until dropped, 1952. Used value, $75 to $80.

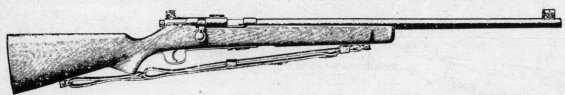

STEVENS Model 416: bolt-action, target model; .22 LR only; 26" heavy barrel; 5-rd. detachable box magazine; unchecked walnut target-type stock; sling swivels, sling; receiver peep sight, hooded front. Introduced in 1937; dropped, 1949. Used value, $145 to $165.

*Model 15Y*

STEVENS-Springfield Model 15: bolt-action, takedown single-shot; .22 LR, long, short; 22" barrel; unchecked pistol-grip stock; open rear sight, bead front. Introduced in 1937; dropped, 1948. Used value, $35 to $45.

Stevens Model 15 has identical specifications to Stevens-Springfield Model 15, except for substitution of 24"

barrel, redesigned stock, including black forearm tip. Introduced in 1948; dropped, 1965. Used value, $45 to $50.

Model 15Y, the so-called Youth Model, has same specifications as standard Stevens Model 15, except for 21" barrel, shorter buttstock. Introduced in 1958; dropped, 1965. Used value, $45 to $50.

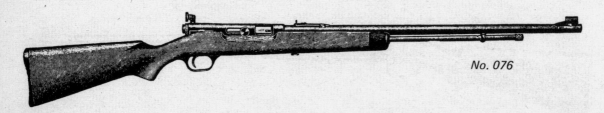

*No. 076*

STEVENS Buckhorn No. 76: takedown autoloader; .22 LR only; 24" barrel; 15-rd. tube magazine; unchecked sporter-style stock, black forearm tip; open rear sight, plain bead front. Introduced in 1938; dropped, 1948. Used value,

$70 to $75.

No. 076 has same specifications as No. 76, except for peep receiver sight, open middle sight, hooded front. Introduced in 1938; dropped, 1948. Used value, $75 to $85.

*Model 87*

**STEVENS Model 87:** takedown autoloader; .22 LR only; 24" barrel until late 60s, current production has 20" barrel; uncheckered pistol-grip stock, black forearm tip; open rear sight; bead front. Marketed as Springfield Model 87 from 1938 to 1948, until trade name dropped. Dropped, 1976.

**STEVENS Buckhorn No. 57:** takedown autoloader; has the same specifications as No. 76, except for 5-rd. detachable box magazine. Introduced in 1939; dropped, 1948. Used value, $65 to $75.

Used value, $60 to $65.
 **Model 087,** Springfield designation, has same specs as Model 87, except for peep rear sight, hooded front. Introduced in 1938; redesignated, 1948. Used value, $60 to $65.
 **Model 87-S** is Stevens designation for 087, as of 1948. Dropped, 1953. Used value, $60 to $65.

**No. 057** has the same specifications as the No. 57. Also introduced in 1939; dropped, 1948. Used value, $65 to $75.

*Model 84S*

**STEVENS-Springfield Model 84:** bolt-action, takedown repeater; has the same specifications as the Model 86, except for 5-rd. detachable box magazine. Introduced in 1940 as Springfield Model 84; when trade name was dropped in 1948, it was redesignated as Stevens Model 84 and continued until dropped, 1965. Used value, $50 to $55.
 **Model 084** has the same specifications as Springfield

Model 84, except for substitution of rear peep sight, hooded front. Introduced in 1940; when trade name was dropped in 1948, it was redesignated. Used value, $50 to $55.
 **Model 84S** is exactly the same as Model 084, but designation was changed when Springfield name was dropped. Marketed as Stevens Model 84-S from 1948 until dropped, 1952. Used value, $50 to $55.

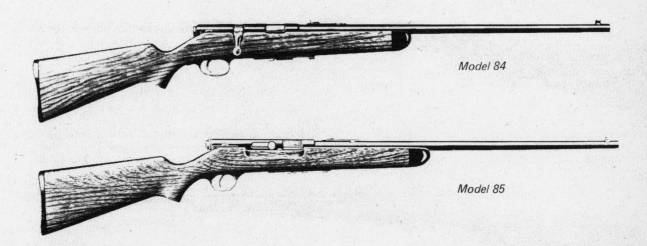
*Model 84*

*Model 85*

**STEVENS-Springfield Model 85:** has the same specifications as Model 87, except for 5-rd. detachable box magazine. From introduction in 1939 until 1948, was designated as Springfield Model 85. Has been Stevens Model 85 since 1948; dropped, 1976. Used value, $65 to $75.
 **Model 085** is same as Model 85, except for peep rear

sight, hooded front. This designation was used on Springfield brand rifles from 1939 until 1948. Used value, $65 to $75.
 **Model 85-S** is exactly the same as Model 085, but carries Stevens name since 1948; dropped, 1976. Used value, $65 to $75.

**STEVENS Model 322:** bolt-action carbine; .22 Hornet only; .21'' barrel; 4-rd. detachable box magazine; unchecked walnut pistol-grip stock; open rear sight, ramp front. Introduced in 1947; dropped, 1950. Used value, $105 to $115.

**Model 322-S** has the same specifications as the Model 322, except for substitution of a peep rear sight. Introduced in 1947; dropped, 1950. Used value, $115 to $120.

**STEVENS Model 325:** bolt-action carbine; .30-30 only; 21'' barrel; 3-rd. detachable box magazine; unchecked pistol-grip stock; open rear sight, bead front. Introduced in 1947; dropped, 1950. Used value, $95 to $110.

**Model 325-S** has same specifications as Model 325, except for substitution of peep rear sight. Introduced in 1947; dropped, 1950. Used value, $100 to $115.

# WALTHER

*Olympic*

**WALTHER Olympic Model:** bolt-action, single-shot; .22 LR; 26'' heavy barrel; extension micrometer rear sight, interchangeable front; hand-checkered pistol-grip target stock of European walnut; full rubber-covered beavertail forend; thumbhole, palm rest, adjustable buttplate; sling swivels. Manufactured in Germany prior to WWII. Used value, $400 to $425.

*Model 2*

**WALTHER Model 1:** autoloader; .22 LR, 5, 9-rd. detachable box magazine; 20'' barrel; tangent curve rear sight, ramp front; hand-checkered European walnut sporting stock; pistol grip; grooved forend; sling swivels. Has bolt-action feature, making it possible to fire as autoloader, single-shot or as bolt-operated repeater. Manufactured prior to WWII. Used value, $250 to $275.

**Model 2** has same basic specs as Model 1, except for 24½'' barrel, heavier stock. Used value, $250 to $275.

*Model V*

**WALTHER Model V:** bolt-action, single-shot; .22 LR; 26'' barrel; open rear sight, ramp front; unchecked European walnut pistol-grip sporting stock, grooved forend; sling swivels. Manufactured prior to World War II. Used value, $190 to $200.

**Model V Meisterbusche** has same general specs as standard model, except for checkered pistol grip, micrometer open rear sight. Used value, $210 to $225.

*Model KKJ*

**WALTHER Model KKJ:** bolt-action; .22 LR, .22 magnum, .22 Hornet; 24'' medium-heavy target barrel; 5-rd. clip checkered European walnut pistol-grip stock, forearm; high, tapered comb; sling swivels. Imported originally by Interarms. Introduced in 1957; .22 Hornet still in production. Used value, $320 to $335.

*Model KKM*

**WALTHER Model KKM Match Model:** bolt-action; single-shot; .22 LR only; 28" barrel; fully adjustable match trigger; micrometer rear sight, Olympic front with post, aperture inserts; European walnut stock with adjustable hook butt plate, hand shelf, ball-type offset yoke palm rest.

Imported from Germany by Interarms. Introduced in 1957; still in production. Used value, $525 to $575.

Model KKM-S has same specs as Model KKM, except for adjustable cheekpiece. Used value, $430 to $450.

**Model KKJ-Ho** has same specs as KKJ, except chambered for .22 Hornet cartridge. Used value, $240 to $250.

**Model KKJ-Ma** has same specs as KKJ, except chambered for .22 WRFM. Used value, $240 to $250.

*U.I.T. Match Model*

**WALTHER U.I.T. Match Model:** bolt action; single-shot; .22 LR only; 25½" barrel; conforms to NRA, UIT rules; fully adjustable trigger; micrometer rear sight; interchange-able post or aperture front; European walnut stock adjustable for length, drop; forearm guide rail for sling or palm rest. Imported from Germany by Interarms. Introduced in 1966; still in production. Used value, $425 to $450.

*Moving Target Match*

**WALTHER Moving Target Model:** bolt-action; single shot; .22 LR only; 23.6" barrel; micrometer rear sight, globe front; especially designed for running boar competition; receiver grooved for dovetail scope mounts; European walnut thumb-hole stock; stippled forearm, pistol grip; adjustable cheekpiece, buttplate. Imported from Germany by Interarms. Introduced in 1972; still in production. Used value, $420 to $435.

*Prone 400*

**WALTHER Prone 400 Model:** bolt action; single-shot; .22 LR only; has the same general specifications as U.I.T. Match Model except for scope blocks, split stock for cheek-piece adjustment; especially designed for prone shooting. Introduced in 1972; still in production. Used value, $440 to $465.

*Model SSV*

**WALTHER Model SSV:** bolt-action, single-shot; .22 LR, .22 Hornet; 25½" barrel; no sights; European walnut Monte Carlo stock; high cheekpiece, full pistol grip, forend. Used value, $300 to $320.

Model GX-1

**WALTHER Model GX-1:** bolt-action, single-shot; .22 LR; 25½" heavy barrel; free rifle design; micrometer aperture rear sight; globe front; European walnut thumbhole stock; adjustable cheekpiece, buttplate; removable butt hook; accessory rail; hand stop, palm rest, counter-weight, sling swivels. Used value, $475 to $500.

# WEATHERBY

Deluxe Magnum

**WEATHERBY Deluxe Magnum:** Roy Weatherby's first rifle; bolt-action in .220 Rocket, .257 Weatherby magnum, .270 Weatherby magnum, 7mm Weatherby magnum, .300 Weatherby magnum and .375 Weatherby magnum. Mauser Brevex actions were built to Weatherby's specs by FN; some Springfield actions were used; barrel length was 24" on all but .375WM, which had 26" barrel; Monte Carlo stock with cheekpiece; hand-checkered pistol grip, forearm; black grip cap, forearm tip; quick-detachable sling swivels. Introduced in 1948; dropped, 1955. Used value, $350 to $365.

Deluxe 378 Magnum

**WEATHERBY Deluxe .378 Magnum:** has same specs as Deluxe Magnum, except in .378 Weatherby magnum only; 26" barrel. Action is Schultz & Larsen to Weatherby specs. Dropped, 1955. Used value, $400 to $425.

**WEATHERBY Deluxe:** same specs as Deluxe Magnum, except chambered for .270 Winchester, .30/06. Dropped 1955. Used value, $266.50 to $279.50.

**WEATHERBY Mark V Deluxe:** bolt-action in .22/250, .30/06, .224 Weatherby Varmintmaster and Weatherby magnum chamberings of .240, .257, .270, 7mm, .300, .340, .378 and .460. Mark V action available in right or left-hand model; some actions made by Sauer in Germany to Weatherby specs; depending on caliber, box magazine holds 2 to 5 rds.; 24" barrels; no sights; drilled, tapped for scope mounts; Monte Carlo stock, cheekpiece; skip checkering on pistol grip, forearm; forearm tip, pistol grip cap, recoil pad;

Mark V Deluxe

quick-detachable sling swivels. Introduced in 1958, made in U.S. from 1958 to 1960, then production transferred to Germany; still in production. Left-hand action worth $25 more than right-hand. Used values, for right-hand models, .460 Weatherby magnum, $600 to $625; .378 Weatherby magnum, $525 to $550; other calibers, $435 to $450.

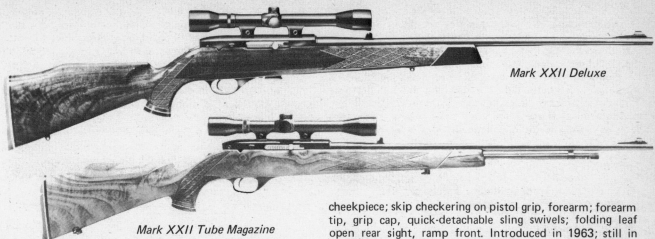

*Mark XXII Deluxe*

*Mark XXII Tube Magazine*

**WEATHERBY Mark XXII Deluxe:** .22 LR; semi-automatic 24'' barrel, 5, 10-shot clip magazines; Monte Carlo stock, cheekpiece; skip checkering on pistol grip, forearm; forearm tip, grip cap, quick-detachable sling swivels; folding leaf open rear sight, ramp front. Introduced in 1963; still in production. Used value, $140 to $160.

**XXII Tubular Magazine** version introduced 1973, still in production. Made in Japan. Used value, $140 to $160.

*Vanguard*

**WEATHERBY Vanguard:** bolt-action; .25/06, .243, .270, .30/06, .308, .264, 7mm, .300 Win. magnum; 3 or 5-rd. magazines, depending on caliber; 24'' barrel, adjustable trigger; no sights; receiver drilled, tapped for scope mounts; hinged floor plate; American walnut stock; pistol-grip cap; forearm tip; hand-checkered forearm, pistol-grip. Introduced in 1970; still in production. Used value, $245 to $260.

# WINCHESTER

*Model 73 Rifle*

*Model 73 Carbine*

**WINCHESTER Model 73:** lever-action; .22RF, .32-20, .38-40, .44-40; 6, 12, 15 or 17-rd. tubular magazine; 24'' barrel; open rear sight, bead or blade front; uncheckered American walnut straight-grip stock, forend. Manufactured 1873 to 1924. Collector value. Used value, $950 to $1100.

**WINCHESTER Low-Wall Sporter:** lever-action, single-shot; .22 RF; 28'' round, octagonal barrel; solid frame; open rear

**Model 73 Carbine** has same general specs as rifle, except for 20'' barrel, 12-rd. magazine. Collector value. Used value, $1350 to $1500.

**Model 73 Special Sporter** has same specs as standard rifle, except for octagon barrel only, color case-hardened receiver, select American walnut pistol-grip stock. Collector value. Used value, $1750 to $1950.

sight, blade front; uncheckered American walnut straight stock, forend. Manufactured 1885 to 1920. Collector value. Used value, $300 to $350.

**WINCHESTER High-Wall Sporter:** lever-action, single-shot; .22 RF through .50; solid frame or takedown; light 30" barrel; open rear sight, blade front; uncheckered American walnut straight-grip stock, forend. Manufactured 1885 to 1920. Collector value. Used value, $450 to $500.

**High-Wall Special Grade** has same specs as standard high-wall, except for better wood; hand-checkered stock, forend. Collector value. Used value, $700 to $750.

**High-Wall Schuetzen** has same basic action as standard high-wall; solid frame or takedown; spur lever; double-set trigger; 30" octagonal barrel; Vernier rear tang peep sight, wind-gauge front; European walnut Schuetzen-type stock; hand-checkered forend, pistol grip; Schuetzen buttplate, adjustable palm rest. Collector value. Used value, $1750 to $1900.

**High-Wall Winder Musket** has same basic specs of other high-wall models; chambered for .22 Short, .22 LR; 28" round barrel; solid frame or takedown; musket-type rear sight, blade front; straight-grip military-type stock, forend. Collector value. Used value, $400 to $450.

*Model 1886*

**WINCHESTER Model 1886:** lever-action repeating rifle; it is more a collector's item than practical rifle; of 10 black powder calibers in which it was made, all are obsolete but .45/70; has 8-shot tube magazine or 4-shot half magazine; 26" barrel, round, half-octagonal, octagonal; open rear sight; bead or blade front sight; plain straight stock, forearm. Introduced in 1886; discontinued, 1935. Price when discontinued, $53.75; used value, $575 to $650.

**Model 1886 Carbine** is same as rifle but with 22" barrel. Used value, $735 to $775.

*Model 90*

**WINCHESTER Model 90:** slide-action repeater, with visible hammer; tubular magazine holds 15 .22 rimfire shorts, 12 longs, 11 LR rds; also chambered for .22 WRF; magazine holds 12 of these. 24" octagonal barrel; plain, straight stock, grooved slide handle; open rear, bead front sight; originally solid frame design, after serial No. 15,499, all were takedowns. Introduced in 1890; discontinued, 1932. Retail when discontinued, $22.85; used value, $225 to $250.

*Model 92*

**WINCHESTER Model 92:** lever-action repeater; 24" barrel, round; half-octagonal, octagonal; 13-shot tube magazine, 7-shot half-magazine, 10-shot two-thirds magazine; available in .25-20, .32-40, .38-40, .44-40; plain, straight stock, forearm; open rear, bead front sight. Introduced in 1892; dropped, 1941. Price when discontinued, $22.80; used value, $400 to $500.

**Model 92 Carbine** had 20" barrel, 11 or 5-shot magazine. Used value, $500 to $600.

**Model 92 was redesignated as Model 53** in 1924, with modifications, including 6-shot tube half magazine in solid frame, 7-shot in takedown. Barrel was 22" nickel steel; open rear sight, bead front; straight stock; pistol grip stock optional; forearm was redesigned. Introduced in 1924; dropped, 1932. Used value, $400 to $425.

*Model 94 Antique*

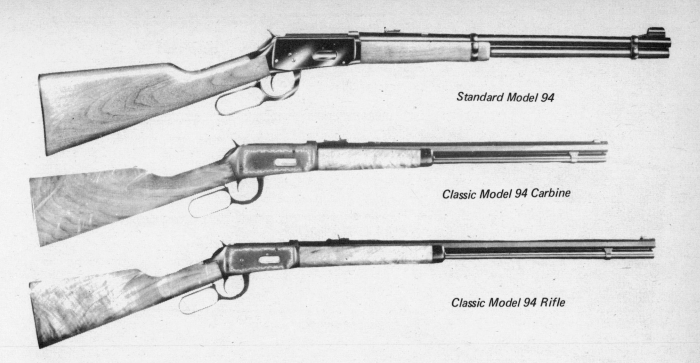

*Standard Model 94*

*Classic Model 94 Carbine*

*Classic Model 94 Rifle*

**WINCHESTER Model 94:** Carbine, center-fire lever-action. Originally available in .30-30, .32 Special, .25-35 Winchester, .32-40, .38-55, .44 magnum added in 1967. Originally introduced in rifle length, but discontinued in 1936. Currently made only in .30-30. Rifles had 22", 26" barrels; carbine, 20" barrel; carbine has full-length tube magazine with 6-rnd capacity, half-length magazine with 4-rnd capacity; plain, uncheckered American walnut stock; open rear sight; blade front on early versions; ramp front sight introduced in 1931. Production of receiver mechanism revised from 1964 to 1971. Post-'71 version has redesigned steel carrier with sturdier block design, redesigned lever camming slot, improved loading port; barrel band on forearm; saddle ring. Introduced in 1894; still in production. Used values, pre-1964 version, $265 to $275; pre-1971 version, $95 to $100; post-1971 version, $95 to $110.

**Model 94 Magnum** carbine has same general specifications as the standard Model 94, except that magazine holds 10 .44 magnum cartridges. Introduced in 1968; dropped, 1972. Used value, $240 to $275.

**Model 94 Classic** has same general specifications as standard Model 94, except for octagonal barrel in 20", 26" lengths; steel butt plate, semi-fancy American walnut stock, forearm; scroll work on receiver; .30-30 only. Introduced in 1957; dropped, 1970. Used values: carbine, $150 to $165; rifle length, $165 to $175.

**Model 94 Antique** has same general specifications as standard Model 94, except for case-hardened receiver with scrollwork. Introduced in 1968; dropped, 1974. Used value, $140 to $165.

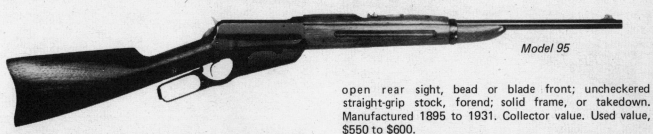

*Model 95*

**WINCHESTER Model 95:** lever-action; .30-40 Krag, .30 Gov't. (03), .30 Gov't. (06), .303 British, .35 Winchester, .38-72, .405 Winchester, .40-72; .30-40, .303 have 5-rd. box magazine, 4 rds. for other calibers; 24", 26", 28" barrel; open rear sight, bead or blade front; uncheckered straight-grip stock, forend; solid frame, or takedown. Manufactured 1895 to 1931. Collector value. Used value, $550 to $600.

**Model 95 Carbine** has same specs as Model 95 rifle, except for carbine stock, solid frame only, 22" barrel; chambered for .30-40, .30-30, .30/06 (see above), .303 British. Collector value. Used value, $750 to $800.

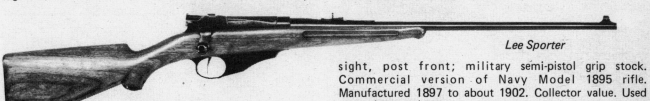

*Lee Sporter*

**WINCHESTER-Lee Musket:** bolt-action; 6mm (.236 USN); 5-rd. clip-loaded box magazine; 28" barrel; folding leaf rear sight, post front; military semi-pistol grip stock. Commercial version of Navy Model 1895 rifle. Manufactured 1897 to about 1902. Collector value. Used value, $600 to $625.

**Lee Sporter** has same specs as musket, except for sporter stock, 24" barrel, open rear sight, bead front. Manufactured 1897 to about 1902. Collector value. Used value, $650 to $700.

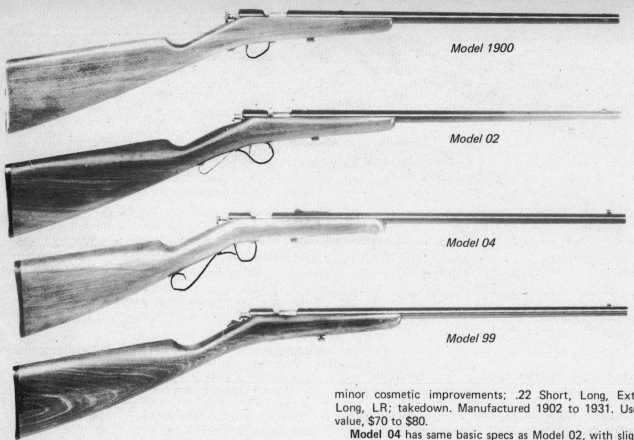

*Model 1900*

*Model 02*

*Model 04*

*Model 99*

**WINCHESTER Model 1900:** bolt-action, single-shot; .22 Short, Long; 18″ round barrel; takedown; open rear sight, blade front; straight-grip one-piece American walnut stock. Manufactured 1899 to 1902. Some collector interest. Used value, $75 to $90.

**Model 02** has same basic specs as Model 1900, with

minor cosmetic improvements; .22 Short, Long, Extra Long, LR; takedown. Manufactured 1902 to 1931. Used value, $70 to $80.

**Model 04** has same basic specs as Model 02, with slight changes in stock design; .22 Short, Long, Extra Long, LR; 21″ round barrel. Manufactured 1904 to 1931. Used value, $70 to $80.

**Thumb Trigger Model 99** has same specs as Model 02, except button at rear of cocking piece serves as trigger. Manufactured 1904 to 1923. Some collector interest. Used value, $225 to $240.

*Model 03*

**WINCHESTER Model 03:** self-loader; .22 Winchester Auto RF; 10-rd. tubular magazine in butt; 20″ barrel; takedown; open rear sight, bead front; uncheckered straight-grip stock,

forend. Manufactured 1903 to 1932. Collector value. Used value, $275 to $300.

*Model 05*

**WINCHESTER Model 05:** self-loader; .32 Win. Self-Loading, .35 Win. Self-Loading; 5, 10-rd. box magazine, 22″ barrel; takedown; open rear sight, bead

front; uncheckered American walnut pistol-grip stock, forend. Manufactured 1905 to 1920. Collector value. Used value, $325 to $350.

**Model 07** has same general design specs as Model 05, except chambered for .351 Win Self-Loading only; 20″

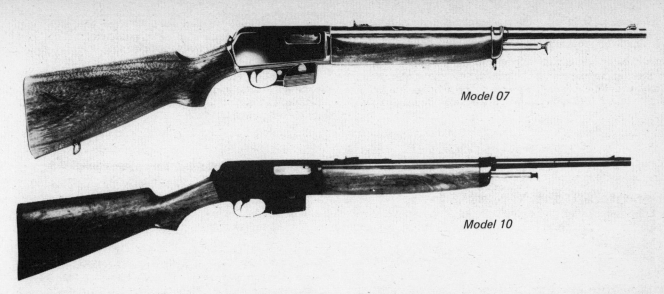

Model 07

Model 10

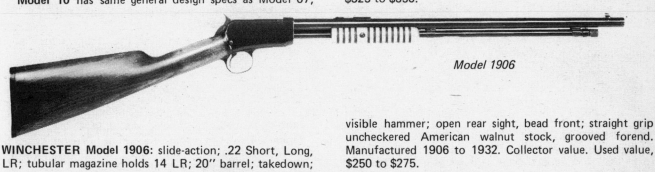

Model 1906

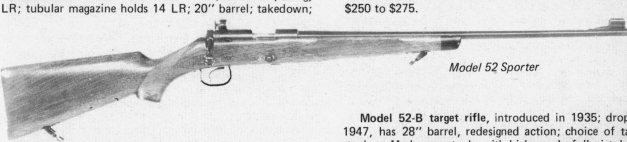

Model 52 Sporter

barrel. Manufactured 1907 to 1957. Collector value. Used value, $325 to $350.

**Model 10** has same general design specs as Model 07, except chambered for .401 Win. Self-Loading. Manufactured 1910 to 1936. Collector value. Used value, $325 to $350.

**WINCHESTER Model 1906:** slide-action; .22 Short, Long, LR; tubular magazine holds 14 LR; 20" barrel; takedown; visible hammer; open rear sight, bead front; straight grip uncheckered American walnut stock, grooved forend. Manufactured 1906 to 1932. Collector value. Used value, $250 to $275.

**WINCHESTER Model 52:** bolt-action rifle. Like taxes, this rifle just goes on, some models being dropped to be replaced by updates; there have been no less than 14 variations, one — Model 52-D — still in production. Model 52 target rifle was introduced in 1919; dropped in 1937. Had standard barrel, 28"; .22 LR, 5-shot box magazine; folding leaf peep rear sight, blade front sight, with options available; scope bases; originally had semi-military stock; pistol grip; grooves on forearm; later versions had higher comb, semi-beavertail forearm; slow lock model was replaced in 1929 by speed lock; last arms of model bore serial number followed by letter "A." Used value, slow lock style, $200 to $215; speed lock, $225 to $235.

**Model 52 heavy barrel** model had speed lock; same general specs as standard model, except for heavy barrel; a Lyman 17G front sight. Dropped, 1939. Used value, $265 to $275.

**Model 52 sporting rifle;** same as standard model, except for 24" lightweight barrel; deluxe sporting stock, checkered, with black forend tip; cheekpiece; has Lyman No. 48 receiver sight, gold bead on hooded ramp at front. Dropped, 1958. Used value, $690 to $750.

**Model 52-B target rifle,** introduced in 1935; dropped, 1947, has 28" barrel, redesigned action; choice of target stock or Marksman stock, with high comb, full pistol grip, beavertail forearm; wide variety of sights was available at added cost. Used value, sans sight, $225 to $240.

**Model 52-B heavy barrel** has same specs as standard 52-B, except for heavier barrel. Used value, $235 to $250.

**Model 52-B bull gun** has extra-heavy barrel, Marksman stock; other specs are same as standard Model 52-B. Used value, $265 to $295.

**Model 52-B sporting rifle** is same as first type Model 52 sporting rifle, except that it utilizes Model 52-B action. Dropped, 1961. Used value, $690 to $750.

**Model 52-C target rifle** — and others in "C" series — introduced in 1947; dropped, 1961. Target rifle has improved action, trigger mechanism, with new Marksman stock, heavy barrel; various sight combinations available at added cost; other specs are same as original model. Used value, sans sights, $245 to $265.

**Model 52-C standard** model has same specs as the original Model 52 heavy barrel, but with the standard barrel. Used value, $215 to $225.

**Model 52-C bull gun** has same general specs as Model 52 heavy barrel model, but has extra-heavy bull barrel, giving gun weight of 12 lbs. Used value, $250 to $265.

**Model 52-D target rifle** was introduced in 1961; continues in production. Action has been redesigned as single-shot only for .22 LR; has 28" free-floating standard or heavy barrel; blocks for standard target scopes; redesigned Marksman stock; rubber butt plate; accessory channel in stock with forend stop. Used value, sans sights, $265 to $275.

**Model 52 International Match Rifle** introduced in 1976, features laminated international-style stock with aluminum forend assembly, adjustable palm rest. Used values, sans sights: with ISU trigger, $425 to $435; with Kenyon trigger, $500 to $525.

**Model 52 International Prone Rifle**, introduced in 1976, has same features as International Match model, except for oil finished stock with removable roll-over cheekpiece for easy bore cleaning. Used value, sans sights, $340 to $360.

*Model 55*

**WINCHESTER Model 55 Center-fire:** lever-action; .25-35, .30-30, .32 Win. Special; 3-rd. tubular magazine. 24" round barrel; open rear sight, bead front; uncheckered American walnut straight-grip stock, forend. Based on Model 94 design. Collector value. Manufactured 1924 to 1932. Used value, $550 to $600.

*Model 54 Improved Sporter*

**WINCHESTER Model 54:** bolt-action center-fire. This is another of those models that verged on being an empire. There were numerous models and styles, in spite of the fact that it had a relatively short life. What the manufacturer calls the "first type" was made from 1925 to 1930; the improved type, from 1930 to 1936.

The early type sporting rifle had a 24" barrel, 5-shot box magazine and was in .270 Win. 7x57mm, .30-30, .30/06, 7.65mmx53mm, 9x57mm; two-piece firing pin; open rear sight, bead front. Stock was checkered, pistol grip design; scored steel butt plate, checkered from 1930 on; forearm tapered. Retail, when dropped 1936, $59.75; used value, $275 to $350.

**Model 54 carbine** — first type — was added in 1927; it had plain stock, grasping grooves on forearm, 20" barrel. Used value, $350 to $375.

**Model 54 super grade** was same as the early sporter, except for deluxe stock with pistol grip cap, cheekpiece, black forend tip. Came with quick-detachable sling swivels one-inch leather sling. Used value, $425 to $450.

**Model 54 sniper's rifle** has heavy 26" barrel, Lyman No. 48 rear peep sight, blade front sight; semi-military type stock; only in .30/06. Used value, $400 to $425.

**Model 54 sniper's match rifle** sort of gilds the lily; it is the same as the early sniper-model, but with Marksman target stock, scope bases and the same variety of calibers as standard model. Used value, $465 to $475.

**Model 54 National Match** rifle differs from standard model only in that it has Lyman sights, Marksman target stock, scope bases. Used value, $375 to $400.

**Model 54 target rifle** is same as standard model, but has 24" medium-weight barrel, 26" in .220 Swift; has Marksman target stock, Lyman sights, scope bases. Used value, $425 to $435.

**Model 54 improved sporter** has speed lock, one-piece firing pin; NRA-type stock; checkered pistol grip, forearm; 5-shot box magazine; in .22 Hornet, .220 Swift, .250-3000, .257 Roberts, .270 Win, 7x57mm, .30/06; has 24" barrel, except for 26" for .220 Swift. Used value, $325 to $375.

**Model 54 improved carbine** is same as improved sporter, but has 20" barrel; stock may be NRA type or lightweight stock used on original version. Used value, $385 to $400.

*Model 56*

**WINCHESTER Model 56:** bolt-action .22 rimfire, choice of .22 shorts, or LRs; 5, 10-shot magazines; 22" barrel; uncheckered pistol grip stock, schnabel-type forearm; open rear sight, bead front. Introduced in 1926; dropped, 1929. Retail when discontinued, $21; used value, $115 to $125.

*Model 57*

**WINCHESTER Model 57:** bolt-action target rifle; same as Model 56, but with semi-military-type target stock, swivels, web sling; Lyman peep sight, blade front; .22 LR, but avail-able until 1930 in .22 short. Introduced in 1926; dropped, 1936. Retail when discontinued, $25; used value, $125 to $150.

*Model 58*

**WINCHESTER Model 58:** bolt-action, single-shot; .22 Short, Long, LR; 18" barrel; open rear sight, blade front sight; uncheckered straight-grip hardwood stock. Same general specs as Model 02. Manufactured 1928 to 1931. Used value, $55 to $65.

*Model 59*

**WINCHESTER Model 59:** bolt-action, single-shot; .22 long, short, LR; 23" barrel; pistol grip, uncheckered one-piece stock; open rear sight, blade front; takedown configuration. Produced only in 1930. Retail price, $8.45; used value, $65 to $75.

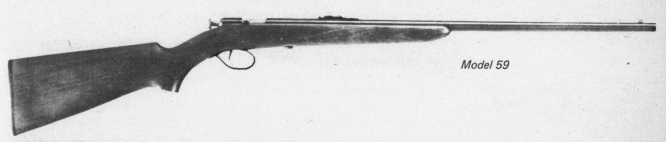

*Model 60*

**WINCHESTER Model 60:** bolt-action, single-shot redesign-ed Model 59; .22 short, long, LR; introduced in 1931; dis-continued, 1934. 23" barrel, until 1933; 27" thereafter; plain, pistol grip stock; open rear sight, blade-type front. Retail when discontinued, $5.50; used value, $65 to $75.

*Model 60A*

**WINCHESTER Model 60A:** same as Model 60, except for Lyman rear peep sight, square-top front; has semi-military target stock, web sling; introduced in 1933; discontinued, 1939. Retail price when discontinued, $8; used value, $100 to $125.

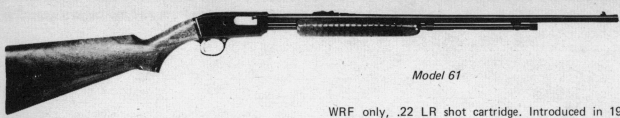

*Model 61*

**WINCHESTER Model 61**: hammerless slide-action, take-down repeater; .22 short, long, LR; tubular magazine holds 20 shorts, 16 longs, 14 LRs; 24" barrel, open rear sight, bead front; uncheckered pistol grip stock, grooved semi-beavertail slide handle. Also available with 24" octagonal barrel, chambered for .22 shorts only, .22 LR only, .22 WRF only, .22 LR shot cartridge. Introduced in 1932; dropped, 1963. Retail when discontinued, $70; used value, $245 to $275.

    **The Model 61 Magnum** introduced in 1960; dropped, 1963, differs from the standard model only in that it is chambered for .22 rimfire magnum; magazine holds 12 rds. Used value, $325 to $350.

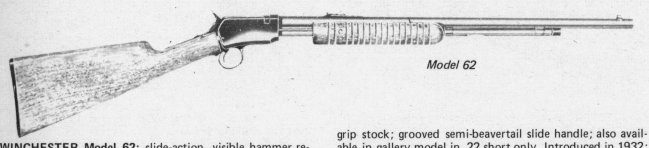

*Model 62*

**WINCHESTER Model 62**: slide-action, visible hammer repeater; chambered for .22 short, long, LR; tube magazine holds 20 shorts, 16 longs, 14 LRs; 23" barrel; plain, straight grip stock; grooved semi-beavertail slide handle; also available in gallery model in .22 short only. Introduced in 1932; dropped, 1959. Retail when discontinued, $53; used value, $225 to $250.

*Model 63*

**WINCHESTER Model 63**: takedown, self-loading rifle; .22 LR, .22 LR Super Speed; 23" barrel; 10-shot tube magazine in butt stock; open rear sight, bead front; plain pistol grip stock, forearm; available in early series with 20" barrel. Introduced in 1933; discontinued, 1958. Retail when discontinued, $85; used value, $245 to $265.

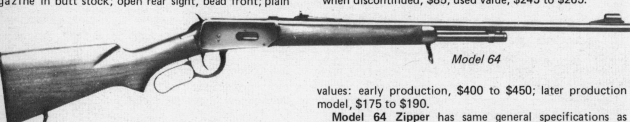

*Model 64*

**WINCHESTER Model 64**: lever-action; .25-35, .30-30, .32 Winchester Special; 20", 24" barrel; open rear sight, ramped bead front; uncheckered American walnut pistol-grip stock, forend. Improved version of Model 55. Originally manufactured 1933 to 1957; additional production with .30-30 chambering only, 24" barrel, 1972 to 1973. Collector value on original production. Used values: early production, $400 to $450; later production model, $175 to $190.

    **Model 64 Zipper** has same general specifications as original Model 64, but with peep rear sight, 26" barrel, chambered for .219 Zipper only. Manufactured 1938 to 1941. Collector value. Used value, $550 to $600.

    **Model 64 Deer Rifle** has same specs as standard original model, except for hand-checkered pistol-grip stock, forend, 1" sling swivels, sling; checkered steel buttplate; chambered only for .30-30, .32 Winchester. Manufactured 1933 to 1956. Collector value. Used value, $450 to $500.

*Model 65*

**WINCHESTER Model 65**: improvement on the Model 53, it's a lever-action solid frame repeater, in .25-20, .32-20; has 22" barrel, 7-shot tube half magazine; open rear sight, bead front on ramp base. Plain pistol grip stock, forearm. Introduced in 1933; dropped, 1947. Price when discontinued, $70; used value, $375 to $395.

**Model 65 .218 Bee** introduced in 1939; dropped, 1947. It is same as standard model, except for 24" barrel, peep rear sight. Used value, $520 to $550.

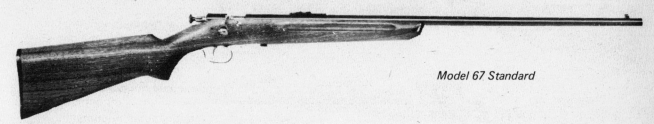

*Model 67 Standard*

**WINCHESTER Model 67:** bolt-action, takedown, single-shot; in .22 short, long, LR, .22 WRF; also made with smoothbore for shot; 27" barrel; open rear sight, bead front; unchecked pistol grip stock; early models had grooved forearm. Introduced in 1934; dropped, 1963.

Retail price when discontinued, $22; used value, $75 to $90.
**Model 67 Boy's Rifle** is the same as standard model, but has shorter stock, 20" barrel. Used value, $65 to $80.

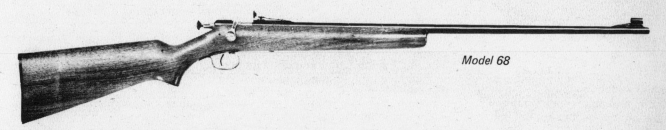

*Model 68*

**WINCHESTER Model 68:** bolt-action, single-shot takedown; the same as the Model 67, except for being equipped with rear peep sight. Introduced in 1934; discontinued,

1946. Retail price, when discontinued, $6.95; used value, $100 to $125.

*Model 69 Standard*

**WINCHESTER Model 69:** bolt-action, takedown repeater; .22 short, long, LR, detachable 5, 10-rd. box magazine; 25" barrel. Peep or open rear sight; bead ramp front; unchecked pistol grip stock. Introduced in 1935; discontinued, 1963. Retail price, when discontinued, $36; used value, $120 to $125.

**Model 69 Target Rifle** is same as standard Model 69, except for rear peep sight, blade front sight, sling swivels. Used value, $125 to $135.
**Model 69 Match Rifle** differs from the target model only in that it has Lyman No. 57EW receiver sight. Used value, $125 to $135.

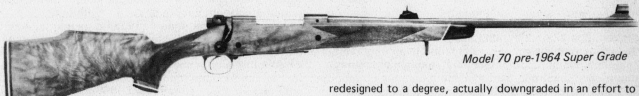

*Model 70 pre-1964 Super Grade*

**WINCHESTER Model 70:** this bolt-action center-fire repeating rifle is a versatile longarm, having been produced in more variations and configurations than any other of the manufacturer's firearms. The rifle is divided into roughly three historical categories, the original variations having been made from 1936 to 1963; at that time the rifle was

redesigned to a degree, actually downgraded in an effort to meet rising costs, but to hold the retail price. This series of variations was produced from 1964 until 1972, at which time the rifle was upgraded and the retail price increased.
**Model 70 Standard Grade (1936-1963);** available in .375 H&H magnum, 8x57mm, .300 H&H magnum, .308 Win., .30/06, 7x57mm, .270 Win., .257 Roberts, .250-3000, .243 Win., .220 Swift, .22 Hornet (other rare calibers exist, including 9x57mm, .35 Rem., and .300 Savage). 4-shot box magazine in magnum calibers, 5-shot for others; for a short period, a 20" barrel was available; standard was 24", with

*Model 70 Magnum (1964)*

*Model 70 Deluxe (1964)*

*Model 70 Mannlicher (1964)*

*Model 70 African (1972)*

*Model 70 Varmint (1972)*

*Model 70 Target (1972)*

26″ for .300 magnum, .220 Swift; 25″ for .375 H&H magnum; hooded ramp front sight, open rear; hand-checkered walnut stock; later production had Monte Carlo comb as standard. Retail price when introduced, $62; used value, $250 to $400 in standard calibers; $1500 to $2750 in rare calibers.

**Model 70 Standard Grade (1964-1971)**; available in .30/06, .308 Win., .270, .243, .225, .22-250, .222 Rem.; 24″ barrel, 5-shot box magazine; hooded ramp front sight, open rear, Monte Carlo cheekpiece, impressed checkering; sling swivels. Used value, $165 to $175.

**Model 70 Standard Grade (1971 to present)**; available in .30/06, .308, .270, .243, .25/06, .222, .22-250; 22″ swaged, floating barrel; walnut Monte Carlo stock; cut checkering on pistol grip, forearm; has removable hooded ramp bead front sight, open rear; receiver tapped for scope mounts; steel grip cap; sling swivels. Used value, $175 to $200.

**Model 70 Target Model (1937-1963)**; same as standard model of period, except for scope bases, 24″ medium-weight barrel, Marksman stock; when introduced, it was available in same calibers as standard model; when discontinued, only in .30/06, .243 Win. Used value, $425 to $850, depending upon caliber.

**Model 70 Target Model (1964-1971)**; .30/06, .308 Win.; 24″ barrel, 5-shot box magazine; target scope blocks, no sights; high-comb Marksman stock; aluminum handstop; swivels. Used value, $215 to $235.

**Model 70 Target Model (1972 to present)**; same as current standard model, except has 24″ heavy barrel; contoured aluminum handstop for either left or right-handed shooter; high-comb target stock; clip slot in receiver; tapped for micrometer sights. Used value, $245 to $265.

**Model 70 Super Grade (1937-1960)**; same as standard model of early production period, except for deluxe stock, cheekpiece, black forearm tip, sling, quick-detachable sling swivels; grip cap. Used value, $650 to $1000 in standard calibers.

**Model 70 Super Grade (current production)**; .300 Win. magnum; .30/06, .270, .243; .300 magnum has recoil pad; same as standard model, except for semi-fancy, presentation-checkered walnut stock; ebony forearm tip with white spacer, pistol grip; nonslip rubber butt plate, knurled bolt handle. Used value, $345 to $375.

Model 70 National Match; same as early standard model, except for Marksman target stock; scope bases; .30/06 only; discontinued, 1960. Used value, $425 to $475.

Model 70 Featherweight Sporter; introduced in 1952; dropped, 1963; same as standard model of period, but has redesigned stock, aluminum trigger guard, butt plate, floor plate; 22" barrel; .358 Win., .30/06, .308 Win., .270 Win., .264 Win. magnum, .243 Win. Used value, $325 to $400.

Model 70 Featherweight Super Grade same as Featherweight Sporter, but with deluxe stock, cheekpiece, sling, quick-detachable swivels, black pistol grip cap, forearm tip; discontinued, 1960. Used value, $675 to $750.

Model 70 Varmint (1956-1963); same as early standard model, except with 26" heavy barrel; varminter stock; scope bases; .243 Win., .220 Swift. Used value, $375 to $425.

Model 70 Varmint (1974 to present); same as earlier version, but in .243, .22-250, .222 only. Used value, $200 to $220.

Model 70 Bull Gun; same as early model, except for 28" extra heavy barrel, scope bases; Marksman stock, .30/06, .300 H&H magnum; discontinued, 1963. Used value, $465 to $500.

Model 70 African (1956-1963); same as super grade of the era, but with 24" barrel, 3-shot magazine; recoil pad, Monte Carlo stock; .458 Win. magnum only. Used value, $775 to $850.

Model 70 African (1964-1971); same as original version, except for special sights, 22" barrel; hand-checkered stock; twin stock-reinforcing bolts, Monte Carlo stock, ebony forearm tip; recoil pad; quick-detachable swivels. Used value, $325 to $350.

Model 70 African (1971 to present); same as earlier version, except for floating heavy barrel. Used value, $375 to $385.

Model 70 Alaskan (1960-1963); same as early standard model, except for 25" barrel, recoil pad; 3-shot magazine in .338 Win., 4-shot in .375 H&H magnum. Used value, $450 to $500.

Model 70 Westerner (1960-1963); same as standard model of era, except for 26" barrel in .264 Win. magnum, 24" barrel in .300 Win. magnum. Used value, $400 to $425.

Model 70 Deluxe (1964-1971); in .243, .270 Win., .30/06, .300 Win. magnum; 3-shot box magazine, 24" barrel in magnum caliber, 5-shot magazine, 22" barrel in others; hooded ramp front sight, open rear; recoil pad on magnum, hand-checkered forearm, pistol grip, Monte Carlo walnut stock, ebony forearm tip. Used value, $275 to $295.

Model 70 Magnum (1964-1971); in .375 H&H magnum, .338, .300, .264 Win. magnum, 7mm Rem. magnum; 24" barrel, 3-shot magazine; twin stock-reinforcing bolts, recoil pad, swivels, checkered Monte Carlo stock; hooded ramp front sight, open rear. Used value, .375 H&H magnum, $225 to $240; other calibers, $175 to $185.

Model 70 Mannlicher (1969-1971); Mannlicher-type stock with Monte Carlo comb, cheekpiece, quick-detachable swivels, checkered wood, steel forearm cap, hooded ramp front sight, open rear; in .30/06, .308 Win., .270, .243; 19" barrel; 5-shot box magazine. Used value, $345 to $375.

Model 70 International Army Match; produced in 1971 only; .308 Win.; 5-shot box magazine, 24" heavy barrel; externally adjustable trigger; International Shooting Union stock; forearm rail for accessories; adjustable butt plate; optional sights. Used value, sans sights, $325 to $375.

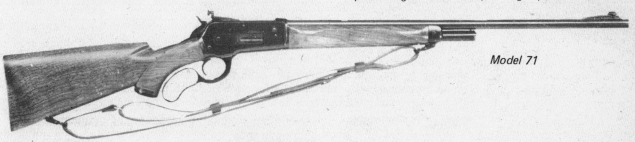

Model 71

WINCHESTER Model 71: solid frame lever-action repeating rifle; 20", 24" barrel; .348 Win; 4-rd. tubular magazine; open rear sight, bead front on ramp with hood; plain walnut stock, forearm. Introduced in 1936; dropped, 1957.

Retail when discontinued, $138; used value, $525 to $575.

Model 71 Special is same as standard grade, but has checkered stock, forearm; grip cap, quick-detachable sling swivels, leather sling. Used value, $725 to $750.

Model 77

WINCHESTER Model 77: semi-auto, solid-frame, clip type; .22 LR only; 8-shot clip magazine; 22" barrel; bead front sight, open rear; plain, one-piece hardwood stock; pistol grip. Introduced, 1955; dropped, 1963. Retail when dropped, $40; used value, $90 to $100.

Model 77, tubular magazine type; same as clip-type Model 77, except for 15-rd. tube magazine. Retail when dropped, $40. Used value, $90 to $100.

WINCHESTER Model 677: similar to standard Model 67, except for no sights; scope mounts were mounted on barrel; fired .22 shorts, longs, LRs interchangeably. Enjoyed little success due to poor scope mounting system. Introduced in 1937; dropped, 1939. Enjoys some value as a collectors item, as only 2239 were produced. Retail price, when dropped, $5.95. Used value, $150 to $165.

**WINCHESTER Model 697:** similar to standard Model 69, except that there were no sight cuts in barrel; scope bases were attached to barrel; no sights; rifle fired .22 short, long, LR cartridges interchangeably; came equipped with choice of 2¾ or 5X scope; 25" round barrel. Introduced, 1937; dropped, 1941. Retail when dropped, $12.50. Collector interest. Used value, $175 to $185.

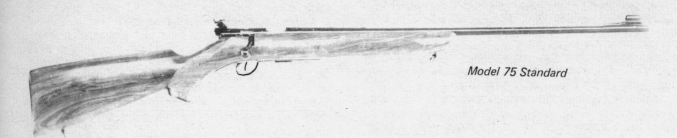

*Model 75 Standard*

**WINCHESTER Model 75:** solid-frame sporting model fires .22 LR ammo; 5-rd. box magazine; 24" barrel; bolt-action repeater, cocked with opening movement of bolt; checkered select walnut stock, pistol grip; hard rubber grip cap; swivels; checkered steel butt plate. Introduced in 1939; dropped, 1958. Retail, when dropped, $70.95; used value, $350 to $375.

**Model 75 Target Model;** same as standard model, but equipped with target scope or variety of sights; predated sporting model. Introduced in 1938; dropped, 1958; uncheckered walnut stock, semi-beavertail forearm; pistol grip, checkered steel butt plate; came with 1" army-type leather sling. Retail price, when dropped, $80.55. Used value, $145 to $175.

*Model 72*

**WINCHESTER Model 72:** bolt-action takedown repeater; tubular magazine holds 22 shorts, 16 longs, 15 LRs; 25" barrel; peep or open rear sight, bead front; uncheckered pistol grip stock. Introduced in 1938; dropped, 1959. Price when discontinued, $38.45. Used value, $100 to $115.

*Model 74*

**WINCHESTER Model 74:** self-loading, takedown; chambered for .22 short only or .22 LR only; tube magazine in butt stock holds 20 shorts, 14 LR rds. 24" barrel; open rear sight, bead front; uncheckered one-piece pistol grip stock. Introduced in 1939; discontinued, 1955. Price when dropped, $39.20. Used value, $85 to $95.

*Model 43 Standard*

**WINCHESTER Model 43:** bolt-action sporting rifle; .218 Bee, .22 Hornet; .25-20, .32-20; last two dropped, 1950. 24" barrel; 3-shot detachable box magazine; open rear sight, bead front on hooded ramp; uncheckered pistol grip stock with swivels. Introduced in 1949; dropped, 1957. Retail when dropped, $75. Used value, $235 to $250.

**Model 43 Special Grade;** same as standard Model 43, except for grip cap, checkered pistol grip, forearm; open rear sight or Lyman 59A Micrometer. Used value, $300 to $325.

*Model 47*

**WINCHESTER Model 47:** bolt-action single-shot; .22 short, long, LR; 25" barrel; uncheckered pistol grip stock; peep or open rear sight; bead front. Introduced in 1949; dropped, 1954. Price when discontinued, $24.25. Used value, $85 to $100.

*Model 88*

**WINCHESTER Model 88:** lever-action rifle; available in .243 Winchester, .284 Winchester, .308 Winchester, .358 Winchester; barrel length, 22"; weighs 6½ lbs.; measures 39½" overall; fitted with hooded bead front sight, folding leaf rear sight. Stock is one-piece walnut with steel-capped pistol grip, fluted comb, carbine barrel band, sling swivels. Has four-shot detachable magazine of staggered, box-type, held with double latches. Hammerless action, with three-lug bolt, cross-bolt safety; side ejection. Introduced in 1955; dropped, 1974. Latest retail price, $169.95. Used value, $165 to $175.

*Model 55*

**WINCHESTER Model 55:** automatic single-shot; .22 shorts, longs, LRs; 22" barrel; open rear sight, bead front; one-piece uncheckered walnut stock. Introduced in 1957; dropped, 1961. Retail price when discontinued, $20.45. Used value, $110 to $125.

*Model 100*

**WINCHESTER Model 100:** semi-auto, gas-operated carbine; available in .243 Winchester, .284 Winchester, .308 Winchester. Barrel is 22"; weight, 7½ lbs.; measures 42½" overall. In 1967, barrel length was reduced to 19". Stock is one-piece walnut with checkered pistol grip and forearm, sling swivels. Magazine holds 4 rds., except .284, which holds 3 rds.; tapped for receiver sights or scope mounts; equipped with hooded bead front sight, folding leaf rear. Introduced in 1960; dropped in 1974. Last retail price, $179.95. Used value, $165 to $175.

**WINCHESTER Model 250:** .22 rimfire lever-action rifle; standard and deluxe models; 20½" barrel; tubular magazine, with capacity of 21 shorts, 17 longs, 15 LR cartridges, chambered to handle these interchangeably. Stock is walnut-finished hardwood; receiver of aluminum alloy, grooved for tip-off scope mounts; sights include a front square post on a streamlined ramp; square notch sight in rear, adjustable for windage and elevation; cross lock safety is located on front of the trigger guard; weight, 5 lbs. Deluxe model included select walnut stock, fluted comb, cheek piece, basket weave

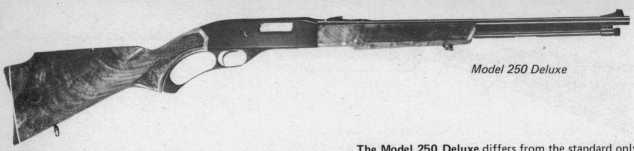

*Model 250 Deluxe*

checkering, white spacers between butt plate and stock, sling swivels. Introduced in 1963; discontinued, 1974. Used value, $85 to $90.

**The Model 250 Deluxe** differs from the standard only in that it has a fancy walnut Monte Carlo stock, forearm and has sling swivels. It was manufactured from 1965 to 1971. Used value, $95 to $100.

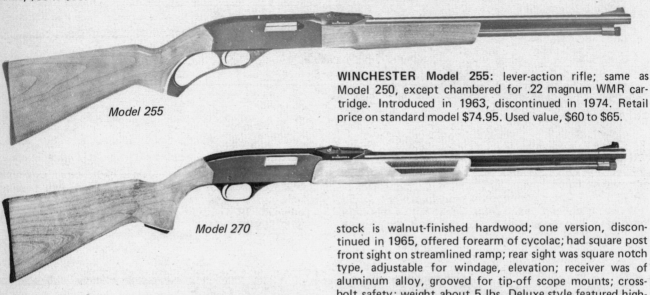

*Model 255*

*Model 270*

**WINCHESTER Model 255:** lever-action rifle; same as Model 250, except chambered for .22 magnum WMR cartridge. Introduced in 1963, discontinued in 1974. Retail price on standard model $74.95. Used value, $60 to $65.

**WINCHESTER Model 270:** slide-action rifle; .22 rimfire; available in standard and deluxe models; 20½" barrel; tubular magazine with capacity of 21 shorts, 17 longs, 15 LRs; chambered to handle all three interchangeably; stock is walnut-finished hardwood; one version, discontinued in 1965, offered forearm of cycolac; had square post front sight on streamlined ramp; rear sight was square notch type, adjustable for windage, elevation; receiver was of aluminum alloy, grooved for tip-off scope mounts; crossbolt safety; weight about 5 lbs. Deluxe style featured high-gloss Monte Carlo stock of walnut with fluted comb, basketweave checkering, cheekpiece. Introduced in 1963, dropped in 1974. Last retail price for standard version, $72.95. Used value for standard, $75 to $80.

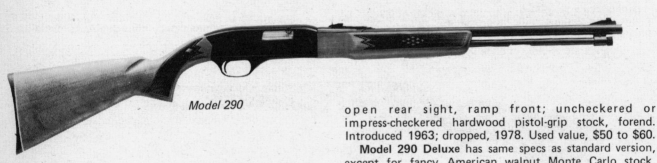

*Model 290*

**WINCHESTER Model 290:** semi-automatic; .22 Short, Long, LR; tubular magazine holds 15 LR rds.; 20½" barrel; open rear sight, ramp front; uncheckered or impress-checkered hardwood pistol-grip stock, forend. Introduced 1963; dropped, 1978. Used value, $50 to $60.

    **Model 290 Deluxe** has same specs as standard version, except for fancy American walnut Monte Carlo stock, forend. Manufactured 1965 to 1973. Used value, $75 to $85.

*Model 275*

**WINCHESTER Model 275:** slide-action rifle; same as Model 270, but chambered for .22 rimfire magnum cartridge. Introduced in 1964, dropped in 1974. Last retail price for standard model, $77.95. Used value for standard $75 to $80.

*Model 121 Standard*

**WINCHESTER Model 121:** single-shot; .22 rimfire; fires shorts, longs, LRs; barrel length is 20½"; weighs 5 lbs.; one-piece stock is of American hardwood with modified Monte Carlo profile; sights are standard ramped post bead, adjustable V at rear. Receiver is steel, with front locking bolt; grooved to accommodate tip-off mounts for scope sight. Introduced in 1967; discontinued, 1973. Available in three versions, a **Youth Model** with short buttstock and **Standard Model**, both at $23.95; a **Deluxe Version** with Monte Carlo, fluted comb and sling swivels at $27.95. Used value for Youth model, $40 to $45; Standard model, $40 to $45; Deluxe, $55 to $60.

*Model 131*

**WINCHESTER Model 131:** bolt-action, clip loading .22 rimfire; 20" barrel, overall weight about 5 lbs.; stock is one-piece American hardwood with fluted comb, modified Monte Carlo profile; ramped bead post front, adjustable rear sight; clip-type magazine holds 7 rds., short, long, LR; steel receiver is grooved for telescopic sight mounts; barrel has 1-in-16" twist ratio; front locking bolt; red safety and red cocking indicator. Introduced in 1967; dropped, 1973; last retail price $38.45. Used value, $45 to $55.

*Model 135*

**WINCHESTER Model 135:** same as Model 131, except .22 magnum. Introduced in 1967; dropped, 1973; last retail price, $41.45. Used value, $65 to $75.

*Model 141*

**WINCHESTER Model 141:** bolt-action; .22 rimfire; hidden tubular magazine holds 19 shorts, 15 longs, 13 LR cartridges interchangeably; barrel is 20½"; weight, 5 lbs.; stock is American hardwood with fluted comb, modified Monte Carlo; front locking bolt, ramped bead post front and adjustable rear sight; red cocking indicator and red-marked safety. Introduced in 1967; dropped in 1973. Last retail price, $41.95; used value, $45 to $55.

*Model 150*

**WINCHESTER Model 150:** lever-action carbine; .22 rim-fire; has 20½″ barrel, weighs 5 lbs; stock is walnut-finished American hardwood; forearm has frontier-style barrel band; straight grip; no checkering; tube magazine holds 21 shorts, 17 longs, 15 LR cartridges; receiver is aluminum alloy, grooved for scope sight. Introduced in 1967; dropped, 1974. Retail price $53.95; used value, $55 to $65.

*Model 770 Standard*

**WINCHESTER Model 770:** bolt-action; available in .222 Remington, .22-250, .243 Winchester, .270 Winchester, .308 Winchester, .30/06; also in .264 Winchester magnum, 7mm Remington magnum, .300 Winchester magnum. Available with 22″ barrel for standard calibers, 24″ for magnums; weighs 7½ lbs. Stock is walnut with high comb Monte Carlo, undercut cheekpiece; has front sight ramp and hood with adjustable rear sight. Magazine capacities vary, depending upon caliber. Standard models have composition butt plates, magnums, rubber recoil pads. There is a red cocking indicator, serrated trigger. Pistol grip is capped, and grip and forearm checkered. This rifle was designed as a lower echelon Model 70, but failed to meet acceptance, thus was dropped after only four years in the line, being replaced by Model 70A. Introduced, 1969; dropped, 1973; retailed at $139.95 for standard models, $154.95 for magnums. Used value for standards, $145 to $150; magnums, $175 to $185.

*Model 310*

**WINCHESTER Model 310:** bolt-action; single-shot; .22 rimfire, 22″ barrel; weighs 5-5/8 lbs.; 39″ overall in length; 13½″ length of pull; stock is American walnut with Monte Carlo, fluted comb; checkered pistol grip, forearm. Has ramped bead post front sight, adjustable rear sight; receiver is grooved for scope sight; also drilled, tapped for micrometer rear sight. Is equipped with sling swivels, serrated trigger, positive safety lever. Introduced in March 1971; dropped, 1974. Last retail price, $44.95; used value, $50 to $55.

*Model 320*

**WINCHESTER Model 320:** bolt action; .22 rimfire; 22″ barrel; weighs 5-5/8 lbs.; measures 39½″ overall; stock is American walnut, with Monte Carlo, fluted comb; checkered pistol grip and forearm; ramped bead post front sight, adjustable rear; grooved for scope mounts; drilled, tapped for micrometer rear sight; magazine holds 5 rds. of .22 short, long, LR. Is equipped with sling swivels, serrated trigger, positive safety. Introduced in March 1971; dropped, 1974. Last retail price, $57.50; used value, $60 to $65.

*Model 70A*

**WINCHESTER Model 70A:** bolt-action rifle; available in .222 Remington; .22-250; .243 Winchester; .270 Winchester, .30/06, .308 Winchester with 22" barrels, 24" barrels in .264 Winchester magnum, 7mm Remington magnum and .300 Winchester magnum. Incorporates features of Model 70 rifle; action is of chrome molybdenum steel; three-position safety; serrated trigger; engine-turned bolt; rear sight is adjustable leaf with white diamond for quick sighting; front sight is hooded ramp type; stock is dark American walnut with high comb Monte Carlo, undercut cheekpiece. Introduced in 1972, as replacement for Model 770, more closely following style of Model 70. Current retail, standard model, $245.95; magnum model, $261.95. Used value, $180 to $185; magnum used value, $185 to $195.

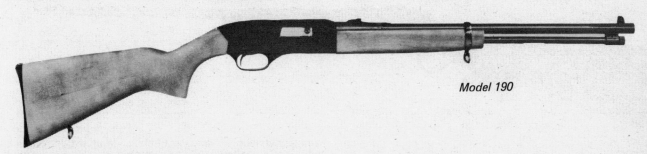

*Model 670*

**WINCHESTER Model 670:** bolt-action; available in carbine style with 19" barrel, sporting rifle, with 22", magnum version with 24" barrel; sporting rifle, carbine held 4 rds. in magazine; magnum, 3 rds.; carbine chambered for .243 Winchester, .270 Winchester, .30/06; sporting rifle, .225, .243, .270, .308 Winchester, .30/06; magnum version, .264 Winchester magnum, .300 Winchester magnum. Has non-detachable box magazine; front sight is bead on ramp, rear, open, adjustable type; both sights easily detached for scope mounting; stock is hardwood with walnut finish, high comb Monte Carlo style; redesigned in 1972, with only 22" version being produced in .243 and .30/06. Dropped in 1974. Last retail price, $134.95; used value, $135 to $145.

*Model 9422 Standard*

**WINCHESTER Model 9422:** lever-action; duplicates appearance of Model 94; in .22 short, long, long rifle and magnum. Has 20½" barrel; weighs 6½ lbs.; stock, forearm are of American walnut, with steel barrel band around latter; front sight is ramp, dovetail bead and hood, with adjustable semi-buckhorn at rear. Standard model holds 21 shorts, 17 longs, 15 LRs, interchangeable. Magnum model holds 11 .22 rimfire cartridges. Receiver is of forged steel, with all-steel action. Both styles are grooved for scope mounts. Both styles were introduced in 1972. Current retail prices are $184.95, standard; $190.95, magnum; used value, $130 to $135 for standard; $140 to $145 for magnum.

*Model 190*

**WINCHESTER Model 190:** semi-auto carbine; .22 rimfire; 20½" barrel with 1-in-16" twist. American hardwood stock, with plain, uncapped pistol grip; forearm encircled with barrel band; tube magazine with capacity of 21 shorts, 15 LRs; sights include bead post front, adjustable V at rear; aluminum alloy receiver is grooved for scope mounts. Weight is approximately 5 lbs, overall length, 39"; sling swivels included. Introduced in 1974. Current retail price, $78.75. Used value, $45 to $55.

*Model 490*

**WINCHESTER Model 490:** semi-automatic; .22 LR; 5-rd. clip magazine; 22" barrel; folding leaf rear sight, hooded ramp front; impress-checkered American walnut pistol-grip stock, forend. Introduced 1975, dropped 1977. Used value, $90 to $100.

# MISCELLANEOUS RIFLES
## U.S.-MADE

*AR-7 Explorer*

**ARMALITE AR-7 Explorer:** survival rifle originally designed for use by U.S. Air Force; .22 LR, semi-automatic; takedown; 8-rd. box magazine; 16" cast aluminum barrel, with steel liner; moulded plastic stock, hollow for storing action, barrel, magazine; designed to float; peep rear sight; blade front. Introduced in 1959; still in production, but manufactured since 1973 by Charter Arms Corporation. Used value, $70 to $75.

**ARMALITE Custom AR-7:** same specs as AR-7 Explorer, except with walnut stock; pistol grip, cheekpiece; not designed to float. Introduced in 1964; dropped, 1970. Used value, $90 to $95.

**BUFFALO NEWTON Sporter:** bolt-action; .256, .30/06, .35 Newton; 5-rd. box magazine; 24" barrel; reversed set trigger; hand-checkered pistol grip. Introduced in 1922; dropped, 1932. Manufactured by Newton Arms Co., Buffalo, New York. Used value, primarily as collector item, $455 to $465.

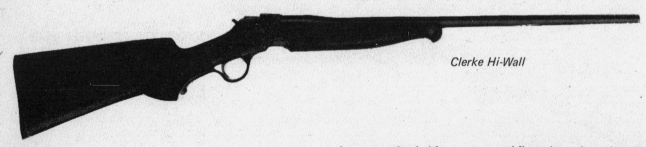

*Clerke Hi-Wall*

**CLERKE Hi-wall:** single-shot; .223, .22-250, .243, 6mm Rem., .250 Savage, .257 Roberts, .25/06, .264 Win., .270, 7mm Rem. Magnum, .30-30, .30/06, .300 Win., .375 H&H, .458 Win., .45-70; barrel, 26" medium-weight; walnut pistol-grip stock, forearm; no checkering; black butt plate; no sights; drilled, tapped for scope mounts; exposed hammer; schnabel forearm, curved finger lever. Introduced in 1970; dropped, 1975. Used value, $200 to $215.

**Deluxe Hi-Wall:** same specs as standard model, except for half-octagon barrel, adjustable trigger, checkered pistol grip, forearm, cheekpiece; plain or double set trigger. Used value, single trigger, $265 to $275; double set trigger, $285 to $300.

**COMMANDO Mark III:** semi-automatic; .45 Auto; 16½″ barrel; 15 or 30-rd. magazine; muzzle brake, cooling sleeve; peep-type rear sight, blade front; walnut stock and forearm; available with choice of vertical or horizontal foregrip. Manufactured 1969 to 1976. Used value, $110 to $120.

**Mark 9** has the same specifications as Mark III, except chambered for 9mm Luger, redesigned trigger housing. Introduced 1976, still in production. Used value, $115 to $125.

**Mark 45** has same specifications as Mark 9, but chambered for .45 Auto; choice of 5, 15, 30, 90-rd. magazines. Introduced 1976, still in production. Used value, $115 to $125.

*Daisy VL No. 0003*

*Daisy VL Presentation*

**DAISY V/L:** single-shot; under-lever action; .22 V/L caseless cartridge; 18″ barrel; adjustable open rear sight, ramp blade front; stock of wood-grained Lustran plastic. Manufactured 1968 to 1969; only 19,000 produced. Used value, $65 to $75.

**V/L Presentation Grade** has same specifications as standard model, except for American walnut stock. Manufactured 1968 to 1969; only 4000 produced. Used value, $110 to $120.

**V/L Collector Kit** includes Presentation Grade rifle, gold plate engraved with owner's name, gun's serial number; included gun case, brass wall hangers for gun, 300 rounds of V/L ammo. Manufactured 1968 to 1969; only 1000 produced. Some collector value. Used value, $200 to $225.

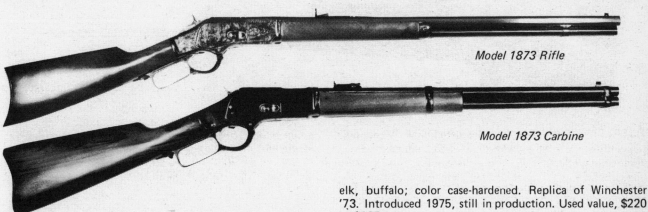

*Model 1873 Rifle*

*Model 1873 Carbine*

**DIXIE Model 1873:** lever-action; .44-40; 11-rd. tubular magazine; 23½″ octagonal barrel; leaf rear sight, blade front; walnut stock, forearm; receiver engraved with scrolls, elk, buffalo; color case-hardened. Replica of Winchester '73. Introduced 1975, still in production. Used value, $220 to $235.

**Model 1873 Carbine** has same general specifications as rifle version, except no engraving or color case-hardening; 20″ barrel. Used value, $165 to $175.

**IVER JOHNSON Model X:** bolt-action, single-shot; takedown; .22 LR, .22 long, .22 short; 22″ barrel; open rear sight, blade front; hardwood pistol-grip stock; knob forearm tip; uncheckered. Introduced in 1928; dropped, 1932. Used value, $29 to $31.50.

*Model 2X*

**IVER JOHNSON Model 2X:** same general specs as Model X, but has larger stock, without forearm knob; heavier 24″ barrel. Introduced in 1932; dropped, 1955. Used value, $65 to $75.

**NEWTON-Mauser Sporter:** bolt-action; .256 Newton; 5-rd. box magazine; double-set triggers; 24" barrel; Mauser

**NEWTON Standard Sporter (Type I):** bolt-action; .22, .256, .280, .30, .33, .35 Newton; .30/06; 24" barrel; open rear sight, ramp front; hand-checkered pistol grip stock; Newton action. Manufactured 1916 to 1918. Collector value. Used value, $320 to $330.

**Standard Sporter (Type II)** has same general specs as

action; hinged floorplate; open rear sight, ramp front; American walnut pistol-grip stock. Manufactured 1914 to 1915. Used value, $55 to $65.

Type I, except improved design; .256, .30, .35 Newton, .30/06; 5-rd. box magazine; reversed set-trigger, Enfield-design bolt handle. Collector value. Manufactured 1921 to 1922. Used value, $320 to $330.

**Buffalo Newton Sporter** has same specs as Type II, but manufactured by Buffalo Newton Rifle Co. Collector value. Manufactured 1922 to 1924. Used value, $320 to $330.

*Omega III*

**OMEGA III:** bolt-action; .25/06, .270, .30/06, 7mm Rem. magnum, .300 Win. magnum, .338 Win. magnum, .358 Norma magnum; barrels, 22", 24"; choice of Monte Carlo, Classic or thumbhole varminter; claro walnut English laminated or laminated walnut/maple; no sights; right or

left-hand action; octagonal bolt; square locking system, enclosed bolt face; rotary magazine holds 5 standard or 4 belted cartridges; fully adjustable trigger. Introduced in 1973; dropped, 1976. Used value, $375 to $395.

*3000*

**PEDERSEN 3000:** bolt-action, Mossberg Model 800 action; .270, .30/06, 7mm Rem. magnum, .338 Win. magnum; 3-rd. magazine; barrels 22" in .270, .30/06; 24", all other calibers; American walnut stock, roll-over cheekpiece; hand-checkered pistol grip, forearm; no sights; drilled, tapped for

scope mount; adjustable trigger; sling swivels. Grades differ in amount of engraving and quality of stock wood. Introduced in 1972; dropped, 1975. Used values, Grade I, $700 to $725; Grade II, $435 to $455; Grade III, $390 to $415.

**PEDERSEN 3500:** bolt-action; .270 Win., .30/06, 7mm Rem. mag.; 22" barrel in standard calibers, 24" for 7mm mag.; 3-rd. magazine; drilled, tapped for scope mounts; hinged steel floor plate; damascened bolt; adjustable trigger;

hand-checkered black walnut stock, forearm; rosewood pistol-grip cap, forearm tip. Introduced in 1973; dropped, 1975. Used value, $325 to $350.

**PEDERSON Model 4700:** lever-action; .30-30, .35 Remington; 5-rd. tubular magazine; 24" barrel; Mossberg

Model 472 action; open rear sight, hooded ramp front; black walnut stock, beavertail forearm; barrel band swivels. Manufactured 1975. Used value, $160 to $170.

*Plainfield Standard Carbine*

*Military Sporter*

*Deluxe Sporter*

**PLAINFIELD M-1 Carbine:** same as U.S. military carbine, except available in 5.7mm, as well as standard .30 M-1; early models had standard military fittings, some from surplus parts; current model has ventilated metal hand guard, not bayonet lug. Introduced in 1960; dropped, 1976. Used value, $135 to $145.

**M-1 Military Sporter Carbine** is same as M-1 Carbine, but with unslotted buttstock; has wood hand guard. Used value, $135 to $145.

**M-1 Carbine, Commando Model,** is same as M-1, except with telescoping wire stock, pistol grips front and rear. Used value, $165 to $175.

**Deluxe Sporter** is same as M-1, except for Monte Carlo sporting stock. Introduced in 1960; dropped, 1973. Used value, $145 to $155.

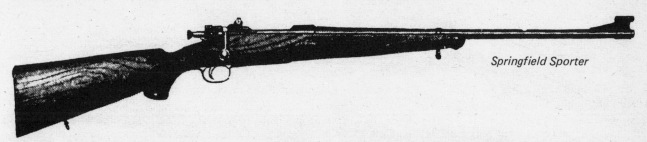

*Springfield Sporter*

**SEDGLEY Springfield Sporter:** built on Springfield 1903 bolt-action; .218 Bee, .22-3000, .220 Swift, .22-4000, .22 Hornet, .22-35, .250-3000, .257 Roberts, .270 Win., .30/06, 7mm; 24" barrel; hand-checkered walnut stock; sling swivels, grip cap; Lyman No. 48 rear sight, bead front on matted ramp. Introduced in 1928; discontinued, 1941. Used values, $400 to $425; left-hand model, $415 to $435; Mannlicher stock, 20" barrel, $450 to $475.

*DGA Sporter*

**SHILEN DGA Model:** bolt-action; .17 Rem., .222 Rem., .223 Rem., .22-250, .220 Swift, 6mm Rem., .243 Win., .250 Savage, .257 Roberts, .284 Win., .308 Win., .358 Win.; 3-rd. magazine; 24" barrel; no sights; uncheckered Claro walnut stock; cheekpiece; pistol grip; sling swivels. Introduced 1976, still in production. Used value, $425 to $440.

**DGA Varminter** has same specs as standard model, except for 25" heavy barrel. Introduced 1976, still in production. Used value, $425 to $440.

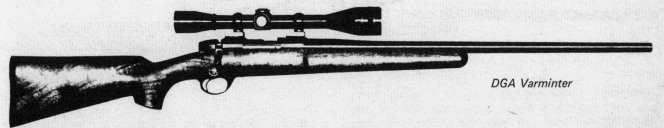

*DGA Varminter*

**DGA Benchrest Model** is single-shot bolt-action, but built on same basic specs as standard model; has 26" medium or heavy barrel; classic or thumbhole walnut or fiberglass stock. Introduced 1977, still in production. Used value, $450 to $500.

*M1A*

**SPRINGFIELD ARMORY M1A:** semi-automatic, gas-operated; .308 Win. (7.62 NATO); 5, 10, 20-rd. box magazine; 25-1/16" barrel, flash suppressor; adjustable aperture rear sight, blade front; walnut, birch or fiberglass stock; fiberglass hand guard; sling swivels, sling. Same general specs as military M14 sans full-auto capability. Maker is private Illinois firm, not a U.S. Government

**STANDARD Model G:** semi-automatic, gas-operated; .25-35, .30-30, .25 Rem., .30 Rem., .35 Rem.; magazine holds 4 rds. in .35, 5 rds. in other calibers; hammerless; takedown; 22-3/8" barrel; open rear sight, ivory bead front; gas port, when closed, required manual slide action;

facility. Introduced 1974, still in production. Used values, fiberglass stock, $260 to $270; birch stock, $165 to $275; walnut, $290 to $300.

**Match M1A** has same general specs as standard model, except for National Match grade barrel, sights; better trigger pull, modified gas system, mainspring guide; glass-bedded American walnut stock. Used value, $350 to $375.

**Super Match M1A** has same specs as Match model, except for heavier, premium-grade barrel. Used value, $390 to $400.

American walnut buttstock, slide handle-type forearm. Manufactured 1910. Some collector value. Used value, $300 to $325.

**Model M** has same general specs as Model G, sans gas-operating feature; operates as slide-action. Manufactured 1910. Used value, $190 to $215.

*Standard Carbine*

*Deluxe Carbine*

**UNIVERSAL .30 Carbine:** same as .30 M-1 military carbine, but sans bayonet lug; 5-rd. clip magazine; made for short period in mid-1960s with Teflon-coated barrel, action; matted finish on metal. Introduced in 1964; still in production. Used value, $145 to $155.

**Deluxe .30 Carbine** is same as standard model, except for choice of gold-finished, nickel or blued metal parts; Monte Carlo stock; dropped, 1973. Used value, gold-finish, $175 to $185; nickel, $145 to $155; blue, $125 to $135.

**Ferret Semi-auto** rifle is the same as Universal deluxe .30

Carbine, except for blued finish only, .256 caliber only, no iron sights, equipped with 4X Universal scope. Dropped, 1973. Used value, $165 to $175.

In 1974, models were revised and redesignated by model numbers.

**Universal 1000** is same as military issue, except for better walnut stock, receiver tapped for scope mounts; dropped, 1977. Used value, $135 to $145.

**Model 1002** is the same as Model 1000, except it has blued metal military type perforated hand guard; dropped, 1977. Used value, $140 to $150.

*'76 Standard*

**WICKLIFFE Model '76:** single-shot; .22 Hornet, .223 Rem., .22-250, .243 Win., .25/06, .308 Win., .30/06, .45-70; 22" lightweight, 26" heavy sporter barrel; no sights; American walnut Monte Carlo stock; cheekpiece, pistol grip, semi-beavertail forend; falling-block action. Introduced 1976, dropped 1979. Used value, $220 to $235.

**Model '76 Deluxe** has same specs as standard model, except .30/06 only; 22" barrel; high-luster blue finish; nickel-silver grip cap, better wood. Introduced 1976, dropped 1979. Used value, $270 to $300.

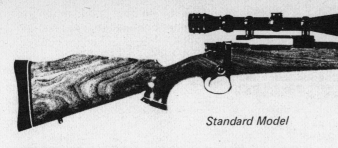

*Standard Model*

**WINSLOW Bolt-Action:** chambered in all standard and magnum center-fire calibers; 24" barrel, 26" for magnums; choice of 3 stock styles; hand-rubbed black walnut, hand-checkered pistol grip, forearm; 4-rd. blind magazine; no sights, receiver tapped for scope mounts; recoil pad; quick detachable swivel studs, ebony forearm tip, pistol-grip cap. Introduced, 1963; dropped, 1978. Used value, $375 to $415; varmint model in .17/222, .17/223, .415 to $450; left-hand models, add $60.

# FOREIGN-MADE

**BERETTA Sporting Carbine:** .22 LR, 4, 8 or 20-rd. magazine; 20½" barrel; 3-leaf folding rear sight, Patridge-type front; European walnut stock, sling swivels, hand-checkered pistol grip. When bolt handle is dropped, acts as conventional bolt action; with bolt handle raised, fires semiauto. Produced in Italy following World War II. Used value, $140 to $150.

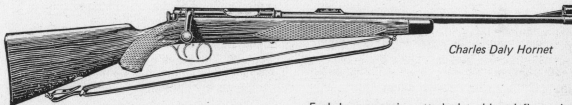

*Charles Daly Hornet*

**CHARLES DALY Hornet:** originally made by Franz Jaeger Co. of Germany; miniaturized Mauser action; .22 Hornet only; 24" barrel, double set triggers; walnut stock; hand-checkered pistol grip, forearm; leaf rear sight, ramp front; 5-rd. box magazine attached to hinged floor plate. Introduced 1931; importation discontinued, 1939. Imported by Charles Daly. (Note: Same model was imported by A.F. Stoeger and sold as Herold rifle.) Collector interest. Used value, $725 to $750.

*Finnish Lion Match*

**FINNISH Lion Match Model:** bolt-action; single-shot; .22 LR; 28¾" barrel; extension-type rear peep sight, aperture front; European walnut free rifle-type stock; full pistol grip, beavertail forearm, thumbhole, palm rest, hand stop, hooked buttplate, swivel. Manufactured 1937 to 1972. Used value, $280 to $300.

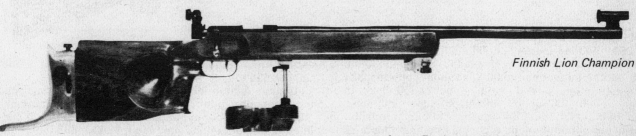

*Finnish Lion Champion*

**FINNISH Lion Champion:** bolt-action; single-shot; free rifle design; .22 LR; 28¾" barrel; extension-type rear peep sight, aperture front; European walnut free-rifle stock; full pistol grip, beavertail forearm, thumbhole, palm rest, hand stop, hooked buttplate, swivel. Manufactured 1965 to 1972. Used value, $350 to $374.

**FINNISH Lion ISU Target Model:** bolt-action; single-shot; .22 LR; 27½″ barrel; extension-type rear peep sight, aperture front; European walnut target-design stock;

*Deluxe Mauser*

**F.N. Deluxe Mauser:** bolt-action; .220 Swift, .243 Winchester, .244 Remington, .257 Roberts, .250/3000, .270 Winchester, 7mm, .300 Savage, .308 Winchester, .30/06; 5-rd. box magazine; 24″ barrel; Tri-range rear sight, hooded ramp front; hand-checkered European walnut

hand-checkered beavertail forearm, full pistol grip, adjustable buttplate, swivel. Manufactured 1966 to 1977. Used value, $190 to $215.

stock, pistol grip; cheekpiece; sling swivels. Manufactured in Belgium 1947 to 1963. Also manufactured in several European calibers. Used value, $425 to $450.

**Presentation Grade** has same general specifications as Deluxe Mauser, except for engraved receiver, trigger guard, barrel breech, floorplate; selected walnut stock. Manufactured 1947 to 1963. Used value, $725 to $750.

*Supreme Mauser*

**F.N. Supreme Mauser:** bolt-action; .243 Winchester, .270 Winchester, 7mm, .308 Winchester, .30/06; 22″ barrel; 4-rd. magazine in .243, .308; 5 rds. in other calibers; Tri-range rear sight, hooded ramp front; hand-checkered European walnut stock; pistol grip, Monte Carlo

cheekpiece, sling swivels. Manufactured 1957 to 1975. Used value, $425 to $450.

**Supreme Magnum** has same general specifications as Supreme Mauser, except chambered for .264 Winchester magnum, 7mm Remington magnum, .300 Winchester magnum; 3-rd. magazine. Manufactured 1957 to 1973. Used value, $450 to $475.

*Model A2*

**GEVARM Model A2:** autoloader; blowback action; takedown; .22 LR only; 21½″ barrel; 8-rd. clip magazine; no firing pin (as such) or extractor; fires from open bolt; ridge on bolt face offers twin ignition; tangent rear sight, hooded

globe front; unchecked walnut stock, schnabel forearm. Imported by Tradewinds, Inc., beginning in 1958; dropped, 1963. Used value, $55 to $65.

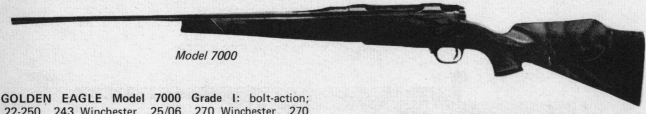

*Model 7000*

**GOLDEN EAGLE Model 7000 Grade I:** bolt-action; .22-250, .243 Winchester, .25/06, .270 Winchester, .270 Weatherby magnum, 7mm Remington magnum, .30/06, .300 Weatherby magnum, .300 Winchester magnum, .338 Winchester magnum; 4-rd. magazine for .22-250, 3 rds. in other calibers; 24″ or 26″ barrels; no sights; checkered American walnut stock, contrasting grip cap, forend tip, golden eagle head inset in grip cap; recoil pad. Made in

Japan. Introduced in 1976; dropped, 1979. Used value, $275 to $290.

**Grade I African Model** has same general specifications, but is chambered for .375 Holland & Holland magnum, .458 Winchester magnum; furnished with sights. Introduced in 1976; dropped, 1979. Used value, $300 to $325.

**GREIFELT Sport Model:** bolt-action; .22 Hornet; 5-rd. box magazine; 22″ barrel; 2-leaf rear sight, ramp front;

hand-checkered European walnut stock; pistol grip; made in Germany prior to World War II. Used value, $625 to $650.

*Monte Carlo*

*Deluxe*

**CARL GUSTAF Standard Model:** bolt-action; 6.5x55, 7x54, 9.3x62mm, .270 Winchester, .308 Winchester, .30/06; 4-rd. magazine for the 9.3x62mm, 5 rds. for other calibers; folding leaf rear sight, hooded ramp front; sling swivels; Classic style French walnut stock; hand-checkered pistol grip, forearm. Available in left-hand model also. Manufactured in Sweden 1970 to 1977. Used value, $315 to $325.

**Monte Carlo Model** has same general specifications as Standard model, except for addition of 7mm Remington magnum chambering, Monte Carlo-style stock with cheekpiece. Manufactured 1970 to 1977. Used value, $340 to $350.

**CARL GUSTAF Varmint-Target Model:** bolt-action; .222 Remington, .22-250, .243 Winchester, 6.5x55mm;

**Model II** has same specifications as Monte Carlo model, except for chambering, select walnut stock, rosewood forend tip. Chambered for .22-250, .243 Winchester, .25/06, .270 Winchester, 6.5x55mm, 7mm Remington magnum, .308 Winchester, .30/06, .300 Winchester magnum; 3-rd. magazine in magnum calibers. Manufactured 1970 to 1977. Used value, $425 to $440.

**Model III** has same specifications as Monte Carlo model, except for higher grade wood, high-gloss finish, rosewood forend tip, no sights. Chambered for .22-250, .25/06, .270 Winchester, 6.5x55mm, 7mm Remington magnum, .308 Winchester, .30/06, .300 Winchester magnum; 3-rd. magazine in magnum calibers. Manufactured 1970 to 1977.

**Deluxe Model** has same general specifications as Monte Carlo; chambered for 6.5x55mm, .308 Winchester, .30/06, 9.3x62mm; engraved trigger guard, floorplate; top grade French walnut stock, rosewood forend tip. Manufactured 1970 to 1977. Used value, $600 to $625.

adjustable trigger; 26¾" barrel; no sights; target-style stock, French walnut. Introduced 1970, still in production. Used value, $425 to $450.

*Grand Prix*

**CARL GUSTAF Grand Prix:** single-shot target model; .22 LR; single-stage adjustable trigger; 26¾" barrel, adjustable

weight; adjustable cork buttplate; no sights; uncheckered French walnut target-style stock. Introduced 1970, still in production. Used value, $425 to $450.

**HAENEL Mauser-Mannlicher:** bolt-action; 7x57, 8x57, 9x57mm; 5-rd. Mannlicher-type box magazine; 22" or 24" barrel, half or full octagon; raised matted rib; action based on Model 88 Mauser; double-set trigger; leaf open rear sight, ramp front; hand-checkered European walnut sporting

stock cheekpiece, schnabel tip, pistol grip, sling swivels. Manufactured in Germany prior to WWII. Used value, $260 to $275.

**'88 Mauser Sporter** has the same general specifications, except for 5-rd. Mauser box magazine. Manufactured in Germany prior to WWII. Used value, $260 to $275.

*Model HK300*

**HECKLER & KOCH Model HK 300:** semi-automatic; .22 WRFM; 5 or 15-rd. detachable box magazine; 19.7'' barrel; V-notch rear sight, ramp front; hand-checkered European walnut cheekpiece stock; drilled, tapped for scope mounts. Manufactured in Germany. Introduced 1977, still in production. Used value, $160 to $170.

**HECKLER & KOCH Model HK91-A-2:** semi-automatic; .308 Winchester; 5 or 20-rd. detachable box magazine; 19'' barrel; V and aperture rear sight, post front; plastic buttstock, forearm; delayed roller-lock blow-back action. Introduced 1978, still in production. Primarily for law enforcement use in this country. Used value, $240 to $250.

    **Model HK-91-A-3** has same specifications as A-2, except for collapsible metal buttstock. Introduced 1978, still in production. Used value, $260 to $270.

**HECKLER & KOCH Model HK-93-A-2:** semi-automatic; .223 Remington; has the same general specifications as Model HK-91-A-2, except for 16.13'' barrel. Primarily for law enforcement. Introduced 1978, still in production. Used value, $240 to $250.

    **Modek HK-93-A-3** has same specifications as A-2, except for collapsible metal buttstock. Introduced 1978, still in production. Used value, $260 to $270.

*Royal*

**HOLLAND & HOLLAND Royal:** hammerless sidelock double rifle; actually a special-order rifle in the realm of semi-production, with original buyer's options available; .240 Apex, 7mm Holland & Holland magnum, .300 Holland & Holland magnum, .375 Holland & Holland magnum, .458 Win., .465 Holland & Holland; 24'', 26'', 28'' barrels; two-piece choice European stock; hand-checkered pistol grip, forearm; folding leaf rear sight, ramp front; swivels; custom-engraved receiver. Still in production. Used values, pre-WWII model, $7250 to $7500; post-war, $6250 to $6500.

    **No. 2 Model** has the same specifications as H&H Royal, except for less ornate engraving, less figure in stock. Still in production. Used value, pre-WWII, $5500 to $5750; post-war, $5250 to $5500.

    **Model Deluxe** has the same specifications as Royal Model, except for more ornate engraving, better grade European walnut in stock; better fitting. Still in production. Used value, pre-WWII, $9500 to $9750; post-war, $8000 to $8250.

*Best Quality*

**HOLLAND & HOLLAND Best Quality:** bolt-action; built on Mauser or Enfield action; .240 Apex, .300 Holland & Holland magnum, .375 Holland & Holland magnum; 24'' barrel; 4-rd. box magazine; cheekpiece stock of European walnut; hand-checkered pistol grip, forearm; folding leaf rear sight, hooded ramp front; sling swivels, recoil pad. Still in production. Used value, pre-WWII, $2500 to $2750; post-war, $2250 to $2500.

**HOLLAND & HOLLAND Deluxe Magazine Model:** bolt-action; has the same specifications as Best Quality model, except for higher quality engraving, exhibition grade European walnut stock. Introduced following World War II, still in production. Used value, $2600 to $2700.

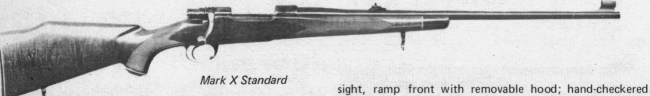

*Mark X Standard*

**INTERARMS Mark X:** bolt-action; .22-250, .243 Win., .270 Win., .308 Win., .25/06, .30/06, 7mm Rem. mag., .300 Win. mag.; 24'' barrel; sliding safety; hinged floor plate; adjustable trigger at added cost; adjustable folding-leaf rear sight, ramp front with removable hood; hand-checkered European walnut Monte Carlo stock, forearm; white spacers on grip cap, butt plate, forearm tip. Imported from Czechoslovakia. Introduced in 1972; still in production. Four additional variations have appeared since 1974. Used values, standard model, $185 to $195; with adjustable trigger, $200 to $215.

*Interarms Mark X Viscount*

**Mark X Cavalier** has same specs as Mark X, but with roll-over cheekpiece, rosewood grip cap and forend tip, recoil pad. Introduced 1974, still in production. Used value, $200 to $210.

**Mark X Viscount** has same specs as Mark X, except for hand-checkered field stock, plainer wood. Introduced 1974, still in production. Used value, $150 to $160.

**Mark X Mannlicher Carbine** has same specs as Mark X, except for Mannlicher-type stock, 20" barrel; made only in .270 Winchester, .308 Winchester, .30/06, 7x57mm. Introduced 1976, still in production. Used value, $200 to $210.

**Mark X Alaskan** has same specifications as Mark X, except for stock crossbolt, heavy-duty recoil pad; made in .375 H&H magnum, .458 Winchester magnum. Introduced 1976, still in production.

*Krico Sporter*

**KRICO Sporter:** bolt-action; .22 Hornet, .222 Remington; 4-rd. clip magazine; 22", 24", 26" barrel lengths; miniature Mauser-type action; single or double-set trigger; open rear sight, hooded ramp front; hand-checkered European walnut stock, cheekpiece, pistol grip, forend tip; sling swivels. Manufactured in Germany 1956 to 1962. Used value, $415 to $425.

**Krico Carbine** has same specs as Sporter model, except for Mannlicher-type stock, 22" barrel. Manufactured 1956 to 1962. Used value, $415 to $425.

**Krico Varmint Model** has same specs as Sporter, except for heavy barrel, no sights; .222 Remington only. Manufactured 1956 to 1962. Used value, $415 to $425.

*Krico Model 311*

**KRICO Model 311:** bolt-action; .22 LR; 5 ot 10-rd. clip magazine; 22" barrel; open rear sight, hooded ramp front; single or double-set trigger; hand-checkered European walnut stock, pistol grip, cheekpiece; sling swivels. Also available with Kaps 2½X scope. Manufactured 1958 to 1962. Used values: iron sights, $214 to $225; with scope, $285 to $300.

*Krieghoff Teck*

**KRIEGHOFF Teck:** over/under; 7x57R, 7x64, 7x65R, .308 Winchester, .30/06, .300 Winchester magnum, 9.8x74R, .375 H&H magnum, .458 Winchester magnum, 25" barrel; box lock; Kersten action, double crossbolt, double underlugs; Express rear sight, ramp front; hand-checkered European walnut stock, forearm. Manufactured in West Germany. Introduced 1967, still in production. Used values: standard calibers, $2000 to $2100; magnum calibers, $2200 to $2350.

**KRIEGHOFF Ulm:** over/under; has same general specs, caliber range as Teck model, except for side lock, leaf arabesque engraving. Introduced 1963, still in production. Used value, $2900 to $3000.

*Ulm*

**KRIEGHOFF Ulm-Primus:** over/under; has same general specs as Ulm model, except for deluxe modifications including higher grade of engraving, wood, detachable sidelocks. Introduced 1963, still in production. Used value, $3350 to $3500.

*Premier*

**MUSGRAVE Premier NR5:** bolt-action; .243 Winchester, .270 Winchester, .30/06 .308 Winchester, 7mm Remington magnum; 5-rd. magazine; 25½" barrel; no sights; European walnut stock, Monte Carlo, cheekpiece; hand-checkered pistol grip, forearm; pistol-grip cap, forend tip; recoil pad; sling swivel studs. Introduced 1972, importation stopped 1973. Still being made in South Africa. Used value, $240 to $250.

*Valiant*

**MUSGRAVE Valiant NR6:** bolt-action; .243 Winchester, .270 Winchester, .30/06, .308 Winchester, 7mm Remington magnum; has same general specs as NR5, except for 24" barrel, straight comb stock, skip checkering, sans grip cap, forend tip; leaf rear sight, hooded ramp front. Introduced 1972, importation stopped 1973. Used value, $180 to $190.

*RSA*

**MUSGRAVE RSA NR1:** bolt-action, single-shot; .308 Winchester; 26-2/5" barrel; target configuration; aperture rear sight, tunnel front; European walnut target stock; barrel band; rubber buttplate; sling swivels. Introduced 1972, importation stopped 1973. Used value, $220 to $230.

*Mauser*

**MUSKETEER Mauser:** FN Mauser, bolt-action sporter; .243, .270, .25/06, .264 Magnum, .308, .30/06, 7mm Magnums, .300 Winchester Magnum; magazine capacity, 3 rds., magnum, 5, standard calibers; 24" barrel; sling swivels; checkered pistol grip, forearm, Monte Carlo stock. Introduced in 1963; dropped, 1972. Imported by Firearms International. Used value, $250 to $265.

*Model N-900*

**NORRAHAMMAR Model N-900:** bolt-action; Husqvarna action; .243 Win., .270 Win., .308 Win., .30/06; 20¼" barrel; single-stage trigger; ebony grip cap, butt plate; side safety; hinged floor plate; hand-checkered European walnut pistol-grip stock, forearm; hooded front sight, adjustable rear; sling swivels. Manufactured in Sweden. Originally imported by Tradewinds, Inc., in 1957; importation dropped, 1967. Used value, $175 to $185.

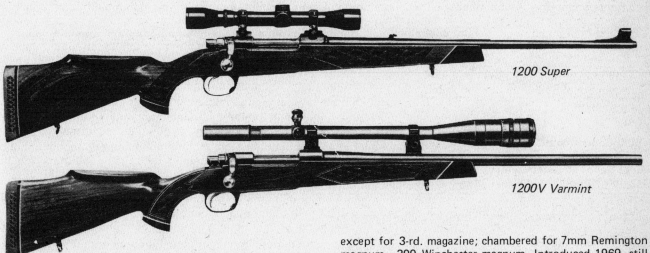

*1200 Super*

*1200V Varmint*

**PARKER-HALE 1200 Super:** bolt-action; .22-250, .243 Winchester, 6mm Remington, .25/06, .270 Winchester, .30/06, .308 Winchester; 4-rd. magazine; 24" barrel; Mauser-design action; folding open rear sight, hooded ramp front; checkered European walnut pistol-grip stock; Monte Carlo cheekpiece; recoil pad; sling swivels. Introduced 1968, still in production. Manufactured in England. Used value, $180 to $190.

**1200 Super Magnum** has same specs as 1200 Super, except for 3-rd. magazine; chambered for 7mm Remington magnum, .300 Winchester magnum. Introduced 1969, still in production. Used value, $200 to $210.

**1200P Presentation** has same general specs as 1200 Super, sans sights; has engraved action, floorplate, trigger guard; detachable sling swivels; chambered for .243 Winchester, .30/06. Manufactured 1969 to 1975. Used value, $225 to $235.

**1200V Varminter** has same general specs as 1200 Super, sans sights; 24" heavy barrel; chambered for .22-250, 6mm Remington, .25/06, .243 Winchester. Introduced 1969, still in production. Used value, $200 to $210.

*Double Rifle*

**PURDEY Double Rifle:** side-lock action; .375 Flanged Nitro Express, .500-465 Nitro Express, .470 Nitro Express, .577 Nitro Express; hammerless, ejectors; 25" 25½" barrel; folding leaf rear sight, hooded ramp front; hand-checkered European cheekpiece stock; sling swivels; recoil pad. Introduced prior to World War I, still in production. Used value, $1200 to $1300.

**PURDEY Big Game Sporter:** bolt-action; 7x57, .300 H&H magnum, .375 H&H magnum, 10.75x73; 3-rd. magazine; 24" barrel; Mauser-design action; folding leaf rear sight, hooded ramp front; hand-checkered European walnut pistol-grip stock. Introduced post-World War I, still in production. Used value, $2300 to $2500.

**ROSS Model 10:** bolt-action; .280 Ross, .303 British; 4 or 5-rd. magazines; interrupted screw lugs; 22", 24", 26" barrels; 2-leaf open rear sight, bead front; hand-checkered American walnut sporting stock. Manufactured in Canada 1910 to 1918. Some collector value. May be unsafe to fire. Used value, $200 to $225.

*Bronco*

**ROSSI Bronco:** single-shot; swing-out chamber; .22 LR, long, short; 16½" barrel; skeletonized crackle-finished alloy stock; cross-bolt safety; instant takedown; adjustable rear sight; blade front. Introduced in 1970; dropped 1975. Marketed by Garcia. Used value, $35 to $40.

*Gallery Model*

**ROSSI Gallery Model:** slide action; takedown; .22 LR, long, short, .22 magnum; 22½" barrel; tube magazine; 14 LR, 16 long, 20 short cartridge capacity; adjustable rear sight, fixed front; uncheckered straight-grip walnut stock,

model, $110 to $115.

**Gallery Model Carbine** has same specs as standard Gallery Model except for 16¼" barrel. Introduced 1975, still in production. Used value, $85 to $95.

**Gallery Model Magnum** has same specs as standard version, except for 10-rd. magazine, chambering for .22 WRFM. Manufactured 1975. Used value, $120 to $125.

**SAUER Mauser Sporter:** bolt-action; 7x57, 8x57, .30/06; other calibers on special order; 5-rd. box magazine; 22", 24" half-octagon barrels, matted raised rib; double-set trigger; three-leaf open rear sight, ramp front; hand-chceckered pistol-grip European walnut stock, raised side panels, Schnabel tip; sling swivels; also manufactured with full-length stock, 20" barrel. Manufactured prior to WWII. Used value, $350 to $375.

**SCHULTZ & LARSEN Model 47:** bolt-action, single shot; .22 LR; 28½" barrel; set trigger; micrometer receiver sight, globe front; free-rifle style European walnut stock; cheekpiece, thumbhole, buttplate, palm-rest, sling swivels. Manufactured in Germany. Used value, $425 to $450.

**SCHULTZ & LARSEN Model 54:** bolt-action, single-shot; 6.5x55mm, American calibers were available on special order; 27½" barrel; micrometer receiver sight, globe front; free-rifle style European walnut stock; adjustable buttplate; cheekpiece; palm rest, sling swivels. Used value, $550 to $600.

**SCHULTZ & LARSEN Model 54J:** bolt-action; .270 Win., .30/06, 7x61 Sharpe & Hart; 3-rd. magazine; 24", 26" barrels; hand-checkered European walnut sporter stock; Monte Carlo comb, cheekpiece. Used value, $325 to $350.

*Model A*

**SMITH & WESSON Model A:** bolt-action; .22-250, .243 Win., .270 Win., .308 Win., .30/06, 7mm Rem. magnum, .300 Win. magnum; 5-rd. magazine in standard calibers, 3 rds. for magnums; 23¾" barrel; folding leaf rear sight, hooded ramp front; hand-checkered European walnut stock; Monte Carlo, rosewood pistol grip cap, forend tip; sling swivels. Manufactured in Sweden by Husqvarna. Imported 1969 to 1972. Used value, $300 to $325.

**Model B** has same specs as Model A, except for 20¾" light barrel, Schnabel forend tip; chambered for .243 Win.,

Model B

Model C

Model D

Model E

.270 Win., .30/06. Imported 1969 to 1972. Used value, $275 to $300.

Model C has same specifications as Model B, except for straight comb stock. Imported 1969 to 1972. Used value, $275 to $300.

Model D has same specs as Model C, except for full-length Mannlicher-type stock. Imported 1969 to 1972. Used value, $290 to $310.

Model E has same specs as Model B, except for full-length Mannlicher-type stock. Imported 1969 to 1972. Used value, $290 to $310.

Model 125

SMITH & WESSON Model 125: bolt-action; .270 Win., .30/06; 5-rd. magazine; 24″ barrel; step adjustable rear sight, hooded ramp front; action drilled, tapped for scope mounts; thumb safety. Standard grade has hand-checkered stock of European walnut; deluxe grade adds rosewood forearm tip, pistol grip cap. Introduced in 1973; dropped, 1973. Used value, standard grade, $165 to $175; deluxe grade, $185 to $195.

Model 14D

SQUIRES BINGHAM Model 14D: bolt-action; .22 LR; 5-rd. box magazine; 24″ barrel; V-notch rear sight, hooded ramp front; grooved receiver for scope mounts; exotic hand-checkered wood stock, contrasting forend tip, pistol-grip cap. Manufactured in the Philippines. Not currently imported. Used value, $50 to $60.

Model 15 has same specs as Model 14D, except chambered for .22 WRFM. Used value, $55 to $65.

**SQUIRES BINGHAM Model M16:** semi-automatic; .22 LR; 19½" barrel, muzzle brake/flash hider; has general appearance of military M-16; integral rear sight, ramped post front; black painted mahogany buttstock, forearm. Not currently imported. Used value, $50 to $60.

**SQUIRES BINGHAM Model M20D:** semi-automatic; .22 LR; 15-rd. detachable box magazine; 19½" barrel, muzzle brake/flash hider; V-notch rear sight, blade front; grooved receiver for scope mount; hand-checkered exotic wood stock; contrasting pistol-grip cap, forend tip. Not currently imported. Used value, $50 to $60.

*Rolling Block*

**STAR Rolling Block Carbine:** single-shot; .30-30, .357 magnum, .44 magnum; 20" barrel; rolling-block action; folding leaf rear sight; ramp front; straight-grip European walnut stock, forearm; metal buttplate, barrel band. Manufactured in Spain 1973 to 1975. Not imported. Used value, $110 to $120.

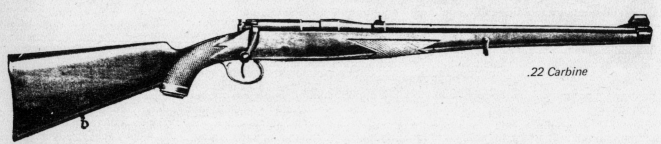

*.22 Carbine*

**STEYR Carbine:** bolt-action; .22 LR; 5-rd. detachable box magazine; 19" barrel; leaf rear sight, hooded bead front; hand-checkered European walnut Mannlicher-type stock; sling swivels, buttplate. Manufactured in Austria, 1953 to 1967. Used value, $265 to $275.

**UNIQUE T66:** bolt-action, single-shot; .22 LR; 25½" barrel; micrometer aperture rear sight, globe front; stippled-grip French walnut target stock; Monte Carlo comb; bulky target forearm; adjustable buttplate; adjustable swivel; accessory track on forearm. Manufactured in France. Introduced 1966, still in production. Used value, $350 to $375.

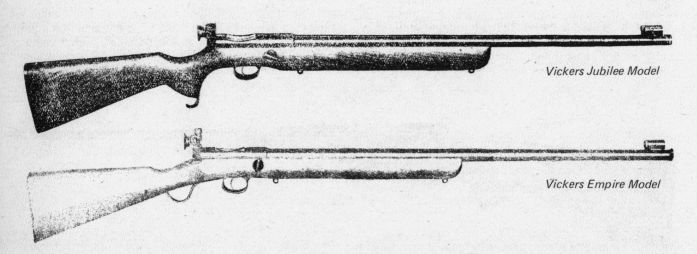

*Vickers Jubilee Model*

*Vickers Empire Model*

**VICKERS Jubilee Model:** Martini-type action; single-shot; .22 LR; 28" heavy barrel; Perfection rear peep sight, Parker-Hale No. 2 front; single-piece European walnut target stock, full pistol grip, forearm. Manufactured prior to World War II. Used value, $275 to $300.

**Empire Model** has same general specs as Jubilee, except for straight-grip stock, 27", 30" barrels. Manufactured prior to WWII. Used value, $220 to $240.

*Magazine Model*

**WESTLEY RICHARDS Magazine Model:** built on Mauser or magnum Mauser action; .30/06, 7mm High Velocity, .318 Accelerated Express, .375 magnum, .404 Nitro Express, .425 magnum; barrels, 22″ for 7mm, 25″ for .425, 24″ for all other calibers; leaf rear sight, hooded front; sporting stock of French walnut; hand-checkered pistol grip, forearm; cheekpiece; horn forearm tip; sling swivels. Used value, $1150 to $1250.

*Double Model*

**WESTLEY RICHARDS Double:** double rifle favored for African big game; box-lock action; hammerless, ejectors; hand-detachable locks; .30/06, .318 Accelerated Express, .375 magnum, .425 Magnum Express, .465 Nitro Express, .470 Nitro Express; 25″ barrels; leaf rear sight, hooded front; French walnut stock; hand-checkered pistol grip, forearm; cheekpiece; horn forearm tip; sling swivels. Used value, $1750 to $2250.

*Express*

**WHITWORTH African Express:** bolt-action; .375 H&H magnum, .458 Win. magnum; 3-rd. magazine; 24″ barrel; Mauser-type action; 3-leaf open rear sight, hooded ramp front; European walnut English-style cheekpiece stock; hand-checkered pistol grip, forend; forend tip; recoil pad; sling swivels. Manufactured in England. Imported 1974 to present by Interarms. Used value, $340 to $360.

# RIFLE NOTES

# RIFLE NOTES

# SHOTGUNS

## In Buying A Used Shotgun, There Are Many Items To Seek Out To Determine Whether You Are Buying Wisely!

IN THE PAST, the rule of thumb for used shotguns that are currently manufactured has been roughly fifty percent of retail value, assuming the gun is in good mechanical condition with half or more of the original finish remaining. Due to the high demand for good used shotguns, this must be changed to around seventy percent of retail price, almost equal to wholesale price. So, a gun that retails for $200 new, may have sold for $100 a few years ago in goood used condition in the past, but now a $140 to $160 price tag can be expected. The percentage, incidentally, varies from one geographic area to another.

Naturally, the overall condition of a used shotgun plays an important role in arriving at a final price. One owner will clean the gun after each shoot, adding a drop or two of lubrication as needed. He transports the gun in a case and avoids unnecessary damage to the gun such as using the gun to hold down a barbed-wire fence while crossing. Normally, such a person may own and use a gun for a dozen years without decreasing the value in excess of normal. The gun will give the overall outward appearance of being well used but also well cared for by the owner.

The second type owner will destroy value

This Remington Sportsman 48 has been badly rusted through neglect, exposure to salt water, lack of cleaning, oiling.

rapidly through sheer negligence. His gun is usually dirty, rusty and with the action full of old accumulated powder residue. Usually the metal parts of the gun will have a light coat of "pepper rust," although he may have added a coat of oil just before the proposed sale. Heavily worn bluing is also a sure sign of hard use and neglect.

The wood will also give a good account of the overall usage. If it has minor scratches or dents

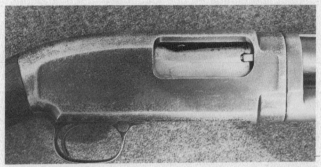

Most of the bluing has been worn off Winchester Model 12 through hard use and a lack of preventative maintenance.

with seventy-five percent of the original finish remaining, chances are that this is just normal wear. On the other hand, if most of the finish is gone and deep scratches and gouges are evident, chances are that the complete gun has experienced neglect of the worst kind.

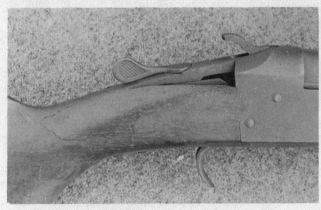

Because of crack in pistol grip, Western Field single barrel is all but worthless for shooting in the field.

Some gunowners are of the opinion that, if a few drops of oil is good, a bath of oil is even better. Beware of the oil-flooded shotgun! It may be a last ditch effort to hide neglect. Oil-soaked

Dark spots on L.C. Smith pistol grip are not figure in the wood but result of excess oil; it can rot the wood.

wood, especially where the wood joins the metal, is generally a sign of rushed maintenance. In addition, such oil-soaked wood eventually may have to be replaced.

One of the best ways to really examine a used shotgun is to inspect it in strong sunlight. Artificial light cannot compare in revealing tell-tale evidence. A gun that has most of its bluing, but covered with pepper rust that is hidden by a heavy last-minute coat of oil will appear normal under artificial light. Strong sunlight, on the other hand, will reveal every speck of rust! A worn wood finish with a heavy coat of wax also may go undetected under artificial light, but offers a completely different story in sunlight!

The first step is to examine the exterior surfaces of the gun slowly and carefully. Watch for rust,

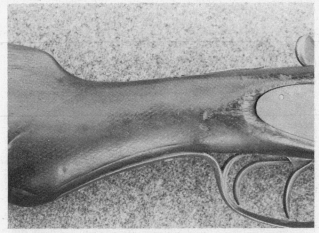

*Extensive use over the years has resulted in diminishing of the original checkering pattern on L.C. Smith grip area.*

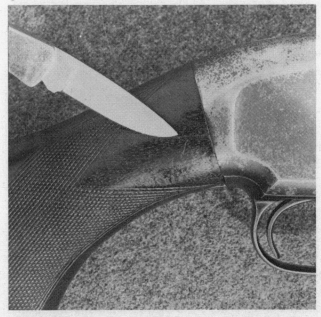

*Minute crack in Model 12 stock is seen easily in bright sunlight. Stock must be repaired or replaced for shooting.*

powder residue, heavily worn wood and metal finish. Wood cracks, gouges and heavy dents reveal a gun that has been neglected. Any split or crack in either stock or forend may necessitate expensive replacement. Bad nicks in the metal or a shiny worn finish will reduce the gun's value.

Now, slowly open the gun action. Look for heavy wear resulting in loose major components. If the shotgun is the break-open type, double check for wear between the receiver and the barrel. A little known trick is to remove the forend as its spring tension may hold the barrel firmly to the receiver thus hiding overall looseness. While the forearm is off, look at the metal finish that is hidden when the forend is attached. This section receives little wear and will retain the original metal finish. Compare this section finish with the other metal parts to arrive at the percent of the remaining original finish.

Closely check the function of the extractors or ejectors. A gun fitted with automatic ejectors should be examined more closely. Both ejectors should initially move out an equal distance. Dry

*Inspection reveals protruding firing pin, which could detonate primer when action is closed; an unsafe factor.*

fire one barrel, then open the action slowly. The first movement should be to provide primary extraction followed by tripping the ejector mechanism. Check the other ejector the same way, then both ejectors in full operation. If possible, check their function with fired shotshell cases.

An extractor-fitted break-open gun should lift a fired case sufficiently for easy finger extraction. If you plan to buy a used gun, several fired empty cases will help you evaluate any gun.

With a pump or autoloader, check the operation of the mechanism. Dummy shotshells, available from gunsmith supply houses, are worth the effort to thoroughly check the action cycle, loading, extraction and ejection.

On any shotgun, check the function of the safety. A malfunction or loose safety means extra dollars for replacement. Check the trigger pull, especially on double guns which should give five pounds of pull per trigger. If one of the single trigger variety, check the trigger reset for firing the second barrel.

Finally, inspect the bore or bores of the barrel. Again, sunlight is the answer. For pumps or semi-auto, open the action and insert a piece of white paper to reflect the light through the bore.

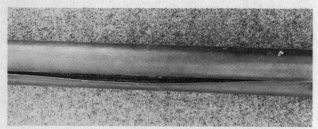

*Old double guns are prone to have loose ribs. Bottom rib on this L.C. Smith is in need of professional repair.*

Insist on a clean bore, even if you have to do the cleaning! The bores should be bright and devoid of any pits or scratches. If not, the price drops in proportion to the damage. Inspect the shell chamber in strong sunlight. A rusty chamber is a sign of neglect and will also decrease the value.

Next on the list is any alteration. Recoil pads will not detract, unless the gun is an antique. It is a matter of opinion when it comes to a choke device. The main point is whether the device presents any

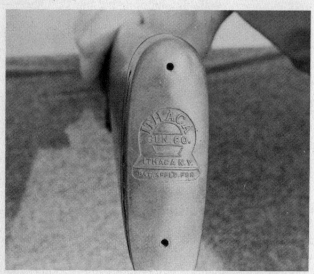

*Ithaca recoil pad installed on Winchester Model 12 skeet gun makes it obvious that this gun is not all original.*

problem to the new owner. If acceptable, the overall price should not change. However, any and all alterations from the factory original opens the door to lower price negotiation.

Finally, check the barrel length for alterations. Most American produced guns have 20, 22, 24, 26,

28, 30, 32 or 34-inch barrels. Foreign guns use the metric designation, but barrel length should end on an even metric scale. A pocket U.S./metric tape will prove invaluable as any shortened barrel

*Weaver choke installed on Model 12 with solid mat rib may be versatile in the field, but collector value diminishes.*

decreases value. Check the choke designation on the barrel as it may have been changed from original.

All of the foregoing has been with shotguns still in current production as most buying and selling concerns these guns. However, the same basic rules apply to a good usable shotgun that is currently not manufactured.

There is one main difference. If the first type requires a trip to the gunsmith, then replacement parts are no problem. Usually a manufacturer maintains a parts inventory for five years after discontinuing a model. After this, replacement parts may present an expensive problem. Even if a gunsmith can locate the needed part, cost will usually be doubled. If the part has to be fabricated, cost can easily be four hundred percent above normal.

For this reason, a shotgun no longer in production should receive a more careful and thorough inspection. It is always a good idea to have a qualified gunsmith inspect these guns for mechanical damage prior to purchase. Five bucks spent for such an inspection is money well spent, as it can save the potential buyer hundreds of dollars in an unwise purchase.

Now we come to the so-called classic shotguns. There are no established hard and fast rules as to what determines a classic. Basically they are double-barrel guns such as the Parker, L.C. Smith, Fox Sterlingworth, et cetera. However, a few other guns fall into this basic category such as the Winchester Model 12 pump and the Remington Model 11 semi-auto. These are the guns that demand a high price due to the heavy demand.

Why such a demand? Snob appeal has a lot to do with it, as some hunters are just not happy until they own one of the classics. These individuals are willing to part with a good supply of dollars to acquire one. True, the classics are usually well built guns, and if given good care and maintenance, will provide a lot of pleasure and actually increase in market value. If you wanted to narrow down the ownership reason, it would probably have to do with pride of ownership.

The prices for the shootable classic shotguns change so much that it is difficult to pin down. The best source of current information is attendance at a large gun show. Just about every major dealer will have several of the classic shotguns for sale. Such gun shows are always an education on all gun values.

Many people are starting to collect shotguns both for pleasure and investment. We know of one individual who purchased over three hundred of the shooting classic shotguns as an investment program as opposed to stocks and bonds! In five years, his investment value had more than doubled.

Another individual collected Damascus barrel rabbit ear doubles of well known names. These once were available in abundance at $25 to $40 each. He sold his two-hundred-gun collection recently for $40,000! This group does not include the cheap trade brand guns but rather the Parkers, Fox, et al. It still is possible to locate these guns, if you know what to buy and the current values.

Trade brand name shotguns are simply well known models and manufacturers built specifically for a large marketing company. The knowledgeable buyer can identify both the manufacturer and the more well known model. Such guns often are sleepers when it comes to value, as the less known name and model usually means a lower asking price. While there is no cross reference list, most good gunsmiths know and can identify the cross reference compatible model, thus providing the buyer with the necessary knowledge for a bargain purchase.

Does refinishing and restoration increase or decrease value? It all depends on the skill of the gunsmith doing the work. If the gun shows heavy abuse, most of the finish is gone and a loose mechanism is obvious, a good gunsmith actually can increase the shotgun's value by restoration of the shooting classics. A true antique may require more thought and skill, therefore cost of

Matching proof marks on receiver and barrel indicate barrel was fitted to receiver at Winchester factory.

restoration becomes a major factor in the final decision.

Most shotguns of current manufacture or good shooting guns of recently discontinued models fall into another category. Almost without exception, these guns can be refinished to new condition without value loss. Normally, it also extends the usable life of such guns.

Metal refinishing to factory specifications costs roughly $40 to $50 for a quality job. Wood refinishing is $30 to $40 average. If done correctly on a shotgun in good mechanical condition, the gun's increased value about equals the refinishing cost.

# AYA

**AYA Matador:** side-by-side, hammerless double-barrel; 10, 12, 16, 20, 20-ga. magnum; barrels, 26", 28", 30", 32"; any standard choke combo; European walnut stock, forearm; checkered pistol grip, beavertail forearm; Anson & Deeley box-lock; single selective trigger; selective automatic ejectors. Imported as Model 400E by Firearms International. Introduced in 1955; dropped, 1963. Used value, $340 to $350.

Matador II has same general specs as Matador I, except

**AYA Bolero:** side-by-side, hammerless double-barrel; has the same general specifications as standard Matador, except for nonselective ejectors, trigger; 12, 16, 20, 28-ga., .410.

**AYA Model 37 Super:** sidelock over/under; 12, 16, 20, 28, .410 gauges; 26", 28", 30" barrels; any standard choke combo; vent rib; single selective trigger; automatic ejectors;

**AYA Model 56:** sidelock, triple-bolting side-by-side; 12, 20 gauges; barrel length, chokes to customer's specs; European walnut stock to customer's specs; semi-custom manufacture. Matted rib; automatic safety, ejectors; cocking indi-

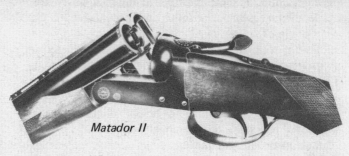
*Matador II*

for better wood, vent-rib barrel. Manufactured 1964 to 1969. Used value, $350 to $375.

Imported as Model 400 by Firearms International. Introduced in 1955; dropped, 1963. Used value, $235 to $250.

hand-checkered stock, forearm; choice of pistol-grip or straight stock; heavily engraved. Introduced in 1963; still in production. Used value, $1750 to $1900.

cators; gas escape valves; folding front trigger; engraved receiver. Introduced in 1972; still in production. Imported by Wm. Larkin Moore. Used value, $900 to $940.

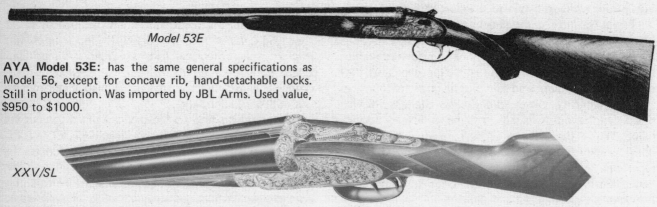
*Model 53E*

**AYA Model 53E:** has the same general specifications as Model 56, except for concave rib, hand-detachable locks. Still in production. Was imported by JBL Arms. Used value, $950 to $1000.

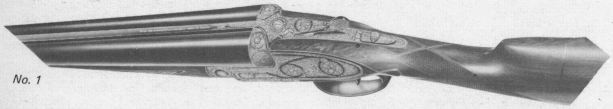
*XXV/SL*

**AYA XXV/SL:** has the same general specifications as Model 56, except is in 12-ga. only; 25" barrels; narrow top rib.

Still in production. Imported by Wm. Larkin Moore. Used value, $750 to $780.

*No. 1*

**AYA No. 1:** has the same general specifications as Model 56, except for concave rib, double bolting, lightweight

frame. Still in production. Was imported by JBL Arms. Used value, $1100 to $1150.

*No. 2*

**AYA No. 2:** has the same general specifications as AYA No. 1, except does not have folding trigger, cocking indicators. Still in production. Imported by Wm. Larkin Moore. Used value, $650 to $685.

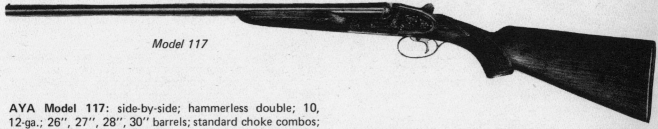

*Model 76*

**AYA Model 76:** side-by-side; hammerless double; 12, 20-ga.; 26", 28", 30" barrels; standard choke combos; hand-checkered European walnut stock, beavertail forend; Anson & Deeley box-lock; selective single trigger; auto ejectors. Still in production. Used value, $400 to $425.

**Model 76 410:** has same general specs as standard model, except chambered for 3" .410 shell; has extractors, 26" barrels; double triggers; straight-grip English-style stock. Still in production. Used value, $350 to $380.

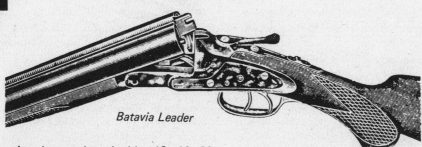

*Model 117*

**AYA Model 117:** side-by-side; hammerless double; 10, 12-ga.; 26", 27", 28", 30" barrels; standard choke combos; hand-checkered European walnut stock, beavertail forend; Holland & Holland-design detachable sidelocks; selective single trigger; auto ejectors. Still in production. Imported by Interarms. Used value, $600 to $625.

# BAKER

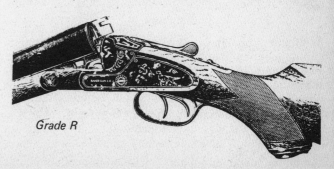

*Batavia Leader*

**BAKER Batavia Leader:** hammerless double; 12, 16, 20 gauges; 26" to 32" barrel, any standard choke combo; sidelock; automatic ejectors or plain extractors; hand-checkered pistol grip, forearm; American walnut stock. Introduced in 1921; discontinued, 1930. Manufactured by Baker Gun Co., Batavia, New York. Used value, with automatic ejectors, $425 to $450; plain extractors, $300 to $325.

**BAKER Black Beauty Special:** same specs as Batavia Leader, but with higher quality finish; dropped, 1930. Used

**BAKER Grade S:** side-by-side; hammerless double; 12, 16-ga.; 26", 28", 30", 32" barrels; same general specs as Batavia Leader, but with finer finish, Flui-tempered steel

**Batavia Special** has same specs as Batavia Leader, except for plain extractors, less expensive finish; 12-ga. only. Used value, $275 to $295.

**Batavia Ejector** has same specs as Leader, except for inferior finish; Damascus or forged steel barrels; standard auto ejectors; 12, 16-ga. only. Used value, $450 to $475.

value, with auto ejectors, $625 to $675; plain extractors, $465 to $490.

barrels; scroll, line engraving; hand-checkered European walnut pistol-grip stock, forend. Collector interest. Manufactured 1915 to 1933. Used value, $650 to $750.

**BAKER Grade R:** side-by-side; hammerless double; 12, 16-ga.; 26", 28", 30", 32" barrels; same general specs as Batavia Leader except for Damascus or Krupp steel barrels, more extensive engraving, with game scene; hand-checkered European walnut stock, forend. Manufactured 1915 to 1933. Collector interest. Used value, $700 to $800.

*Grade R*

# BERETTA

Model 409PB

**BERETTA Model 409PB:** hammerless box-lock double; 12, 16, 20, 28 gauges; 27½", 28½", 30" barrels; engraved action; double triggers; plain extractors; improved/ modified, modified/full chokes; hand-checkered European walnut straight or pistol-grip stock, beavertail forearm. Introduced in 1934; dropped, 1964. Used value, $550 to $600.

**BERETTA Model 410:** hammerless box-lock double; 10-ga. magnum only; 27½", 28½", 30" barrels; improved/ modified, modified/full chokes; hand-checkered European walnut straight stock; recoil pad; plain extractors; double triggers. Introduced in 1934; dropped, 1963. Used value, $800 to $835.

Model 410E is a hammerless box-lock double; has the same specifications as Model 409PB except for better wood, finer engraving, automatic ejectors. Introduced in 1934; dropped, 1964. Used value, $950 to $985.

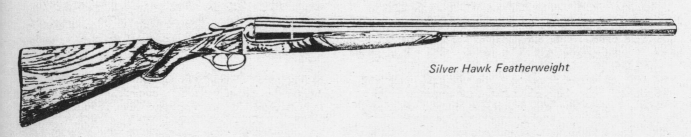

Model 410E

Model 409PB, except for automatic ejectors, side plates and better wood, finer engraving. Introduced in 1934; dropped, 1964. Used value, $985 to $1025.

**BERETTA Model 411E:** hammerless box-lock double; 12, 16, 20, 28 gauges; has the same general specifications as

automatic ejectors; improved/modified, modified/full chokes; hand-checkered pistol-grip stock, forearm. Introduced in 1947; dropped, 1964. Used value, $900 to $935.

**BERETTA Model Asel:** over/under box-lock; 12, 20 gauges; 25", 28", 30" barrels; single nonselective trigger; selective

Silver Hawk Featherweight

**BERETTA Silver Hawk Featherweight:** hammerless box-lock double; 12, 16, 20, 28 gauges; 26" to 32" barrels; plain extractors, double or nonselective single trigger; all standard choke combos; matted rib; hand-checkered European walnut stock, beavertail forearm. Introduced in 1954; dropped, 1967. Used values, single trigger, $375 to

$395; double triggers, $325 to $350.

Silver Hawk Magnum has the same general specifications as Silver Hawk Featherweight, except for recoil pad, 10-ga. only; 3" and 3½" chambers; chrome-plated bores; raised rib; has 30", 32" barrels. Introduced in 1954; dropped, 1967. Used value, single trigger, $400 to $425; double triggers, $350 to $375.

**BERETTA Model 57E:** over/under double; 12, 20, 12 magnum, 20 magnum; has the same general specifications as

Golden Snipe model, but overall quality is higher. Manufactured 1955 to 1967. Used value, $750 to $775.

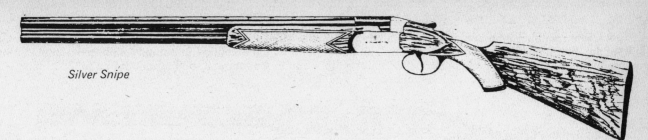

*Silver Snipe*

**BERETTA Silver Snipe:** over/under box-lock; 12, 20 gauges, standard or magnum; 26", 28", 30" barrels; nickel steel receiver; plain or vent rib; improved/modified, modified/

**BERETTA Golden Snipe:** over/under box-lock; 12, 20 gauges standard or magnum; has same general specifications as the Silver Snipe model except for ventilated rib as standard feature; automatic ejectors. Introduced in 1955; dropped, 1975. Used values, selective trigger, $550 to $575;

**BERETTA Grade 100:** over/under double; 12-ga.; 26", 28", 30" barrels, standard choke combinations; side-lock; double triggers; automatic ejectors; hand-checkered straight or pistol-grip European walnut stock, forend. Introduced

full, full/full chokes; selective, nonselective trigger; hand-checkered European walnut pistol-grip stock, forearm. Introduced in 1955; dropped, 1967. Used values, nonselective trigger, $500 to $525; selective trigger, $575 to $600.

nonselective trigger, $600 to $625.
   **Golden Snipe Deluxe** has the same specifications as standard Golden Snipe, except for finer engraving, better walnut; available in skeet, trap models. Introduced in 1955; dropped, 1975. Used value, $575 to $615.

post-World War II, dropped 1960s. Used value, $1650 to $1750.
   **Grade 200** has same general specifications as Grade 100, except for chrome-plated action, bores; improved wood. Used value, $1900 to $2000.

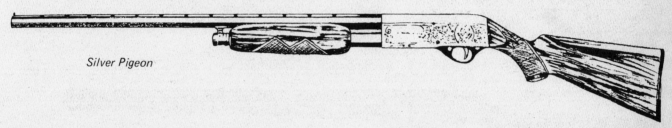

*Silver Pigeon*

**BERETTA Silver Pigeon:** slide-action; 12-ga. only; 26", 30", 32" barrels; standard chokes; hand-checkered walnut pistol-grip stock, matching beavertail forearm; hand-polished, engine-turned bolt; 5-rd. magazine; chromed trigger, light engraving; inlaid silver pigeon. Introduced in 1959; dropped, 1966. Used value, $165 to $175.

**Gold Pigeon** has the same general specifications as Silver Pigeon with vent rib, gold trigger, deluxe engraving, inlaid gold pigeon. Used value, $225 to $250.
   **Ruby Pigeon** has the same specifications as Silver Pigeon, with exception of vent rib, extra deluxe engraving, inlaid gold pigeon with ruby eye. Used value, $300 to $325.

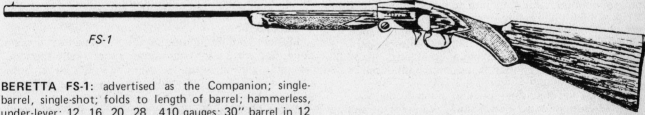

*FS-1*

**BERETTA FS-1:** advertised as the Companion; single-barrel, single-shot; folds to length of barrel; hammerless, under-lever; 12, 16, 20, 28, .410 gauges; 30" barrel in 12 ga., 28" in 16, 20 gauges, 26" in 28, .410 gauges; all full choke; hand-checkered pistol-grip stock, forearm; barrel

release ahead of trigger guard. Introduced in 1959; still in production. Used value, $90 to $100.

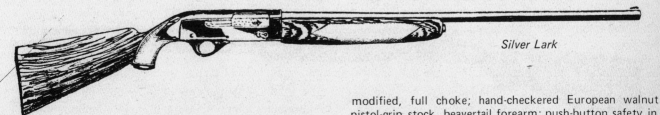

*Silver Lark*

**BERETTA Silver Lark:** autoloader; gas-operated, takedown; 12-ga. only; 26", 28", 30", 32" barrels; improved cylinder,

modified, full choke; hand-checkered European walnut pistol-grip stock, beavertail forearm; push-button safety in trigger guard; all parts hand-polished. Introduced in 1960; dropped, 1967. Used value, $185 to $195.

**Gold Lark** has the same specifications as Silver Lark, except for fine engraving on receiver, ventilated rib. Used value, $250 to $275.

**Ruby Lark** has the same sepcifications as Silver Lark with the exception of a floating rib, stainless steel barrel, profuse engraving. Used value, $350 to $375.

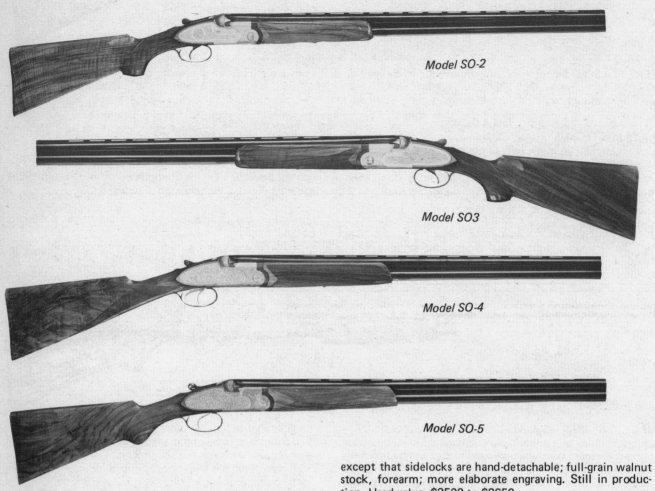

Model SO-2

Model SO3

Model SO-4

Model SO-5

**BERETTA S02 Presentation:** sidelock over/under; listed earlier as 502 Presentation series; 12-ga. only; 26" improved/modified, 28" modified/full barrels standard; skeet, trap models also made; vent rib; straight or pistol-grip stock of hand-checkered European walnut; chrome-nickel receiver; Boehler anti-rust barrels; all interior parts chromed; trigger, safety, top lever checkered; scroll engraving; silver pigeon inlaid in top lever. Introduced in 1965; still in production. Used value, $1500 to $1700.

**Model SO3** has the same specifications as Model SO2, except for fancy selected walnut stock, profuse scroll and relief engraving. Still in production. Used value, $1850 to $2000.

**Model SO4** has the same specifications as SO2 model,

except that sidelocks are hand-detachable; full-grain walnut stock, forearm; more elaborate engraving. Still in production. Used value, $2500 to $2650.

**Model SO5** has the same basic specifications as other SO models, but is virtually handmade, built to customer's specifications. Has Crown grade symbol inlaid in gold in top lever. Still in production on special order basis. Used value, $3250 to $3500.

**Model SO-6** is a side-by-side; hammerless double; 12-ga., 2¾" or 3" chambers; other than barrel placement, has same general specs as over/under SO series guns. Introduced 1948, still in production. Used value, $5700 to $5750.

**Model SO-7** has the same specs as Model SO-6, except for better grade of wood, more elaborate engraving. Introduced 1948, still in production. Used value, $9350 to $9450.

Model BL-1

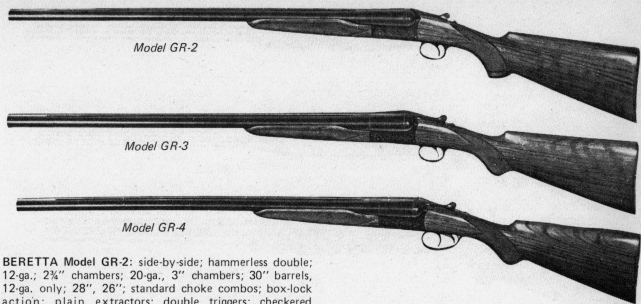

Model GR-2

Model GR-3

Model GR-4

**BERETTA Model GR-2:** side-by-side; hammerless double; 12-ga.; 2¾'' chambers; 20-ga., 3'' chambers; 30'' barrels, 12-ga. only; 28'', 26''; standard choke combos; box-lock action; plain extractors; double triggers; checkered European walnut pistol-grip stock, forend. Manufactured 1968 to 1976. Used value, $425 to $440.

**Model GR-3** has same general specs as Model GR-2, except for single selective trigger, chambering for 3'' 12-ga. shells, recoil pad. Manufactured 1968 to 1976. Used value, $475 to $500.

**Model GR-4** has same specs as Model GR-2, except for automatic ejectors, selective single trigger, higher grade engraving, improved wood; made in 12-ga., 2¾'' chambering only. Manufactured 1968 to 1976. Used value, $575 to $625.

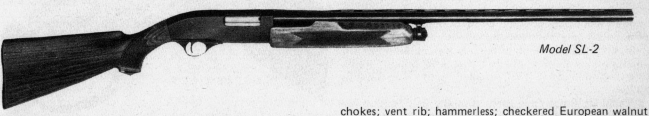

Model SL-2

**BERETTA Model SL-2:** pump action; 12-ga. only; 3-rd. magazine; 26'' improved, 28'' full or modified, 30'' full chokes; vent rib; hammerless; checkered European walnut stock, forend. Manufactured 1968 to 1971. Used value, $220 to $240.

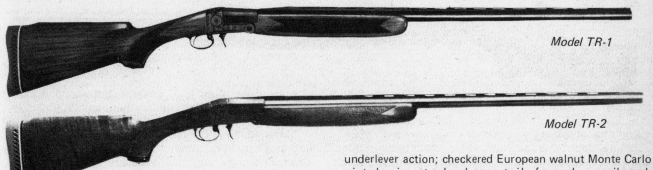

Model TR-1

Model TR-2

**BERETTA Model TR-1:** single-shot trap model; 12-ga. only; 32'' barrel, vent rib; hammerless; engraved frame; underlever action; checkered European walnut Monte Carlo pistol-grip stock, beavertail forend; recoil pad. Manufactured 1968 to 1971. Used value, $150 to $160.

**Model TR-2** has same specs as TR-1, except for extended vent rib. Manufactured 1968 to 1971. Used value, $165 to $175.

**BERETTA BL-1:** box-lock over/under; 12-ga. only; 26'', 28'', 30'' barrels; improved/modified, modified/full chokes; Monoblock design; chrome-moly steel barrels; double triggers; no ejectors; ramp front sight with fluorescent inserts; 2¾'' chambers; automatic safety; hand-checkered European walnut pistol-grip stock, forearm. Introduced in 1969; dropped, 1972. Used value, $300 to $325.

**BL-2** has the same basic specifications as BL-1, except for single selective trigger. Dropped in 1972. Used value, $365 to $380.

**Model BL-2/S** has same general specifications as Model BL-2, except for selective trigger; vent rib; chambered for 2¾'', 3'' shells. Manufactured 1974 to 1976. Used value, $425 to $450.

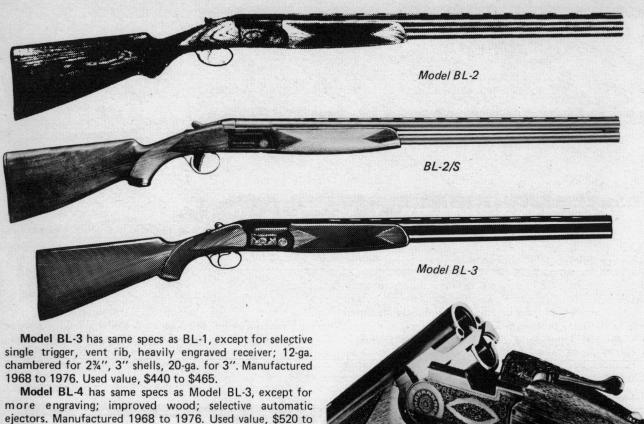

Model BL-2

BL-2/S

Model BL-3

**Model BL-3** has same specs as BL-1, except for selective single trigger, vent rib, heavily engraved receiver; 12-ga. chambered for 2¾'', 3'' shells, 20-ga. for 3''. Manufactured 1968 to 1976. Used value, $440 to $465.

**Model BL-4** has same specs as Model BL-3, except for more engraving; improved wood; selective automatic ejectors. Manufactured 1968 to 1976. Used value, $520 to $550.

**Model BL-5** has same specs as Model BL-4, except for additional engraving, fancier European walnut stock, forend. Manufactured 1968 to 1976. Used value, $690 to $726.

**Model BL-6** has same specs as Model BL-5, except for side plates, more engraving, better wood. Manufactured 1973 to 1976. Used value, $800 to $850.

Model BL-4

Model AL-2

**BERETTA Model AL-2:** autoloader; gas-operated; 12-ga. (2¾'' or 3'') 20-gauge; 26'', 28::, 30'' barrels; full, modified, improved cylinder, skeet chokes; interchangeable barrels; vent rib; medium front bead sight; 3-rd. magazine; European walnut stock, forearm; diamond-point hand

checkering on pistol grip, forearm. Introduced in 1969; still in production. Used values, standard, $225 to $235; trap/skeet, $240 to $250; magnum, $260 to $275.

**Model AL-3** has the same general specifications as AL-2, but with improved wood, hand-engraved receiver; Monte Carlo pistol-grip stock on trap models. Still in production. Used values, standard barrels, $275 to $300; skeet/trap, $350 to $375; 3'' magnum, $350 to $365.

Mark II

**BERETTA Mark II:** single-shot trap model; 12-ga. only; 32'', 34'' barrels; vent rib; box-lock action; automatic ejector; checkered European walnut Monte Carlo pistol-grip

stock, beavertail forend; recoil pad. Manufactured 1972 to 1976. Used value, $425 to $435.

*A-301 Trap*

**BERETTA Model A-301:** autoloader; field model; gas-operated; 12-ga. 2¾" chamber, 20-ga. 3"; 3-rd. magazine; vent rib; 26" improved, 28" full or modified choke barrels; checkered European walnut pistol-grip stock, forearm. Introduced 1977, still in production. Used value, $320 to $340.

A-301 **Magnum** has same specs as field version, except chambered for 12-ga. 3" magnum shells; recoil pad, 30" full choke barrel only. Introduced 1977, still in production. Used value, $350 to $360.

A-301 **Skeet** has same specs as field version, except for 26" barrel, skeet choke, skeet stock, gold-plated trigger. Introduced 1977, still in production. Used value, $320 to $340.

A-301 **Trap** has same specs as field version, except for 30" full choke barrel only, Monte Carlo stock, recoil pad, gold-plated trigger. Introduced 1977, still in production. Used value, $320 to $340.

A-301 **Slug Model** has same specs as field gun except for 22" barrel, slug choke, no rib, rifle sights. Introduced 1977, still in production. Used value, $340 to $350.

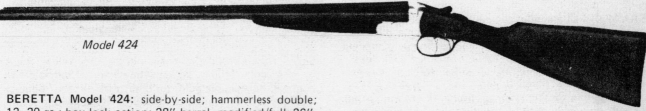

*Model 424*

**BERETTA Model 424:** side-by-side; hammerless double; 12, 20-ga.; box-lock action; 28" barrel, modified/full; 26", improved/modified; plain extractors; border engraving on action; straight-grip checkered European walnut stock, forend. Introduced 1977, still in production. Used value, $500 to $520.

*Model 426E*

**BERETTA Model 426E:** side-by-side; hammerless double barrel; has same general specifications as Model 424, except for selective single trigger, selective auto ejectors, finely engraved action, silver pigeon inlaid in top lever; higher grade wood. Introduced 1977, still in production. Used value, $650 to $675.

*S-58 Trap*

**BERETTA Model S55B:** over/under double barrel; 12-ga., 2¾", 3" chambers, 20-ga., 3" chambers; 26", 28", 30" barrels, standard choke combos; selective single trigger; plain extractors; box-lock action; vent rib; checkered European walnut pistol-grip stock, forend. Introduced 1977, still in production. Used value, $410 to $425.

**Model S56E** has same specs as Model S55B, except for scroll engraving on receiver, selective auto ejectors. Introduced 1977, still in production. Used value, $575 to $600.

**S58 Skeet Model** has same specs as Model S56E, except for 26" barrels; skeet stock, forend; wide vent rib; skeet chokes. Introduced 1977, still in production. Used value, $575 to $600.

**S58 Trap Model** has same specs as skeet version, except for 30" barrels, improved modified/full trap choking; Monte Carlo European walnut stock; recoil pad. Introduced, 1977, still in production. Used value, $575 to $600.

# BERNARDELLI

Roma 3

Roma 4

Roma 6

**BERNARDELLI Roma:** side-by-side; hammerless; Anson & Deeley action; sideplates; 12-ga. only in Roma 3 Model, 12, 16, 20 gauges in others; nonejector standard model; double triggers; 27½", 29½" barrels; modified/full chokes; hand-checkered European walnut stock, forearm; straight or pistol-grip style. Differences in grades are type of engraving, quality of wood, checkering, overall finish. Introduced in 1946; Roma No. 6 still in production; was imported by

Sloans. Others dropped or not imported. Used values, Roma 3, nonejector, $750 to $800; with ejectors, $850 to $900; Roma 4, nonejector, $900 to $950; with ejectors, $950 to $1000; Roma 6, nonejector, $1050 to $1100; with ejectors, $1125 to $1175.

**BERNARDELLI St. Uberto 2:** side-by-side; hammerless; box-lock action; 12, 16 gauges; 26" to 32" barrels; double triggers; all standard choke combos; hand-checkered

European walnut stock, forearm; straight or pistol-grip style. Introduced in 1946; dropped, 1972. Used value, $775 to $825.

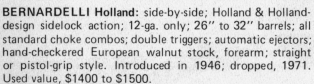

Standard Holland

**BERNARDELLI Holland:** side-by-side; Holland & Holland-design sidelock action; 12-ga. only; 26" to 32" barrels; all standard choke combos; double triggers; automatic ejectors; hand-checkered European walnut stock, forearm; straight or pistol-grip style. Introduced in 1946; dropped, 1971. Used value, $1400 to $1500.

Deluxe Holland model has the same specs as standard Bernardelli Holland, except has beavertail forearm, hunting scene engraved on action. Introduced in 1946; still in production on special order only. Was imported by Sloans. Used value, $4500 to $4650.

**BERNARDELLI Brescia:** side-by-side double barrel; 12, 20-ga.; 25½" improved/modified barrels in 20-ga.; 27½", 29½" modified/full in 12-ga.; sidelock action; exposed hammers; engraved frame; double triggers; plain extractors; checkered European walnut English-style straight stock. Introduced circa 1960, still in production. Used value, $520 to $540.

**Italia Model** has the same specifications as Brescia, except for improved wood, higher grade of engraving. Still in production. Used value, $650 to $675.

Brescia

BERNARDELLI Elio: side-by-side double barrel; 12-ga. only; lightweight game model; has same general specs as Game Cock model, except for automatic ejectors, English-style scroll engraving. Introduced circa 1970, still in production. Used value, $875 to $925.

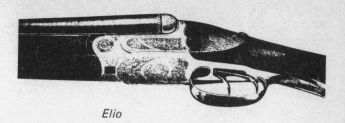

*Elio*

*Standard Gamecock*

*Premier Gamecock*

BERNARDELLI Game Cock: side-by-side; hammerless; box-lock action; 12, 20 gauges; 25″ improved/modified or 28″ modified/full barrels; straight hand-checkered European walnut stock; double triggers on Standard model. Introduced in 1970; still in production. Was imported by Sloans. Used value, $600 to $640.

Deluxe Game Cock model has same specifications as standard, except for light scroll engraving. Used value, $650 to $655.

Premier Game Cock has same specifications as Roma 3 and is same gun by another designation. Price is the same.

# BROWNING

*Auto-5 Magnum 12*

EDITOR'S NOTE: Some models are made in Japan, some in Belgium and some in both countries. Collector interest has increased in Belgium-made models and prices are approximately 25% higher than for Japanese production.

BROWNING Auto-5: autoloader; takedown, recoil-operated; has been made in a wide variety of configurations, grades and gauges. Browning Special or Standard model was introduced in 1900; redesignated as Grade I in 1940. Available in 12, 16 gauges; 26″ to 32″ barrels; 4-rd. magazine; pre-WWII guns were available with 3-rd. magazine also; hand-checkered pistol-grip stock, forearm of European walnut; plain barrel, vent or raised matted rib. Variations still are being manufactured. Used values, with plain barrel, $315 to $325; with raised matted rib, $340 to $350; with vent rib, $375 to $425.

Auto-5 Grade III has the same general specifications as the Grade I or Standard model, except for better wood, checkering and more engraving. Discontinued, 1940. Used values, plain barrel, $550 to $600; with raised matted rib, $650 to $675; with vent rib, $700 to $750.

Auto-5 Grade IV — sometimes called Midas Grade — has

the same general specifications as Grade III, except for profuse inlays of green, yellow gold. Discontinued, 1940. Used values, plain barrel, $1150 to $1250; with raised matted rib, $1350 to $1500; with vent rib, $1800 to $2000.

Auto-5 Trap model, in 12-ga. only, has the same specifications as the Grade I, except for 30″ vent rib barrel, full choke only, trap stock. Used value, $375 to $400.

Auto-5 Magnum 12 has the same general specifications as Grade I, but is chambered for 3″ magnum shell; has recoil pad, plain or vent rib barrel; 28″ barrel is modified or full, 30″ and 32″ are full choke. Introduced in 1958; still in production. Used values, plain barrel, $375 to $400; vent rib, $425 to $450.

Auto-5 Magnum 20 has the same general specifications as the Magnum 12, except is chambered for 20-gauge magnum shell; 26″ barrel is full, modified or improved, 28″ is full or modified; vent rib. Used value, $425 to $450.

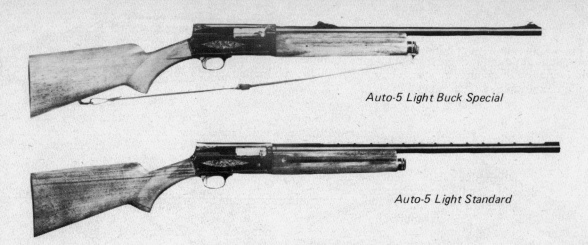

*Auto-5 Light Buck Special*

*Auto-5 Light Standard*

**BROWNING Auto-5 Light:** autoloader; takedown; recoil operated; 12, 16, 20 gauges; same general specifications as Standard Auto-5; 5-rd. magazine, with 3-rd. plug furnished; 2¾'' chamber; 26'', 28'', 30'' barrels, with standard choke choices; receiver is hand engraved; gold plated trigger; double extractors; barrels are interchangeable; made with vent rib only on current models. Introduced in 1948; still in production. Used value, $350 to $375.

**Auto-5 Light Skeet** model has the same specifications as the Light Standard model except for skeet boring; available only in 12, 20 gauges; 28'' barrel, with full or modified choke; 26'' with full, modified or improved cylinder; plain barrel or vent rib; vent rib only on current model. Used value, $350 to $375.

**Auto-5 Light Buck Special** has the same specifications as Standard model, except for 24'' barrel; choked for slugs; adjustable rear sight, gold bead front on contoured ramp; detachable swivels, sling optional on current model. Used value, $345 to $350; with sling, swivels, $350 to $360.

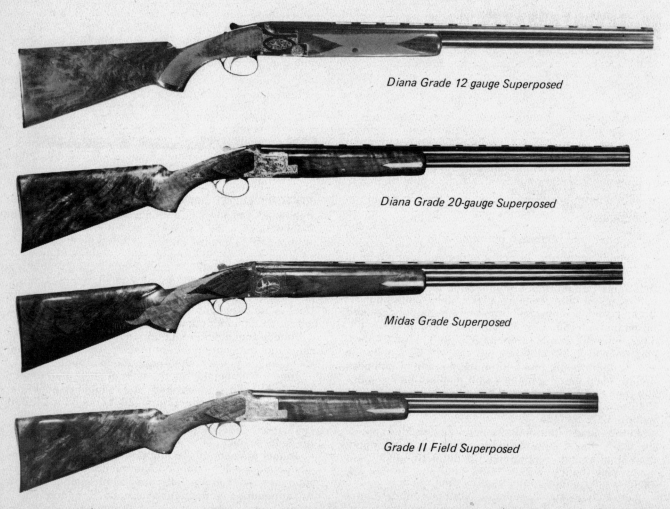

*Diana Grade 12 gauge Superposed*

*Diana Grade 20-gauge Superposed*

*Midas Grade Superposed*

*Grade II Field Superposed*

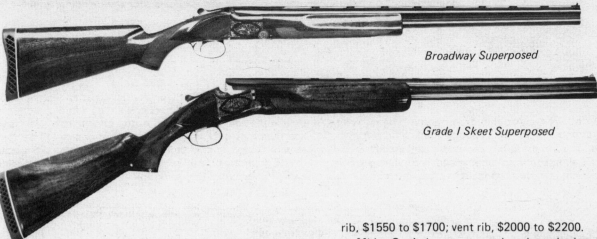

*Broadway Superposed*

*Grade I Skeet Superposed*

**BROWNING Superposed:** over/under; Browning-designed action; 12, 20, 28, .410 gauges; 26½", 28", 30" or 32" barrels; 32" not made since WWII; gun is made in a wide spectrum of variations, grades, choke combinations; early models and pre-WWII had double triggers, twin single triggers or nonselective single trigger. Pre-WWII production ended when Belgium was invaded; hand-checkered stocks, forearms of French walnut; choice of pistol-grip or straight stock. Standard Grade is listed as Grade I, has raised matted rib or vent rib. Introduced in 1928; variations still in production. Used values, with raised matted rib, $700 to $850 to $900; vent rib, $1150 to $1250.

**Lightning Model Grade I** had only matted barrel, no rib before WWII; post-war models have vent rib. Other specifications generally the same as standard Superposed model. Used values, with matted barrel, $950 to $1000; vent rib, $1150 to $1250.

**Pigeon Grade Superposed** was redesignated as Grade II after WWII. Had better wood, finer checkering, more engraving than Standard Superposed model; raised matted rib or vent rib. Used values, with matted rib, $1250 to $1400; vent rib, $1650 to $1750.

**Diana Grade** had either raised matted rib or vent rib before WWII; current models have only vent rib. Has same specs as Pigeon Grade, but with more engraving, better wood, improved general quality. Used values, with matted rib, $1550 to $1700; vent rib, $2000 to $2200.

**Midas Grade** in pre-war versions has raised matted rib or vent rib; current versions have only wide vent rib. Has same general specifications as standard Superposed, but is heavily engraved, gold inlaid. Used values, raised matted rib, $3250 to $3500; vent rib, $4250 to $4500.

**Superposed Magnum** model has the same specifications as Grade I, except is chambered for 12-gauge 3" shells; 30" vent rib barrel, choked full/full or full/modified; recoil pad. Used values, Grade I, $1200 to $1250; Diana Grade, $2250 to $2500; Midas Grade, $4500 to $4750.

**Superposed Lightning Trap** model is 12-ga. only; has 30" barrels; full/full, full/improved, full/modified chokes; straight hand-checkered stock and semi-beavertail forearm of French walnut; ivory bead sights. Used values, Grade I, $1150 to $1250; Diana Grade, $2250 to $2500; Midas Grade, $4500 to $4750.

**Superposed Broadway Trap** model has same specifications as Lightning trap model, except has 30" or 32" barrels; 5/8"-wide Broadway vent rib. Used values, Grade I, $1150 to $1250; Diana Grade, $2250 to $2500; Midas Grade, $4250 to $4500.

**Superposed Skeet** model has the same specifications as Standard Superposed model, except for choice of 26½" or 28" barrels, choked skeet/skeet; made in 12, 20, 28, .410. Used values, Grade I, $1150 to $1250; Pigeon Grade, $1650 to $1750; Diana Grade, $2250 to $2500; Midas Grade, $4250 to $4500.

**BROWNING American Grade I:** autoloader; 12, 16, 20-ga.; 2, 4-rd. tube magazine; recoil-operated; 26", 28", 30", 32" barrel lengths, standard chokes; hand-checkered American walnut pistol-grip stock, forend. Identical to the Remington Model 11A, was manufactured by Remington for Browning, 1940 to 1949. Used value, $160 to $170.

**American Special** has same specs as Grade I, except for either vent rib, or matted raised rib. Manufactured 1940 to 1949. Used values: vent rib, $220 to $235; raised rib, $180 to $195.

**American Special Skeet** version has same specs as Grade I, except for 26" barrel, vent rib, Cutts Compensator. Manufactured 1940 to 1949. Used value, $240 to $250.

**American Field Model** has same specs as Grade I, except for 28" barrel, Poly Choke. Manufactured 1940 to 1949. Used value, $185 to $200.

*Twelvette*

any standard choke; hand-checkered pistol-grip stock, forearm of European walnut; steel receiver; plain or recessed rib barrel; conservative engraving; weight, about 7¾ lbs. Introduced in 1955; dropped, 1961. Used values, with plain barrel, $225 to $250; recessed rib, $250 to $275.

**Twelvette Double Auto** model is same as the standard

**BROWNING Double Auto:** autoloader; takedown; short recoil system; 2-shot; 12-ga. only; 26", 28", 30" barrels;

*Twentyweight*

Double Auto, except for aluminum receiver, barrel with plain matted top or vent rib; receiver is black anodized with gold-wiped engraving; some receivers are anodized in brown, gray or green with silver-wiped engraving; weighs about a pound less than standard model. Introduced in 1955; dropped, 1971. Used values, matted barrel, $250 to $275; vent rib, $325 to $350.

**Twentyweight Double Auto** model has the same specifications as Twelvette model, but weighs 12 oz. less, largely due to thinner stock; 26½" barrel only. Introduced in 1956; dropped, 1971. Used values, matted barrel, $300 to $325; vent rib, $350 to $375.

*BT-99 Grade I*

**BROWNING BT-99 Grade I:** single-shot trap; 12-ga.; 32", 34" barrel; box-lock action; automatic ejector; vent rib; improved, full choke; checkered walnut pistol-grip stock, beavertail forend. Manufactured in Japan. Introduced 1969, still in production. Used value, $315 to $325.

**BT-99 Grade I Competition** has same specifications, except for high wide rib, Monte Carlo-style stock. Introduced, 1976; Competition name dropped 1978. Still in production. Used value, $340 to $350.

*Super-Light Field Grade Superposed*

**BROWNING Superposed Super-Light:** over/under; box-lock action; top lever; 12, 20 gauges; 2¾" chambers; 26½" barrels only; choked modified/full or improved/modified; barrel selector combined with manual tang safety; single selective trigger; straight grip stock of select walnut; hand-checkered grip, forearm; vent rib; enraved receiver. Introduced in 1970; still in production. Used values, Grade I, $900 to $1000; Diana Grade, $2000 to $2250; Midas Grade, $3000 to $3250.

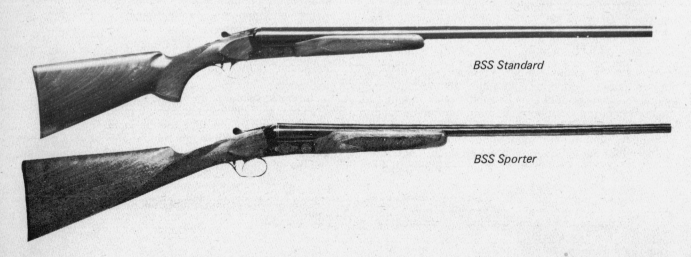

*BSS Standard*

*BSS Sporter*

**BROWNING BSS:** side-by-side double; 12, 20-ga.; 3" chambers; 26", 28", 30" barrels; standard choke combos; box-lock action; hammerless; non-selective single trigger; checkered walnut pistol-grip stock, beavertail forend. Manufactured in Japan. Introduced 1972, still in production. Used value, $260 to $275.

**BSS Sporter** has same specs as BSS 20-ga., except for straight stock, selective trigger. Introduced 1977, still in production. Used value, $270 to $280.

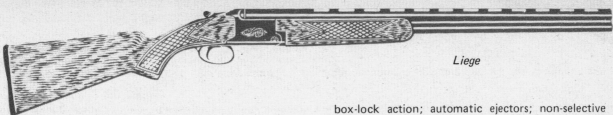

*Liege*

**BROWNING Liege:** over/under; double barrel; 12-ga.; 26½", 28" barrels, chambered for 2¾" shells, 30" for 3"; box-lock action; automatic ejectors; non-selective single trigger; standard choke combos; vent rib; checkered walnut pistol-grip stock, forearm. Manufactured 1973 ro 1975. Used value, $475 to $500.

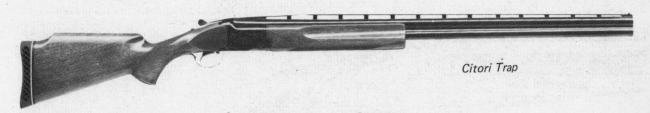

*Citori Trap*

**BROWNING Citori:** over/under; double barrel, 12, 20-ga.; 3" chambers; 26", 28", 30" barrels; improved/modified, modified/full, full/full chokes; automatic ejectors; box-lock action; selective single trigger; checkered pistol-grip stock, semi-beavertail forearm; recoil pad. Manufactured in Japan. Introduced 1973, still in production. Used value, $340 to $350.

**Citori Trap** model has same general specs as standard Citori, except made in 12-ga. only, checkered walnut Monte Carlo stock, beavertail forearm, 30", 32" barrels, standard trap choke combos, vent rib or high-post target wide vent rib. Introduced 1974, still in production. Used values, standard vent rib, $350 to $360; high-post vent rib, $375 to $390.

**Citori Skeet** model has same general specs as standard version, except for skeet stock, forearm; skeet-choked 26", 28" barrels; vent rib or target high-post wide rib. Introduced 1974, still in production. Used values, standard vent rib, $350 to $360; high post vent rib, $375 to $390.

**Citori Sporter** has same general specs as standard model, except made with 26" barrel only; straight-grip stock, Schnabel forend, satin oil finish. Introduced 1978, still in production. Used value, $350 to $360.

*B-2000 Standard*

*B-2000 Skeet*

**BROWNING 2000:** autoloader; gas-operated; 12, 20-ga.; 4-rd. magazine; chambered for 2¾" shells; 26", 28", 30" barrels; choice of standard chokes; vent rib or plain matted barrel; checkered pistol-grip stock of European walnut. Manufactured in Belgium, assembled in Portugal. Introduced 1974, still in production. Used value, $275 to $300.

**2000 Magnum** has same specs as standard model, except 3" chambering, 3-rd. magazine, 26", 28", 30", 32" barrel lengths, vent rib. Introduced 1974, still in production. Used value, $280 to $300.

**2000 Trap** has same specs as standard model, except for Monte Carlo-style stock, recoil pad, 30", 32" barrel lengths; high-post vent rib; modified, improved, full chokes; 12-ga. only, 2¾" chambering. Introduced 1974, still in production. Used value, $325 to $350.

**2000 Skeet** has same specs as standard version, except for skeet stock, 26" skeet-choke barrel; 12, 20-ga.; 2¾" chambering; recoil pad. Introduced 1974, still in production. Used value, $315 to $325.

**2000 Buck Special** has same specs as standard model, except for 24" slug barrel, no rib, open rear sight, front ramp; 12-ga. chambered for 2¾¾" shell, 20-ga., 3". Introduced 1974, still in production. Used value, $280 to $295.

*BPS Standard*

**BROWNING BPS:** pump-action; 12-ga.; 3'' chamber; loads five 2¾'' shells, four 3''; 26'', 28'', 30'' barrels, standard choke choices; take-down; vent rib; checkered walnut pistol-grip stock, semi-beavertail slide handle; recoil pad. Manufactured in Japan. Introduced 1977, still in production. Used value, $165 to $175.

# CHURCHILL

EDITOR'S NOTE: 20, 28-gauges bring 25% to 35% more than prices shown. The .410 is as much as 50% higher.

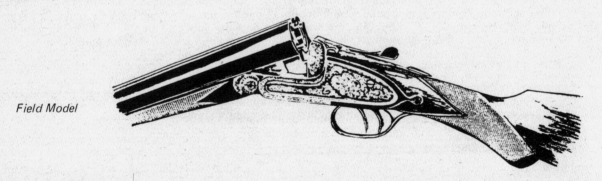

*Premier Quality*

**CHURCHILL Premier Quality:** side-by-side; hammerless; sidelock; 12, 16, 20, 28 gauges; 25'', 28'', 30'', 32'' barrels; any desired choke combo; automatic ejectors; double triggers or single selective trigger; English engraving; hand-checkered European walnut stock, forearm; pistol-grip or straight English style. Introduced in 1900; still marketed. Used values, double triggers, $5750 to $6250; single selective trigger, $6750 to $7000.

*Field Model*

**CHURCHILL Field Model:** side-by-side; hammerless; sidelock; 12, 16, 20, 28 gauges; has the same general design specifications as Premier Model but has lower grade of wood, less engraving, lower overall quality. Introduced in 1900; still marketed. Used values, double triggers, $3000 to $3250; single selective trigger, $3500 to $3700.

*Utility Model*

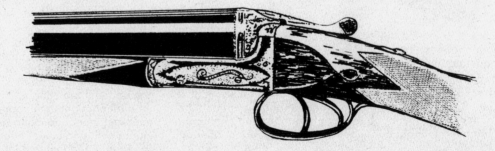

**CHURCHILL Utility Model:** side-by-side; hammerless; sidelock; 12, 16, 20, 28, .410 gauges; 25'', 28'', 30'', 32'' barrels; double triggers or single selective trigger; any desired choke combo; hand-checkered European walnut stock, forearm; pistol-grip or straight English style. Introduced in 1900; still marketed. Used values, double triggers, $2000 to $2250; single selective trigger, $2500 to $2750.

**CHURCHILL Premier Over/Under:** hammerless; sidelock; 12, 16, 20, 28 gauges; 25", 28", 30", 32" barrels; automatic ejectors; double triggers or single selective trigger; English engraving; hand-checkered European walnut stock, forearm; pistol-grip or straight English style. Introduced in 1925; dropped, 1955. Used values, double triggers, $6500 to $6750; single selective trigger, $7250 to $7500. Add $650 for raised vent rib.

*XXV Premiere*

**CHURCHILL XXV Premier:** side-by-side; hammerless double; 12, 20-ga.; 25" barrels; standard choke combos; side-lock; assisted opening feature; auto ejectors; double triggers; narrow rib; checkered walnut straight-grip stock, forearm. Currently produced. Used value, $8250 to $8500.

   **XXV Imperial** has same specs as Premier model, sans the assisted opening feature. Currently produced. Used value, $7500 to $7650.

   **XXV Hercules** has same specs as Premier, except has box-lock action. Currently produced. Used value, $4250 to $4400.

   **XXV Regal** has same specs as XXV Hercules, sans assisted opening feature; made in 12, 20, 28-ga., .410. Currently produced. Used value, $3500 to $3750.

# COGSWELL & HARRISON

**COGSWELL & HARRISON Primac Model:** side-by-side; hammerless; hand-detachable sidelocks; 12, 16, 20 gauges; 25", 26", 27½", 30" barrels; any choke combo; automatic ejectors; double triggers, single or single selective triggers; English-style engraving; hand-checkered European walnut straight-grip stock, forearm. Introduced in 1920s; still in production. Used values, double triggers, $2300 to $2500; single trigger, $2650 to $2900; single selective trigger, $2600 to $2800.

*Victor Model*

**COGSWELL & HARRISON Victor Model:** side-by-side; hammerless; has the same specifications as Primac model except for better finish, finer wood, checkering, engraving patterns. Introduced in 1920s; still in production. Used values, double triggers, $3400 to $3550; single trigger, $3650 to $3850; single selective trigger, $3750 to $4000.

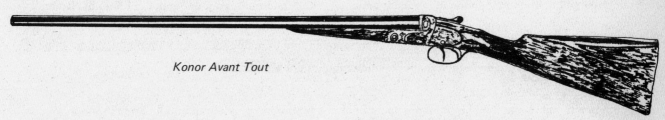

*Konor Avant Tout*

**COGSWELL & HARRISON Konor Avant Tout:** side-by-side; hammerless; box-lock action; 12, 16, 20 gauges; 25", 27½", 30" barrels; any desired choke combo; side plates; double, single or single selective triggers; hand-checkered European walnut straight-grip stock, forearm; pistol-grip stock available on special order; fine checkering, engraving. Introduced in 1920s; still in production. Used values, double triggers, $1500 to $1575; single trigger, $1700 to $1750; single selective trigger, $1775 to $1925.

   **Avant Tout Sandhurst** model has the same specifications as Konor model except for less intricate engraving, checkering, lower grade of wood, overall workmanship. Still in production. Used values, double triggers, $1375 to $1425; single trigger, $1625 to $1675; single selective trigger, $1750 to $1800.

   **Avant Tout Rex** model has the same specifications as Sandhurst model except has no side plates, lower grade wood, checkering, engraving, overall finish. Still in production. Used values, double triggers, $1150 to $1275; single trigger, $1175 to $1250; single selective trigger, $1275 to $1350.

**COGSWELL & HARRISON Huntic Model:** side-by-side; hammerless; sidelock action; 12, 16, 20 gauges; 25", 27½", 30" barrels; any desired choke combo; automatic ejectors; double, single or single selective triggers; hand-checkered European walnut straight-grip stock, forearm; pistol-grip stock on special order. Introduced in late 1920s; still in production. Used values, double triggers, $1150 to $1200; single trigger, $1950 to $2000; single selective trigger, $2050 to $2100.

**COGSWELL & HARRISON Markor Model:** side-by-side; hammerless; box-lock action; 12, 16, 20 gauges; 27½", 30" barrels; any standard choke combo; double triggers; ejector or nonejector; hand-checkered European walnut straight-grip stock, forearm. Introduced in late 1920s; still in production. Used values, ejector model, $1050 to $1125; nonejector, $925 to $1000.

**COGSWELL & HARRISON Ambassador:** side-by-side, hammerless double; 12, 16, 20-ga.; 26", 28", 30" barrels, any choke combo; box-lock action; side plates feature game engraving or rose scroll work; auto ejectors, double triggers; hand-checkered European walnut straight-grip stock, forearm. Introduced 1970, still in production. Used value, $2750 to $3000.

# COLT

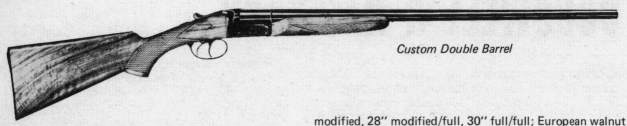

*Custom Double Barrel*

**COLT Custom Double Barrel:** hammerless; box-lock action; 12 (2¾" and 3"), 16 gauges; barrels are 26" improved/modified, 28" modified/full, 30" full/full; European walnut stock; hand-checkered pistol grip, beavertail forearm. Made only in 1961. Used value, $325 to $335.

*Standard Pump*

**COLT Coltsman Pump Model:** slide-action; takedown; 12, 16, 20 gauges; barrels are 26" improved, 28" modified or 30" full choke; magazine holds 4 rds.; European walnut stock; uncheckered pistol grip, forearm. Manufactured for Colt by Manufrance. Introduced in 1961; dropped, 1965.

Used value, $135 to $145.

**Coltsman Custom** pump has the same specifications as standard model, same manufacturer, except has hand-checkered pistol grip, forearm, vent rib. Introduced in 1961; dropped, 1963. Used value, $165 to $175.

*Ultra Light Auto, Standard*

**COLT Ultra Light Auto:** autoloader; takedown; alloy receiver; 12, 20 gauges; chrome-lined barrels are 26" improved or modified, 28" modified or full, 30" full only, 32" full only; 4-rd. magazine; plain barrel, solid or vent rib; European walnut stock; hand-checkered pistol grip, forearm. Manufactured for Colt by Franchi. Introduced in 1964; dropped, 1966. Used values, plain barrel, $165 to $175; solid rib, $185 to $195; vent rib, $200 to $225.

**Ultra Light Custom Auto** is the same as the standard model, except for select walnut stock, forearm; engraved receiver; vent rib only. Introduced in 1964; dropped, 1966. Used values, solid rib, $215 to $225; vent rib, $235 to $250.

**COLT Magnum Auto:** autoloader; takedown; 12, 20 gauges; chambered for 3" magnum shell; other specifications generally the same as those for Ultra Light standard auto. In 12 magnum, barrels are 30" or 32"; 28" in 20 magnum. Produced for Colt by Franchi. Introduced in 1964; dropped, 1966. Used values, plain barrel, $175 to $185; solid rib, $190 to $200; vent rib, $225 to $235.

**Custom Magnum Auto** has same specifications as standard magnum auto, except for select walnut stock, forearm; engraved receiver; vent rib only. Introduced in 1964; dropped, 1966. Used values, solid rib, $200 to $215; vent rib, $235 to $245.

*Sauer Drilling*

**COLT Sauer Drilling:** box-lock action; top lever; crossbolt; .30/06 or .243 Winchester under side-by-side 12-gauge barrels; 25" barrels; set rifle trigger; side safety; shotgun barrels choked modified/full; folding leaf rear sight, blade front with brass bead; cocking indicators; tang barrel selector; automatic sight positioner; oil-finished American walnut stock; hand-checkered pistol grip, forearm; black pistol grip cap; recoil pad. Made for Colt by Sauer in West Germany. Used value, $1850 to $1900.

# CHARLES DALY

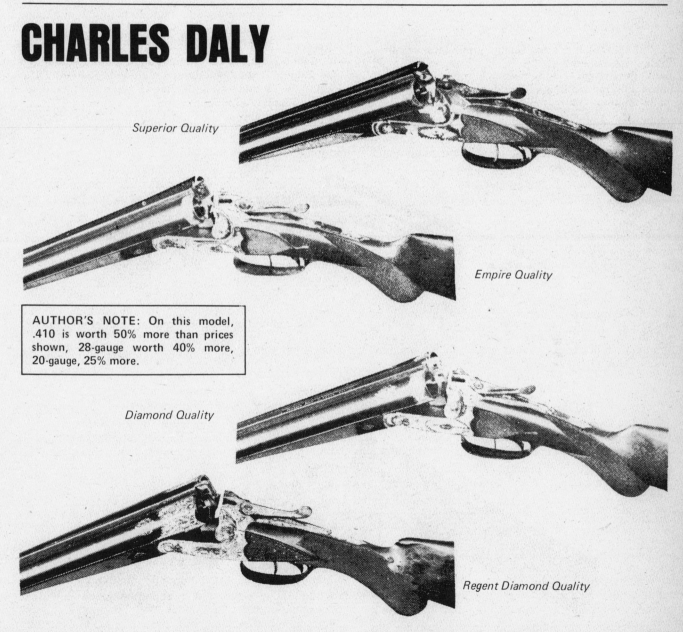

*Superior Quality*

*Empire Quality*

**AUTHOR'S NOTE:** On this model, .410 is worth 50% more than prices shown, 28-gauge worth 40% more, 20-gauge, 25% more.

*Diamond Quality*

*Regent Diamond Quality*

**CHARLES DALY Hammerless Double Barrel:** Anson & Deeley-type box-lock action; 10, 12, 16, 20, 28, .410 gauges; 26" to 28" barrels with any choke combo; walnut stock; checkered pistol grip, forearm; made in four grades; all have automatic ejectors, except Superior Quality; grades differ in grade of wood, checkering, amount of engraving, general overall quality. Made in Suhl, Germany, for Daly. Introduced about 1920; dropped. 1933. Used values, Regent Diamond Quality, $2000 to $2250; Diamond Quality, $1500 to $1750; Empire Quality, $1050 to $1150; Superior Quality, $650 to $700.

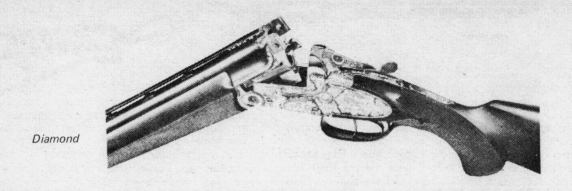

*Diamond*

**CHARLES DALY Empire Quality Over/Under:** Anson & Deeley-type box-lock action; 12, 16, 20 gauges; 26" to 30" barrels; any standard choke combo; European walnut stock; hand-checkered pistol grip, forearm; double triggers; automatic ejectors. Made in Suhl, Germany, for Daly. Introduced about 1920; dropped, 1933. Used value, $1350 to $1500.

**Diamond Quality Over/Under** has the same specifications as Empire Quality, except has more extensive engraving, better wood and improved general overall quality. Used value, $2250 to $2500.

*Empire Quality Trap*

**CHARLES DALY Empire Quality Trap:** single-barrel; Anson & Deeley-type box-lock action; 12-ga. only; 30", 32", 34" vent rib barrel; automatic ejector; European walnut stock; hand-checkered pistol grip, forearm. Made in Suhl, Germany, for Daly in one model only. Introduced about 1920; dropped, 1933. Used value, $1500 to $1750.

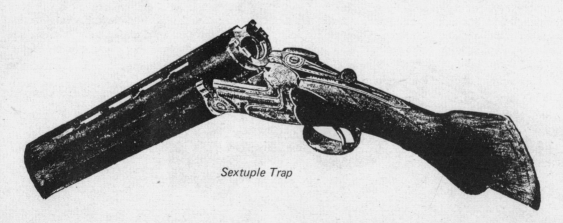

*Sextuple Trap*

**CHARLES DALY Sextuple Trap:** single-barrel; Anson & Deeley-type box-lock action; 12-ga. only; 30", 32", 34" vent rib barrel; six locking bolts; automatic ejector; European walnut stock; hand-checkered pistol grip, forearm. Made in two grades in Suhl, Germany, for Daly; grades differ only in checkering, amount of engraving, grade of wood, improved overall quality. Introduced about 1920; dropped, 1933. Used values, Empire Quality, $1750 to $2000; Regent Diamond Quality, $2500 to $2750.

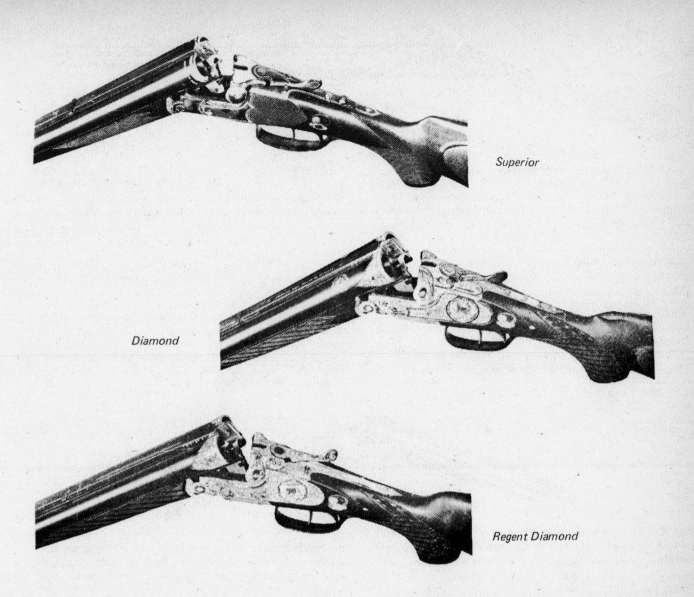

*Superior*

*Diamond*

*Regent Diamond*

**CHARLES DALY Hammerless Drilling:** Anson & Deeley-type box-lock action; 12, 16, 20 gauges; rifle barrel chambered for .25-20, .25-35, or .30-30 cartridges; plain extractors; automatic rear sight operated by selector for rifle barrel; European walnut stock; hand-checkered pistol grip, forearm. Made in three grades in Suhl, Germany, for Daly; grades differ only in checkering, amount of engraving, wood, overall quality. Introduced about 1921; dropped, 1933. Used values, Superior Quality, $950 to $1050; Diamond Quality, $1750 to $2000; Regent Diamond Quality, $2750 to $3000.

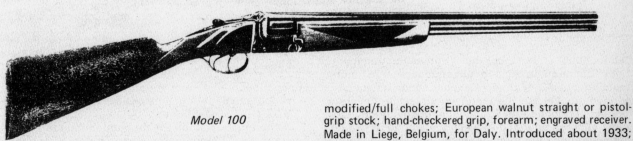

*Model 100*

**CHARLES DALY Model 100 Commander:** over/under; Anson & Deeley-type box-lock action; 12, 16, 20, 28, .410 gauges; 26″, 28″, 30″ barrels; automatic ejectors; double triggers or Miller single selective trigger; improved/modified, modified/full chokes; European walnut straight or pistol-grip stock; hand-checkered grip, forearm; engraved receiver. Made in Liege, Belgium, for Daly. Introduced about 1933; dropped at beginning of WWII. Used values, double trigger, $475 to $500; Miller single trigger, $550 to $600.

**Model 200 Commander** has the same specifications as Model 100, except for better wood, more engraving, improved general overall finish. Used values, double trigger, $625 to $650; single trigger, $700 to $725.

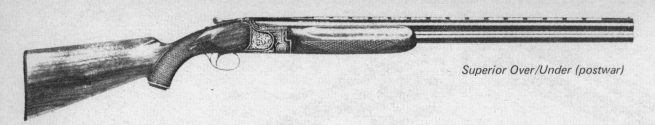

*Superior Over/Under (postwar)*

**CHARLES DALY Field Grade:** over/under; box-lock action; 12 (2¾" or 3"), 20 (2¾" or 3"), 28, .410 gauges; 26", 28" 30" barrels; choked skeet/skeet, improved/modified, modified/full, full/full; vent rib; engraved receiver; selective single trigger; automatic selective ejectors; safety/barrel selector; walnut stock; hand-checkered pistol grip, fluted forearm; recoil pad on 12-ga. magnum version. This, like other Daly shotguns made following WWII, were manu-

factured in Japan. The 12 and 20-ga. standard and magnum guns were introduced in 1963; 28, .410 gauges in 1965. Used value, $400 to $425.

**Superior Grade** over/under has the same general specifications as Field Grade, but is not chambered for magnum shells; other differences include beavertail forearm; selector device to select auto ejection or extraction only. Imported from Japan. Used values, $440 to $450; Superior skeet, $465 to $475; Superior trap, $480 to $490.

**CHARLES DALY Diamond Grade:** over/under; has the same general specifications as the Superior Grade, but is stocked with French walnut, more extensively checkered, engraved receiver, trigger guard. Introduced in 1967; dropped, 1973. Imported from Japan. Used value, $585 to $600.

**Diamond-Regent Grade** over/under has same specifications as Diamond Grade, except for highly figured French walnut stock, profuse engraving, hunting scenes inlaid in gold, silver; firing pins removable through breech face. Introduced in 1967; dropped, 1973. Imported from Japan. Used value, $875 to $900.

*Superior Trap*

**CHARLES DALY Superior Trap:** single-shot, hammerless; 12-ga. only; 32", 34" barrel; full choke; vent rib; box-lock action; auto ejector; checkered walnut Monte Carlo

pistol-grip stock, forearm; recoil pad. Manufactured in Japan, 1968 to 1976. Used value, $375 to $400.

**CHARLES DALY Empire Double:** side-by-side, hammerless; 12, 16, 20-ga.; 3" chambering for 12, 20-ga., 2¾" for 16; 26", 28", 30" barrel lengths; standard choke combos; box-lock action; plain extractors; non-selective

single trigger; checkered walnut pistol-grip stock, beavertail forearm. Manufactured 1968 to 1971. Used value, $260 to $275.

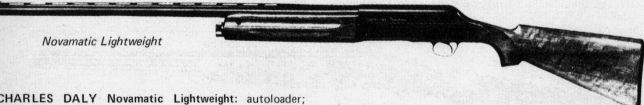

*Novamatic Lightweight*

**CHARLES DALY Novamatic Lightweight:** autoloader; 12-ga.; 3¾" chambering; 4-rd. tubular magazine; 26" barrel, improved cylinder or three-tube Quick-Choke system; plain or vent rib barrel; checkered walnut pistol-grip stock, forearm. Manufactured in Italy by Breda, 1968. Used values, plain barrel, $180 to $190; vent rib, $200 to $210.

**Novamatic Super Lightweight** has same general specs as Lightweight, except standard vent rib, less weight, skeet choke available; 28" barrel in 12-ga.; plain barrel, Quick-Choke available in 20-ga. Manufactured 1968. Used value, $190 to $210.

**Novamatic Super Lightweight 20 Magnum** has same specs as Super Lightweight except for 3" chambering; 3-rd.

magazine; 28" vent-rib barrel, full choke. Manufactured 1968. Used value, $190 to $200.

**Novamatic Trap Model** has same specs as Lightweight, except for 30" vent-rib barrel; full choke; Monte Carlo trap stock; recoil pad. Manufactured 1968. Used value, $210 to $220.

**Novamatic 12 Magnum** has same specs as Lightweight model except for 3" chambering, 3-rd. magazine capacity, 30" vent-rib barrel, full choke, recoil pad. Manufactured 1968. Used value, $210 to $220.

*Venture*

**CHARLES DALY Venture Grade:** over/under; box-lock action; 12, 20 gauges; barrels are 26'' skeet/skeet or improved/modified, 28'' modified/full, 30'' improved/full; checkered walnut pistol-grip stock, forearm; vent rib; manual safety; automatic ejectors; single selective trigger. Imported from Japan. Introduced in 1973. Made in 3 variations. Used values, standard model, $375 to $485; Monte Carlo trap, $385 to $400; skeet, $375 to $390.

*Auto*

**CHARLES DALY Auto:** semi-auto; recoil-operated; 12-ga. only; barrels are 26'' improved, 28'' modified or full, 30'' full; vent rib; walnut stock; hand-checkered pistol grip, forearm; 5-rd. magazine, 3-shot plug furnished; button safety; copy of early Browning patents. Imported from Japan. Introduced in 1973; dropped, 1975. Used value, $200 to $215.

# DAVIDSON

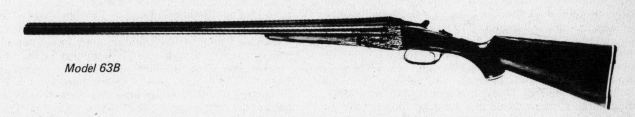

*Model 63B*

**DAVIDSON Model 63B:** double barrel; 12, 16, 20, 28, .410 gauges; Anson & Deely box-lock action; plain extractors, automatic safety; engraved, nickel-plated frame; barrel lengths, 25'' in .410, 26'', 28'' and also 30'' in 12-ga. only; chokes are improved cylinder/modified, modified/full, full/full; hand-checkered walnut stock; pistol grip. Manufactured in Spain; imported by Davidson Firearms Co., Greensboro, North Carolina. Introduced in 1963; still in production, no longer imported. Used value, $180 to $190.

**DAVIDSON Model 63B Magnum:** same specs as standard 63B, except chambered for 3'' 12-ga. magnum shells and 3½'' for 10-ga.; 10-ga. has 32'' full/full barrels; still in production, no longer imported. Used value, 10-ga. magnum, $225 to $235; 12, 20-ga. magnums, $200 to $215.

**DAVIDSON Model 69SL:** double; sidelock action, detachable sideplates; 20, 12 gauges; 26'' barrels, modified/improved; 28'' barrels, modified/full; nickel-plated, engraved action; hand-checkered European walnut stock. Introduced in 1963; still in production, no longer imported. Used value, $235 to $245.

**DAVIDSON Model 73:** side-by-side, hammer double; 12, 20-ga.; 3'' chambers; 20'' barrels; side-lock action, detachable side plates; plain extractors; double triggers; checkered European walnut pistol-grip stock, forearm. Manufactured in Spain. Introduced 1976, still in production, no longer imported. Used value, $185 to $195.

# FOX

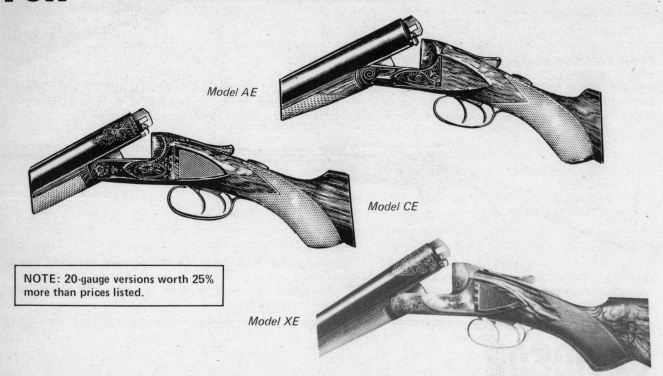

Model AE

Model CE

NOTE: 20-gauge versions worth 25% more than prices listed.

Model XE

**FOX A.H. Fox Model:** hammerless side-by-side; box-lock action; originally made in 12-ga. only with Damascus barrels with 2-5/8″ chambers; steel later changed to Chromex fluid steel and chambers extended to 2¾″ for smokeless powder loads. Guns were made by Fox until firm was absorbed by Savage about 1930. Difference in grades depends upon workmanship, amount of engraving, quality of wood; 12-ga. introduced in 1906; dropped, 1942. With exception of Grade A, all have automatic ejectors. Fox-Kautzky single selective trigger, vent rib were optional at extra cost. Used values, Grade A, $300 to $325; with Kautzky trigger, $400 to $425; with vent rib, $425 to $450; with Kautzky trigger and vent rib, $475 to $500. Grade AE, $350 to $375; with Kautzky trigger, $475 to $500; with vent rib, $475 to $500; with Kautzky trigger

and vent rib, $625 to $650. Grade CE, $425 to $450; with Kautzky trigger, $550 to $575; with vent rib, $550 to $575; with Kautzky trigger and vent rib, $675 to $700. Grade XE, $1000 to $1150; with Kautzky trigger, $1150 to $1250; with vent rib, $1150 to $1250; with Kautzky trigger and vent rib, $1350 to $1500.

**A.H. Fox 16-ga.** has the same specifications as 12-ga., except for chambering. Introduced in 1912; dropped, 1941. Used values are generally the same as for 12-ga., depending upon grade, extras, condition; $325 through $1500.

**A.H. Fox 20-ga.** is a slightly scaled-down version of the 12-ga., but with same general design. Introduced in 1912; dropped, 1946. Used values generally the same as for other gauges, dependent upon grade, extras, condition; $375 to $1750.

Sterlingworth Standard

**FOX Sterlingworth:** side-by-side; hammerless; box-lock action; 12, 16, 20 gauges; 26″, 28″, 30″ barrels; any standard choke combo; double triggers, plain extractors standard; automatic ejectors, single selective trigger extra; has the same general specifications as earlier A.H. Fox doubles, but these were production line guns without much handwork; American walnut stock; hand-checkered pistol

grip, forearm. Introduced in 1910; dropped, 1947. Used values, $325 to $350; with automatic ejectors, $375 to $395; single selective trigger, $375 to $400; with ejectors and selective trigger, $475 to $500.

**Sterlingworth Deluxe** model has the same general specifications as standard model, except it was also available with 32″ barrel; single selective trigger is standard; has Lyman ivory bead sights, recoil pad. Introduced in 1930; dropped, 1946. Used values, $450 to $475; with automatic ejectors, $475 to $500.

**Sterlingworth Skeet** model has the same general specifications as standard model, except for skeet bore only, straight grip stock, 26'' or 28'' barrels; 12-ga. only. Introduced in 1935; dropped, 1946. Used values, $435 to $485; with automatic ejectors, $500 to $525.

**FOX Single-Barrel Trap Model:** box-lock action; 12-ga. only; 30'', 32'' barrel; automatic ejector; vent rib; American walnut stock and forearm, except for Grade M, which had Circassian walnut; hand-checkered pistol grip, forearm; recoil pad optional. Originally made by A.H. Fox, but taken over by Savage about 1930. In 1932, the gun was redesigned, with full pistol-grip stock, Monte Carlo stock.

**FOX Super Fox:** side-by-side; box-lock action; 12-ga. only; chambered for 3'' shells on special order; 30'', 32'' barrels; full choke only; double triggers; engraved action; American

**Sterlingworth Trap** model has the same general specifications as standard Sterlingworth, except for trap stock, 32'' barrels only; 12-ga. only. Introduced in 1917; dropped, 1946. Used values, $400 to $425; with automatic ejectors, $525 to $550.

**Sterlingworth Waterfowl Grade** has the same general specifications as the standard model, except for heavier frame, automatic ejectors; 12-ga. only. Introduced in 1934; dropped, 1939. Used value, $450 to $475.

Of Grade M, only 9 were made, giving it collector value. Difference in grades is based upon quality of wood and amount and quality of engraving on receiver. Introduced in 1919; dropped, 1935. Used values, Grade JE, $575 to $650; Grade KE, $700 to $750; Grade LE, $825 to $875; Grade ME, $4750 to $5000.

walnut stock; hand-checkered pistol grip, forearm; automatic ejectors. Introduced in 1925; dropped, 1942. Used value, $575 to $625.

*Model B*

*Model B-SE*

*Model B-DE*

**FOX Model B:** side-by-side; hammerless; box-lock action; 12, 16, 20, .410 gauges; 26'', 28'', 30'' barrels; double triggers; plain extractors; modified/full, improved/modified, full/full chokes; double triggers; American walnut stock, forearm; hand-checkered pistol grip, forearm; case-hardened frame. Introduced in 1940; still in production. Used value, $135 to $145.

**Model B-ST** has same specs as Fox Model B, except for non-selective single trigger. Manufactured 1955 to 1966. Used value, $170 to $180.

**Model B-DL** has same specs as Model B-ST, except for satin-chrome finished frame, select walnut buttstock, checkered pistol grip, side panels, beavertail forearm. Manufactured 1962 to 1965. Used value, $225 to $250.

**Model B-DE** replaced Model B-DL, with the same general specifications and improvements, but without side panels. Introduced in 1965; dropped, 1966. Used value, $200 to $215.

**Model B-SE** has same specs as Model B, except for single trigger, selective ejectors. Introduced 1966, still in production. Used value, $180 to $190.

**Model B Lightweight** is chambered for 12, 20, .410 gauges; barrels are 24'' (12,20 gauges) improved/modified, 26'' improved/modified, 28'' modified/full, 30'' modified/full in 12-ga. only, 26'' full/full in .410 only; double triggers; select walnut stock; checkered pistol grip, beavertail forearm; vent rib; color case-hardened frame. Introduced in 1973; still in production. Used value, $155 to $165.

# FRANCHI

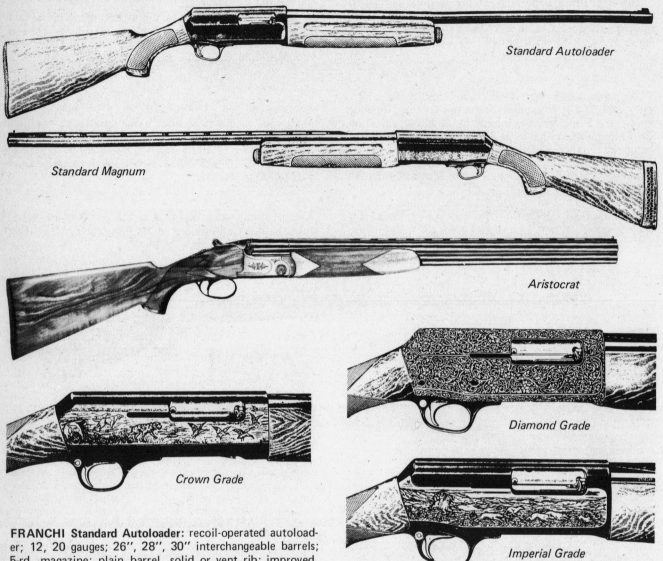

Standard Autoloader

Standard Magnum

Aristocrat

Diamond Grade

Crown Grade

Imperial Grade

**FRANCHI Standard Autoloader:** recoil-operated autoloader; 12, 20 gauges; 26″, 28″, 30″ interchangeable barrels; 5-rd. magazine; plain barrel, solid or vent rib; improved, modified, full chokes; alloy receiver; chrome-lined barrels; simplified takedown; European walnut stock, forearm; pistol grip, forearm hand checkered. Introduced in 1950; still in production. Imported by Stoeger Industries. Used values, plain barrel, $210 to $225; solid rib, $235 to $245; vent rib, $250 to $260.

**Standard Magnum Autoloader** has the same general specifications as Standard model, except it is chambered for 12 or 20-ga., 3″ magnum shotshell; 32″ (12-ga.), 28″ (20-ga.) plain or vent rib barrel; recoil pad. Introduced in 1952; still in production. Imported by Stoeger Industries. Used values, plain barrel, $250 to $260; vent rib, $265 to $275.

**Turkey Gun** has same specs as standard autoloader, except for engraved turkey scene on receiver; 12-ga. only; 26″ matted-rib barrel; extra full choke. Manufactured 1963 to 1965. Used value, $260 to $275.

**Skeet Model** has same specs as standard autoloader except has skeet choke, 26″ vent-rib barrel; fancier walnut stock, forearm. Manufactured 1972 to 1974. Used value, $240 to $250.

**Crown Grade** autoloader has same general specs as standard autoloader, except for hunting scene engraving on the frame. Manufactured 1954 to 1975. Used value, $1000 to $1050.

**Diamond Grade** autoloader has same specs as standard model, except that scroll engraving is silver inlaid. Manufactured 1954 to 1975. Used value, $1200 to $1250.

**Imperial Grade** autoloader features elaborate engraving gold-inlaid hunting scene. Manufactured 1954 to 1975. Used value, $1500 to $1600.

**Aristocrat Magnum** has same specs as field model, except for 3″ chambering; full-choke 32″ barrels; recoil pad. Manufactured 1962 to 1965. Used value, $320 to $340.

**Aristocrat Deluxe Grade** has same specs as standard field, skeet or trap models, but with select walnut stock, forearm; heavy relief engraving on receiver, tang and trigger guard. Manufactured 1960 to 1965. Used value, $550 to $600.

**Aristocrat Supreme Grade** has same specs as Deluxe Grade, except for gold-inlaid game bird figures on receiver. Manufactured 1960 to 1965. Used value, $675 to $725.

**Aristocrat Imperial Grade** was made in field, skeet, trap configurations on a custom basis. Basic specs are the same as for standard models, but wood is top quality European walnut, with exquisite engraving. Manufactured on individual order 1967 to 1969. Used value, $1600 to $1750.

**Aristocrat Monte Carlo Grade** has same general specs as Imperial Grade, except that engraving is more elaborate. Manufactured on individual order 1967 to 1969. Used value, $2100 to $2250.

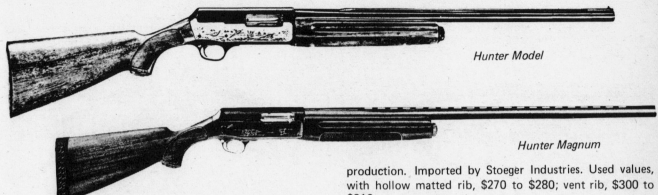

*Hunter Model*

*Hunter Magnum*

**FRANCHI Hunter Model Autoloader:** recoil-operated autoloader; 12, 20 gauges; has the same general specifications as Standard model autoloader, except for better wood, engraved receiver; ribbed barrel only. Introduced in 1950; still in production. Imported by Stoeger Industries. Used values, with hollow matted rib, $270 to $280; vent rib, $300 to $310.

**Hunter Magnum** has same specifications as Hunter model, except is chambered for 12 or 20-ga., 3" magnum shotshell; has 32" (12-ga.), 28" (20-ga.) vent rib, full choke barrel; recoil pad. Introduced in 1955; still in production. Used value, $275 to $285.

*Eldorado*

**FRANCHI Eldorado:** recoil-operated autoloader; 12, 20 gauges; has the same general specifications as Standard model autoloader, but with scroll engraving covering 75% of receiver surfaces; gold-plated trigger; chrome-plated breech bolt; chrome-lined bore; vent rib; select European stock; hand-checkered pistol grip, forearm. Introduced in 1955; still in production. Imported by Stoeger Industries. Used value, $415 to $425.

*Slug Model*

**FRANCHI Slug Gun:** recoil-operated autoloader; 12, 20 gauges; 22" barrel; alloy receiver; same general specifications as Standard autoloader, except for short cylinder bore barrel; raised gold bead front sight, Lyman folding leaf open rear; 5-rd. magazine; sling swivels. Introduced in 1955; still in production. Imported by Stoeger Industries. Used value, $280 to $290.

**FRANCHI Airon Model:** side-by-side; hammerless; Anson & Deeley-type box-lock action; 12-ga. only; all standard barrel lengths, choke combinations; automatic ejectors; straight-grip stock of European walnut; hand-checkered grip and forearm; automatic ejectors; double triggers. Introduced in 1956, special order only; dropped, 1968. Used value, $915 to $935.

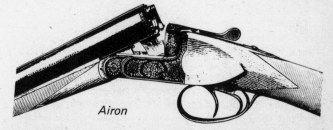

*Airon*

**FRANCHI Astore Model:** side-by-side; hammerless; Anson & Deeley-type box-lock action; 12-ga. only; all standard barrel lengths, choke combinations; plain extractors; double triggers; straight-grip European walnut stock; hand-checkered stock, forearm. Introduced in 1956; special order only; dropped, 1968. Used value, $650 to $700.

Astore S model has the same specifications as standard Astore except for fine engraving on frame. Used value, $1800 to $1850.

Astore II has the same general specs as the Astore S, but is less elaborate; has double triggers, European walnut pistol-grip stock, plain extractors or auto ejectors; 27", 28"

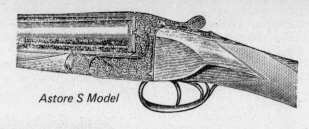

*Astore S Model*

barrels, standard chokes. Currently in production. Used value, $925 to $950.

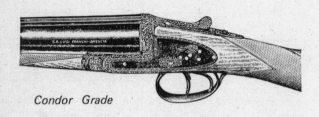

*Condor Grade*

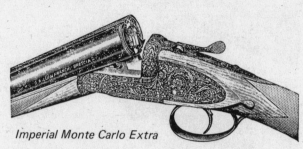

*Imperial Monte Carlo Extra*

**FRANCHI Custom Sidelock Model:** side-by-side; hammerless; 12, 16, 20, 28 gauges; barrel lengths, chokes are to individual customer's requirements; automatic ejectors; hand-detachable locks; straight or pistol-grip stock of European walnut; hand-checkered grip section, forearm; self-opening action, single trigger optional. Made in six grades; variations depending upon quality of wood, amount

of engraving, checkering, overall workmanship. For self-opening action, add $140; for single trigger, add $101. Introduced in 1956, special order only; dropped, 1968. Used values, Condor Grade, $5900 to $6000; Imperial Grade, $7425 to $7500; Imperial S Grade, $672 to $700; Imperial Monte Carlo Grade No. 5, $7425 to $7500; Imperial Monte Carlo Grade No. 11, $11,200 to $11,350; Imperial Monte Carlo Extra, $13,700 to $17,850.

*Deluxe Aristocrat*

**Aristocrat Skeet Model** has the same specifications as trap version, except for 26" barrels choked skeet/skeet, grooved beavertail forearm. Introduced in 1962; dropped, 1968. Used value, $450 to $475.

**Aristocrat Field Model** has same general design specs as other Aristocrat models, including vent rib; 12-ga. only; barrels are 24", cylinder/improved cylinder, 26" improved/modified, 28" modified/full; 30" modified/full; selective automatic ejectors; automatic safety; hand-checkered Italian walnut pistol-grip stock, forearm. English scroll engraving on receiver; blue-black finish only. Introduced in 1960; dropped, 1968. Used value, $400 to $425.

**FRANCHI Aristocrat Trap Model:** over/under; 12-ga. only; 30" barrels; 10mm-wide rib; single selective trigger; automatic ejectors; nonauto safety; selected deluxe grade European walnut stock, beavertail forearm; hand-checkered pistol grip; chrome-lined barrels are improved modified/full; Monte Carlo comb; color case-hardened receiver. Introduced in 1962; dropped, 1968. Used value, $450 to $475.

*Silver King*

**FRANCHI Silver-King Aristocrat:** over/under; 12-ga. only; deluxe version of Aristocrat design; has engraved, bright-finish receiver, selected ultra-deluxe walnut stock, forearm, cut from the same blank for match of grain, color, finish;

hand-checkered pistol grip, forearm; vent rib; barrels are 24" cylinder/improved cylinder, 26" improved/modified, 28" modified/full, 30" modified/full; blue-black finish; chrome-lined barrels. Introduced in 1965; dropped, 1968. Used value, $460 to $475.

**FRANCHI Dynamic 12:** recoil-operated autoloader; 12-ga. only; has the same general specifications and options as Franchi Standard model, except for heavy steel receiver, chrome-plated breech bolt and lifter; European walnut stock, forearm; chrome-lined barrel; 5-rd. magazine; trigger-safety-guard-lifter mechanism detachable as single unit; 3-shot plug furnished; plain or vent rib barrel; also skeet, slug-gun configurations; slug gun has 22″ barrel, sights. Introduced in 1965; dropped, 1970. Used values, with plain barrel, $215 to $225; with vent rib, $250 to $265; slug gun, $300 to $315; skeet model, $300 to $315.

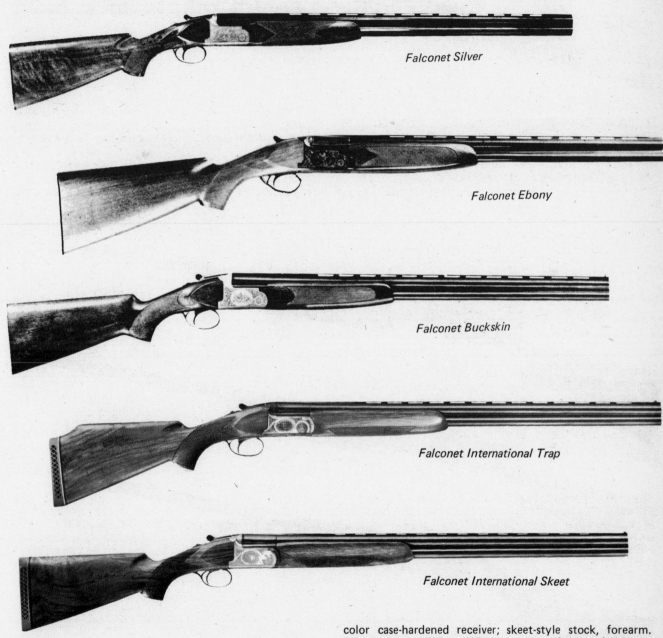

*Falconet Silver*

*Falconet Ebony*

*Falconet Buckskin*

*Falconet International Trap*

*Falconet International Skeet*

**FRANCHI Falconet:** originally introduced as Falcon model; over/under; 12, 20 gauges; 12-ga. has 24″, 26″, 28″, 30″ barrels, with standard choke combos; 20-ga. has 24″, 26″, 28″ barrels; selective single trigger; barrel selector; automatic safety; selective automatic ejectors; alloy receiver, fully engraved; walnut stock, forearm; checkered pistol grip, forearm; epoxy finish. Introduced in 1969; still in production. Imported by Stoeger Industries. Used value, $420 to $448.

**Falconet Skeet Model** has same general specs as field model, except for skeet-choked 26″ barrels; wide vent rib; color case-hardened receiver; skeet-style stock, forearm. Manufactured 1970 to 1974. Used value, $675 to $700.

**Falconet International Skeet Model** has same specs as skeet model except for better finish, improved wood. Manufactured 1970 to 1974. Used value, $725 to $750.

**Falconet Trap Model** has same specs as field model, except for modified/full choke 30″ barrel; 12-ga. only; wide vent rib; color case-hardened receiver; checkered trap-style Monte Carlo stock, forearm; recoil pad. Manufactured 1970 to 1974. Used value, $675 to $700.

**Falconet International Trap Model** has same specs as trap model except for better finish, improved wood; choice of straight stock or Monte Carlo style. Manufactured 1970 to 1974. Used value, $725 to $750.

**FRANCHI Peregrin Model 400:** over/under double; 12-ga.; 26½", 28" barrels, standard choke combos; steel receiver; auto ejectors; selective single trigger; checkered European walnut pistol-grip stock, forearm. Introduced 1975, still in production. Used value, $375 to $400.

**Peregrin Model 451** has same general specs as Model 400, except for alloy receiver. Introduced 1975, still in production. Used value, $340 to $360.

*Franchi 2004 Trap*

**FRANCHI Model 2003 Trap:** over/under double; 12-ga.; 30", 32" barrels, bored modified/full, full/full; high vent rib; box-lock action; single selective trigger; auto ejectors; checkered European walnut straight or Monte Carlo stock, beavertail forearm; recoil pad; marketed with carrying case. Introduced 1976, still in production. Used value, $740 to $765.

**Model 2004** single-barrel trap has same specs as Model 2003, except for 32", 34" full-choke single barrel. Introduced 1976, still in production. Used value, $750 to $765.

**Model 2005 Trap Set** incorporates over/under barrels of Model 2004, single barrel of Model 2004 as interchangeable set. Introduced 1976, still in production. Used value, $1100 to $1200.

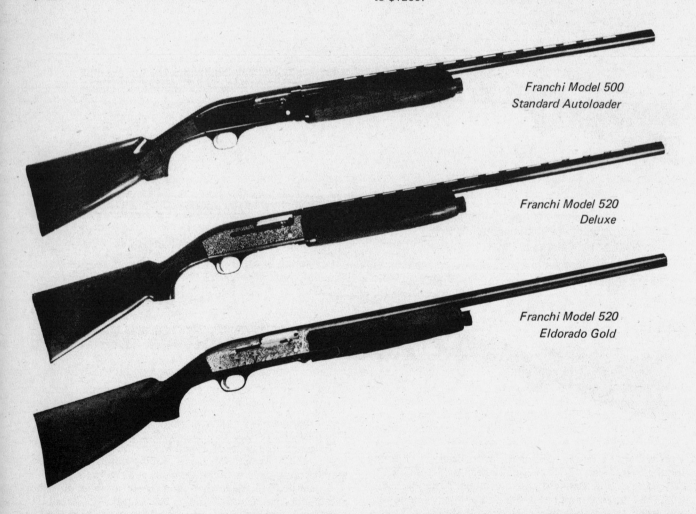

*Franchi Model 500
Standard Autoloader*

*Franchi Model 520
Deluxe*

*Franchi Model 520
Eldorado Gold*

**FRANCHI Model 500:** autoloader; 12-ga.; 4-rd. magazine; gas operated; 26", 28" barrels, vent rib, any standard choke; checkered European walnut pistol-grip stock. Introduced 1976, still in production. Used value, $215 to $225.

**Model 520 Deluxe** has same specs as Model 500, but with engraved receiver, better finish, wood. Introduced 1976, still in production. Used value, $250 to $275.

**Model 520 Eldorado Gold** has same specs as Model 520 Deluxe, except for quality of wood, better engraving, gold-inlays in receiver. Introduced 1977, still in production. Used value, $800 to $850.

# FRANCOTTE

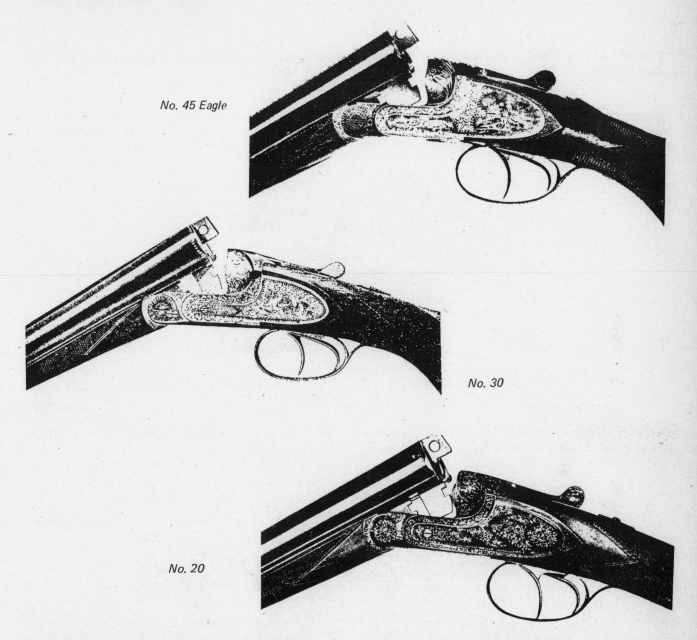

*No. 45 Eagle*

*No. 30*

*No. 20*

**FRANCOTTE A&F Series:** side-by-side; Anson & Deeley type box-lock action; 12, 16, 20, 28, .410 gauges; in 12-ga., 26" to 32" barrels, 26" to 28" in other gauges; any desired choke combo; crossbolt; sideplates on all models except Knockabout; double triggers; automatic ejectors; series was made in seven grades for distribution exclusively in this country by Abercrombie & Fitch; grades varied only in overall quality, grade of wood, checkering and engraving. Introduced prior to World War II, dropped in 1960s. Used values, Knockabout Model, $2350 to $2400; Jubilee Model, $3250 to $3300; No. 14, $3250 to $3300; No. 18, $3000 to $3150; No. 20, $3750 to $3900; No. 25, $4450 to $4500; No. 30, $4700 to $4750; No. 45 Eagle Grade, $5900 to $6000.

**FRANCOTTE Model 6886:** side-by-side; Anson & Deeley box-lock action; 12, 16, 20, 28, .410 gauges; all standard barrel lengths, choke combinations available; automatic ejectors; double triggers; hand-checkered European walnut stock, forearm; straight or pistol-grip design. Manufactured before World War II. Used value, $2000 to $2150.

**FRANCOTTE Model 8446:** side-by-side; Greener crossbolt; side clips; general specifications are the same as Model 6886 except for finish, better construction. Manufactured before World War II. Used value, $2500 to $2600.

**FRANCOTTE Model 6930:** side-by-side; square crossbolt; Anson & Deeley box-lock action; 12, 16, 20, 28, .410 gauges; all standard barrel lengths, choke combos; auto-matic ejectors; double triggers; hand-checkered European walnut stock, forearm; straight or pistol-grip design. Manufactured before World War II. Used value, $2500 to $2600.

**FRANCOTTE Model 4996:** side-by-side; Anson & Deeley box-lock action; side clips; has the same general specifications as Model 8446, except for minor variations in finish, checkering. Manufactured before World War II. Used value, $2500 to $2600.

**FRANCOTTE Model 8457:** side-by-side, Anson & Deeley box-lock action; 12, 16, 20, 28, .410 gauges; all standard barrel lengths, choke combos; Greener-Scott crossbolt; other specifications are the same as those of Model 4996 except for better finish, checkering. Manufactured before World War II. Used value, $2900 to $3000.

*Model 9261*

**FRANCOTTE Model 9261:** side-by-side; Anson & Deeley box-lock action; Greener crossbolt; other specifications are the same as Model 8457. Manufactured before World War II. Used value, $2900 to $3000.

**FRANCOTTE Model 11/18E:** side-by-side; Anson & Deeley box-lock action; side clips; Purdey-type bolt; other specifications are the same as those of Model 9261. Manufactured before World War II. Used value, $2900 to $3000.

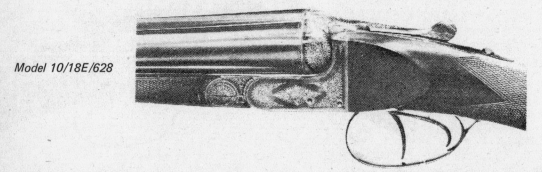

*Model 10/18E/628*

**FRANCOTTE Model 10/18E/628:** side-by-side; Anson & Deeley box-lock action; side clips; Purdey-type bolt; other specifications are the same as Model 11/18E except overall quality is better, including wood, checkering, engraving, finish. Introduced before World War II; still in production. No current importer. Used value, $4000 to $4050.

**FRANCOTTE Model 10594:** side-by-side; Anson & Deeley box-lock action; sideplates; 12, 16, 20, 28, .410 gauges; all standard barrel lengths, choke combos; reinforced frame, side clips; Purdey-type bolt; automatic ejectors; hand-checkered European walnut stock; straight or pistol-grip design. Introduced about 1950; still in production. Used value, $3125 to $3175.

**FRANCOTTE Model 8455:** side-by-side; Anson & Deeley box-lock action; has the same specifications as Model 10594 except for style of engraving, Greener crossbolt. Introduced about 1950; still in production. No current importer. Used value, $3125 to $3175.

*Model 6982*

**FRANCOTTE Model 6982:** side-by-side; Anson & Deeley box-lock action; has the same specifications as Model 10594, except for style of engraving. Introduced about 1950; still in production. No current importer. Used value, $3125 to $3175.

**FRANCOTTE Model 9/40E/38321:** side-by-side; Anson & Deeley box-lock action. Has the same general specifications as Model 6982, except for better quality, fine English engraving. Introduced about 1950; still in production. No current importer. Used value, $4050 to $4150.

**FRANCOTTE Model 120.HE/328:** side-by-side; sidelock; automatic ejectors; double triggers; made in all standard gauges, chokes, barrel lengths to customer's order; hand-checkered European walnut stock, forearm; straight or pistol-grip design. Introduced about 1950; still in production. No current importer. Used value, $8100 to $8250.

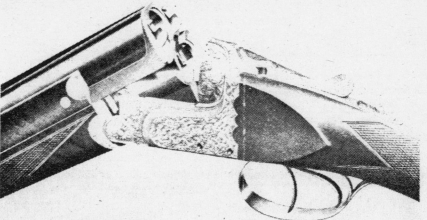

*Model 9/40.SE*

**FRANCOTTE Model 9/40.SE:** over/under; Anson & Deeley box-lock action; 12, 16, 20, 28, .410 gauges; all standard barrel lengths, choke combos; automatic ejectors; double triggers; hand-checkered European walnut stock, forearm; straight or pistol-grip design; elaborate engraving. Introduced about 1950; still in production. No current importer. Used value, $8700 to $8850.

*Model SOB.E/11082*

**FRANCOTTE Model SOB.E/11082:** over/under; Anson & Deeley box-lock action. Same general specifications as Model 9/40SE, but not as profusely engraved. Introduced about 1950; no current importer. Used value, $6350 to $6500.

# GALEF

*Zabala*

**GALEF/ZABALA:** double; 10, 12, 16, 20, 28, .410 gauges; Anson & Deeley-type box-lock action; barrels, 32", 10, 12 gauges only, full/full; 30", 12-ga. only, modified/full; 28", all except .410, modified/full; 26", 12, 20, 28 gauges, improved/modified; 26", .410 only, modified/full; 22", 12-ga. only, improved/improved; hand-checkered European walnut stock; beavertail forearm; recoil pad; automatic safety, plain extractors. Imported from Spain; still in production. Used value, 10-ga., $300 to $310; other gauges, $250 to $360.

*Silver Snipe*

**GALEF/ZOLI Silver Snipe:** over/under; 12, 20 gauges, 3" chambers; Purdey-type double box-lock, cross-bolt action; barrels, 26", improved/modified; 28", modified/full; 30", 12-ga. only, modified/full; 26" skeet, skeet/skeet; 30" trap, full/full; European walnut stock; hand-checkered pistol grip, forearm; automatic safety, except on trap, skeet models; vent rib, single trigger, chrome-lined barrels. Imported from Italy; still in production. Used value, field model, $425 to $450; trap, skeet models, $450 to $475.

**Golden Snipe** over/under has the same specs as Silver Snipe, except for automatic selective ejectors. Still in production. Used value, field model, $500 to $525; trap, skeet, $550 to $575.

*Silver Hawk*

**GALEF/ZOLI Silver Hawk:** side-by-side, hammerless double; 12, 20-ga.; 3" chambers; 26", 28", 30" barrels; improved/modified, modified/full chokes; hand-checkered European walnut pistol-grip stock, beavertail forearm. Manufactured in Italy by Antonio Zoli, 1968 to 1972. Used value, $475 to $500.

**GALEF Companion:** single-shot; 12 magnum, 16, 20 magnum, 28-ga., .410; 26", 28", 30" barrel lengths; has special folding feature; hammerless underlever design; European walnut pistol-grip stock, forearm; plain or vent rib. Manufactured in Italy. Introduced 1968, still in production. Used value, $80 to $90.

*Monte Carlo*

**GALEF Monte Carlo Trap:** single-shot; 12-ga. only; 32" barrel; full choke; vent rib; hammerless underlever design; plain extractor; checkered European walnut pistol-grip stock, beavertail forearm; recoil pad. Manufactured in Italy. Introduced 1968, still in production. Used value, $240 to $250.

# GREENER

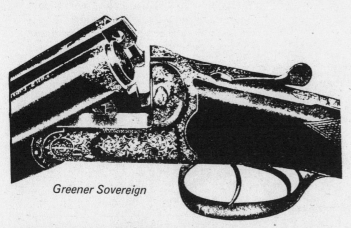

*Greener Sovereign*

**GREENER Jubilee Model:** Grade DH 35; side-by-side; box-lock action; hammerless; 12, 16, 20 gauges; 26", 28", 30" barrels; any choke combo; double triggers; nonselective or selective single trigger at added cost; automatic ejectors; hand-checkered European walnut straight or pistol-grip stock, forearm; engraved action. Introduced in 1875; dropped, 1965. Used value, $1150 to $1250.

**Sovereign Model,** Grade DH40, has the same specifications as Jubilee model except for better overall quality, better wood, checkering, engraving. Used value, $1350 to $1500.

**Crown Model,** Grade DH55 has the same specifications as Sovereign Model except for upgraded overall quality, including finer engraving, checkering and better wood. Used value, $1750 to $1850.

**Royal Model,** Grade DH75 is top of the line for Greener hammerless ejector double style, with same general specifications as others, but with top-quality workmanship, including checkering, engraving and figured walnut in stock, forearm. Used value, $2750 to $2850.

**Note:** On all variations, add $100 to $125 for nonselective single trigger; $175 to $200 for selective trigger.

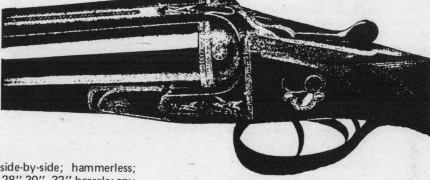

*Greener Far-Killer*

**GREENER Far-Killer Model:** side-by-side; hammerless; box-lock action; 12, 10, 8 gauges; 28" 30", 32" barrels; any desired choke combination; nonejectors; automatic ejectors at added cost; hand-checkered European walnut straight or half-pistol grip stock. Introduced about 1895; dropped, 1962. Used values, 12-ga. nonejector model, $1250 to $1350; with ejectors, $1650 to $1750; 8, 10 gauges, nonejector, $1550 to $1650; with ejectors, $1850 to $1900.

*Greener Empire*

**GREENER Empire Model:** side-by-side; hammerless; box-lock action; 12-ga. only; 28", 30", 32" barrels; any choke combo; hand-checkered European walnut straight or half-pistol grip stock, forearm; nonejector; ejectors at additional cost. Introduced about 1893; dropped, 1962. Used values, nonejector model, $750 to $850; ejector model, $975 to $1150.

**Empire Deluxe Grade** has same general specifications as standard Empire model except has deluxe finish and better craftsmanship. Used values, nonejector model, $850 to $950; ejector model, $1150 to $1250.

**GREENER General Purpose:** single-shot; Martini-type action; takedown; 12-ga. only; 26", 30", 32" barrel; modified, full choke; ejector; hand-checkered European walnut straight grip stock, forearm. Introduced in 1910; dropped, 1964. Used value, $175 to $185.

# GREIFELT

*Grade No. 1*

**GREIFELT Grade No. 1:** over/under; Anson & Deeley box-lock action; 12, 16, 20, 28, .410 gauges; 26", 28", 30", 32" barrels; automatic ejectors; any desired choke combo; solid matted rib standard; vent rib at added cost; hand-checkered European walnut straight or pistol-grip stock, Purdey-type forearm; double triggers standard; single trigger at added cost; elaborate engraving. Manufactured in Germany prior to World War II. Used values, solid matted rib, $3900 to $3950; with vent rib, $4200 to $4275. Add $350 to $375 for single trigger.

**Over/under Combo Model** has same design as Greifelt over/under shotguns; 12, 16, 20, 28-gauge, .410, any standard rifle caliber; 24", 26" barrels; folding rear sight; matted rib; auto or non-auto ejectors. Manufactured prior to World War II. Used values: auto ejectors, $4800 to $5000; non-auto ejectors, $4100 to $4250.

**GREIFELT Grade No. 3:** over/under; Anson & Deeley box-lock action; 12, 16, 20, 28, .410 gauges; same general specifications as Grade No. 1 but engraving is less elaborate, wood has less figure. Manufactured prior to World War II. Used values, solid matted rib, $2550 to $2650; vent rib, $2850 to $2950. Add $350 to $375 for single trigger.

**GREIFELT Model 22:** side-by-side; Anson & Deeley box-lock action; sideplates; 12, 16 gauges; 28", 30" barrels; modified/full choke only; plain extractors; double triggers; hand-checkered stock, forearm; pistol-grip, cheekpiece or straight English style. Introduced about 1950; still in production. No current importer. Used value, $1125 to $1175.

**Model 22E** has the same specifications as standard Model 22 except for addition of automatic ejectors. Introduced about 1950; still in production. No current importer. Used value, $1675 to $1725.

**GREIFELT Model 103:** side-by-side; hammerless; Anson & Deeley box-lock action; 12, 16 gauges; 28", 30" barrels, modified/full chokes; plain extractors; double triggers; hand-checkered European walnut stock, forearm; pistol-grip, cheekpiece or straight English style. Introduced about 1950; still in production. No current importer. Used value, $1125 to $1175.

**Model 103E** has same specifications as Model 103 except for addition of automatic ejectors. Introduced about 1950; still in production. No current importer. Used value, $1675 to $1725.

**GREIFELT Model 143E:** over/under; Anson & Deeley box-lock action; 12, 16, 20 gauges; 26", 28", 30" barrels; has the same general design specifications as the Pre-WWII Grade No. 1, but workmanship is of lower quality. Introduced about 1950; still in production. No current importer. Used values, with raised matted rib, double triggers, $2000 to $2150; vent rib, single selective trigger, $2550 to $2700.

# HARRINGTON & RICHARDSON

*No. 3*

**HARRINGTON & RICHARDSON No. 3:** single barrel, hammerless; takedown; 12, 16, 20, .410 gauges; 26", 28", 30", 32" barrels; automatic ejector; no sights; uncheckered American walnut pistol-grip stock, forearm; full choke only; top-lever break-open action. Introduced in 1908; dropped, 1942. Used value, $45 to $50.

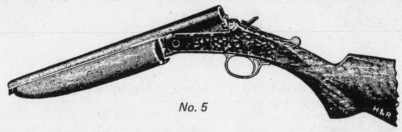

*No. 5*

**HARRINGTON & RICHARDSON No. 5:** single barrel; hammer model; takedown; lightweight configuration; 20, 28, .410 gauges, 26", 28" barrels; full choke only; automatic ejector; uncheckered American walnut pistol-grip stock, forearm; top-lever, break-open action; no sights. Introduced in 1908; dropped, 1942. Used value, $50 to $65.

*No. 6*

**HARRINGTON & RICHARDSON No. 6:** single barrel; hammer model; takedown; heavy breech; 10, 12, 16, 20 gauges; 28", 30", 32", 34", 36" barrels; automatic ejector; uncheckered American walnut pistol-grip stock, forearm; no sights; top-lever, break-open action. Same basic design as No. 5 model except for heavier breech, gauges, barrel lengths. Introduced in 1908; dropped, 1942. Used value, $50 to $65.

*No. 8*

**HARRINGTON & RICHARDSON No. 8:** single barrel; hammer model; takedown; 12, 16, 20, 24, 28, .410 gauges; 26", 28", 30", 32" barrels; full choke only; automatic ejector; uncheckered American walnut pistol-grip stock, forearm; no sights. Same general design as Model 6 except for different forearm design, gauges, et al. Introduced in 1908; dropped, 1942. Used value, $50 to $65.

*Bay State No. 7*

**HARRINGTON & RICHARDSON Bay State No. 7:** Also known as Model No. 9; single barrel; hammer model; takedown; 12, 16, 20, .410 gauges; 26", 28", 30", 32" barrels; full choke only; no sights; uncheckered American walnut pistol-grip stock, forearm. Same specifications as No. 8, except for fuller pistol grip, slimmer forearm. Introduced in 1908; dropped, 1942. Used value, $50 to $65.

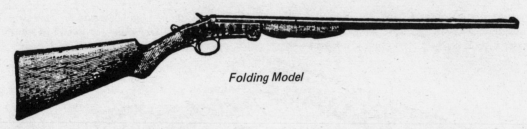

*Folding Model*

**HARRINGTON & RICHARDSON Folding Model:** single barrel; hammer model; gun is hinged at front of frame so barrel folds against stock for storage, transport; full choke only; Light Frame version has 22" barrel only, 28, .410 gauges; Heavy Frame is in 12, 16, 20, 28, .410, 26" barrel; bead front sight; checkered pistol-grip stock, forearm. Introduced about 1910; dropped, 1942. Used value, $65 to $75.

*No. 48 Topper*

**HARRINGTON & RICHARDSON No. 48 Topper:** single barrel; hammer model; takedown; 12, 16, 20, .410 gauges; 26", 28", 30", 32" barrels; modified or full choke; automatic ejector; top-lever, break-open action; specifications similar to those of Model 8. Introduced in 1946; dropped, 1957. Used value, $60 to $65.

**Model 488 Topper Deluxe** has same specifications as No. 48 Topper, except for black lacquered stock, forearm, recoil pad, chrome-plated frame. Introduced in 1946; dropped, 1957. Used value, $70 to $75.

**HARRINGTON & RICHARDSON Model 148 Topper:** single barrel; hammer model; takedown; improved version of No. 48; 12, 16, 20, .410 gauges; in 12-ga., barrels are 30", 32" or 36"; in 16-ga., barrels are 28" or 30"; in 20, .410 gauges, barrels are 28"; full choke only; side lever; uncheckered American walnut pistol-grip stock, forearm; recoil pad. Introduced in 1958; dropped, 1961. Used value, $65 to $75.

**Model 188 Deluxe Topper** has the same specifications as Model 148, except is .410-ga. only; chrome-plated frame; stock, forearm finished with black, red, yellow, blue, green, pink or purple lacquer. Introduced in 1958; dropped, 1961. Used value, $75 to $80.

**HARRINGTON & RICHARDSON Model 480 Jr. Topper:** single barrel; hammer model; has the same general specifications as No. 48 Topper, except for shorter youth stock; 26" barrel only; .410-ga. only. Introduced in 1958; dropped, 1960. Used value, $60 to $65.

**Model 580 Jr. Topper** has the same specifications as Model 480, except for variety of colored stock as with Model 188 Topper. Introduced in 1958; dropped, 1961. Used value, $70 to $75.

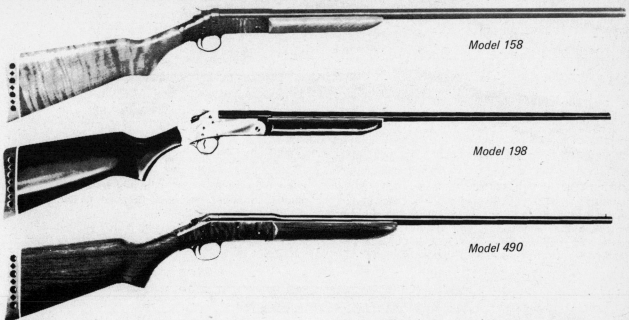

*Model 158*

*Model 198*

*Model 490*

**HARRINGTON & RICHARDSON Model 158 Topper:** single barrel; hammer model; takedown; side-lever, break-open action; improved version of Model 148 Topper; 12, 16, 20, .410 gauges; in 12-gauge, 30″, 32″, 36″ barrels are all full choke; 28″ is full or modified; 16-ga. has 28″ modified barrel only; 20-ga., 28″ full or modified, .410, 28″ full only; no sights; uncheckered hardwood pistol-grip stock, forearm; recoil pad. Introduced in 1962; still in production. Used value, $50 to $55.

**Model 198 Topper Deluxe** has the same specifications as

Model 158, except for black-lacquered stock, forearm; chrome-plated frame; in 20, .410 gauges only. Introduced in 1962; still in production. Used value, $55 to $60.

**Model 490 Topper** has the same specifications as Model 158, except for 26″ barrel only, shorter youth stock; in 20-ga., modified; .410, full choke only. Introduced in 1962; still in production. Used value, $50 to $55.

**Model 590 Topper** has the same specifications as Model 490, except for black-lacquered stock, forearm, chrome-plated frame. Introduced in 1962; dropped, 1963. Used value, $50 to $55.

*Model 159*

**HARRINGTON & RICHARDSON Model 159:** advertised as the Golden Squire model; single barrel; exposed hammer; 12, 20 gauges; in 12-ga., 30″ barrel, 20-ga., 28″ barrel; full choke only; uncheckered hardwood straight grip stock, forearm with schnabel; no sights. Introduced in 1964;

dropped, 1966. Used value, $65 to $70.

**Model 459 Golden Squire Jr.** has same specifications as Model 459, except for shorter youth stock, 26″ full choke barrel; 20, .410 gauges only. Made only in 1964. Used value, $65 to $70.

**HARRINGTON & RICHARDSON Model 348:** advertised as Gamemaster model; bolt-action; takedown; 12, 16 gauges; 28″ barrel; full choke only; 2-rd. tube magazine; uncheckered hardwood pistol-grip stock, forearm. Intro-

duced in 1949; dropped, 1954. Used value, $60 to $65.

**Model 349 Gamemaster Deluxe** has same specifications as Model 348, except for adjustable choke device, 26″ barrel; recoil pad. Introduced in 1953; dropped, 1955. Used value, $70 to $75.

**HARRINGTON & RICHARDSON Model 351:** advertised as the Huntsman model; bolt-action; takedown; 12, 16 gauges; 26″ barrel; Harrington & Richardson variable

choke; push-button safety; 2-rd. tube magazine; uncheckered American hardwood Monte Carlo stock; recoil pad. Introduced in 1956; dropped, 1958. Used value, $70 to $75.

*Model 400*

*Model 402*

**HARRINGTON & RICHARDSON Model 400:** pump action; hammerless; 12, 16, 20 gauges; 28″ full choke barrel only; recoil pad on 12, 16-ga. models; uncheckered pistol-grip stock; 5-rd. tube magazine; grooved slide handle. Introduced in 1955; dropped, 1967. Used value, $110 to $120.

**Model 401** has the same specifications as Model 400 except for addition of Harrington & Richardson variable choke. Introduced in 1956; dropped, 1963. Used value, $120 to $130.

**Model 402** has same general design as Model 400, but is only in .410 bore. Introduced in 1959; dropped, 1963. Used value, $145 to $160.

*Model 403*

**HARRINGTON & RICHARDSON Model 403:** autoloader; takedown; .410 only; 26″ barrel; full choke; 4-rd. tube magazine; uncheckered walnut pistol-grip stock, forearm. Made only in 1964. Used value, $165 to $175.

**HARRINGTON & RICHARDSON Model 404:** double barrel; box-lock action; 12, 20, .410 gauges; in 12-ga., 28″ modified/full barrel; 20-ga., 26″ modified/improved; .410, 25″ full/full; double triggers; plain extractors; checkered hardwood pistol-grip stock, forearm. Made to H&R specifications in Brazil. Introduced in 1968; dropped, 1972. Used value, $175 to $180.

**Model 404C** has same specifications as Model 404 except for Monte Carlo stock. Used value, $185 to $195.

*Model 162*

**HARRINGTON & RICHARDSON Model 162:** single-barrel, slug gun; has same specs as Model 158, except for cylinder bore, rifle sights, 24″ barrel. Introduced 1968, still in production. Used value, $55 to $60.

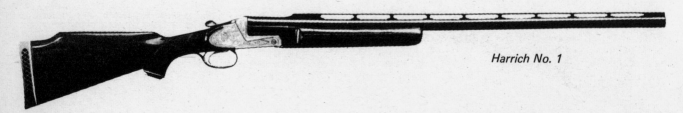

*Harrich No. 1*

**HARRINGTON & RICHARDSON Harrich No. 1:** single-shot top model; 12-ga. only; 32″, 34″ barrel; full choke; high vent rib; Anson & Deeley-type locking, Kersten top locks, double under lugs; hand-checkered European walnut Monte Carlo pistol grip stock, beavertail forearm; recoil pad. Manufactured in Austria 1971 to 1974. Used value, $1750 to $1850.

*Model 440*

**HARRINGTON & RICHARDSON Model 440:** pump action; hammerless; 12, 16, 20 gauges; side ejection; 24", 26", 28" barrels; standard chokes; unchecked American walnut pistol-grip stock, forearm; 4-rd. clip magazine; recoil pad. Introduced in 1972; dropped, 1975. Used value, $125 to $145.

**Model 442** has same specifications as Model 440 except for checkered pistol grip, forearm and full length vent rib. Used value, $160 to $165.

*Model 1212*

**HARRINGTON & RICHARDSON Model 1212:** over/under; 12-ga., 2¾" chambers; 28" barrels; improved/improved modified chokes; box-lock; selective single trigger; plain extractors; vent rib; checkered European walnut pistol-grip stock, fluted forearm. Manufactured in Spain. Introduced in 1976, still in production. Used value, $240 to $250.

**Model 1212 Waterfowler** has same specs as the standard field model except for 30" barrels, modified/full choking; chambering for 3" magnum shells; recoil pad. Introduced 1976, still in production. Used value, $250 to $265.

*Model 176*

**HARRINGTON & RICHARDSON Model 176:** single-shot; hammer type; 10-ga. magnum only; has same general specs as Model 158, except for 36" heavy barrel; walnut stock, full forearm; recoil pad. Introduced 1977, still in production. Used value, $60 to $70.

# HIGH STANDARD

*Supermatic Field 20*

**HIGH STANDARD Supermatic Field Model:** autoloader; 12-ga. gas-operated; 26" improved, 28" modified or full, 30" full barrels; 4-rd. magazine; unchecked American walnut pistol-grip stock, forearm. Introduced in 1960; dropped, 1966. Used value, $155 to $160.

**Field Model 20-ga.** has same general design as 12-ga. but chambered for 3" magnum shell; 3-rd. magazine; 26" improved, 28" modified or full barrels; unchecked pistol-grip stock, forearm. Introduced in 1963; dropped, 1966. Used value, $160 to $165.

*Supermatic Special 20*

**HIGH STANDARD Supermatic Special:** autoloader; 12-ga.; has the same specifications as 12-ga. Field model, except for 27" barrel, adjustable choke. Introduced in 1960; dropped, 1966. Used value, $145 to $150.

**Special 20-ga.** model has same specifications as 20-ga. Field Grade, except for 27" barrel, adjustable choke. Introduced in 1963; dropped, 1966. Used value, $150 to $155.

*Supermatic Trophy 20*

**HIGH STANDARD Supermatic Trophy Model:** autoloader; 12-ga.; has same specifications as Deluxe Rib 12-ga. model, except for 27″ vent rib barrel, adjustable choke. Introduced in 1961; dropped, 1966. Used value, $165 to $170.

**Trophy 20-ga.** has the same specifications as the Deluxe Rib 20, except for 27″ vent rib barrel, adjustable choke. Introduced in 1963; dropped, 1966. Used value, $165 to $175.

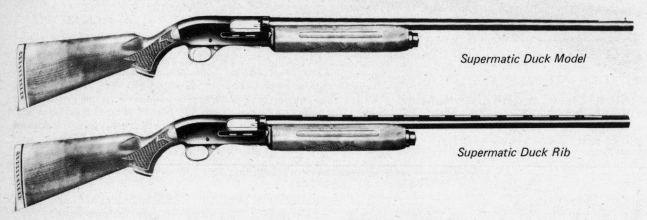

*Supermatic Duck Model*

*Supermatic Duck Rib*

**HIGH STANDARD Supermatic Duck Model:** autoloader; 12-ga. magnum only; has same general specifications as 12-ga. Field model, except for 30″ full choke barrel, recoil pad. Introduced in 1961; dropped, 1966. Used value,

$160 to $165.

**Duck Rib 12 magnum** has the same specifications as the Duck 12 magnum, except for vent rib, checkered stock and forearm. Introduced in 1961; dropped, 1966. Used value, $170 to $175.

**HIGH STANDARD Supermatic Skeet:** autoloader; 12-ga.; 26″ vent rib barrel; skeet choke; other specifications are the same as Deluxe Rib 12 model. Introduced in 1962; drop-

ped, 1966. Used value, $165 to $170.

**Skeet 20-ga.** has same specifications as Deluxe Rib 20 model, except for skeet choke, 26″ vent rib barrel. Introduced in 1964; dropped, 1966. Used value, $165 to $170.

**HIGH STANDARD Supermatic Trap:** autoloader; 12-ga.; 30″ vent rib; full choke only; trap stock; recoil pad. Other

specifications the same as Deluxe Rib 12 model. Introduced in 1962. dropped, 1966. Used value, $170 to $180.

**HIGH STANDARD Supermatic Deer Model:** 12-ga.; cylinder bore; same specs as Supermatic field model, except

for 22″ barrel, rifle sights; checkered stock, forearm; recoil pad. Manufactured 1965. Used value, $150 to $160.

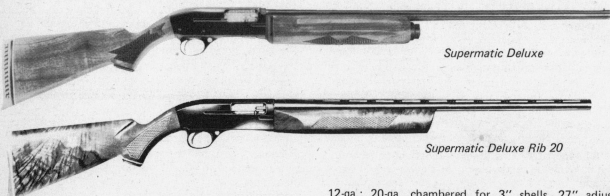

*Supermatic Deluxe*

*Supermatic Deluxe Rib 20*

**HIGH STANDARD Supermatic Deluxe:** 12, 20-ga.; 4-rd. magazine; 27″ adjustable choke barrel (dropped 1970), 26″ improved, 28″ modified, full, 30″ full choke barrels in

12-ga.; 20-ga. chambered for 3″ shells, 27″ adjustable choke barrel (dropped 1970), 26″ improved, 28″ modified or full; checkered American walnut pistol-grip stock, forearm; recoil pad. Differs from original Supermatic; has new checkering, damascened bolt. Manufactured 1966 to

1975. Used values, with adjustable choke, $160 to $165; sans choke, $150 to $155.

**Supermatic Deluxe Rib** has same specs as Supermatic Deluxe, 12, 20-ga.; except for vent rib, no 26" barrel length. Manufactured 1966 to 1975. Used values, with adjustable choke, $160 to $165; sans choke, $150 to $155.

**Supermatic Deluxe Duck Rib** has same specs as Supermatic Deluxe, 12-ga. only, except for 3" magnum chambering, 3-rd. magazine, 30" full choke vent-rib barrel. Manufactured 1966 to 1975. Used value, $190 to $200.

**Supermatic Deluxe Duck** model has same specs as Duck Rib model, sans vent rib. Manufactured 1966 to 1975. Used value, $160 to $170.

**Supermatic Deluxe Skeet** model has same specs as Deluxe Rib version, except was made only with 26" vent-rib barrel, skeet choke; 12, 20-ga. Manufactured 1966 to 1975. Used value, $180 to $195.

**Supermatic Deluxe Trap** model has same specs as Deluxe Rib 12-ga. except has 30" vent-rib barrel, full choke, trap stock. Manufactured 1966 to 1975. Used value, $190 to $200.

*Flite-King Field 20*

**HIGH STANDARD Flite-King Field Model:** slide action; 12-ga.; hammerless; 26" improved cylinder, 28" modified or full, 30" full barrel; 5-rd. magazine; unchecked walnut pistol-grip stock, grooved slide handle. Introduced in 1960; dropped, 1966. Used value, $85 to $95.

**Field model 20-ga.** is chambered for 3" magnum shell; 4-rd. magazine; other specifications, including barrel lengths, chokes are the same as 12-ga. version. Introduced in 1961; dropped, 1966. Used value, $85 to $95.

*Flite-King Special 20*

**HIGH STANDARD Flite-King Special:** slide action; 12-ga.; has the same specifications as Field version, except for 27" barrel, adjustable choke. Introduced in 1960; dropped,

1966. Used value, $100 to $110.

**Special 20-ga.** has same specifications as Field 20, except for 27" barrel, adjustable choke. Introduced in 1961; dropped, 1966. Used value, $100 to $110.

*Flite-King Deluxe Rib 12*

**HIGH STANDARD Flight-King Deluxe Rib:** slide action; 12-ga.; has the same specifications as Field 12 Flite-King except for 28" full or modified, 30" full choke barrel; vent rib; checkered walnut stock, slide handle. Introduced in

1961; dropped, 1966. Used value, $140 to $155.

**Deluxe Rib 20-ga.** has same specifications as Field 20-ga. model, except for 28" full or modified barrel; vent rib; checkered stock, slide handle. Introduced in 1962; dropped, 1966. Used value, $140 to $155.

**HIGH STANDARD Flite-King Trophy:** slide action; 12-ga.; has the same specifications as Deluxe Rib 12-ga., except for 27" vent rib barrel, adjustable choke. Introduced in 1960; dropped, 1966. Used value, $150 to $160.

**Trophy 20-ga.** has the same specifications as Field 20-ga., except for vent rib; 28" modified or full barrel, checkered stock, slide handle. Introduced in 1962; dropped, 1966. Used value, $155 to $165.

**HIGH STANDARD Flite-King Skeet:** slide action, 12-ga.; same specifications as 12-ga. Deluxe Rib except for 26"

skeet-choked barrel, vent rib. Introduced in 1962; dropped, 1966. Used value, $160 to $170.

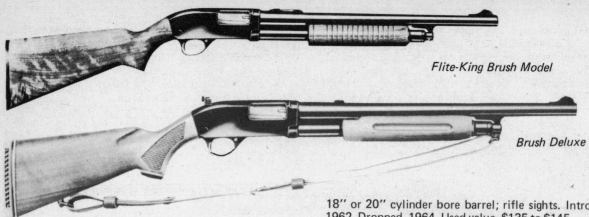

Flite-King Brush Model

Brush Deluxe

**HIGH STANDARD Flite-King Brush Gun:** slide action; 12-ga.; has same specifications as Field model except for

18" or 20" cylinder bore barrel; rifle sights. Introduced in 1962. Dropped, 1964. Used value, $135 to $145.

**Brush Deluxe** model has same specs as Flite-King Brush Gun, except for recoil pad, adjustable peep rear sight; has checkered pistol grip, fluted slide handle, sling swivels, sling; made with 20" barrel only. Manufactured 1964 to 1966. Used value, $160 to $170.

**HIGH STANDARD Flite-King Trap:** slide action; 12-ga.; has the same specifications as Deluxe Rib 12-ga. except for

30" barrel; full choke; vent rib; trap stock; recoil pad. Introduced in 1962; dropped, 1966. Used value, $85 to $90.

**HIGH STANDARD Flite-King 16 Series:** slide action; 16-ga.; has same general specifications as various configurations of Flite-King 12-ga., but not available in

Brush, Skeet or Trap models, nor in 30" barrel lengths. Introduced in 1961; dropped, 1965. Used values, Field, $85 to $90; Special, $125 to $135; Deluxe Rib, $145 to $150; Trophy, $150 to $155.

Flite-King .410 Field

**HIGH STANDARD Flite-King 410 Series:** slide action; 410-ga.; has same specifications as Flite-King 20-ga., but not available in Special and Trophy grades; 26" full choke

barrel only. Introduced in 1962; dropped, 1966. Used values, Field, $85 to $95; Deluxe Rib, $135 to $155; Brush Gun, $110 to $125; Skeet, $140 to $150; Trap, $155 to $165.

Flite-King Deluxe (1966)

**HIGH STANDARD Flite-King Deluxe (1966):** autoloader; 12-ga.; 5-rd. magazine, 26" improved cylinder barrel, 27" with adjustable choke; 28" modified or full; 30" full choke; checkered American walnut pistol-grip stock, forearm; recoil pad. General specifications follow Flite-King series dropped 1966, except for damascened bolt, new checkering design. Manufactured 1966 to 1975. Used values, with adjustable choke, $110 to $115; sans adjustable choke, $95 to $105.

**Deluxe 20 (1966)** has same specs as Deluxe 12-ga., except it is chambered for 3" 20-ga. shells; improved, modified, or full choking. Manufactured 1966 to 1975. Used value, $95 to $105.

**Deluxe 28 (1966)** has same specs as Deluxe 12-ga., except is chambered only modified and full. Manufactured 1966 to 1975. Used value, $95 to $105.

**Deluxe 410 (1966)** has same specs as Deluxe 28, except is chambered for 3" .410 shell; full choke only. Manufactured 1966 to 1975. Used value, $95 to $105.

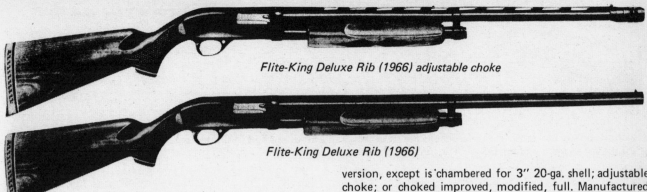

*Flite-King Deluxe Rib (1966) adjustable choke*

*Flite-King Deluxe Rib (1966)*

**HIGH STANDARD Flite-King Deluxe Rib (1966):** 12-ga., has same specs as Flite-King Deluxe 12-ga., except for vent-rib barrel; made in 27″ barrel length with adjustable choke, 28″ modified or full, 30″ full choke. Manufactured 1966 to 1975. Used values, with adjustable choke, $140 to $150; sans adjustable choke, $130 to $140.

**Deluxe Rib 20 (1966)** has same specs as 12-ga. 1966 version, except is chambered for 3″ 20-ga. shell; adjustable choke; or choked improved, modified, full. Manufactured 1966 to 1975. Used values, with adjustable choke, $140 to $150; sans adjustable choke, $130 to $140.

**Deluxe Rib 28 (1966)** has same specs as 20-ga. version, except chambered for 2¾″ shell; no adjustable choke; made with modified, full chokes. Manufactured 1966 to 1975. Used value, $130 to $140.

**Deluxe Rib .410 (1966)** has same specs as 28-ga. version, except chambered for 3″ .410 shell, full choke only. Manufactured 1966 to 1975. Used value, $130 to $140.

*Flite-King Deluxe 28 (1966)*

**HIGH STANDARD Flite-King Deluxe Skeet (1966):** autoloader; 12-ga.; has same specs as standard Deluxe (1966) model except for 26″ vent-rib barrel, skeet choke; optional recoil pad. Manufactured 1966 to 1975. Used value, $130 to $140.

**Deluxe Skeet 20 (1966)** has same specs as 12-ga. except for 20-ga. chambering. Manufactured 1966 to 1975. Used value, $130 to $140.

**Deluxe Skeet 28 (1966)** has same specs as Deluxe Skeet 20, except for 28-ga. chambering. Manufactured 1966 to 1975. Used value, $130 to $140.

**Deluxe Skeet .410 (1966)** has same specs as Deluxe Skeet 20, except for .410 chambering. Manufactured 1966 to 1975. Used value, $130 to $140.

**Deluxe Trap (1966)** has same general specifications as standard Deluxe Rib 12 (1966), except was made only with 30″ vent-rib barrel, full choke, trap stock. Manufactured 1966 to 1975. Used value, $140 to $150.

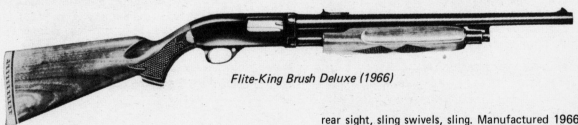

*Flite-King Brush Deluxe (1966)*

**HIGH STANDARD Flite-King Brush Deluxe (1966):** 12-ga.; has same general specs as standard Deluxe 12-ga. (1966) except for 20″ barrel, cylinder bore, adjustable peep rear sight, sling swivels, sling. Manufactured 1966 to 1975. Used value, $130 to $140.

**Flite-King Brush (1966)** has same specs as Brush Deluxe except for rifle sights, no swivels, no sling. Manufactured 1966 to 1975. Used value, $115 to $120.

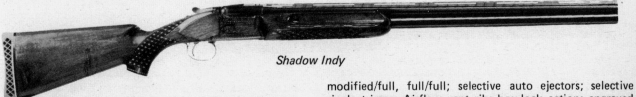

*Shadow Indy*

**HIGH STANDARD Shadow Indy:** over/under; 12-ga., 2¾″ chambering; 27½″ skeet choked barrels; 29¾″ improved modified/full, full/full; selective auto ejectors; selective single trigger; Airflow vent rib; box-lock action; engraved receiver; skip-checkered walnut pistol-grip stock, ventilated forearm; recoil pad. Manufactured in Japan 1974 to 1975. Used value, $550 to $575.

*Shadow Seven*

**Shadow Seven** has same general specs as Shadow Indy, except for less engraving, standard vent rib, forearm; no recoil

**HIGH STANDARD Shadow Auto:** gas-operated; 12, 20-ga.; 2¾", 3" chambering in 12-ga., 3" in 20; magazine holds four 2¾" rounds, three 3¾"; 26" improved cylinder or skeet

pad; 27½" barrels made in improved cylinder/modified, modified/full. Manufactured in Japan 1974 to 1975. Used value, $460 to $495.

barrel, 28" modified, improved modified or full, 30" trap or full; magnum available only with 30" barrel; checkered walnut pistol-grip stock, forearm. Manufactured in Japan 1974 to 1975. Used value, $200 to $215.

# HOLLAND & HOLLAND

> **AUTHOR'S NOTE:** 20-gauge versions are valued at 25% more than indicated prices; 28-gauges, 50% additional.

*Royal Model*

**HOLLAND & HOLLAND Royal Model:** side-by-side; hammerless; 12, 16, 20, 28 gauges; barrel lengths, chokes to customer's specifications; self-opening action; hand-detachable sidelocks; automatic ejectors; double triggers or single nonselective trigger; made in Game, Pigeon, Wildfowl configurations; hand-checkered straight-grip stock, forearm; English engraving. Introduced in 1885; still in production. Used values, double triggers, $6250 to $6500; single trigger, $6750 to $7000.

*Badminton Model*

**HOLLAND & HOLLAND Badminton Model:** side-by-side; hammerless; 12, 16, 20, 28 gauges; has the same specifications as Royal Model side-by-side except action is not self-opening. Introduced in 1890; still in production. Used values, double triggers, $4250 to $4500; single trigger, $4500 to $4750.

**HOLLAND & HOLLAND Model Deluxe:** side-by-side; hammerless; 12, 16, 20, 28 gauges; barrel lengths and chokes to customer's specifications; self-opening action; hand-detachable sidelocks; has the same general specifications as Royal Model, but with much more ornate engraving. Introduced in 1900; still in production. Used values, double triggers, $7500 to $7750; single trigger, $8000 to $8250.

*Royal Under-and-Over*

**HOLLAND & HOLLAND Royal Over/Under:** hammerless; hand-detachable sidelocks; 12-ga. only; barrel lengths, chokes to customer's specifications; automatic ejectors; double triggers or single trigger; made in Game, Pigeon, Wildfowl configurations; hand-checkered European walnut straight-grip stock, forearm. Introduced in 1925; dropped,

1950. Used values, double triggers, $7500 to $7750; single trigger, $8000 to $8250.

**New Royal Model** over/under has the same specifications as original model except for narrower, improved action. Introduced in 1951; dropped, 1965. Used values, double triggers, $8250 to $8500; single trigger, $8750 to $9000.

*Dominion Model*

**HOLLAND & HOLLAND Dominion Model:** side-by-side; hammerless; sidelock; 12, 16, 20 gauges; 25", 28", 30" barrels; choked to customer's specifications; double triggers; automatic ejectors; hand-checkered European walnut straight-grip stock, forearm. Introduced in 1935; dropped, 1965. Used value, $2750 to $3000.

**HOLLAND & HOLLAND Northwood Game Model:** side-by-side; 12, 16, 20, 28-ga.; 28" barrels; any standard choke combo; Anson & Deeley box-lock action; double triggers, automatic ejectors; hand-checkered European walnut straight-grip or pistol-grip stock, forearm. Manufactured prior to World War II until late Sixties. Used value, $2000 to $2150.

**Northwood Wildfowl Model** has same specs as Game Model, except made in 12-ga., 3" chambering only, 30" barrels. Used value, $2000 to $2150.

**Northwood Pigeon Model** has same specs as Game Model, except has more engraving; not offered in 28-ga. Used value, $2000 to $2200.

**HOLLAND & HOLLAND Super Trap:** single-barrel; 12-ga.; 30", 32" barrel; extra-full choke; Anson & Deeley box-lock action; automatic ejector; no safety; Monte Carlo stock of European walnut, full beavertail forearm; recoil pad. Introduced prior to World War II, dropped in late Sixties. Used value, $8150 to $8250.

**Super Trap Deluxe Grade** has same specs as standard model, except for upgraded wood, quality of engraving. Used value, $9150 to $9250.

**Super Trap Exhibition Grade** has same specs as Deluxe Grade, except for better wood, additional engraving. Used value, $10,200 to $10,350.

**HOLLAND & HOLLAND Riviera Model:** side-by-side; hammerless; designed as pigeon gun; has the same specifications as Badminton Model except for double triggers, two sets of interchangeable barrels. Introduced in 1945; still in production. Used value, $5000 to $5250.

# ITHACA

*Hammerless Double Field Grade*

**ITHACA Hammerless Double Field Grade:** side-by-side double barrel; box-lock action; 12, 16, 20, 28, .410 gauges; 26", 28", 30", 32" barrels; any standard choke combination; top-lever breaking; hand-checkered American walnut pistol-grip stock, forearm; pistol-grip cap; various options at additional cost. Introduced with rotary bolt in 1926; dropped, 1948. Used values, standard model, $400 to $425; with automatic ejectors, add $175; with beavertail forearm, add $150; with vent rib, add $250; for 10-ga. magnum, 12-ga. magnum (only 900 made); add $200 to $250.

**Hammerless Double No. 2 Grade** has same general specifications as Field Grade with addition of black walnut stock, forearm, engraving. Various options at added cost. Introduced in 1926; dropped, 1948. Used values, standard version, $475 to $500; with auto ejectors, add $175; with beavertail forearm, add $150; with vent rib, add $275; for 10-ga. magnum, 12-ga. magnum, add $275.

**Hammerless Double No. 4 Grade** has same basic design as Field Grade, but with many custom facets; double triggers are standard; hand engraved with scroll, line engraving; game scenes on frame, top lever, forearm iron, trigger guard; various options at added cost. Introduced in 1926; dropped, 1948. Used values, standard version, $950 to $1000; with single selective trigger, add $200; beavertail

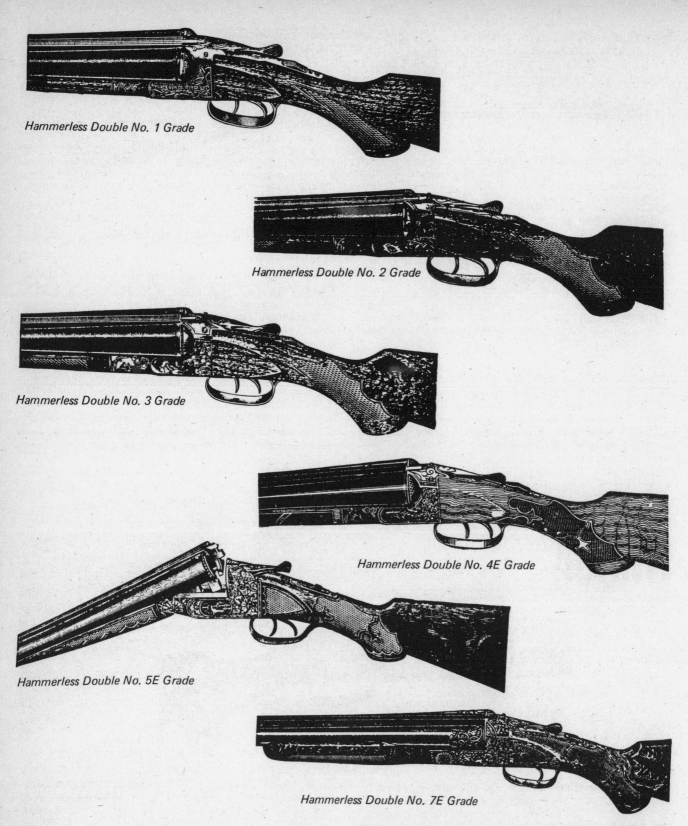

Hammerless Double No. 1 Grade

Hammerless Double No. 2 Grade

Hammerless Double No. 3 Grade

Hammerless Double No. 4E Grade

Hammerless Double No. 5E Grade

Hammerless Double No. 7E Grade

forearm, add $185; vent rib, add $300; 10, 12-ga. magnums, add $300 and $200, espectively.

**Hammerless Double No. 5 Grade** has gold nameplate inset in stock; English pheasant inlaid in gold on left side, woodcock on right; American eagle is engraved on bottom; engraved leaf, flower background; has selective single trigger, beavertail forearm; vent rib extra. Introduced in 1926; dropped, 1948. Used values, $4500 to $5000; with vent rib, add $350; add $750 for 10-ga. magnums; $400 for 12-ga. magnums.

**Hammerless Double No. 7 Grade** has select walnut stock, hand-fitted action, elaborately checkered wood; beavertail forearm with ebony tip; matted vent rib; profusely engraved receiver with oak leaf, acorn design; inlaid designs in green and yellow gold, silver; gold nameplate inset in stock;

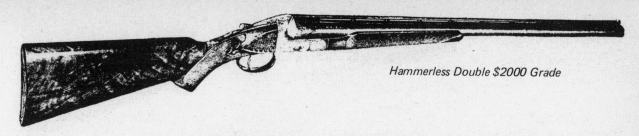

*Hammerless Double $2000 Grade*

single selective trigger is triple gold-plated, hand checkered; automatic ejectors. Introduced in 1926; dropped; 1948. Used value, $5500 to $6000.

**Hammerless Double $2000 Grade** has same specifica-

tions as other grades, but is inlaid with gold in elaborate designs; selective single trigger, vent rib, beavertail forearm. Prior to World War II, was listed as $1000 Grade. Introduced in 1926; dropped, 1948. Used value, $7500 to $8000.

*One Barrel Trap 4E Grade*

**ITHACA One Barrel Trap Gun:** single-shot, hammerless; box-lock action; 12-ga. only; 30", 32", 34" barrels; vent rib; hand-checkered American walnut pistol-grip stock, forearm; recoil pad; made in four grades, differing only in quality of workmanship, grade of wood, amount of engrav-

ing, checkering. $5000 Grade was designated as $1000 model prior to World War II. Introduced in 1922; still in production. Used values, No. 4-E, $2250 to $2500; No. 5-E, $3500 to $3750; No. 7-E, $6000 to $6500; $5000 Grade, $7500 to $8000.

**ITHACA Single-Barrel Victory Model:** single-shot, hammerless; box-lock action; 12-ga. only; 34" barrel; has same general specifications as other One Barrel models, but less

extensive engraving, checkering, lower grade of wood. Introduced in 1922; dropped about 1938. Used value, $800 to $875.

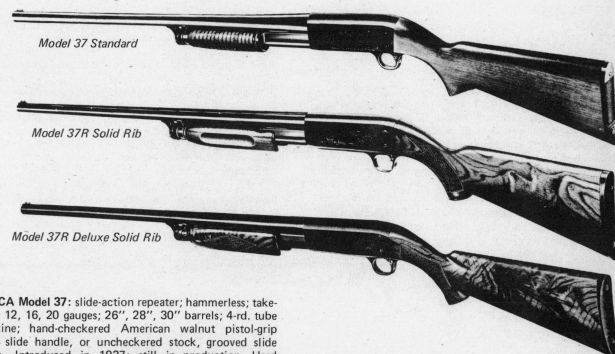

*Model 37 Standard*

*Model 37R Solid Rib*

*Model 37R Deluxe Solid Rib*

**ITHACA Model 37:** slide-action repeater; hammerless; takedown; 12, 16, 20 gauges; 26", 28", 30" barrels; 4-rd. tube magazine; hand-checkered American walnut pistol-grip stock, slide handle, or uncheckered stock, grooved slide handle. Introduced in 1937; still in production. Used values, with checkered pistol grip, slide handle, $155 to $165; with plain stock, grooved slide handle, $140 to $150.

**Model 37R** has the same general specifications as standard Model 37 except for raised solid rib. Introduced in 1937; dropped, 1967. Used values, with checkered pistol grip, slide handle, $165 to $175; uncheckered stock, grooved slide handle, $140 to $145.

**Model 37S Skeet Grade** has same general specifications as standard model, except for vent rib, extension slide handle. Introduced in 1937; dropped, 1955. Used value, $275 to $300.

**Model 37T Trap Grade** has same general specifications as Model 37S except for straight trap stock of selected walnut,

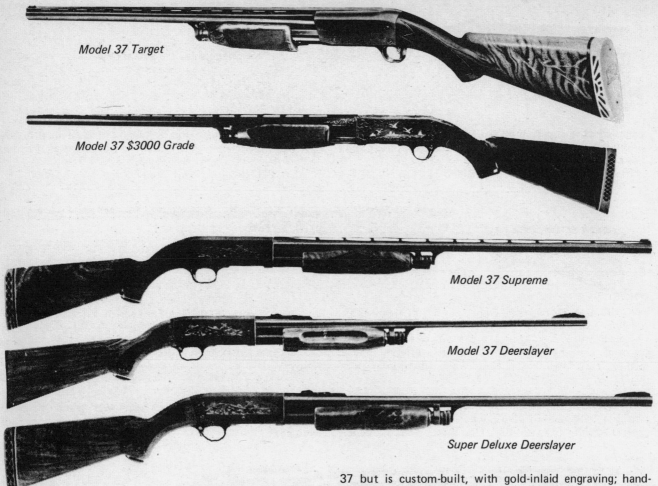

Model 37 Target

Model 37 $3000 Grade

Model 37 Supreme

Model 37 Deerslayer

Super Deluxe Deerslayer

recoil pad. Introduced in 1937; dropped, 1955. Used value, $300 to $325.

**Model 37T Target Grade** replaced Model 37S Skeet Grade and Model 37T Trap Grade. Has same general specifications as standard Model 37 except for hand-checkered stock, slide handle of fancy walnut; choice of skeet or trap stock; vent rib. Introduced in 1955; dropped, 1961. Used value, $325 to $350.

**Model 37 Supreme Grade** has same general specifications as Model 37T, but available in skeet or trap configuration. Manufactured 1967 to 1979. Used value, $275 to $285.

**Model 37 $3000 Grade** was listed as $1000 Grade prior to World War II. Has same basic design as standard Model

37 but is custom-built, with gold-inlaid engraving; hand-finished parts; hand-checkered pistol-grip stock, slide handle of select figured walnut; recoil pad. Introduced in 1937; dropped, 1967. Used value, $4250 to $4500.

**Model 37R Deluxe** has same general specifications as standard Model 37R except for hand-checkered fancy walnut stock, slide handle. Introduced in 1955; dropped, 1961. Used value, $185 to $200.

**Model 37 Deerslayer** has same specifications as standard Model 37 except for 20″ or 26″ barrel bored for rifled slugs; open rifle-type rear sight, ramp front. Introduced in 1969; still in production. Used value, $150 to $165.

**Model 37 Super Deerslayer** has same specs as standard Deerslayer, except for improved wood in stock, slide handle. Manufactured 1962 until 1979. Used value, $180 to $190.

Model 66

**ITHACA Model 66 Supersingle:** lever-action single-shot; manually cocked hammer; 12, 20, .410 gauges; 30″ full choke barrel or 28″ full or modified in 12-ga., 28″ full or modified in 20-ga., 26″ full in .410. Checkered straight stock, uncheckered forearm. Introduced in 1963; dropped

1979. Used value, $65 to $75.

**Model 66 Youth Model** has same specifications as standard Model 66 except for shorter stock, recoil pad, 25″ barrel; 20, .410 gauges only. Introduced in 1965; dropped 1979. Used value, $65 to $75.

**Model 66 Vent Rib** has same specifications as standard model, except for vent-rib barrel; made in 20-ga. only with checkered stock, recoil pad. Manufactured 1969 to 1974. Used value, $85 to $95.

Model 66 Long Tom has same specs as standard 66, except for 36" full choke barrel; 12-ga. only; checkered

*Model 66RS*

stock; recoil pad. Manufactured 1969 to 1974. Used value, $75 to $80.

Model 66RS Buck Buster has 22" barrel, cylinder bore, rifle sights; 12, 20-ga. Introduced 1967; 12-ga. dropped, 1970; discontinued, 1979. Used value, $75 to $80.

*Model 100*

ITHACA-SKB Model 100: side-by-side, double barrel; box-lock action; 12, 20 gauges; in 12-ga., 30" full/full barrels, 28", full/modified, 26", improved/modified; in 20-ga., 25"

improved/modified only; single selective trigger; plain extractors; automatic safety; hand-checkered pistol-grip stock, forearm. Made in Japan. Introduced in 1967; dropped, 1976. Used value, $350 to $375.

Ithaca-SKB Model 150 has same specs as Model 100, except for more ornate scroll engraving, beavertail forearm. Manufactured 1972 to 1974. Used value, $565 to $590.

*Model 200E Standard*

ITHACA-SKB Model 200E; side-by-side, double barrel; box-lock action; has the same general specifications as Model 100 except for automatic selective ejectors, engraved, silver-plated frame, gold-plated nameplate, trigger; beavertail forearm. Introduced in 1967; dropped, 1977. Used value, $500 to $525.

Model 200E Skeet Grade has the same specifications as standard model except for 25" barrel in 12-ga., 25" in 20-ga.; skeet/skeet; nonautomatic safety; recoil pad. Introduced in 1967; dropped, 1976. Used value, $600 to $625.

Ithaca-SKB Model 280 has same specs as Model 200E, except for English type straight stock, game scene engraved on frame; not made with 30" barrels; quail gun has 25" barrels in improved cylinder. Imported 1971 to 1979. Used value, $550 to $575.

*Model 500 Standard*

ITHACA-SKB Model 500: over/under; hammerless; top lever, box-lock action; 12, 20 gauges; in 12-ga., 25" barrels have improved/modified choke combo, 28", improved/modified or modified/full, 30", modified/full; in 20-ga., 26" barrels have improved/modified, 28", modified/full;

gold-plated single selective trigger; automatic ejectors, non-automatic safety; chrome-lined barrels, action; Raybar front sight; scroll-engraved border on receiver; hand-checkered walnut pistol-grip stock, forearm; pistol-grip cap; fluted comb. Introduced in 1967; dropped, 1976. Used value, $500 to $525.

Model 500 Magnum has same specifications as standard Model 600 except for magnum chambering. Used value, $525 to $540.

*Model 600 Skeet*

ITHACA-SKB Model 600 Trap Grade: over/under; hammerless; box-lock action; 12-ga. only; 30", 32" barrels full/full or full/improved; straight or Monte Carlo stock; recoil pad;

other specifications are the same as those of Model 500. Introduced in 1967; dropped, 1976. Used value, $625 to $650.

Model 600 Skeet Grade has the same specifications as Model 500 except for 26", 28" skeet/skeet barrels, recoil pad. Introduced in 1967; dropped, 1976. Used value, $625 to $650.

*Model 700*

**ITHACA-SKB Model 700:** over/under; hammerless; box-lock action; in both skeet, trap styles; has the same specifications as Model 600 except for select oil-finished walnut stock, heavily engraved receiver. Introduced in 1967; dropped, 1976. Used value, $650 to $675.

**ITHACA MX-8:** over/under trap model; box-lock action; 12-ga.; 30", 32" barrels bored for international claybird competition; single nonselective trigger; interchangeable trigger/hammer groups; hand-checkered European walnut pistol-grip stock, forearm; oil or lacquer wood finish; vent rib. Introduced in 1968; still in production. Used value, $1850 to $2000.

*Mirage*

**ITHACA Mirage:** over/under; box-lock action; 12-ga.; 32", 30", 28" barrels; extra-full/modified, skeet/skeet boring; interchangeable hammer-trigger groups; single selective trigger; hand-checkered walnut pistol-grip stock, schnabel forearm; recoil pad. Introduced in 1968; still in production but no longer imported. Used value, $2000 to $2250.

*Competition 1 Trap*

**ITHACA Competition I:** over/under trap gun; box-lock action; 12-ga.; 30", 32" barrels; interchangeable hammer/trigger group; single nonselective trigger; improved/modified choke combo; vent rib; standard or Monte Carlo stock design; hand-checkered American walnut pistol-grip stock, forearm. Introduced in 1968; dropped, 1974. Used value, $1150 to $1250.

**Competition I Skeet** model has same general specifications as trap gun except for skeet stock, 26¾" skeet/skeet barrels; leather-faced recoil pad. Introduced in 1968; dropped, 1974. Used value, $1150 to $1250.

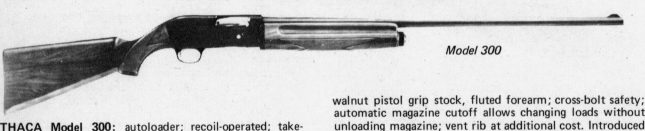

*Model 300*

**ITHACA Model 300:** autoloader; recoil-operated; takedown; 12-ga. only; 30" full choke barrel, 28" full or modified, 26" improved cylinder; checkered American walnut pistol grip stock, fluted forearm; cross-bolt safety; automatic magazine cutoff allows changing loads without unloading magazine; vent rib at additional cost. Introduced in 1969; dropped, 1973. Used values, plain barrel, $135 to $150; vent rib, $155 to $165.

*Model 900 Deluxe Standard*

**ITHACA Model 900 Deluxe:** autoloader; recoil-operated; takedown; 12, 20 gauges; 30" full choke barrel in 12-ga. only; 28" full or modified, 25" improved cylinder; vent rib; hand-checkered American walnut pistol grip stock, forearm; white spacers on grip cap, butt plate; interchangeable barrels, cross-bolt safety; gold-filled engraving on receiver, gold-plated trigger, nameplate inlaid in stock. Introduced in 1969; dropped, 1973. Used value, $185 to $195.

**Model 900 Deluxe Slug Gun** has same specifications as standard model except for 24" barrel, rifle sights. Introduced in 1969; dropped, 1973. Used value, $160 to $165.

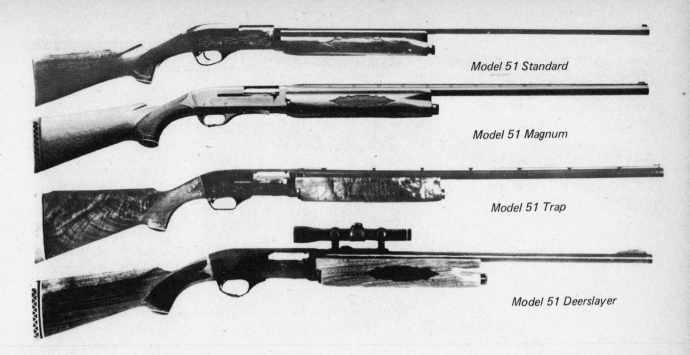

*Model 51 Standard*

*Model 51 Magnum*

*Model 51 Trap*

*Model 51 Deerslayer*

**ITHACA Model 51:** autoloader; gas-operated; takedown; 12-ga.; 30″ full choke barrel, 28″ full, modified or skeet, 26″ improved or skeet; Raybar front sight; hand-checkered American walnut pistol-grip stock; white spacer on pistol grip; 3-rd. tube magazine; reversible safety; engraved receiver; vent rib at added cost. Introduced in 1970; still in production. Used values, plain barrel, $210 to $225; vent rib, $250 to $260.

**Model 51 Magnum** has same specifications as standard model except for 3″ chambers. Used value, $250 to $260.

**Model 51 Trap** has same specifications as standard model except for 30″, 32″ barrel, trap stock, trap recoil pad, vent rib. Used value, $300 to $325.

**Model 51 Skeet** has same specifications as standard model except for skeet stock, skeet recoil pad, vent rib. Used value, $275 to $285.

**Model 51 Deerslayer** is in 12, 20-gauge; 24″ special bore barrel for slugs; has Raybar front sight, open adjustable rear; sight base grooved for scope. Used value, $270 to $280.

**Model 51 20-ga.** has same general design as standard Model 51; 26″ improved cylinder or skeet barrel; 28″ full or modified; vent rib; magnum chambering at extra cost. Used values, standard model, $215 to $225; with vent rib, $250 to $260; standard magnum, $235 to $240; magnum with vent rib, $255 to $260; skeet version, $260 to $265.

*LSA-55 Turkey Gun*

**ITHACA LSA-55 Turkey Gun:** over/under combo; 12-ga./.222 Remington; 24½″ ribbed barrels; plain extractor; single trigger; exposed hammer; folding leaf rear sight, bead front; checkered walnut Monte Carlo stock, forearm. Imported by Ithaca from Finland 1970 to 1979. Used value, $320 to $340.

*Light Game Model*

**ITHACA Light Game Model:** over/under; box-lock action; 12-ga.; 27-5/8″ barrel; modified/full, improved/full, improved/modified; interchangeable hammer/trigger group; single nonselective trigger; hand-checkered French walnut pistol-grip stock, schnabel forearm; case-hardened frame; hand engraved. Introduced in 1971; dropped, 1974. Used value, $1750 to $2000.

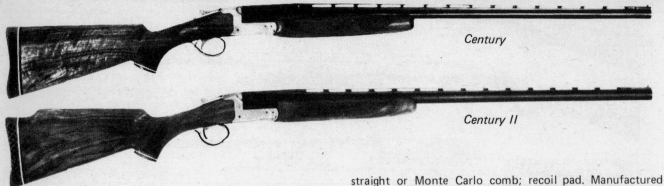

Century

Century II

**ITHACA SKB Century:** single-barrel trap; 12-ga.; 30″, 32″ barrels, vent rib, full choke, auto ejector; box-lock action; checkered pistol-grip walnut stock, beavertail forearm; straight or Monte Carlo comb; recoil pad. Manufactured 1973 to 1974. Used value, $420 to $440.

**Century II** has same specs as Century, except for redesigned locking iron, reverse-taper forearm, higher stock. Manufactured 1975 to 1979. Used value, $430 to $450.

Model XL300

**ITHACA Model XL 300:** autoloader; gas-operated; 12, 20 gauges; in 12-ga., 30″ full choke barrel, 28″ full or modified, 26″ improved cylinder; in 20-ga., 30″ full or modified, 28″ full or modified, 26″ improved or skeet; checkered American walnut pistol-grip stock, fluted forearm; self-compensating gas system; reversible safety; vent rib at additional cost. Introduced in 1973; dropped, 1976. Used values, plain barrel, $170 to $175; vent rib, $185 to $200.

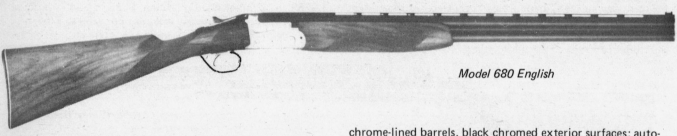

Model 680 English

**ITHACA-SKB Model 680 English:** over/under; hammerless; box-lock action; 12, 20 gauges; 26″, 28″ barrels, full/modified or modified/improved; single selective trigger; chrome-lined barrels, black chromed exterior surfaces; automatic selective ejectors; Bradley sights; vent rib; straight-grip stock; wraparound checkering. Introduced in 1973; dropped, 1976. Used value, $435 to $350.

Model XL 900 Standard

**ITHACA Model XL 900:** autoloader; gas-operated; 12, 20 gauges; 5-rd. tube magazine; in 12-ga., barrels are 30″ full choke, 28″ full or modified, 26″ improved cylinder; in 20-ga., 28″ full or modified, 26″ improved; trap version has 30″ full or improved choke; skeet version, 26″ skeet; Bradley-type front sight on target grade guns, Raybar front sight on vent rib field grades; uncheckered walnut-finished stock; self-compensating gas system; reversible safety; action release button. Introduced in 1973; dropped 1978. Used values, vent rib, $235 to $245; skeet grade, $245 to $250; trap grade (12-ga. only), $250 to $260.

**Model XL 900 Slug Gun** has same specifications as standard Model XL 900 except for 24″ slug barrel, rifle sights. Introduced in 1973; dropped 1978. Used value, $225 to $230.

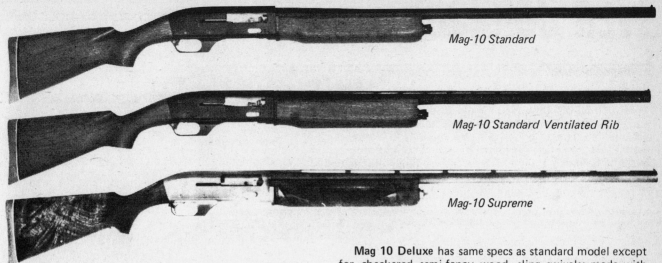

*Mag-10 Standard*

*Mag-10 Standard Ventilated Rib*

*Mag-10 Supreme*

**ITHACA Mag 10:** autoloader; gas-operated; 10-ga.; 3 rds. 3½" magnum shells; full choke; plain or vent rib barrel; walnut stock, forearm; recoil pad. Introduced 1977; still in production. Used value, $290 to $315.

**Mag 10 Deluxe** has same specs as standard model except for checkered semi-fancy wood, sling swivels; made with vent rib only. Introduced 1977, still in production. Used value, $400 to $425.

**Mag 10 Supreme** has same specs as Deluxe model, except for more fancy wood. Introduced 1974, still in production. Used value, $465 to $490.

*Model 880 Crown Grade*

**ITHACA-SKB Model 880 Crown Grade:** over/under; box-lock action; side plates; 12, 20 gauges; 32" full/improved barrel, 30" full/improved, 26" skeet/skeet in 12-ga.; 28" skeet/skeet in 20-ga.; Bradley-type front sight; trap or skeet stock; hand-checkered fancy French walnut pistol-grip stock, forearm; hand-honed action; engraved receiver; gold-inlaid crown on bottom of frame. Introduced in 1973; dropped, 1976. Used value, $1150 to $1200.

*High quality engraving and inlay work has been an outstanding feature of Ithaca's top-grade guns.*

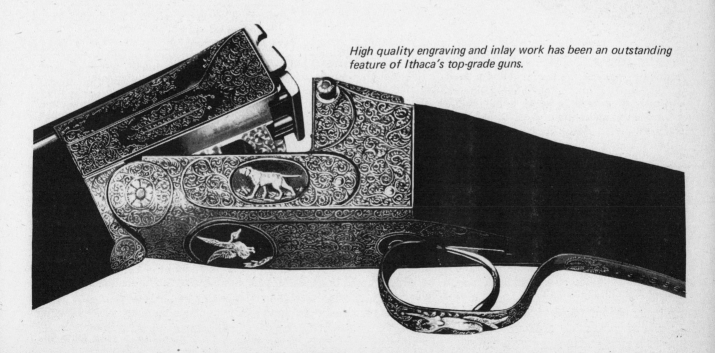

# IVER JOHNSON

*Champion Grade*

**IVER JOHNSON Champion Grade:** single barrel; hammer gun; 12, 16, 20, .410 gauges; 26", 28", 30", 32" barrels; full choke only; top-lever breaking; automatic ejector; uncheckered American walnut pistol-grip stock, forearm; bead front sight. Introduced in 1909; dropped 1976. Used value, $65 to $75.

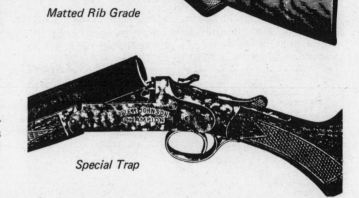

*Matted Rib Grade*

**IVER JOHNSON Matted Rib Grade:** single barrel; hammer gun; 12, 16, 20, .410 gauges; has the same general specifications as Champion Grade, except for raised vent rib, hand-checkered pistol grip, forearm. Introduced about 1910; dropped, 1948. Used value, $100 to $125.

*Special Trap*

**IVER JOHNSON Special Trap Model:** single barrel; hammer gun; 12-ga. only; 32" barrel only; other specifications are the same as those of Matted Rib Grade. Introduced about 1912; dropped, 1949. Used value, $285 to $295.

*Hercules*

> **NOTE: 20-gauge is worth 25% more than prices listed; .410 50% higher.**

**IVER JOHNSON Hercules Grade:** double barrel; box-lock action; hammerless; 12, 16, 20, .410 gauges; 26", 28", 30", 32" barrels; full/full, modified/full chokes; double triggers; single nonselective or selective trigger at extra cost; automatic ejectors at additional cost; hand-checkered straight or pistol-grip stock, forearm. Introduced about 1920; dropped, 1948. Used values, double trigger, plain extractor model, $225 to $250; double triggers, auto ejectors, $275 to $300; plain extractors, nonselective trigger, $275 to $300; nonselective trigger, auto ejectors, $325 to $350; selective single trigger, plain extractors, $335 to $365; selective single trigger, auto ejectors, $375 to $400.

*Skeeter Model*

**IVER JOHNSON Skeeter Model:** double barrel; box-lock action; hammerless; 12, 16, 20, 28, .410 gauges; 26" or 28" barrels; beavertail forearm. Other specifications the same as Hercules grade, with the same options. Introduced about 1920; dropped, 1949. Used values, double triggers, plain extractors, $400 to $425; double triggers, auto ejectors, $450 to $475; nonselective trigger, auto ejectors, $500 to $525; selective single trigger, plain extractors, $525 to $550; selective trigger, auto ejectors, $575 to $625.

*Super Trap*

**IVER JOHNSON Super Trap Model:** double barrel; hammerless; box-lock action; 12-ga. only; 32" barrel, full choke only; vent rib; hand-checkered pistol-grip stock, beavertail forearm; recoil pad. Introduced about 1924; dropped, 1949. Used values, double triggers, $525 to $550; nonselective single trigger, $575 to $600; single selective trigger, $650 to $700.

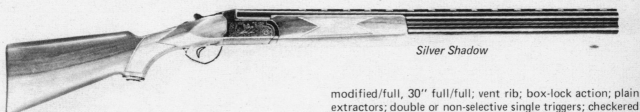

*Silver Shadow*

**IVER JOHNSON Silver Shadow:** over/under; 12-ga.; 3" chambers; 26" improved cylinder/modified barrels, 28" modified/full, 30" full/full; vent rib; box-lock action; plain extractors; double or non-selective single triggers; checkered European walnut pistol-grip stock, forend. Manufactured in Italy. Introduced 1973, still in production. Used values, single trigger, $200 to $215; double triggers, $190 to $200.

# KRIEGHOFF

*Trumpf Drilling*

**KRIEGHOFF Trumpf:** drilling: 12, 16, 20-ga.; last with 2¾" or 3" chambering; rifle barrel chambered for .243 Winchester, 6.5x57R, 7x57R, 7x65R, .30/06, other calibers available on special order; box-lock action; steel or dural receiver; slit extractor or ejector for shotgun barrels; double triggers; 25" barrels; solid rib; folding leaf rear sight, post or bead front; checkered European walnut pistol-grip stock; cheekpiece, forend; sling swivels. Introduced 1953, still in production. Used value, $1900 to $2000.

**Neptun** drilling: has the same specs as Trumpf model, except for sidelocks, engraved hunting scene. Introduced 1960, still in production. Used value, $2850 to $3000.

**Neptun-Primus** drilling: has same specs as Neptun model, except for detachable sidelocks, fancier figured walnut, higher grade of engraving. Introduced 1962, still in production. Used value, $3550 to $3700.

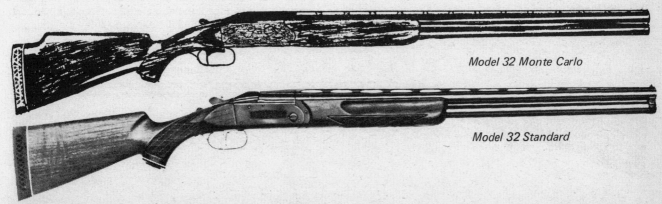

*Model 32 Monte Carlo*

*Model 32 Standard*

**KRIEGHOFF Model 32:** over/under; 12, 20, 28-ga., .410; 26½", 28", 30", 32" barrels; any choke combo; box-lock action; single trigger; auto ejectors; checkered European walnut pistol-grip stock, forend; manufactured in field, skeet, trap configurations; patterned after Remington Model 32. Introduced 1958, still in production. Used values, standard model, $1650 to $1700; low-rib two-barrel trap, $2200 to $2250; high-rib Vandalia two barrel trap, $2700 to $2750.

**Model 32 Single-Barrel Trap** model has same specs as over/under except 12-ga. only, 32", 34" barrels; modified, improved modififed, full chokes; high vent rib; checkered Monte Carlo stock, beavertail forend; recoil pad. Introduced 1959, still in production. Used value, $1350 to $1400.

**Model 32 Skeet Set** has four sets of matched barrels (12, 20, 28-ga., .410); skeet chokes, stock design; marketed in fitted case in six grades, price depending upon quality of wood, amount and quality of engraving. Used values, Standard Grade, $3900 to $4000; Munchen Grade, $5000 to $5150; San Remo Grade, $5750 to $5900; Monte Carlo Grade, $11,000 to $11,250; Crown Grade, $11,400 to $11,650; Super Crown Grade, $12,750 to $13,000; Exhibition Grade, $22,000 to $22,500.

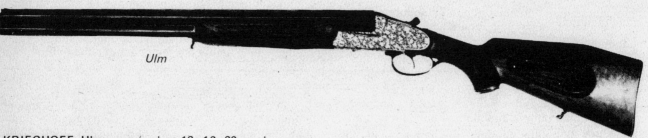

*Ulm*

**KRIEGHOFF Ulm:** over/under; 12, 16, 20-ga.; has same specs as Teck Model over/under, except has sidelocks, arabesque engraving. Introduced 1958, still in production. Used value, $2300 to $2400.

**Ulm Combo** has same specs, gauges, calibers as Teck combo except for sidelocks, arabesque engraving. Introduced 1963, still in production. Used value, $2300 to $2400.

**Ulm-Primus** over/under has same specs as Ulm over/under, except for detachable sidelocks, fancier figured walnut, higher grade engraving. Introduced 1958, still in production. Used value, $3000 to $3200.

**Ulm-Primus Combo** has same specs as Ulm combo, except for detachable sidelocks, fancier walnut, higher grade engraving. Introduced 1963, still in production. Used value, $3000 to $3200.

*Teck*

**KRIEGHOFF Teck:** over/under; 12, 16, 20-ga.; last chambered for 2¾" or 3" shells; 28" vent rib barrel; modified/full choke; box-lock action; Kersten double crossbolt; auto ejectors; double or single triggers; checkered European walnut pistol-grip stock, forend. Manufactured in West Germany. Introduced 1967, still in production. Used value, $1600 to $1700.

**Teck Combo** has same general specs as Teck over/under, except receiver is steel or dural; slit extractor or ejector for shotgun barrel; rifle barrel in .22 Hornet, .222 Remington, .222 Remington magnum, 7x57R, 7x64, 7x65R, .30-30, .300 Winchester magnum, .30/06, .308, 9.3x74R; 25" barrels; solid rib; folding leaf rear sight, post or bead front; checkered European walnut pistol-grip stock; cheekpiece, semi-beavertail forend; sling swivels. Introduced 1967, still in production. Used value, $1600 to $1700.

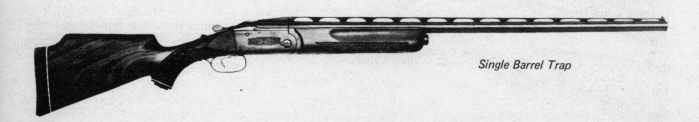

*Single Barrel Trap*

**KRIEGHOFF Single Barrel Trap:** single-shot; box-lock action; 12-ga. only; 32" or 34" full choke barrel; thumb safety; vent rib; hand-checkered Monte Carlo pistol-grip stock of European walnut, grooved beavertail forearm. Available in five grades, price depending upon grade of wood, decoration. Manufactured in West Germany. Introduced in 1970; still in production. Used values, standard grade, $1000 to $1150; Sam Remo Grade, $2250 to $2500; Monte Carlo Grade, $4500 to $4750; Crown Grade, $4750 to $5000; Super Crown Grade, $6000 to $6250.

**KRIEGHOFF Vandalia Trap:** single-barrel or over/under; box-lock action; 12-ga. only; 30", 32", 34" barrels; three-way safety; selective single trigger; ejectors; vent rib; hand-checkered European walnut pistol-grip stock, beavertail forearm. Available at additional cost with silver, gold inlays, relief engraving, fancier wood. Manufactured in West Germany. Introduced in 1973; dropped, 1976. Used value for standard model, $1250 to $1500.

---

# LEFEVER

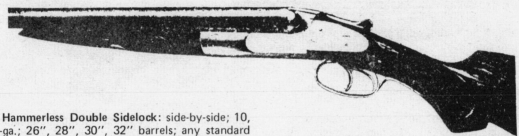

*H Grade*

**LEFEVER Hammerless Double Sidelock:** side-by-side; 10, 12, 16, 20-ga.; 26", 28", 30", 32" barrels; any standard choke combo; plain extractors or auto ejectors, depending upon model (suffix E guns, A, AA, Optimus, Thousand Dollar Grade models have auto ejectors); double or single selective triggers; DS, DSE Grade models are sans cocking indicators; hand-checkered American walnut straight grip or pistol-grip stocks, forends. Grades — 20 of them — differ in workmanship, quality of engraving, checkering, figure of wood, et al. Manufactured 1885 to 1919. Collector value. Used values, DS Grade, $400 to $425; DSE, $550 to $575; H Grade, $500 to $525; HE, $625 to $650; G Grade, $600 to $625; GE, $750 to $775; F Grade, $850 to $875; FE, $1000 to $1050; E Grade, $1100 to $1200; EE, $1200 to $1300; D Grade, $1300 to $1400; DE, $1500 to $1600; C Grade, $1600 to $1750; CE, $1750 to $1850; B Grade, $2250 to $2400; BE, $2400 to $2550; A Grade, $2750 to $3000; AA Grade, $3250 to $3500; Optimus Grade, $4250 to $4500; Thousand Dollar Grade, $8300 to $8600.

*No. 5, Grade B*

**D.M. LEFEVER Double Hammerless:** side-by-side; 12, 16, 20-ga.; any barrel length, choke combo; box-lock action; auto ejector; double or single selective triggers; hand-cehckered American walnut straight-grip or pistol-grip stock, forend. Produced in seven grades, differing primarily in workmanship, quality of wood, checkering, engraving, et al. Marketed as New Lefever. Collector value. Manufactured 1904 to 1906. Used values, O Excelsior Grade (plain extractors), $525 to $575; O Excelsior (auto ejector), $725 to $775; No. 9, F Grade, $950 to $1000; No. 8, E Grade, $1200 to $1300; No. 6, C Grade, $1600 to $1700; No. 5, B Grade, $2100 to $2250; No. 4, AA Grade, $3150 to $3300; Uncle Dan Grade, $5200 to $5300.

**D.M. LEFEVER Single-Barrel Trap:** single-shot; 12-ga.; 26", 28", 30", 32" barrels; full choke only; box-lock action; auto ejector; hand-checkered American walnut pistol-grip stock, forend. Collector value. Manufactured 1904 to 1906. Used value, $525 to $550.

*Nitro Special*

NOTE: 20-gauge 25% higher than prices shown; .410 50% higher.

**LEFEVER Nitro Special:** side-by-side double barrel; box-lock action; 12, 16, 20, .410 gauges; 26", 28", 30", 32" barrels; standard choke combos; double triggers; single non-selective trigger at added cost; plain extractors; hand-checkered American walnut pistol-grip stock, forearm. Introduced in 1921; dropped, 1948. Used values, double triggers, $225 to $275; single trigger, $300 to $350.

*Single Barrel Trap*

**LEFEVER Single Barrel Trap:** single-shot; box-lock action; hammerless; 12-ga. only; 30", 32" barrels; ejector; full choke only; vent rib; bead front sight; hand-checkered American walnut pistol-grip stock, forearm; recoil pad. Introduced about 1923; dropped, 1942. Used value, $250 to $350.

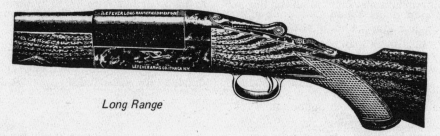

*Long Range*

**LEFEVER Long Range:** single-shot; box-lock action; hammerless; 12, 16, 20 gauges; 26", 28", 30", 32" barrels; standard chokes; bead front sight; no recoil pad; field stock; other specifications similar to those of single-barrel trap model. Introduced about 1923; dropped, 1942. Used value, $150 to $200.

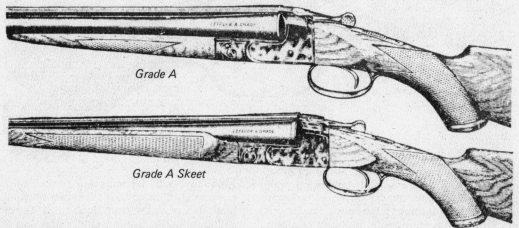

*Grade A*

*Grade A Skeet*

**LEFEVER Grade A:** side-by-side; hammerless; 12, 16, 20-ga., .410; 26", 28", 30", 32" barrels; standard choke combos; box-lock action; plain extractors or auto ejectors; double, single triggers; hand-checkered American walnut pistol-grip stock, forend. Manufactured in Ithaca plant, 1934 to 1942. Used value, plain extractors, double triggers, $325 to $350; auto ejector, double triggers, $400 to $425; plain extractors, single trigger, $400 to $425; auto ejectors, single triggers, $450 to $500.

**Grade A Skeet** model has same specs as standard Grade A, except for integral auto ejector, single trigger, 26" barrels, skeet chokes, beavertail forend. Manufactured 1934 to 1942. Used value, $525 to $550.

# MARLIN

**MARLIN Model 1898:** slide action; 12-ga.; 5-rd. tubular magazine; 26", 28", 30", 32" barrels; standard chokes; takedown; visible hammer; American walnut pistol-grip stock, grooved slide handle; checkering on higher grades.

**MARLIN Model 16:** slide action; 16-ga.; 5-rd. tubular magazine; 26", 28" barrels, standard chokes; takedown; American walnut pistol-grip stock, grooved slide handle. Manufactured in four grades, differing in quality of wood;

Grades differ in quality of wood, amount of engraving. Marlin's first shotgun was manufactured 1898 to 1905. Collector value. Used values, Grade A, $375 to $400; Grade B, $450 to $475; Grade C, $625 to $650; Grade D, $1250 to $1300.

engraving and checkering on Grades C, D; visible hammer. Manufactured 1904 to 1910. Used values, Grade A, $275 to $300; Grade B, $325 to $350; Grade C, $475 to $500; Grade D, $950 to $1000.

*Model 17 Standard*

**MARLIN Model 17:** slide action; 12-ga.; 5-rd. tubular magazine; 30", 32" barrels; full choke only; solid frame; uncheckered American walnut straight-grip stock, grooved slide handle, visible hammer. Collector value. Used value, $225 to $250.

**Model 17 Riot Gun** has same specs as standard model,

except for 20" barrel, cylinder bore. Manufactured 1906 to 1908. Some collector interest. Used value, $210 to $225.

**Model 17 Brush** model has same specs as standard version, except for 26" barrel, cylinder bore. Manufactured 1906 to 1908. Some collector value. Used value, $230 to $240.

**MARLIN Model 19:** slide action; 12-ga.; 5-rd. tubular magazine; has same general specs as Model 1898, except is lighter in weight, has two extractors, matted sighting groove on top of receiver; visible hammer. Made in four grades,

differing in quality of workmanship and wood, amount of engraving. Manufactured 1906 to 1907. Collector value. Used values, Grade A, $250 to $265; Grade B, $325 to $350; Grade C, $425 to $450; Grade D, $925 to $950.

**MARLIN Model 21 Trap:** slide action; 12-ga.; has the same general specifications as Model 19, except for straight-grip stock; visible hammer. Made in four grades, differing in

workmanship, quality of wood, engraving. Manufactured 1907 to 1909. Collector interest. Used values, Grade A, $250 to $265; Grade B, $325 to $350; Grade C, $425 to $450; Grade D, $925 to $950.

**MARLIN Model 24:** slide action; 12-ga.; has same general specs as Model 19, but features solid matted rib attached to frame, automatic recoil safety lock, improved takedown.

Made in four grades. Manufactured 1908 to 1915. Used values, Grade A, $275 to $300; Grade B, $350 to $375; Grade C, $450 to $500; Grade D, $950 to $1000.

**MARLIN Model 26:** slide action; 12-ga.; has same general specs as Model 24, Grade A, except for straight-grip stock, solid frame, 30", 32" full choke barrel; visible hammer. Manufactured 1909 to 1915. Used value, $225 to $235.

**Model 26 Riot** model has same specs as standard Model

26, except for 20" barrel, cylinder bore. Manufactured 1909 to 1915. Used value, $215 to $225.

**Model 26 Brush** model has same specs as standard version except for 26" cylinder-bore barrel. Manufactured 1909 to 1915. Used value, $240 to $250.

*Model 30 Grade D*

**MARLIN Model 30:** slide action; has same general specs as Model 16, except for improved takedown, auto recoil safety lock, solid matted rib on frame; visible hammer. Manufactured in four grades, depending upon quality of wood, amount and quality of engraving. Manufactured

1910 to 1915. Used values, Grade A, $275 to $300; Grade B, $325 to $350; Grade C, $440 to $460; Grade D, $950 to $980.

**Model 30 Field** has same specs as Grade B, except for 25" barrel, modified choke, straight-grip stock. Manufactured 1913 to 1914. Used value, $325 to $350.

*Model 28B*

**MARLIN Model 28:** slide action; 12-ga.; 5-rd. tubular magazine; 26", 28", 30", 32" barrels, standard chokes; takedown; hammerless; made in four grades; all have matted barrel top, except for 28D which has solid matted rib. Differences in grades are quality of wood, amount of engraving on 28C, 28D. Three grades manufactured 1913 to 1915; Model 28A manufactured 1913 to 1922. Used values, Model 28A, $275 to $300; 28B, $375 to $400; 28C, $550 to $600; 28D, $1000 to $1100.

**Model 28T Trap** has same specs as Model 28A, except for 30" barrel, matted rib; full choke; hand-checkered straight-grip walnut stock, high fluted comb; fancier wood. Manufactured 1915. Used value, $450 to $475.

**Model 28TS** has same specs as Model 28T, except for stock of plainer walnut, matted-top barrel instead of rib. Manufactured 1915. Used value, $265 to $275.

**MARLIN Model 31A:** slide action; 16, 20-ga.; 25", 26", 28" barrel; hammerless; scaled-down version of Model 28; matted top barrel; standard chokes; uncheckered American walnut pistol-grip stock, grooved slide handle. Manufactured 1915 to 1922. Used value, $265 to $275.

**Model 31B** has same general specs as 31A, except for hand-checkered stock. Manufactured 1915 to 1917. Used value, $375 to $390.

**Model 31C** has same specs as Model 31B, except for improved wood, better checkering quality. Manufactured 1915 to 1917. Used value, $525 to $550.

**Model 31D** has same specs as Model 31C, except for improved wood, straight-grip stock optional. Manufactured 1915 to 1917. Used value, $950 to $1050.

**Model 31F** has same specs as Model 31B, except for 25" barrel, modified choke, optional straight or pistol-grip stock. Manufactured 1915 to 1917. Used value, $365 to $375.

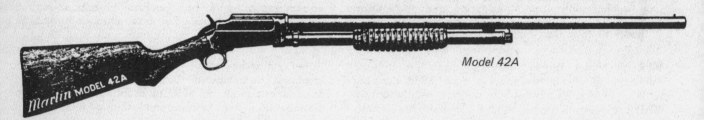

*Model 42A*

**MARLIN Model 42A:** slide-action repeater; takedown; 12-ga. only; 26" cylinder bore, 28" modified, 30" or 32" full choke; visible hammer; 5-rd. magazine; uncheckered American walnut pistol-grip stock, grooved slide handle; bead front sight. Introduced in 1922; dropped, 1934. Used value, $150 to $165.

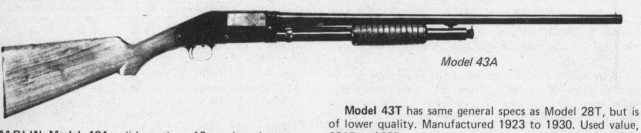

*Model 43A*

**MARLIN Model 43A:** slide action; 12-ga.; has the same general specifications as Model 28, but lower in overall quality. Manufactured 1923 to 1930. Used value, $190 to $200.

**Model 43T** has same general specs as Model 28T, but is of lower quality. Manufactured 1923 to 1930. Used value, $315 to $325.

**Model 43TS** has same specs as Model 28TS, but is of lower quality. Manufactured 1923 to 1930. Used value, $200 to $215.

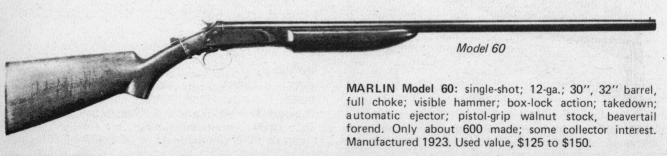

*Model 60*

**MARLIN Model 60:** single-shot; 12-ga.; 30", 32" barrel, full choke; visible hammer; box-lock action; takedown; automatic ejector; pistol-grip walnut stock, beavertail forend. Only about 600 made; some collector interest. Manufactured 1923. Used value, $125 to $150.

**MARLIN Model 44A:** slide action; 20-ga.; hammerless; has same general specs as Model 31A, except is of slightly lower quality. Manufactured 1923 to 1935. Used value, $215 to $225.

**MARLIN Model 49:** slide action repeater; has same general specs as Model 42A, except not as well or expensively made. Used by Marlin as a premium, with purchase of four

**Model 44S** has same specs as Model 44A, except for hand-checkered American walnut stock; stock and slide handle of better quality wood. Manufactured 1932 to 1935. Used value, $315 to $325.

shares of corporate stock; less than 3000 made. Some collector value. Manufactured 1925 to 1928. Used value, $190 to $200.

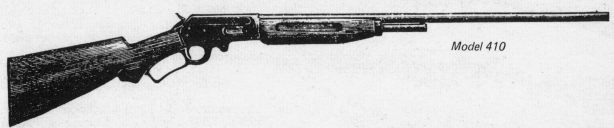

*Model 410*

**MARLIN Model 410:** lever-action; .410, 2½" shell; 4-rd. tubular magazine; 22", 26" barrels; full choke; solid frame;

visible hammer; unchecked American walnut pistol-grip stock, grooved beavertail forend. Manufactured 1929 to 1932. Collector interest. Used value, $325 to $350.

*Model 53*

**MARLIN Model 53:** slide action; 12-ga.; has same general specs as Model 43A, except for redesigned tubular

**MARLIN Model 63A:** slide action; 12-ga.; has same general specifications as Model 43A, replacing it in line. Manufactured 1931 to 1935. Used value, $190 to $200.

**Model 63T** has same specs as Model 43T. Manufactured

magazine, slide handle. Manufactured 1929 to 1930. Used value, $165 to $175.

1931 to 1935. Used value, $315 to $325.

**Model 63TS Trap Special** has same specs as Model 63T, except that stock dimensions were to special order. Manufactured 1931 to 1935. Used value, $320 to $335.

*Model 90-DT*

Introduced in 1937; dropped during WWII. Used values, double trigger style, $325 to $350; single trigger, $425 to $450.

**Model 90-DT** is post-WWII version of Model 90 with double triggers, no rib between barrels, no recoil pad. Introduced in 1949; dropped, 1958. Used value, $325 to $350.

**Model 90-ST** is post-war single nonselective trigger version; no rib between barrels, no recoil pad. Introduced in 1949; dropped, 1958. Used value, $425 to $450.

**MARLIN Model 90:** standard over/under; hammerless; boxlock action; 12, 16, 20, .410 gauges; 28", 30" barrels; improved/modified, modified/full choke combos; full-length rib between barrels; double triggers; single nonselective trigger at extra cost; hand-checkered American walnut pistol-grip stock, forearm; recoil pad; bead front sight.

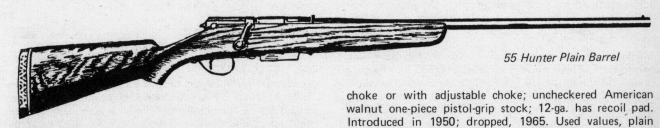

*55 Hunter Plain Barrel*

choke or with adjustable choke; unchecked American walnut one-piece pistol-grip stock; 12-ga. has recoil pad. Introduced in 1950; dropped, 1965. Used values, plain barrel, $55 to $65; adjustable choke, $65 to $70.

**Model 55-G** was marketed as Marlin-Glenfield model.

**MARLIN Model 55 Hunter:** bolt-action; takedown; 12, 16, 20 gauges; 28" barrel in 12, 16 gauges, 26" in 20; full

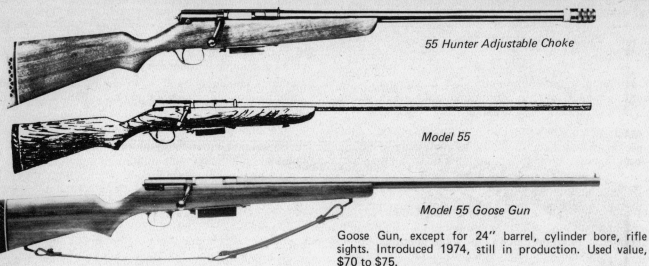

*55 Hunter Adjustable Choke*

*Model 55*

*Model 55 Goose Gun*

Has same specifications as Model 55, except for walnut-finished hardwood stock. Used values, plain barrel, $55 to $60; with adjustable choke, $65 to $70.

**Model 55 Swamp Gun** has same specifications as Model 55 Hunter except for 20½" barrel, chambered for 3" 12-ga. magnum shell; adjustable choke; sling swivels. Introduced in 1963; dropped, 1965. Used value, $75 to $85.

**Model 55S Slug** version has same specs as Model 55

Goose Gun, except for 24" barrel, cylinder bore, rifle sights. Introduced 1974, still in production. Used value, $70 to $75.

**Model 55 Goose Gun** bolt-action repeater; takedown; 12-ga. only; 36" barrel; full choke only; 2-rd. detachable clip magazine; thumb safety; unchecked one-piece walnut pistol-grip stock; recoil pad; sling swivels; leather carrying strap; double extractors; tapped for receiver sights. Introduced in 1964; still in production. Used value, $85 to $95.

**Model 5510** has same general specs as Model 55, except chambered for 10-ga. 3½" magnum shell; 34" heavy barrel; full choke. Introduced 1976, still in production. Used value, $115 to $125.

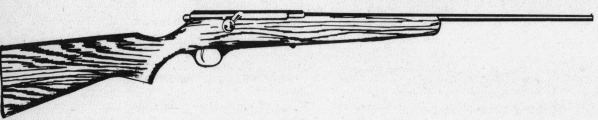

**MARLIN Model 59 Olympic:** single-shot, bolt-action; takedown; .410 only; 2½" or 3" shells; 24" barrel; full choke only; bead front sight; self-cocking bolt; automatic thumb

safety; unchecked one-piece walnut pistol-grip stock; also available with Junior stock with 12" length of pull. Introduced in 1960; dropped, 1962. Used value, $75 to $85.

**MARLIN-Glenfield Model 60-G:** single-shot, bolt-action; takedown; .410 only; has exactly the same specifications as

Model 59, except for walnut-finished hardwood stock. Introduced in 1961; dropped, 1962. Used value, $75 to $85.

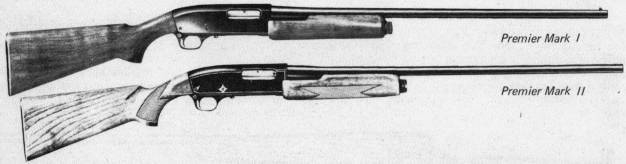

*Premier Mark I*

*Premier Mark II*

**MARLIN Premier Mark I:** slide-action repeater; takedown; hammerless; 12-ga. only; 3-rd. magazine; 26" improved or skeet, 28" modified, 30" full choke barrels; side ejection; cross-bolt safety; French walnut pistol-grip stock, forearm; bead front sight. Introduced in 1961; dropped, 1963. Used value, $115 to $125.

**Premier Mark II** has the same specifications as Premier Mark I, except for scroll-engraved receiver, checkered pistol

grip, forearm. Introduced in 1961; dropped, 1963. Used value, $135 to $155.

**Premier Mark IV** has the same specifications as Premier Mark II, except for full coverage engraved receiver, engraved trigger guard, fine checkering, better wood, pistol-grip cap, vent rib at added cost. Introduced in 1961; dropped, 1963. Used values, plain barrel, $200 to $225; vent rib, $235 to $250.

*Model 50*

**MARLIN Model 50:** bolt-action repeater; takedown; 12, 20 gauges; 28″ barrel in 12-ga., 26″ in 20-ga.; 12-ga. has recoil pad; other specifications are the same as Goose Gun, except 12-ga. was available with adjustable choke. Introduced in 1967; dropped, 1975. Used values, plain barrel, $75 to $85; with adjustable choke, $85 to $95.

*Standard 120 Magnum*

**MARLIN Model 120 Magnum:** slide action; hammerless; 12-ga.; 2¾″ or 3″ chamber, 26″ improved cylinder barrel, 28″ modified, 30″ full choke; vent rib; checkered walnut pistol-grip stock, semi-beavertail forearm; slide release button; cross-bolt safety; interchangeable barrels; side ejection. Introduced in 1974; still in production. Used value, $135 to $150.

**Model 120 Trap** has same basic specifications as 120 Magnum, except for hand-checkered Monte Carlo stock, full forearm; 30″ full or modified trap choke. Introduced in 1974; still in production. Used value, $185 to $195.

# MAUSER-BAUER

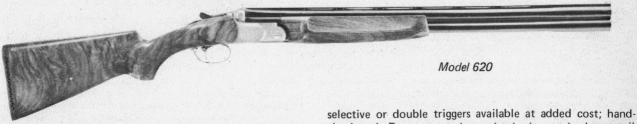

*Model 620*

**MAUSER-BAUER Model 620:** over/under; Greener cross-bolt action; 12 ga.; 28″ barrels, modified/full; improved/modified, skeet/skeet, 30″, full/modified; single nonselective adjustable triggers; vent rib, automatic ejectors; selective or double triggers available at added cost; hand-checkered European walnut pistol-grip stock, beavertail forearm; recoil pad. Produced in Germany by Mauser. Introduced in 1972; dropped, 1974. Used values, standard model, $600 to $625; single-selective trigger, $675 to $700; double triggers; $675 to $700.

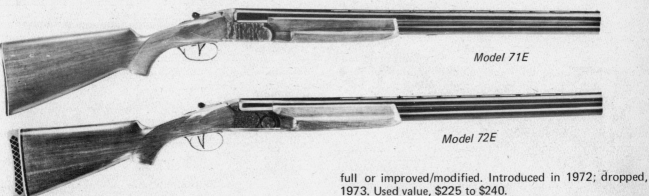

*Model 71E*

*Model 72E*

**MAUSER-BAUER Model 71E:** over/under field model; has the same general specifications as the Model 620 except for double triggers only; no recoil pad; 28″ barrels, modified/full or improved/modified. Introduced in 1972; dropped, 1973. Used value, $225 to $240.

**Model 72E** has the same general specifications as Model 71E, except for wider rib, engraved receiver. Trap version has 30″ trap/trap bored barrel; skeet has 28″ full/modified. Introduced in 1972; dropped, 1973. Used value, $300 to $325.

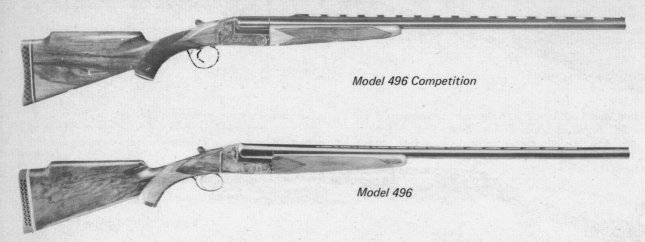

*Model 496 Competition*

*Model 496*

**MAUSER-BAUER Model 496:** single-barrel trap model; single-shot; Greener crossbolt box-lock action; 12 ga; 32'' modified; 34'' full choke barrel; double underlocking blocks; matted vent rib; color case-hardened action; scroll engraving; hand-checkered European walnut Monte Carlo stock, forearm; automatic ejector, auto safety; recoil pad.

Introduced in 1972; dropped, 1974. Used value, $320 to $345.

**Model 496 Competition Grade** has same general specifications as standard model except for high ramp rib; front, middle sight beads; hand finishing on wood and metal parts. Introduced in 1973; dropped, 1974. Used value, $450 to $475.

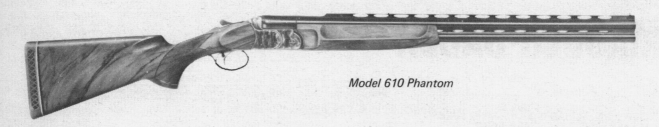

*Model 610 Phantom*

**MAUSER-BAUER Model 610 Phantom:** over/under; 12 ga.; 30'', 32'' barrels; standard choke combinations; raised rib; vent rib between barrels for heat reduction; color case-hardened action; coil springs throughout working parts; hand-checkered European walnut stock, forearm; recoil pad. Introduced in 1973; dropped, 1974. Used value, $575

to $600.

**Model 610 Skeet** version has same general specifications as standard Model 610 except has set of Purbaugh tubes to convert gun for all-gauge competition. Tubes convert to 20, 28, .410 gauges. Introduced in 1973; dropped, 1974. Used value, $800 to $825.

*Model 580*

**MAUSER-BAUER Model 580:** advertised as St. Vincent model; side-by-side; side-lock Holland & Holland action; 12 ga.; 28'', 30'', 32'' barrels; standard choke combos; split

sear levers; coil hammer springs; single or double triggers; scroll engraved receiver; hand-checkered European walnut straight stock, forearm. Introduced in 1973; dropped, 1974. Used value, $700 to $725.

# MERKEL

**MERKEL Model 100:** over/under; hammerless; box-lock action; 12, 16, 20 gauges; standard barrel lengths, choke combos; Greener crossbolt safety; double triggers; plain extractors; plain barrel; ribbed barrel at added cost; hand-checkered European walnut stock, forearm; pistol-grip and cheekpiece or straight English type. Manufactured in Germany prior to World War II. Used values, plain barrel, $800 to $1000; ribbed barrel, $1000 to $1250.

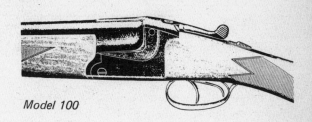

*Model 100*

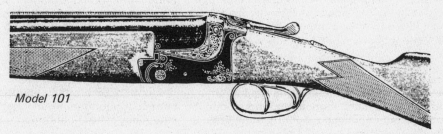

*Model 101*

**MERKEL Model 101:** over/under; hammerless; box-lock action; has the same general specifications as Model 100 except for English engraving motif, standard ribbed barrel, separate extractors. Manufactured in Germany prior to World War II. Used value, $1000 to $1250.

Model 101E has the same specifications as Model 101 except for ejectors. Used value, $1250 to $1350.

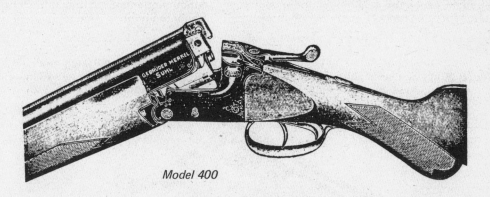

*Model 400*

**MERKEL Model 400:** over/under; hammerless; box-lock action; has the same general specifications as Model 101 except for Arabesque engraving on receiver, Kersten double crossbolt, separate extractors. Manufactured in Germany prior to World War II. Used value, $1000 to $1250.

Model 400E has the same specifications as Model 400 except for ejectors. Used value, $1250 to $1350.

**MERKEL Model 401:** over/under; hammerless; box-lock action; has the same general specifications as Model 400 except for finer overall workmanship, hunting scene engraving on receiver. Manufactured in Germany prior to World War II. Used value, $1250 to $1500.

Model 401E has the same general specifications as Model 400 except for Merkel ejectors. Used value, $1500 to $1750.

**MERKEL Model 200:** over/under; hammerless; box-lock action; 12, 16, 20, 24, 28, 32 gauges; Kersten double crossbolt; scalloped frame; Arabesque engraving; separate extractors; double triggers; standard barrel lengths, choke combinations; ribbed barrels; hand-checkered European walnut stock, forearm; pistol-grip and cheekpiece or straight English style. Manufactured in Germany prior to World War II. Used value, $1000 to $1250.

Model 200E has the same general specifications as Model 200 except for ejectors; double, single or single selective trigger. Introduced prior to World War II; still in production; 24, 28, 32 gauges dropped during WW II. Importation dropped by Champlin, 1979; J.J. Jenkins currently imports. Used values, double triggers, $1150 to $1250; single trigger, $1250 to $1350; single selective trigger, $1350 to $1500.

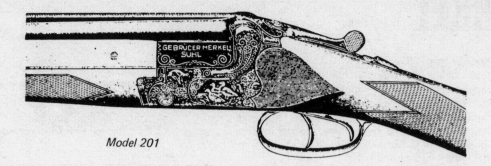

*Model 201*

**MERKEL Model 201:** over/under; hammerless; box-lock action; has the same general specifications as Model 200 except for better engraving, wood, checkering, overall quality. Manufactured in Germany prior to World War II. Used value, $1250 to $1350.

**MERKEL Model 202:** over/under; hammerless; box-lock action; has the same general specifications as Model 201 except for better engraving, dummy side plates, finer wood, checkering. Manufactured in Germany prior to World War

**MERKEL Model 203:** over/under; hammerless; hand-detachable side locks; 12, 16, 20 gauges; ribbed barrels in standard lengths, choke combos; Kersten double crossbolt; automatic ejectors; Arabesque or hunting scene engraving; hand-checkered European walnut stock, forearm; pistol-

**MERKEL Model 204E:** over/under; hammerless; 12, 16, 20 gauges; has the same general specifications as Model 203E

**Model 201E** has the same specifications as Model 201 except for ejectors; double, single or single selective trigger. Still in production. Currently imported by J.J. Jenkins. Used values, double triggers, $1350 to $1450; single trigger, $1450 to $1550; single selective trigger, $1550 to $1650.

II. Used value, $1500 to $1650.
**Model 202E** has the same specifications as Model 202 except for ejectors. Manufactured prior to World War II. Used value, $1650 to $1750.

grip, cheekpiece or straight English style. Introduced in Germany prior to World War II. Currently imported by J.J. Jenkins. Used values, double triggers, $1500 to $1650; single trigger, $1650 to $1750; single selective trigger, $1750 to $1850.

except for fine English-style engraving, double triggers only, Merkel side locks. Manufactured in Germany prior to World War II. Used value, $2500 to $2750.

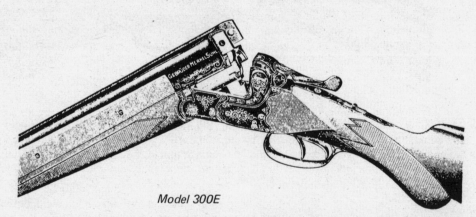

*Model 300E*

**MERKEL Model 300:** over/under; hammerless; Merkel-Anson box-lock; 12, 16, 20, 24, 28, 32 gauges; standard barrel lengths, choke combos; Kersten double crossbolt; two underlugs; scalloped frame; Arabesque or hunting scene engraving; separate extractors; ribbed barrels; hand-

**MERKEL Model 301:** over/under; hammerless; Merkel-Anson box-lock action; has the same general specifications as Model 300 except for better engraving, wood, checker-

checkered European walnut pistol-grip, cheekpiece or straight English style stock. Manufactured in Germany prior to World War II. Use;d value, $1500 to $1600.
**Model 300E** has the same general specifications as Model 300 except for automatic ejectors. Used value, $1650 to $1750.

ing. Manufactured in Germany prior to World War II. Used value, $1750 to $1850.
**Model 301E** has the same specifications as Model 301 except for automatic ejectors. Used value, $1850 to $1950.

**MERKEL Model 302:** over/under; hammerless; has the same general specifications as Model 301E except for dummy side plates. Manufactured in Germany prior to World War II. Used value, $2150 to $2250.

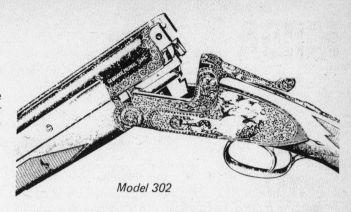
*Model 302*

**MERKEL Model 303E:** over/under; hammerless; Holland & Holland-type hand-detachable side locks; Kersten crossbolt, double underlugs, automatic ejectors. Has same general

design specifications as Model 203E but is of better quality throughout. Introduced prior to World War II; still in production. Currently imported by J.J. Jenkins. Used value, $3250 to $3550.

**MERKEL Model 304E:** over/under; hammerless; Holland & Holland-type hand-detachable side locks; has virtually the same specifications as 303E except for better workmanship and quality. Introduced in Germany prior to World War II. Still in production, but not imported at this time. Used value, $4750 to $5000.

*Model 304E*

**MERKEL Model 130:** side-by-side; hammerless; box-lock action; 12, 16, 20, 28, .410 gauges; standard barrel lengths, choke combos; Anson & Deeley-type action; side plates; double triggers; automatic ejectors; elaborate Arabesque or hunting scene engraving; hand-checkered European walnut stock, forearm; pistol-grip, cheekpiece or straight English style. Manufactured in Germany prior to World War II. Used value, $2850 to $3000.

*Model 130*

**MERKEL Model 127:** side-by-side; hammerless; Holland & Holland-type action; hand-detachable side locks; 12, 16, 20, 28, .410 gauges; standard barrel lengths, choke combos; elaborately engraved with Arabesque or hunting scene; hand-checkered European walnut stock, forearm; pistol-grip, cheekpiece or straight English style. Manufactured in Germany prior to World War II. Used value, $5000 to $5250.

*Model 127*

**MERKEL Model 475:** side-by-side; hammerless; side locks; 12, 16, 20 gauges; 3'' chamber available; all standard barrel lengths, choke combos; double hook bolting; Greener-type breech; double, single or single selective trigger; cocking indicators; English Arabesque engraving; hand-checkered

European walnut stock, forearm; pistol-grip, cheekpiece or straight English style. Introduced prior to World War II; still in production. Currently imported by Champlin Firearms. Used values, double triggers, $700 to $725; single trigger, $725 to $750; single selective trigger, $775 to $800.

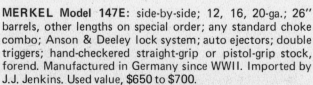
*Model 147E*

**MERKEL Model 147E:** side-by-side; 12, 16, 20-ga.; 26'' barrels, other lengths on special order; any standard choke combo; Anson & Deeley lock system; auto ejectors; double triggers; hand-checkered straight-grip or pistol-grip stock, forend. Manufactured in Germany since WWII. Imported by J.J. Jenkins. Used value, $650 to $700.

**Model 147S** has same specs as Model 147E, except for side-lock action, engraved hunting scene on action.

Manufactured since WWII. Used value, $1350 to $1400.

**Model 47S** has same specs as Model 147S, except for less elaborate engraving pattern. Manufactured since WWII. Used value, $1050 to $1100.

# MIIDA

*Model 612*

**MIIDA Model 612:** over/under; 12-ga.; 26" improved cylinder/modified, 28" modified/full barrels; box-lock action; auto ejectors; single selective trigger; engraving; checkered walnut pistol-grip stock, forearm. Manufactured in Japan, imported by Marubeni America Corp., 1972 to 1974. Used value, $400 to $425.

*Model 2100*

**MIIDA Model 2100 Skeet:** over/under; 12-ga.; 27" vent rib barrels; skeet choke; selective single trigger; box-lock action; auto ejectors; skeet stock, forearm of select walnut; 50% of frame engraved. Imported 1972 to 1974. Used value, $475 to $500.

**MIIDA Model 2200T Trap:** over/under; 12-ga.; 29¾" improved modified/full choke barrels; vent rib; checkered fancy walnut trap stock, semi-beavertail forearm; recoil pad; 60% engraving coverage on frame. Imported 1972 to 1974. Used value, $525 to $550.

**Model 2200S Skeet** has same general specs as 2200T, except for 27" skeet-choked barrel; skeet stock, no recoil pad. Imported 1972 to 1974. Used value, $525 to $550.

*Model 2300*

**MIIDA Model 2300T Trap:** has the same general specs as Model 2200T, except for 70% coverage of frame with engraving. Imported 1972 to 1974. Used value, $575 to $600.

**Model 2300S Skeet** has same specs as Model 2200S, except for 70% engraving coverage of frame. Imported 1972 to 1974. Used value, $575 to $600.

*Grandee GRT*

**MIIDA Grandee GRT Trap:** over/under; 12-ga.; 29" full choke barrels; box-lock action, sideplates; gold inlaid; fully engraved frame, breech ends of barrels, locking lever, trigger guard; single selective trigger; auto ejectors; wide vent rib; extra fancy walnut trap stock, semi-beavertail forearm; recoil pad. Imported 1972 to 1974. Used value, $1225 to $1250.

**Model GRS Skeet** has same general specs as GRT except for 27" skeet-choked barrels, skeet stock, no recoil pad. Imported 1972 to 1974. Used value, $1225 to $1250.

# MOSSBERG

*Model 83D*

**MOSSBERG Model 83D:** bolt-action; takedown; .410-ga. only; 23″ barrel; interchangeable modified, full choke tubes; 2-rd. fixed top loading magazine; unchecked one-piece finger-grooved pistol-grip stock. Introduced in 1940; replaced in 1947 by Model 183D. Used value, $60 to $65.

*Model 85D*

**MOSSBERG Model 85D:** bolt-action; takedown; 20-ga. only; 25″ barrel, with interchangeable choke tubes for full, modified, improved cylinder; 2-rd. detachable box magazine; unchecked one-piece finger-grooved pistol grip stock, black plastic butt plate. Introduced in 1940; replaced in 1947 by Model 185D. Used value, $60 to $65.

*Model 183K*

**MOSSBERG Model 183D:** bolt-action; takedown; .410-ga. only; 24″ barrel; all other specifications are the same as Model 83D. Introduced in 1947; dropped, 1971. Used value, $60 to $65.

**Model 183K** has the same specifications as Model 183D, except for C-Lect-Choke instead of interchangeable tubes. Introduced in 1953; still in production. Used value, $65 to $70.

*Model 185K*

**MOSSBERG Model 185D:** bolt-action; takedown; 20-ga. only; has same specifications as Model 85D, except for 26″ barrel, full, improved cylinder choke tubes. Introduced in 1947; dropped, 1971. Used value, $60 to $65.

**Model 185K** has the same specifications as Model 185D except for variable C-Lect-Choke replacing interchangeable tubes. Introduced in 1950; dropped, 1963. Used value, $70 to $75.

*Model 190 D*

**MOSSBERG Model 190D:** bolt-action; takedown; 16-ga. only; 26" barrel; other specifications are identical to those of Model 185D, including full, improved cylinder choke tubes. Introduced in 1955; dropped, 1971. Used value, $60 to $65.

**Model 190K** has the same general specifications as Model 185K except for 16-ga. chambering. Introduced in 1956; dropped, 1963. Used value, $70 to $75.

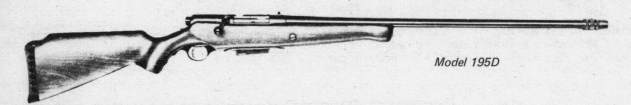

*Model 195D*

**MOSSBERG Model 195D:** bolt-action; takedown; 12-ga. only; 26" barrel; interchangeable chokes; other specifications are the same as those of Model 185D. Introduced in 1955; dropped, 1971. Used value, $60 to $65.

**Model 195K** has the same general specifications as the Model 185K except is in 12-ga. only; C-Lect-Choke. Introduced in 1956; dropped, 1963. Used value, $70 to $75.

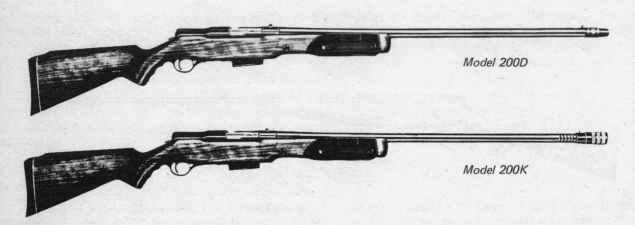

*Model 200D*

*Model 200K*

**MOSSBERG Model 200D:** slide action; 12-ga. only; 28" barrel; interchangeable choke tubes; 3-rd. detachable box magazine; uncheckered, walnut-finished hardwood, pistol-grip stock with grooved forearm; black nylon slide handle; recoil pad. Introduced in 1955; dropped, 1959. Used value, $65 to $70.

**Model 200K** has the same specifications as Model 200D except for substitution of C-Lect-Choke. Introduced in 1955; dropped, 1959. Used value, $75 to $85.

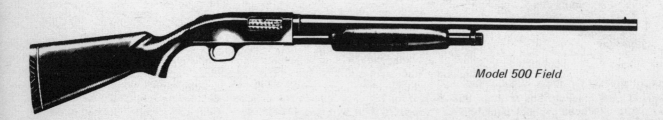

*Model 500 Field*

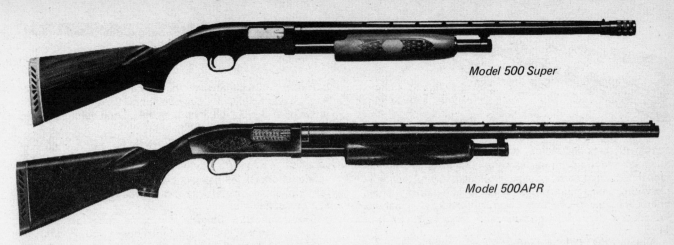

Model 500 Super

Model 500APR

MOSSBERG Model 500 Field Grade: slide action; hammerless; takedown; 12, 16, 20 gauges; 24" Slugster barrel with rifle sights in 12-ga. only, 26" improved or with adjustable C-Lect-Choke; 28" modified/full; 30" full choke in 12-ga. only; 6-rd. tube magazine; 3-shot plug furnished; uncheckered American walnut pistol-grip stock; grooved slide handle; recoil pad. Introduced in 1961; still in production. Used values, standard barrel, $115 to $120; Slugster barrel, $120 to $130; C-Lect-Choke barrel, $125 to $135; heavy magnum barrel, $135 to $145.

Model 500 Super Grade has the same basic specifications as standard Model 500 except for checkered pistol grip, slide handle; vent rib barrel. Introduced in 1961; still in production. Used values, standard barrel, $145 to $150;

MOSSBERG Model 385K: bolt-action; takedown; 20-ga. only; 26" barrel; C-Lect-Choke; walnut-finished hardwood

MOSSBERG Model 390K: bolt-action; takedown; 16-ga. only; 28" barrel; other specifications are the same as those

C-Lect-Choke, $150 to $155; heavy magnum barrel, $150 to $160.

Model 500E has the same general specifications as standard Model 500 but is chambered for .410 only; 26" barrel; full, modified, improved chokes; tube magazine holds 6 standard rds., 5 magnum rds.; uncheckered walnut pistol-grip stock, grooved forearm, fluted comb; recoil pad. Used values, standard barrel, $125 to $135; skeet barrel with vent rib, checkering, $175 to $200.

Model 500APR Pigeon Grade trap gun has the same specifications as standard Model 500 except for vent rib 30" barrel; full choke only; checkered walnut Monte Carlo stock, beavertail slide handle; recoil pad. Introduced in 1968; still in production. Used value, $150 to $160.

Monte Carlo stock; 2-rd. detachable clip magazine; recoil pad. Introduced in 1963; still in production. Used value, $60 to $65.

of Model 385K. Introduced in 1963; still in production. Used value, $60 to $65.

Model 395K

MOSSBERG Model 395K: bolt-action; takedown; 12-ga. only; 28" barrel; other specifications are the same as those

of Model 385K. Introduced in 1963; still in production. Used value, $60 to $65.

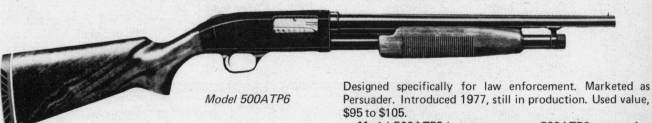

Model 500ATP6

MOSSBERG Model 500ATP6 has same general specs as pre-1977 Model 500 field grade, except 12-ga. only; 18½", 20" barrel; cylinder bore; 6-rd. magazine; uncheckered pistol-grip stock, grooved slide handle; shotgun or rifle sights.

Designed specifically for law enforcement. Marketed as Persuader. Introduced 1977, still in production. Used value, $95 to $105.

Model 500ATP8 has same specs as 500ATP6, except for 8-rd. magazine. Introduced 1977, still in production. Used value, $100 to $110.

Model 500TP8-SP has same specs as 500ATP8, except for bayonet lug, Parkerized finish. Introduced 1977, still in production. Used value, $115 to $125.

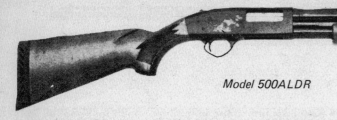

Model 500ALDR

MOSSBERG Model 500ALD: pump-action; 12-ga.; 28'', 30'', 32'' plain barrel; has same general specs as pre-1977 Model 500 field version, except for game scene etched in receiver; also available with Accu-choke, three interchangeable choke tubes; restyled stock, slide handle. Introduced 1977, still in production. Used value, $110 to $115.

Model 500ALDR has same specs as 500ALD, except for vent rib. Introduced 1977, still in production. Used value, $120 to $125.

Model 500ALMR has same specs as 500ALDR, except designated as Heavy Duck Model, chambered for 12-ga. magnum shells. Introduced 1977, still in production. Used value, $125 to $135.

Model 500ALS Slugster has same specs as Model 500 ALD except for 24'' cylinder bore barrel, rifle sights. Introduced 1977, still in production. Used value, $115 to $125.

Model 500CLD has same specs as Model 500ALD, except in 20-ga. Introduced 1977, still in production. Used value, $105 to $110.

Model 500CLDR has same specs as 500CLD, except for vent rib. Introduced 1977, still in production. Used value, $120 to $125.

Model 500CLS Slugster has same specs as 500ALS Slugster, except is 20-ga. Introduced 1977, still in production. Used value, $115 to $125.

Model 500EL has same general specs as 500ALD, except made as .410. Introduced 1977, still in production. Used value, $105 to $110.

Model 500ELR has same specs as Model 500EL, except for vent rib. Introduced 1977, still in production. Used value, $115 to $125.

# NEW HAVEN

Model 290

NEW HAVEN Model 290: bolt-action; takedown; 16-ga.; 28'' barrel; detachable full choke tube; other choke tubes available at added cost; 2-rd. detachable clip; thumb safety; oil-finished American walnut Monte Carlo-style pistol-grip stock. Manufactured by Mossberg. Introduced in 1960; dropped, 1965. Used value, $40 to $45.

NEW HAVEN Model 295: bolt-action; takedown; 12-ga.; other specifications are the same as those of Model 290.

Introduced in 1960; dropped, 1965. Used value, $40 to $45.

NEW HAVEN Model 283: bolt-action; takedown; .410-ga.; 25'' barrel; 3'' chamber. Other specifications are the same

as those of Model 290. Introduced in 1960; dropped, 1965. Used value, $40 to $50.

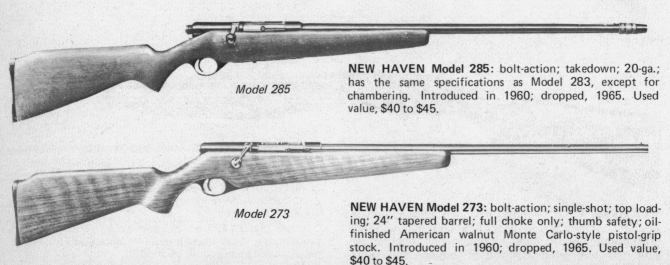

Model 285

NEW HAVEN Model 285: bolt-action; takedown; 20-ga.; has the same specifications as Model 283, except for chambering. Introduced in 1960; dropped, 1965. Used value, $40 to $45.

Model 273

NEW HAVEN Model 273: bolt-action; single-shot; top loading; 24'' tapered barrel; full choke only; thumb safety; oil-finished American walnut Monte Carlo-style pistol-grip stock. Introduced in 1960; dropped, 1965. Used value, $40 to $45.

**NEW HAVEN Model 600:** slide action; takedown; 12-ga.; 26" improved cylinder barrel, 28" full or modified, 30" full choke; 6-rd. magazine; choice of standard or 3" magnum barrel; safety on top of receiver; unchecked walnut pistol-grip stock, extension slide handle. Same general design as Mossberg Model 500. Introduced in 1962; dropped, 1965. Used value, $70 to $75.

**Model 600K** has the same specifications as Model 600, except for C-Lect-Choke feature. Used value, $70 to $80.

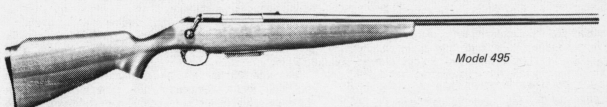

*Model 495*

**NEW HAVEN Model 495:** bolt-action; takedown; 12-ga.; 28" full choke barrel; 2-rd. detachable clip; thumb safety; Monte Carlo-design, unchecked, walnut-finished hard-wood pistol-grip stock. Introduced in 1964; dropped, 1965. Used value, $45 to $50.

# NOBLE

**NOBLE Model 40:** slide action; 12-ga. only; 28" barrel; solid frame; 6-rd. magazine; Multi-Choke; recoil pad; unchecked American walnut pistol-grip stock, grooved fore-arm; push-button safety. Introduced in 1952; dropped, 1956. Used value, $45 to $50.

**NOBLE Model 50:** slide action; 12-ga. only; 28" barrel; solid frame; has the same specifications as Model 40, except without recoil pad and Multi-Choke. Introduced in 1954; dropped, 1956. Used value, $45 to $50.

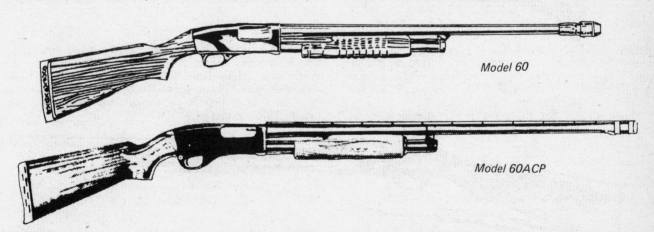

*Model 60*

*Model 60ACP*

**NOBLE Model 60:** slide action; 12, 16 gauges; 28" barrel; solid frame; cross-bolt safety; 5-rd. magazine; unchecked American walnut pistol-grip stock; grooved slide handle, Vari-Chok choke; recoil pad. Introduced in 1957; dropped, 1969. Used value, $60 to $65.

**Model 60AF** has the same specifications as Model 60, except for selected steel barrel, damascened bolt, select walnut stock with fluted comb. Introduced in 1965; dropped, 1966. Used value, $50 to $55.

**Model 60ACP** replaced Model 60, Model 60 AF; has same general specifications, except receiver is machined from single block of steel, all lock surfaces are hardened. Introduced in 1967; dropped, 1971. Used value, $70 to $75.

**Model 66 RCLP** has the same specifications as Model 60 ACP, except for checkered pistol grip, slide handle. Introduced in 1967; dropped, 1971. Used value, $80 to $85.

*Model 65*

**NOBLE Model 65:** slide action; 12, 16 gauges, 28" barrel; solid frame; has same specifications as Model 60, except without recoil pad, Vari-Chok choke. Introduced in 1957; dropped, 1969. Used value, $55 to $60.

*Model 602*

**NOBLE Model 602:** slide action; 20-ga. only; solid frame; 28″ barrel; adjustable choke; 5-rd. magazine; top safety; side ejection; uncheckered American walnut pistol-grip stock; grooved slide handle; recoil pad. Introduced in 1963; dropped, 1971. Used value, $100 to $110.

Model 602RCLP has same general specs as Model 602, except for key lock safety mechanism, vent rib, checkered

**NOBLE Model 70:** slide action; .410 gauge only 26″ barrel; full choke; solid frame; top safety; uncheckered walnut pistol-grip stock; grooved forearm. Introduced in 1959; dropped, 1967. Used value, $60 to $70.

Model 70X replaced Model 70; specifications are the same, except has side ejection, damascened bolt. Introduced in 1967; dropped, 1971. Used value, $80 to $90.

Model 70CLP has same general specs as Model 70, except for adjustable choke. Manufactured 1958 to 1970.

pistol-grip stock, slide handle. Manufactured 1967 to 1970. Used value, $135 to $145.

Model 602RLP has same specs as 602RCLP except is sans adjustable choke; full or modified choke. Manufactured 1967 to 1970. Used value, $120 to $125.

Model 602CLP has same specs as 602RCLP, except for plain barrel. Manufactured 1958 to 1970. Used value, $110 to $115.

Model 602XL has same specs as Model 602RCLP, except for plain barrel, no recoil pad, only slide handle is checkered, full or modified choke. Manufactured 1958 to 1970. Used value, $100 to $105.

Used value, $110 to $115.

Model 70XL has same specs as Model 70CLP, sans adjustable choke; checkered buttstock. Manufactured 1958 to 1970. Used value, $100 to $105.

Model 70RCLP has same specs as Model 70CLP, except for vent rib. Manufactured 1967 to 1970. Used value, $130 to $140.

Model 70RLP has same specs as Model 70CLP, but sans adjustable choke. Manufactured 1967 to 1970. Used value, $120 to $125.

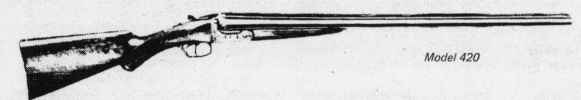

*Model 420*

**NOBLE Model 420:** double barrel; hammerless; 12, 16, 20 gauges; 28″ barrels; full/modified only; top lever; double triggers; automatic safety; matted rib; checkered pistol-grip stock, forearm. Introduced in 1959; dropped, 1971. Used value, $85 to $95.

Model 420EK has the same general specifications as

Model 420, except for demi-block with triple lock; automatic selective ejectors, hand-checkered Circassian walnut pistol-grip stock; beavertail forearm; recoil pad; hand-engraved action; front and middle bead sights; gold inlay on top lever. Made only in 1968 under this designation. Used value, $110 to $120.

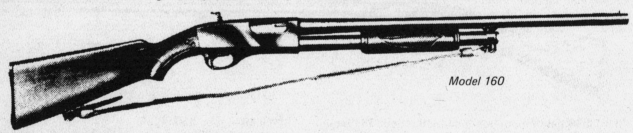

*Model 160*

**NOBLE Model 160 Deergun:** slide action; 12, 16 gauges; specifications the same as Model 60, except for 24″ barrel; hard rubber butt plate; sling swivels; detachable carrying strap; Lyman adjustable peep rear sight, ramp post front; tapped for scope. Introduced in 1965; dropped, 1966. Used

value, $60 to $75.

Model 166L Deergun replaced Model 160; general specifications are the same, except for improved workmanship. Introduced in 1967; dropped, 1971. Used value, $75 to $80.

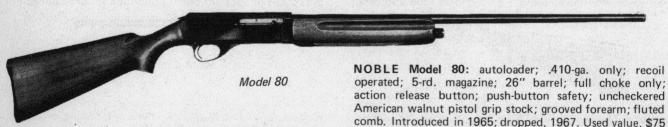

*Model 80*

**NOBLE Model 80:** autoloader; .410-ga. only; recoil operated; 5-rd. magazine; 26″ barrel; full choke only; action release button; push-button safety; uncheckered American walnut pistol grip stock; grooved forearm; fluted comb. Introduced in 1965; dropped, 1967. Used value, $75 to $80.

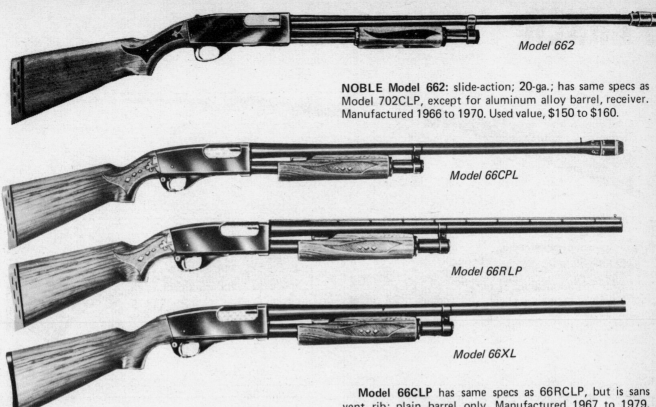

*Model 662*

*Model 66CPL*

*Model 66RLP*

*Model 66XL*

**NOBLE Model 662:** slide-action; 20-ga.; has same specs as Model 702CLP, except for aluminum alloy barrel, receiver. Manufactured 1966 to 1970. Used value, $150 to $160.

**NOBLE Model 66RCLP:** slide-action; 12, 16-ga.; 3" chamber in 12-ga.; 5-rd. tubular magazine; 28" vent rib barrel; adjustable choke; solid frame; key lock safety mechanism; checkered American walnut pistol-grip stock, slide handle; recoil pad. Manufactured 1967 to 1970. Used value, $130 to $140.

**Model 66RLP** has same specs as 66CLP, sans adjustable choke; choked modified or full. Manufactured 1967 to 1970. Used value, $110 to $115.

**NOBLE Model 450E:** double barrel; 12, 16, 20 gauges; 28" barrel; modified/full chokes; demi-block with triple lock;

**NOBLE Series 200:** slide action; 20-ga. only; 28" barrel, modified or full choke; solid frame; 5-rd. magazine; tang safety; side ejection; impressed checkering on slide handle;

**NOBLE Series 300:** slide action; 12-ga. only; 28" barrel; modified or full choke; solid frame; tang safety; side ejection; American walnut stock, slide handle; impressed check-

**NOBLE Series 400:** slide action; .410-ga. only; 25" barrel; modified or full choke; solid frame, tang safety; side ejection; American walnut stock, slide handle; impressed check-

**NOBLE Model 390 Deergun:** slide action; 12-ga. only; 24" rifled slug barrel; sling swivels; detachable carrying strap; Lyman adjustable peep rear sight, ramp post front; solid

**NOBLE Model 757:** slide action; 20-ga. only; 5-rd. magazine; solid frame; 28" barrel of aircraft alloy; adjustable choke; barrel, receiver black anodized; decorated receiver;

**Model 66CLP** has same specs as 66RCLP, but is sans vent rib; plain barrel only. Manufactured 1967 to 1979. Used value, $110 to $115.

**Model 66XL** has same specs as Model 66RCLP, sans vent rib; no adjustable choke; bored modified or full; only slide handle is checkered; no recoil pad. Manufactured 1967 to 1970. Used value, $100 to $105.

**Model 166L Deer Gun** has same general specs as Model 66CLP, except for 24" slug-bored barrel, rifle sights, receiver dovetailed for scope mounts; sling swivels, carrying strap. Manufactured 1967 to 1970. Used value, $120 to $125.

double triggers; all specifications the same as Model 420EK, which it replaced. Introduced in 1969; dropped, 1971. Used value, $105 to $115.

American walnut stock, slide handle; recoil pad. Made in 1972 only. Used values, standard model, $75 to $80; with Vari-Chek choke, $80 to $85; with vent rib, $80 to $85; Vari-Chek and vent rib, $95 to $105.

ering; 6-rd. magazine, 3-shot plug furnished. Made only in 1972. Used values, standard model, $75 to $80; with Vari-Chek, $75 to $80; with vent rib, $85 to $90; Vari-Chek and vent rib, $95 to $100.

ering on pistol grip, slide handle; damascened bolt. Made only in 1972. Used values, standard model, $70 to $75; with Vari-Chek, $85 to $90; with vent rib, $85 to $90; Vari-Chek and vent rib, $95 to $100.

frame; tang safety; American walnut stock, slide handle; impressed checkering. Made only in 1972. Used value, $85 to $90.

tang safety; side ejection; American walnut stock; impressed checkering on slide handle, pistol grip. Made only in 1972. Used value, $95 to $100.

# PARKER

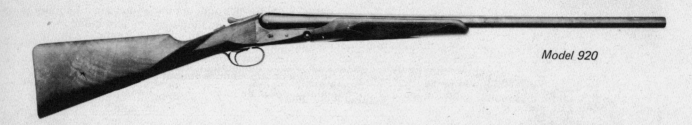

*Model 920*

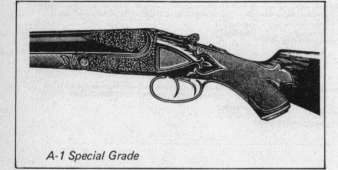

*A-1 Special Grade*

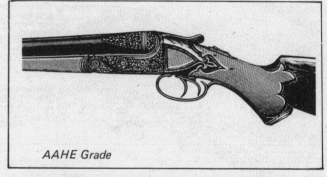

*AAHE Grade*

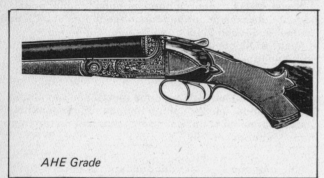

*AHE Grade*

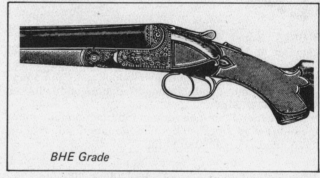

*BHE Grade*

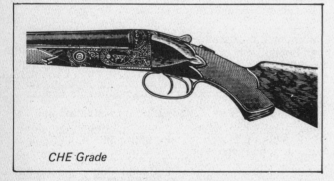

*CHE Grade*

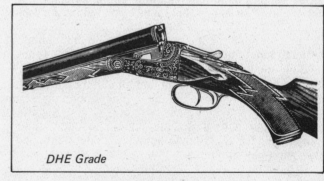

*DHE Grade*

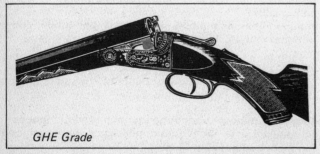

*GHE Grade*

*VHE Grade UHE*

**PARKER Model 920 Hammerless:** after Parker Brothers was absorbed by Remington Arms in 1934, shotgun was designated as Remington Parker Model 920; prior to that, it was known simply as Parker Hammerless Double; side-by-side double; 10, 12, 16, 20, 28, .410 gauges; 26" to 32" barrels; any standard choke combo; box-lock action; automatic ejectors; choice of straight, half or pistol-grip stock; hand-checkered pistol grip, forearm of select walnut; double or selective single trigger. Because of the wide variations in styles and extras, as well as the number of grades — differing in engraving, checkering and general workmanship — there is a wide range of values. The selective trigger was introduced in 1922, with the raised vent rib; the beavertail forend was introduced in 1923; all add to used value. Prior to 1920, model was built with Damascus barrels, today considered collector items. For all practical purposes, the shootable model was introduced in 1920, dropped in 1940, but some guns were put together from available parts stocks

by Remington until 1942. Grades are in descending values, with the A-designated model being worth several times that of the V model. Nonejector models —pre-1934 — are worth about 30% less than values shown for ejector models; if gun has interchangeable barrels, it is worth 30 to 35% more than shown. Those in 20, 28, .410 also have more value. Prices shown are for 12, 16-ga. configurations. Used values, A-1 Special Grade, $10,000 to $12,000; AAHE, $8500 to $9000; AHE, $7500 to $8000; BHE, $6000 to $6500; CHE, $4250 to $4500; DHE, $3000 to $3500; GHE, $2000 to $2500; VHE, $1250 to $1500.

With single selective trigger, add $200 to $300 to base price shown. For raised vent rib, add $325 to $350. For beavertail forearm addition, in grades VHE, GHE, DHE, CHE, add $200 to $250 to base price; for grades BHE, AHE, AAHE, add $450 to $500 to base; for A-1 Special, add $500 to $750.

*Trojan*

**PARKER Trojan:** hammerless double barrel; 12, 16, 20 gauges; 26", 28" barrels, modified/full choke, 30" full; American walnut stock; hand-checkered pistol grip, forearm; box-lock action; plain extractors; double or single

triggers. Introduced in 1915; dropped, 1939. Used values, double trigger, 12, 16 gauges, $700 to $750; 20-ga., $950 to $1000; single trigger, 12, 16 gauges, $800 to $850; 20-ga., $1150 to $1250.

*Single-Barrel Trap*

**PARKER Single-Barrel Trap:** after absorption of Parker by Remington, model was listed as Remington Parker Model 930. In 12-ga. only; 30", 32", 34" barrels; any designated choke; vent rib; ejector; hammerless box lock action; straight, half or pistol-grip stock of select American walnut;

hand-checkered pistol grip, forearm. Various grades differ with amount of workmanship, checkering, engraving, et al. General specifications are the same for all variations. Introduced in 1917; dropped, 1942. Used values, SA-1 Special, $7000 to $7500; SAA, $4500 to $5000; SA, $3500 to $3750; SB, $2500 to $2750; SC, $1500 to $1750.

# PEDERSEN

*Grade I*

**PEDERSEN 1000 Series Grade I:** over/under; box-lock action; 12, 20 gauges; barrel lengths, stock dimensions to customer specifications; hand-checkered American walnut pistol-grip stock, forearm; rubber recoil pad; vent rib; automatic ejectors; single selective trigger; hand-engraved, gold-filled receiver. Introduced in 1973; dropped, 1975. Used value, $725 to $750.

Series 1000 Grade II has the same specifications as Grade I except for standard stock dimensions, no gold filling, less extensive engraving on receiver, less fancy wood in stock, forearm. Introduced in 1973; dropped, 1975. Used value, $475 to $500.

Series 1000 Grade III has the same specifications as Grade II except for no receiver engraving; has gold-plated trigger, forearm release. Introduced in 1973; dropped, 1975. Used value, $400 to $450.

Model 1000 Magnum Grade I has same specs as Model 1000 Grade I, except for 12-ga. magnum 3" shell chambering, 30" barrels, improved modified/full chokes. Manufactured 1973 to 1975. Used value, $1450 to $1500.

Model 1000 Magnum Grade II has same specs as Magnum Grade I, except for lower grade wood, less engraving, fewer silver inlays. Manufactured 1973 to 1975. Used value, $1250 to $1300.

Model 1000 Trap Grade I has same specs as Model 1000 Grade I, except made in 12-ga. only; 30", 32" barrels; modified/full or improved modified/full chokes; Monte Carlo trap stock. Manufactured 1973 to 1975. Used value, $1450 to $1500.

Model 1000 Trap Grade II has same specs as Grade I, except for lower grade wood, less engraving, fewer silver inlays. Manufactured 1973 to 1975. Used value, $1250 to $1300.

Model 1000 Skeet Grade I has same specs as basic Model 1000 Grade I, except 12-ga. only; 26", 28" barrels; skeet stock, skeet chokes. Manufactured 1973 to 1975. Used value, $1450 to $1500.

Model 1000 Skeet Grade II has same specs as Grade I, except has lower grade wood, less engraving, fewer silver inlays. Manufactured 1973 to 1975. Used value, $1250 to $1300.

*Model 1500*

**PEDERSEN 1500:** over/under; box-lock action; 12-ga. only; 26", 28", 30", 32" barrels; hand-checkered European walnut pistol-grip stock, forearm; rubber recoil pad; field version of Series 1000; automatic selective ejectors; vent rib; choice of sights. Introduced in 1973; dropped, 1975. Used value, $400 to $425.

**PEDERSEN Series 2000 Grade I:** side-by-side double barrel; box-lock action; 12, 20 gauges; barrel length, stock dimensions to customer's specifications; hand-checkered American walnut pistol-grip stock, forearm; automatic selective ejectors; barrel selector/safety; single selective trigger; automatic safety; gold-filled, hand-engraved receiver.

Model 1500 Trap has same specs as basic Model 1500, except for 30", 32" barrels; modified/full or improved modified/full chokes; Monte Carlo trap stock. Manufactured 1973 to 1975. Used value, $400 to $425.

Model 1500 Skeet has same specs as standard Model 1500, except for 27" barrels, skeet choke, skeet stock. Manufactured 1973 to 1975. Used value, $390 to $410.

Introduced in 1973; dropped, 1975. Used value, $725 to $750.

Series 2000 Grade II has same specifications as Grade I except for standard stock dimensions, less extensive engraving, less fancy wood. Introduced in 1973; dropped, 1975. Used value, $450 to $475.

*Model 2500 Grade III*

**PEDERSEN 2500 Grade III:** side-by-side double barrel; box-lock action; 12, 20 gauges; has the same specifications as 2000 series but is field version. Hand-checkered pistol grip, beavertail forearm; European walnut stock; standard stock dimensions; no receiver engraving. Introduced in 1973; dropped, 1975. Used value, $225 to $245.

*Model 4000*

**PEDERSEN Model 4000:** slide-action; 12, 20-ga., .410; 3" chambers; 26", 28", 30" barrels, standard chokes; based upon Mossberg Model 500; full-coverage engraving on receiver; checkered select American walnut stock, slide

**PEDERSEN Model 4500:** slide-action; has same general specs as standard Model 4000, except less engraving on receiver. Manufactured 1975. Used value, $165 to $175.

handle. Manufactured 1973. Used value, $220 to $240.

**Model 4000 Trap** has same specs, except made in 12-ga. only, 30" full choke barrel, recoil pad, Monte Carlo trap stock. Manufactured 1975. Used value, $235 to $250.

**Model 4500 Trap** has same specs as Model 4000 Trap, except less engraving. Manufactured 1975. Used value, $175 to $190.

# PERAZZI

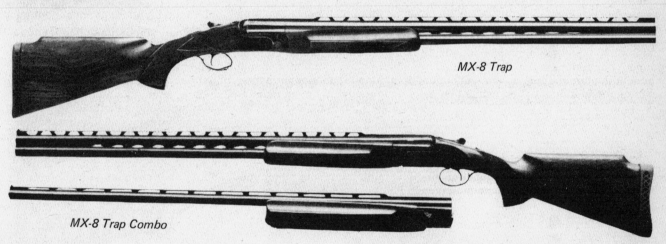

*MX-8 Trap*

*MX-8 Trap Combo*

**PERAZZI MX-8 Trap:** over/under; 12-ga.; 30", 32" barrels; high vent rib; box-lock action, auto selective ejectors; non-selective single trigger; improved modified/full chokes; checkered European walnut Monte Carlo stock, forend;

recoil pad. Made in Italy. Imported by Ithaca 1969 to 1978. Used value, $1626 to $1650.

**MX-8 Combo Trap** model has same specs as MX-8 trap gun, except for extra single 32", 34" barrel; full choke; vent rib; forend; two trigger groups. Imported 1973 to 1978 by Ithaca. Used value, $2500 to $2550.

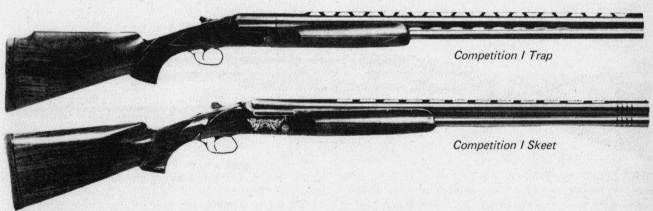

*Competition I Trap*

*Competition I Skeet*

**PERAZZI Competition I Trap:** over/under; 12-ga.; 30", 32" barrels; vent rib; improved modified/full chokes; box-lock action, auto ejectors; single trigger; checkered

European walnut pistol grip stock, forend, recoil pad. Imported by Ithaca 1969 to 1974. Used value, $1150 to $1200.

**Competition I Skeet** model has same specs as trap

version, except for 26¾" barrels; integral muzzle brakes; skeet chokes; skeet stock, forend. Imported by Ithaca 1969 to 1974. Used value, $1150 to $1200.

**Competition I Single-Barrel Trap** model has same general specs as over/under trap model, except for single 32", 34" barrel; full choke; checkered Monte Carlo stock, beavertail forend. Imported by Ithaca 1973 to 1978. Used value, $1300 to $1350.

*Single Barrel Trap*

**PERAZZI Single-Barrel Trap:** single-shot; 12-ga.; 34" barrel; full choke; vent rib; box-lock action; auto ejector; checkered European walnut pistol-grip stock, forend; recoil pad. Imported by Ithaca 1971 to 1972. Used value, $1150 to $1200.

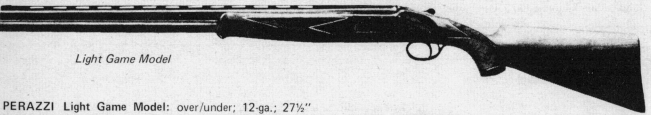

*Light Game Model*

**PERAZZI Light Game Model:** over/under; 12-ga.; 27½" barrels; modified/full, improved cylinder/modified chokes; single trigger; box-lock action; auto ejectors; checkered European walnut field stock, forend. Imported by Ithaca 1972 to 1974. Used value, $1150 to $1200.

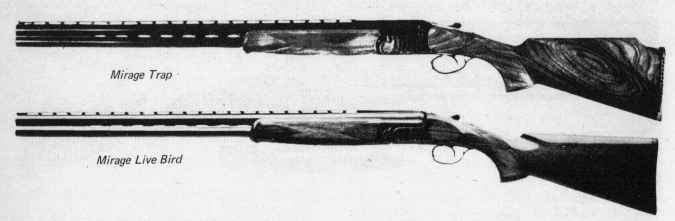

*Mirage Trap*

*Mirage Live Bird*

**PERAZZI Mirage Trap:** over/under; 12-ga.; has the same general specs as MX-8 trap model, except for a tapered vent rib. Imported by Ithaca 1973 to 1978. Used value, $1650 to $1700.

**Mirage Live Bird** model has same specs as Mirage trap, except for modified/extra full 28" barrels; redesigned stock, forend for live bird competition. Imported by Ithaca 1973 to 1978. Used value, $1650 to $1700.

**Mirage Skeet** version has same specs as Mirage trap except for 28" barrels, integral muzzle brakes, skeet chokes; skeet stock, forend. Imported by Ithaca 1973 to 1978. Used value, $1650 to $1700.

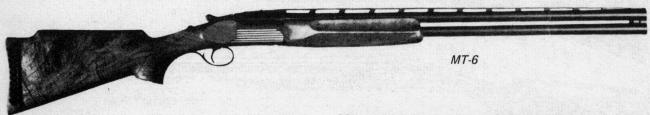

*MT-6*

**PERAZZI MT-6 Trap:** over/under; 12-ga.; 30", 32" separated barrels; wide vent rib; five interchangeable choke tubes; non-selective single trigger; box-lock action; auto selective ejectors; checkered European walnut pistol-grip stock, forend; recoil pad; marketed in fitted case. Imported by Ithaca 1976 to 1978. Used value, $2000 to $2150.

**MT-6 Skeet** has same specs as trap version, except for 28" barrels; choke tubes include skeet and skeet; skeet stock, forend. Imported by Ithaca 1976 to 1978. Used value, $2000 to $2150.

**MT-6 Trap Combo:** same as MT-6 trap model, except has extra single under-barrel, high aluminum vent rib; 32", 34" barrels; seven interchangeable choke tubes. Marketed in fitted case. Imported by Ithaca 1977 to 1978. Used value, $3250 to $3400.

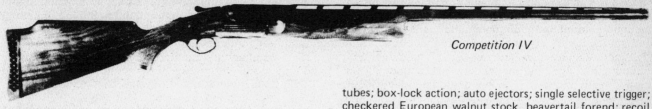

*Competition IV*

**PERAZZI Competition IV:** single-barrel trap; 12-ga.; 32", 34" barrels; high, wide vent rib; four interchangeable choke tubes; box-lock action; auto ejectors; single selective trigger; checkered European walnut stock, beavertail forend; recoil pad. Marketed in fitted case. Imported by Ithaca 1977 to 1978. Used value, $1600 to $1650.

# PREMIER

*Ambassador*

**PREMIER Ambassador:** double; 12, 16, 20, .410 gauges; triple Greener crossbolt action; barrels, 22", except in .410, 26"; all gauges, modified/full chokes; European walnut stock, hand-checkered pistol grip, forearm; double triggers, cocking indicators; automatic safety. Imported from Europe by Premier Shotguns. Still in production. Used value, $165 to $175.

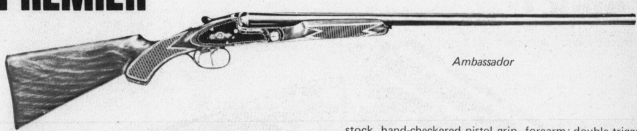

*Continental*

**PREMIER Continental:** same as Ambassador model except for outside hammers; not available in .410. Other specs identical. Used value, $160 to $170.

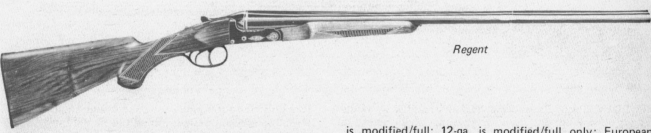

*Regent*

**PREMIER Regent:** double; 12, 16, 20, 28, .410 gauges; triple Greener crossbolt action; barrels, 26", improved/modified, except in 28, .410, which are modified/full; 28", is modified/full; 12-ga. is modified/full only; European walnut stock, hand-checkered pistol grip, forearm; matted tapered rib; double triggers; automatic safety. Still in production. Used value, $150 to $165.

*Brush King*

**PREMIER Brush King:** double; same as Premier Regent model, except in 12, 20 gauges only; 22" barrels, improved/modified. Still in production. Used value, $150 to $170.

**PREMIER Magnum:** double; similar to Premier Regent; 10, 12 gauges only; 10 with 32" barrel, 12 has 30"; choked full/full; recoil pad; European walnut stock, hand-checkered pistol grip, forearm; beavertail forearm. Still in production. Used values, 10-ga., $160 to $170; 12-ga., $145 to $165.

**PREMIER Monarch Supreme:** side-by-side; 12, 20-ga.; 2¾" chambers in 12-ga.; 3" in 20; box-lock action; double triggers; auto ejectors; 26" improved cylinder/modified, 28" modified/full barrels; checkered European fancy walnut pistol-grip stock, beavertail forearm. Introduced 1959, still in production. Used value, $300 to $325.

**PREMIER Presentation Custom Grade:** has the same general specs as Monarch Supreme, but is made only to customer's order; has higher grade wood, engraved hunting scene, gold and silver inlays. Introduced 1959, still in production. Used value, $700 to $725.

# PURDEY

*Hammerless Double*

**PURDEY Hammerless Double Model:** side-by-side; sidelock; 12, 16, 20 gauges; 26", 27", 28", 30" barrels, last in 12-ga. only; double triggers or single trigger; any choke combo desired; choice of rib style; automatic ejectors; hand-checkered European walnut straight-grip stock, forearm standard; pistol-grip stock on special order; made in several variations including Game Model, Featherweight Game, Pigeon Gun, with side clips; Two-Inch Model for 2" shells. Prices are identical for all. Introduced in 1880; still in production. Used values, double triggers, $6250 to $6500; single trigger, $7250 to $7500.

*Single Barrel Trap*

**PURDEY Single Barrel Trap Model:** single-barrel, single-shot; Purdey action; 12-ga. only; barrel length, choke to customer's specifications; vent rib; engraved receiver; hand-checkered European walnut stock, forearm; straight English style or pistol-grip design. Introduced in 1917; still in production. Used value, $7500 to $7750.

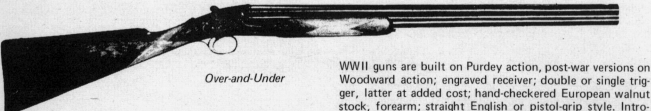

*Over-and-Under*

**PURDEY Over-and-Under Model:** sidelock action; 12, 16, 20 gauges; 26", 27", 28" barrels, last in 12-ga. only; any choke combo; any rib style to customer's preference; Pre-WWII guns are built on Purdey action, post-war versions on Woodward action; engraved receiver; double or single trigger, latter at added cost; hand-checkered European walnut stock, forearm; straight English or pistol-grip style. Introduced in 1925; still in production. Used values, with Purdey action, double triggers, $8000 to $8500; Purdey action with single trigger, $9000 to $9500; Woodward action, double triggers, $10,000 to $12,500; Woodward action, single trigger, $12,500 to $14,000.

# REMINGTON

*Model 1882*

**REMINGTON Model 1882:** side-by-side; 10, 12, 16-ga.; 28", 30", 32" steel or damascus barrels; visible hammers; double triggers; hand-checkered American walnut pistol-grip stock, forearm. Manufactured 1882 to 1910. Collector value. Used value, $325 to $350.

*Model 1889*

**REMINGTON Model 1889:** side-by-side; 10, 12, 16-ga.; 28", 30", 32" steel or damascus barrels; visible hammers; double triggers; hand-checkered American walnut stock, slim forend. Manufactured 1889 to 1908. Collector value. Used value, $475 to $500.

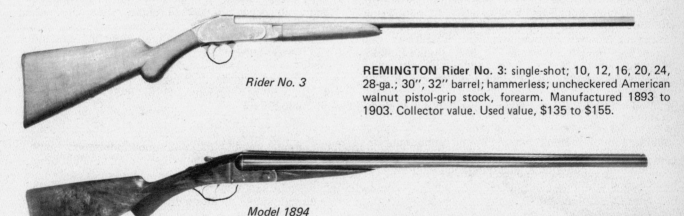

*Rider No. 3*

**REMINGTON Rider No. 3:** single-shot; 10, 12, 16, 20, 24, 28-ga.; 30", 32" barrel; hammerless; uncheckered American walnut pistol-grip stock, forearm. Manufactured 1893 to 1903. Collector value. Used value, $135 to $155.

*Model 1894*

**REMINGTON Model 1894:** side-by-side; 10, 12, 16-ga.; 28", 30", 32" barrels; double triggers, box-lock action; auto ejector; hammerless; hand-checkered American walnut straight-grip stock, forearm. Manufactured 1894 to 1910. Collector value. Used value, $500 to $525.

**Model 1894 Trap** has same specs as standard model, except for trap stock, 32" full choke barrel. Manufactured 1894 to 1910. Collector value. Used value, $550 to $600.

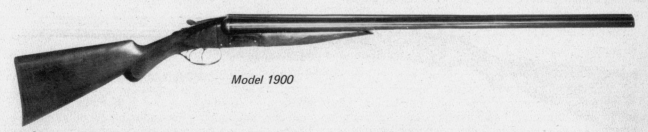

*Model 1900*

**REMINGTON Model 1900:** side-by-side; 10, 12, 16-ga.; had the same general specifications as Model 1894, but improved in quality, with heavier forearm. Manufactured 1900 to 1910. Collector value. Used value, $525 to $550.

**Model 1900 Trap** has same general specs as Model 1894 Trap, but is of somewhat higher quality in wood and finish. Manufactured 1900 to 1910. Collector value. Used value, $550 to $600.

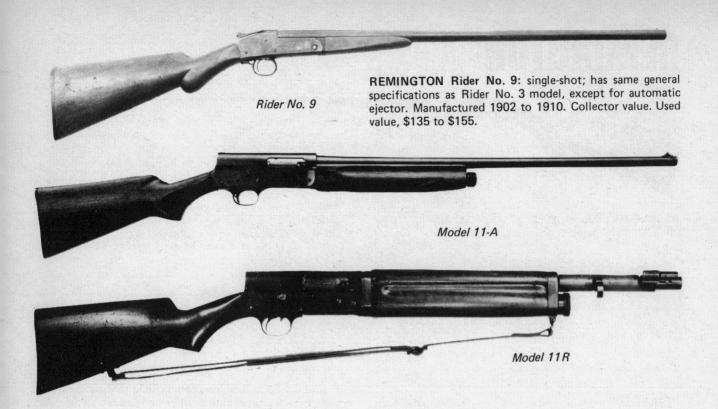

*Rider No. 9*

**REMINGTON Rider No. 9:** single-shot; has same general specifications as Rider No. 3 model, except for automatic ejector. Manufactured 1902 to 1910. Collector value. Used value, $135 to $155.

*Model 11-A*

*Model 11R*

**REMINGTON Model 11A:** hammerless, takedown, Browning-type autoloader; 5-rd. capacity; tube magazine; 12, 16, 20 gauges; barrel lengths, 26″, 28″, 30″, 32″; full, modified, improved, cylinder bore, skeet chokes; checkered pistol grip, forearm. Introduced in 1905; dropped, 1949. Was replaced by Model 11-48. Used values with plain barrel, $165 to $175; solid rib, $175 to $200; vent rib, $225 to $250.

**Model 11R Riot Gun** has same specifications as Model 11A, except that it is 12-ga. only; has sling swivels, 20″ barrel. Introduced in 1921; dropped, 1948. Used value, $175 to $200.

**Model 11 custom grades**, Expert, Special, Tournament and Premier styles, differ from Model 11A only in grade of walnut used in stock, forearm, engraving, checkering. Used values, Special grade (11B), $325 to $350; Tournament (11D), $550 to $600; Expert (11E), $800 to $900; Premier, $1000 to $1250.

*Model 10A*

**REMINGTON Model 10A:** slide-action repeater; hammerless, takedown; barrel lengths, 26″, 28″, 30″, 32″; full, modified, cylinder bore; grooved slide handle; uncheckered pistol-grip stock; 12-ga. only; 6-rd. capacity; tube magazine. Introduced, 1907; dropped, 1929. Used value, $175 to $225.

*Model 17A*

**REMINGTON Model 17A:** slide-action repeater; hammerless, takedown; 5-rd. capacity; 20-ga. only; tube magazine; barrel lengths, 26″, 28″, 30″, 32″; modified, full, cylinder bore choke choice, grooved slide handle, uncheckered stock, with pistol grip; Browning design. Introduced in 1921; dropped, 1933. Used value, $240 to $250.

*Model 29*

**REMINGTON Model 29:** hammerless, takedown slide-action repeater; 12-ga. only; tubular magazine, 5-shot capacity; Model 29A has plain barrel, 26″, 28″, 30″, 32″; full, modified, cylinder bore; hand-checkered slide handle, pistol-grip stock; made from 1929 to 1933. Used value, $235 to $265.

**Model 29T Target Gun** differs from Model 29A only in ventilated rib, longer slide handle, straight grip on trap stock. Used value, $325 to $350.

*Model 31A*

**REMINGTON Model 31:** this model is one of those successes that leads to numerous versions. In all, there are ten variations, all introduced in 1931, dropped in 1949.

**Model 31A,** the standard grade slide-action repeater, is a hammerless, takedown model, with either 3 or 5-shot capacity; early models had checkered pistol-grip stock, slide handle; later styles had plain stock, grooved slide handle. Barrels, with choice of plain surface, solid rib or vent rib, were in 26″, 28″, 30″, 32″ lengths, choked full, modified, improved, cylinder bore, skeet. Made in 12, 16, 20 gauges. Used value, with plain barrel, $175 to $200; solid rib, $250 to $275; vent rib, $300 to $325.

**Model 31 Custom Grades** are Special Tournament, Expert and Premier, differing from Model 31A only in the grade of wood, amount and fineness of checkering and the amount and quality of engraving. Other specifications remain the same. Used values, Special grade (31B), $325 to $350; Tournament (31D), $650 to $675; Expert (31E), $950 to $1000; Premier (31F), $1150 to $1250.

**Model 31TC Trap Grade** is same as standard model, but in 12-ga. only, with 30″, 32″ vent rib barrel, full choke, trap stock, pistol grip, recoil pad; extension beavertail forend; stock, forend are checkered. Used value, $450 to $475.

**Model 31S Trap Special** has same specs as Model 31TC, except half-pistol grip stock, forend of standard walnut, solid rib barrel. Used value, $435 to $450.

**Model 31H Hunter's Special** differs from Model 31S only in that it has a sporting stock with more drop and shorter length. Used value, $375 to $400.

**Model 31R Riot Gun** is same as Model 31A, but in 12-ga. only, with 20″ barrel. Used value, $200 to $225.

*Model 32 Standard*

**REMINGTON Model 32:** this hammerless, takedown over/under is another of those on which the manufacturer built a lengthy reputation, making the model in its various configurations for a decade. Introduced in 1932; dropped, 1942. However, the nostalgia and demand resulted in the basic model which, with modern manufacturing techniques, was reintroduced in 1972 as the Model 3200.

**The Model 32A Standard Grade** has automatic ejectors and the earlier model had double triggers; later, it was available only with a single selective trigger; in 12-ga. only, barrels are 26″, 28″, 30″, 32″; standard chokes are full, modified, but options were offered for full, modified, improved, cylinder bore, skeet; choice of plain barrel, raised matted solid rib, vent rib; stock was walnut with checkered pistol grip, forend. Used value, with double triggers, $750 to $800; single trigger, $900 to $1000; with vent rib, add $175 to $200; with raised solid rib, $75 to $100.

**Model 32 Skeet Grade** has same specs as Model 32A, except for choice of 26″, 28″ barrel, skeet boring; selective trigger only, beavertail forend. Used value, with plain barrels, $1100 to $1150; vent rib, $1300 to $1350; raised solid rib, $1175 to $1200.

**Model 32 Custom** stylings included Tournament, Expert and Premier grades, differing from standard 32A model only in engraving, fineness of checkering, grade of walnut used. Other specs are the same. Used value, Tournament grade (32D), $1750 to $2000; Expert (32E), $2750 to $3000; Premier (32F), $3250 to $3500.

**Model 32TC Trap Grade** has same specs as Model 32A, except for 30″, 32″ vent rib barrel, trap stock with checkered beavertail forend, pistol grip; either double or single selective triggers; full choke only. Used value, with double triggers, $1150 to $1250; single trigger, $1300 to $1350.

*Model 11-48 Standard*

**REMINGTON Model 11-48A:** autoloader; half-pistol grip; hand-checkered stock, forend; 5-shot capacity in 12, 16, 20 gauges; 4-shot in 28, .410; redesigned version of Model 11; introduced in 1949; dropped, 1969; hammerless, takedown; tube magazine; 26" barrel, choked improved cylinder; 28", modified or full; 30", full, in 12-ga. only; plain barrel, matted top surface, ventilated rib choices. Used value, $145 to $170; Special grade (11-48B), Tournament grade (11-48D) and Premier grade (11-48F) had higher grades of wood, more and finer-line checkering, engraving. Used values, Special, $250 to $275; Tournament, $700 to $750; Premier, $1150 to $1250.

**Model 11-48A .410** was introduced in 1954, 28-ga., 1952; both discontinued, 1969. Used value with plain barrel, $175 to $750; with matted top surface, $225 to $250; vent rib, $275 to $300.

**Model 11-48SA Skeet** model is same as 28-ga. standard model, except for vent rib, skeet choke, 25" barrel; 28-ga. introduced, 1952; .410, 1954. Used value, $275 to $300.

**Model 11-48A Riot Gun** is same as standard model, but in 12-ga. only, with 20" plain barrel. Used value, $150 to $185.

*Sportsman 48A*

**REMINGTON Sportsman 48A:** autoloader; 12, 16, 20-ga.; 26" improved cylinder, 28" modified or full, 30" full choke barrel; vent rib, matted barrel, plain barrel available; hammerless; takedown; 2-rd. tubular magazine; streamlined receiver; hand-checkered American walnut pistol-grip stock, grooved forend. Manufactured 1949 to 1959. Used values, vent rib, $215 to $225; matted barrel, $170 to $180; plain barrel, $160 to $170.

**Sportsman 48B Special Grade** has same general specs as standard 48A, except for higher quality wood, checkering; engraved receiver. Manufactured 1949 to 1959. Used value, $240 to $250.

**Sportsman 48D Tournament Grade** has same specs as 48B, except for improved wood, finer checkering, more engraving. Manufactured 1949 to 1959. Used value, $525 to $550.

**Sportsman 48F Premier Grade** has same specs as 48D, but features top quality wood, fully engraved receiver. Manufactured 1949 to 1959. Used value, $1050 to $1100.

**Sportsman 48SA Skeet** has same specs as 48A, except for 26" barrel with matted surface or vent rib, skeet choke, ivory bead front sight, metal bead rear. Manufactured 1949 to 1960. Used values, vent rib, $215 to $225; matted barrel, $180 to $190.

*Model 870SA*

**REMINGTON Model 870:** made in 14 styles, this slide-action model has variations even within the styles. This model verged on being an empire, with some still in the line, and the life of even the least popular being extended for the 13 years from 1950 to 1963.

**Model 870AP** Wingmaster was the standard grade. A hammerless takedown, it had tube magazine, total capacity of 5 rds.; plug furnished with gun; barrels were 25" improved cylinder; 28", modified or full; 30", full, the last in 12-ga. only; choice of plain, matted top surface vent rib; walnut stock, no checkering, grooved slide handle. Introduced in 1950; dropped, 1963. Used values, plain barrel, $150 to $175; matted surface, $175 to $200; vent rib, $200 to $225.

**Model 870 Wingmaster Field Gun,** still in production, was introduced, 1964. Specs are same as 870AP, except for checkered stock, slide handle. Used value, plain barrel, $150 to $175; vent rib, $175 to $200.

**Model 870 Wingmaster Custom Grades** include Tournament, Premier stylings. Only difference from Model 870AP is grade of walnut, amount of engraving, checkering; other specs are same. Introduced in 1960; still in production.

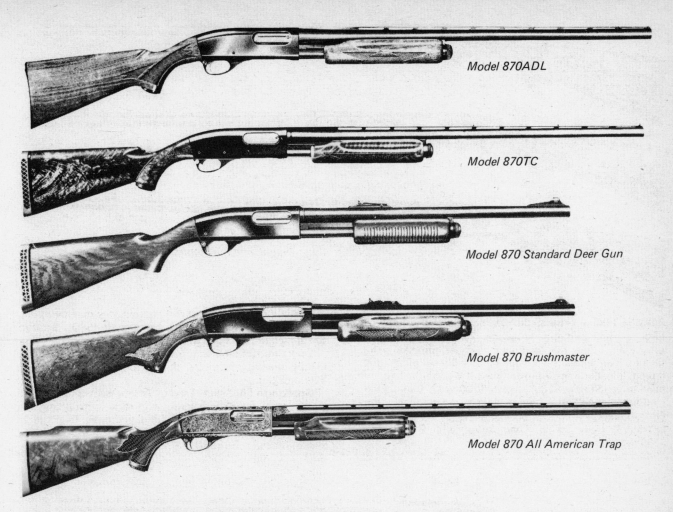

Model 870ADL

Model 870TC

Model 870 Standard Deer Gun

Model 870 Brushmaster

Model 870 All American Trap

Used values, Tournament (870D), $700 to $725; Premier, $1150 to $1250; Premier gold inlaid, $2000 to $2250.

**Model 870ADL** Wingmaster is the deluxe grade of the 870AP with the same general specs, except for fine-checkered beavertail forend, pistol-grip stock; choice of matted top surface barrel, vent rib. Introduced in 1950; dropped, 1963. Used values, matted surface, $200 to $225; vent rib, $235 to $265.

**Model 870BDL** Wingmaster varies from 870ADL only in selected American walnut for stock, forend. Introduced in 1950; dropped, 1963. Used value, with matted top surface barrel, $225 to $250; vent rib, $275 to $285.

**Model 870SA** Wingmaster Skeet gun is same as 870AP, except for 26″ barrel, vent rib, skeet boring, ivory bead front sight, metal bead in rear; has extension beavertail slide handle, pistol-grip stock, both fine-checkered. Introduced in 1950; still in production. Used values, Skeet grade (870SA), $225 to $250; Skeet Target (870SC), $275 to $300; Skeet Tournament (870SD), $650 to $700; Skeet Premier grade (870SF), $1150 to $1250.

**Model 870TB** Wingmaster Trap Special has same specs as standard model, except for 28″, 30″ vent rib barrel, full choke, no rear sight, metal bead front; checkered trap stock, slide handle. Introduced in 1950; still in production. Used value, $185 to $225.

**Model 870TC** Wingmaster Trap grade is same as 870TB, except for both front, rear sights, higher grade of walnut. Introduced in 1950; still in production. Used values, Trap grade (870TC), $300 to $325; Trap Tournament (870TD), $700 to $750; Trap Premier, $1150 to $1250.

**Model 870 Wingmaster Magnum;** same as 870AP, except

in 12-ga. 3″ magnum only; 30″ full choke barrel; recoil pad. Introduced in 1955; discontinued, 1963. Used value, $185 to $225.

**Model 870 Magnum Deluxe** is same as standard 870 Magnum, including lifetime, except for checkered extension beavertail slide handle, stock, matted top surface barrel. Used value, $225 to $250.

**Model 870 Magnum Duck Gun** has same specs as 870 field gun, except chambered for 3″ 12, 20-ga. magnum shells only; 28″, 30″ barrel, plain vent rib, modified, full choke recoil pad. Introduced in 1964; still in production. Used values, with plain barrel, $175 to $200; vent rib, $225 to $250.

**Model 870 Wingmaster Field Gun** has specs of 870AP standard model, except for checkered stock, slide handle. Introduced in 1964; still in production. Used values, with plain barrel, $165 to $175; vent rib, $185 to $200.

**Model 870 Deer Gun;** standard configuration is same as 870 riot model, except for Winchester rifle-type sights. Used value, $165 to $185.

**Model 870 Brushmaster Deluxe** deer gun is same as standard deer gun, but has recoil pad, checkered stock, slide handle; available in 12, 20 gauges. Used value, $175 to $200.

**Model 870 All American Trap** has same specs as Model 870TB, except for custom-grade engraved receiver, trigger guard, barrel; straight comb or Monte Carlo stock, forend of fancy American walnut; manufactured only with 30″ full choke barrel. Introduced 1972, still in production. Used value, $450 to $485.

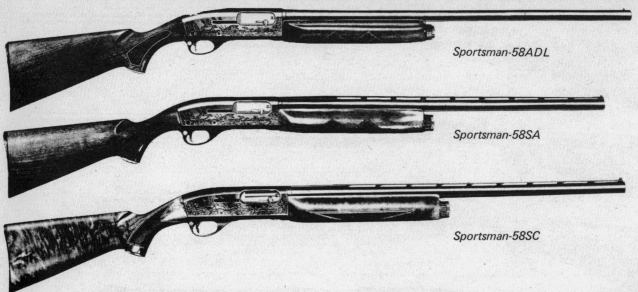

*Sportsman-58ADL*

*Sportsman-58SA*

*Sportsman-58SC*

**REMINGTON Sportsman-58ADL:** gas-operated autoloader; 12-ga. only; 3-shot tube magazine; 26″, 28″, 30″ barrels, with plain, vent rib; improved cylinder, modified, full choke, Remington skeet boring, checkered pistol grip, forend. Introduced in 1956; dropped, 1964. Used values, with plain barrel, $175 to $185; vent rib, $200 to $225.

**Sportsman-58BDL** Deluxe Special grade is same as 58ADL, except walnut wood is of select grade; manufactured during same period. Used values, with plain barrel, $200 to $225; vent rib, $250 to $275.

**Sportsman-58 Tournament and Premier** grades are same as 58ADL, except for vent rib, improved wood, checkering, engraving. Used values, Tournament grade (58D), $700 to $750; Premier, $1150 to $1250.

**Sportsman-58SA Skeet** gun has the same specs as 58-ADL, except for vent rib, special skeet stock, forend. Used value, $200 to $225.

**Sportsman-58 Skeet Target, Tournament and Premier** grades verge on custom guns; with same general specs as Model 58SA, they have better wood, engraving, finer checkering. Used values, Skeet Target grade (58SC), $350 to $375; Skeet Tournament (58D), $700 to $750; Premier grade (58SF), $1150 to $1250.

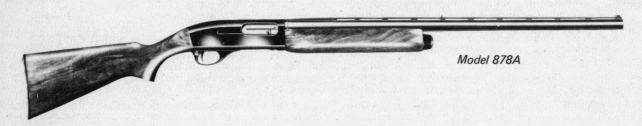

*Model 878A*

**REMINGTON Model 878A Automaster:** gas-operated autoloader; 12-ga. only; 3-shot tube magazine; plain or vent rib; uncheckered pistol-grip stock, forend; barrels, 26″ improved cylinder; 28″ modified, 30″ full choke. Introduced in 1959; dropped, 1962. Used value, $150 to $175.

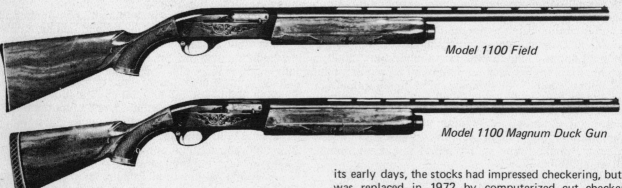

*Model 1100 Field*

*Model 1100 Magnum Duck Gun*

**REMINGTON Model 1100:** a gas-operated, hammerless takedown, autoloader, this model was introduced in 1963 in several configurations, all of them still in production. In its early days, the stocks had impressed checkering, but this was replaced in 1972 by computerized cut checkering; crossbolt safety; alloy receiver.

The **Model 1100 Field Gun** has plain barrel or vent rib, in 12, 16, 20 gauges; barrels 30″ full, 28″ modified or full, 26″ improved cylinder; black plastic butt plate, white

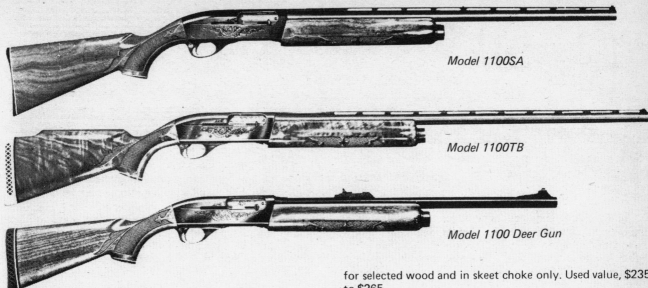

Model 1100SA

Model 1100TB

Model 1100 Deer Gun

spacer. Used value, with plain barrel, $175 to $185; vent rib, $225 to $250.

**The Model 1100 Magnum Duck Gun** is same as field model, except for chambering for 3'' 12, 20-ga. magnum shells only; 20-ga. has 28'' full or modified barrel; 12-ga., 30'' barrel; 12-ga., 30'' full, modified; recoil pad. Used value, plain barrel, $175 to $200; vent rib, $235 to $265.

**Model 1100SA** Skeet model; 12, 20 gauges; same as 1100 field gun, except for 26'' barrel, vent rib, skeet choke or Cutts compensator. Used value, with skeet choke, $225 to $250; Cutts compensator, $200 to $225.

**Model 1100SB** skeet gun is the same as 1100SA, except for selected wood and in skeet choke only. Used value, $235 to $265.

**Model 1100TB** trap model; same as 1100 field style, except for trap stock, Monte Carlo or straight comb choice; 30'' barrel, full, modified trap choke; vent rib; 12-ga. only; recoil pad. Used value, straight stock, $235 to $265; Monte Carlo stock, $250 to $275.

**Model 1100 Tournament, Premier Grades** are same as standard models, except for grade of walnut; amount, fineness of checkering; engraving, gold inlays. Used values, Tournament (1100D), $650 to $700; Premier (1100F), $1150 to $1250; Premier, gold inlaid, $2000 to $2250.

**Model 1100 Deer Gun;** same as field gun, but with 22'' barrel; 12, 20 gauges; improved cylinder; rifle sights; recoil pad. Used value, $190 to $200.

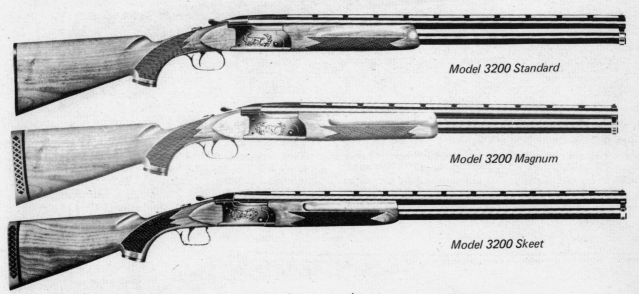

Model 3200 Standard

Model 3200 Magnum

Model 3200 Skeet

**REMINGTON Model 3200:** over/under; 12-ga.; 2¾'' chambering; 26'' improved cylinder/modified, 28'' modified/full, 30'' modified/full barrels; vent rib; box-lock action; auto ejectors; selective single trigger; checkered American walnut pistol-grip stock, forearm. Bears resemblance to earlier Model 32. Introduced 1973, still in production. Used value, $800 to $850.

**Model 3200 Magnum** has same specs as standard model, except chambered for 3'' magnum shell; 30'' barrels,

modified/full or full/full. Introduced 1973, still in production. Used value, $850 to $875.

**Model 3200 Skeet** has same specs as standard 3200, except for skeet-choked 26'', 28'' barrels, skeet stock, full beavertail forearm. Introduced 1973, still in production. Used value, $900 to $950.

**Model 3200 Competition Skeet** has same specs as 3200 Skeet, except for engraved forend latch plate, trigger guard; gilt scrollwork on frame; select walnut wood. Introduced 1973; still in production. Used value, $950 to $1000.

Model 3200 Competition Skeet

Model 3200 Trap

**Model 3200 Special Trap** has same specs as 3200 Trap, except for higher grade select walnut woodwork. Introduced 1973, still in production. Used value, $625 to $650.

**Model 3200 Trap** has same specs as standard 3200, except for straight comb or Monte Carlo trap stock, beavertail forearm; 30″, 32″ improved modified/full or full/full chokes. Introduced 1973, still in production. Used value, $575 to $600.

**Model 3200 Competition Trap** has same specs as Model 3200 Trap, except for engraved forend latch plate, trigger guard; gilt scrollwork on frame; select fancy walnut wood. Introduced 1973, still in production. Used value, $700 to $725.

# RICHLAND

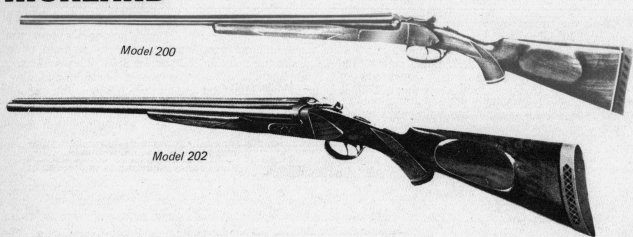

Model 200

Model 202

**RICHLAND Model 200:** side-by-side field gun; hammerless; Anson & Deeley type box-lock action; 12, 16, 20, 28, .410 gauges; 26″ improved/modified, 28″ modified/full; in .410 only; 26″ modified/full, 20-ga. only, 22″ improved/modified; double triggers; plain extractors; hand-checkered European walnut pistol-grip stock, beavertail forearm; cheekpiece; recoil pad. Imported from Spain. Introduced in

1963; still in production. Used value, $190 to $195.

**Model 202** has same specifications as Model 200, but comes with two sets of barrels in same gauge. In 12-ga., barrels are 30″ full/full with 3″ chambers, 26″ improved/modified; in 20-ga., barrels are 26″ modified/full, 22″ improved/modified with 3″ chambers. Introduced in 1963; importation dropped, 1971. Used value, $280 to $290.

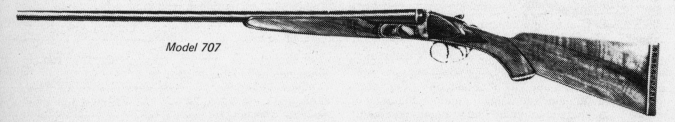

Model 707

**RICHLAND Model 707 Deluxe:** side-by-side field gun; hammerless; box-lock action; 12, 20 gauges; in 12-ga., barrels are 28″ modified/full, 26″ improved/modified; in 20-ga., barrels are 30″ full/full, 28″ modified/full; 26″

improved/modified; triple bolting system; double triggers; plain extractors; hand-checkered European walnut stock, forearm; recoil pad. Imported from Spain. Introduced in 1963; dropped, 1972. Used value, $280 to $290.

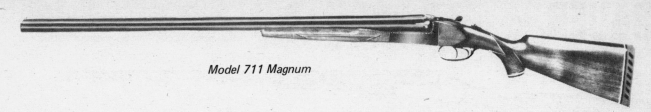

*Model 711 Magnum*

**RICHLAND Model 711 Magnum:** advertised as Long Range Waterfowl Magnum; side-by-side; hammerless; Anson & Deeley box-lock-type action; Purdey-type triple lock; 10, 12 gauges; 10-ga. has 3½" chambers, 12-ga., 3"; 32" full/ full barrels in 10-ga., 30" full/full in 12-ga; double triggers; plain extractors; automatic safety; hand-checkered European walnut pistol-grip stock, forearm; recoil pad. Imported from Spain. Introduced in 1963; still in production. Used value, $225 to $235.

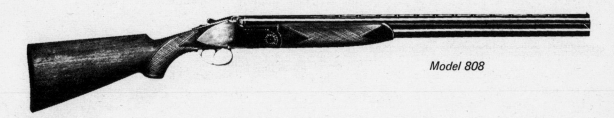

*Model 808*

**RICHLAND Model 808:** over/under; box-lock action; 12-ga. only; 30" full/full, 28" modified/full, 26" improved/modified barrels; plain extractors; nonselective single trigger; hand-checkered European walnut stock, forearm; vent rib. Imported from Italy. Introduced in 1963; importation dropped, 1968. Used value, $310 to $320.

*Model 828*

**RICHLAND Model 828:** over/under; box-lock action; color case-hardened receiver; 28-ga. only; 26" improved/modified, 28" full/modified barrels; sliding crossbolt lock; non-automatic safety; plain extractors; vent rib; rosette engraving; hand-checkered European walnut stock, quick-detachable forearm. Imported from Italy. Introduced in 1971; available on special order only. Used value, $265 to $275.

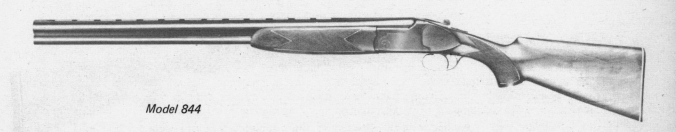

*Model 844*

**RICHLAND Model 844:** over/under; nickel-chrome steel box-lock action; 12-ga., 12-ga. mag.; 26" improved/modified, 28" modified/full, 30" full/full barrels; plain extractors; non-selective single trigger; hand-checkered European walnut pistol-grip stock, forearm. Imported from Italy. Introduced in 1971; Magnum Model still available. Used value, $190 to $190.

# SAUER

*Royal Model*

**SAUER Royal Model:** side-by-side; Anson & Deeley-type box-lock action; 12, 20 gauges; 30" full/full barrels in 12-ga. only, 28" modified/full, 26" improved/modified in 20-ga. only; Greener crossbolt; single selective trigger; automatic ejectors; automatic safety; double underlugs; scalloped frame; Arabesque engraving; hand-checkered European walnut pistol-grip stock, beavertail forearm; recoil pad. Introduced in 1950s; still in production. No current importer. Used value, $600 to $650.

*Artemis Grade II*

**SAUER Artemis Model:** side-by-side; Holland & Holland-type sidelock action; 12-ga. only; 28" modified/full barrels; Greener-type crossbolt; double underlugs; double sear safeties; automatic ejectors; single selective trigger; hand-checkered European walnut pistol-grip stock, beavertail forearm; recoil pad. Grade I has fine line engraving; Grade II has English Arabesque motif. Introduced in 1950s; still in production. No current importer. Used values, Grade I, $2500 to $2750; Grade II, $2900 to $3200.

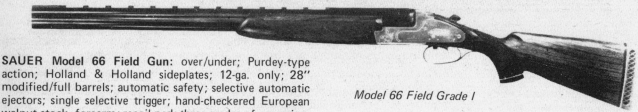

*Model 66 Field Grade I*

**SAUER Model 66 Field Gun:** over/under; Purdey-type action; Holland & Holland sideplates; 12-ga. only; 28" modified/full barrels; automatic safety; selective automatic ejectors; single selective trigger; hand-checkered European walnut stock, forearm; recoil pad; three grades of engraving. Introduced in 1950s; still in production. No current importer. Used values, Grade I, $850 to $900; Grade II, $1050 to $1100; Grade III, $1550 to $1600.

**Model 66 Trap** has same general specifications as field model except for 30" full/full or modified/full barrels; trap stock; wide vent rib; non-automatic safety; ventilated beavertail forearm. Introduced in 1960s; still in production.

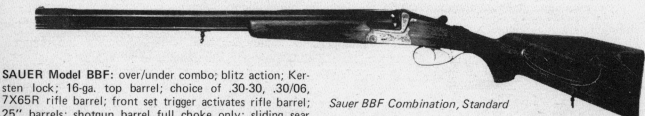

*Sauer BBF Combination, Standard*

**SAUER Model BBF:** over/under combo; blitz action; Kersten lock; 16-ga. top barrel; choice of .30-30, .30/06, 7X65R rifle barrel; front set trigger activates rifle barrel; 25" barrels; shotgun barrel full choke only; sliding sear safety; folding leaf rear sight; hand-checkered European walnut pistol-grip stock, forearm; modified Monte Carlo comb, cheekpiece; sling swivels; Arabesque engraving pattern. Introduced in 1950s; still in production. No current importer. Used value, $1050 to $1100.

# SAVAGE

*Model 28A*

**SAVAGE Model 28A:** slide action; takedown; hammerless; 12-ga. only; 26″, 28″, 30″, 32″ plain barrel; 5-rd. tube magazine; modified, cylinder, full choke; uncheckered American walnut pistol-grip stock, grooved slide handle; black plastic butt plate. Introduced in 1920s; dropped about 1940. Used value, $140 to $145.

**Model 28B** has the same general sepcifications as Model 28A except has raised matted rib. Used value, $150 to $165.

**Model 28D** trap gun has the same specifications as Model 28A except for full-choke barrel, matted rib; hand-checkered pistol-grip, trap stock, checkered slide handle. Used value, $200 to $225.

*Model 420*

**SAVAGE Model 420:** over/under; box-lock action; takedown; hammerless; 12, 16, 20 gauges; 26″, 28″, 30″ barrels, last in 12-ga. only; double triggers; single non-selective trigger at extra cost; automatic safety; choked modified/full or cylinder/improved; uncheckered American walnut pistol-grip stock, forearm. Introduced in early 1930s; dropped, 1942. Used values, double triggers, $250 to $275; single trigger, $325 to $350.

*Model 430*

**SAVAGE Model 430:** over/under; box-lock action; takedown; hammerless; has the same specifications as Model 420 except for hand-checkered American walnut stock, forearm; recoil pad; matted top barrel. Introduced in early 1930s; dropped, 1942. Used values, double triggers, $275 to $300; single trigger, $375 to $385.

*Model 720*

**SAVAGE Model 720:** autoloader; Browning design; takedown; 12, 16 gauges; 26″, 28″, 30″, 32″ barrels, last in 12-ga. only; 4-rd. tube magazine; cylinder, modified, full chokes; hand-checkered American walnut pistol-grip stock, forearm; black plastic butt plate. Introduced in 1930; dropped, 1949. Used value, $165 to $185.

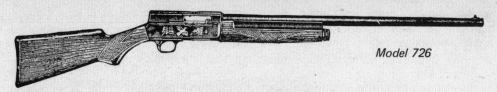

*Model 726*

**SAVAGE Model 726:** autoloader; takedown; 12, 16 gauges; has the same specifications as Model 720 except tube

magazine has 2-rd. capacity. Introduced in 1930; dropped, 1949. Used value, $150 to $155.

**SAVAGE Model 740C:** autoloader; skeet gun; takedown; 12, 16 gauges; has the same specifications as Model 726,

except for skeet stock, beavertail forearm, Cutts Compensator; 24½" barrel. Introduced in late 1930s; dropped, 1949. Used value, $175 to $185.

**SAVAGE Model 745:** autoloader; takedown; 12-ga. only; 28" barrel; has the same general specifications as Model 720

except for alloy receiver; 3-rd. or 5-rd. tube magazine. Introduced in 1946; dropped, 1949. Used value, $150 to $160.

*Model 220 Standard*

**SAVAGE Model 220:** single-barrel; single-shot; takedown; hammerless; 12, 16, 20, .410 gauges; 28" to 36" barrels in 12-ga.; 28" to 32" in 16-ga.; 26" to 32" in 20-ga., 28" in .410; full choke only; automatic ejector; uncheckered American walnut pistol-grip stock, forearm. Introduced about 1947; dropped, 1965. Used value, $70 to $80.

**Model 220AC** has the same specifications as standard Model 220 except for Savage adjustable choke. Used value, $75 to $85.
**Model 220P** has the same specifications as standard Model 220 except for Poly Choke; 12-ga. has 30" barrel only, 16 and 20 gauges have 28" barrel; not made in .410; recoil pad. Used value, $75 to $85.

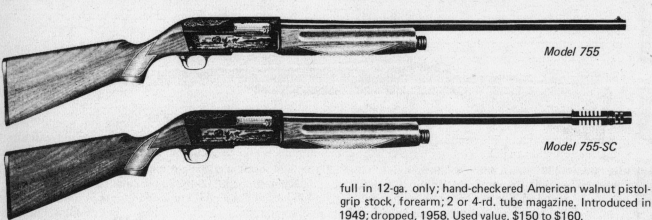

*Model 755*

*Model 755-SC*

full in 12-ga. only; hand-checkered American walnut pistol-grip stock, forearm; 2 or 4-rd. tube magazine. Introduced in 1949; dropped, 1958. Used value, $150 to $160.
**Model 755-SC** has same general specifications as standard Model 755, except for 25" barrel, adjustable Savage Super Choke. Used value, $160 to $170.

**SAVAGE Model 755:** autoloader; takedown; 12, 16 gauges; 26" improved cylinder barrel; 28" full or modified, 30"

*Model 24 Standard*

**SAVAGE Model 24:** over/under combo; top barrel, .22 LR, long, short; lower barrel, .410 3" shotshell; full choke bottom barrel; 24" barrels; open rear sight, ramp front rifle sight; uncheckered walnut pistol-grip stock; sliding button selector; single trigger. Introduced in 1950; dropped, 1965. Used value, $65 to $85.

**Model 24-M** has the same specifications as Model 24 except that top barrel is chambered for .22 rimfire magnum cartridge. Used value, $90 to $100.

**Model 24-DL** has same specifications as standard Model 24 except checkered stock has Monte Carlo comb, beavertail forearm; in 20, .410-ga. lower barrel; satin chrome-finished receiver, trigger guard. Used value, $115 to $125.

**Model 24-MDL** has same specifications as Model 24-DL except upper barrel is chambered for .22 rimfire magnum cartridge. Used value, $125 to $135.

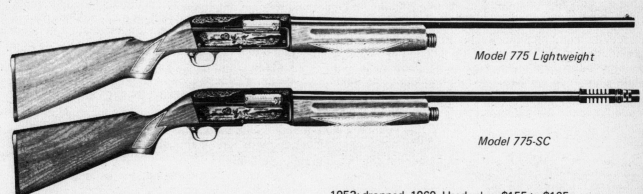

Model 775 Lightweight

Model 775-SC

**SAVAGE Model 775 Lightweight:** autoloader; takedown; 12, 16 gauges; has the same general specifications as standard Model 755 except for alloy receiver. Introduced in 1953; dropped, 1960. Used value, $155 to $165.

**Model 755-SC** has same specifications as Model 775 Lightweight except for 26" barrel, Savage Super Choke. Used value, $165 to $170.

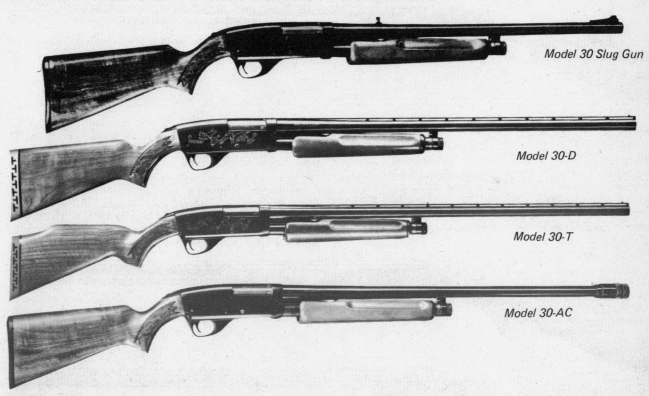

Model 30 Slug Gun

Model 30-D

Model 30-T

Model 30-AC

**SAVAGE Model 30:** slide action; hammerless; solid frame; 12, 20, .410 gauges; 26", 28", 30" barrels; improved modified, full chokes; 5-rd. magazine in 12, 20 gauges, 4-rd. in .410; uncheckered American walnut stock, grooved slide handle; hard rubber butt plate. Introduced in 1958; still in production. Used value, $105 to $115.

**Model 30-AC** has the same specifications as standard Model 30 except for 26" barrel, adjustable choke; 12-ga. only. Introduced in 1959; dropped, 1975. Used value, $115 to $125.

**Model 30-ACL** has same specifications as Model 30-AC but ejection port, safety are on left side. Introduced in 1960; dropped, 1964. Used value, $125 to $130.

**Model 30-T** has the same specifications as standard model except for 30" full choke barrel only; 12-ga. only; Monte Carlo trap stock, recoil pad. Introduced in 1964; dropped, 1975. Used value, $145 to $155.

**Model 30 Slug Gun** has the same specifications as standard Model 30 except for 22" slug barrel, rifle sights; 12, 20 gauges. Introduced in 1964; still in production. Used value, $125 to $135.

**Model 30-D** has same specifications as standard model except is chambered for 12, 20, .410 3" magnum shells; checkered pistol-grip, fluted extension slide handle; alloy receiver; etched pattern on receiver; recoil pad. Introduced in 1972; still in production. Used value, $120 to $125.

*Model 750 Standard*

**SAVAGE Model 750:** autoloader; Browning design; take-down; 12-ga. only; 26" improved, 28" full or modified barrel; 4-rd. tube magazine; checkered American walnut pistol-grip stock, grooved forearm. Introduced in 1960; dropped, 1963. Used value, $165 to $175.

**Model 750-SC** has same specifications as standard Model 750 except for 26" barrel only, Savage Super Choke. Introduced in 1962; dropped, 1963. Used value, $165 to $175.

**Model 750-AC** has same specifications as Model 750 except for 26" barrel only, adjustable choke. Introduced in 1964; dropped, 1967. Used value, $165 to $175.

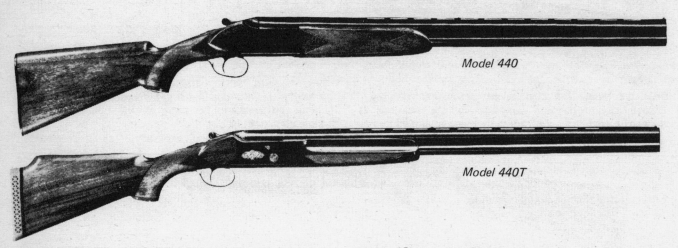

*Model 440*

*Model 440T*

**SAVAGE Model 440:** over/under; 12, 20-ga.; 2¾" chambers in 12-ga., 3" in 20; 26" barrel with improved cylinder/modified or skeet chokes, 28" modified/full, 30 ' modified/full; box-lock action; single selective trigger; plain extractors; checkered American walnut pistol-grip stock, forearm. Manufactured 1968 to 1972. Used value, $375 to $400.

**Model 440T Trap** has same specifications as Model 440,

except 12-ga. only; 30" barrels, improved modified/full chokes; wide vent rib; checkered select American walnut trap-type Monte Carlo stock, semi-beavertail forearm; recoil pad. Manufactured 1969 to 1972. Used value, $435 to $450.

**Model 444 Deluxe** has same general specs as Model 440, except for auto ejectors, select walnut stock, semi-beavertail forearm. Manufactured 1969 to 1972. Used value, $435 to $450.

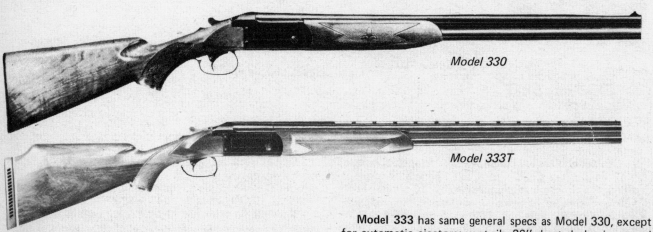

*Model 330*

*Model 333T*

**Model 333** has same general specs as Model 330, except for automatic ejectors; vent rib; 26" skeet choke, improved cylinder/modified barrels; 28" modified/full; 30" modified/full, fuller forearm. Imported 1973, dropped 1979. Used value, $390 to $415.

**Model 333T Trap** has same specs as Model 330, except 12-ga. only; 30" vent rib barrel; improved modified/full chokes; Monte Carlo trap stock; recoil pad. Imported 1972; dropped 1979. Used value, $375 to $390.

**SAVAGE Model 330:** over/under; 12, 20-ga.; 2¾" chambers for 12-ga., 3" for 20; 26" improved cylinder/modified barrel, 28" modified/full, 30" modified/full; box-lock action; selective single trigger; plain extractors; checkered European walnut pistol-grip stock, forearm. Manufactured in Finland by Valmet. Imported 1969; dropped, 1979. Used value, $315 to $325.

*Model 550*

**SAVAGE Model 550:** side-by-side; 12, 20-ga.; 2¾" chambers in 12-ga.; 3" in 20; 26" improved cylinder/modified barrels, 28" modified/full, 30" modified/full; hammerless; box-lock action; non-selective single trigger; auto ejectors; checkered American walnut pistol-grip stock, semi-beavertail forearm. Manufactured 1971 to 1973. Used value, $185 to $200.

*Model 2400 Combo*

**SAVAGE Model 2400 Combo:** over/under; 12-ga. full choke top barrel, .308 Winchester or .222 Remington lower barrel; box-lock action based on Model 330, 23½" barrel; solid matted rib; blade front sight, folding leaf rear; dovetail for scope mounting; checkered European walnut Monte Carlo pistol-grip stock, semi-beavertail forearm; recoil pad. Imported 1975; dropped 1979. Used value, $400 to $425.

*Model 242*

**SAVAGE Model 242:** over/under; .410; 24" barrels; full choke; based upon design of Model 24D combo gun. Introduced 1977, still in production. Used value, $85 to $95.

# L.C. SMITH

*Field Grade*

**L.C. SMITH Single-Barrel:** single-shot; box-lock; hammer-less; 12 ga. only; automatic ejector; 32", 34" barrels; vent rib; walnut stock; hand-checkered pistol grip, forearm; recoil pad. Made in 7 grades, original retail depending upon the quality of workmanship, engraving, quality of wood. Specialty Grade, introduced in 1917; dropped, 1948. Used value, $565 to $625. Eagle Grade, introduced in 1919; dropped, 1931. Used value, $1300 to $1350. Crown Grade, introduced in 1919; dropped, 1946. Used value, $1500 to $1750. Monogram Grade, introduced in 1919; dropped, 1946. Used value, $2750 to $3000. Olympic Grade, introduced in 1928; dropped, 1951. Used value, $500 to $550. Premier Grade, introduced in 1931; dropped, 1946. Used value, $4250 to $4500. Deluxe Grade, introduced in 1931; dropped, 1946. Used value, $7000 to $7250.

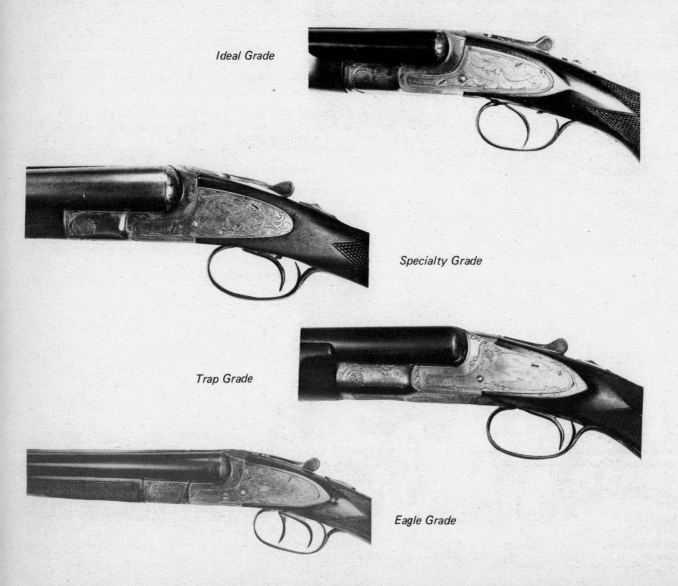

*Ideal Grade*

*Specialty Grade*

*Trap Grade*

*Eagle Grade*

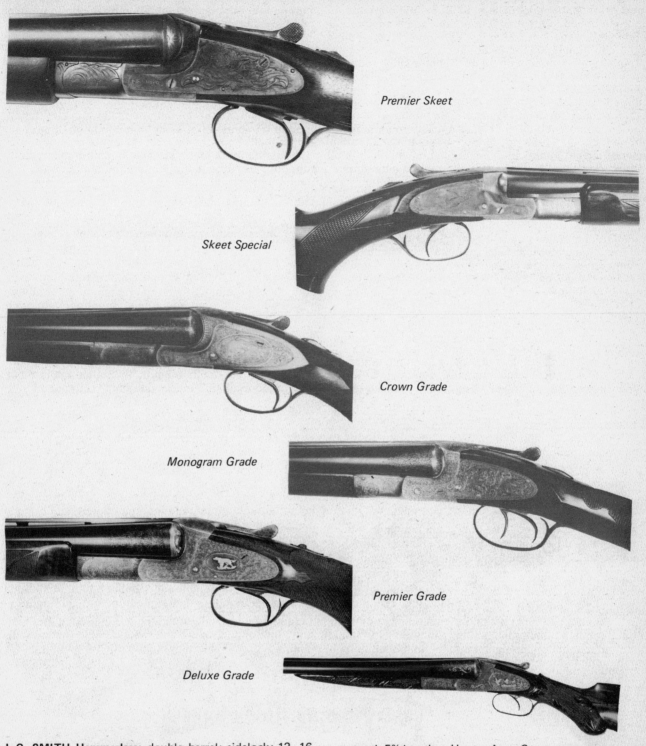

*Premier Skeet*

*Skeet Special*

*Crown Grade*

*Monogram Grade*

*Premier Grade*

*Deluxe Grade*

**L.C. SMITH Hammerless:** double barrel; sidelock; 12, 16, 20, .410 gauges; 26″ to 32″ barrels; standard choke combos; hand-checkered walnut stock, forearm; choice of straight stock, half or full pistol grip; beavertail or standard forearm; general specifications are the same on all grades, but grades depend upon quality of workmanship, checkering, engraving and wood. Guns were made by ·Hunter Arms from 1913 until 1945; by L.C. Smith from 1945 to 1951. Values shown are for 12-ga. guns; 16-ga. are worth 5% less than 12s; 20-ga. guns are worth about 20% more than 12s; .410 guns are worth 50 to 75% more than 12-ga. guns; models made by L.C. Smith Gun Company are

worth 5% less than Hunter Arms Company guns:

**Field Grade,** introduced in 1913; dropped, 1951; double triggers, plain extractors. Used value, $325 to $350; with automatic ejectors, $400 to $425; with non-selective single trigger, plain extractors, $375 to $400; single trigger, automatic ejectors, $475 to $500.

**Ideal Grade,** introduced in 1913; dropped, 1951; double triggers, plain extractors, $475 to $500; double triggers, automatic ejectors, $550 to $600; single non-selective trigger, plain extractors, $452 to $463; single selective trigger, automatic ejectors, $650 to $675.

**Specialty Grade,** introduced in 1913; dropped, 1951;

double triggers, plain extractors, $650 to $675; double triggers, automatic ejectors, $750 to $785; single selective trigger, plain extractors, $725 to $750; single selective trigger, auto ejectors, $825 to $850.

**Trap Grade,** introduced in 1913; dropped, 1939; made only with single selective trigger, automatic ejectors. Used value, $825 to $850.

**Eagle Grade,** introduced in 1913; dropped, 1939; double triggers, plain extractors, $1450 to $1500; double triggers, automatic ejectors, $1400 to $1450; single selective trigger, plain extractors, $1400 to $1450; single trigger, auto ejectors, $1600 to $1650.

**Crown Grade,** introduced in 1913; dropped, 1945; double triggers, automatic ejectors, $1750 to $1800; single selective trigger, auto ejectors; $2000 to $2250.

**Monogram Grade,** introduced in 1913; dropped, 1945; selective single trigger, automatic ejectors, $2500 to $2750.

**Premier Grade,** introduced in 1913; dropped, 1941; single selective trigger, automatic ejectors, $3750 to $4000.

**Deluxe Grade,** introduced in 1913; dropped, 1945; $7500 to $8000.

**Skeet Special,** introduced in 1913; dropped, 1942; selective or nonselective single trigger, automatic ejectors, $565 to $585.

**Premier Skeet Grade,** introduced in 1949; dropped, 1951; single selective trigger, automatic ejectors, $575 to $600.

*Marlin Deluxe Grade*

**L.C. SMITH Marlin:** double barrel; hammerless; sidelock action; Field Grade is 12 ga. only; 28" barrels; modified/full only; double triggers; case-hardened frame; vent rib; standard extractors; automatic tang safety; checkered pistol-grip stock of select walnut; pistol-grip cap. Deluxe Grade has same specifications as Field Grade, except for better wood, full beavertail forearm, Simmons floating vent rib. Introduced in 1968; dropped, 1972. Used values, Field Grade, $365 to $375; Deluxe Grade, $475 to $500.

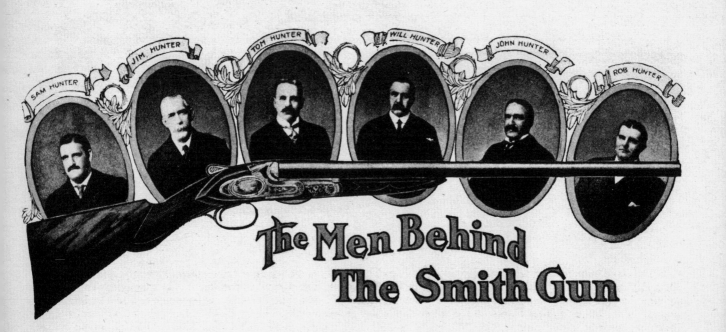

*In early days of L.C. Smith manufacture, family members of the Hunter Gun Co. took credit for success in advertisements.*

# STEVENS

*Model 620*

**STEVENS Model 620:** slide action; hammerless; 12, 16, 20 gauges; 26'', 28'', 30'', 32'' barrels; takedown; 5-rd. tube magazine; cylinder, improved, modified, full chokes; hand-checkered American walnut pistol-grip stock, slide handle; black plastic butt plate. Introduced in 1927; dropped, 1953. Used value, $125 to $135.

**STEVENS Model 621:** slide action; hammerless; 12, 16, 20 gauges; has the same specifications as the Model 620 except for raised solid matted rib. Introduced in 1927; dropped, 1953. Used value, $135 to $150.

*Model 311*

**STEVENS-Springfield Model 311:** side-by-side; hammerless; box-lock action; 12, 16, 20, .410 gauges; 26'', 28'', 30'', 32'' barrels; modified/full, cylinder/modified, full/full chokes; early guns had uncheckered American walnut pistol-grip stock, forearm; current production has walnut-finished hardwood stock, fluted comb; double triggers; plastic butt plate. Introduced in 1931; still in production as Savage-Stevens Model 311. Used value, $145 to $165.

*Model 59*

**STEVENS Model 59:** bolt-action repeater; takedown; .410-ga. only; 24'' barrel, full choke only; 5-rd. tube magazine; uncheckered one-piece walnut-finished hardwood pistol-grip stock; plastic butt plate. Introduced in 1934; dropped, 1973. Used value, $65 to $85.

*Model 530ST*

**STEVENS Model 530:** side-by-side; hammerless; box-lock action; 12, 16, 20, .410 gauges; 26'', 28'', 30'', 32'' barrels; modified/full, cylinder/modified, full choke combos; double triggers; early models have recoil pads; hand-checkered American walnut pistol-grip stock, forearm. Introduced in 1936; dropped, 1954. Used value, $165 to $195.

**Model 530M** has the same specifications as Model 530 except stock, forearm are of Tenite plastic. Introduced before World War II; dropped, 1947. Used value, $135 to $155.

**Model 530ST** has the same specifications as Model 530 except for single selective trigger. Introduced in 1947; dropped, 1954. Used value, $200 to $225.

*Model 58*

**STEVENS Model 58:** bolt-action repeater; takedown; .410-ga. only; 24″ barrel; full choke only; 3-rd. detachable box magazine; unchecked one-piece walnut-finished hard- wood pistol-grip stock; plastic butt plate; current model has machine-checkering on grip, forearm. Introduced in 1937; still in production as Savage-Stevens Model 58. Used value, $45 to $55.

*Model 258*

**STEVENS Model 258:** bolt-action repeater; takedown; 20-ga. only; 25″ barrel, full choke only; double triggers; unchecked hardwood one-piece pistol-grip stock; black plastic forearm cap, butt plate. Introduced in 1937; dropped, 1965. Used value, $55 to $65.

*Model 107*

**STEVENS Model 107:** single-barrel; single-shot; hammer gun; takedown; 12, 16, 20, .410 gauges; 28″, 30″ barrels in 12, 16 gauges, 28″ in 20-ga., 26″ in .410; full choke only; automatic ejector; unchecked walnut-finished hardwood pistol-grip stock, forearm. Introduced in 1937; dropped, 1953. Used value, $55 to $70.

*No. 22-410*

**STEVENS Model 22-410:** over/under combo gun; .22 LR, long, short barrel over .410 shotgun barrel; visible hammer; takedown; 24″ barrels; full choke shotgun barrel; single trigger; open rear sight, rifle-type ramp front; original models had unchecked American walnut pistol-grip stock, forearm; later production had Tenite plastic stock, forearm. Introduced in 1938; dropped, 1950. Still in production by Savage Arms as Model 24, with variations. Used values, walnut stock, $75 to $100; plastic stock, $65 to $75.

*Model 240*

**STEVENS Model 240:** over/under; hammer gun; takedown; .410-ga. only; 26" barrels, full choke only; double triggers; early models had uncheckered American walnut pistol-grip stock, forearm; later versions had stock, forearm of Tenite plastic. Introduced in 1939; dropped, 1942. Used values, walnut stock, $250 to $275; plastic stock, $190 to $225.

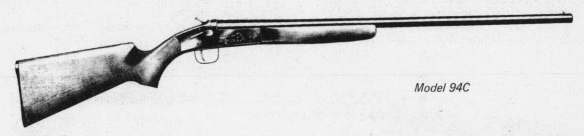

*Model 94C*

**STEVENS Model 94C:** single-barrel; single-shot; hammer gun; 12, 16, 20, .410 gauges; full choke only; 28", 30", 32", 36" barrels; automatic ejector; top lever breaking; walnut-finished hardwood pistol-grip stock, forearm; machine checkering on current models; color case-hardened frame. Introduced before World War II; still in production as Savage-Stevens Model 94C. Used value, $55 to $60.

**STEVENS-Springfield Model 5151:** side-by-side; hammerless; box-lock action; 12, 16, 20, .410 gauges; has the same general specifications as Stevens Model 311 except for hand-checkered pistol grip, forearm; recoil pad; two Ivoroid sights. Manufactured prior to World War II. Used value, $165 to $185.

Model 5151-ST has the same specifications as Model 5151 except for non-selective single trigger. Used value, $175 to $195.

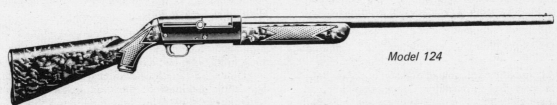

*Model 124*

**STEVENS Model 124:** autoloader; solid frame, hammerless; 12-ga. only; 28" barrel; improved, modified, full chokes; 2-rd. tube magazine; checkered Tenite plastic stock, forearm. Introduced in 1947; dropped, 1952. Used value, $85 to $95.

*Model 77 Standard*

**STEVENS Model 77:** slide action repeater; solid frame; hammerless; 12, 16 gauges; 26" barrel improved; 28" modified or full choke; 5-rd. tube magazine; uncheckered walnut-finished hardwood stock, grooved slide handle. Introduced in 1954; dropped, 1971. Used value, $120 to $130.

Model 77SC has the same specifications as standard Model 77, except for Savage Super Choke. Used value, $140 to $150.

# UNIVERSAL FIREARMS

**UNIVERSAL Model 101:** single-shot, external hammer; takedown; 12-ga. only; 28", 30" full-choke barrel; 3" chamber; top-breaking action; unchecked pistol-grip stock, beavertail forearm. Introduced in 1967; dropped, 1969. Replaced by Single Wing model. Used value, $50 to $65.

**UNIVERSAL Model 202:** side-by-side double barrel; box-lock action; 12, 20 gauges; 26" improved/modified barrels, 28" modified/full; 3" chambers; top breaking; double triggers; hand-checkered European walnut pistol-grip stock, European-style forearm. Introduced in 1967; dropped, 1969. Replaced by Double Wing model. Used value, $125 to $135.

**Model 203** has the same specifications as Model 202, except is chambered for 3½" 10-ga. shells; has 32" full/full barrels. Introduced in 1967; dropped, 1969. Used value, $200 to $225.

*Double Wing*

**UNIVERSAL Double Wing:** side-by-side; box-lock; top-breaking action; 12, 20 gauges; 26" improved/modified barrels, 28" and 30" modified/full; double triggers; recoil pad; checkered European walnut pistol-grip stock, beavertail forearm. Introduced in 1970; dropped, 1974. Used value, $150 to $175.

**UNIVERSAL Model 2030:** side-by-side; top-breaking box-lock action; has the same general specifications as Double Wing Model except chambered for 3½" 10-ga. shells; 32" full/full barrels only. Introduced in 1970; dropped, 1974. Used value, $200 to $225.

**UNIVERSAL Auto Wing:** autoloader; recoil operated; takedown; 12-ga. only; 5-shot magazine, 3-shot plug furnished; 2¾" chamber; 25", 28", 30" barrel; improved, modified, full chokes; vent rib; ivory bead front, middle sights; crossbolt safety; interchangeable barrels; checkered European walnut pistol-grip stock, grooved forearm. Introduced in 1970; dropped, 1974. Used value, $135 to $155.

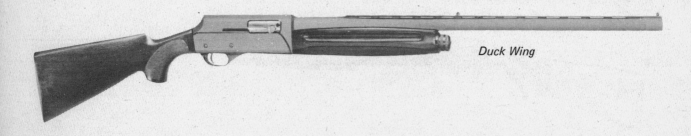

*Duck Wing*

**UNIVERSAL Duck Wing:** autoloader; recoil operated; takedown; 12-ga. only. Has the same specifications as Auto Wing model except has 28", 30" barrel only; full choke only; exposed metal parts coated with olive green Teflon-S. Introduced in 1970; dropped, 1972. Used value, $150 to $175.

*Over Wing*

**UNIVERSAL Over Wing:** over/under; hammerless; box-lock; top-breaking action; 12, 20 gauges; 3" chambers; 26" improved/modified, 28" or 30" modified/full barrels; vent rib; front, middle sights; checkered European walnut pistol-grip stock, forearm; recoil pad; double triggers; single trigger model with engraved receiver at added cost. Introduced in 1970; dropped, 1974. Used values, double trigger model, $175 to $200; single trigger, $225 to $250.

**UNIVERSAL Single Wing:** single-shot; external hammer; top-breaking action; 12-ga. only; 3" chamber; takedown; 28" full or modified barrel; uncheckered European walnut pistol-grip stock, beavertail forearm; automatic ejector. Introduced in 1970; dropped, 1974. Used value, $50 to $65.

**UNIVERSAL BAIKAL MC-21:** autoloader; takedown; 12-ga. only; 5-rd. magazine; 26" improved, 28" modified, 30" full choke barrels; vent rib; hand-checkered European walnut cheekpiece stock; white spacers at pistol grip, butt plate; hand-rubbed finish; grooved forearm; chrome-lined barrel, chamber; reversible safety; target grade trigger. Manufactured in Russia. Introduced in 1973. Used value, $265 to $275.

*Baikal TOZ-66*

**UNIVERSAL BAIKAL TOZ-66:** side-by-side; exposed hammers; 12-ga. only; 2¾" chambers; 20" improved/modified, 28" modified/full barrels; hand-checkered European hardwood pistol-grip stock, beavertail forearm; chrome-lined barrels, chambers; hand-engraved receiver; extractors. Manufactured in Russia. Introduced in 1973. Used value, $150 to $175.

*Baikal IJ-58M*

**UNIVERSAL BAIKAL IJ-58M:** side-by-side; hammerless; 12-ga. only; 2¾" chambers; 26" improved/modified, 28" modified/full barrels; hand-checkered European walnut pistol-grip stock, beavertail forearm; hinged front double trigger; chrome-lined barrels, chambers; hand-engraved receiver; extractors. Manufactured in Russia. Introduced in 1973; Used value, $175 to $200.

**UNIVERSAL BAIKAL MC-10:** side-by-side; hammerless; 12, 20 gauges; 2¾" chambers; 12-ga. has 28" modified/full barrels, 20-ga., 26" improved/modified; hand-checkered fancy European walnut stock, semi-beavertail forearm; choice of pistol grip or straight stock; chrome-lined barrels, chambers, internal parts; raised solid rib; double triggers; auto safety; extractors or selective ejectors; receiver engraved with animal bird scenes; engraved trigger guard, tang. Manufactured in Russia. Introduced in 1973. Used value, $500 to $525.

**UNIVERSAL BAIKAL IJ-25:** over/under; 12-ga. only; 2¾" chambers; 26" skeet/skeet barrels, 28" modified/full, 30" improved/full; hand-checkered European walnut pistol-grip stock, ventilated forearm; white spacers at pistol-grip

cap, recoil pad; single non-selective trigger; chrome-lined barrels, chambers, internal parts; vent rib; hand-engraved, silver inlaid receiver, forearm latch, trigger guard. Manufactured in Russia. Introduced in 1973. Used value, $400 to $425.

*IJ-27*

**UNIVERSAL IJ-27:** over/under; 12-ga. only; has the same general specifications as IJ-25, except for double triggers, automatic safety, non-selective ejectors. Introduced in 1973;

Used value, $250 to $275.
   **Universal Baikal IJ-27E** has same specifications as the IJ-27, except for substitution of selective ejectors. Used value, $250 to $300.

**UNIVERSAL BAIKAL MC-5:** over/under; 12-ga. only; 2¾" chambers; 26" improved/modified, skeet/skeet barrels; fancy hand-checkered European walnut stock; choice of straight or pistol-grip stock, with or without cheekpiece;

non-removable forearm; engraved receiver; double triggers; extractors; hand-fitted solid rib; hammer interceptors; chrome-lined barrels, chambers, internal parts. Manufactured in Russia. Introduced in U.S. in 1973. Used value, $400 to $425.

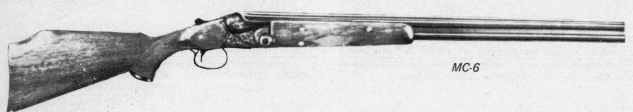

*MC-6*

**UNIVERSAL BAIKAL MC-6:** over/under; 12-ga. only; has the same specifications as MC-5, except is skeet model, with

single nonselective trigger, raised rib. Used value, $650 to $700.

**UNIVERSAL BAIKAL MC-7:** over/under; 12, 20 gauges; 2¾" chambers; 12-ga., 28" modified/full, 20-ga., 26" improved/modified barrels; hand-checkered European walnut straight or pistol-grip stock, beavertail forearm;

double triggers; selective ejectors; solid raised rib; chrome-lined barrels, chambers, internal parts; hand-chiseled, engraved reciever. Manufactured in Russia. Introduced in U.S. in 1973. Used value, $1250 to $1350.

*MC-8*

**UNIVERSAL BAIKAL MC-8:** over/under; 12-ga. only; 2¾" chambers; 26" special skeet barrels; 28" modified/full; two-barrel set; fancy hand-checkered European walnut Monte Carlo pistol-grip stock, non-removable forearm;

double triggers; extractors; hand-fitted vent rib; blued, engraved receiver; chrome-lined barrels, chambers, internal parts; single selective trigger, selective ejectors available at no extra cost. Manufactured in Russia. Introduced in U.S. in 1973. Used value, $525 to $550.

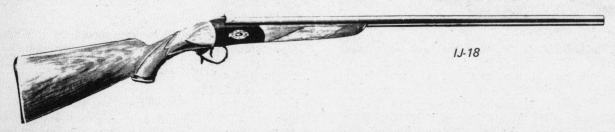

*IJ-18*

**UNIVERSAL BAIKAL IJ-18:** single-barrel, single-shot; 12, 20 gauges; 2¾" chamber; in 12-ga., 28" modified, 30" full choke barrel, 20-ga., 26" modified; hand-checkered European walnut pistol-grip stock, forearm; white spacers

at pistol grip, plastic butt plate; cross-bolt safety in trigger guard; cocking indicator; chrome-lined barrel, chamber. Manufactured in Russia. Introduced in U.S. in 1973; Used value, $45 to $65.

# WESTLEY RICHARDS

**WESTLEY RICHARDS Best Quality:** side-by-side; double barrel; hammerless; box-lock action; 12, 16, 20 gauges; barrel lengths, chokes to order; hand-detachable locks; hinged lockplate; selective ejectors; hand-checkered walnut stock, forearm; choice of straight, half-pistol grip; double or single selective trigger. Introduced in 1890; dropped, 1965. Used values, double trigger model, $3450 to $3625; single selective trigger, $4250 to $4500.

Best Quality Pigeon or Wildfowl Model has same specifications as standard model except for stronger action, triple bolting, 12-ga. only, chambered for 2¾", 3" shells; 28", 30" full choke barrels. Introduced in 1900; still in production. Used values, double trigger model, $4500 to $5000; single selective trigger, $5250 to $5500.

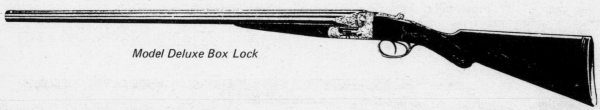

*Model Deluxe Box Lock*

**WESTLEY RICHARDS Model DeLuxe Quality:** side-by-side double barrel; hammerless; box-lock action; hand-detachable locks; triple-bite lever work; other specifications are same as Best Quality model, except for better workmanship throughout. Available in Pigeon or Wildfowl Model at same price. Introduced in 1890; still in production. Used values, double trigger model, $6250 to $6500; single selective trigger, $6500 to $7000.

*Model Deluxe Sidelock*

**WESTLEY RICHARDS Sidelock Model DeLuxe Quality:** side-by-side double barrel; hammerless; hand-detachable side locks; 12, 16, 20 gauges; barrel lengths, chokes to order; selective ejectors; double triggers, single selective triggers; hand-checkered European stock, forearm; straight or half-pistol grip available in Pigeon or Wildfowl Model at same price. Introduced in 1910; still in production. Used values, double trigger model, $7000 to $7250; single selective trigger, $7250 to $7500.

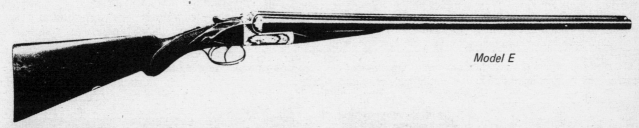

*Model E*

**WESTLEY RICHARDS Model E:** side-by-side double barrel; hammerless; Anson & Deeley box-lock action; 12, 16, 20 gauges; barrel lengths, choking to order; selective ejector or non-ejector; double triggers; hand-checkered European walnut stock, forearm; straight or half-pistol grip; Pigeon or Wildfowl Model available at same price. Introduced in late 1920s; still in production. Used values, ejector model, $2500 to $2750; nonejector, $2250 to $2500.

**WESTLEY RICHARDS Ovundo:** over/under; hammerless; box-lock action; 12-ga. only; barrel lengths, chokes to order; hand-detachable locks, dummy side plates; single selective trigger; hand-checkered European walnut stock, forearm; straight or half-pistol grip. Introduced in 1920; dropped, 1945. Used value, $8750 to $9500.

# WINCHESTER

*Model 1887*

**WINCHESTER Model 1887:** lever action; 10, 12-ga.; 4-rd. tubular magazine; 30", 32" barrel, full choke; solid frame; uncheckered American walnut pistol-grip stock, forend. Collector value. Manufactured 1887 to 1901. Used value, $350 to $400.

   **Deluxe Model 1887** has same specs as standard model, except has damascus barrel, hand-checkered stock, forend. Manufactured 1887 to 1901. Used value, $400 to $425.

*Model 1901*

**WINCHESTER Model 1901:** lever action; 10-ga.; has same general specifications as Model 1887, except for re-design features. Replaced Model 1887 in line. Collector interest. Manufactured 1901 to 1920. Used value, $425 to $450.

*Model 97*

**WINCHESTER Model 97:** slide-action shotgun; visible hammer, takedown or solid frame in 12, 16 gauges, 5-shot tube magazine. Barrel lengths: 26", 28", 30", 32"; last in 12-ga. only; choked full, modified, cylinder bore, with intermediate chokes introduced in 1931. Gun, introduced in 1897, was revamp of Model 1893. Numerous variations were introduced, discontinued over the years, with model discontinued, 1957. Standard grade has plain stock and grooved slide handle, side ejection port. Retail price when discontinued, $89.95; used value, $250 to $265.

   Model 97 also was available in higher grade trap, tournament, pigeon grades. Stocks on higher grades were of better walnut, checkered. On these, slide handles also were of better wood, checkered, in standard or semi-beavertail configuration, without the deep wood grooves of standard model. Higher grades were discontinued 1939. Used value on trap grade, $400 to $425; tournament grade, $525 to $550; pigeon grade, $825 to $950.

   Model 97 also was offered as riot gun with same specifications as standard model, takedown or solid frame. In 12-ga. only, it had 20" cylinder bore barrel. Trench gun, the same as riot model, was issued with bayonet by U.S. government in 1917-18. Used value on riot model, $250 to $275; trench model, $350 to $375.

*Model 1911*

**WINCHESTER Model 1911:** autoloading shotgun was hammerless, takedown, in 12-ga. only. Barrels were plain in 26", 28", 30", 32"; standard chokes; 4-shell tubular magazine; stock and forearm plain or checkered. Intro- duced in 1911; discontinued, 1925. Considered unsafe; recalled by factory for refund or new Model 12. Collector value only. Original retail price, $61.50; used value, $220 to $235.

*Model 12 Standard*

*Model 12 Trap*

*Model 12 Pigeon*

*Model 12 Super Pigeon Skeet*

*Model 12 Super Pigeon Trap*

**WINCHESTER Model 12:** slide-action shotgun; in 12, 16, 20 and 28 gauges, in three standard versions; has blued receiver of chrome-moly steel, engine-turned bolt and carrier, ventilated rib; butt stock and slide handle are walnut with fine-line hand checkering; magazine capacity, 5 rds. Field gun has 26", 28", 30" barrels, with choice of improved cylinder, modified or full, full chokes, respectively. Model 12 trap gun is full choke only with 30" barrel, choice of standard or Monte Carlo stock, recoil pad; skeet gun is skeet choked, with 26" barrel, fitted stock, recoil pad. Introduced originally in 1912; dropped from line in 1965; reintroduced in 1972; retail price on current models starts at $875, depending upon style. Price in 1965, when dropped was $237.50, for skeet model, for 1972 model, $290 to $360, depending on style; for pre-1965 models, $185. Nostalgia has resulted in older Model 12s often selling for more than original retail price. As an example of supply and demand, in 1965, price for pigeon grade was $372.50. One year later — with Model 12 discontinued and considered a custom gun, price leaped to $825.

Prior to discontinuance in 1965, there were many variations of Model 12 and an even wider variation of used values. Model 12 Featherweight, made from 1959 to 1962, had plain barrel, modified takedown, alloy guard, in 12-ga. only; available in 26", improved cylinder; 28", modified or full; 30", full. Used value, $275 to $300. Standard version with matted rib, discontinued after WWII, has used value of $450 to $500. Standard grade, with vent rib, also discontinued after WWII, was 12-ga. only with 26¾" or 30" barrel. Used value, $650 to $700. Manufactured from 1918 to 1963 was Model 12 riot model, in 12-ga., with 20" cylinder bore barrel. Used value, $275 to $300.

The Model 12 has appeared in several skeet configurations. The standard skeet model, discontinued after WWII, was in 12, 16, 20, 28 gauges, with 5-shot tube magazine, 26" barrel, skeet choke. Featured red or ivory bead front sight, 94B mid-sight. Pistol grip was checkered as was extension slide handle. Used value, $575 to $600. Skeet model with plain barrel, sans sights, was manufactured from 1937 to 1947; used value, $575 to $600. Style featuring Cutts Compensator, with plain barrel, was discontinued, 1954; used value, $450 to $500. Discontinued in 1965, skeet style with ventilated rib was 12, 20 gauges; used value, $650 to $700 for 12-ga., $800 to $1250 for 20-ga.

Of trap configurations, original was discontinued after WWII. It had specs of standard Model 12, plus extension slide handle, recoil pad, straighter stock, checkered pistol

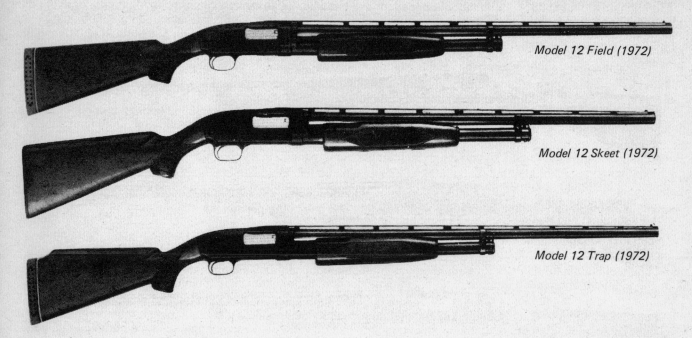

*Model 12 Field (1972)*

*Model 12 Skeet (1972)*

*Model 12 Trap (1972)*

grip, recoil pad, 30" matted rib barrel; 12-ga., full choke only. Used value, $600 to $650. Trap model with ventilated rib was same as standard trap otherwise; used value, $650 to $750. Model 12 trap with Monte Carlo stock and vent rib; used value, $700 to $800.

Model 12 also was produced in two styles for duck hunters. The heavy duck gun, in 12-ga. only, handled 3" shells, had 3-shot magazine, recoil pad, 30" or 32" barrel lengths, full choke only. Discontinued, 1964; used value, $475 to $500. Same style, with matted rib, was discontinued, 1959; used value, $600 to $650.

Model 12 pigeon grade guns virtually constitute an empire unto themselves. These were deluxe versions of the standard, field, duck, skeet or trap guns made on special order only. Pigeon grade guns had finer finishes, hand-worked actions, engine-turned bolts, carriers. Stock dimensions were to specs of individual, with top grade walnut, fancy hand-checkering. At added cost from $50 to $250 or more, engraving and carving could be added. This particular grade was discontinued, 1965; prices are based upon variations, sans added engraving and carving. Range of used values is: field gun, plain barrel, $600 to $625; with vent rib, $1200 to $1225; skeet gun, matted rib, $725 to $750; vent rib, $1200 to $1250; skeet, Cutts Compensator, $750 to $775; trap gun, matted rib, $825 to $850; with vent rib, $1200 to $1500.

Used values for Winchester Model 12 Super Pigeon grade can be no more than an approximation, since these are rare as pearls and, like pearls, are worth what the buyer wants to pay. Super Pigeon grade, introduced, 1965, still is produced in conjunction with the Model 12, reintroduced to the trade in 1972. Custom Model 12 has the same general specs as standard models; available in 12-ga. only, with any standard choke and barrel length choice of 26", 28", or 30", with vent rib. Receiver is engraved; hand-honed and fitted action. Stocks, forearm are fancy walnut and made to individual order. Used value starts at $1250. After that, you're on your own.

**Model 12 (1972)** has same general specs as standard Model 12, except for engine-turned bolt, carrier; 12-ga. only; 26", 28", 30" standard choke barrels; vent rib, hand-checkered American walnut stock, slide handle. Manufactured 1972 to 1975. Used value, $400 to $425.

**Model 12 Skeet (1972)** has same specs as standard Model 12 (1972), except for 26" skeet-choked barrel; hand-checkered skeet stock, slide handle; recoil pad. Manufactured 1972 to 1975. Used value, $425 to $450.

**Model 12 Trap (1972)** has same specs as standard Model 12 (1972); 30" full choke vent rib barrel only; straight or Monte Carlo trap stock, recoil pad. Manufactured 1972 to present. Used value, $425 to $450.

*Model 20*

**WINCHESTER Model 20:** single-shot shotgun. Takedown hammer gun, .410 only, for 2½" shell. Only in 26", full choke barrel; checkered pistol grip, forearm. Introduced in 1919; discontinued, 1924. Retail when discontinued, $16.50; used value, $235 to $265.

*Model 36*

**WINCHESTER Model 36:** single-shot bolt-action takedown shotgun. Cocks by pulling rearward on knurled firing-pin head, the same mechanism used in some Winchester single-shot rifles. Shot 9mm short or long shot or ball cartridges interchangeably. Has one-piece plain wood stock, forearm, special trigger guard that forms the pistol grip, composition butt plate. Round 18" barrel. No guns were serialized. Introduced in 1920; discontinued, 1927. Price at time discontinued, $7.05; used value, $150 to $175.

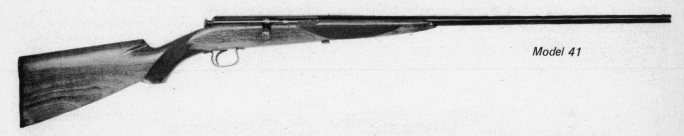

*Model 41*

**WINCHESTER Model 41:** single-shot bolt-action shotgun. Standard takedown style only, with 24" full choke barrel, firing .410-ga., 2½" ammo. Chambering was changed in 1933 for 3" shell. Stock is plain one-piece walnut; pistol grip; hard rubber butt plate. Straight grip was optional at no increase in price; checkered stocks on special order. Model 41s were not numbered serially; increase in value reflects interest as a collector item. Introduced in 1920; discontinued, 1934. Original retail, $9.95; used value, $225 to $250.

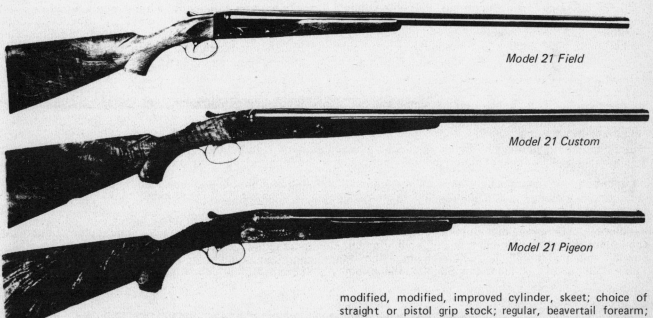

*Model 21 Field*

*Model 21 Custom*

*Model 21 Pigeon*

**WINCHESTER Model 21:** double barrel hammerless field gun; boxlock; automatic safety. Early models have double triggers, non-selective ejection; post WWII guns have selective single trigger, selective ejection. Made in 12, 16, 20, 28 gauges, .410, with 20", 28", 30", 32" barrels, last only in 12-ga. raised matted or ventilated rib. Chokes are full, improved modified, modified, improved cylinder, skeet; choice of straight or pistol grip stock; regular, beavertail forearm; checkered walnut. Introduced in 1931; discontinued, 1959. Retail when discontinued, $425; used value with double triggers, non-selective ejection, $1000 to $1250; double triggers, selective ejection, $1250 to $1400; selective single trigger, non-selective ejection, $1500 to $1750; selective single trigger, selective ejection, $1750 to $1850; with ventilated rib, add $275 to $350.

**Model 21 Skeet Gun** is same general design as standard

*Model 21 Grand American*

model, but has 26″, 28″ barrels only; skeet chokes; red bead front sight; selective single trigger, selective ejection, non-auto safety, checkered French walnut stock, beavertail forearm; wooden butt is checkered without pad or butt plate; discontinued, 1958. Used value, with matted rib, $1650 to $1850; with ventilated rib, $1850 to $2250.

**Model 21 Trap** model differs from standard with 30″ or 32″ barrels, full choke, selective trigger, non-auto safety, selective ejection; pistol grip or straight stock, beavertail forearm of checkered walnut. Discontinued, 1958. Used value, with matted rib, $1500 to $1750; with vent rib, $1850 to $2250.

**Model 21 Duck Gun** has same general specs as field gun, but is chambered for 3″, 12-ga. shells; has 30″, 32″ barrels, full choke; selective ejection, selective single trigger, recoil pad, checkered beavertail forearm, pistol grip stock. Discontinued, 1958; used value, with matted rib, $1700 to $1850; with vent rib, $2000 to $2250.

As with the Model 12, the Winchester Model 21 has become a special order gun. Since 1960, it has been offered only in custom, pigeon and Grand American grades. General specs are as for the standard Model 21, but these have full fancy American walnut stocks, forearms, with fancy checkering, hand-honed working parts. Carved woodwork, gold inlays and engraving are available at added cost. The custom trio still is being manufactured. Used value, custom grade, $3500 to $3750; pigeon grade, $4500 to $5000; Grand American, $6500 to $7000.

*Model 42*

**WINCHESTER Model 42**: hammerless slide-action shotgun; .410 only; 26″ or 28″ barrel, full or modified choke; chambered for 3″ shells; available with plain walnut stock, no checkering; slide handle grooved; capacity of 6 shells in 2½″ length, 5 shells in 3″ length; weight, 5-7/8 to 6 lbs. Trap grade had full fancy wood and checkering, until dropped in 1940. Introduced in May, 1933; dropped in 1963; last retail price, $101.95; used value, $450 to $650.

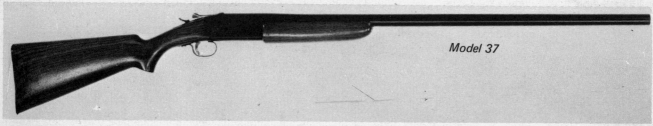

*Model 37*

**WINCHESTER Model 37**: single-shot shotgun; is top lever, breakdown construction with automatic ejector, semi-hammerless action; plain barrel only in 12, 16, 20, .410 gauges; barrel lengths, 28″, 30″, 32″ in all but .410, with choice of 26″ or 28″; all full choke. Stock is plain walnut with composition butt plate, pistol grip, semi-beavertail forearm. On special order, at no extra charge, barrels could be modified or cylinder choke. Introduced in 1936, discontinued, 1963. Last retail price was $35; used value, $85 to $140.

*Model 24*

**WINCHESTER Model 24:** hammerless double-barrel shotgun in 12, 16, 20 gauges. With 26" barrels, chokes were improved/modified; 28", modified/full and improved/modified; 30" barrels, modified/full, in 12-ga. only. Stock is plain walnut, with pistol grip, semi-beaver-tailed forearm, composition butt plate; straight stock at no added charge; a breakdown model, it has double triggers, automatic ejectors. Introduced in 1940; discontinued, 1957. Price when discontinued, $96.20; used value, $300 to $350; 20-ga., $400 to $450.

*Model 40 Skeet*

**WINCHESTER Model 40:** autoloading shotgun; 12-ga. only, with streamlined receiver, hammerless action; 4-rd. tube magazine; 28" or 30" barrels; choke, modified or full. Had plain pistol-grip stock, semi-beavertail forearm, ramp bead front sight. Introduced, 1940; discontinued, 1941. Retail, when discontinued, $68.15. Used value, $250 to $300.

**Model 40 Skeet** model had 24" barrel, with Cutts compensator; checkering on pistol grip, forearm; grip cap. Collector interest. Original price, $73.50; used value, $280 to $325.

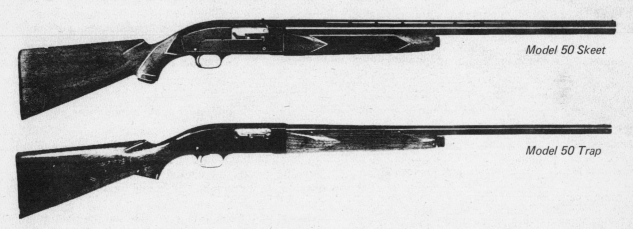

*Model 50 Skeet*

*Model 50 Trap*

**WINCHESTER Model 50:** autoloading shotgun; field grades available in 12 and 20 gauges; skeet, 12; trap, 12; 12-gauge barrels were 30" full choke, 28" full or modified, 28" improved or skeet. There were numerous options, including a ventilated rib and gun could fire field or high-velocity loads, without adjustment; stock was of American walnut, hand-checkered with fluted comb, composition butt plate; magazine tube was below barrel, with two-shell capacity, side ejection. Featherweight model was adopted in 1958. Weight for standard was 7¼ lbs. for 12-gauge, 7 lbs. for Featherweight, 5¾ lbs. for 20-gauge. Pigeon grade gun was available with any combination of barrel lengths and chokes. Barrels interchangeable, with bead front sight. Gun worked on short recoil principle. When fired, floating chamber moved rearward to start the action moving to the rear. Bolt continued to rear, extracting and ejecting spent shell, lifting new one into position. Introduced in late 1954; discontinued in 1961. Retailed at $144.95 for standard grade; used value, $260 to $300.

**The Model 50 Field** gun is the same as the standard, except for ventilated rib; used value, $300 to $325. Skeet version has 26" barrel vent rib, skeet stock in selected walnut, skeet choke; used value, $300 to $335. Model 50 trap, 12-ga. only; full choke 30" vent rib barrel; Monte Carlo stock of select walnut; used value, $375 to $400.

*Model 25*

**WINCHESTER Model 25:** slide-action repeating shotgun; solid frame; hammerless; 12-ga. only, with 4-rd. tubular magazine. Made with 28" plain barrel in improved cylinder, modified or full choke; metal bead front sight. Stock, grooved slide handle are walnut, with pistol grip. Introduced, 1950; discontinued, 1953. Used value, $275 to $325.

Model 25 was made in riot model from 1949 to 1955; only change from standard was a 20" cylinder choke barrel. Used value, $225 to $275.

*Model 59*

**WINCHESTER Model 59:** autoloading shotgun; 12-ga. only. Had checkered stock, forearm. Choices were 26″ barrel, improved cylinder; 28″, modified or full; 30″ full choke. Special order 26″ barrel has Versalite choke system of cylinder tubes (introduced in 1961) to allow any choke variation. Barrel was fiberglass-wrapped steel tube. Introduced in 1959; discontinued, 1965. Retail price when discontinued, $160; used value, $250 to $300.
*(Winchester also made a Model 59 rimfire rifle in 1930 — don't be confused by the model numbers.)*

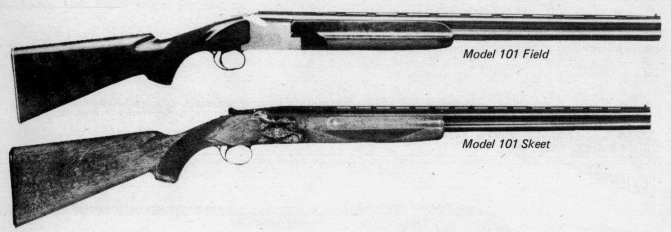

*Model 101 Field*

*Model 101 Skeet*

**WINCHESTER Model 101:** field gun with box-lock action, engraved receiver, automatic ejectors, single selective trigger, combo barrel selector, safety; vent ribbed barrels. Model 101 is virtually an empire in itself, being made in various configurations and styles. Handles 2¾″ shells in 12, 28 gauges, 3″ in 20, .410; 30″ barrels on 12 only, choked modified/full; 28″, modified/full; 26″, 12-ga. only, and 26½″, choked improved/modified. Stock, forearm are checkered French walnut. Made in Japan by Olin Kodensha. The 12-ga. was introduced in 1963; other gauges, 1966. Still manufactured, Used value, 12, 20 gauges, $450 to $475; 28, .410, $525 to $550.

**Model 101 Magnum Field** gun is same as standard field gun, but chambered for 12 and 20-ga., 3″ magnum shells. The 30″ barrels are choked full/full, modified/full; has recoil pad. Introduced, 1966, still in production; used value, $475 to $500.

**Model 101 Skeet** gun is the same as the field model, except for skeet stock, forearm; barrels for 12-ga. are 26″, for 20-ga., 26½″; 28, .410, 28″; all gauges skeet choked. Introduced in 1966, still in production; used value for 12, 20 gauges, $485 to $500; 28, .410, $550 to $575.

**Model 101 Trap** gun has trap stock, Monte Carlo or straight; recoil pad; 12-ga. only; barrels are 30″, 32″, improved modified/full, full/full. Introduced in 1966, still produced. Used value, straight stock, $550 to $575; Monte Carlo, $575 to $585.

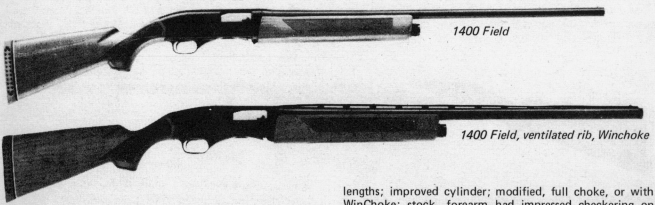

*1400 Field*

*1400 Field, ventilated rib, Winchoke*

**WINCHESTER Model 1400:** field gun; gas-operated take-down autoloader; 2-shot magazines; 2¾″ chamber for 12, 16, 20 gauges; plain barrel or with vent rib in 26″, 28″, 30″ lengths; improved cylinder; modified, full choke, or with WinChoke; stock, forearm had impressed checkering on walnut; recoil pad was available with recoil reduction system and Cycolac stock. Introduced in 1964; dropped in 1968 to be replaced by Model 1400 Mark II. Original price,

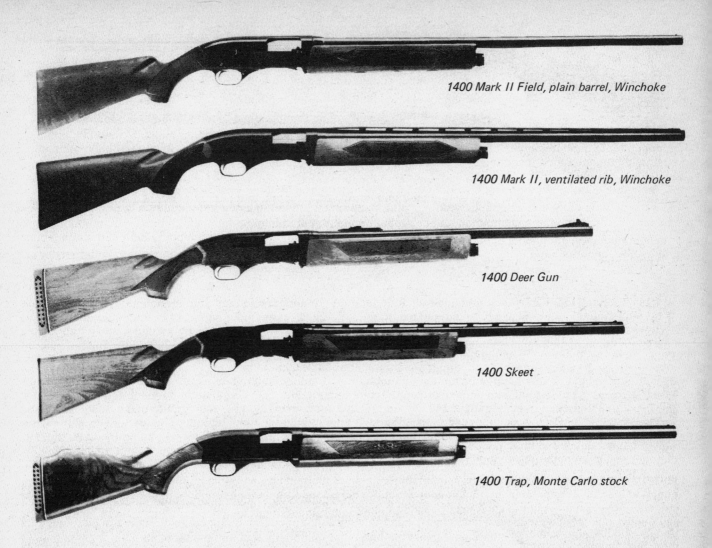

1400 Mark II Field, plain barrel, Winchoke

1400 Mark II, ventilated rib, Winchoke

1400 Deer Gun

1400 Skeet

1400 Trap, Monte Carlo stock

$149.95; used value, with plain barrel, $120 to $135; with vent rib, $136 to $141; with WinChoke, add $8 to $10; with recoil reduction system, add $50 to $60.

**Model 1400 Mark II**, introduced in 1968, has restyled stock, forearm, push-button carrier release; has front-locking, rotating bolt locking into barrel extension. Self-compensating gas system for standard and 2¾" loads; aluminum receiver, engine-turned bolt, push-button action release, cross-bolt safety. Used value, plain barrel, $140 to $150; vent rib, $165 to $175.

**Model 1400 Deer Gun**, made from 1965 to 1968, was same as standard Model 1400, but had 22" barrel, rifle sights for slugs or buckshot. Used value, $140 to $150.

**Model 1400 Skeet** gun, is 12, 20 gauges only; has 26" vent rib barrel, skeet choke; stock, forearm are semi-fancy walnut; stock is Cycolac when recoil reduction system is used. Introduced in 1965, discontinued, 1968; used value, $200 to $210; with recoil reduction system, add $50 to $60.

**Model 1400 Trap** gun, made from 1965 to 1968, 12-ga. 30" vent rib barrel, full choke; has semi-fancy walnut stock or recoil reduction system. Used value, with trap stock, $185 to $195; with Monte Carlo, $210 to $225; with recoil reduction system, add $50 to $60.

Model 1200

**WINCHESTER Model 1200:** slide action takedown shotgun, with front-lock rotary bolt; 4-rd. magazine; in 12, 16, 20 gauges, with 2¾" chambers; plain or vent barrels, 26", 28", 30" in length; improved cylinder, modified, full choke choice, or with interchangeable WinChoke tubes for cylinder, modified or full. Stock, slide handle are press-checkered; walnut stock; recoil pad. Introduced in 1964. Model with Winchester recoil reduction system, introduced with Cycolac stock, introduced in 1966, discontinued, 1970. Original plain model was priced at $185. Used value,

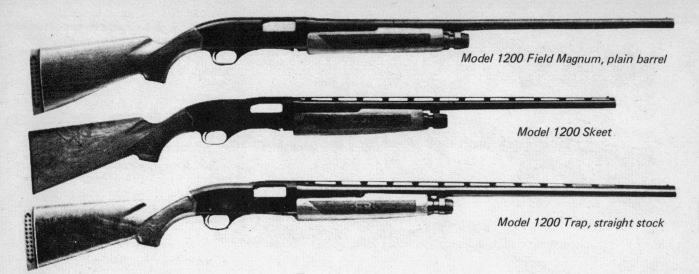

*Model 1200 Field Magnum, plain barrel*

*Model 1200 Skeet*

*Model 1200 Trap, straight stock*

with plain barrel, $120 to $125; with vent rib barrel, $120 to $130; with WinChoke, add $8 to $10; with recoil reduction system, add $50 to $60.

The **Model 1200 Magnum Field** gun was introduced in 1966; same as standard Model 1200 field gun, but chambered for 3" magnum shells in 12, 20 gauges; choice of plain or vent rib; 28", 30" full choke barrels. Used value, with plain barrel, $130 to $140; with vent rib barrel, $150 to $160; for recoil reduction system, add $50 to $60.

The **Model 1200 Deer** model appeared from 1965 to 1974. Same as standard model, has rifle-type sights on 22" barrel. It was meant for rifled slugs or buckshot; 12-ga. only, with sling swivels. Used value, $125 to $135.

**Model 1200 Skeet** gun, made from 1965 to 1973, was 12, 20 gauges only, with 2-shot magazine, tuned trigger; 26" vent rib barrel; semi-fancy walnut stock, forearm; skeet choke. Used value, $190 to $200; with Winchester recoil system, add $50 to $60.

**Model 1200 Trap** gun was in 12-ga. only; 2-shot magazine; 30" full choke vent rib barrel; 28" with WinChoke; regular or Monte Carlo trap stock of semi-fancy walnut; made from 1965 to 1973. Used value, with regular trap stock, $185 to $195; Monte Carlo stock, $200 to $215; with Winchester recoil reduction system, add $50 to $60; with WinChoke, add $8 to $10.

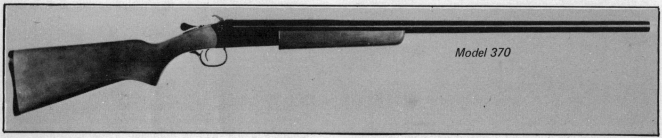

*Model 370*

**WINCHESTER Model 370:** single-barrel shotgun; available in 12-gauge in 36", 32" and 30" barrel lengths; in 16-gauge with 32" and 30"; 20 and 28-gauge, 28" barrel, .410 with 26" barrel. All are chambered for 3" shells, except 16 and 28 gauges, which use 2¾" shells. Weight varies with gauges and barrel length, ranges from 5½ to 6¼

lbs. Break-open type, it has automatic ejection, plain American hardwood stock; uncapped pistol grip and hard rubber butt plate. In full choke only; with bead front sight. Introduced in 1968; discontinued, to be replaced by Model 37A. Last retail price, $35.95; used value, $40 to $45.

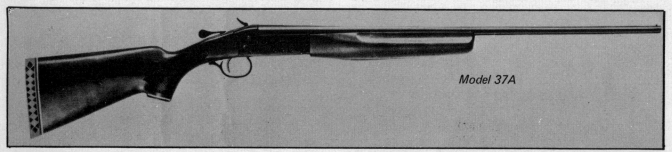

*Model 37A*

**WINCHESTER Model 37A:** single-shot shotgun; available in all gauges from 12 through .410, with choice of barrel in 25", 28", 30", 36"; with exception of 16 and 28 gauges, all are chambered for 3" shells; all full chokes. Also available in Youth model with 26" barrel in 20 and .410 gauges in improved-modified and full chokes respectively;

stock is of walnut-stained hardwood with checkering on bottom of forearm and sides of capped pistol grip; features top lever opening to right or left, concave hammer spur; white spacer between grip cap and butt plate. Introduced in 1973; retail price, $68.95 for 12-gauge with 36" barrel and Youth model; all others, $62.95; used value, $45 to $50.

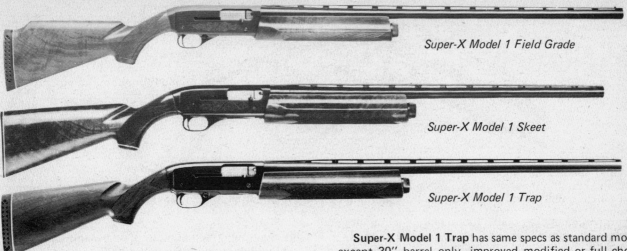

*Super-X Model 1 Field Grade*

*Super-X Model 1 Skeet*

*Super-X Model 1 Trap*

**WINCHESTER Super-X Model 1:** autoloader; gas-operated; 12-ga.; 2¾'' chamber; 4-rd. magazine; 26'' improved cylinder, 28'' modified, full, 30'' full choke barrels; takedown; checkered American walnut pistol-grip stock, forearm. Introduced 1974, still in production. Used value, $215 to $235.

**Super-X Model 1 Trap** has same specs as standard model, except 30'' barrel only, improved modified or full choke; straight or Monte Carlo trap stock, forearm of select American walnut; recoil pad. Introduced 1974, still in production. Used value, $310 to $325.

**Super-X Model 1 Skeet** has same specs as standard model, except for skeet stock, 26'' skeet choke barrels. Introduced 1974, still in production. Used value, $310 to $325.

# MISCELLANEOUS SHOTGUNS
## U.S.-MADE

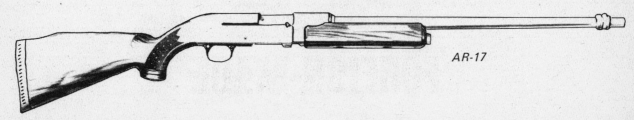

*AR-17*

**ARMALITE AR-17 Golden Gun:** 12-ga. only; 2-shot only; recoil operated, semi-auto; barrel, receiver housing of aluminum alloy; 24'' barrel; interchangeable choke tubes for improved, modified, full chokes; polycarbonate stock, forearm; recoil pad; gold-anodized finish; also with black-anodized finish. Introduced, 1964; discontinued, 1965. Some collector value, as only 2000 made. Used value, $400 to $475.

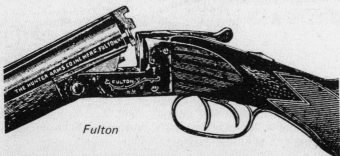

*Fulton*

**HUNTER Fulton:** hammerless, double; box-lock; 12, 16, 20 gauges; 26'' to 32'' barrels, standard choke combos, double triggers, or non-selective single trigger; walnut stock, hand-checkered pistol grip, forearm. Introduced, 1920; dropped, 1948. Manufactured by Hunter Arms Company, Fulton, New York. Used value, single trigger, $435 to $450; double triggers, $350 to $375.

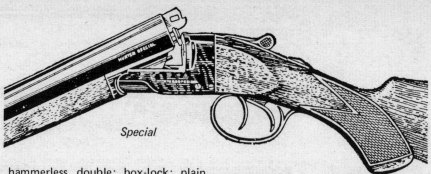

*Special*

**HUNTER Special:** hammerless double; box-lock; plain extractors; 12, 16, 20 gauges; 26 to 30" barrels, standard choke combos; walnut stock, hand-checkered pistol grip, forearm; dropped, 1948. Used value, single trigger, $575 to $600; double triggers, $475 to $500.

**KESSLER Three-Shot Repeater:** bolt-action, takedown; 12, 16, 20 gauges; 28" barrel in 12, 16 gauges, 26" in 20-ga.; 2-rd. detachable box magazine; full choke only; unchecker-ed one-piece pistol-grip stock; recoil pad. Introduced in 1951; dropped, 1953. Made by Kessler Arms Corp., Silver Creek, New York. Used value, $45 to $65.

**KESSLER Lever-Matic:** lever-action repeater; takedown; 12, 16, 20 gauges; 26", 28", 30" barrels, full choke only; 3-rd. magazine; unchecked pistol-grip stock; recoil pad; dropped, 1953. Used value, $75 to $95.

**MORONNE Model 46:** over/under; 12, 20-ga.; 26" improved cylinder/modified, 28" modified/full barrels; box-lock action; non-selective single trigger; plain extractors; checkered straight or pistol-grip stock; plain barrel or vent rib. Some collector value; fewer than 500 manufactured by Rhode Island Arms 1949 to 1953. Used values, 12-ga., plain barrels, $525 to $550; 12-ga., vent rib, $675 to $700; 20-ga., plain barrels, $675 to $700; 20-ga., vent rib, $750 to $800.

*Red Label*

**RUGER Red Label:** over/under; 20-ga.; 3" chambers; 26" vent rib barrels; improved cylinder/modified, skeet chokes; box-lock action; single selective trigger; auto ejectors; checkered American walnut pistol-grip stock, forearm. Introduced 1977, still in production. Used value, $375 to $400.

**WESTERN ARMS Long Range Hammerless:** double, box-lock; double or single trigger; plain extractors; in 12, 16, 20, .410 gauges; barrels, 26" to 32", modified/full chokes; uncheckered walnut stock, forearm. Introduced in 1924; discontinued, 1942. Made by Western Arms Corp., later absorbed by Ithaca Gun Co. Used value, with single trigger, $275 to $300; double triggers, $225 to $250.

# FOREIGN-MADE

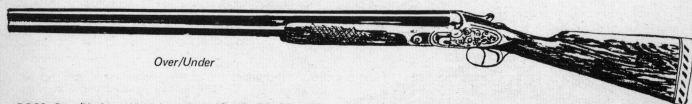

*Over/Under*

**BOSS Over/Under:** sidelock action; 12, 16, 20, 28, .410 gauges; 26", 28", 30", 34" barrels; any desired choke combo; automatic ejectors; double or non-selective single trigger; selective single trigger extra; hand-checkered European walnut stock, forearm; recoil pad; matted or vent rib. Introduced about 1952; still in production. Not currently imported. English made. Used values, double triggers, $6000 to $6500; non-selective single trigger, $6500 to $7500; selective single trigger, $7500 to $9000.

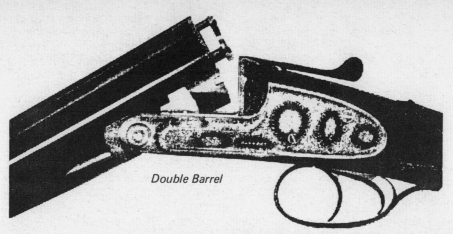

*Double Barrel*

**BOSS Double Barrel:** side-by-side; sidelock; 12, 16, 20, 28, .410 gauges; 26", 28", 30", 32" barrels; any desired choke combo; automatic ejectors; double or non-selective single trigger; selective single trigger extra; hand-checkered European walnut stock, forearm; straight or pistol-grip stock. Introduced after WWI; still in production. Not currently imported. Used values, double triggers, $5500 to $6000; non-selective single trigger, $6500 to $7000; selective single trigger, $8000 to $8500.

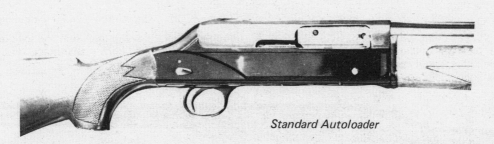

*Standard Autoloader*

**BREDA Autoloader:** takedown autoloader; 12-ga. only; 4-rd. tube magazine; 25½", 27½" barrels; chromed bore; plain or with matted rib; hand-checkered European walnut stock, forearm; straight or pistol-grip style; available in three grades with chromed receivers, engraving. Grade, value depends upon amount of engraving, quality of wood. Introduced in 1946; still in production. Made in Italy. Used values, Standard, with plain barrel, $160 to $180; with matted rib, $175 to $190; Grade I, $305 to $320; Grade II, $360 to $390; Grade III, $390 to $420.

**Magnum 12 Autoloader** model has the same specs as Standard Breda Autoloader, except is chambered for 12-ga. 3" magnum shell. Introduced in 1950; still in production. Used values, with plain barrel, $175 to $190; with matted rib, $185 to $200.

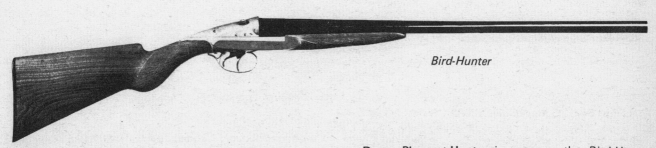

*Bird-Hunter*

**DARNE Bird-Hunter:** double, 20, 12 gauges; sliding breech action; double triggers; automatic selective ejection; 25½" barrels; improved cylinder, modified; raised rib; deluxe walnut stock, hand-checkered forearm; case-hardened receiver. Manufactured in France; was imported by Firearms Center, Victoria, Texas, but manufacture now discontinued. Used value, $375 to $390.

**Darne Pheasant-Hunter** is same as the Bird-Hunter, except for highly engraved receiver, fancy walnut stock, forearm; 12-ga. only, 27½" barrels, modified and full chokes. Used value, $485 to $500.

**Darne Quail-Hunter Supreme** is same as Bird-Hunter model, except for premium grade engraving, extra-fancy wood; 20, 28 gauges only; 25½" barrels, improved/modified chokes. Used value, $675 to $700.

**FERLACH Constant Companion:** side-by-side double barrel; Anson & Deeley-type action; 12, 16, 20 gauges; 28", 30" barrels; tapered boring; quadruple Greener bolt; auto safety; ejectors; engraved receiver; double triggers; hand-checkered black walnut pistol-grip stock; cheekpiece. Manufactured in Austria. Originally imported by Flaig's. Introduced in 1956; dropped, 1958. Used value, $300 to $350.

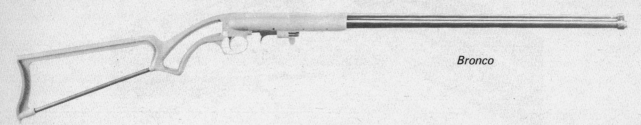

*Bronco*

**GARCIA Bronco:** single-shot; .410; swing-out action; one-piece metal frame stock, receiver; crackle finish; 18½" barrel. Italian made. Manufactured 1968 to 1978. Used value, $40 to $45.

*Bronco 22/410*

**GARCIA Bronco 22/410:** over/under combo; swing-out action; takedown; .22 LR top barrel, .410 lower; 18½" barrel; one-piece metal frame stock, receiver; crackle finish. Manufactured 1976 to 1978. Italian made. Used value, $45 to $60.

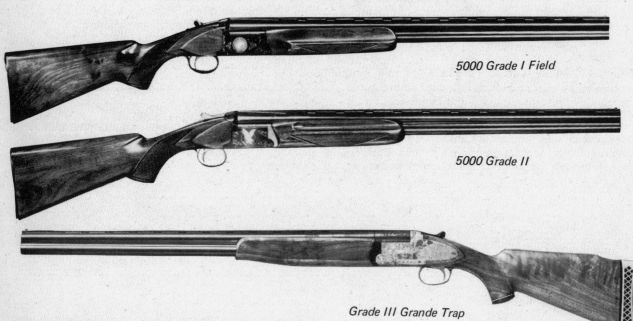

*5000 Grade I Field*

*5000 Grade II*

*Grade III Grande Trap*

**GOLDEN EAGLE Model 5000 Grade I Field:** over/under; 12, 20-ga.; 2¾", 3" chambers in 12-ga., 3" in 20; 26", 28", 30" barrels; box-lock action; selective single trigger; auto ejectors; improved/modified, modified/full choking; vent rib; engraved receiver; gold eagle head inlaid in frame; checkered walnut pistol-grip stock, semi-beavertail forearm. Manufactured in Japan; imported 1975 to 1980. Used value, $500 to $520.

**Model 5000 Grade I Trap** has same specs as field model, except 30", 32" barrels; modified/full, improved modified/full, full/full choking; wide vent rib, trap style stock; recoil pad. Imported 1975 to 1980. Used value, $600 to $625.

**Model 5000 Grade I Skeet** has same specs as field model except for 26", 28" skeet-choked barrels, vent rib. Imported 1975 to 1980. Used value, $540 to $560.

**Model 5000 Grade II Field** has same specs as Grade I field model, except for more elaborate engraving, spread-wing eagle inlaid in gold, fancier wood. Imported 1975 to 1980. Used value, $560 to $575.

**Model 5000 Grade II Trap** has same specs as Grade I trap model, except for more elaborate engraving, spread-wing eagle gold inlay, vent side ribs, inertia trigger, fancier wood. Imported 1975 to 1980. Used value, $680 to $700.

**Model 5000 Grade II Skeet** has same specs as Grade I skeet model, except for more elaborate engraving, spread-wing eagle gold inlay, inertia trigger, vent side ribs, fancier wood. Imported 1975 to 1980. Used value, $620 to $640.

**Model 5000 Grade III** is available in field, trap, skeet versions. Same specs as lower grades, except has game scene engraving, scroll-engraved frame, barrels, side plates, fancy wood; trap model has Monte Carlo comb, full pistol grip, recoil pad. Imported 1976 to 1980. Used value, $1850 to $2000.

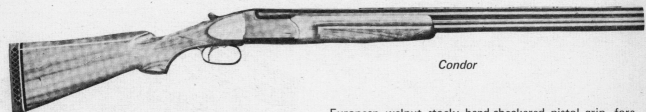

*Condor*

**KLEINGUENTHER Condor:** over/under; 12, 20 gauges; Purdey-type double-lock action; barrels, 26" improved/modified or skeet/skeet; 28", full/modified or modified/modified; 30", 12-ga. only, full/modified, full/full; European walnut stock; hand-checkered pistol grip, forearm; single selective trigger; automatic ejectors, vent rib; skeet model has extra-wide rib. Imported from Italy; still in production. Used value, field grade, $290 to $315; skeet, $325 to $340.

**KLEINGUENTHER Condor Trap:** has same specs as field grade, except for wide vent rib, Monte Carlo stock; 12-ga. only; barrels, 28", full/modified; 30", 32", modified/full or full/full. Still in production. Used value, $350 to $375.

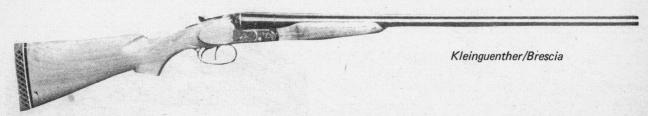

*Kleinguenther/Brescia*

**KLEINGUENTHER/BRESCIA:** double; 12, 20 gauges; Anson & Deeley-type action; barrels, 28", full/modified or improved/modified, chrome-lined; European walnut stock; hand-checkered pistol grip, forearm; recoil pad; double triggers; engraved action. Still in production. Imported from Italy. Used value, $190 to $200.

*Rigby Regal*

**RIGBY Sidelock Double:** side-by-side; in all gauges, barrel lengths, chokes to customer's specifications; automatic ejectors; double triggers; hand-checkered European walnut straight-grip stock, forearm; English engraving; two grades, differing in overall quality, amount of engraving. English made. Introduced in 1885; dropped, 1955. Used values, Sandringham Grade, $3000 to $3200; Regal Grade, $4500 to $5000. Add $500 to $750 for fitted case.

**RIGBY Box-lock Double:** side-by-side; in all gauges, barrel lengths, chokes to customer's desires; automatic ejectors; double triggers; hand-checkered European walnut straight-grip stock, forearm; English engraving; in two grades, differing in amount and nature of engraving, overall quality. Introduced in 1900; dropped, 1955. Used values, Chatsworth Grade, $2750 to $3000; Sackville Grade, $2250 to $2500. Add $500 to $750 for fitted case.

*Model 4*

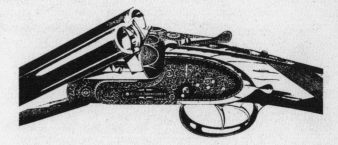

*Model 6E*

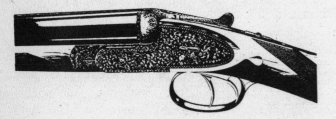

*Model 7E*

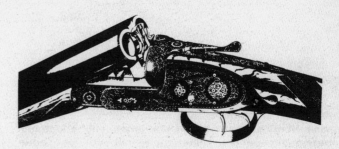

*Model 10*

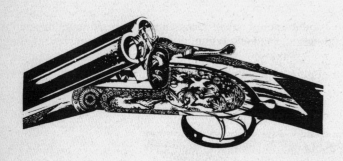

*Model 11*

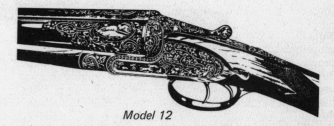

*Model 12*

**SARASQUETA Sidelock Double:** side-by-side; hammerless; 12, 16, 20, 28 gauges; barrel lengths, choke combinations to customer's order; double triggers; hand-checkered European walnut straight-grip stock, forearm. Gun is made in 13 grades; except for No. 6 and No. 7, all have automatic ejectors. Grades differ in quality of wood, checkering, and amount and quality of engraving. Spanish manufacture. Used values, No. 4, $400 to $425; No. 4E, $475 to $500; No. 5, $450 to $475; No. 5E, $500 to $525; No. 6, $325 to $350; No. 6E, $600 to $625; No. 7, $650 to $675; No. 7E, $675 to $700; No. 8, $550 to $575; No. 9, $675 to $700; No. 10, $1000 to $1100; No. No. 11, $1525 to $1575; No. 12, $1500 to $1600.

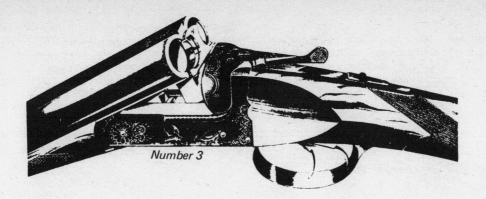

Number 3

**SARASQUETA No. 2:** side-by-side; hammerless, box-lock action; 12, 16, 20, 28 gauges; manufactured in all standard barrel lengths, choke combinations; plain extractors; double triggers; hand-checkered European walnut straight-grip stock, forearm; Greener crossbolt; engraved. Introduced in mid-1930s; still in production. Used value, $300 to $325.

No. 3 has same specifications as No. 2, but no Greener crossbolt; engraving style is different. Still in production. Used value, $300 to $325.

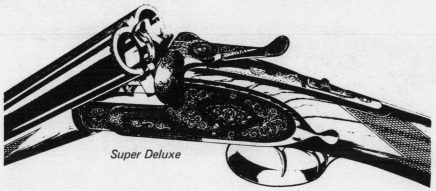

Super Deluxe

**SARASQUETA Super Deluxe:** side-by-side; sidelock action; hammerless; 12-ga. only; barrel lengths, choke combos to customer's order; automatic ejectors; double triggers; hand-checkered European walnut pistol-grip stock, forearm; engraved action. Introduced in 1930s; still in production. Used value, $1000 to $1100.

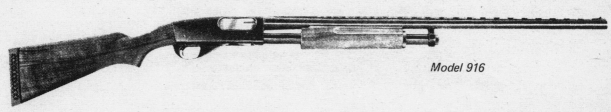

Model 916

**SMITH & WESSON Model 916:** slide action; 12, 16, 20 gauges; 6-shot; barrel lengths, 20″ cylinder choke, 26″ improved cylinder, 28″ modified, full or adjustable choke; 30″ full; vent rib on 26″ and 28″ barrels available; unchecked walnut stock; fluted comb, grooved slide handle; satin-finished steel receiver, no-glare top. Introduced in 1973; dropped 1980. Japanese made. Used value, plain barrels, sans recoil pad, $85 to $90; plain barrel with adjustable choke, $90 to $95; plain barrel, recoil pad, $85 to $90; with vent rib, recoil pad, $100 to $115.

Model 916T has same general specifications as Model 916, except 12-ga. only; takedown; not made with 20″ barrel; plain or vent rib. Introduced 1976, dropped 1980. Used values, vent rib, $115 to $125; plain barrel, $100 to $110.

Model 1000

**SMITH & WESSON Model 1000:** gas-operated autoloader; 12-ga. only, 2¾" chamber, 4-rds.; barrel lengths, 26" skeet, improved cylinder, 28" improved, modified, full; walnut stock, checkered pistol grip, forearm; crossbolt safety; vent rib; front, middle beads; engraved alloy receiver; pressure compensator. Introduced in 1973; still in production. Manufactured in Japan. Used value, $200 to $225.

**Model 1000 Magnum** has same specs as standard Model 1000, except chambered for 12-ga. 3" shell only; 30" modified or full choke barrel; recoil pad. Imported 1977 to present. Used value, $220 to $235.

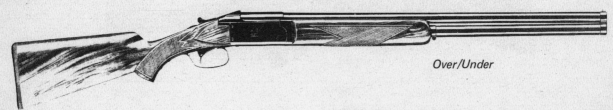

*Over/Under*

**VALMET Over/Under:** box-lock action; 12-ga. only; single selective trigger; plain extractors; barrels, 26", improved/modified; 28", modified/full; 30", modified/full or full/full; hand-checkered walnut stock. Imported 1951-1967 by Firearms International, dropped 1967. From 1968 to 1979 the similar Model 330 has been imported by Savage. Manufactured in Finland. Used value, $293 to $310.

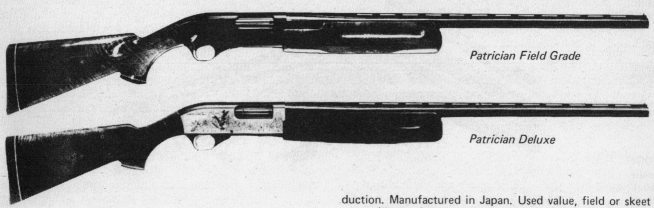

*Patrician Field Grade*

*Patrician Deluxe*

**WEATHERBY Patrician:** slide-action repeater; 12-ga. only, 2¾" chamber; barrels, 26", modified, improved or skeet; 28", full or modified; 30", full; vent rib; walnut stock; hand-checkered pistol-grip, forearm; recoil pad; hidden magazine cap; cross-bolt safety. Introduced in 1970; still in production. Manufactured in Japan. Used value, field or skeet grade, $210 to $220; trap grade, $230 to $245.

**Patrician Trap** has same specs as standard Patrician, except for trap stock, 30" full choke barrel. Imported 1972 to present. Used value, $200 to $215.

**Patrician Deluxe** has same specs as standard grade, except for fancy grade wood, etched receiver. Imported 1972 to present. Used value, $225 to $240.

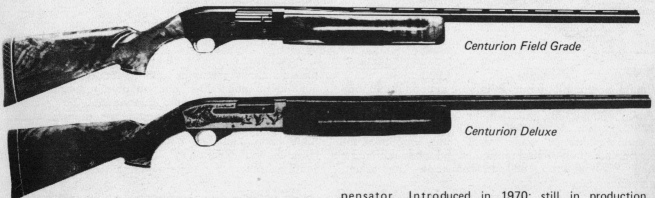

*Centurion Field Grade*

*Centurion Deluxe*

**WEATHERBY Centurion:** autoloader; 12-ga. only, 2¾" chamber; barrels, 26", skeet or improved cylinder; 28", improved, modified, full; 30", full; American walnut stock; hand-checkered pistol grip, forearm; vent rib with front, middle bead sights; engraved alloy receiver; pressure compensator. Introduced in 1970; still in production. Manufactured in Japan. Used value, $210 to $218.50.

**Centurion Trap** model has same specs as standard Centurion, except for trap stock, 30" full choke barrel. Imported 1972 to present. Used value, $235 to $250.

**Centurion Deluxe** has same specs as standard version, except for fancy grade wood, etched receiver. Imported 1972 to present. Used value, $250 to $265.

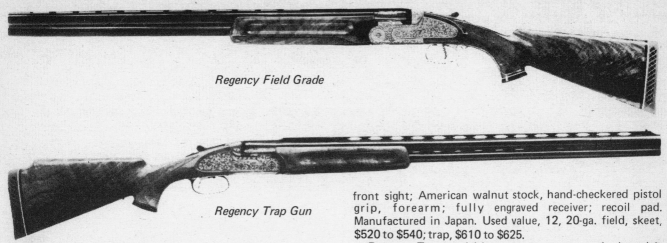

*Regency Field Grade*

*Regency Trap Gun*

**WEATHERBY Regency:** over/under; 12, 20 gauges; box-lock action with simulated sidelocks; selective automatic ejectors, single selective trigger; barrels, 28" only, full/modified, modified/improved, skeet/skeet; vent rib, bead front sight; American walnut stock, hand-checkered pistol grip, forearm; fully engraved receiver; recoil pad. Manufactured in Japan. Used value, 12, 20-ga. field, skeet, $520 to $540; trap, $610 to $625.

**Regency Trap** model has same specs as standard model, except has trap stock, straight or Monte Carlo comb; 30", 32" barrels, modified/full, improved modified/full, full/full chokes; vent side ribs, vent top rib. Imported 1965 to present. Used value, $625 to $650.

*Special Trap Over/Under*

**WOODWARD Over/Under:** marketed as Woodward Best Quality; built to customer order in any standard gauge, barrel length, choke; sidelock action; double or single triggers; auto ejectors; plain barrel or vent rib. Manufactured 1909 to World War II. Collector value. English manufacture. Used values, single trigger, $17,250 to $17,500; double triggers, $16,250 to $16,500.

**WOODWARD Single Barrel Trap:** special order; has same general mechanical specs as over/under model; vent rib; 12-ga. only. Manufactured prior to World War II. Collector value. Used value, $15,250 to $15,500.

**WOODWARD Double:** side-by-side; marketed as Woodward Best Quality Hammerless; built to customer order in any standard gauge, barrel length, choke; sidelock action; double or single triggers; automatic ejectors; produced in field, wildfowl, skeet or trap configurations. Manufactured prior to World War II. Collector value. Used values, single trigger, $12,000 to $12,250; double triggers, $11,000 to $11,250.

# SHOTGUN NOTES

# COMMEMORATIVES

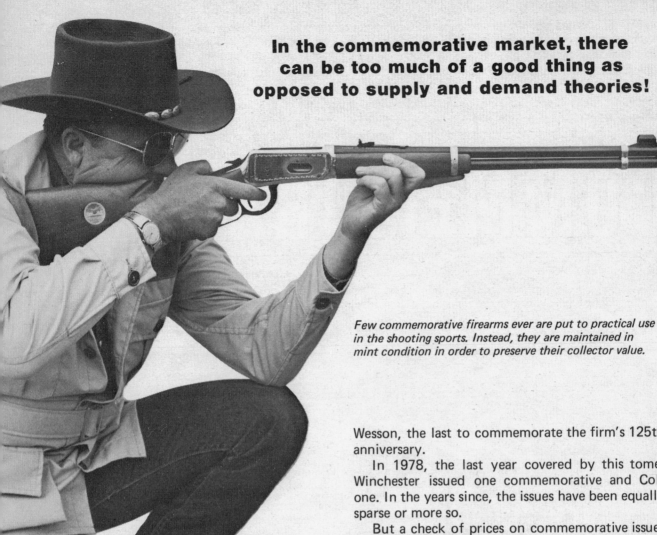

## In the commemorative market, there can be too much of a good thing as opposed to supply and demand theories!

*Few commemorative firearms ever are put to practical use in the shooting sports. Instead, they are maintained in mint condition in order to preserve their collector value.*

THERE IS some concern in collecting circles as to whether the bloom is off the rose on the commemorative scene. One has only to take a look at the number of commemoratives issued the past few years to realize that the manufacturers who were turning out such items ultimately realized that they had gotten carried away.

The last big year of commemoratives — as one might expect — was the Bicentennial year, when a number of firms climbed on the bandwagon. Oddly, for an event that was supposed to instill pride in our national heritage, it is amazing how many of those commemorative models were made overseas and imported to be sold here. One has only to check the listings in the following section to take note of this fact.

In 1977, only three commemoratives were issued: one each by Winchester, Colt and Smith &

Wesson, the last to commemorate the firm's 125th anniversary.

In 1978, the last year covered by this tome, Winchester issued one commemorative and Colt one. In the years since, the issues have been equally sparse or more so.

But a check of prices on commemorative issues may give us a hint to what has been happening. Rarity still appears to be the basis for value. For example, in 1961, early in the days of the commemorative fad, Cherry's Sporting Goods out of Genesee, Illinois, ordered 104 No. 4 Colt Derringer replicas with appropriate wording to commemorate the town's 125th anniversary. The original retail price of those little guns, complete with gold plating and cased in a velvet/satin-lined case, was $27.50. Today, these little handguns go for $600 up. Because of the fact that Bob Cherry had only 104 made, the rarity is certain to cause the value to increase.

That same year, Colt celebrated its 125th anniversary and came up with a special issue of the Colt Single Action Army model, with some gold-plating, a proper inscription on the barrel, and a velvet-lined box. Only 7390 of these were made and they sold originally for $150. Today, the price is around $600 for one in mint condition.

Also in 1961, Colt offered a Pony Express Centennial model, a dressed-up Frontier Scout, which retailed for $80, with only 1007 being made. Current value is well upward of $500. The Kansas Statehood Centennial was celebrated that same year with a Colt Frontier Scout. With the additional dressing, it retailed for $75, but there were 6201 of them made. Current value is in the vicinity of $300.

If you look at the original prices, the number made in each instance and the current value, the correlation is obvious: the fewer the number made, the greater the current value.

But somewhere along the way, some of the manufacturers came to the conclusion that if a little of a good thing is profitable, loading the market should be even more profitable. It just ain't necessarily so.

Winchester moved into the commemorative market with their familiar Model 94 carbine in 1964, issuing 1500 Wyoming Diamond Jubilee commemoratives for distribution exclusively by an in-state hardware firm. The original retail price on these was $100; today, they go for around $1000 — ten times their original cost!

By 1971, Winchester was turning out such items as the National Rifle Association Commemorative in carload lots. The original price on this one was $149.95. Today, it sells for a bit more than $400, which is not a bad gain, but it had a tough time catching on. There were just too many of them available and at one point, about 1973, they were being offered in discount stores!

Collecting commemoratives was all the rage for a few years. That does not mean that the values have not increased; they will continue to increase simply because of the fact that they were made in limited numbers. In the case of some, the run was limited to 20,000 guns, but it still is limited. However, those variations where that many were turned out are not gaining nearly as rapidly in value as the shorter runs.

In some of the heyday years, Colt, as an example, was turning out nearly a dozen different commemoratives. In 1969, they issued ten different variations, but in each instance, the runs were limited. For example, their Texas Ranger issue of that year featured two hundred custom guns and eight hundred standard models, all based upon the .45 SAA design. The custom guns are out of sight, and since they were put together to customer's order, few are ever for sale. The standard version originally sold for $650 and today brings upward of $1000.

The recent announcement by Colt that the venerable old Single Action Army is to be discontinued from the line no doubt will cause the value of commemoratives based upon this particular model to skyrocket in price, along with the standard SAA model.

The fact that Winchester has cut back considerably on its production of commemoratives and Colt has done the same in recent years doesn't mean that they are running out of things to celebrate. There will continue to be commemoratives offered by these and other manufacturers, we're certain, but we suspect the numbers are going to be limited. Prices on commemoratives of today's manufacture are considerably higher than in the early days, because manufacturing costs have increased in line with standard models. The limited runs also will be prompted by the fact that a man who once would pay $150 for a commemorative is not likely to pay $1000 for a variation of the same model today. That means that the market is going to be smaller; hence the limited runs.

# 1960

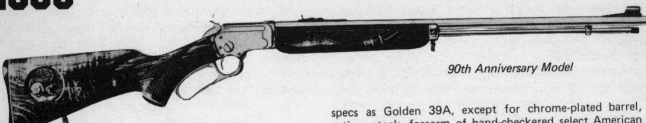

*90th Anniversary Model*

**MARLIN 90th Anniversary Model:** Model 39A rifle commemorating firm's ninth decade. Has same general specs as Golden 39A, except for chrome-plated barrel, action; stock, forearm of hand-checkered select American walnut; squirrel figure carved on right side of buttstock. Manufactured 1960; only 500 made. Used value, $425 to $440.

# 1961

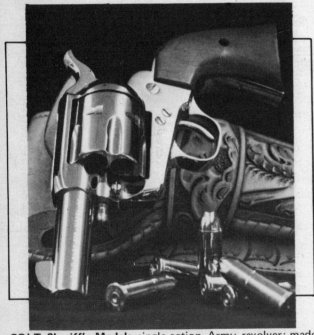

**COLT Sheriff's Model:** single-action Army revolver; made exclusively for Centennial Arms Corp.; "Colt Sheriff's Model .45" on left side of 3" barrel; .45 Colt only; walnut grips without medallions; 25 made with nickel finish; 478, blued; made only in 1961. Original price, nickel, $139.50; blued, $150. Current values, nickel, $3250 to $3350; blued, $1200 to $1250.

**COLT 125th Anniversary Model:** single-action Army revolver; "125th Anniversary — SAA Model .45 Cal." on left side of 7½" barrel; .45 Colt only; varnished walnut grips; gold-plated Colt medallions; gold-plated hammer, trigger, trigger guard; balance blued; originally cased in red velvet-lined box; 7390 made in 1961 only. Original retail, $150. Current value, $550 to $595.

**COLT Kansas Statehood Centennial:** Frontier Scout revolver; "1861 — Kansas Centennial — 1961" on left side of 4¾" barrel; .22 LR only; walnut grips; no medallions; gold-plated in entirety; originally cased in velvet-lined box with Kansas State seal inlaid in lid; 6201 made in 1961 only. Original retail, $75. Current value, $285 to $300.

**COLT Geneseo Anniversary:** No. 4 Derringer replica; "1836 — Geneseo Anniversary Model — 1961" on left side of 2½" barrel; .22 short only; walnut grips; gold-plated in entirety; originally cased in velvet/satin-lined box; made especially for Cherry's Sporting Goods, Geneseo, Ill.; 104 made in 1961 only. Original retail, $27.50; current value, $600 to $625.

**COLT Pony Express Centennial:** Frontier Scout revolver; "1860-61 — Russell, Majors and Waddell/Pony Express Centennial Model — 1960-61" on left side of 4¾" barrel; .22 LR only; varnished walnut grips; gold-plated Colt medallions; gold-plated in entirety; originally cased in rosewood box with gold-plated centennial medallion in lid; 1007 made in 1961 only. Original retail, $80. Current value, $500 to $525.

**COLT Civil War Centennial:** single-shot replica of Colt Model 1860 Army revolver; "Civil War Centennial Model — .22 Caliber Short" on left side of 6" barrel; .22 short only; varnished walnut grips; gold-plated Colt medallions; gold-plated frame, backstrap, trigger guard assembly, balance blued; originally in Leatherette case; 24,114 made in 1961 only. Original retail, $32.50. Current value, $125 to $135.

# 1962

**COLT Rock Island Arsenal Centennial:** single-shot version of Colt Model 1860 Army revolver; "1862 — Rock Island Arsenal Centennial Model — 1962" on left side of 6" barrel;

.22 short only; varnished walnut grips; blued finish; originally in blue and gray Leatherette case; 550 made in 1962 only. Original retail, $38.50. Current value, $200 to $220.

**COLT Columbus, Ohio, Sesquicentennial:** Frontier Scout revolver; "1812 — Columbus Sesquicentennial — 1962" on left side of 4¾" barrel; .22 LR only; varnished walnut grips with gold-plated medallions; gold-plated in entirety; originally cased in velvet/satin-lined walnut case; 200 made in 1962 only. Original retail, $100. Current value, $600 to $625.

**COLT Fort Findlay, Ohio, Sesquicentennial:** Frontier Scout revolver; "1812 — Fort Findlay Sesquicentennial — 1962" on left side of 4¾" barrel; .22 LR, .22 magnum; varnished walnut grips; gold plated in entirety; originally cased in red velvet/satin-lined walnut box; 110 made in 1962 only. Original retail, $89.50. Current value, $600 to $625. Cased pair, .22LR, .22 magnum, 20 made in 1962. $3200 to $3250.

**COLT New Mexico Golden Anniversary:** Frontier Scout revolver; "1912 — New Mexico Golden Anniversary — 1962" wiped in gold on left side of 4¾" barrel; .22 LR only; varnished walnut grips; gold-plated medallions; barrel, frame, base pin screw, ejector rod, rod tube plug and screw, bolt and trigger, hammer screws blued; balance gold plated; originally cased in redwood box with yellow satin/velvet lining; 1000 made in 1962 only. Original retail, $79.95. Current value, $325 to $340.

**COLT West Virginia Statehood Centennial:** Frontier Scout revolver; "1863 — West Virginia Centennial — 1963" wiped in gold on left side of 4¾" barrel; .22 LR only; pearlite grips, gold-plated medallions; blued, with gold-plated backstrap, trigger guard assembly and screws, stock screw; originally cased in blonde wood box with gold velvet/satin lining; 3452 made in 1962 only. Original retail, $75. Current value, $250 to $290.

**West Virginia Statehood Centennial single-action Army** revolver has same legend on barrel as .22 version; 5½" barrel; .45 Colt only; same blue/gold finish as Scout version; same type of casing; 600 made in 1963 only. Original retail, $150. Current value, $625 to $650.

# 1963

**COLT Fort McPherson, Nebraska, Centennial:** No. 4 Derringer replica; "Fort McPherson/1863 — Centennial — 1963" wiped in gold on left side of 2½" barrel; .22 short only; Ivorylite grips, no medallions; gold plated with blued barrel, bolt, trigger screw, hammer and screw, trigger and stock screw; originally cased in walnut-finished box, with gold velvet/satin lining; 300 made in 1963 only. Original retail, $28.95. Current value, $320 to $325.

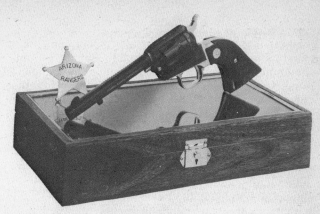

**COLT Arizona Territorial Centennial:** Frontier Scout revolver; "1863 — Arizona Territorial Centennial — 1963" wiped in gold on left side of 4¾" barrel; .22 LR only; Pearlite grips, gold-plated medallions; gold plated, with blue barrel, frame, base pin screw, ejector rod, rod tube, tube plug and screw, bolt and trigger screws, hammer and hammer screw; originally cased in blonde-finished box, with yellow velvet/satin lining; 5355 made in 1963 only. Original retail, $75. Current value, $285 to $300.

**Arizona Territorial Centennial single-action Army** revolver has same legend on barrel as Scout version; 5½" barrel; .45 Colt only; same blue/gold-plated finish as Scout; same type case; 1280 made in 1963 only. Original retail, $150. Current value, $600 to $625.

**COLT Carolina Charter Tercentenary:** Frontier Scout revolver; "1663 — Carolina Charter Tercentenary — 1963" wiped in gold on left side of 4¾" barrel; .22 LR only; walnut grips; gold-plated medallions; gold plated, with barrel, frame, cylinder, base pin screw, ejector rod, rod tube, tube plug, tube screw, bolt, trigger and hammer screws blued; originally cased in blonde-finished box with yellow velvet/satin lining; 300 made in 1963 only. Original retail, $75. Current value, $375 to $385.

**Carolina Charter Tercentenary .22/.45 combo set** includes Frontier Scout described above, single-action Army revolver, with same legend on 5½" barrel, .45 Colt only; same finish on grips as Frontier version; larger case to fit both guns; 251 sets made in 1963 only. Original retail for set, $240. Current Value, $800 to $850.

**COLT H. Cook 1 of 100:** Frontier Scout/single-action Army revolvers, sold as set; "H. Cook 1 of 100" on left side of barrels; Scout has 4¾" barrel, .22 LR only; SA Army has 7½" barrel, .45 Colt only; Pearlite grips; nickel-plated medallions; both nickel plated with blued frame, base pin, trigger and hammer screws; originally cased in silver-colored box with blue satin/velvet lining; 100 sets made in 1963 only for H. Cook Sporting Goods, Albuquerque, N.M. Original retail for set, $275. Current value, $925 to $975.

**COLT Fort Stephenson, Ohio, Sesquicentennial:** Frontier Scout revolver; "1813 — Fort Stephenson Sesquicentennial — 1963" wiped in silver on left side of 4¾" barrel; .22 LR only; laminated rosewood grips, nickel-plated medallions; nickel-plated finish, with blued barrel, frame, base pin screw, ejector rod, rod tube, tube plug and screw, bolt and trigger and hammer screws; originally cased in blonde-finished wood, with yellow velvet/satin lining; 200 made only in 1963. Original retail, $75. Current value, $625 to $650.

**COLT Battle of Gettysburg Centennial:** Frontier Scout revolver; "1863 — Battle of Gettysburg Centennial — 1963" wiped in gold on left side of 4¾" barrel; .22 LR only; walnut grips; gold-plated medallions; gold plated with blued barrel, frame, base pin screw, ejector rod tube, tube plug and screw, and bolt, trigger and hammer screws; originally cased in blonde-finished wood with yellow velvet in bottom, blue satin in lid; 1019 made in 1963 only. Original retail, $89.95. Current value, $285 to $300.

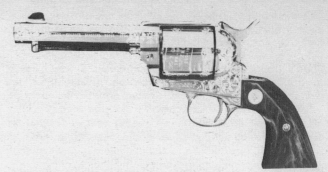

**COLT Idaho Territorial Centennial:** Frontier Scout revolver; "1863 — Idaho Territorial Centennial — 1963" wiped in silver on left side of 4¾" barrel; .22 LR only; pearlite grips; nickel-plated medallions; nickel plated with blue frame, barrel, base pin screw, ejector rod tube, tube plug and screw, and bolt, trigger and hammer screws; originally cased in blonde-finished wood, with gold velvet/satin lining; 902 made in 1963 only. Original retail, $75. Current value, $375 to $400.

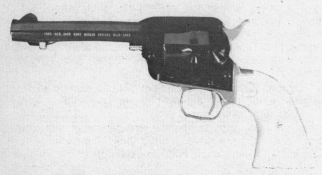

**COLT General John Hunt Morgan Indian Raid:** Frontier Scout revolver; "1863 — Gen. John Hunt Morgan Indian Raid — 1963" wiped in gold on left side of 4¾" barrel; .22 LR; Pearlite grips, gold-plated medallions; gold plated with blued frame, barrel, cylinder, base pin screw, ejector rod, rod tube, tube plug and tube screw and bolt and trigger screws; originally cased in blonde-finished wood, with gold velvet/satin lining; 100 made in 1963 only. Original retail, $74.50. Current value, $825 to $850.

# 1964

**COLT Cherry's Sporting Goods 35th Anniversary:** Frontier Scout/single-action Army revolvers, sold as set; "1929 — Cherry's Sporting Goods — 1964" on left side of barrel; Scout has 4¾" barrel, .22 LR only; SA Army has 4¾" barrel, .45 Colt only; both have laminated rosewood grips; gold-plated medallions; gold plated in entirety; originally

cased in embossed black Leatherette, with black velvet/satin lining; 100 sets made in 1964 only. Original retail, $275. Current value, $1100 to $1150.

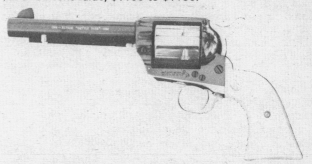

**COLT Nevada Statehood Centennial:** Frontier Scout revolver; "1864 — Nevada Centennial — 1964" wiped in silver on left side of 4¾" barrel; .22 LR only; Pearlite grips; nickel-plated medallions; nickel-plated finish, with blued barrel, frame, base pin screw, cylinder, ejector rod, rod tube, tube plug and tube screw, hammer, bolt, trigger screws; originally cased in gray-finished wood with blue velvet-lined bottom, silver satin-lined lid; 3984 made in 1964 only. Original retail, $75. Used value, $285 to $300.

**Nevada Statehood Centennial single-action Army** revolver has same legend on barrel as Frontier Scout; 5½" barrel; .45 Colt only; grips, medallions, finish identical to Scout; same casing motif; 1688 made in 1964 only. Original retail, $150. Current value, $625 to $750.

**Nevada State Centennial Frontier Scout/single-action Army set** includes the two handguns described above in oversized case; 189 standard sets were made, plus 577 sets featuring extra engraved cylinders; made in 1964 only. Original retail, standard set, $240; with extra engraved cylinders, $350. Current values, standard set, $925 to $950; with extra engraved cylinders, $1200 to $1250.

**COLT Nevada Battle Born Commemorative:** Frontier Scout revolver; "1864 — Nevada 'Battle Born' — 1964" wiped in silver on left side of 4¾" barrel; .22 LR only; Pearlite grips; nickel-plated medallions; nickel plated, with blued frame, barrel, base pin screw, ejector rod, tube, tube plug and screw, bolt, trigger and hammer screws; cased in blue-finished wood box, with blue velvet/satin lining; 981 made in 1964 only. Original retail, $85. Current value, $285 to $300.

**Nevada Battle Born Commemorative single-action Army** revolver has same legend on barrel as Frontier Scout version; 5½" barrel; .45 Colt only; same grips, finish, casing as Frontier Scout; 80 made in 1964 only. Original retail, $175. Used value, $1350 to $1375.

**Nevada Battle Born Commemorative Frontier Scout/single-action Army set** includes the two handguns previously described in oversize case; 20 sets were made in 1964 only. Original retail, $265. Current value, $1800 to $1850.

**COLT Montana Territory Centennial:** Frontier Scout revolver; "1864 — Montana Territory Centennial — 1964" on left side of barrel, "1889 — Diamond Jubilee Statehood — 1964" on right side; both markings wiped in gold; 4¾" barrel; .22 LR only; rosewood or Pearlite grips; gold-plated medallions; gold-plated finish, except for blued barrel, frame, base pin screw, cylinder, ejector rod, rod tube, tube plug and tube screw, bolt, and trigger and hammer screws; originally cased in walnut-finished box with red velvet/satin lining; 2300 made in 1964 only. Original retail, $75. Current value, $285 to $300.

**Montana Territory Centennial single-action Army** revolver has same barrel markings as Frontier Scout version; 7½" barrel, .45 Colt only; same grips, finish, except frame is color case-hardened; same casing as Frontier Scout; 851 made in 1964 only. Original retail, $150. Current value, $600 to $625.

**COLT Wyoming Diamond Jubilee:** Frontier Scout revolver; "1890 — Wyoming Diamond Jubilee — 1965" on left side of barrel; 4¾" barrel; .22 LR only; rosewood grips, nickel-plated medallions; nickel-plated finish, except for blued barrel, frame, ejector rod, rod tube, tube plug and plug screw. Cased in blonde-finished box, with blue velvet bottom lining, silver satin-lined lid; 2357 made in 1964 only. Original retail, $75. Current value, $285 to $300.

**COLT General Hood Centennial:** Frontier Scout revolver; "1864 — General Hood's Tennessee Campaign — 1964" on left side of 4¾" barrel; .22 LR only; laminated rosewood grips, gold-plated medallions; gold-plated finish, except for blued trigger, hammer, base pin, ejector rod, rod head and

screw and screws for base pin, hammer, trigger, backstrap and trigger guard; originally cased in blonde-finished wood box, with green velvet/satin lining; 1503 made in 1964 only. Original retail, $75. Current value, $285 to $300.

**COLT New Jersey Tercentenary:** Frontier Scout revolver; "1664 — New Jersey Tercentenary — 1964" on left side of barrel; 4¾" barrel; .22 LR only; laminated rosewood grips; nickel-plated medallions; blued finish, with nickel-plated barrel, frame, ejector rod tube, tube plug and screw; originally cased in blonde-finished box with blue velvet lining in bottom, silver satin in lid; 1001 made in 1964 only.

Original retail, $75. Current value, $285 to $300.

**New Jersey Tercentenary single-action Army** revolver has same legend on barrel; 5½" barrel, .45 Colt only; grips, medallions, finish the same as on Frontier Scout version; same casing; 250 made in 1964 only. Original retail, $150. Current value, $765 to $800.

**COLT St. Louis Bicentennial:** Frontier Scout revolver; "1764 — St. Louis Bicentennial — 1964" wiped in gold on left side of 4¾" barrel; .22 LR only; laminated rosewood grips; gold-plated medallions; gold plated, except for blued frame, barrel, cylinder, ejector rod, rod tube, tube plug and screw; nonfluted cylinder; originally cased in blonde-finished wood box; yellow velvet/satin lining; 802 made in 1964 only. Original retail, $75. Current value, $285 to $300.

**St. Louis Bicentennial single-action Army** revolver has same legend on barrel as Frontier Scout version; 5½" barrel, .45 Colt only; same grips, medallions, finish, casing as Scout version; 200 made in 1964 only. Original retail, $150. Current value, $650 to $700.

**St. Louis Bicentennial Frontier Scout/single-action Army set** includes the two handguns described above in oversize case; 200 sets made in 1964 only. Original retail, $240. Current value, $850 to $900.

**COLT California Gold Rush Commemorative:** Frontier Scout revolver; "California Gold Rush Model" on left side of 4¾" barrel; .22 LR only; Ivorylite grips; gold-plated medallions; gold plated in entirety; originally cased in blonde wood box; blue velvet lining in bottom, gold in lid; 500 made in 1964 only. Original retail, $79.50. Current value, $350 to $365.

**California Gold Rush single-action Army** has same barrel legend as Frontier Scout version; 5½" barrel, .45 Colt only; same finish, grips, casing; 130 made in 1966 only. Original retail, $175. Current value, $950 to $975.

**COLT Pony Express Presentation:** single-action Army revolver; "Russell, Majors and Waddell — Pony Express Presentation Model" on left side of barrel. Various Pony Express stop markings on backstraps; 7½" barrel; .45 Colt; walnut grips; nickel-plated medallions; nickel plated in entirety; originally cased in walnut-finished wood with transparent Lucite lid; lined with burgundy velvet; 1004 made in 1964 only. Original retail, $250. Current value, $900 to $925.

**COLT Chamizal Treaty Commemorative:** Frontier Scout revolver; "1867 Chamizal Treaty — 1964" wiped in gold on left side of 4¾" barrel, .22 LR only; Pearlite grips; gold-plated medallions; gold-plated finish; blued frame, barrel, ejector rod, ejector tube, rod plug and screw, base pin and base pin screw and hammer, trigger and bolt screws; originally cased in blonde-finished wood; yellow velvet/satin lining; 450 made in 1964. Original retail, $85. Current value, $340 to $360.

   **Chamizal Treaty single-action Army revolver** has same legend on 5½" barrel; .45 Colt only; same grips, finish as Frontier Scout version; same type of case; 50 made in 1964. Original retail, $170. Current value, $1300 to $1350.

   **Chamizal Treaty Frontier Scout/single-action Army combo** includes the two guns described above in one over-size case; 50 pairs made in 1965. Original retail, $280. Current value, $1950 to $2000.

**COLT Col. Sam Colt Sesquicentennial Presentation:** single-action Army revolver; "1815 — Col. Saml Colt Sesquicentennial Model — 1964" on left side of 7½" barrel; .45 Colt only; rosewood grips; roll-engraved scene on cylinder; nickel-plated medallions; silver-plated finish, with blued frame, barrel, ejector rod tube and screw, hammer and trigger; originally cased in varnished walnut box, with 12 dummy nickel-plated cartridges in cartridge block; burgundy velvet lining; 4750 made in 1964 only. Original retail, $225. Current value, $760 to $790.

   **Sam Colt Sesquicentennial Deluxe** has the same specifications as standard presentation model, except grips are hand-fitted rosewood with escutcheons rather than medallions; hand-engraved cylinder; case has plate marked "1 of 200"; 200 made in 1964 only. Original retail, $500. Current value, $1550 to $1650.

   **Custom Deluxe** model has same specifications as Deluxe, except for facsimile of Samuel Colt's signature engraved on backstrap, lid of case engraved with "1 of 50", name of purchaser engraved when requested; 50 made in 1965. Original retail, $1000. Used value, $2975 to $3050.

**COLT Wyatt Earp Buntline:** single-action Army revolver; "Wyatt Earp Buntline Special" on left side of 12" barrel; .45 Colt only; laminated black rosewood grips; gold-plated medallions; gold plated in entirety; originally cased in black-finished wood, lined with green velvet/satin; 150 made only in 1964. Original retail, $250. Used value, $1575 to $1600.

**COLT Wichita Commemorative:** Frontier Scout revolver; "1864 — Kansas Series — Wichita — 1964" wiped in silver on left side of 4¾" barrel; .22 LR only; Pearlite grips; gold-plated medallions; gold plated in entirety; originally cased in blonde-finished wood; lined with red velvet/satin; 500 made in 1964 only. Original retail, $85. Current value, $325 to $350.

**ITHACA Model 49 St. Louis Bicentennial:** lever-action single-shot; hand-operated rebounding hammer; .22 LR, long, short; 18" barrel; Western carbine-style straight stock; open rear sight, ramp front. Only 200 manufactured in 1964. Original retail, $34.95. Current value, $155 to $165.

**REMINGTON Montana Centennial:** Model 600 carbine; bolt action; 6mm Remington only; deviates from standard Model 600 specifications only in better walnut, commemorative medallion inlaid into the stock; barrel inscription reads, "1864-1964/75th Anniversary"; 1000 made in 1964 only. Original retail, $124.95. Current value, $420 to $440.

**WINCHESTER Wyoming Diamond Jubilee Commemorative:** Model 94 carbine; .30-30 only; 1500 made, distributed exclusively by Billings Hardware Co.; same as standard M94, except for color case-hardened, engraved receiver, commemorative inscription on barrel; brass saddle ring, loading gate; state medallion imbedded in stock; made only in 1964, with retail of $100. Current value, $950 to $1000.

# 1965

**COLT Dodge City Commemorative:** Frontier Scout revolver; "1864 — Kansas Series — Dodge City — 1964" wiped in silver on left side of 4¾" barrel; .22 LR only; Ivorylite grips, gold-plated medallions; gold-plated finish, with blued base pin and screw, ejector rod, ejector rod head, bolt and trigger screw, hammer and hammer screw, trigger; originally cased in blonde-finished wood; lined with kelly green velvet/satin; 500 made in 1965 only. Original retail, $85. Current value, $250 to $265.

**COLT Colorado Gold Rush Commemorative:** Frontier Scout revolver; "1858 — Colorado Gold Rush — 1878" wiped in silver on left side of 4¾" barrel; .22 LR only; laminated rosewood grips; nickel-plated medallions; gold-plated finish, with nickel-plated hammer, base pin and screw, ejector rod head, hammer and trigger screws, trigger, grip screw; originally cased in blonde-finished wood; black velvet/satin lining; 1350 made in 1965 only. Original retail, $85. Current value, $290 to $315.

**COLT Oregon Trail Commemorative:** Frontier Scout revolver; "Oregon Trail Model," wiped in gold, on left side of 4¾" barrel; .22 LR only; Pearlite grips; gold-plated medallions; blued finish with gold-plated backstrap and trigger guard assembly and screws, hammer, trigger and screws, base pin, base pin screw and ejector rod head; originally cased in blonde-finished wood; lined with blue velvet in bottom, gold satin in lid; 1995 made only in 1965. Original retail, $75. Current value, $285 to $300.

**COLT Joaquin Murrieta 1 of 100:** Frontier Scout/single-action Army combo; both have "Joaquin Murrietta 1 of 100" on left side of barrels; Scout has 4¾" barrel, .22 LR only; SAA has 5½" barrel, .45 Colt only; grips on both are Pearlite, with gold-plated medallions; finish for both is gold-plate with blued barrels, frames, ejector rod tubes; originally in one oversize case of walnut-finished wood; blue velvet/satin lining; 100 sets made in 1965 only. Original retail, $350. Current value, $1050 to $1100.

**COLT Forty-Niner Miner:** Frontier Scout revolver; "The '49er Miner" wiped in gold on left side of 4¾" barrel, .22 LR only; laminated rosewood grips; gold-plated medallions; gold-plated finish with blued barrel, frame, backstrap and trigger guard assembly, ejector rod, tube and tube plug, ejector tube screw; originally cased in walnut-finished wood; lined with velvet in bottom, blue satin in lid; 500 made only in 1965. Original retail, $85. Current value, $285 to $300.

**COLT Old Fort Des Moines Reconstruction Commemorative:** Frontier Scout revolver; "Reconstruction of Old Fort Des Moines" wiped in silver on left side of 4¾" barrel; .22 LR only; Pearlite grips; gold-plated medallions; gold-plated in entirety; originally cased in white-finished wood; royal purple velvet lining in bottom, white satin in lid; 700 made in 1965 only. Original retail, $89.95. Current value, $325 to $340.

Old Fort Des Moines Reconstruction single-action Army revolver; has same legend on 5½" barrel; .45 Colt only; grips, finish the same as on Frontier Scout version; same casing; 100 made in 1965 only. Original retail, $169.95. Current value, $725 to $750.

Old Fort Des Moines Frontier Scout/single-action Army combo has the same specifications as those for two guns described above, in one oversize case; 100 sets made in 1965 only. Original retail, $289.95. Current value, $1150 to $1200.

**COLT Appomattox Centennial:** Frontier Scout revolver; "1865 — Appomattox Commemorative Model — 1965" wiped in silver on left side of 4¾" barrel; .22 LR only; laminated rosewood grips; nickel-plated medallions; nickel-plated finish, with blued barrel, frame, backstrap and trigger guard screws, ejector rod tube, tube plug and tube screw; originally cased in blonde-finished wood lined with blue velvet in bottom, gray satin in lid; 1001 made in 1965 only. Original retail, $75. Current value, $275 to $290.

Appomattox Centennial single-action Army has same legend on 5½" barrel; .45 Colt only; grips, finish, casing the same as for Frontier Scout version; 250 made in 1965. Original retail, $150. Current value, $625 to $650.

Appomattox Centennial Frontier Scout/single-action Army Combo consists of two guns described above in one oversize case; 250 sets made in 1965 only. Original retail, $240. Current value, $900 to $925.

**COLT General Meade Campaign Commemorative:** Frontier Scout revolver; "Gen. Meade Pennsylvania Campaign Model" wiped in gold on left side of 4¾" barrel; .22 LR only; Ivorylite grips, gold-plated medallions; gold-plated finish; blued frame, barrel, cylinder, ejector rod tube, tube plug and screw, hammer and trigger screws; originally cased in walnut-finished wood; blue velvet lining in bottom, gold satin in lid; 1197 made in 1965 only. Original retail, $75. Current value, $275 to $290.

General Meade Campaign single-action Army revolver has same legend on the 5½" barrel; .45 Colt only; same finish, casing as Frontier Scout version; 200 made in 1966 only. Original retail, $165. Current value, $750 to $765.

**COLT St. Augustine Quadricentennial:** Frontier Scout revolver; "1565 — St. Augustine Quadricentennial — 1965" wiped in gold on left side of 4¾" barrel; .22 LR only; Pearlite grips; gold-plated medallions; gold-plated finish, with blued barrel, base pin, ejector rod, tube, tube plug and screw, frame, hammer and trigger screws, backstrap and trigger guard assembly and screws; cased in blonde-finished wood; gold velvet/satin lining; 500 made in 1965 only. Original retail, $85. Current value, $315 to $325.

# 1966

**COLT Oklahoma Territory Commemorative:** Frontier Scout revolver; "1890 — Oklahoma Diamond Jubilee — 1965" wiped in gold on left side of 4¾" barrel; .22 LR only; laminated rosewood grips; gold-plated medallions; blued finish with gold-plated backstrap and trigger guard assembly and screws, cylinder, ejector rod head, base pin and screw, bolt and trigger cased in blonde-finished wood; red velvet/satin lining; 1343 made only in 1966. Original retail, $85. Current value, $275 to $290.

**COLT Dakota Territory Commemorative:** Frontier Scout revolver; "1861 — Dakota Territory — 1889" wiped in gold on left side of 4¾" barrel; .22 LR only; laminated rosewood grips; gold-plated medallions; blued finish with gold-plated backstrap and trigger guard assembly and screws, ejector rod and head, base pin, trigger, hammer, stock screw; originally cased in blonde-finished wood; red velvet/satin lining; 1000 made in 1966 only. Original retail, $85. Current value, $275 to $290.

**COLT Abercrombie & Fitch Trailblazer:** New Frontier single-action Army revolver; "Abercrombie & Fitch Co." wiped in gold on left side of 7½" barrel; .45 Colt only; rosewood grips; gold-plated medallions; gold-plated finish, blued barrel, cylinder, hammer, sights, ejector rod tube, ejector rod screw, case-hardened frame; roll-engraved, non-fluted cylinder; originally cased in varnished American walnut with brass-framed glass cover; bottom lined with crushed blue velvet; 200 made in 1966 with "New York" marked on butt, 100 with "Chicago" butt marking; 200 with "San Francisco" butt marking. Original retail, $275. Current value, $1675 to $1750.

**COLT Indiana Sesquicentennial:** Frontier Scout revolver; "1816 — Indiana Sesquicentennial — 1966" wiped in gold on left side of 4¾" barrel; .22 LR only; Pearlite grips; gold-plated medallions; blued finish, with gold-plated back-strap and trigger guard assembly, base pin and screw, ejector rod head, cylinder, bolt and trigger screw, hammer and hammer screw, trigger, stock screw; originally cased in blonde-finished wood; bottom lined with gold velvet, lid with blue satin; 1500 made in 1966 only. Original retail, $85. Current value, $275 to $290.

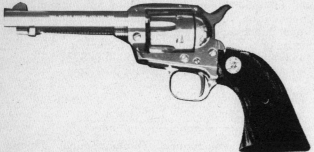

**COLT Abilene Commemorative:** Frontier Scout revolver; "1866 – Kansas Series – Abilene – 1966" wiped in silver on left side of 4¾" barrel; .22 LR only; laminated rosewood grips; gold-plated medallions; gold plated in entirety; originally cased in blonde-finished wood; blue velvet/satin lining; 500 made in 1966 only. Original retail, $95. Current value, $325 to $340.

**REMINGTON 150th Anniversary Model 1100 SA:** autoloading skeet shotgun; 12-ga. only; 26" barrel; vent rib; specifications the same as standard Model 1100, except for stamp-engraved legend on left side of receiver: "Remington Arms Company, Inc., 1816-1966, 150th Anniversary" with corporate logo; 1000 made in 1966 only. Original retail, $185. Current value, $300 to $325.

Model 1100 TB 150th Anniversary commemorative has same specifications as skeet version, except for recoil pad, 30" barrel, trap stock; same stamp-engraved legend on receiver; 1000 made in 1966 only. Original retail, $220. Current value, $325 to $375.

**REMINGTON 150th Anniversary Model 870 SA:** pump action skeet gun; 12-ga. only; 26" barrel; vent rib; specifications the same as standard Model 870, except for stamp-engraved legend on left side of receiver: "Remington Arms, Company Inc., 1816-1966, 150th Anniversary" with corporate logo; 1000 made in 1966 only. Original retail, $130. Current value, $300 to $325.

Model 870 TB 150th Anniversary commemorative has same specifications as skeet version, except for recoil pad,

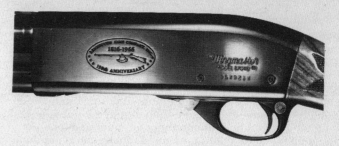

30" barrel, trap stock; same stamp-engraved legend on receiver; 1000 made in 1966 only. Original retail, $165. Current value, $350 to $375.

**REMINGTON 150th Anniversary Model 742 ADL:** autloading rifle; .30/06 only; impressed basket weave checkering; has same specifications as standard 742 ADL, except for stamp-engraved legend on left side of receiver: "Remington Arms Company Inc., 1816-1966, 150th Anniversary" with corporate logo; 1000 made in 1966 only. Original retail, $150. Current value, $325 to $350.

**REMINGTON 150th Anniversary Model 760 ADL:** pump action rifle; .30/06 only; has the same specifications as standard 760 BDL Deluxe model, except for stamp-engraved legend on left side of receiver: "Remington Arms Company Inc., 1816-1966, 150th Anniversary," with corporate logo; 1000 made in 1966 only. Original retail, $135. Current value, $300 to $325.

**REMINGTON 150th Anniversary Model 552A:** autoloading rifle; .22 LR, long, short; has same specifications as standard Model 552, except for stamp-engraved legend on left side of receiver: "Remington Arms Company Inc., 1816-1966, 150th Anniversary," with corporate logo; 1000 made in 1966 only. Original retail, $58. Current value, $100 to $115.

**REMINGTON 150th Anniversary Model 572A:** pump action rifle; .22 LR, long, short; has same specifications as standard Model 572, except for stamp-engraved legend on left side of receiver; "Remington Arms Company Inc., 1816-1966, 150th Anniversary," with corporate logo; 1000 made in 1966 only. Original retail, $60. Current value, $100 to $115.

**REMINGTON 150th Anniversary Nylon 66:** autoloading rifle; .22 LR; has same specifications as standard Nylon 66 Apache Black model, except for stamp-engraved legend on left side of receiver: "Remington Arms Company Inc., 1816-1966, 150th Anniversary," with corporate logo; 1000 made in 1966 only. Original retail, $50. Current value, $95 to $105.

**WINCHESTER Nebraska Centennial Commemorative:** Model 94 carbine; .30-30 only; same as standard M94 except for gold-plated loading gate, butt plate, barrel band, hammer; commemorative inscription on barrel, medallion in stock; only 2500 made and distributed only in Nebraska; made only in 1966. Original retail, $100. Current value, $850 to $900.

**WINCHESTER Centennial '66 Commemorative:** Model 94; rifle and carbine versions commemorate Winchester's 100th anniversary; produced in 1966 only; 100,478 were made; .30-30 only; rifle version has 26" ½-octagon barrel; full-length, 8-rd. magazine; gold-plated forearm cap, receiver; post front sight, open rear; walnut stock, forearm with epoxy finish; saddle ring; brass butt plate; commemorative inscription on barrel and top tang. Retail price, $125; used value, $425 to $435. Carbine differs only in shorter forearm, 20" barrel, 6-rd. magazine. Used value, $425 to $435. Matched set, with consecutive serial numbers, current value, $850 to $875.

# 1967

**COLT Bat Masterson:** Frontier Scout revolver; "Lawman Series — Bat Masterson" on left side of 4¾" barrel; .22 LR only; checkered rubber eagle grips; nickel-plated finish; cased originally in black Leatherette; red velvet/satin lining; 3000 made in 1967 only. Original retail, $90. Current value, $325 to $340.

**Bat Masterson single-action Army** has same legend on 4¾" barrel, .45 Colt only; grips, finish, casing are the same as for Frontier Scout version; 500 made in 1967 only. Original retail, $180. Current value, $675 to $700.

**COLT Alamo Commemorative:** Frontier Scout revolver; "Alamo Model," flanked by stars, wiped in gold on left side of 4¾" barrel; .22 LR only; Ivorylite grips, with inlaid gold-plated Texas star below screw on left grip. Gold-plated finish; blued barrel, frame, ejector rod tube, tube plug and screw; originally cased in blonde-finished wood box; blue velvet/satin lining; 4250 made in 1967 only. Original retail, $85. Current value, $290 to $315.

**Alamo Commemorative single-action Army** has same legend on barrel; same grips, finish, but with blued barrel, frame and ejector rod tube and tube screw; same casing; 750 made in 1967 only. Original retail, $165. Current value, $650 to $675.

**Alamo Commemorative Frontier Scout/single-action Army combo.** Includes two guns described above in one oversize case; 250 sets made in 1967 only. Original retail, $265. Current value, $950 to $1000.

**COLT Coffeyville Commemorative:** Frontier Scout revolver; "1866 — Kansas Series — Coffeyville — 1966" wiped in silver on left side of 4¾" barrel; .22 LR only; walnut grips; gold-plated medallions; gold-plated finish; blued backstrap and trigger guard assembly screws, base pin and screw, ejector rod, ejector rod head, hammer and hammer screw, trigger; originally cased in blonde-finished wood; black velvet/satin lining; 500 made in 1967 only. Original retail, $95. Current value, $325 to $350.

**COLT Chisholm Trail Commemorative:** Frontier Scout revolver; "1867 — Kansas Series — Chisholm Trail — 1967" wiped with silver on left side of 4¾" barrel; .22 LR; Pearlite grips; nickel-plated medallions; blued finish, with nickel-plated backstrap and trigger guard assembly and screws, trigger, hammer, base pin, ejector rod head, stock screw; originally cased in blonde-finished wood, gold velvet/satin lining; 500 made in 1967 only. Original retail, $100. Current value, $290 to $315.

**COLT Chateau Thierry Commemorative:** automatic, Model 1911A1; "1917 World War I Commemorative 1967" on right side of slide; roll-engraved scene on left depicting WWI battle; 5" barrel; .45 auto; checkered walnut grips; inlaid commemorative medallions; left grip inlaid with Chateau Thierry battle bar; blued finish with slide scene, serial number, banner, Colt markings wiped in gold; several features including no trigger finger relief cuts, non-grooved trigger, safety lever, adapted from original Model 1911 design; Standard model cased in olive drab box; Deluxe and Custom models have oiled, waxed teak cases; Deluxe model case inscribed "One of Seventy-Five/Deluxe Engraved/

chester's Model 64 boy's rifle, discontinued in 1963. Canadian commemorative is in .30-30 caliber, with octagonal 26'' rifle or 20'' carbine barrel; black-chromed receiver is engraved with maple leaf motif; forearm tip is black chromed; straight stock is finished with ''antique-gloss.'' Both versions have a dovetail bead-post front sight, buckhorn rear. Carbine is equipped with saddle ring, has 6-shot magazine, the rifle, 8. Gold-filled inscription on barrel reads, ''Canadian Centennial 1867-1967.'' Introduced in 1967. Original price for rifle or carbine, $125; matching set, with consecutive serial numbers, $275. Current value, rifle, $400 to $450; carbine, $400 to $450; matched set, $900 to $1000.

Chateau Thierry Commemoratives''; Custom model case inscribed ''One of Twenty-Five/Custom Engraved/Chateau Thierry Commemoratives''; gun bears gold-filled signature of A.A. White engraver; 7400 Standard versions made in 1967-68, 75 Deluxe, 25 Custom. Original retail prices: Standard, $200; Deluxe, $500; Custom, $1000. Current values: Standard, $425 to $500; Deluxe, $1200 to $1300; Custom, $2500 to $2750.

**REMINGTON Canadian Centennial:** Model 742 rifle; autoloader; .30/06 only; same as standard model except for impressed checkering on pistol grip. Left side of receiver is engraved with maple leaves, special insignia, ''1867-1967 — Canadian Centennial Gun,'' wiped in white; serial number is preceded by letter C; 1000 made in 1967 only. Original retail, $119.95. Current value, $275 to $325.

**WINCHESTER Alaskan Purchase Centennial:** Model 94 rifle; sold only in Alaska; receiver is engraved in 19th Century filigree for ''antique'' appeal; centered in stock is the official Alaskan Purchase centennial medallion with totem pole symbol of the state; barrel is 26'', with magazine capacity of 8 rds.; other facets are standard of Model 94. Introduced, 1967. Original price, $125. Current value, $950 to $1000.

**WINCHESTER Canadian Centennial:** Model 64; action, obviously, is the Model 94; not to be confused with Win-

# 1968

**COLT Nebraska Centennial:** Frontier Scout revolver; ''1867 — Nebraska Centennial — 1967'' on left side of 4¾'' barrel; .22 LR; Pearlite grips; gold-plated barrel, frame, hammer, trigger, ejector rod head, stock screw; originally cased in blonde-finished wood; lined with blue velvet in bottom, gold satin in lid; 7001 made in 1968 only. Original retail, $100. Current value, $280 to $300.

**COLT Gen. Nathan Bedford Forrest:** Frontier Scout revolver; ''General Nathan Bedford Forrest'' on left side of 4¾'' barrel; .22 LR only; laminated rosewood grips; gold-plated medallions; gold-plated finish; blued cylinder, backstrap and trigger guard assembly; originally cased in dark brown Leatherette; red velvet/satin lining; 3000 made in 1968-69. Original retail, $110. Current value, $280 to $300.

**COLT Pawnee Trail Commemorative:** Frontier Scout revolver; ''1868 — Kansas Series — Pawnee Trail — 1968'' wiped in silver on left side of 4¾'' barrel; .22 LR; laminated rosewood grips; nickel-plated medallions; blued finish; nickel-plated backstrap and trigger guard assembly and screws, cylinder, base pin, ejector rod head, trigger, hammer, stock screw; originally cased in blonde-finished wood; lined with blue velvet in bottom, silver satin in lid; 501 made in 1968. Original retail, $110. Current value, $280 to $300.

**COLT Pat Garrett Commemorative:** Frontier Scout revolver; ''Lawman Series — Pat Garrett'' on right side of 4¾'' barrel; .22 LR only; Pearlite grips; gold-plated medallions; gold-plated finish; nickel-plated barrel, frame, backstrap and trigger guard assembly, ejector rod; loading gate is gold plated; originally cased in black Leatherette with gold velvet/satin lining; 3000 made in 1968 only. Original retail, $110. Current value, $325 to $340.

**Pat Garrett single-action Army revolver** has same barrel legend; 5½'' barrel; .45 Colt only; same grips, finish, casing as Frontier Scout version; 500 made in 1968. Original retail, $220. Current value, $650 to $675.

**COLT Santa Fe Trail Commemorative:** Frontier Scout revolver; "Kansas Series — Santa Fe Trail — 1968" wiped in silver on left side of 4¾" barrel; .22 LR; Ivorylite grips; nickel-plated medallions; blued finish with nickel-plated backstrap and trigger guard assembly and screws, hammer, trigger, stock screw, base pin, ejector rod head; originally cased in blonde-finished wood; green velvet/satin lining; 501 made in 1968-69. Original retail, $120. Current value, $280 to $300.

**COLT Belleau Wood Commemorative:** automatic; Model 1911A1; "1917 World War I Commemorative 1967" on right side of slide; roll engraved scene on left side of machine gun battle; 5" barrel; .45 auto only; rosewood grips inlaid with commemorative medallions; left grip inlaid with Belleau Wood battle bar; blued finish; slide scene, serial number, banner, Colt markings wiped in gold on Standard model; Deluxe version has slide, frame hand engraved, serial numbers gold-inlaid; Custom has more elaborate engraving; the same features of 1911 model adapted to Chateau Thierry model are incorporated; cases are same as Chateau Thierry model, with brass plate for Deluxe engraved "One of Seventy-Five/Deluxe Engraved/Belleau Wood Commemorative"; plate on Custom model reads "One of Twenty-Five/Custom Engraved/Belleau

Wood Commemoratives"; production began in 1968, with 7400 Standard types, 75 Deluxe, 25 Custom. Original retail: Standard, $200; Deluxe, $500; Custom, $1000. Current values: Standard, $425 to $450; Deluxe, $1250 to $1350; Custom, $2500 to $2750.

**WINCHESTER Buffalo Bill Commemorative:** Model 94; available with either 20" or 26" barrel, both with bead-post front sights, semi-buckhorn rear sights. Hammer, trigger, loading gate, forearm tip, saddle ring, crescent butt plate are nickel plated. Barrel, tang are inscribed respectively, "Buffalo Bill Commemorative" and "W.F. Cody — Chief of Scouts." Receiver is embellished with scrollwork. American walnut stock has Buffalo Bill Memorial Assn. medallion imbedded; rifle has 8-rd. tubular magazine, carbine, 6 rds. Introduced, 1968. Original price, $129.95. Current value, rifle, $375 to $400; carbine, $375 to $400.

**WINCHESTER Illinois Sesquicentennial:** Model 94; standard design, except for words, "Land of Lincoln," and a profile of Lincoln engraved on the receiver, with gold-filled inscription on barrel, "Illinois Sesquicentennial, 1818-1968"; gold plated metal butt plate, trigger, loading gate and saddle ring. Official souvenir medallion is imbedded in the walnut stock. This was the first state commemorative to be sold outside the celebrating state by Winchester. Introduced in 1968. Original price, $110. Current value, $390 to $415.

**FRANCHI Centennial:** semi-automatic takedown rifle, .22 LR only; commemorates 1868-1968 centennial of S.A. Luigi Franchi; centennial seal engraved on receiver; 21" barrel, 11-rd. butt stock magazine; hand-checkered European walnut stock, forearm; open rear sight, gold bead front on ramp. Deluxe model has better grade wood, fully engraved receiver. Made only in 1968. Original retail: deluxe, $124.95; standard, $86.95. Current values, deluxe model, $325 to $350; standard model, $235 to $250.

# 1969

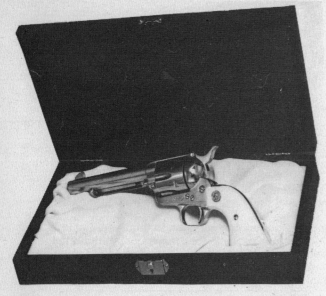

**COLT Alabama Sesquicentennial:** Frontier Scout revolver; "1819 — Alabama Sesquicentennial — 1969" on left side of 4¾" barrel; .22 LR only; Ivorylite grips; gold-plated medallions; gold-plated finish; nickel-plated loading gate, cylinder, ejector rod, rod head and tube, base pin and screw, bolt and trigger guard assembly screws, hammer and screw, trigger; originally cased in red leatherette-covered wood box; white velvet lining in bottom, red satin in lid; 3001 made in 1969. Original retail, $110. Current value, $290 to $310.

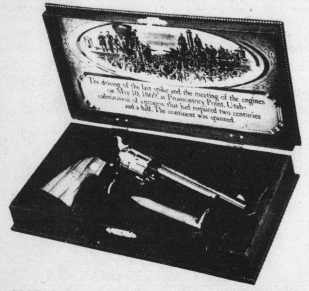

**COLT Golden Spike:** Frontier Scout revolver; "1869 — Golden Spike — 1969" on right side of 6" barrel, standard barrel markings on left, both wiped in gold; .22 LR only; sand-blasted walnut-stained fir grips; gold-plated medallions; gold-plated finish; blued barrel, frame, backstrap and trigger guard assembly and ejector tube plug and screw; originally cased in hand-stained, embossed simulated mahogany; 11,000 made in 1969. Original retail, $135. Current value, $290 to $310.

**COLT Wild Bill Hickok Commemorative:** Frontier Scout revolver; "Lawman Series — Wild Bill Hickok" wiped in silver on right side of 6" barrel; .22 LR only; nonfluted cylinder; Pearlite grips; nickel-plated medallions; nickel-plated finish; blued barrel, frame, ejector tube screw; originally cased in black Leatherette-covered box; bottom lined in blue velvet, lid in silver satin; 3000 made, production began in 1969. Original retail, $116.60. Current value, $325 to $340.

Wild Bill Hickok Commemorative single-action Army has the same legend on 7½" barrel; .45 Colt only; same finish as Frontier Scout version, except for nickel-plated loading gate; same casing; 500 made, production beginning in 1969. Original retail, $220. Current value, $650 to $665.

**COLT Second Battle of the Marne Commemorative:** automatic, Model 1911A1; "1917 World War I Commemorative 1967" on right side of slide; roll-engraved combat scene on left side of slide; 5" barrel, .45 auto; white French holly grips; inlaid commemorative medallions; left grip inlaid with 2nd Battle of the Marne battle bar; blue finish, with slide engraving, serial number on Standard, banner, other markings wiped in gold; Deluxe and Custom models are hand engraved, with serial numbers gold inlaid; work on Custom model is in greater detail; cases are same as others in series, except Deluxe case has brass plate inscribed "One of Seventy-Five/Deluxe Engraved/2nd Battle of the Marne Commemorative"; Custom case has same type of plate inscribed "One of Twenty-five/Custom Engraved/2nd Battle of the Marne Commemorative"; 7400 Standard guns made in 1969, 75 Deluxe, 25 Custom. Original retail, Standard, $220; Deluxe, $500; Custom, $1000. Current values, Standard, $425 to $475; Deluxe, $1150 to $1250; Custom, $2500 to $2650.

**COLT Shawnee Trail Commemorative:** Frontier Scout revolver; "1869 — Kansas Series — Shawnee Trail — 1969" wiped in silver on left side of 4¾" barrel; .22 LR only; laminated rosewood grips; nickel-plated medallions; blued finish; nickel-plated backstrap and trigger guard assembly and screws, cylinder, base pin, ejector rod head, hammer, trigger and stock screw; originally cased in blonde-finished wood; red velvet/satin lining; 501 made in 1969 only. Original retail, $120. Current value, $290 to $315.

**COLT Texas Ranger Commemorative:** single-action Army revolver; "Texas Ranger Commemoratives/One Riot-One Ranger" wiped in silver on left side of barrel; "Texas Rangers" roll engraved on backstrap; sterling silver star, wreath on top of backstrap behind hammer; YO Ranch brand stamped on bottom of backstrap; 7½" barrel; .45 Colt only; Standard model has rosewood grips, silver miniature Ranger badge inlaid in left grip; blued finish; case-hardened frame; nickel-plated trigger guard, base pin and screw, ejector rod and head, ejector tube screw; gold-plated stock screw, stock escutcheons, medallions. First 200 are custom models, with finish, decoration to customer's desires at increasing prices; custom-finished guns had deluxe engraved serial numbers, ivory grips with star inlay; originally cased in special hand-rubbed box with drawers, glass top; red velvet lining; 200 Custom, 800 Standard guns made; production began in 1969. Original values, Custom, varying with customer's desires; Standard, $650. Current value, Standard, $1000 to $1150.

**COLT Arkansas Territorial Sesquicentennial:** Frontier Scout revolver; "1819 — Arkansas Territory Sesquicentennial — 1969" on left side of 4¾" barrel; .22 LR only; laminated rosewood grips; gold-plated medallions; aluminum frame; blued frame, backstrap and trigger guard assembly, ejector rod head; gold-plated stock screw nut; originally cased in blonde-finished baswood; red velvet/satin lining; 3500 made; production began in 1969. Original retail, $110. Current value, $250 to $265.

**COLT Meuse Argonne Commemorative:** automatic, Model 1911A1; "1917 World War I Commemorative 1967" on right side of slide; left has roll-engraved charge on pillbox on Standard; slides, frames on Deluxe, Custom models are hand engraved, serial numbers inlaid in gold; Custom model is more elaborately engraved, inlaid; 5" barrel, .45 auto only; varnished crotch walnut grips; inlaid commemorative medallions; left grip inlaid with Meuse Argonne battle bar; blued finish; engraving, numbers, et al., gold wiped on Standard model; same case as earlier WWI Commemoratives; brass plate for Deluxe reads "One of Seventy-Five/Deluxe Engraved/Meuse Argonne Commemoratives"; plate on Custom case is inscribed "One of Twenty-Five/Custom Engraved/Meuse Argonne Commemoratives"; production began in 1969; 7400 Standard, 75 Deluxe, 25 Custom. Original retail, Standard, $220; Deluxe, $500; Custom, $1000. Current values, Standard, $425 to $450; Deluxe, $1150 to $1250; Custom, $2250 to $2500.

**COLT California Bicentennial:** Frontier Scout revolver; "1769 — California Bicentennial — 1969" on left side of 6" barrel; .22 LR only; laminated rosewood grips; gold-plated medallions; gold-plated finish; all screws nickel-plated, except base pin, grip screws; hammer, trigger also nickel plated; originally cased in California redwood; black velvet/satin lining; 5000 made in 1969-70. Original retail, $135. Current value, $290 to $315.

**COLT Fort Larned Commemorative:** Frontier Scout revolver; "1869 — Kansas Series — Fort Larned — 1968" on left side of 4¾" barrel; .22 LR; Pearlite grips; nickel-plated medallions; nickel-plated finish; blued backstrap and trigger guard assembly, base pin and screw, cylinder, ejector rod head and tube screw, hammer and stock screw, bolt and trigger screw; originally cased in blonde-finished wood; blue velvet lining in bottom, silver satin in lid; 500 made in 1969-70. Original retail, $120. Current value, $290 to $315.

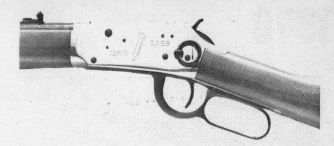

**WINCHESTER Golden Spike:** Model 94; features 20" barrel with twin barrel bands plated in yellow gold; yellow gold receiver, engraved with decorative scrolled border on right side, inscribed on other side with railroad spike flanked by dates, 1859 and 1969. Barrel carries "Golden Spike Commemorative" inscription; upper tang bears words, "Oceans United By Rail." Butt stock, forearm are straight-line design of satin-finished American walnut, with fluted comb. Inset in stock is centennial medallion of engines of Central Pacific, Union Pacific meeting on May 10, 1969. It has straight brass butt plate, blued saddle ring; chambered for .30-30, weight is 7 lbs. Introduced in 1969. Original retail price, $119.95. Current value, $400 to $425.

**WINCHESTER Theodore Roosevelt Commemorative:** Model 94 rifle and carbine; made in 1969 only; 49,505 manufactured; .30-30 only; rifle has 26" octagonal barrel; 6-rd. half-magazine; forearm cap, upper tang, receiver plated with white gold; receiver engraved with American eagle, "26th President 1901-1909," Roosevelt's facsimile signature; contoured lever, half-pistol grip; medallion in stock. Retail price, $125; used value, $250 to $265. Carbine differs from rifle in shorter forearm, full-length 6-rd. tubular magazine; 20" barrel. Current value, $400 to $425. Matched set with consecutive serial numbers, $825 to $875.

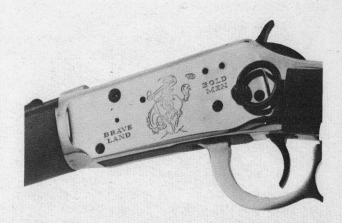

**WINCHESTER Cowboy Commemorative:** Model 94; receiver, upper and lower tang, lever, barrel bands are nickel plated; butt plate is stainless steel, with tang that extends over top of stock for square comb look; stock is straight grip with extended forearm of American walnut; imbedded in right side of stock is medallion of cowboy roping a steer; etched on left side of receiver, "Brave Land — Bold Men." Opposite side is engraved with coiled lariat, spurs; barrel is 20", carrying "Cowboy Commemorative"; upper tang has inscription, "Winchester Model 1894." Has adjustable semi-buckhorn rear sight, blued saddle ring; in .30-30 only. Introduced in 1969; original retail price, $125. Current value, $400 to $425.

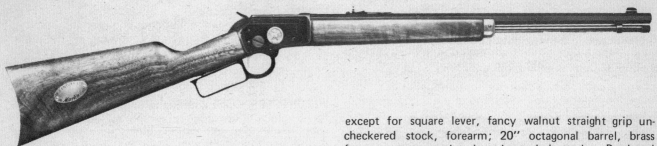

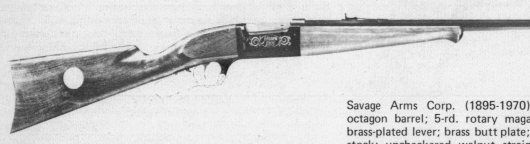

**MARLIN Model 39 Century Ltd:** marking Marlin Centennial, 1870-1970, specs are same as standard Model 39A, except for square lever, fancy walnut straight grip uncheckered stock, forearm; 20" octagonal barrel, brass forearm cap; nameplate inset in stock, butt plate. Produced only in 1970. Original retail, $125. Current value, $200 to $235.

**SAVAGE Anniversary Model 1895:** replica of Savage Model 1895; hammerless lever-action; marks 75th anniversary of Savage Arms Corp. (1895-1970); .308 Win. only; 24" octagon barrel; 5-rd. rotary magazine; engraved receiver, brass-plated lever; brass butt plate; brass medallion inlaid in stock; uncheckered walnut straight-grip stock, schnabel-type forearm. Made only in 1970; 9,999 produced. Original retail, $195. Current value, $285 to $310.

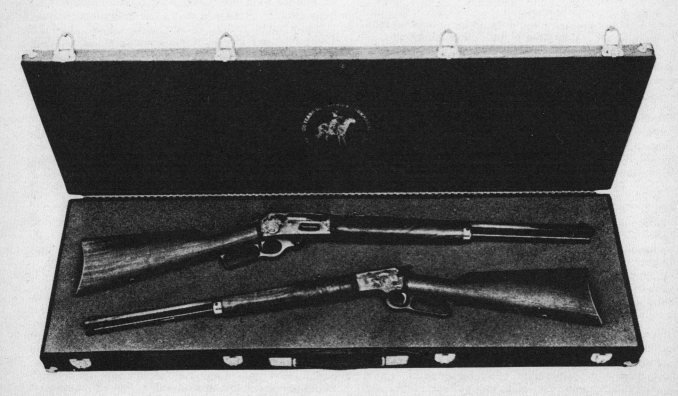

**MARLIN Centennial Matched Pair:** combines presentation-grade Model 336 centerfire, rimfire Model 39, in luggage-type case; matching serial numbers, for additional collector value. Both rifles have fancy walnut straight-grip stocks, forearms; brass forearm caps, brass butt plates, engraved receivers with inlaid medallions. Model 336 is chambered for .30-30 only, Model 39 for .22 LR, .22 long, .22 short cartridges. Only 1000 sets were manufactured in 1970. Original retail, $750. Current value, $1450 to $1490.

**COLT World War II/European Theater:** automatic, Model 1911A1; slide is marked "World War II Commemorative/European Theater of Operations" on left side; right side is roll-engraved with major sites of activity; 5" barrel; .45 auto only; bird's-eye maple grips; gold-plated medallions; nickel-plated finish in entirety; originally cased in oak box with oak cartridge block; lid removable; 7 dummy cartridges included; infantry blue velvet lining; 11,500 made; production began in 1970. Original retail, $250. Current value, $425 to $475.

**COLT World War II/Pacific Theater:** automatic, Model 1911A1; slide is marked "World War II Commemorative/Pacific Theater of Operations" on right side; left side roll-engraved with names of 10 major battle areas; both sides of slide bordered in roll marked palm leaf design; 5" barrel; .45 auto only; Brazilian rosewood grips; gold-plated medallions; nickel plated in entirety; originally cased in Obichee wood; light green velvet lining; 7 nickel-plated dummy cartridges in cartridge block; 11,500 made; production began in 1970. Original retail, $250. Current value, $425 to $475.

**COLT Maine Sesquicentennial:** Frontier Scout revolver; "1820 — Maine Sesquicentennial — 1970" on left side of 4¾" barrel; .22 LR only; nonfluted cylinder; Pearlite grips; gold-plated medallions; gold-plated finish; nickel-plated backstrap and trigger guard assembly, cylinder, base pin screw, hammer and hammer screw, ejector rod, ejector rod head, ejector tube screw, bolt and trigger screw; originally cased in natural knotty white pine; lined with royal blue velvet in bottom, light blue satin in lid; 3000 made in 1970. Original retail, $120. Current value, $280 to $300.

**COLT Missouri Territorial Sesquicentennial:** Frontier Scout revolver; "1820 — Missouri Sesquicentennial — 1970" wiped in gold on left side of 4¾" barrel; .22 LR only; walnut grips; gold-plated medallions; blued finish; gold-plated cylinder, loading gate, base pin, ejector rod head, ejector tube, tube screw, bolt and trigger screw, hammer, trigger, stock screw, top backstrap screws; originally cased in natural finish willow, lined in red velvet; 3000 made in 1970. Original retail, $125. Current value, $280 to $300.

**Missouri Territorial Sesquicentennial single-action Army** has same legend on the 5½" barrel, .45 Colt only; grips, medallions, finish and plating are same as Frontier Scout version, except for case-hardened frame, loading gate; same casing; 900 made; production started in 1970. Original retail, $220. Current value, $565 to $590.

**COLT Wyatt Earp Commemorative:** Frontier Scout revolver; "Lawman Series — Wyatt Earp" on right side of barrel; standard model markings on left side; 12" Buntline barrel; .22 LR only; walnut grips; nickel-plated medallions; blued finish; nickel-plated barrel, cylinder, ejector tube plug, ejector tube screw, rod head, base pin and base pin screw, hammer, trigger and backstrap and trigger guard assembly; originally cased in black Leatherette-covered box; bottom lined with burgundy velvet, lid with red satin; 3000 made; production started in 1970. Original retail, $125. Current value, $350 to $365.

**Wyatt Earp single-action Army** has same legend on barrel, but wiped in silver; 16-1/8" barrel; .45 Colt only; same grips, medallions as Frontier Scout version; blued finish; case-hardened frame; nickel-plated hammer, trigger, base pin, base pin crosslatch assembly; same casing as Frontier Scout; 500 made; production began in 1970. Original retail, $395. Current value, $1575 to $1600.

**COLT Fort Riley Commemorative:** Frontier Scout revolver; "1870 — Kansas Series — Fort Riley — 1970" wiped in black on left side of 4¾" barrel; .22 LR only; Ivorylite grips; nickel-plated medallions; nickel-plated finish; blued backstrap and trigger guard assembly, cylinder, base pin and screw, ejector rod head and tube screw, bolt and trigger screw, hammer and screw, trigger, stock screw; originally cased in blonde-finished wood; black velvet/satin lining; 500 made in 1970. Original retail, $130. Current value, $280 to $300.

**COLT Fort Hays Commemorative:** Frontier Scout revolver; "1870 — Fort Hays — 1970" wiped in silver on left side of 4¾" barrel; .22 LR only; hard rubber grips; nickel-plated finish; blued barrel, backstrap and trigger guard assembly screws, cylinder, base pin screw, ejector tube screw, bolt and trigger screw, hammer screw, trigger; originally cased in blonde-finished wood; bottom lined with blue velvet, gold satin in lid; 500 made in 1970. Original retail, $130. Current value, $280 to $300.

**WINCHESTER Lone Star Commemorative:** Model 94; produced in rifle version with 26" barrel and carbine with 20" length. Receiver, upper and lower tang, lever, forearm cap, magazine tube cap all are gold plated; butt plate is crescent shaped, solid brass. Stocks are American walnut with half-pistol grip, fluted comb; commemorative medal with faces of Sam Houston, Stephen F. Austin, William Travis, Jim Bowie and Davy Crockett is inset in right side of stock. Left side of receiver is engraved with star and dates, 1845, 1970; both sides are bordered with series of stars; barrel carries inscription, "Lone Star Commemorative." Upper tang has "Under Six Flags," referring to banners of Spain, France, Mexico, Texas Republic, Confederacy and United States, which have flown over territory. It has bead-post front sight, semi-buckhorn rear, plus saddle ring. Introduced in 1970; original price, $140 for either rifle or carbine; $305 for matched set with consecutive serial numbers. Current values, carbine, $400 to $425; rifle, $400 to $425; matched set, $825 to $875.

---

# 1971

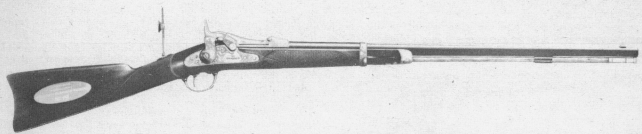

**HARRINGTON & RICHARDSON Anniversary Model 1873:** replica of Officer's Model 1873 trapdoor Springfield commemorating 100th anniversary of H&R (1871-1971). Single-shot action; .45-70 only; 26" barrel; engraved receiver, breech block, hammer, lock, band, butt plate; hand-checkered walnut stock with inlaid brass commemorative plate; peep rear sight, blade front; ramrod. Made only in 1971. Production limited to 10,000. Current value, $375 to $400.

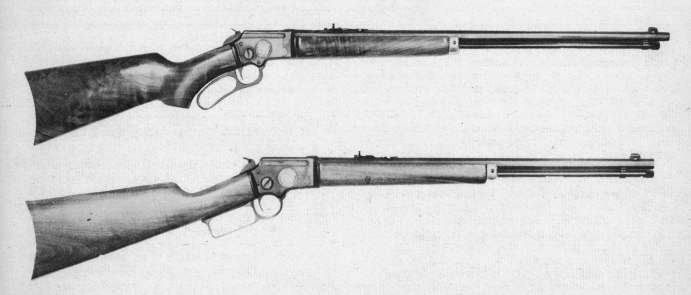

**MARLIN 39A Article II:** same general specs as Model 39A; commemorates National Rifle Association Centennial, 1871-1971. Medallion with legend "The Right to Bear Arms" set on blued receiver; 24" octagonal barrel; tube magazine holds 19 LR, 21 longs, 25 shorts; fancy un-checkered walnut pistol-grip stock, forearm; brass butt plate, forearm cap. Produced only in 1971. Original retail, $135. Current value, $225 to $250.

**Article II carbine** is same as Article II rifle, except it has straight-grip stock, square lever, shorter magazine, reduced capacity; 20" octagonal barrel. Produced only in 1971. Original retail, $135. Current value, $235 to $265.

**SAVAGE Model 71:** single-shot lever-action; replica of Stevens favorite, issued as commemorative to Joshua Stevens, founder of Stevens Arms Co.; .22 LR only; 22" octagon barrel; brass-plated hammer, lever; uncheckered straight-grip stock, schnabel forearm; brass commemorative medallion inlaid in stock; brass butt plate; open rear sight, brass blade front; made in 1971 only; 10,000 produced. Original retail, $75. Current value, $130 to $135.

**WINCHESTER National Rifle Association Centennial Model:** Introduced in two versions: musket and rifle, both on Model 94 actions; musket resembles Model 1895 NRA musket with military lever to meet requirements for NRA match competition at turn of century; has 26" tapered, round barrel; full length American walnut forearm; black-chromed steel butt plate; rear sight has calibrated folding rear leaf sight, blade front sight; magazine holds 7 rds.

Rifle model resembles Model 64, also made on 94 action. Has half magazine holding 5 rds., 24" tapered round barrel, hooded ramp and bead-post front sight, adjustable semi-buckhorn rear sight, contoured lever, blued steel forearm cap.

Both models are .30-30, have quick detachable sling swivels; receivers are black-chromed steel; NRA seal in silver-colored metal is set in right side of stocks; left side of receivers inscribed appropriately with "NRA Centennial Musket" or "NRA Centennial Rifle." Both were introduced in 1971; retail price on each was $149.95; matched set with consecutive serial numbers, $325. Current values, musket, $400 to $425; rifle, $400 to $425; cased set, $825 to $850.

**COLT Fort Scott Commemorative:** Frontier Scout revolver; "1871 — Kansas Series — Fort Scott — 1971" on left side of 4¾" barrel; .22 LR only; checkered rubber, eagle-style grips; nickel-plated finish; blued barrel, cylinder, base pin screw, ejector tube screw, bolt and trigger screw, hammer, hammer screw, trigger; originally cased in blonde-finished wood; gold velvet/satin lining; 500 made in 1971. Original retail, $130. Current value, $200 to $210.

escutcheons; originally cased in walnut, with inlaid NRA plate; gold velvet/satin lining; 2412 .357 magnums, 4131 .45 Colts made; production began in 1971. Original retail, $250. Current value, $500 to $525.

**COLT NRA Centennial Commemorative:** single-action Army; "1871 NRA Centennial 1971" wiped in gold on left side of 4¾", 5½", or 7½" barrels; .357 magnum, .45 Colt; goncalo alves grips; gold-plated NRA medallion inlays; blued finish; case-hardened frame; nickel-silver grip screw

**COLT NRA Centennial Commemorative:** automatic; Gold Cup National Match model; "1871 NRA Centennial 1971/The First 100 Years of Service/.45 Automatic Caliber" wiped in gold on left side of slide; MK IV barrel; Eliason rear sight; 5" barrel; .45 auto only; checkered walnut grips; gold-plated NRA medallion inlays; blued; has same type of case as NRA commemorative SAA; 2500 made; production began in 1971. Original retail, $250. Current value, $450 to $500.

# 1972

**COLT Florida Territorial Sesquicentennial:** Frontier Scout revolver; "1822 — Florida Territory — 1972" on left side of 4¾" barrel; .22 LR only; cypress wood grips; gold-plated medallions; blued finish; case hardened frame, loading gate; gold-plated base pin, base pin screw, ejector rod head and screws, hammer, trigger and trigger screws; originally cased in cypress box; gold velvet/satin lining; 2001 made; production began in 1972. Original retail, $125. Current value, $290 to $310.

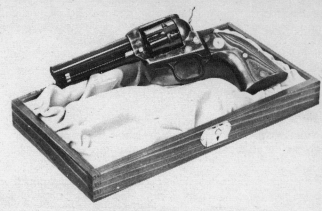

**MARLIN Model 336 Zane Grey:** same specs as Model 336A, except in .30-30 only; 22" octagonal barrel. Commemorates centennial of Zane Grey's birth, 1872-1972; commemorative medallion attached to receiver; selected un- checkered walnut pistol-grip stock, forearm; brass forearm cap, butt plate; 10,000 produced with special serial numbers, ZG1 through ZG10,000. Produced only in 1972. Original retail, $150. Current value, $235 to $265.

# 1973

**SAKO Golden Anniversary Model:** has same specifications as Sako long action Deluxe Sporter; 7mm Remington magnum only; floor plate, trigger guard, receiver feature gold oak leaf, acorn decoration; hand-checkered select European walnut stock, hand-carved oak leaf pattern. Commemorates firm's 50th anniversary; only 1,000 made in 1973. Current value, $1300 to $1350.

**WINCHESTER Texas Ranger Commemorative:** Model 94; features stock, forearm of semi-fancy walnut, with the butt stock having square comb, metal butt plate. Chambered in .30-30, tube magazine holds 6 rds.; a facsimile of Texas Ranger star badge is imbedded in the stock; saddle ring is included. Of standard grade, only 4850 were released in April 1973, all of them in the state of Texas. Another 150 so-called Special Edition guns, at $1000 each, were released, in presentation cases, only to the Texas Ranger Association. These were hand-checkered, with full fancy walnut stocks, barrel and receiver highly polished. Magazine holds only 4 rds.; gun has 16" barrel, weighs 6 lbs; standard model weighs 7 lbs; has 20" barrel. With Special Edition guns, commemorative star is mounted inside the presentation case instead of in the stock. Also introduced April 1973. Original price, standard model, $134.95. Current value, $750 to $800; Special Edition model, original price, $1000. Current value, $2500 to $3000.

**CHURCHILL One of One Thousand:** .270 Winchester, 7mm Remington magnum, .308, .30/06, .300 Winchester magnum, .375 Holland & Holland magnum, .458 Winchester magnum; 5-rd. magazine in standard calibers, 3 rds. for magnums; made on Mauser-type action; classic French walnut stock; hand-checkered pistol-grip, forearm; recoil pad, cartridge trap in butt; sling swivels. Manufactured in England in 1973 to commemorate Interarms' 20th anniversary. Only 1,000 made. Current value, $1100 to $1150.

**COLT Arizona Ranger Commemorative:** Frontier Scout revolver; "Arizona Ranger Commemorative" on left side of 4¾" barrel; .22 LR only; laminated rosewood grips; nickel-plated medallions; blued finish; case-hardened frame; nickel-plated backstrap and trigger guard assembly, hammer, trigger, base pin, base pin assembly, screw for backstrap/trigger guard assembly, grips; originally cased in walnut with glass window lid; replica Arizona Ranger badge included in case; lined with maroon velvet; 3001 made; production began in 1973. Original retail, $135. Current value, $280 to $300.

**COLT Peacemaker Centennial:** single-action Army revolver, Frontier Six Shooter configuration; "The Frontier Six-Shooter" etched on left side of barrel, "1873 Peacemaker Centennial 1973" roll marked on right side; 7½" barrel; .44-40 only; checkered rubber eagle-style grips; nickel-plated in entirety; originally cased in leather-covered wood box; brown velvet lining; 1500 made; production began in 1973. Original retail, $300. Current value, $425 to $450.
   **Peacemaker Centennial in .45 Colt Peacemaker** configuration has "1873 Peacemaker Centennial 1973" roll marked on left side of 7½" barrel, .45 Colt only; one-piece varnished walnut grip; blued finish; case-hardened frame, hammer; originally cased in oiled walnut with brass-framed glass cover; maroon velvet lining; 1500 made; production began in 1973. Original retail, $300. Current value, $650 to $675.
   **Peacemaker Centennial .45 Colt/.44-40 combo** includes both guns described above in oversize case of walnut-stained willow; lined with dark maroon velvet; matching serial numbers on guns; 500 sets made in 1973. Original retail, $625. Current value, $1700 to $1750.

**REMINGTON 1973 Ducks Unlimited Commemorative:** Model 1100 autoloading shotgun; 12-ga. only; 30" barrel;

full choke; vent rib. Other specifications the same as standard Model 1100, except that serial number is preceded by DU; Ducks Unlimited medallion, surrounded by gilded scrollwork, is attached to left side of receiver; 500 made in 1973. only. Original retail, $230. Current value, $375 to $450.

**SMITH & WESSON Texas Ranger Commemorative:** Model 19 .357 Combat Magnum; 4" barrel; sideplate stamped with Texas Ranger commemorative seal; uncheckered goncalco alves stocks; marketed with specially designed Bowie-type knife in presentation case. Commemorated the 150th anniversary of the Texas Rangers. Reported 8,000 sets made in 1973. Current value, $450 to $475.

# 1974

**CHARLES DALY Wildlife Commemorative:** over/under; 12-ga.; trap and skeet models only; has same general specs as Diamond Grade over/under; fine scroll work on left side of receiver, duck scene engraved on right side. Manufactured in Japan 1974. Reported 500 guns made. Current value, $850 to $900.

# 1976

**BROWNING Bicentennial Superposed:** over/under, 12-ga.; same basic specs as standard Superposed shotgun, but sideplates have engraved, gold inlaid turkey hunting scene on right side, U.S. flag, bald eagle on left. State markings are in gold on blue background; handcheckered American walnut straight-grip stock, Schnabel forearm; marketed in velvet-lined walnut presentation case. Only 51 made; one for each state and District of Columbia. Manufactured in Belgium 1976. Current value, $8200 to $8250.

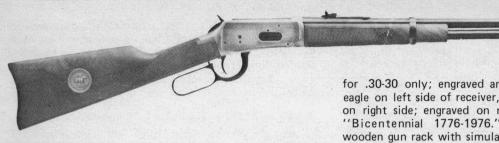

**WINCHESTER Bicentennial '76 Carbine:** Model 94; has same general specs as standard model, except chambered for .30-30 only; engraved antique silver finish; American eagle on left side of receiver, "76" encircled with 13 stars on right side; engraved on right side of barrel is legend "Bicentennial 1776-1976." Originally marketed with wooden gun rack with simulated deer antlers, gold-colored identification plate. Reported 20,000 made in 1976. Original price, $325. Current value, $350 to $365.

**REMINGTON Bicentennial Model 742:** has the same specs as standard Model 742 Woodsmaster, except for Bicentennial commemorative inscription etched on receiver; different checkering pattern. Manufactured 1976 only. Current value, $190 to $200.

**REMINGTON Bicentennial Model 760:** has same specifications as standard Model 760 Gamemaster, except for Bicentennial commemorative inscription etched on receiver; different checkering pattern. Manufactured 1976 only. Current value, $165 to $175.

**COLT Bicentennial Set:** includes Colt SAA revolver, Python revolver and 3rd Model Dragoon revolver, with accessories; all have rosewood stocks, matching roll-engraved unfluted cylinders, blued finish, silver medallion bearing the Seal of the United States; Dragoon has silver grip frame; all revolvers in set have matching serial numbers, 0001 through 1776. Marketed with deluxe three-drawer walnut presentation case, reproduction volume of "Armswear." Made only in 1976. Current value for set, $2350 to $2500.

**BROWNING Bicentennial 78:** single-shot Model 78; .45-70; same specs as standard model, except for bison and eagle engraved on receiver, scroll engraving on lever, both ends of barrel, buttplate, top of receiver; high grade walnut stock, forearm. Manufactured in Japan. Marketed with engraved hunting knife, commemorative medallion, alder presentation case. Gun and knife serial numbers match, beginning with 1776. Only 1,000 sets made. Manufactured only in 1976. Current value for set, $1900 to $1950.

**ITHACA Bicentennial Model 37:** slide action; 12-ga.; has basic specs of Model 37 Supreme, except for Bicentennial design etched into receiver, serialized USA 0001 to USA 1976; full fancy walnut stock, slide handle. Only 1,976 guns made in 1976. Marketed in presentation case. Current value, $550 to $590.

**WICKLIFFE '76 Commemorative:** single-shot; has same specs as '76 Deluxe model, except for filled etching on sidewalls of receiver; 26" barrel only; U.S. silver dollar inlaid in stock; marketed in presentation case. Manufactured 1976 only. Only 100 made. Current value, $450 to $475.

# 1977

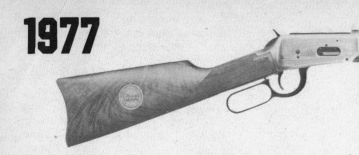

**WINCHESTER Wells Fargo Model 94:** has same specs as standard Model 94, except .30-30 only; antique silver-finish engraved receiver; nickel-silver stagecoach medallion inset in buttstock; checkered fancy American walnut stock; forearm; curved buttplate. Reported 20,000 made in 1977. Current value, $375 to $390.

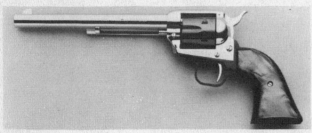

**COLT Second Amendment Commemorative:** Peacemaker Buntline revolver; .22 rimfire; 7½" barrel bears inscription, "The Right To Keep And Bear Arms;" polished nickel-plated barrel, frame, ejector rod assembly, hammer, trigger; blued cylinder, backstrap, trigger guard; black pearlight stocks; fluted cylinder; specially serial numbered; marketed in special presentation case, carrying reproduction copy of Second Amendment to the Constitution. Reported 3,000 made in 1977. Original price, $194.95. Current value, $260 to $275.

**SMITH & WESSON 125th Anniversary:** Model 25 revolver; .45 Colt chambering; 6½" barrel; blued finish; goncalco alves stocks; "Smith & Wesson 125th Anniversary" gold-filled on barrel; sideplate has gold-filled anniversary seal; marketed in case bearing nickel-silver anniversary seal. Included is book, *125 Years With Smith & Wesson.* Reported 9,950 issued in 1977. Current value, $375 to $400.

   **Deluxe Edition 12th Anniversary** has same specs as standard issue, except has Class A engraving, ivory stocks; anniversary medallion on box is sterling silver, book is leather-bound. Reported 50 issued in 1977. Current value, $1600 to $1650.

# 1978

**WINCHESTER Legendary Lawman:** Model 94 Carbine; .30-30 only; has same specs as standard model, except for 16" barrel, full length tube magazine; antique silver-finish barrel bands; right side of barrel bears silver-colored inscription, "Legendary Lawman"; extended forearm, straight-grip stock; nickel-silver medallion set in buttstock features sheriff standing on Western street. Reported 20,000 manufactured in 1978. Original price, $375. Current value, $385 to $395.

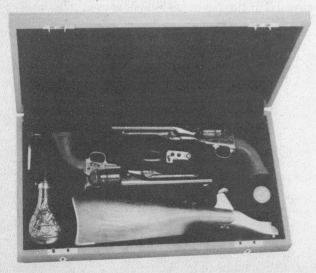

**COLT U.S. Cavalry Commemorative:** based on 1860 Single Action Army design; commemorates 200th anniversary of U.S. Cavalry, 1777 to 1977; blued barrel, ejector rod assembly, cylinder, backstrap, trigger; frame, hammer color case-hardened; brass trigger guard; one-piece walnut stocks; naval engagement scene roll marked on non-fluted cylinder; marketed with detachable walnut shoulder stock, accessories, in oiled American walnut presentation case. Reported 3,000 units manufactured 1978. Original price, $995. Current value, $1000 to $1050.